www.wadsworth.com

www.wadsworth.com is the World Wide Web site for
Wadsworth and is your direct source to dozens of online
resources.

At *www.wadsworth.com* you can find out about
supplements, demonstration software, and student
resources. You can also send email to many of our authors
and preview new publications and exciting new
technologies.

www.wadsworth.com
Changing the way the world learns®

ON HUMAN NATURE

AN INTRODUCTION TO PHILOSOPHY

Thomas F. Wall
Emmanuel College

THOMSON

™

WADSWORTH

Australia • Canada • Mexico • Singapore • Spain
United Kingdom • United States

THOMSON
™
WADSWORTH

Publisher: Holly J. Allen
Philosophy Editor: Steve Wainwright
Assistant Editors: Lee McCracken, Anna Lustig
Editorial Assistant: Barbara Hillaker
Marketing Manager: Worth Hawes
Advertising Project Managers: Bryan Vann, Vicky Wan
Print/Media Buyer: Lisa Claudeanos
Permissions Editor: Stephanie Lee

Production Service: Shepherd, Inc.
Copy Editor: Francine Banwarth
Cover Designer: Yvo Riezebos
Cover Image: Picasso: *Three Women.*
  Scala/Art Resource, NY
Compositor: Shepherd, Inc.
Printer: Banta—Harrisonburg

Printed in the United States of America

1 2 3 4 5 6 7 08 07 06 05 04

For more information about our products, contact us at:
Thomson Learning Academic Resource Center
1-800-423-0563

For permission to use material from this text or product, submit a request online at *http://www.thomsonrights.com.* Any additional questions about permissions can be submitted by email to thomsonrights@thomson.com.

Library of Congress Control Number: 2004104985

ISBN 0-534-62478-2

Thomson Wadsworth
10 Davis Drive
Belmont, CA 94002-3098
USA

Asia
Thomson Learning
5 Shenton Way #01-01
UIC Building
Singapore 068808

Australia/New Zealand
Thomson Learning
102 Dodds Street
Southbank, Victoria 3006
Australia

Canada
Nelson
1120 Birchmount Road
Toronto, Ontario M1K 5G4
Canada

Europe/Middle East/Africa
Thomson Learning
High Holborn House
50/51 Bedford Row
London WC1R 4LR
United Kingdom

Latin America
Thomson Learning
Seneca, 53
Colonia Polanco
11560 Mexico D.F.
Mexico

Spain/Portugal
Paraninfo
Calle Magallanes, 25
28015 Madrid, Spain

*This book is dedicated to Nancy, Kathy, Susan,
and Kevin: siblings by nature, dearest friends by choice.*

Contents

Preface

This textbook is designed for use in a course that introduces students to philosophy. The core question that it addresses is, *What is human nature?* This question may be understood in both a narrow and a broad sense. In its *narrow* sense it is a factual question about the innate tendencies shared by all human beings. The various authors discussed here ask if there are any such natural tendencies—tendencies to think in certain ways, or to desire certain things, or to have certain sorts of feelings and emotions, or even to behave in one particular way or another. Natural tendencies are present simply because we come into this world constructed as the kinds of beings that we are, and not as the result of a process of learning.

Do we all have natural tendencies to be selfish, for example, or are we basically altruistic by nature? Are the lives of all human beings driven especially by reason, or rather by emotion or conscious and even unconscious desires? Are we slaves to the forces of nature or of culture, or are we able to guide our lives by our own free choices? Are we products of evolution, cousins to all other creatures on this planet, or do we have unique minds, emotions, desires, and conscious experiences that set us apart from the rest of nature? These and related questions are discussed by each of the authors considered in this text.

The question of human nature may also be understood in a *broad* sense. In addition to a list of innate tendencies, an answer to the broader question of human nature also requires consideration of background **assumptions,** especially those about knowledge and reality. Understanding the general view of the world and how we come to know it of each author is essential for a deeper, more detailed understanding of his or her view of human nature. Only by locating a discussion of human nature in the context of the author's worldview can a "theory" of human nature be constructed which explains what human beings are and why we behave as we do. In addition to examining these basic assumptions, this text also investigates the **consequences** of holding a particular theory of human nature. These consequences are very practical ones, and include what follows from a particular view of human nature about such issues as the degree to which we are free, the nature of morality, the best type of society, the existence of God, the possibility of life after death, and the existence and nature of gender differences.

Since this textbook on human nature discusses not only human nature itself but also questions of epistemology, metaphysics, philosophy of mind, ethics, philosophy of religion, political and social philosophy, and so on, it is quite suitable for use as an introductory text in philosophy. It includes all of the standard topics of such an introductory course, and it centers the discussion of them on very concrete, very real, very practical questions for students—Who am I, what is the point of this life that I am living, and how should I live it?

Theories of human nature originate from many sources. For example, various *religions* have contributed heavily to the discussion of human nature for many centuries, and some of their views will be discussed in this text. Various *sciences,* a great many of them in fact, are currently working feverishly especially on the narrow question of human nature. We will examine some of these views in the chapters to come. *Philosophers*, of course, have also addressed the question of human nature, and have done so since the beginning of philosophy itself. Many of their theories will be discussed in this text, beginning with those constructed by the ancient Asian and Greek philosophers over twenty-five hundred years ago. Whatever their origin, however, at some point theories of human nature become philosophical theories, and thus become subject to philosophical scrutiny. That is why this is a philosophy book, not a religious studies or science text—because it discusses theories of human nature in a philosophical manner.

The theories of human nature discussed in this text are presented in more or less chronological order, and each follows the same outline. First, I present a fairly extensive overview of the theory, which begins with a brief discussion of the life and times of the author, then examines the relevant background assumptions, collectively referred to as the author's "worldview." The core question of human nature is next addressed, followed by a consideration of the practical consequences which follow from adopting such a view. This comprehensive introduction is followed by selections from the author's writings, which comprise about 50 percent of the book.

Generally speaking, the writings of each author are so extensive that only a fraction of primary source material may be included in a course whose plan is to consider many theories. So extensive introductions to each theory are provided to describe the overall view of the author and to provide the larger context within which his or her selected readings may be examined more meaningfully. Within these introductions to each theory the selected writings of the author are referenced, their contents briefly described, and their contribution to the author's broader view identified. My suggestion is that you read these introductions first, get a general idea of what each view says, and then read what the author himself or herself has to say. Why the primary source material if the text explains things clearly? Because, in the end, the best source of what the author means are the original words of the author, not those of one who simply interprets what he thinks the author meant.

One final point, an important point, on how matters of *gender* are treated in this text. The issue of whether and to what degree men and women have different natures is an extremely important one. For many, if men and women have different natures then it becomes acceptable to treat men and women differently. Historically, women often have been viewed as having inferior natures, a "fact" that was used to justify their inferior treatment in the home and society. In more modern times, these sexist views have been combated especially by feminist authors, whose insights have been used in the battle for equal rights and equal treatment for women. To understand the history of the suppression and liberation of women it is important to understand the various ways in which the nature of women has been construed as different from men, and thus this text takes up the issue throughout.

Despite the importance of this issue, there is no separate chapter in this text with a title such as "The Feminist Perspective on Human Nature." This is because the question of natural differences between men and women is a controversial issue itself, even among feminist authors, so there is no one perspective shared by all. Since the differences between feminist authors often parallel the differences between the competing theories of human nature which are included in this text, the matter of a feminist perspective is best addressed within the context of each chapter. This happens within the introductions, in the section called "Gender," and sometimes in one or more of the selected writings. This approach allows the assumptions and consequences of a particular "feminist" perspective on human nature better to be understood and evaluated. The current debate among feminists on this important question is formed more clearly in this manner, since each different view may be seen as arising within the general theory it accepts.

Acknowledgments

I would like to thank Steve Wainwright, Philosophy and Religion editor at Wadsworth, for his wise guidance and enthusiastic encouragement. I would also like to thank my colleague, Russ Sullivan, for his helpful comments on an earlier version of the manuscript, and Susan Von Daum Tholl, who provided valuable research assistance. I wish to thank those who reviewed this text for their many helpful comments: Karin Brown, San Jose State University; William Glod, Tulane University; Richard A. Richards, University of Alabama; Edrie Sobstyl, University of Texas at Dallas; Andrew Tallon, Marquette University; and Andrew Ward, Georgia Institute of Technology. Finally, I would like to thank my wife, Kay. Despite her own busy schedule, she always managed to find the time to support and encourage me throughout this project.

Part 1

Introduction

This book is designed to introduce beginning students to philosophy. There are many ways to be introduced to philosophy, just as there are many ways to be introduced to art or music or the law, for example. If philosophy is thought of in terms of its *method*, then emphasis might be placed on training students to think like philosophers, just as a legal education might focus on training students to think like lawyers.[1] If this approach is taken, choices have to be made about which thinking skills to develop and to which problems they are to be applied. If, on the other hand, the focus is on the *content* of philosophy, as it is in this text, then choices must be made about which areas of this vast content to emphasize.

The history of philosophy has a more central role in the study of philosophy than is true in most other disciplines. So one choice to make in an introductory philosophy book which emphasizes content is which historical and contemporary philosophers to study. In addition, since philosophers spend a lot of time trying to solve problems, another choice to be made is which problem or problems to examine. This text focuses on one central problem, the problem of understanding human nature. In the chapters to follow it presents a wide variety of solutions to this problem, solutions that are called "Theories of Human Nature." In the process of coming to understand these various theories, these answers to one of the most central of all philosophical questions, you will learn a great deal about the content of philosophy.

The Nature of Philosophy

It is important at the start to get an idea of what philosophy is and what philosophers do. Some time will be spent in this book examining views of human nature that did not arise from Western philosophy. However, because so many of the theories discussed here are a product of Western thought, it is the nature of Western philosophy that will be addressed in this *Introduction*. Western philosophy, like so much of Western culture, began in ancient Greece over twenty-five hundred years ago. The word "philosophy" comes from two Greek words, "philein" (to love) and "sophia" (wisdom). Originally, then, philosophy was the *love of wisdom*, and philosophers were people who spent their lives attempting to become wise. To be wise was to have a general understanding of all things— nature, ourselves, society, God, morality, and the meaning of life and death. Wisdom was not identified with any sort of practical knowledge, what we might call "professional training" or "career preparation" today. It was considered by ancient philosophers to be much more valuable than practical knowledge, even to the point of constituting the very goal of life itself. A person who was wise was as close to happiness as he or she could be.

Philosophy has retained some of this original meaning, at least insofar as it is still concerned with a general understanding of the basic issues mentioned previously. But most philosophers today draw a sharper distinction than did their predecessors between knowledge of the world and knowledge of how we *think* about the world. Most philosophers today do not think of what they do as acquiring factual knowledge, knowledge of how things are. That task has long been relinquished to the various natural and behavioral sciences that have developed since the original definition of philosophy was introduced by the Greeks. Now philosophers see themselves as concerned with ideas, not things; with conceptual questions, not empirical ones; with understanding or interpreting facts, not discovering them. Philosophers do not perform experiments or send out surveys or make observations to settle their questions. They think.

The Subject Matter of Philosophy

What philosophers think about are basic beliefs. These constitute much of the **subject matter** of philosophy. A *belief* is a thought that can be expressed in a declarative sentence. "The earth is flat," is a belief, though a false one. "The right thing to do is to look out for yourself," is a moral belief, though a very controversial one. We have commonsense beliefs, scientific and mathematical beliefs, religious beliefs, and many other sorts of beliefs about the world, ourselves, and others. Since beliefs are composed of concepts, concepts are also included in what philosophy studies, and so are systems of beliefs, such as scientific and philosophical theories.

Philosophers are not concerned with just any beliefs, but focus on beliefs that are basic. A belief is *basic* if its truth or falsity determines the truth or falsity of lots of other beliefs. As a weak foundation undermines the entire house, so a false basic belief undermines the structure of beliefs built upon it. The basic belief of religion, for example, may be identified as the belief that God exists. If this belief is false, lots of other religious beliefs that depend upon its truth become false, or at least need to be reinterpreted. Morality based upon God's word, for example, or liturgical celebrations of the special relationships between humans and God, no longer have firm support. Sometimes philosophers refer to these basic beliefs as "fundamental issues" or "big questions" and in other similar ways that mean essentially the same thing as basic beliefs.

Some basic beliefs are embedded in our everyday thinking. Some of these we are conscious of possessing while others are held less consciously, as deep assumptions. Beliefs about God and some of our moral beliefs about right and wrong are examples of the former. Most of us have beliefs about these matters of which we are aware. Beliefs about the existence and nature of the world are examples of beliefs that we may have but not find on the surface of our thinking. These beliefs serve as background assumptions that are necessary for us to function in life, but rarely are identified, let alone called into question. Can you imagine how it would change your life, for example, if you came to believe that the world around you was simply a creation of your own imagination and that nothing and no one in it really existed? This unusual belief shows us by contrast what our basic belief about the existence of the material world really is, namely that it really does exist.

Other basic beliefs are also held as underlying assumptions that we may become aware of perhaps more frequently as various circumstances bring them into question. If someone close to us dies, for example, we may hope that she lives on after death in some form. We may wonder about the degree to which anybody is free and responsible for their actions when we hear about someone who seemed trapped in miserable circumstances committing a terrible crime. Other basic beliefs are found as assumptions within various disciplines and the study of them is often very technical, requiring a good deal of knowledge about specialized disciplines. Examining the basic beliefs of mathematics or quantum mechanics requires this sort of specialized knowledge. Every science has basic beliefs that it assumes to be true and upon which it builds its theories. Some have competing basic beliefs, such as psychology, for example, which has more than one basic belief about the nature of the mind.

The Method of Philosophy

If philosophers are concerned with basic beliefs, if that is their subject matter, we still have to understand what it means to "think" about these beliefs to be clear about the nature of philosophy. While there are different opinions among philosophers about the method of philosophy, most would agree on the following points. Philosophical thinking, the **method** of philosophy, involves several aspects. Often philosophical thinking begins with the awareness that there are several competing basic beliefs, several different ways to think about the same thing. In this text, for example, several theories of human nature are presented as true, even though they are often at great odds with each other. Now this presents a problem. Which of these several competing theories should a reasonable person accept? Philosophical thinking is a type of problem solving. It first requires a clear grasp of the nature of the problem. This, in turn, often requires clarification of the basic concepts in terms of which the problem is presented. If the problem, for example, is whether or not it is reasonable to believe that God exists, it is important to be clear about the concept of God.

Philosophical thinking also requires an understanding of the various possible solutions to the problem under consideration. In the case of the existence of God, for example, these would include theism, atheism, and agnosticism, among others. Perhaps most importantly, philosophers spend a great deal of time giving reasons why some possible solution should be thought of as preferable to others. That is, they present arguments for their views. They do not simply present their ideas as opinions, but philosophers try to persuade others that their views ought to be accepted by any reasonable person. As a lawyer might argue for the guilt or innocence of his or her client, so philosophers argue for the truth of basic beliefs or theories. In addition, they often defend their positions by arguing against competing views. Much of what philosophers do, then, is to engage in rational persuasion, attempting to convince any rational person that what they claim is more reasonable than the alternatives.

To understand philosophy it is important to understand the difference between philosophical problems and scientific ones. Scientific problems are those that can be answered by gathering information through observation and experimentation. Philosophical problems, on the other hand, arise after the facts are known. For example, the various entities in the world might be experienced as fitting together to form an orderly place, a universe that functions according to laws discovered by science. But what should we make of this? What can we infer from it? How do we interpret its significance? Was the order of the world as we know it produced by some sort of intelligence, for example, as is the case with things like watches or TV sets? Or rather is its design the result of the natural forces of evolution that allow only adaptive beings to survive? What should such order mean to us?

The design of the universe is compatible with either an intelligent cause or a nonintelligent cause. So which is the correct way to think about the origin of its design? This is the problem. It is not a scientific problem because such questions as these cannot be solved simply by discovering more facts. More discoveries of design in the universe are neither necessary nor helpful for understanding the significance of its design. Instead, it is a philosophical problem, a problem about how to interpret already known facts. In this case it is a problem about how best to understand the origin and significance of the design of the universe. Instead of gathering more information, solving philosophical problems requires us to argue that one interpretation of the already known facts, one possible solution, is superior to another. Simply put, to "argue" means to "provide reasons" that support the truth of one possible solution over another.

Other sorts of philosophical problems arise because of insufficient information. More facts would help to settle these sorts of problems. Whether or not we should think of ourselves as like computers, for example, may very well have to do with advances in the cognitive sciences, and with the results of artificial intelligence research. But very often currently unknown facts will continue to remain unavailable, or at least not become available in a manner sufficient to settle the issue. With these sorts of problems it is often the task of philosophy to think about what such discoveries *would* mean, if they were true. If we *could* construct computers that *could* perform all the essential human behaviors as well as humans do, could we then argue that we have created a person? Would such computers have rights? Would we then be nothing but various types of computers ourselves?

Sometimes the major benefit of such speculation is to focus our thinking on the nature of our current beliefs. If we ask, for example, what a computer would have to be able to do, and how it would have to look, for us to think of it as like ourselves, we are asking about what is essential to being a person like ourselves. If we ask what a truly just society would look like, we might better understand our own society by contrast, by how far it falls short of such an ideal. The point for now, however, is that this second type of problem is like the first, insofar as both require us to argue for some interpretation of the facts, some possible solution, as superior to its alternatives. In the first sort of problem, all the important facts are already in. In the second, they are not. So in the second case what these facts might be has to be imagined by thought experiments. In both cases, real or imagined facts cry out for further interpretation, thus giving rise to philosophical problems and to the need for hard thinking to solve them. In the chapters to follow, it will be helpful for you to understand that the various theories of human nature proposed for our acceptance are all based on facts, but all go beyond the facts. Even the so-called scientific theories that are examined in the end include interpretations of the facts which go well beyond the facts. Whether these theories arise from religion, philosophy, or science, they all involve interpretations of facts. In short, they are all philosophical theories.

The Divisions of Philosophy

It may help you to get a better idea about the subject matter of philosophy if we say a few words about its major divisions, each of which studies particular basic beliefs. In general, to study the "philosophy of" anything is to think critically about the basic beliefs of that area. Among the most important branches of philosophy are the following:

The *philosophy of reality,* also called *metaphysics,* is concerned with basic beliefs about the existence and nature of the world.

The *philosophy of knowledge,* also called *epistemology,* examines basic beliefs about the nature, origin, extent, and justification of knowledge.

The *philosophy of mind* is especially concerned with our basic beliefs about the nature of persons, how minds relate to bodies and personal identity.

The *philosophy of religion* thinks critically about basic beliefs concerned with the existence and nature of God.

The *philosophy of morality* or *ethics,* is concerned with our basic beliefs about right and wrong, good and evil.

Social and political philosophy are concerned with our basic beliefs about such matters as the legitimacy of government, the extent of governmental authority over individual freedom, and the nature of a just society.

Logic studies the proper methods of reasoning.

In addition, there is also the philosophy of science (in general and for specific sciences), the philosophy of mathematics, the philosophy of law, the philosophy of language, the philosophy of history, the philosophy of art (also called aesthetics), and others as well, such as the many areas of applied ethics. "Human nature" itself is not a separate division of philosophy, because its study involves several areas.

Historical Periods of Philosophy

Since many of the theories of human nature come from the distant past of philosophy, it is helpful to have a brief and general idea of the shape of its past. Western philosophy, like so much of Western culture, began in ancient Greece sometime in the sixth century B.C.E. with the Presocratic philosophers, a group that included Thales, Heraclitus, Parmenides, and many others. From this time to about 300 C.E. is called the *Ancient* period of philosophy. Major figures during this time include Socrates (470–399) and his most famous student, Plato (427–348), and Plato's most famous student, Aristotle (384–322). For almost two thousand years the writings of Plato and Aristotle were synonymous with human wisdom. Plato's school, the Academy, was the first university-like educational institution in Western history.

The *Medieval* period dates from the time of St. Augustine (354–430 C.E.) to 1600. During this time philosophy was said to be the "handmaiden of theology." This was a time when most Europeans were Christians and accepted the authority of the Roman Catholic Church. Answers to many of the big questions were provided by what was taken to be the revealed word of God as found in the Old and New Testaments. One of the central functions of philosophy during this period was to help make clear what God's word meant. During this period much original philosophy was produced but there was also a heavy reliance by theologians on the writings of Plato and Aristotle. Some important figures of the Medieval period, in addition to St. Augustine, were St. Anselm (1033–1109) and especially St. Thomas Aquinas (1225–1274).

During the *Modern* or *Classical Modern* period, from 1600 to 1900, philosophy began to rely less on faith and more on human reason. Much of its agenda was inspired by the development of the natural sciences. Questions about the nature and limits of knowledge and the nature of reality became important, as did political and social questions. Descartes (1596–1650), Spinoza (1632–1677), Leibniz (1646–1716), Kant (1724–1804), and Hegel (1770–1831) were all important continental philosophers during this period. Important English speaking philosophers were Locke (1632–1704), Berkeley (1685–1753), and David Hume (1711–1776).

The *Contemporary* period of philosophy includes philosophers from 1900 to the present. Its major areas have been existentialism, analytic philosophy, and pragmatism. Existentialism is primarily a European philosophical movement which focuses upon the subjective self. Early representatives include the Danish philosopher, Soren Kierkegaard (1813–1855) and the German philosopher, Friedrich Nietzsche (1844–1900), while contemporary existentialists include the French philosopher, Jean-Paul Sartre (1905–1980) and the German philosopher, Martin Heidegger (1889–1976).

Analytic philosophy, especially that version of it called "Ordinary Language" philosophy, is primarily a British philosophical movement among whose major contributors have been Ludwig Wittgenstein (1889–1951), Gilbert Ryle (1900–1976), and John Austin (1911–1960). These philosophers were concerned with showing how the misuse of language is often at the root of philosophical problems, and how clarifying ordinary language is usually sufficient to eliminate them. Pragmatism is a North American philosophical movement heavily influenced by science, whose many themes include the belief that truth is provisional and that the meaning of concepts is to be identified with the logical, psychological, and social consequences to which using them leads. Those who formulated the leading themes of pragmatism include Charles S. Peirce (1830–1914), William James (1842–1910) and John Dewey (1859–1952).

The Value of Philosophy

Finally, a word or two on why it is important to study philosophy. Philosophy is valuable for several reasons.

Philosophy is necessary. Human beings are built in such a way that they require their experience and behavior to be meaningful. To be meaningful we must understand our experience and have a point to our behavior. Ultimately, this requires a system of philosophical beliefs, a worldview, that operates in our lives as a set of background assumptions. Most of us acquire such a philosophical outlook uncritically. When we study philosophy we become aware of it and examine it critically. In either case we *must* have such a view to lead our lives with meaning. The only issue is whether we absorb it from our society uncritically or examine it carefully and adopt it critically.

Philosophy produces self-knowledge. Socrates actually chose death over a life where he was forbidden by the Athenian Senate to question freely and publicly the meaning of life. At his trial Socrates explained why he would not stop asking philosophical questions and accept the lesser sentence of exile that was offered to him. It was because ". . . to discourse about virtue, and of those other things about which you hear me examining myself and others . . . is the greatest good of man, and that the unexamined life is no life for a human being . . ."[2] The critical examination of the basic ideas that shape who we are and why we have the goals that we do—*understanding* the point of living, not just living—is what Socrates finds so valuable. It is liberating in the truest sense that its study frees us to understand ourselves and thus allows us to begin to create who we are.

Philosophy expands our ego-centric perspective. Philosophy helps us to make the journey from the *village* of our ego-centric perspective to cognitive citizenship in the wider *universe*. It expands our thinking. As the famous British philosopher and mathematician Bertrand Russell put it, the person "who has no tincture of philosophy goes through life imprisoned in the prejudices derived from common sense, from the habitual beliefs of his age or nation, and from convictions which have grown up in his mind without the co-operation or consent of his deliberate reason." But one who engages in philosophical thinking is not so trapped, because struggling with philosophical questions will "enlarge our conception of what is possible, enrich our intellectual imagination and diminish the dogmatic assurance which closes the mind against speculation; but above all because, through the greatness of the universe which philosophy contemplates, the mind is rendered also great, and becomes capable of that union with the universe which constitutes its highest good."[3]

Philosophy has practical value. Philosophy majors score among the highest on standardized tests, tests that require reasoning skills, tests that are used as important criteria for admission to medical school, law school, and graduate programs. Acquiring this ability to think carefully is also much better job preparation for the twenty-first century than narrow training in a particular field, training that emphasizes mastery of content. Content changes so rapidly that such training soon becomes obsolete. Moreover, several career changes will be the norm for most future workers, and many jobs available in the future have yet to be defined, so it is rather difficult to prepare for a career except by building skills. Studying philosophy helps to build the thinking skills that will be essential for the next century. Thinking for yourself and thinking well will be among the most valued qualities of any employee. So philosophy has some utilitarian value, even though most students of philosophy have been drawn to it for other, more intrinsic reasons. At the very least, philosophy is fun and exciting. But that, of course, is a judgment you will have to make for yourself.

The Question of Human Nature

The philosophical problem to be examined in this text is, *What is human nature?* Let us understand this question to be about the structure and the innate tendencies shared by all human beings. Our common **structure** includes our physical, chemical, and biological make-up, but here it especially refers to the nature and function of our minds. Our **innate tendencies,** should we have any, are those that we all share simply because we are members of the human species. We will look for them especially in the areas of reason, emotion, and desire. These are not tendencies which we have learned—since different people in different places at different times learn different things. Rather, they are tendencies that are ours from birth, tendencies possessed by any human being, whatever his or her location in time or space.

At first glance the question of human nature seems to be straightforward enough, one that ought to have an answer acceptable to everyone. Do we not answer such questions about other living things, such as dogs or birds or snakes? If I want to buy a dog, for example, and need advice in selecting a breed that is most compatible with my lifestyle, I may consult books, or breeders, or veterinarians, or other experts who are able to tell me about the "natures" of various breeds. This, in fact, was how I selected my border collie—by understanding in advance something about his innate tendencies. I wanted a smart, high energy, athletic dog. I wanted a dog with a nature like his.

If the nature of animals may be discovered by observation, why is it not the same for our understanding of human nature? Why do we not simply go to the "experts" and have them tell us about our common structures and innate tendencies, as other experts can tell us about the nature of border collies or other animals? Why do we have *theories* of human nature—and so many of them—instead of simply having a description of human nature? Why do we not have, for example, a simple description that says, "All human beings are _____ ,"where the blank is filled in with words naming our various innate tendencies? In short, why is not the question of human nature a straightforward factual question, one that can be answered by making observations, those of daily life, and especially those of science?

A Commonsense Question

There are some who do, in fact, think that human nature can be discovered by observation. They believe that the problem of human nature is indeed a factual problem. For example, if we think of *common sense* as our everyday understanding of the world, then we do seem to have a commonsense idea of human nature which is based upon observation. We talk about people as having a certain temperament, or being driven by certain emotions or desires, such as greed or anger or jealousy. "He's a quiet guy, always has been," or "She really has a temper," or "It's just not his nature to lie," are some commonly used statements that seem to describe human nature.

However, we use these statements not so much to describe a universal human nature, but to distinguish between various tendencies of different human beings to act in one way or another. We say such things as, "he is friendly," "he is aloof," "she is a liar," "she is a caring person," and so on. Moreover, when we speak this way of general character traits of individuals, we do not necessarily rule out that these are learned behaviors. So, many of our commonsense descriptions of human nature are neither descriptions of a universal human nature, nor of human "nature" at all.

In fairness to our everyday wisdom, sometimes when we say things like, "It's human nature," or "It's only natural," we *are* talking about a universal trait and one that is innate. However, there are so many different opinions about what these traits are, that we can hardly say that there is anything like a commonsense consensus about human nature. Some believe, for example, that human beings are innately selfish, while others believe that we are naturally altruistic. Some believe that we are rational beings, while others believe that we are driven by desire to do the things that we do. Some believe that we are aggressive by nature, while others believe that aggression is learned, and that if we did not learn it we would be peace loving creatures. Some believe that there is no such thing at all as human nature, and that our structures and tendencies and the behaviors which they produce are all molded by the environment. At the same time, others believe that many more of our tendencies and traits than formerly believed are "hard-wired" into us by nature. The opinions held in our daily lives about human nature are many indeed.

A Scientific Question

If there is no generally accepted idea of human nature to be found in our everyday lives, then perhaps we might expect to find it in science. Surely it is reasonable to expect that experts in the areas of science that study human beings should agree on what sorts of tendencies we share, and which of these are innate and which are learned. This is especially true today, since so many sciences in the past two or three decades have turned their attention to the study of human nature. Here are just some of the sciences and combined areas of research that are currently engaged in the study of human nature: anthropology, archeology, artificial intelligence, behavior genetics, cognitive science, developmental psychology, economics, ethology, evolutionary biology, evolutionary psychology, linguistics, primatology, psychiatry, sociology, and sociobiology. In addition, there are many newly formed offshoots of these sciences, many of which contain the prefix "neuro," because they search for the neurological underpinnings of their subject matter. These include neurobiology, neurolinguistics, neuropsychiatry, neuropsychology, and many others.

Many of these sciences provide an explanation of human nature by appealing to how culture, what we learn, shapes what we do, while others appeal to the natural ways of behaving we are born with and the genes that determine them. It seems clear that both elements, nature and nurture, genes and culture, are involved in shaping our behavior. A full scientific account of human nature would have to include an account of how these two components—our natural ways of behaving and what we learn—interact. If human nature is the hardware of behavior, culture may be thought of as its software. Human beings can be "programmed" in a great number of ways by various cultures to acquire a vastly more rich and complex repertoire of behaviors than nature itself allows. The point for now is that if solving the problem of human nature is understood to be a purely factual matter, something to be achieved by observation alone, then scientific observations of our genetic determinants have to be supplemented with accounts of how culture extends our behavior, and thus our selves, beyond these determinants.

Perhaps science will some day be able to develop a complete picture of human nature. As an electronics engineer might explain how the hardware of a computer is built from its component parts, and as a software engineer might explain the various programs that such a machine could run, so too, science may be able to explain how evolution has designed human beings and how various cultures interact with this design to produce various behaviors. Even if that day finally arrives, however, which seems very unlikely, there is more to human nature than a complete factual account of our structure and our innate tendencies, and how they get expressed in various cultures would explain. There is more involved in understanding ourselves than simply understanding the sorts of machines that we are and the kinds of "programs" we can run. Many other questions must be answered as well.

A Philosophical Question

Included among these other questions are those typically answered by the humanities. For example, we value greatly the aesthetic dimension of ourselves. No explanation of human nature would be complete if it ignored the role that it plays in our lives. Science cannot provide this explanation. It is difficult to understand, for example, what may be the reproductive or survival value possessed by a deeply moving poem, or a beautiful work of art, or the sweet sound of a violin in the background, as the fiery red sun sets over the cool ocean air. We also have a spiritual dimension that cries out for greater understanding than simply its survival value. These are dimensions of human nature that have more to do with thriving than surviving, and they are beyond the scope of science to explain. It appears that describing and explaining human nature is a task both for science and for the humanities. We come to understand as much about ourselves through art, music, poetry, religion and especially through the stories that we tell about lives, as we do through science.

Among the humanities, understanding human nature is especially a job for philosophy, and this for several reasons. First, philosophy has specifically addressed this question for centuries. There is a gold mine of wisdom in what philosophers have said about what it means to be a human being, most of which was written long before current scientific accounts of human nature. Second, in addition to having a long history of discussing this problem, philosophy continues to be necessary for a full discussion of human nature today. This is because solving the problem of human nature involves not simply the narrow task of discovering facts—a job especially for science—but also is a matter of *interpreting* the facts discovered, of figuring out what they mean for our understanding of ourselves. To interpret facts is to see them in a broader context and to give reasons why their meaning or significance should be taken in one way rather than another.

For example, if it is true that some of our behavior is directed by our genes, does that mean that we are not free to choose our thoughts, behaviors, feelings and desires? Does it mean that we are slaves to a genetically determined human nature? If so, then how do we explain the existence of various cultures? How do the same genetically based tendencies give rise to so many different ways of living? And if we are the products of our genes, or even if we are the products of our cultures alone, what sense does morality have? Does it make any sense to say that people are obliged to do certain things and refrain from doing others, if they cannot help doing what they do? If their genes or their cultures make them behave as they do? If this is not enough, how do these concepts of human nature change our religious ideas, our notions, for example, that we are made in the image of God? It should be clear that a full account of human nature must include not only scientific facts, but also both interpretations of these facts and consideration of their significance for other important dimensions of human nature. This is what philosophy does, it interprets the broader significance of facts.

The third, and perhaps the most important reason why the problem of human nature should be seen as primarily a philosophical problem, is because understanding human nature requires just as much an understanding of what we *can* be, even what we *ought to* be, as it requires us to understand what we are. Even if science could provide a coherent view of what human nature is, it could not provide an understanding of what it could be. Philosophers are especially adept at constructing such ideals. They are good at bridging the gap between the descriptive and the normative, between what is and what could be or even should be. It is one thing to know that we have aggressive or selfish tendencies, for example, that conflict with our altruism and our reason. It is quite another thing to see that these conflicting tendencies should blend together and to present a plan as how they could do so in such a way as to lead human beings to a higher, more noble, more fulfilling kind of life. In the end, knowledge of what we might aspire to become may turn out to be the most important knowledge that we have about human nature.

Evaluating Philosophical Theories

Theories are sets of interrelated beliefs that explain particular facts. Scientists are continually constructing, revising, and evaluating theories that explain various segments of this complex, wonderful world in which we live. In philosophy, too, we construct theories to help us to interpret the facts that we discover in science and daily life. In this text we will examine various theories of human nature, all of which try to understand the significance of the commonsense, philosophical, religious, and scientific data that has been discovered about human beings. Since more than one theory exists which claims to explain the facts in question, you will have to decide which one, or which combination of more than one, does the best job of explaining what it means to be a human being. But how do you judge between competing philosophical theories?

Reasoned Judgments

One of the dangers of presenting one theory of human nature after another is that you may come to believe that no one of them is any better than any other. Unlike "facts," which must be accepted by any reasonable person, you may begin to believe that theories are simply collections of "opinions" that may be accepted or not as you wish. You may view them as similar to tastes, for example, which are merely subjective matters. However, while the theories of human nature presented here are not simply lists of facts, they are not mere matters of opinion either. They provide evidence to support their various claims, factual evidence, inferences based on facts, and reasonable interpretations. Because of this they may be evaluated rationally, on the basis of the strengths of their evidence. To evaluate them is to form a **reasoned judgment** about their relative merits, as a jury does when it evaluates the cases made by the prosecution and the defense.

During the process of evaluation, try to give each theory a fair hearing. There is something of importance to be learned from each one. As you examine more and more of the theories included here, you will be in a better position to compare and contrast their strengths and weaknesses. Some theories may be just right on some matters and wrong on others; some may overinflate the importance of one human characteristic and ignore other ones of importance; and some may omit altogether what others consider to be essential elements of human nature. It is important to know that there are rules for making these sorts of evaluative judgments. It is not merely a matter of which view "feels" right to you. The rules that are used to judge the adequacy of philosophical theories are similar to those used to evaluate scientific theories. These rules, sometimes called criteria, state that one theory is better than another if it (1) accounts for all the facts, or least for more facts than its rivals, and (2) is more consistent, and (3) simpler than its competing theories. Let us examine these three criteria in turn.

Universality

A good scientific theory should be able to explain all of the facts that it was designed to explain. Let's use an example to see how this rule works in judging one scientific theory to be superior to another. According to this rule, the theory of evolution is superior to its creationist competitors for lots of reasons, but one of them is that it explains more of the known facts than creationism does. Creationism is the view that the world was created more or less as described in the Biblical account of creation, an account which is found in the "Book of Genesis," in the Old Testament. Here it says, in effect, that the world was created some six thousand years ago with all the species that now exist having been created at that time. Unfortunately, this leaves unexplained all the fossils that have been unearthed, fossils which dramatically predate the biblical date of creation. The theory of evolution explains more facts than creationism, so at least according to rule (1) it is a better theory.

This criterion works in a similar way to evaluate philosophical theories. One philosophical theory is better than another according to this first criterion, if it explains more facts than its competitors. If it explains "all" the facts that it is supposed to, we say that it is *universal*. Some critics complain, for example, that theories of the mind which equate the mind with the brain are not universal. They leave many facts unexplained, such as all the facts of conscious experience. It seems to many that the brain cannot be the source of consciousness, since consciousness experiences seem to be very different sorts of things than brain events. Many of them go on to conclude that minds are not made of matter, and that human beings are composed of both material "stuff" (our bodies) and nonmaterial "stuff" (our minds).

Consistency

The second criterion says that one theory is better than another if it is more *consistent*. Consistency refers to two properties of a theory. First, in an acceptable theory the statements which constitute the theory are all consistent with one another. They contain no contradictions or inconsistencies. We will call this *internal* consistency. Second, the theory itself must be consistent with generally accepted facts and other scientific theories. A scientific theory, for example, must "fit in" with what the rest of reliable science says about the world. We will call this *external* consistency.

Suppose a scientist wrote an article explaining the shape of the Milky Way Galaxy by saying that God was located at its center and acted as a spiritual magnet, attracting all the stars and planets and moons and asteroids, and so on. Suppose further that such a theory explains just as many facts as the "black hole" theory, and that all the statements it contains are consistent with all the others. Nevertheless, this article would never be published in any reputable scientific journal. It is not an acceptable theory because appealing to God to explain how the Galaxy operates does not fit in with the way that science works. Such a theory is externally inconsistent. Science does not accept untestable hypotheses or spiritual being hypotheses as legitimate explanations.

The way that this rule works to test philosophical theories is similar. Philosophical theories also have to be compatible with things outside of themselves. This includes scientific theories, since any philosophical theory that contradicted well-tested scientific theories would be less acceptable for that reason. For many, philosophical theories must be consistent with commonly accepted beliefs as well. For example, if I put forward an ethical theory which claims that the right thing to do is to harm as many people as I can, as often as I can, such a theory would be rejected. It flies in the face of well-established moral beliefs, such as the belief that morality requires us at a minimum to do no harm to others.

Simplicity

The third criterion says that for any two theories that are equally universal and consistent, the one to be preferred is the one that is more *simple*. For one theory to be simpler than another does not necessarily mean that it is less complicated. Rather, for one theory to be simpler than another means that it uses fewer items in its explanations. For example, suppose that the members of some primitive tribe of people still believe that mental illness is due to possession by the devil. Now suppose a team of scientists tries to convince them that such illnesses are caused by chemical imbalances in the brain. They administer drugs to mentally ill people and, lo and behold, these people begin to behave normally. They are cured. The chief of the tribe may still claim that devils cause the illness by caus- ing the chemical imbalance, and that the drugs chase off the devil by restoring the necessary balance of chemicals.

He may say that, but he too would not get an article to that effect published in a reputable scientific journal. Devils are unnecessary. Chemical imbalances are enough. We do not need both of them when one will do the job. In philosophy we also prefer theories which contain fewer entities. For example, a materialist theory of the mind may have trouble explaining some facts, such as how con- sciousness can be produced by the brain. However, it does have the benefit of being simpler, of explaining human beings solely in terms of matter, not matter plus some sort of nonmaterial mind.

Many times in philosophy we will find ourselves unable to decide which the- ory is to be preferred over another, even after applying these criteria. This is because one theory may be superior according to some criteria, but not others. Even when this happens, however, understanding these criteria will help us to understand what remains to be done for a theory to be adequate. In this way, the process of selecting one theory over another may be seen to be a matter of reason, not simply a matter of preference. The best theory, the one that it is most reasonable to adopt, is the one which explains the most, is the most consistent with the facts and other theories, and requires the fewest types of entities to do its job.

Descriptive and Normative Theories

One important consideration to keep in mind as you judge the adequacy of theories of human nature is the distinction between descriptive and normative theories. **Descriptive theories,** as the name suggests, are primarily concerned with describing and explain what human nature *is*. Such theories place great emphasis on facts, and are often based on a scientific foundation. Other theories are **normative theories.** They are concerned more with what human beings can be, even *ought to be,* than with what we are. Often, theories based on religious and philosophical beliefs include a great deal of discussion of how to develop our natures to their fullest.

It would be convenient if we could say that science tells us what we are while philosophy and religion tell us what we ought to be. In this way we neatly blend scientifically based theories of human nature with religious and philo- sophical ones. The truth of the matter is not so simple, however. Each theory contains both descriptive and normative elements, though with different degrees of emphasis on one element or the other. In practice, this means that sometimes your evaluation will have to focus on the adequacy of factual evi- dence presented. At other times it will be directed toward the goals set by the theory, the achievement of which the author believes to be required for a full, rich, human life.

The Structure of This Text

Each chapter of this text has the following structure. First there is an *Introduction*, which discusses briefly the life and times of the author and a brief orientation to the ideas to follow. Next is a section called *Worldview*. Here the basic beliefs about reality and knowledge accepted by the author are examined. Also discussed here briefly are the contributions of some of those who have had a significant influence in shaping these beliefs. This is an important section since very often general beliefs about knowledge and reality heavily influence the author's theory of human nature. The third section is called *Human Nature*, and it is here that the core question of human nature is answered. Then the consequences of holding the particular view of human nature are examined in the next section called *Consequences.* Some of the consequences of adopting the recommended view of human nature include the degree of freedom allowed by the view, the type of ethical principles it allows, its idea of the good life, the type of society with which it is most compatible, whether or not it allows for the existence of God and life after death, and what it has to say about differences between male and female human natures. The last section of each chapter is called *Readings.* Here will be found extensive original readings of the authors discussed in the chapter.

The *Human Nature* Website

No textbook on such a large, complex issue as human nature can contain enough material to suit everyone. Of necessity, many important authors, issues, and perspectives had to be excluded. To partially compensate for this, however, a website has been established to supplement the text. In it you will find discussions of such issues as the influence of Socrates and the Presocratic philosophers on Plato; the contribution of Arab and Jewish philosophers during the medieval period, feminist perspectives on human nature, and African concepts of human nature. In addition, contemporary topics of importance to our investigations are surveyed, such as the nature of ethical theories, the issue of freedom and determinism, and the possibility of immortality—among others.

There you will also find possible exam questions, bibliographical material, and a mini-course on critical thinking. The website will be updated as needed. Your suggestions for additions and corrections are most welcome. You may forward them to me at my email address: wall@emmanuel.edu.

Part 2

Theories of Human Nature

Chapter 1

Ancient Asian Philosophers: The Buddha and Confucius

Most of the theories on human nature to be found in this text have been constructed by Western thinkers. Yet our search for an understanding of human nature begins by examining the views of two of the most influential Eastern thinkers who ever lived. One is the Indian philosopher Siddhartha Gautama, known as the **Buddha;** the other is the extremely influential Chinese moral philosopher, K'ung Fu-tzu, known as **Confucius.** The teachings of these men pre-date the earliest Western philosophers that we are to examine. Sometimes what they have to say about human nature is similar to their early Western counterparts, but often it is quite different. This is a benefit for us, since the contrasts between Eastern and Western views will help us better to understand each.

One of the ways in which Eastern thought differs is in its failure to maintain the sharp distinction between religion and philosophy that is usually found in Western thought. Comments about God and heaven, for example, are often intermingled with those about nature and consciousness and other "secular" notions. In fact, later versions of Buddhism are more often than not thought of as religions. Despite this difference, the title of this chapter refers to both men as philosophers, since their essential teachings are based on human experience and reason more than on divine inspiration or religious teachings.

Another difference is that Eastern philosophers seldom present arguments for their views, preferring instead simply to offer advice and guidelines for how to live, allowing the listener the choice to accept their words or not. This is because their teachings are based on their personal experiences, which were profound and entirely convincing to them and their followers. They viewed their task to be the passing on of this acquired wisdom to all who had ears to hear.

Siddhartha Gautama, the Buddha

Introduction

We begin this chapter by discussing how the Buddha answers the broad question of human nature. While the Buddha now is understood by some religious Buddhists to be a divine being, the historical Buddha was Siddartha Gautama. It is a matter of some uncertainty just when he lived, though his dates are usually given as around 560–480 B.C.E. He was born in northeast India, in what is currently Nepal. His father was a wealthy prince. The story of his birth and life is filled with more myth than fact. One account has it that his birth was miraculous. His mother dreamed that she was approached by a white elephant carrying a lotus flower. The elephant entered her side. This dream was interpreted by the court priests to mean that she had conceived a son who would be a famous teacher. Because of this she named him "Siddartha," which means "wish fulfilling." She died one week after his birth.

Because there was a prophecy that his son would suffer from the knowledge of human misery, Siddartha's father tried to protect him from exposure to such misery. He kept Siddartha confined to the palace and to a princely life of luxury. He married and was expected to succeed his father as ruler of the region. Instead, he grew restless and wandered at night into the surrounding city with his servant. What he found there was the other side to life from which he had been protected for his first thirty years—the suffering and misery and death of ordinary people. He was so moved by the revelation that the ultimate end of life was misery and death, that he renounced his position of wealth and status and began a seven-year quest for wisdom and salvation. He wandered through India seeking out and studying with teachers of many sorts, until he finally adopted the ascetic life as his answer to the existence of human misery.

Asceticism is the practice of denial. Ascetics deny their bodily desires and pleasures in order to overcome them, to be stronger than them, to control them. Often asceticism is coupled with meditation and prayer and withdrawal from ordinary life. For many years Siddartha became a monk and practiced an extreme form of asceticism, nearly starving himself to death. Finally he realized that neither his former life of self-indulgence nor this opposite extreme of self-denial was the way to live one's life. Instead, he searched for a "middle way." One day at the age of thirty-five he is said to have rested under a large tree, later called a Bodi tree, a tree of wisdom. He decided not to move until he had either found the wisdom that he searched for or he died. For forty-nine days he meditated under that tree, until finally he had his "awakening." The meaning of the term "Buddha" is "the one who woke up." His enlightenment, gained through deep meditation, gave him both insight into the nature of reality, including the nature of human beings, and a practice whereby this knowledge could be used to escape suffering. For the next forty-five years he taught others this way to live and gained many followers.[1]

Worldview

The teachings of the Buddha are best seen against the background of some of the themes of Indian religion that existed at his time, especially some of the foundational ideas of the ancient Indian religion, **Hinduism.** While Hinduism did not develop fully until the first century B.C.E., its seeds were sown two thousand years earlier, and its roots began to take hold in about 1500 B.C.E., about a thousand years before the time of Siddhartha. At that time India was invaded by a group called Aryans, who probably came from the central Eurasian plain. Their language was Sanskrit and their writings included four collections of hymns, called the *Vedas,* and later commentaries on these hymns, the most influential of which were the *Upanishads.* The main ideas found in the dialogues called the *Upanishads* are those of brahman, atman, moksha, samsara, and karma. Since the Buddha's views of the true way to live presupposed these ideas, and often were formulated in direct odds with some of them, it is important to understand their meaning.

The Influence of Hinduism

The **brahman**, referred to in the *Vedas* as "that one thing," is the Hindu concept of absolute reality. Brahman is not a particular sort of thing; it is not even a god in the personal sense. It is perhaps best thought of as the self-existent, unchanging, eternal, cosmic consciousness or world spirit. It is the supreme being upon which every creature, every particular thing, is dependent. Individuals are dependent upon brahman in two senses. First, they were created by brahman. One myth used in the *Upanishads* to explain creation refers to brahman's loneliness and desire. Brahman was the only being; it was alone and lonely and wanted companionship. So it breathed forth from itself the universe and all of its creatures.

If all particular, concrete things are dependent on brahman for their creation, they are also dependent on this supreme being for their continued existence. As the hair growing on the head of a person is dependent upon that person for its life and being, so all creation is dependent upon brahman for its reality. In fact, particular beings are themselves merely various forms of brahman, as clay figures are all various forms of clay. In this way there is no separation of brahman and the world, but the fleeting and transitory things of the world all reflect in their own way the underlying permanent reality of brahman. In addition, since all particular beings are just various partial manifestations of brahman, all creatures are united as just so many forms of the same underlying reality. All creatures are connected both to each other and to the ultimate source or ground of being. Brahman is thus at once a transcendent being, a being beyond the particular beings of this world, and an imminent being, a being within this world.

In addition to this concept of reality, early Hindu thought also had much to say about human nature. The Hindu concept of **atman** is the concept of the self or soul. This is not the personal, day-to-day self with which we are all familiar. It is not our bodies or our social selves; it is not even our psychological selves, which we experience as the collection of all of our thoughts and feelings and memories and so on. Instead, it is a deeper self within each of us, a spiritual, non-physical self. *Reading 1,* a selection from the *Upanishads,* describes the Hindu concept of self as permanent, unchanging, and even infinite. It is a self that may be known only through a long process of ascetic discipline, withdrawal from the world, and deep meditation. To describe atman in this way makes it appear like brahman itself. In fact, one of the leading themes of the *Upanishads* is that atman is identical with brahman. If this is so, then brahman may be known not only through studying the wisdom found in holy books and that possessed by great teachers, but also through the process of coming to know our own deeper, essential selves. But how can brahman and atman be identical?

The way that this is *explained* is to understand atman as consciousness itself. Think about being conscious of an apple on the table for example, or an image of your mother's face. Usually we are aware of the object of consciousness, the apple or image, but not the activity of consciousness, let alone pure consciousness itself. This consciousness is the self behind the scenes of ordinary consciousness, the entity that always escapes detection since we are aware of it only as it is focused on particular objects. If brahman is understood to be mind, or the consciousness of the world, then atman may be understood as a portion of this mind of consciousness within each of us. As the water scooped from a lake in a bucket is the same as the water in the lake, so we are at our very core all identical with brahman. Our essential human nature is itself divine. In coming to know ourselves we not so much come to *know* brahman, but actually come to *realize* brahman.

The way that we *experience* the identity of atman and brahman is through deep meditation which takes us through various **levels of consciousness.** In addition to waking consciousness, there is the deeper level of dream consciousness. Beyond this lies dreamless sleep consciousness, which contains no objects. Finally, there is the deepest level of meditative consciousness, where the individual seems to be absorbed into absolute reality. Here is where atman and brahman are experienced as identical, as one in the sea of consciousness; a consciousness which contains no objects, no differentiated reality, no things. Hindus teach that the experience of this "no-thingness" is the goal of life, our highest state of being. This is because such an experience is where our liberation or salvation is to be found. To understand the nature of this liberation requires that we examine the meaning of the concepts of samsara and karma.

The doctrine of **samsara** or reincarnation was accepted by most Hindus. This is the process of life, death, and rebirth which continues eternally or until the soul gets liberated. According to the doctrine of samsara, upon the death of an individual his or her deeper self, the atman, gets reborn into a new body. While such rebirth within this world may seem to be a blessing, in truth being chained to the wheel of life is really a form of bondage. This is especially true if a person is reborn as a lower form of life than a human being. At what level of life rebirth occurs is depends upon how well or poorly a person has led his or her current life. It is determined by **karma,** the law that requires us to pay for the consequences of our deeds. If we have led a good life, we will be reborn into a higher life form, thereby increasing our chances of escape from samsara. If we have not, we are born into a lower life form, which increases our struggle for release and thus our time spent in the world of multiple finite existences. The most fortunate are those reborn as seekers of brahman and atman. Once gained, the experience of atman being united with brahman liberates us forever from the cycle of life and death and rebirth. This liberation is called **moksha.** Once liberated, we return to brahman, eternally absorbed into its supreme being.

The Buddha's Worldview

These are the underlying ideas of early Hindu religion, ideas with which Siddartha would certainly have been familiar. Many of them he absorbed into his own pathway to salvation; many he rejected and replaced with those discovered by his own experience. Chief among the many differences between Buddhism and Hinduism is the Buddha's attitude toward knowledge of ultimate reality. Ultimate reality for the Buddha, as it was for Hindus, is not the everyday reality of our commonsense world. It cannot be known through the senses, through observation. For Hindus, it is important to understand it through the mind, through reason, or through the holy books. An understanding of reality as it was expressed in the holy books was required for salvation. In these scriptures is to be found boundless speculation about things that are beyond experience, such as the origin of the universe, the nature and lives of the gods, the nature of life after liberation, and so on. Many of these accounts were clothed in complex myths which gave birth to a multitude of elaborate rituals. In addition to this mythological speculation, the early Hindus also valued abstract thinking, believing strongly that important aspects of reality could be captured in the abstract concepts of metaphysics. These concepts were the product of the mind speculating about the true nature of reality.

For the Buddha, however, mythological and metaphysical thinking distorts rather than reveals what is real. For him, reality is not describable in concepts. This is primarily because concepts divide reality into many different sorts of things, while true reality itself is one and undifferentiated. Just as containers artificially form water into various shapes and sizes, so concepts artificially divide a unified reality into what appears to be a multiplicity of beings. So the Buddha did not attempt to construct any theories—either metaphysical or epistemological. Whenever he did offer some guidance about reality and knowledge, it was always as a way to help the seeker of wisdom to *experience* reality.

Since reality is beyond ordinary knowledge and even abstract metaphysical knowledge, the only way for reality to be known is by personal experience. Reality is to be encountered in deep meditative states of consciousness; it is not to be understood by the mind. The Buddha was more concerned with practical matters than speculative ones, especially with discovering how to escape from the suffering that pervades all lives. He was not concerned, nor did he want his followers to be concerned with esoteric philosophical questions about the origin of the universe, the existence of God, the dualism of body and soul, or the nature of life after death.

While he rejected metaphysical speculation, however, he did have a sort of working definition of reality in order to construct guidelines for his followers. The basic belief of his "theory" of reality was similar in some respects to the Hindu idea. Reality is the permanent, unchanging, undifferentiated one which the Buddha had found upon his awakening or enlightenment. This is something like brahman, but a brahman stripped of all of its properties and various forms of manifestation. The other significant claim about reality is that all things in this world continually change. Nothing which can be perceived to exist in this world is permanent. All is in flux. Whatever something is for one moment, it is something else soon after. There are no unchanging forms or essences of things, only properties which come and go, combining and recombining into various combinations. One consequence of this view is that in this world of things constantly becoming something else, there is nothing permanent. If nothing is permanent, then nothing is of value in itself. If this is so, then lives based upon the pursuit of worldly goods and the pleasures they supposedly bring are doomed to failure. Another consequence of his belief in the impermanence of all beings is that we ourselves are also impermanent. The Buddhist notion of human nature is especially built upon this insight, one of the most important in all of Buddhist thought.

Human Nature

The most significant divergence from Hindu thought in the teachings of the Buddha lies in his claim that at the root of human nature there is no atman, no permanent, enduring self. Instead, there is only **anatman**, the not-self. *Reading 2* is a description of this not-self by a well-known contemporary follower of the

Buddha, the Zen Buddhist Thich Nhat Hanh. The Buddha acknowledges that we do experience our "selves" in our daily lives. He also agrees with Hindu thought that such a self is simply an ever changing collection of various elements, strung together by the continuity of mental and physical actions. Hindus think that there is a deeper self, atman, lying beneath or behind our experienced selves. This self is nonphysical, unchanging, permanent, and essentially the same in all human beings. It is what survives our deaths, only to be reborn again in yet another body, until we escape the wheel of rebirth. It may be known through study and especially through prayer, ascetic practices, and deep meditation. For the Buddha, however, there is no such self. Instead, we are merely a *collection* of our bodies and mental states—our thoughts and feelings, our desires and emotions, our memories and our perceptions—with nothing that these are states "of." If these actions and mental events are constantly changing, then our selves are constantly changing, impermanent beings.

Buddha denies the existence of atman. In doing so he denies a dualistic conception of human beings. He denied, that is, that we have a soul, a nonphysical self that is our essential self. This denial is also a denial of what is sometimes called **essentialism** with respect to human nature. Essentialism is the view that there is a common essence or nature shared by all human beings. Instead of being permanent, nonphysical "things," the Buddha believed that our selves are not things at all, but rather unique mental and physical processes of becoming. During this process we create the sorts of beings that we are to become. To say that we are unique combinations of mental and physical elements does not mean that there are no common factors shared by all human beings. In fact, the basic condition of all human beings is suffering. This is what is natural, this is what is common to all, this is what is the lot of all human beings. This is human nature as it is. This is what the young Buddha, despite his protective environment, discovered life to be at its root.

The primary purpose of the Buddha in rejecting the doctrine of atman seems to have been practical more than metaphysical. He wanted to warn each of his followers of the dangers of becoming too attached to their own self, with all of its fleeting desires and worldly concerns. In denying a self, however, there remained for him a serious problem. Buddha accepted the doctrine of samsara, but without the doctrine of a self as a soul it seems difficult to explain what it is that gets reborn. If we are just a collection of various elements, and if in our next life there is a different collection, then it would appear that it is not "me" that gets reborn but someone else. Moreover, Buddha also accepts from Hindu thought the idea of karma, the belief that our actions have consequences for which we remain responsible over our entire series of lifetimes. But if it is not "me" that goes from one life to another, then how can "I" be said to have moral responsibly in the next life for the good and evil actions performed in this one?

The Buddha used various metaphors to explain both the continued identity of a person and responsibility in the next life for his or her actions in this life. One of these is of a candle passing on its flame to another candle, thus creating the same flame in different candles. The flame is not the soul, however, while the candle is the body, as Hindus taught. Rather, the flame is karma itself, while the candle is a new self, a new combination of bodily actions and mental events. The Buddha reversed the order of explanation, and simply took it as a given that our moral responsibility, our karma remains from one life to another. This is what explains the continuity of life, not sameness of self or soul. For me to get reincarnated is for a new body with new mental states to begin to exist with the karma of my former self. As usual, the Buddha was not as interested in rational consistency as he was in practical efficacy. He wanted to stress the importance of living the sort of life that would create good karma so that a person might escape this world of suffering.

Consequences

Freedom

The question of freedom for both Hindus and the Buddha has not so much to do with our freedom *to* choose and to perform certain actions, but rather with freedom *from* the human condition. For Hindus, we human beings are in bondage to the wheel of birth, death, and rebirth. While this is true also for the Buddha, the fact that we are prisoners of human suffering during these lives is what interested him most. This suffering is the result of natural causal processes which inevitably lead to sickness, death, and other sorts of human misery. It is also the result of a moral process, karma, the requirement that we must be held responsible for our deeds from one lifetime to another. A morally bad life not only increases suffering in this lifetime, but also in the next. It does this by prolonging the cycle of life, death, and rebirth at a lower, more painful level of existence. A morally good life, on the other hand, places us in a position to escape from our bondage. But what is a morally good life and how is escape possible?

Ethics

Ethics is the study of morality. It focuses on two central areas. One, called **theory of obligation,** concerns how to tell right from wrong. Many philosophers today focus on this area of ethics. The other, called **value theory,** is about what is truly valuable in itself. It is an examination of what constitutes moral goodness and is especially an examination of what counts as the **good life,** the life of happiness. The Buddha did not develop a set of rules defining right and wrong behaviors. In general, however, he thought of wrong actions as those which cause suffering to oneself or others. A principle like "Do no harm," might be his guide in deciding between right and wrong. Some of his advice about leading a morally good life may be found in *Reading 3.* More important to him than formulating elaborate moral rules was the clarification of the good life, a life in which following moral rules was simply one element. In particular, he was concerned to formulate general guidelines to direct his followers along the path that leads to escape from suffering, to liberation and happiness. Among the most important of these guidelines are what the Buddha called the **Four Noble Truths.** *Reading 4* contains two of his sermons. In the first sermon he declares that the four noble truths are:

1. A necessary part of human existence is suffering (*duhkha*).

2. Suffering is caused by ignorant craving (*trishna*).

3. Suffering may be rooted out by overcoming desire.

4. Following the Eightfold Path is the way to overcome desire.

The first of these truths informs us of the human condition that is common to all—we all suffer. In addition to the suffering caused by disease, injury, and old age, about which we can do little, there is another form of suffering about which we can do a great deal. This is the suffering caused by loss, and truth (2) tells us that this suffering is caused by ourselves. It is our ignorant craving, our desire that is undirected and undisciplined by knowledge, that causes this type of suffering. Our greed, our possessiveness, and our egocentric perspective on life are what lead to this type of suffering that lies at the root of our unhappiness. We want things. When we do not get them or when they prove to be unsatisfying, as they always do, we become unhappy; we suffer. To avoid this suffering truth (3) prescribes a difficult course of action—it tells us to stop wanting. It tells us that the best way to deal with the inescapable pain and suffering of life is to detach ourselves from our desires, especially our desires to hold on to things that we believe will make us happy. We desire things for the pleasure and status they bring; we desire to retain our youth and our health; we crave wealth and fame; we desperately want to establish and maintain relationships with other people— all the while believing that doing so will make us happy. But these transitory things make us happy only for fleeting moments. They inevitably fall away from us, causing pain and suffering and unhappiness.

The secret to happiness is not to get what we want—since these impermanent things, even if achieved, will surely be lost. It is, rather, not to want them in the first place. Once we rid ourselves of our desires for these ever changing things and states of being we are ready to find true happiness. Truth (4) states that ridding ourselves of our desires for the fleeting things of life may be achieved by following what Buddhists call the **Noble Eightfold Path.** The "Fire Sermon" found in *Reading 4* describes this path, which is the closest thing to a positive ethic found in the Buddha's teaching, as follows:

1. Right Views (free from superstition or delusion)

2. Right Aspirations (high, worthy of the intelligent man)

3. Right Speech (kind, open, truthful)

4. Right Conduct (peaceful, honest, pure)

5. Right Livelihood (harming or endangering no living thing)

6. Right Effort (in self-training and self-control)

7. Right Mindfulness (the active, aware mind)

8. Right Rapture (in deep meditation on the realities of life)

The first two steps involve understanding the Buddhist way of detachment; the next three have to do with the moral life; and the last three with preparing oneself for, and entering into, deep meditative states. It should be noted that for Buddhists who are not monks, only the first five requirements are recommended. The hope is that in later lives the laity who follow these five steps will become monks capable of moving on to higher levels of existence. For monks who practice asceticism and meditation, however, all eight steps must be followed if suffering is to be escaped.

It is in deep meditation that our salvation lies. It is here that the "awakening" occurs; it is here that we become enlightened. It is here that we find the ultimate goal of life for the Buddhist. As moksha is the name that Hindus have for the liberating experience of oneness with reality, the enlightened state of the Buddhists is called **nirvana.** Nirvana is not a place, like "heaven," nor a god or anything divine. It is a deep meditative state of consciousness in which the everyday world is experienced for what it really is, mere illusion. While the world is ordinarily understood by us to contain a multiplicity of things, and to contain our selves as separate from these things and from other selves, from the enlightened perspective these are all merely appearances of a deeper reality. The experience of this deeper reality is an experience of the oneness of all Being. What appear to be distinct bits of reality, things and selves, are as drops in the ocean of Being, the one and undivided reality.

In the deepest meditation we are aware only of consciousness itself, not any objects of consciousness. There is nothing experienced but pure consciousness itself. Things disappear; even our so-called selves disappear, even our mental states disappear. We experience no-self, no-thing, no psychological states, only pure consciousness itself. It is at once the pure consciousness of all reality and of no-things, or nothingness. As a result of this experience we realize that there is no self and that the world is merely a world of appearances. It is especially this realization that frees us from wanting and thus from suffering. If there is no self and if the world is an illusion, then there is no point to want things for ourselves, and thus no pain when such wants prove futile.

Here in this deep meditative state is where complete detachment from desire is achieved; here in this deep meditative state is where release from samsara is to be found and where suffering is finally conquered. This is the good life, the fulfillment of human nature at it highest level. It requires that we understand our life to be a continuing series of lives which are bound together by the ties of karma and which point toward the experience of nirvana. In this "awakening" experience we find at once our longed-for release from suffering and our highest bliss.

Society

The philosophical Buddhism of Siddhartha Gautama does not obviously prefer one type of society over another. With its stress on the individual and withdrawal from life, it has little to say about how society should be structured. For the Buddha, enlightenment is found by the individual, each for themselves. The group is not essential to happiness. While there was indifference to political and social structures, however, there was no indifference to their degree of **justice.** The India of Siddhartha's time had established a rigid caste system. This system had originally divided people into four classes. There were rulers, who were the priestly class, warriors, merchants, and slaves. These four groups later grew in number and division, with each caste having more or less of the goods and privileges of society. Members of lower castes were discriminated against quite harshly. There were even groups of people who fit into no caste, called "untouchables." They were perceived as less than human and treated with the greatest disdain. The Buddha enraged even many of his own followers when he accepted an untouchable as a follower. For the Buddha, however, this was an action which assumed that all people are equal in the deepest sense, in their natural ability to suffer and to escape from suffering.

God and Immortality

It is clear that the Buddha found no place for a God or a plurality of gods in his teaching. It was not so much that he denied the existence of divine powers, but more that he found them to be irrelevant to his concerns. As with everything else in this life, he believed that the gods, too, are changing, impermanent instances of becoming. Individuals must journey their own paths in life toward nirvana, without the help of the gods. The teachings of the original Buddha amounted to a *philosophy* of life, but his ideas were later incorporated by many of his followers into religious systems. Some later religious interpretations of Buddhist thought have even made the Buddha himself an object of divine worship. If the teachings of Siddhartha are to be classified as a religion at all, however, then they would surely be a religion without a God.

The question of immortality was not addressed completely by the Buddha, especially the question of what happens after the death of someone who attains nirvana. This should not be surprising, since he had little interest in such speculations. Hindu thought had two possible interpretations of what happens at death. For those who have not attained moksha there is the inevitable return of their soul to another birth, into another body. If they had made progress toward moksha, this accumulated progress remained with them, enabling them to come even closer to brahman in their next life. For those who have realized the brahman through meditation, however, upon their death there is once and for all escape from samsara and the eternal bliss of the absorption of their soul into the cosmic consciousness called brahman.

While the Buddha would agree that those who do not reach nirvana do not escape from suffering and samsara, he seems to have left open the question of what happens to those who have. Does one escape suffering in *this* life only to be reborn again into a new life where desire must again be conquered? If so, does reaching enlightenment in this life carry over to the next? Or does the attainment of nirvana free the awakened one once and for all from future lives, from samsara? If this is so, does that mean he ceases to exist altogether, or is nirvana a final transcendence of the space-time world into another timeless and blissful form of existence?

Certainly some later Buddhists interpreted nirvana in this latter way, even speaking of a sort of "nirvana world" in contrast to this world. The Buddha himself seems to have been unconcerned with these questions, however, and this for three reasons. First, what happens to an enlightened one after his or her death cannot be known. Second, and perhaps more importantly, such questions reveal attachments to one's own much desired happiness. Therefore, they are themselves obstacles to the very attainment of detachment. Third, whether there is escape from suffering and the attainment of bliss only in this life, or such benefits exist also in future rebirths or even eternally in a transcendent world, all of these possibilities are blessings. So why worry about which is true? Perhaps it is best to understand the Buddha's teaching to be that this world and the nirvana world are merely different perspectives of one and the same thing.

Gender

Since probably about half of the readers of this text are female and half male, it is important to discuss whether or not the concept of human nature developed by each author applies equally well to males and females. Obviously there are biological differences between men and women, but are there differences in rational, spiritual, psychological, moral, social, or other natural tendencies that are sufficiently significant to say that men and women are different by nature? In most societies until fairly recently, women were not given access to the same educational, financial, political, and social opportunities and resources as men. This is why, again until fairly recently, the vast majority of views about human nature have been constructed by men. In examining what these men have to say about human nature, keep in mind what they have to say about the natural abilities and roles of women, and why they claim what they do. In a later chapter contemporary women philosophers and scientists will have the opportunity to respond and to develop their own views.

Generally speaking, the Asian view of women before Buddhism was that women were inferior to men, and that their chief role in life was to serve men. This was certainly the view to be found in early Hinduism and in Confucianism as well. Breaking from this tradition, The Buddha seemed to treat men and women as equals. They were certainly equal, he believed, in their ability to suffer and in their participation in samsara. Women were also assumed by the Buddha to have the necessary intelligence, motivation, and discipline to become followers of his. The Buddha thought that not only monks, but also nuns were capable of following the eightfold path to salvation. While women had essentially the same nature as men, however, their sexual natures were a concern for the Buddha. Because women were considered to be the source of sexual pleasure, and because pleasures of all sorts, and sexual pleasures in particular, were to be avoided, their bodies were seen as morally inferior to those of men.

Readings

1. The Hindu Concept of Self

Editor's Note: The following is a conversation between a young man, Nachiketas, and the god of death. It is found in the Katha Upanishad.

PART 1

DEATH: Choose now the third boon.

NACHIKETAS: When a man dies, this doubt arises: some say "he is" and some say "he is not." Teach me the truth.

DEATH: Even the gods had this doubt in times of old; for mysterious is the law of life and death. Ask for another boon. Release me from this.

NACHIKETAS: This doubt indeed arose even to the gods, and you say, O Death, that it is difficult to understand; but no greater teacher than you can explain it, and there is no other boon so great as this.

DEATH: Take horses and gold and cattle and elephants; choose sons and grandsons that shall

From The Upanishads, *trans. by Juan Mascaro. (New York: Penguin, 1965), pp. 56–66. Reprinted with permission.*

live a hundred years. Have vast expanses of land, and live as many years as you desire.

Or choose another gift that you think equal to this, and enjoy it with wealth and long life. Be a ruler of this vast earth. I will grant you all your desires.

Ask for any wishes in the world of mortals, however hard to obtain. To attend on you I will give you fair maidens with chariots and musical instruments. But ask me not, Nachiketas, the secrets of death.

NACHIKETAS: All these pleasures pass away, O End of all! They weaken the power of life. And indeed how short is all life! Keep thy horses and dancing and singing.

Man cannot be satisfied with wealth. Shall we enjoy wealth with you in sight? Shall we live whilst you are in power? I can only ask for the boon I have asked.

When a mortal here on earth has felt his own immortality, could he wish for a long life of pleasures, for the lust of deceitful beauty?

Solve then the doubt as to the great beyond. Grant me the gift that unveils the mystery. This is the only gift Nachiketas can ask.

PART 2

DEATH: There is the path of joy, and there is the path of pleasure. Both attract the soul. Who follows the first comes to good; who follows pleasure reaches not the End.

The two paths lie in front of man. Pondering on them, the wise man chooses the path of joy; the fool takes the path of pleasure.

You have pondered, Nachiketas, on pleasures and you have rejected them. You have not accepted that chain of possessions wherewith men bind themselves and beneath which they sink.

There is the path of wisdom and the path of ignorance. They are far apart and lead to different ends. You are, Nachiketas, a follower of the path of wisdom: many pleasures tempt you not.

Abiding in the midst of ignorance, thinking themselves wise and learned fools go aimlessly hither and thither, like blind led by the blind.

What lies beyond life shines not to those who are childish, or careless, or deluded by wealth.

"This is the only world: there is no other," they say; and thus they go from death to death.

Not many hear of him; and of those not many reach him. Wonderful is he who can teach about him; and wise is he who can be taught. Wonderful is he who knows him when taught.

He cannot be taught by one who has not reached him; and he cannot be reached by much thinking. The way to him is through a Teacher who has seen him: He is higher than the highest thoughts, in truth above all thought.

This sacred knowledge is not attained by reasoning; but it can be given by a true Teacher. As your purpose is steady you have found him. May I find another pupil like you.

I know that treasures pass away and that the Eternal is not reached by the transient. I have thus laid the fire of sacrifice of Nachiketas, and by burning in it the transient I have reached the Eternal.

Before your eyes have been spread, Nachiketas, the fulfillment of all desire, the dominion of the world, the eternal reward of ritual, the shore where there is no fear, the greatness of fame and boundless spaces. With strength and wisdom you have renounced them all.

When the wise rests his mind in contemplation on our God beyond time, who invisibly dwells in the mystery of things and in the heart of man, then he rises above pleasures and sorrow.

When a man has heard and has understood and, finding the essence, reaches the Inmost, then he finds joy in the Source of joy. Nachiketas is a house open for thy Atman, thy God.

NACHIKETAS: Tell me what you see beyond right and wrong, beyond what is done or not done, beyond past and future.

DEATH: I will tell you the Word that all the *Vedas* glorify, all self-sacrifice expresses, all sacred studies and holy life seek. That Word is OM.

That Word is the everlasting Brahman: that Word is the highest End. When that sacred Word is known, all longings are fulfilled.

It is the supreme means of salvation: it is the help supreme. When that great Word is known, one is great in the heaven of Brahman.

Atman, the Spirit of vision, is never born and never dies. Before him there was nothing, and he is ONE for evermore. Never-born and eternal, beyond times gone or to come, he does not die when the body dies.

If the slayer thinks that he kills, and if the slain thinks that he dies, neither knows the ways of truth. The Eternal in man cannot kill: the Eternal in man cannot die.

Concealed in the heart of all beings is the Atman, the Spirit, the Self; smaller than the smallest atom, greater than the vast spaces. The man who surrenders his human will leaves sorrows behind, and beholds the glory of the Atman by the grace of the Creator.

Resting, he wanders afar; sleeping, he goes everywhere. Who else but my Self can know that God of joy and of sorrows?

When the wise realize the omnipresent Spirit, who rests invisible in the visible and permanent in the impermanent, then they go beyond sorrow.

Not through much learning is the Atman reached, not through the intellect and sacred teaching. It is reached by the chosen of him—because they choose him. To his chosen the Atman reveals his glory.

Not even through deep knowledge can the Atman be reached, unless evil ways are abandoned, and there is rest in the senses, concentration in the mind and peace in one's heart.

Who knows in truth where he is? The majesty of his power carries away priests and warriors, and death itself is carried away.

PART 3

In the secret high place of the heart there are two beings who drink the wine of life in the world of truth. Those who know Brahman, those who keep the five sacred fires and those who light the threefold fire of Nachiketas call them "light" and "shade."

May we light the sacred fire of Nachiketas, the bridge to cross to the other shore where there is no fear, the supreme everlasting Spirit!

Know the Atman as Lord of a chariot; and the body as the chariot itself. Know that reason is the charioteer; and the mind indeed is the reins.

The horses, they say, are the senses; and their paths are the objects of sense. When the soul becomes one with the mind and the senses he is called "one who has joys and sorrows."

He who has not right understanding and whose mind is never steady is not the ruler of his life, like a bad driver with wild horses.

But he who has right understanding and whose mind is ever steady is the ruler of his life, like a good driver with well-trained horses.

He who has not right understanding, is careless and never pure, reaches not the End of the journey; but wanders on from death to death.

But he who has understanding, is careful and ever pure, reaches the End of the journey, from which he never returns.

The man whose chariot is driven by reason, who watches and holds the reins of his mind, reaches the End of the journey, the supreme everlasting Spirit.

Beyond the senses are their objects, and beyond the objects is the mind. Beyond the mind is pure reason, and beyond reason is the Spirit in man.

Beyond the Spirit in man is the Spirit of the universe, and beyond is Purusha, the Spirit Supreme. Nothing is beyond Purusha: He is the End of the path.

The light of the Atman, the Spirit, is invisible, concealed in all beings. It is seen by the seers of the subtle, when their vision is keen and is clear.

The wise should surrender speech in mind, mind in the knowing self, the knowing self in the Spirit of the universe, and the Spirit of the universe in the Spirit of peace.

Awake, arise! Strive for the Highest, and be in the Light! Sages say the path is narrow and difficult to tread, narrow as the edge of a razor.

The Atman is beyond sound and form, without touch and taste and perfume. It is eternal, unchangeable, and without beginning or end: indeed above reasoning. When consciousness of the Atman manifests itself, man becomes free from the jaws of death.

The wise who can learn and can teach this ancient story of Nachiketas, taught by Yama, the god of death, finds glory in the world of Brahman. . . .

PART 5

. . . I will now speak to you of the mystery of the eternal Brahman; and of what happens to the soul after death.

The soul may go to the womb of a mother and thus obtain a new body. It even may go into trees or plants, according to its previous wisdom and work.

There is a Spirit who is awake in our sleep and creates the wonder of dreams. He is Brahman, the Spirit of Light. Who in truth is called the Immortal. All the worlds rest on that Spirit and beyond him no one can go:

This in truth is That.

PART 6

. . . The whole universe comes from him and his life burns through the whole universe. In his power is the majesty of thunder. Those who know him have found immortality.

From fear of him fire burns, and from fear of him the sun shines. From fear of him the clouds and the winds, and death itself, move on their way.

If one sees him in this life before the body passes away, one is free from bondage; but if not, one is born and dies again in new worlds and new creations.

Brahman is seen in a pure soul as in a mirror clear, and also in the Creator's heaven as clear as light; but in the land of shades as remembrance of dreams, and in the world of spirits as reflections in trembling waters.

When the wise man knows that the material senses come not from the Spirit and that their waking and sleeping belong to their own nature, then he grieves no more.

Beyond the senses is the mind, and beyond mind is reason, its essence. Beyond reason is the Spirit in man, and beyond this is the Spirit of the universe, the evolver of all.

And beyond is Purusha, all-pervading, beyond definitions. When a mortal knows him, he attains liberation and reaches immortality.

His form is not in the field of vision: no one sees him with mortal eyes. He is seen by a pure heart and by a mind and thoughts that are pure. Those who know him attain life immortal.

When the five senses and the mind are still, and reason itself rests in silence, then begins the Path supreme.

This calm steadiness of the senses is called Yoga. Then one should become watchful, because Yoga comes and goes.

Words and thoughts cannot reach him and he cannot be seen by the eye. How can he then be perceived except by him who says "He is"?

In the faith of "He is" his existence must be perceived, and he must be perceived in his essence. When he is perceived as "He is," then shines forth the revelation of his essence.

When all desires that cling to the heart are surrendered, then a mortal becomes immortal, and even in this world he is one with Brahman.

When all the ties that bind the heart are unloosened, then a mortal becomes immortal. This is the sacred teaching.

One hundred and one subtle ways come from the heart. One of them rises to the crown of the head. This is the way that leads to immortality; the others lead to different ends. Always dwelling within all beings is the Atman, the Purusha, the Self, a little flame in the heart. Let one with steadiness withdraw him from the body even as an inner stem is withdrawn from its sheath. Know this pare immortal light; know in truth this pure immortal light.

And Nachiketas learnt the supreme wisdom taught by the god of after-life, and he learnt the whole teaching of inner-union, of Yoga. Then he reached Brahman, the Spirit Supreme, and became immortal and pure. So in truth will anyone who knows his Atman, his higher Self.

2. The Buddhist Concept of Not-Self

THE BUDDHIST REVOLUTION

BUDDHISM WAS BORN TOWARD THE end of the sixth century B.C.E. The word "Buddhism" comes from the Sanskrit verb *Budh*, which in the Vedic scriptures foremostly signifies "to know," then "to wake up." The one who *knows*, the one who *wakes up*, is called a buddha. The Chinese have translated the word "buddha" as "an awakened person." *Buddhism is, therefore, a doctrine of awakening, a doctrine of insight and understanding.*

But the Buddha made it known from the beginning that this awakening, this understanding, can only be acquired by the practice of the "Way" and not by studies or speculation. Liberation, in Buddhism, comes about through understanding and not by grace or merit.

The rise of Buddhism in India must be considered a new vision of humanity and life. This vision was expounded first as a reaction against the Brahmanic practices and beliefs that dominated the society of the time. What was this society? From the intellectual standpoint, the authority of the Brahmanic tradition dominated all: the Vedic revelation, the divine supremacy of Brahma, and the miraculous power of sacrifice were the three fundamentals one could not dispute. From the standpoint of belief, Brahma, Vishnu, and Shiva were the object of all the schools. From the philosophical standpoint, the thoughts of the Vedas and Upanishads were the basis of all philosophical concepts. Sankhya, Yoga, and the six philosophical schools were born and developed on this basis. Buddhism was thoroughly opposed to absolute Vedic authority and to all the points of view stemming from it. From the standpoint of belief, Buddhism rejected all deisms and all forms of sacrifice. From the social point of view, Buddhism combated the caste system, accepting untouchables in the order at the same level as a king. (Buddha, having met an untouchable who carried night soil, brought him to the edge of the river to wash him, then accepted him into the Buddhist community, despite the extreme protests of the others.) From the intellectual standpoint, it rigorously rejected the notion of a Self *(Atman)*, which is the very heart of Brahmanism.

One can see how Buddha reacted against the currents of thought of his time by reading, for example, the *Brahmajalasutta*, which is found in the *Dighanikaya (Long Discourses)*. His opposition to Brahmanic thought must be regarded primarily as a reaction, a revolt, rather than as an effort to present the Buddhist point of view. It does not mean that all the thoughts contained in the Vedas and Upanishads are erroneous or contrary to truth. This opposition is a clap of thunder aimed at giving a great shock in order to change the customs, manners, and modes of thought that had brought society to an impasse.

Because Brahmanism considers the concept of Atman (Self) as a basis for its methodology and its ontology, Buddha posited the doctrine of the *Anatman* (not-self). What did he mean? *This self of which you speak, whether it is the great self or the small self, is only a concept that does not correspond to any reality.*

If we think in ontological terms, we might say the doctrine of not-self was considered by the Buddha as a truth opposing the doctrine of self, but this is not correct. If we think in methodological terms, we see immediately that the notion of not-self is an antidote aimed at liberating us from the prison of dogma. Before examining the question of truth and falsehood, it is necessary to examine the attitudes and methods. This allows us to say that the notion of not-self was born in reaction to the Brahmanic notion of the self, and not as a discovery independent of the thought of the time. It was a simple reaction that later served as the point of departure for a new understanding.

NOT-SELF

Drastic methods are frequently used in Buddhism to uproot habits and prejudices. This characteristic trait of Buddhism is manifested most energetically in Zen.

The Buddha used the notion of the not-self to upset and to destroy. Later, he used it to expound his teaching of awakening. It can thus be said that the notion of not-self is the point of departure of Buddhism.

Buddhist scriptures often speak of the "not-self" nature of all phenomena. Things do not possess a self (*Sarva dharmas nairatmya*). Nothing in itself contains an absolute identity. This means a rejection of the principle of identity, which is the basis of formal logic. According to this principle, A must be A, B must be B, and A cannot be B. The doctrine of not-self says: A is not A, B is not B, and A can be B. This is something that shocks people and invites them to reexamine themselves.

In order to understand not-self, the concept of impermanence (*anitya*) in Buddhism must also be considered. All is impermanent. Everything is in a state of perpetual change. Nothing remains the same for two consecutive *ksanas* (the shortest imaginable periods of time). It is because things transform themselves ceaselessly that they cannot maintain their identity, even during two consecutive ksanas. Not being able to fix their identity, they are not-self; that is to say, devoid of absolute identity. Not having a fixed identity, A is no longer the A of the preceding ksana; this is why one says that A is not A. Impermanence is another name for not-self. In time, things are impermanent, in space they are devoid of a fixed identity. Not only are physical phenomena impermanent and without a separate self, but the same is true of physiological phenomena, for example our body, mental phenomena, and feelings.

Many people think that anatman and anitya are the basis for a pessimistic moral doctrine. They say, "If all things are impermanent and devoid of a fixed identity, why bother to struggle so hard to obtain them?" This is a misunderstanding of the Buddha's teaching. Buddhism aims at liberation through understanding. It is therefore necessary to examine the teachings of the Buddha from the point of view of understanding, and not to take his words too literally without understanding their meaning. Impermanence and not-self are important principles that lead to deep understanding.

THINGS AND CONCEPTS

The principle of not-self brings to light the gap between things themselves and the concepts we have of them. Things are dynamic and alive, while our concepts are static. Look, for example, at a table. We have the impression that the table itself and our concept of it are identical. In reality, what we believe to be a table is only our concept. The table itself is quite different. Some notions—wood, brown, hard, three feet high, old, etc.—give rise to a concept of table in us. The table itself is always more than that. For example, a nuclear physicist will tell us that the table is a multitude of atoms whose electrons are moving like a swarm of bees, and that if we could put these atoms next to each other, the mass of matter would be smaller than one finger. This *table*, in reality, is always in transformation; in time as well as in space it is made only of *non-table* elements. It depends on these elements so much that if we were to remove them from the table, there would be nothing left.

The forest, the tree, the saw, the hammer, and the cabinetmaker are non-table elements, as are the parents of the cabinetmaker, the bread that they eat, the blacksmith who makes the hammer, and so on. If we know how to look deeply at the table, we can see the presence of all these non-table elements in it. The existence of the table demonstrates the existence of all non-table elements, in fact, of the entire universe. This idea is expressed in the Avatamsaka system of Buddhism by the notion of interbeing.

THE INTERBEING OF THINGS

Genesis in Buddhism is called interbeing. The birth, growth, and decline of things depend upon multiple causes and conditions and not just a single one. The presence of one thing (*dharma*) implies the presence of all other things. The enlightened man or woman sees each thing not as a separate entity but as a complete manifestation of reality. The twelfth-century Vietnamese Zen monk, Dao Hanh, said, "If one thing exists, everything exists, even a speck of dust. If one thing is empty, everything is empty, even the whole universe."

The doctrine of not-self aims at bringing to light the *interbeing nature of things,* and, at the same time, demonstrates to us that the concepts we have of things do not reflect and cannot convey reality. The world of concepts is not the world of reality. Conceptual knowledge is not the perfect instrument for studying truth. Words are inadequate to express the truth of ultimate reality.

THE VANITY OF METAPHYSICS

These preliminary remarks are the point of departure of Zen Buddhism. If concepts do not represent reality, then conceptual knowledge of reality can be considered erroneous. That is demonstrated many times in Buddhism. The Buddha always told his disciples not to waste their time and energy in metaphysical speculation. Whenever he was asked a metaphysical question, he remained silent. Instead, he directed his disciples toward practical efforts. Questioned one day about the problem of the infinity of the world, the Buddha said, "Whether the world is finite or infinite, limited or unlimited, the problem of your liberation remains the same." Another time he said, "Suppose a man is struck by a poisoned arrow and the doctor wishes to take out the arrow immediately. Suppose the man does not want the arrow removed until he knows who shot it, his age, his parents, and why he shot it. What would happen? If he were to wait until all these questions have been answered, the man might die first." Life is so short. It must not be spent in endless metaphysical speculation that does not bring us any closer to the truth.

But if conceptual knowledge is fallible, what other instrument should we use to grasp reality? According to Buddhism, we only reach reality through direct experience. Study and speculation are based on concepts. In conceptualizing we cut reality into small pieces that seem to be independent of one another. This manner of conceiving things is called *imaginative and discriminative knowledge (vikalpa)* according to the Vijñanavadin school of Buddhism. The faculty that directly experiences reality without passing through concepts is called *non-discriminative and non-imaginative wisdom (nirvikalpajñana).* This wisdom is the fruit of meditation. It is a direct and perfect knowledge of reality, a form of understanding in which one does not distinguish between subject and object. It cannot be conceived by the intellect nor expressed by language.

EXPERIENCE ITSELF

Suppose I invite you to join me for a cup of tea. You receive your cup, taste the tea, and then drink a little more. You seem to be enjoying it. Then you put your cup on the table and we have a conversation.

Now, suppose I ask you to describe the tea. You use your memory, your concepts, and your vocabulary to describe the sensations. You may say, "It is very good tea, the best Tieh Kuan Ying tea, manufactured in Taipei. I can still taste it in my mouth. It is very refreshing." You could express your sensation in many other ways. But these concepts and these words *describe your direct experience* of the tea; *they are not the experience itself.* Indeed, in the direct experience of the tea, you do not make the distinction that you are the subject of the experience and that the tea is its object; you do not think that the tea is the best, or the worst, of the Tieh Kuan Ying of Taipei. There is no concept or word that can frame this pure sensation resulting from experience. You can offer as many descriptions as you like, but only you have had a direct experience of the tea. When someone listens to you, she can re-create for herself certain sensations, based on experiences that she might have had, but that is all. And you yourself, when you are describing the experience, are already no longer in it. In the experience, you were one with the tea. There was no distinction between subject and object, no evaluation, and no discrimination. That pure sensation is an example of *non-discriminative wisdom,* which introduces us to the heart of reality.

3. Buddhist Ethics

Editor's Note: The Dhammapada is a work that has become part of Buddhist scriptural tradition. While its origin is unknown, it does appear to have existed in pre-Christian times. More importantly, it is purported to express the teachings of the Buddha.

CHAPTER I
THE TWIN-VERSES

1. All that we are is the result of what we have thought: it is founded on our thoughts, it is made up of our thoughts. If a man speaks or acts with an evil thought, pain follows him, as the wheel follows the foot of the ox that draws the carriage.

2. All that we are is the result of what we have thought: it is founded on our thoughts, it is made up of our thoughts. If a man speaks or acts with a pure thought, happiness follows him, like a shadow that never leaves him.

3. 'He abused me, he beat me, he defeated me, he robbed me,'—in those who harbour such thoughts hatred will never cease.

4. 'He abused me, he beat me, he defeated me, he robbed me,'—in those who do not harbour such thoughts hatred will cease.

5. For hatred does not cease by hatred at any time: hatred ceases by love, this is an old rule.

6. The world does not know that we must all come to an end here;—but those who know it, their quarrels cease at once.

7. He who lives looking for pleasures only, his senses uncontrolled, immoderate in his food, idle, and weak, Mâra (the tempter) will certainly overthrow him, as the wind throws down a weak tree.

8. He who lives without looking for pleasures, his senses well controlled, moderate in his

food, faithful and strong, him Mâra will certainly not overthrow, any more than the wind throws down a rocky mountain.

19. The thoughtless man, even if he can recite a large portion (of the law), but is not a doer of it, has no share in the priesthood, but is like a cowherd counting the cows of others.

20. The follower of the law, even if he can recite only a small portion (of the law), but, having forsaken passion and hatred and foolishness, possesses true knowledge and serenity of mind, he, caring for nothing in this world or that to come, has indeed a share in the priesthood.

CHAPTER II
ON EARNESTNESS

21. Earnestness is the path of immortality (Nirvâna), thoughtlessness the path of death. Those who are in earnest do not die, those who are thoughtless are as if dead already.

22. Those who are advanced in earnestness, having understood this clearly, delight in earnestness, and rejoice in the knowledge of the Ariyas (the elect).

23. These wise people, meditative, steady, always possessed of strong powers, attain to Nirvâna, the highest happiness.

CHAPTER IV
FLOWERS

44. Who shall overcome this earth, and the world of Yama (the lord of the departed), and the world of the gods? Who shall find out the

Selections from The Dhammapada, *as reprinted in* World Scriptures *by Kenneth Kramer (New York: Paulist Press, 1986; www.paulistpres.com), pp. 90–94. Reprinted with permission of Paulist Press.*

plainly shown path of virtue, as a clever man finds out the (right) flower?

45. The disciple will overcome the earth, and the world of Yama, and the world of the gods. The disciple will find out the plainly shown path of virtue, as a clever man finds out the (right) flower.

46. He who knows that this body is like froth, and has learnt that it is as unsubstantial as a mirage, will break the flower-pointed arrow of Mâra, and never see the king of death.

47. Death carries off a man who is gathering flowers and whose mind is distracted, as a flood carries off a sleeping village.

48. Death subdues a man who is gathering flowers, and whose mind is distracted, before he is satiated in his pleasures.

58, 59. As on a heap of rubbish cast upon the highway the lily will grow full of sweet perfume and delight, thus the disciple of the truly enlightened Buddha shines forth by his knowledge among those who are like rubbish, among the people that walk in darkness.

CHAPTER VI
THE WISE MAN

85. Few are there among men who arrive at the other shore (become Arhats); the other people here run up and down the shore.

86. But those who, when the law has been well preached to them, follow the law, will pass across the dominion of death, however difficult to overcome.

87, 88. A wise man should leave the dark state (of ordinary life), and follow the bright state (of the Bhikshu). After going from his home to a homeless state, he should in his retirement look for enjoyment where there seemed to be no enjoyment. Leaving all pleasures behind, and calling nothing his own, the wise man should purge himself from all the troubles of the mind.

CHAPTER VII
THE VENERABLE (ARHAT)

90. There is no suffering for him who has finished his journey, and abandoned grief, who has freed himself on all sides, and thrown off all fetters.

91. They depart with their thoughts well-collected, they are not happy in their abode; like swans who have left their lake, they leave their house and home.

92. Men who have no riches, who live on recognised food, who have perceived void and unconditioned freedom (Nirvâna), their path is difficult to understand, like that of birds in the air.

93. He whose appetites are stilled, who is not absorbed in enjoyment, who has perceived void and unconditioned freedom (Nirvâna), his path is difficult to understand, like that of birds in the air.

94. The gods even envy him whose senses, like horses well broken in by the driver, have been subdued, who is free from pride, and free from appetites.

95. Such a one who does his duty is tolerant like the earth, like Indra's bolt; he is like a lake without mud; no new births are in store for him.

CHAPTER X
PUNISHMENT

129. All men tremble at punishment, all men fear death; remember that you are like unto them, and do not kill, nor cause slaughter.

130. All men tremble at punishment, all men love life; remember that thou art like unto them, and do not kill, nor cause slaughter.

131. He who seeking his own happiness punishes or kills beings who also long for happiness, will not find happiness after death.

132. He who seeking his own happiness does not punish or kill beings who also long for happiness, will find happiness after death.

133. Do not speak harshly to anybody; those who are spoken to will answer thee in the same way. Angry speech is painful, blows for blows will touch thee.

134. If, like a shattered metal plate (gong), thou utter not, then thou hast reached Nirvâna; contention is not known to thee.

CHAPTER XI
OLD AGE

146. How is there laughter, how is there joy, as this world is always burning? Why do you not seek a light, ye who are surrounded by darkness?

147. Look at this dressed-up lump, covered with wounds, joined together, sickly, full of many thoughts, which has no strength, no hold!

148. This body is wasted, full of sickness, and frail; this heap of corruption breaks to pieces, life indeed ends in death.

149. Those white bones, like gourds thrown away in the autumn, what pleasure is there in looking at them?

150. After a stronghold has been made of the bones, it is covered with flesh and blood, and there dwell in it old age and death, pride and deceit.

151. The brilliant chariots of kings are destroyed, the body also approaches destruction, but the virtue of good people never approaches destruction,—thus do the good say to the good.

152. A man who has learnt little, grows old like an ox; his flesh grows, but his knowledge does not grow.

153, 154. Looking for the maker of this tabernacle, I shall have to run through a course of many births, so long as I do not find (him); and painful is birth again and again. But now, maker of the tabernacle, thou hast been seen; thou shalt not make up this tabernacle again. All thy rafters are broken, thy ridge-pole is sundered; the mind, approaching the Eternal

(visankhâra, nirvâna), has attained to the extinction of all desires.

155. Men who have not observed proper discipline, and have not gained treasure in their youth, perish like old herons in a lake without fish.

156. Men who have not observed proper discipline, and have not gained treasure in their youth, he, like broken bows, sighing after the past.

CHAPTER XII
SELF

157. If a man hold himself dear, let him watch himself carefully; during one at least out of the three watches a wise man should be watchful.

158. Let each man direct himself first to what is proper, then let him teach others; thus a wise man will not suffer.

159. If a man make himself as he teaches others to be, then, being himself well subdued, he may subdue (others); one's own self is indeed difficult to subdue.

160. Self is the lord of self, who else could be the lord? With self well subdued, a man finds a lord such as few can find.

CHAPTER XIII
THE WORLD

167. Do not follow the evil law! Do not live on in thoughtlessness! Do not follow false doctrine! Be not a friend of the world.

168. Rouse thyself! do not be idle! Follow the law of virtue! The virtuous rests in bliss in this world and in the next.

169. Follow the law of virtue; do not follow that of sin. The virtuous rests in bliss in this world and in the next.

170. Look upon the world as a bubble, look upon it as a mirage: the king of death does not see him who thus looks down upon the world.

171. Come, look at this glittering world, like unto a royal chariot; the foolish are immersed in it, but the wise do not touch it.

CHAPTER XIV
THE BUDDHA (THE AWAKENED)

179. He whose conquest is not conquered again, into whose conquest no one in this world enters, by what track can you lead him, the Awakened, the Omniscient, the trackless?

180. He whom no desire with its snares and poisons can lead astray, by what track can you lead him, the Awakened, the Omniscient, the trackless?

181. Even the gods envy those who are awakened and not forgetful, who are given to meditation, who are wise, and who delight in the repose of retirement (from the world).

182. Difficult (to obtain) is the conception of men, difficult is the life of mortals, difficult is the hearing of the True Law, difficult is the birth of the Awakened (the attainment of Buddhahood).

183. Not to commit any sin, to do good, and to purify one's mind, that is the teaching of (all) the Awakened.

184. The Awakened call patience the highest penance, long-suffering the highest Nirvâna; for he is not an anchorite (pravragita) who strikes others, he is not an ascetic (sramana) who insults others.

185. Not to blame, not to strike, to live restrained under the law, to be moderate in eating, to sleep and sit alone, and to dwell on the highest thoughts,—this is the teaching of the Awakened.

186. There is no satisfying lusts, even by a shower of gold pieces; he who knows that lusts have a short taste and cause pain, he is wise;

187. Even in heavenly pleasures he finds no satisfaction, the disciple who is fully awakened delights only in the destruction of all desires.

188. Men, driven by fear, go to many a refuge, to mountains and forests, to groves and sacred trees.

189. But that is not a safe refuge, that is not the best refuge; a man is not delivered from all pains after having gone to that refuge.

190. He who takes refuge with Buddha, the Law (Dhamma), and the Church (Sangha); he who, with clear understanding, sees the four holy truths:—

191. Viz. pain, the origin of pain, the destruction of pain, and the eightfold holy way that leads to the quieting of pain;—

192. That is the safe refuge, that is the best refuge; having gone to that refuge, a man is delivered from all pain.

193. A supernatural person (a Buddha) is not easily found, he is not born everywhere. Wherever such a sage is born, that race prospers.

CHAPTER XX
THE WAY

273. The best of ways is the eightfold; the best of truths the four words; the best of virtues passionlessness; the best of men he who has eyes to see.

274. This is the way, there is no other that leads to the purifying of intelligence. Go on this way! Everything else is the deceit of Mâra (the tempter).

275. If you go on this way, you will make an end of pain! The way was preached by me, when I had understood the removal of the thorns (in the flesh).

276. You yourself must make an effort. The Tathâgatas (Buddhas) are only preachers. The thoughtful who enter the way are freed from the bondage of Mâra.

277. 'All created things perish,' he who knows and sees this becomes passive in pain; this is the way to purity.

278. 'All created things are grief and pain,' he who knows and sees this becomes passive in pain; this is the way that leads to purity.

279. 'All forms are unreal,' he who knows and sees this becomes passive in pain; this is the way that leads to purity.

CHAPTER XXIV
THIRST

334. The thirst of a thoughtless man grows like a creeper; he runs from life to life, like a monkey seeking fruit in the forest.

348. Give up what is before, give up what is behind, give up what is in the middle, when thou goest to the other shore of existence; if thy mind is altogether free, thou wilt not again enter into birth and decay.

351. He who has reached the consummation, who does not tremble, who is without thirst and without sin, he has broken all the thorns of life: this will be his last body.

352. He who is without thirst and without affection, who understands the words and their interpretation, who knows the order of letters (those which are before and which are after), he has received his last body, he is called the great sage, the great man.

353. 'I have conquered all, I know all, in all conditions of life I am free from taint; I have left all, and through the destruction of thirst I am free; having learnt myself, whom shall I teach?'

369. O Bhikshu, empty this boat! if emptied, it will go quickly; having cut off passion and hatred, thou wilt go to Nirvâna.

370. Cut off the five (senses), leave the five, rise above the five. A Bhikshu, who has escaped from the five fetters, he is called Oghatinna, 'saved from the flood.'

371. Meditate, O Bhikshu, and be not heedless! Do not direct thy thought to what gives pleasure, that thou mayest not for thy heedlessness have to swallow the iron ball (in hell), and that thou mayest not cry out when burning, 'This is pain.'

CHAPTER XXVI
THE BRÂHMANA (ARHAT)

383. Stop the stream valiantly, drive away the desires, O Brâhmana! When you have understood the destruction of all that was made, you will understand that which was not made.

384. If the Brâhmana has reached the other shore in both laws (in restraint and contemplation), all bonds vanish from him who has obtained knowledge.

385. He for whom there is neither this nor that shore, nor both, him, the fearless and unshackled, I call indeed a Brâhmana.

414. Him I call indeed a Brâhmana who has traversed this miry road, the impassable world and its vanity, who has gone through, and reached the other shore, is thoughtful, guileless, free from doubts, free from attachment, and content.

415. Him I call indeed a Brâhmana who in this world, leaving all desires, travels about without a home, and in whom all concupiscence is extinct.

416. Him I call indeed a Brâhmana who, leaving all longings, travels about without a home, and in whom all covetousness is extinct.

420. Him I call indeed a Brâhmana whose path the gods do not know, nor spirits (Gandharvas), nor men, whose passions are extinct, and who is an Arhat (venerable).

421. Him I call indeed a Brâhmana who calls nothing his own, whether it be before, behind, or between, who is poor, and free from the love of the world.

422. Him I call indeed a Brâhmana, the manly, the noble, the hero, the great sage, the conqueror, the impassible, the accomplished, the awakened.

423. Him I call indeed a Brâhmana who knows his former abodes, who sees heaven and hell, has reached the end of births, is perfect in knowledge, a sage, and whose perfections are all perfect.

4. Sermons of the Buddha

THE FIRST SERMON

THESE TWO EXTREMES, O MONKS, are not to be practiced by one who has gone forth from the world. What are the two? That conjoined with the passions, low, vulgar, common, ignoble, and useless, and that conjoined with self-torture, painful, ignoble, and useless. Avoiding these two extremes the Tathagata has gained the knowledge of the Middle Way, which gives sight and knowledge, and tends to calm, to insight, enlightenment, *nirvana.*

What, O monks, is the Middle Way, which gives sight . . . ? It is the noble Eightfold Path, namely, right views, right intention, right speech, right action, right livelihood, right effort, right mindfulness, right concentration. This, O monks, is the Middle Way. . . .

1. Now this, O monks, is the noble truth of pain: birth is painful, old age is painful, sickness is painful, death is painful, sorrow, lamentation, dejection, and despair are painful. Contact with unpleasant things is painful, not getting what one wishes is painful. In short the five *khandhas* of grasping are painful.

2. Now this, O monks, is the noble truth of the cause of pain: that craving which leads to rebirth, combined with pleasure and lust, finding pleasure here and there, namely, the craving for passion, the craving for existence, the craving for non-existence.

3. Now this, O monks, is the noble truth of the cessation of pain: the cessation without a remainder of that craving, abandonment, forsaking, release, non-attachment.

4. Now this, O monks, is the noble truth of the way that leads to the cessation of pain: this is the noble Eightfold Path, namely, right views, right intention, right speech, right action, right livelihood, right effort, right mindfulness, right concentration. . . .

As long as in these noble truths my threefold knowledge and insight duly with its twelve divisions was not well purified, even so long, O monks, in the world with its gods, Mara, Brahma, with ascetics, *brahmins*, gods, and men, I had not attained the highest complete enlightenment. Thus I knew.

But when in these noble truths my threefold knowledge and insight duly with its twelve divisions was well purified, then, O monks, in the world . . . I had attained the highest complete enlightenment. Thus I knew. Knowledge arose in me; insight arose that the release of my mind is unshakable; this is my last existence; now there is no rebirth.

THE FIRE-SERMON

Then The Blessed One, having dwelt in Uruvela as long as he wished, proceeded on his wanderings in the direction of Gaya Head, accompanied by a great congregation of priests, a thousand in number, who had all of them aforetime been monks with matted hair. And there in Gaya, on Gaya Head, The Blessed One dwelt, together with the thousand priests.

And there The Blessed One addressed the priests:—

"All things, O priests, are on fire. And what, O priests, are all these things which are on fire?

"The eye, O priests, is on fire; forms are on fire; eye-consciousness is on fire; impressions received by the eye are on fire; and whatever sensation, pleasant, unpleasant, or indifferent, originates in dependence on impressions received by the eye, that also is on fire.

"And with what are these on fire?

"With the fire of passion, say I, with the fire of hatred, with the fire of infatuation; with birth, old age, death, sorrow, lamentation, misery, grief, and despair are they on fire.

From Buddhism in Translation, *trans. by Henry Clarke Warren (Cambridge, MA: Harvard University Press, 1896).*

"The ear is on fire; sounds are on fire; . . . the nose is on fire; odors are on fire; . . . the tongue is on fire; tastes are on fire; . . . the body is on fire; things tangible are on fire; . . . the mind is on fire; ideas are on fire; . . . mind-consciousness is on fire; impressions received by the mind are on fire; and whatever sensation, pleasant, unpleasant, or indifferent, originates in dependence on impressions received by the mind, that also is on fire.

"And with what are these on fire?

"With the fire of passion, say I, with the fire of hatred, with the fire of infatuation; with birth, old age, death, sorrow, lamentation, misery, grief, and despair are they on fire.

"Perceiving this, O priests, the learned and noble disciple conceives an aversion for the eye, conceives an aversion for forms, conceives an aversion for eye-consciousness, conceives an aversion for the impressions received by the eye; and whatever sensation, pleasant, unpleasant, or indifferent, originates in dependence on impressions received by the eye, for that also he conceives an aversion. Conceives an aversion for the ear, conceives an aversion for sounds, . . . conceives an aversion for the nose, conceives an aversion for odors, . . . conceives an aversion for the tongue, conceives an aversion for tastes, . . . (conceives an aversion for the body, conceives an aversion for things tangible, . . . conceives an aversion for the mind, conceives an aversion for ideas, conceives an aversion for mind-consciousness, conceives an aversion for the impressions received by the mind; and whatever sensation, pleasant, unpleasant, or indifferent, originates in dependence on impressions received by the mind, for this also he conceives an aversion. And in conceiving this aversion, he becomes divested of passion, and by the absence of passion he becomes free, and when he is free he becomes aware that he is free; and he knows that rebirth is exhausted, that he has lived the holy life, that he has done what it behooved him to do, and that he is no more for this world."

Now while this exposition was being delivered, the minds of the thousand priests became free from attachment and delivered from the depravities.

Study Questions

1. What does the Buddha mean by the not-self, and how does this differ from the Hindu concept of atman?

2. Why does the Buddha hold the understanding of reality in such low esteem?

3. What is the primary cause of the suffering that lies at the heart of human nature, and how can this suffering be overcome?

4. What does it mean to say that the laws of karma determine the form of life into which a person gets reborn?

5. Explain the Buddhist concept of nirvana.

Confucius

Introduction

The oldest continuous civilization in the world is that of China, tracing its history back even further than the four and one-half millennia of Indian civilization. One of the two most influential Chinese thinkers was **Lao Tzu,** who lived probably in the sixth century B.C.E. He was the founder of **Taoism** (pronounced "*Dow*-ism"), and he was especially interested in how we should live our lives in harmony with nature. His very famous and only written work is the *Tao Te Ching (Classic of the Way and Its Power)*, a short, very influential book consisting of poetically expressed insights. *Reading 1* consists of selections from the *Tao*, which has been translated into English over forty times, and has been the object of nearly a thousand commentaries. It may be necessary to use one of these commentaries to understand fully what each of these brief and compact comments mean.

A brief introduction to Taoism is presented in the next section, both for its own intrinsic interest and also because it was often at odds with the ideas of the other major philosopher, and perhaps the most influential of all Chinese moral philosophers, **Confucius** (551–479 B.C.E.). "Confucius" is the Western pronunciation of the Chinese name, K'ung Fu-tzu. "K'ung" is the family name, and "Fu-tzu," meaning "great master," is the honorary title given to Confucius. He was given this title partly because he had established a school which became a very influential model in Chinese education. Its curriculum concentrated especially on applying ethics to social issues. The title was also in recognition of the contributions of his later life, during which he traveled throughout China, teaching his many disciples and offering his instruction to many rulers. The overriding concern of Confucius was to discover and teach others how we should live our lives in harmony with each other in society.

Confucius lived during one of the worst periods of the nine-hundred year Chou dynasty. Chinese life was beset with corruption, violence, numerous vicious wars between feudal lords, and a near breakdown of the moral order. Confucius worked as a minor government official in his early life and saw all of this misery firsthand. As a result, it became his mission in life to restore order and goodness to society. This was to be accomplished primarily through teaching others about the nature and purpose of a morally good society. His major written work is the *Analects*, a collection of brief remarks or "sayings" that may have been composed by his followers. *Reading 2* consists of selections from the *Analects.* Each of these sayings is usually a brief summary of one or more of his major ideas.

Both Confucius and Lao Tzu were familiar with the ancient wisdom of China found in the leading *ching* (Classic) texts. Among these was a text on poetry, the *Shih ching*, a book on history, the *Shu ching*, the *I ching*, which described the universe as a single, interrelated system, and the *Li chi*, a book describing various rites and ceremonies. These and other ancient texts had helped to shape Chinese culture by presenting a number of ideas and images that came to be part of the common store of knowledge of the educated person. They would surely be known to Lao Tzu and Confucius, and had a significant influence on their teachings. In fact, after his death, the *Analects* of Confucius was added to this list of Classics, as was *The Book of Mencius*, written by one of his most influential followers.

Worldview

Among the commonly known themes found in the Classics and known throughout Chinese culture were the following:[2]

(a) **Heaven:** This was not so much a supernatural world which contained gods and other spirits, but rather the cosmos above the earth, and especially the moral laws inherent in the universe to which human beings must submit in order to live excellent lives.

When ceremonies were performed to the heavens it was to recognize the place of humans in the vast cosmological order more than to acknowledge a personal god or gods. Even though there is much discussion of heaven by both, the teachings of Lao Tzu and Confucius are best thought of as forms of secular belief.

(b) **The mandate of heaven:** This is the sanction of heaven granted to a ruler. This mandate imposed certain benefits and duties on a ruler. The main benefit was the increased authority and social force it gave to the ruler. If he was seen as ruling in accordance with this mandate then his word had great authority and must be obeyed. On the other hand, the mandate from heaven also imposed on the ruler the general duty of ruling in the interest of the people, not himself. It also required him to perform certain ceremonies and rituals. These rituals and ceremonies were important, because they drew the community together and gave it an identity and cohesion. Since a good and stable society is the most important goal of life for many Chinese thinkers, even more important than the lives of individuals, the performance of ceremonies and rituals was an extremely important duty.

(c) **Tao:** Meaning "way" or "path." For Taoists it was especially the way of nature. To follow the Tao is to align yourself with the order of the universe, and thus to achieve a happy life; to deviate from its path is to court disaster and misery, the lot of most people. For others, Tao was not so much the way of nature but rather the way of morality, or some other pathway to a good life—such as the way of *ching* or of wise men.

(d) **Yin and Yang:** These are the opposing components of all things in nature and society. Yin is the passive, weak, destructive, female principle, while yang is the active, strong, constructive, male principle. Each are a necessary compliment to one another. As a hill in the daytime has a dark (yin) and a light (yang) side, so are all things and relationships composed of these two principles. The *I ching* contains many analysis of natural objects and events in terms of their yin and yang components.

(e) **Family reverence:** The strength of the family was based on respect for the father and other older members of the extended family. This was important since the basic social unit in all Chinese history had always been the family. In fact, reverence was especially paid to the ancestors of living family members, even to the point of offering prayers and sacrifices and asking for guidance. Honoring tradition in the guise of the "way of the fathers" has been a powerful force for conservatism throughout Chinese history.

The Influence of Taoism

Taoism was built upon (c) and (d), while the teachings of Confucius were built especially upon (a), (b), and (e). The central concept of Taoism is that of the "Way." As Hinduism was unable to describe brahman in language, so Taoism is unable to say what the Way is. It may be said in general that it is the pattern or order of nature, but this path is beyond the ability of ordinary language to describe in detail. Instead, it can only be spoken of indirectly, through various metaphorical and even paradoxical expressions. A "paradox" is an apparently contradictory statement that nevertheless expresses a truth. The *Tao Te Ching* is filled with such statements. Knowledge of the Way comes not through reason, but through experience, especially through mystical experiences that are the result of meditation.

If the Way is the way of nature, then to live fully is to live in harmony with nature. To live in harmony with nature requires that we understand nature to be one coherent, dynamic system which is composed of the opposing forces, yin and yang. These forces ceaselessly join together and separate, causing the regular flow of nature, the cycles of life and death, summer and winter, cold and warm, male and female, and so on. To live in harmony with nature is to adapt to these orderly changes of opposites, understanding that nothing is permanent except nature itself. The wise man does not fret during a drought, since he knows that rain will soon appear; he does not grieve at death, since he knows that it is part of life; he does not shrink in the face of evil, for he knows that good will eventually follow.

One of the central practices of Taoism is referred to as **wu wei,** the doctrine of "inaction." This does not mean doing nothing, but seems rather to mean doing nothing that is opposed to nature. In particular, it means refraining from the attempt to control things that are beyond a person's control. This includes the behavior and feelings that others have for you, the attempt by governments to control the behavior of its subjects, and even our attempt to control nature through technology. Instead, we should step back, be calm and strong, maintain our own values in the midst of chaos, and allow events to unfold according to nature's way—the way of the Tao.

The Confucian Worldview

For Lao Tzu, living in harmony with nature requires either that we withdraw from society completely or at least live simply, in small rural communities, with little regard for the trappings of society or the guidance of government. This is directly opposed to the teachings of Confucius, who thought that it was not harmony with nature, but rather membership in a morally good society that offered the best way to live. Confucius shunned theories of reality and knowledge in favor of very practical considerations of morality. In fact, when Confucius did have something to say about the universe in general, it was to claim that the most basic truths about it had more to do with morality than with metaphysics. What is most real is the moral order of the universe, not any supposed rational order that it might possess.

Morality is not simply an invention of human societies for Confucius. Rather, it originates in heaven and is present in the world in the form of the mandate from heaven. This mandate is a set of moral guidelines and virtues which define the life of moral perfection. Further, this moral system, this mandate from heaven, is not known through any special method of knowledge, such as intuition or meditation or reasoning. Instead, it can be known by studying what the great men and teachers of the past have said about it. The central claim of Confucius is that the true Way is the life of moral perfection. Moral perfection is not simply a necessary condition to attain some other good. We are not morally good in order to achieve a life of wisdom, for example, or mystical experience. Moral perfection itself is the ultimate goal. This perfection may be attained by any person who lives in a good society and conforms his or her behavior to the mandate of heaven as it is revealed through the ancient Classics.

Human Nature

Confucius believed that all human beings, whatever their social status, have a similar nature. The "nature" that concerned him was not so much our physical or biological nature, nor was it even our rational or psychological nature. Instead, it was our moral nature that was most important. To say that we have a moral nature is to deny that morality is simply the creation of human society. Instead, for Confucius our innate moral tendencies are given to us all alike by heaven. Our moral nature is part of the universe that created us all to be as we are. For Confucius, this means that every one of us is capable of moral perfection. Although our human nature is *capable* of moral perfection, however, very, very few ever attain it. As was evidenced by the terrible state of affairs in China during his lifetime, the more common path of humanity is toward vice, not virtue. Is this because human nature is itself corrupt and easily led astray? Or is human nature basically good, but corrupted by evil rulers?

In the writings of Confucius we are offered little help in answering this basic question. One thing seems to be clear, however. Confucius believed that *human nature is essentially social.* Whether it is inclined more to the good or to the evil, it is shaped mostly by the social environment. Human nature is pliable. With the proper conditions, it may be bent toward either the good or the evil. This is why it is so important to establish morally good societies, because it is society that makes us who we are. Two hundred years or so after the death of Confucius a dispute arose among his followers about the exact teachings of Confucius on human nature. On one side stood **Mencius** (371–289 B.C.E.), who believed that human nature is essentially good; on the other was **Hsun-tzu** (298–239 B.C.E.), who believed that we are evil by nature. If anyone won this debate it was Mencius, whose view became the prevalent one among followers of Confucius. His view of human nature may be found in *Reading 3.*

Hsun-tzu took as his point of departure the belief of Confucius that the reason for human misery is selfishness and ignorance. Because people from the most common of men to the most exalted rulers are ignorant of the Way, they are driven by desire, not knowledge. Since the goods which they desire are finite and desired by others as well, selfishness inevitably leads to envy, hatred, and violence. At their very core people are indifferent to the fate of one another. No more than nature cares about whom it rains upon or strikes down with sickness, do human beings care about those people who are harmed by their actions. There is no place for altruism in human nature. Given this as our human condition, the only way to gain moral perfection is through proper training and control by a strong ruler. It is not *self*-discipline, but the discipline and training forced upon a person by a strong society that is the only foil to selfishness and ignorance. People must be taught the Way, and they must be forced by society to adopt it. This discipline, motivated by threats and fear, is the only hope for channeling our egotistic human nature into a civilized condition.

Mencius, on the other hand, was much more optimistic about human nature. We do help each other, he believed, and we do feel a sense of guilt and shame when we act selfishly, even though there is no one present to blame us for failing to act altruistically. Following the lead of Confucius that all human beings are capable of becoming morally perfected, it was the belief of Mencius that human nature was essentially good from the start. We are all born with virtuous inclinations, and thus we are all innately good. Heaven has instilled in us all the innate knowledge of right from wrong. We know in our hearts what counts as virtue and vice. Heaven has also given us a sense of shame for our misdeeds, which acts as an immediate, emotional check on our vices. In addition, it has built into our hearts a sense of compassion for the suffering of our fellow humans.

But if we are innately good, why are there so many evil persons and evil deeds in this world? Mencius, in apparent agreement with Hsun-tzu, says that it is because we are also born with desires whose strength can often overcome virtue. It is therefore essential that our innate goodness be nurtured and our desires tempered. Training and guidance is required to develop this moral nature of ours, to be sure. But it needs to be much less harsh and strict than that envisaged by Hsun-tzu. The lesson to be learned is that human nature, whatever its starting point, may be bent either in the direction of good or evil—as Confucius had said many decades earlier. The key is to establish a society in which the native impulses of human beings are channeled in the direction of moral perfection, and not in the direction of selfishness and ignorance.

Consequences

Freedom

It was clear that Confucius believed in the ability of human beings to choose either the life of selfishness or the life of moral perfection. At the same time, however, he also believed that some things which were important to our lives were not subject to our control. In particular, Confucius seemed to believe that our social status was predetermined by heaven, and thus well beyond our control. There was nothing that could be done to change our social position in life, so we should simply accept it and direct our efforts to things that are under our control, especially the attainment of moral perfection.

Ethics

Ethics is about right and wrong and the motives which drive us to do one or the other. It is also about good and evil. This includes moral goodness, especially what are the most important virtues to develop and vices to avoid, and what are the proper motives for action. It also includes discovering what is the good life, which very often means what human nature could be when it is most fully developed. For most of the people discussed in this text, moral goodness may be part of what makes a life good, but only part. For Confucius, however, the good life *is* the life of moral perfection. For him, the ideal life to strive for was what he called **chun tzu**, translated as "man at his best," and sometimes as "the gentleman." Such a life brings joy all by itself, and thus is to be prized for its own sake. Moral goodness is its own reward. It requires at least three things. It requires that we do what is right and avoid actions that are wrong; it requires that we do so with the correct motive; and it requires that we develop a good moral character, one that will keep us aligned with moral goodness.

The ethics of Confucius was an ethics of virtue. According to this approach, right and wrong actions are those that stem from a morally good character. A morally good character is a set of good habits or good dispositions to behave; a set of virtues in other words. Virtuous behavior includes doing what is right, but it also includes doing so for the right reason or intention, and with the correct motive. For Confucius, we act with the correct intention when we do what is right simply because it is right. Being moral to please others, to gain a good reputation, to avoid punishment, or to gain wealth and fame, for example, are not worthy intentions. A man of moral perfection understands the value of a good moral character and acts in accordance with it simply because it is the right thing to do. For Confucius, having a good moral character is its own reward.

In addition, the correct motive is always what Confucius calls **jen**. This means "benevolence" or "kind-heartedness," and for Confucius it ought to be at the root of all human relationships. We ought to strive for moral perfection because it is the right thing to do (our intention) and do so because it is an expression of love and kindness among and between human beings (our motive). But which are the good moral habits (virtues) that express benevolence? Confucius tells us that we should follow the principle of **shu**, or reciprocity. This is something like the golden rule, which requires us to treat people as we would want them to treat us. This is how we tell what is a virtue, at least in general. An individual will develop a morally good character if he or she follows shu, because it is the way to express jen to others.

Society

Confucius taught that individual moral perfection is the key to a stable society. However, it is difficult for individuals to develop a good moral character in the face of strong competition from their selfish desires and passions. In fact, for Confucius chun tzu is unthinkable apart from the social training and discipline that is required to foster and sustain it. A good society can foster good individuals, who then in turn sustain the stability and benevolence of the society. A society riddled with selfish and greedy actions, however, will produce nothing but chaos and suffering. Driven by the conviction that human society—not nature, not gods, and not metaphysical wisdom—is the most important reality, Confucius taught constantly that it is a good human society that we ought to seek above all else.

A good society nurtures virtue in general and also in particular circumstances. As a person learns to speak a language in a social context, so he or she learns to identify and perform social roles in such a context as well. This is primarily what society passes on from one generation to another, how to be and act well within certain types of social relationships. It teaches the young how to be good sons and daughters, for example, and the older how to be good mothers and fathers. Thus, through proper training and education, the wisdom of the past may be transferred to the next generation, and from them to their sons and daughters, and so on. As it is society that primarily shapes the attitudes and behavior of individuals, so society should be designed to produce benevolent, virtuous subjects.

Perhaps the major contribution of Confucius and his followers was to spell out in some detail just how human social relationships ought to be structured if they are to be in accordance with his basic moral principles of jen and shu. To this end, Confucius sought to instruct rulers and subjects alike about the conditions required to produce a good society. Many of his teachings were basically of this nature: "This is how you should act in these circumstances, and why you should do so, if you are to encourage virtuous lives for yourselves and others." Among these conditions are those expressed in the concepts of *li, hsiao, chih* and *cheng ming*.[3]

Li refers to rites and ceremonies and means something like "decorum" or "good form." Confucius knew that it is not enough to have a general sense of benevolence to have a good moral character, or even to have a general idea of reciprocity. In addition, there must be some notion of what type of action in specific circumstances expresses these attitudes and principles. While the rites and ceremonies may first appear to be simply the external trappings of morality, they play the extremely important role in moral education of showing just what actions are virtuous. Each one of the rites and ceremonies is designed to demonstrate how particular actions and social roles ought to be performed. At its heart, each li is an experience of self-discipline, of surrendering self-interest to benevolence and virtue. These rites and ceremonies express ancient Chinese moral wisdom, which itself ultimately derives from the mandate of heaven. There were rites and ceremonies for every occasion, from birth to funerals, from youthful games to marriage. Always the purpose was the same, to demonstrate how to act benevolently and virtuously.

Chih means knowledge, another crucial element of a good society. While it refers to all sorts of academic knowledge, especially knowledge of the good life, it especially means for Confucius the application of such knowledge to human affairs. What Confucius has in mind especially is the knowledge of the ancient Chinese Classics, which themselves express the mandate of heaven, and the application of this wisdom to human affairs by a wise and benevolent ruler. A good society must have a good ruler, one who is motivated by benevolence, not greed, and one who is informed about the nature of virtue. In addition, the good ruler must understand how to apply this general knowledge in his laws, policies, educational programs, and in his general dealings with his subjects. As we have seen, much of the curriculum in the school founded by Confucius was designed to produce just such wise and good rulers. Most importantly, in the good society rulers must themselves be living examples of chun tzu in order to teach and inspire others to follow the Way.

In order to pass on to the next generation the wisdom of li and chih there must be an acceptance on their part to receive it. This acceptance is found in societies which recognize the ancient practice of hsiao. **Hsiao** means "respect," even a feeling of reverence, for one's father in particular and for all elders in general. As the family is the building block of society, respect for one's parents, especially the respect of a son for his father, is the cement of the family. Good fathers will pass on the wisdom of the past. It is in this wisdom that both the stability and virtue of society is to be found. Since the respect and reverence of a son for his father will produce an acceptance of this wisdom in the son, a society in which such respect is present has within it the basis for stability and virtue. In addition, the attitudes which support good family relationships also lie at the basis of other human relationships. From filial piety, for example, the son himself learns to be a kind father and an honorable husband. Even benevolent rulers and loyal subjects derive their humaneness from the reverential bond formed between parent and child.

Finally, in addition to the presence of hsiao, the observation of li, and the presence of chih, jen, and shu in the ruler, any good society must also contain **cheng ming**, "the reification of names." For Confucius, the social discord of his time was caused especially by selfishness and ignorance of the Way. Selfishness is to be controlled by the discipline of li, ignorance overcome by hsiao and chih, and the lives of individuals and human society reformed by the acceptance of jen and shu. There was another plague on society as well, however, one so widespread that Confucius considered it to need his special attention. It concerned the lack of trust between people, especially between ruler and subject. Rulers lied as a matter of course to their subjects. This gap between word and deed destroyed the trust that is necessary for establishing loyalty in subjects, and thus for establishing good and stable societies. Cheng ming requires there to be agreement between names and the things or deeds that they name. The good ruler and the loyal subject alike are people who say what they mean and mean what they say. They keep their word; they allow no discrepancy between word and deed.

God and Immortality

Generally speaking, Confucius dismissed speculations about gods and an after-life in favor of his real concern, the establishment of guidelines for the formation of good societies. He seems to be open to belief in life after death, since he accepted rituals which included sacrifices to ancestors. He also seemed to be open to belief in various deities, since he treated the belief that others had in the official gods of society with respect. However, he did not directly answer when questions about these matters were addressed to him. Instead, he preferred to suspend his judgment about them, to remain agnostic in their regard.

Gender

There is a long tradition of sexism in China. Even today a male child is much more highly valued than a female child. The writings of Confucius fall squarely into this tradition. Confucius had little to say about women in his writings, but what he did have to say left it clear that he considered them to be inferior to men. They were to be excluded from education, for example, presumably because they had neither the intelligence nor self-discipline it required. All of his writings refer only to men as those capable of the knowledge and virtue required for the good life. "*Man* at his best," or the "gentle*man*" is attainable only by males. In theory, Confucianism can be broadened to include women as equals, but such inclusiveness was not something achieved or even desired by Confucius.

Readings

1. The Wisdom of Taoism

1. A WAY CAN BE A GUIDE

A way can be a guide, but not a fixed path;
names can be given, but not permanent labels.
Nonbeing is called the beginning of heaven and
    earth;
being is called the mother of all things.
Always passionless, thereby observe the subtle;
ever intent, thereby observe the apparent.
These two come from the same source but
    differ in name;
both are considered mysteries.
The mystery of mysteries
is the gateway of marvels.

2. EVERYONE KNOWS

When everyone knows beauty is beauty,
this is bad.
When everyone knows good is good,
this is not good.
So being and nonbeing produce each other:
difficulty and ease complement each other,
long and short shape each other,
high and low contrast with each other,
voice and echoes conform to each other,
before and after go along with each other.
So sages manage effortless service
and carry out unspoken guidance.
All beings work, without exception:
if they live without possessiveness,
act without presumption,
and do not dwell on success,
then by this very nondwelling
success will not leave.

3. NOT EXALTING CLEVERNESS

Not exalting cleverness
causes the people not to contend.
Nor putting high prices on hard-to-get goods
causes the people not to steal.
Not seeing anything to want
causes the mind not to be confused.
Therefore the government of sages
empties the mind and fills the middle,
weakens the ambition and strengthens the bones,
always keeping the people innocent and
    passionless.
It makes the sophisticated not dare to contrive;
action being without contrivance,
nothing is disordered.

4. THE WAY IS UNIMPEDED HARMONY

The Way is unimpeded harmony;
its potential may never be fully exploited.
It is as deep as the source of all things:
it blunts the edges,
resolves the complications,
harmonizes the light,
assimilates to the world.
Profoundly still, it seems to be there:
I don't know whose child it is,
before the creation of images.

5. HEAVEN AND EARTH

Heaven and earth are not humane;
they regard all beings as straw dogs.
Sages are not humane;
they see all people as straw dogs.

Eighteen selections, as submitted, from The Essential Tao, *translated and presented by Thomas Cleary (New York: Harper-Collins, 1991). Copyright © 1991 by Thomas Cleary. Reprinted by permission of HarperCollins Publishers Inc.*

The space between heaven and earth
is like bellows and pipes,
empty yet inexhaustible,
producing more with movement.
The talkative reach their wits' end
again and again;
that is not as good as keeping centered.

7. HEAVEN IS ETERNAL, EARTH IS EVERLASTING

Heaven is eternal, earth is everlasting.
The reason they can be eternal and everlasting
is that they do not foster themselves;
that is why they can live forever.
For this reason sages put themselves last,
and they were first;
they excluded themselves,
and they survived.
Was it not by their very selflessness
that they managed to fulfill themselves?

8. HIGHER GOOD IS LIKE WATER

Higher good is like water:
the good in water benefits all,
and does so without contention.
It rests where people dislike to be,
so it is close to the Way.
Where it dwells becomes good ground;
profound is the good in its heart,
benevolent the good it bestows.
Goodness in words is trustworthiness,
goodness in government is order;
goodness in work is ability,
goodness in action is timeliness.
But only by noncontention
is there nothing extreme.

9. TO KEEP ON FILLING

To keep on filling
is not as good as stopping.
Calculated sharpness
cannot be kept for long.
Though gold and jewels fill their houses,
no one can keep them.
When the rich upper classes are haughty,

their legacy indicts them.
When one's work is accomplished honorably,
to retire is the Way of heaven.

10. CARRYING VITALITY AND CONSCIOUSNESS

Carrying vitality and consciousness,
embracing them as one,
can you keep them from parting?
Concentrating energy,
making it supple,
can you be like an infant?
Purifying hidden perception,
can you make it flawless?
Loving the people, governing the nation,
can you be uncontrived?
As the gate of heaven opens and closes,
can you be impassive?
As understanding reaches everywhere,
can you be innocent?
Producing and developing,
producing without possessing,
doing without presuming,
growing without domineering:
this is called mysterious power.

25. SOMETHING UNDIFFERENTIATED

Something undifferentiated was born before
heaven and earth;
still and silent, standing alone and unchanging,
going through cycles unending,
able to be mother to the world.
I do not know its name;
I label it the Way.
Imposing on it a name,
I call it Great.
Greatness means it goes;
going means reaching afar;
reaching afar means return.
Therefore the Way is great,
heaven is great,
earth is great,
and kingship is also great.
Among domains are four greats,
of which kingship is one.

Humanity emulates earth,
earth emulates heaven,
heaven emulates the Way,
the Way emulates Nature.

36. SHOULD YOU WANT TO CONTAIN

Should you want to contain something,
you must deliberately let it expand.
Should you want to weaken something,
you must deliberately let it grow strong.
Should you want to eliminate something,
you must deliberately allow it to flourish.
Should you want to take something away,
you must deliberately grant it.
This is called subtle illumination.
Flexibility and yielding
overcome adamant coerciveness.
Fish shouldn't be taken from the depths;
the effective tools of the nation
shouldn't be shown to others.

37. THE WAY IS ALWAYS UNCONTRIVED

The Way is always uncontrived,
yet there's nothing it doesn't do.
If lords and monarchs could keep to it,
all beings would evolve spontaneously.
When they have evolved and want to act,
I would stabilize them with nameless simplicity.
Even nameless simplicity would not be wanted.
By not wanting, there is calm,
and the world will straighten itself.

42. THE WAY PRODUCES ONE

The Way produces one;
one produces two,
two produce three,
three produce all beings:
all beings bear yin and embrace yang,
with a mellowing energy for harmony.
The things people dislike
are only to be alone, lacking, and unworthy;
yet these are what monarchs call themselves.
Therefore people may gain from loss,

and may lose from gain.
What others teach,
I also teach.
The strong cannot master their death:
I take this to be the father of teachings.

43. WHAT IS SOFTEST IN THE WORLD

What is softest in the world
drives what is hardest in the world.
Nonbeing enters where there is no room;
that is how we know noncontrivance enhances.
Unspoken guidance and uncontrived enhancement
are reached by few in the world.

48. FOR LEARNING YOU GAIN DAILY

For learning you gain daily;
for the Way you lose daily.
Losing and losing,
thus you reach noncontrivance;
be uncontrived, and nothing is not done.
Taking the world is always done
by not making anything of it.
For when something is made of it,
that is not enough to take the world.

57. GOVERN NATIONS BY NORMALCY

Use straightforwardness for civil government,
use surprise for military operations;
use noninvolvement to take the world.
How do I know this?
The more taboos there are in the world,
the poorer the populace is;
the more crafts the people have,
the more exotic things are produced;
the more laws are promulgated,
the greater the number of thieves.
Therefore the sage says,
I contrive nothing,
and the people are naturally civilized;
I am fond of tranquility,
and the people are naturally upright.
I have nothing to do,

and the people are naturally enriched;
I have no desire,
and the people are naturally simple.

63. DO NONDOING

Do nondoing,
strive for nonstriving,
savor the flavorless,
regard the small as important,
make much of little,
repay enmity with virtue;
plan for difficulty when it is still easy,
do the great while it is still small.
The most difficult things in the world
must be done while they are easy;
the greatest things in the world
must be done while they are small.
Because of this sages never do great things;
that is why they can fulfill their greatness.
If you agree too easily, you'll be little trusted;
if you take it easy a lot, you'll have a lot of
      problems.
Therefore it is through difficulty
that sages end up without problems.

64. WHAT IS AT REST IS EASY TO HOLD

What is at rest
is easy to hold.
What has not shown up
is easy to take into account.

What is frail
is easy to break.
What is vague
is easy to dispel.
Do it before it exists;
govern it before there's disorder.
The most massive tree grows from a sprout;
the highest building rises from a pile of earth;
a journey of a thousand miles begins with a step.
Those who contrive spoil it;
those who cling lose it.

Thus sages contrive nothing,
and so spoil nothing.
They cling to nothing,
and so lose nothing.

Therefore people's works
are always spoiled on the verge of completion.
Be as careful of the end
as of the beginning,
and nothing will be spoiled.

Thus sages want to have no wants;
they do not value goods hard to get.
They learn not learning
to recover from people's excesses,
thereby to assist
the naturalness of all beings,
without daring to contrive.

2. Teachings of Confucius

BOOK I

2. Master Yu said, Those who in private life behave well towards their parents and elder brothers, in public life seldom show a disposition to resist the authority of their superiors. And as for such men starting a revolution, no instance of it has ever occurred. It is upon the trunk that a gentleman works. When that is firmly set up, the Way grows. And surely proper behavior toward parents and elder brothers is the trunk of Goodness?

Reprinted from The Analects of Confucius, *trans. by Arthur Waley. Copyright © 1938 by George Allen & Unwin Ltd., with permission from Scribner, an imprint of Simon & Schuster Adult Publishing Group and from Routledge, London.*

6. The Master said, A young man's duty is to behave well to his parents at home and to his elders abroad, to be cautious in giving promises and punctual in keeping them, to have kindly feelings toward everyone, but seek the intimacy of the Good. If, when all that is done, he has any energy to spare, then let him study the polite arts.

7. Tzu-yu asked about the treatment of parents. The Master said, 'Filial sons' nowadays are people who see to it that their parents get enough to eat. But even dogs and horses are cared for to that extent. If there is no feeling of respect, wherein lies the difference?

14. The Master said, A gentleman who never goes on eating till he is sated, who does not demand comfort in his home, who is diligent in business and cautious in speech, who associates with those that possess the Way and thereby corrects his own faults—such a one may indeed be said to have a taste for learning.

16. The Master said, (the good man) does not grieve that other people do not recognize his merits. His only anxiety is lest he should fail to recognize theirs.

BOOK II

12. The Master said, A gentleman is not an implement.

13. Tzu-kung asked about the true gentleman. The Master said, He does not preach what he practices till he has practiced what he preaches.

14. The Master said, A gentleman can see a question from all sides without bias. The small man is biased and can see a question only from one side.

15. The Master said, 'He who learns but does not think, is lost.' He who thinks but does not learn is in great danger.

16. The Master said, He who sets to work upon a different strand destroys the whole fabric.

17. The Master said, Yu, shall I teach you what knowledge is? When you know a thing, to recognize that you know it, and when you do not know a thing, to recognize that you do not know it. That is knowledge.

19. Duke Ai asked, What can I do in order to get the support of the common people? Master K'ung replied, If you 'raise up the straight and set them on top of the crooked,' the commoners will support you, But if you raise the crooked and set them on top of the straight, the commoners will not support you.

20. Chi K'ang-tzu asked whether there were any form of encouragement by which he could induce the common people to be respectful and loyal. The Master said, Approach them with dignity, and they will respect you. Show piety towards your parents and kindness toward your children, and they will be loyal to you. Promote those who are worthy, train those who are incompetent; that is the best form of encouragement.

21. Someone, when talking to Master K'ung, said, How is it that you are not in the public service? The Master said, The Book says: 'Be filial, only be filial and friendly towards your brothers, and you will be contributing to government.' There are other sorts of service quite different from what you mean by 'service.'

BOOK IV

2. The Master said, Without Goodness a man

    Cannot for long endure adversity,

    Cannot for long enjoy prosperity.

    The Good Man rests content with Goodness; he that is merely wise pursues Goodness in the belief that it pays to do so.

3, 4. Of the adage 'Only a Good Man knows how to like people, knows how to dislike them,' the Master said, He whose heart is in the smallest degree set upon Goodness will dislike no one.

5. Wealth and rank are what every man desires; but if they can only be retained to the detriment of the Way he professes, he must relinquish them. Poverty and obscurity are what every man detests; but if they can only be

avoided to the detriment of the Way he professes, he must accept them. The gentleman who ever parts company with Goodness does not fulfill that name. Never for a moment does a gentleman quit the way of Goodness. He is never so harried but that he cleaves to this; never so tottering but that he cleaves to this.

6. The Master said, I for my part have never yet seen one who really cared for Goodness, nor one who really abhorred wickedness. One who really cared for Goodness would never let any other consideration come first. One who abhorred wickedness would be so constantly doing Good that wickedness would never have a chance to get at him. Has anyone ever managed to do Good with his whole might even as long as the space of a single day? I think not. Yet I for my part have never seen anyone give up such an attempt because he had not the *strength* to go on. It may well have happened, but I for my part have never seen it.

7. The Master said, Every man's faults belong to a set. If one looks out for faults it is only as a means of recognizing Goodness.

8. The Master said, In the morning, hear the Way; in the evening, die content!

9. The Master said, A Knight whose heart is set upon the Way, but who is ashamed of wearing shabby clothes and eating coarse food, is not worth calling into counsel.

10. The Master said, A gentleman in his dealings with the world has neither enmities nor affections; but wherever he sees Right he ranges himself beside it.

11. The Master said, Where gentlemen set their hearts upon moral force *(tê)*, the commoners set theirs upon the soil. Where gentlemen think only of punishments, the commoners think only of exemptions.

12. The Master said, Those whose measures are dictated by mere expediency will arouse continual discontent.

16. The Master said, A gentleman takes as much trouble to discover what is right as lesser men take to discover what will pay.

17. The Master said, In the presence of a good man, think all the time how you may learn to equal him. In the presence of a bad man, turn your gaze within!

24. The Master said, A gentleman covets the reputation of being slow in word but prompt in deed.

25. The Master said, Moral force *(tê)* never dwells in solitude; it will always bring neighbors.

26. Tzu-yu said, In the service of one's prince repeated scolding can only lead to loss of favor; in friendship, it can only lead to estrangement.

BOOK V

28. Tzu-kung said, If a ruler not only conferred wide benefits upon the common people, but also compassed the salvation of the whole State, what would you say of him? Surely, you would call him Good? The Master said, It would no longer be a matter of 'Good.' He would without doubt be a Divine Sage. Even Yao and Shun could hardly criticize him. As for Goodness—you yourself desire rank and standing; then help others to get rank and standing. You want to turn your own merits to account; then help others to turn theirs to account—in fact, the ability to take one's own feelings as a guide—that is the sort of thing that lies in the direction of Goodness.

BOOK VII

15. The Master said, He who seeks only coarse food to eat, water to drink and bent arm for pillow, will without looking for it find happiness to boot. Any thought of accepting wealth and rank by means that I know to be wrong is as remote from me as the clouds that float above.

19. The Master said, I for my part am not one of those who have innate knowledge. I am simply one who loves the past and who is diligent in investigating it.

22. The Master said, Heaven begat the power *(tê)* that is in me. What have I to fear from such a one as Huan T'ui?

24. The Master took four subjects for his teaching: culture, conduct of affairs, loyalty to superiors and the keeping of promises.

25. The Master said, A Divine Sage I cannot hope ever to meet; the most I can hope for is to meet a true gentleman. The Master said, A faultless man I cannot hope ever to meet; the most I can hope for is to meet a man of fixed principles. Yet where all around I see Nothing pretending to be Something, Emptiness pretending to be Fullness, Penury pretending to be Affluence, even a man of fixed principles will be none too easy to find.

29. The Master said, Is Goodness indeed so far away? If we really wanted Goodness, we should find that it was at our very side.

35. The Master said, Just as lavishness leads easily to presumption, so does frugality to meanness. But meanness, is a far less serious fault than presumption.

36. The Master said, A true gentleman is calm and at ease; the Small Man is fretful and ill at ease.

BOOK VIII

4. When Master Tsêng was ill, Mêng Ching Tzu came to see him. Master Tsêng spoke to him saying, When a bird is about to die its song touches the heart. When a man is about to die, his words are of note. There are three things that a gentleman, in following the Way, places above all the rest: from every attitude, every gesture that he employs he must remove all trace of violence or arrogance; every look that he composes in his face must betoken good faith; from every word that he utters, from every intonation, he must remove all trace of coarseness or impropriety. As to the ordering of ritual vessels and the like, there are those whose business it is to attend to such matters.

13. The Master said, Be of unwavering good faith, love learning, if attacked be ready to die for the good Way. Do not enter a State that pursues dangerous courses, nor stay in one where the people have rebelled. When the Way prevails under Heaven, then show yourself; when it does not prevail, then hide. When the Way prevails in your own land, count it a disgrace to be needy and obscure; when the Way does not prevail in your land, then count it a disgrace to be rich and honoured.

BOOK IX

4. There were four things that the Master wholly eschewed: he took nothing for granted, he was never over-positive, never obstinate, never egotistic.

7. The Master said, Do I regard myself as a possessor of wisdom? Far from it. But if even a simple peasant comes in all sincerity and asks me a question, I am ready to thrash the matter out, with all its pros and cons, to the very end.

17. The Master said, I have never yet seen anyone whose desire to build up his moral power was as strong as sexual desire.

24. The Master said, First and foremost, be faithful to your superiors, keep all promises, refuse the friendship of all who are not like you; and if you have made a mistake, do not be afraid of admitting the fact and amending your ways.

25. The Master said, You may rob the Three Armies of their commander-in-chief, but you cannot deprive the humblest peasant of his opinion.

28. The Master said, he that is really Good can never be unhappy. He that is really wise can never be perplexed. He that is really brave is never afraid.

29. The Master said, There are some whom one can join in study but whom one cannot join in progress along the Way; others whom one can join in progress along the Way, but beside whom one cannot take one's stand; and others again beside whom one can take one's stand, but whom one cannot join in counsel.

BOOK XI

3. The Master said, Hui was not any help to me; he accepted everything I said.

11. Tzu-lu asked how one should serve ghosts and spirits. The Master said, Till you have learnt to serve men, how can you serve ghosts? Tzu-lu then ventured upon a question about the dead. The Master said, Till you know about the living, how are you to know about the dead?

19. Tzu-chang asked about the Way of the good people. The Master said, He who does not tread in the tracks cannot expect to find his way into the Inner Room.

BOOK XII

1. Yen Hui asked about Goodness. The Master said, 'He who can himself submit to ritual is Good.' If (a ruler) could for one day 'himself submit to ritual,' everyone under Heaven would respond to his Goodness. For Goodness is something that must have its source in the ruler himself; it cannot be got from others.

   Yen Hui said, I beg to ask for the more detailed items of this (submission to ritual). The Master said, To look at nothing in defiance of ritual, to listen to nothing in defiance of ritual, to speak of nothing in defiance of ritual, never to stir hand or foot in defiance of ritual. Yen Hui said, I know that I am not clever; but this is a saying that, with your permission, I shall try to put into practice.

2. Jan Jung asked about Goodness. The Master said, Behave when away from home as though you were in the presence of an important guest. Deal with the common people as though you were officiating at an important sacrifice. Do not do to others what you would not like yourself. Then there will be no feelings of opposition to you, whether it is the affairs of a State that you are handling or the affairs of a Family.

   Jan Yung said, I know that I am not clever; but this is a saying that, with your permission, I shall try to put into practice.

4. Ssu-ma Niu asked about the meaning of the term Gentleman. The Master said, The Gentleman neither grieves nor fears. Ssu-ma Niu said, So that is what is meant by being a gentleman—neither to grieve nor to fear? The Master said, On looking within himself he finds no taint; so why should he either grieve or fear?

8. Chi Tzu-ch'êng said, A gentleman is a gentleman in virtue of the stuff he is made of. Culture cannot make gentleman. Tzu-kung said, I am sorry, Sir, that you should have said that. For the saying goes that 'when a gentleman has spoken, a team of four horses cannot overtake his words.'

   Culture is just as important as inborn qualities; and inborn qualities, no less important than culture. Remove the hairs from the skin of a tiger or panther, and what is left looks just like the hairless hide of a dog or sheep.

11. Duke Ching of Ch'i asked Master K'ung about government. Master K'ung replied saying, Let the prince be a prince, the minister a minister, the father a father and the son a son. The Duke said, How true! For indeed when the prince is not a prince, the minister not a minister, the father not a father, the son not a son, one may have a dish of millet in front of one and yet not know if one will live to eat it.

16. The Master said, The gentleman calls attention to the good points in others; he does not call attention to their defects. The small man does just the reverse of this.

17. Chi K'ang-tzu asked Master K'ung about the art of ruling. Master K'ung said, Ruling (*chêng*) is straightening (*chêng*). If you lead along a straight way, who will dare go by a crooked one?

19. Chi K'ang-tzu asked Master K'ung about government, saying, Suppose I were to slay those who have not the Way in order to help on those who have the Way, what would you think of it? Master K'ung replied saying, You are there to rule, not to slay. If you desire what is good, the people will at once be good. The essence of the gentleman is that of wind; the

essence of small people is that of grass. And when a wind passes over the grass, it cannot choose but bend.

BOOK XIII

3. Tzu-lu said, If the prince of Wei were waiting for you to come and administer his country for him, what would be your first measure? The Master said, It would certainly be to correct language. Tzu-lu said, Can I have heard you aright? Surely what you say has nothing to do with the matter. Why should language be corrected? The Master said, Yu! How boorish you are! A gentleman, when things he does not understand are mentioned, should maintain an attitude of reserve. If language is incorrect, then what is said does not concord with what was meant; and if what is said does not concord with what was meant, what is to be done cannot be effected. If what is to be done cannot be effected, then rites and music will not flourish. If rites and music do not flourish, then mutilations and lesser punishments will go astray. And if mutilations and lesser punishments go astray, then the people have nowhere to put hand or foot.

   Therefore the gentleman uses only such language as is proper for speech, and only speaks of what it would be proper to carry into effect. The gentleman, in what he says, leaves nothing to mere chance.

6. The Master said. If the ruler himself is upright, all will go well even though he does not give orders. But if he himself is not upright, even though he gives orders, they will not be obeyed.

19. Fan Ch'ih asked about Goodness. The Master said, In private life, courteous, in public life, diligent, in relationships, loyal. This is a maxim that no matter where you may be, even amid the barbarians of the east or north, may never be set aside.

23. The Master said, The true gentleman is conciliatory but not accommodating. Common people are accommodating but not conciliatory.

BOOK XIV

13. Tzu-lu asked what was meant by 'the perfect man.' The Master said, If anyone had the wisdom of Tsang Wu Chung, the uncovetousness of Mêng Kung Ch'o, the valour of Chuang Tzu of P'ien and the dexterity of Jan Ch'iu, and had graced these virtues by the cultivation of ritual and music, then indeed I think we might call him 'a perfect man.'

    He said, But perhaps to-day we need not ask all this of the perfect man. One who, when he sees a chance of gain, stops to think whether to pursue it would be right; when he sees that (his prince) is in danger, is ready to lay down his life; when the fulfilment of an old promise is exacted, stands by what he said long ago—him indeed I think we might call 'a perfect man.'

24. The Master said, The gentleman can influence those who are above him; the small man can only influence those who are below him.

BOOK XV

17. The Master said, The gentleman who takes the right as his material to work upon and ritual as the guide in putting what is right into practice, who is modest in setting out his projects and faithful in carrying them to their conclusion, he indeed is a true gentleman.

23. Tzu-kung asked saying, Is there any single saying that one can act upon all day and every day? The Master said, Perhaps the saying about consideration: 'Never do to others what you would not like them to do to you.'

27. The Master said, When everyone dislikes a man, inquiry is necessary; when everyone likes a man, enquiry is necessary.

29. The Master said, To have faults and to be making no effort to amend them is to have faults indeed!

30. The Master said, I once spent a whole day without food and a whole night without sleep, in order to meditate. It was no use. It is better to learn.

31. The Master said, A gentleman, in his plans, thinks of the Way; he does not think how he is going to make a living. Even farming sometimes entails times of shortage; and even learning may incidentally lead to high pay. But a gentleman's anxieties concern the progress of the Way; he has no anxiety concerning poverty.

32. The Master said, He whose wisdom brings him into power, needs Goodness to secure that power. Else, though he get it, he will certainly lose it. He whose wisdom brings him into power and who has Goodness whereby to secure that power, if he has not dignity wherewith to approach the common people, they will not respect him. He whose wisdom has brought him into power, who has Goodness whereby to secure that power and dignity wherewith to approach the common people, if he handles them contrary to the prescriptions of ritual, is still a bad ruler.

36. The Master said, From a gentleman consistency is expected, but not blind fidelity.

BOOK XVI

5. Master K'ung said, There are three sorts of pleasure that are profitable, and three sorts of pleasure that are harmful. The pleasure got from the due ordering of ritual and music, the pleasure got from discussing the good points in the conduct of others, the pleasure of having many wise friends is profitable. But pleasure got from profligate enjoyments, pleasure got from idle gadding about, pleasure got from comfort and ease is harmful.

14. The wife of the ruler of a State is referred to by the ruler as 'That person.' She refers to herself as Little Boy. The people of the country call her 'That person of the Prince's.' When speaking of her to people of another State the ruler calls her 'This lonely one's little prince.' But people of another State likewise call her 'That person of the Prince's.'

BOOK XVII

3. The Master said, It is only the very wisest and the very stupidest who cannot change.

8. The Master said, Yu, have you ever been told of the Six Sayings about the Six Degenerations? Tzu-lu replied, No, never. (The Master said) Come, then; I will tell you. Love of Goodness without love of learning degenerates into silliness. Love of wisdom without love of learning degenerates into utter lack of principle. Love of keeping promises without love of learning degenerates into villainy. Love of uprightness without love of learning degenerates into harshness.

25. The Master said, Women and people of low birth are very hard to deal with. If you are friendly with them, they get out of hand, and if you keep your distance, they resent it.

BOOK XX

2. Tzu-chang asked Master K'ung, saying, What must a man do, that he may thereby be fitted to govern the land? The Master said, He must pay attention to the Five Lovely Things and put away from him the Four Ugly Things. Tzu-chang said, What are they, that you call the Five Lovely Things? The Master said, A gentleman 'can be bounteous without extravagance, can get work out of people without arousing resentment, has longings but is never covetous, is proud but never insolent, inspires awe but is never ferocious.'

Tzu-chang said, What is meant by being bounteous without extravagance? The Master said, If he gives to the people only such advantages as are really advantageous to them, is he not being bounteous without extravagance? If he imposes upon them only such tasks as they are capable of performing, is he not getting work out of them without arousing resentment? If what he longs for and what he gets is Goodness, who can say that he is covetous? A gentleman, irrespective of whether he is dealing with many persons or with few, with the small or with the great, never presumes to slight them. Is not this indeed being 'proud without insolence'? A gentleman sees to it that his clothes and hat are put on straight, and imparts such dignity to his gaze that he imposes on others. No sooner do they see him from afar than they are in awe. Is not this indeed inspiring awe without ferocity?

Tzu-chang said, What are they, that you call the Four Ugly Things? The Master said, Putting men to death, without having taught them (the Right); that is called savagery. Expecting the completion of tasks, without giving due warn-ing; that is called oppression. To be dilatory about giving orders, but to expect absolute punctuality, that is called being a tormentor. And similarly, though meaning to let a man have something, to be grudging about bringing it out from within, that is called behaving like a petty functionary.

3. The Master said, He who does not understand the will of Heaven cannot be regarded as a gentleman. He who does not know the rites cannot take his stand. He who does not under-stand words, cannot understand people.

3. On Human Nature

MENCIUS SAID: ALL MEN HAVE a certain sympathy toward their fellows. The great monarchs of old had this human sympathy, and it resulted in their government being sympathetic. Having this feel-ing of sympathy for his fellows, he who acts upon it in governing the Empire will find that his rule can be conducted as it were in the palm of his hand. What I mean by this feeling of sympathy which all men possess is this: If anyone were to see a child falling into a well, he would have a feeling of horror and pity, not because he happened to be an intimate friend of the child's parents, nor because he sought the approbation of his neigh-bours and friends, nor yet because he feared to be thought inhumane. Looking at the matter in the light of this example, we may say that no man is devoid of a feeling of compassion, nor of a feeling of shame, nor of a feeling of consideration for oth-ers, nor of a feeling of plain right and wrong. The feeling of compassion is the origin of benevolence; the feeling of shame is the origin of righteousness; the feeling of consideration for others is the origin of good manners; the feeling of right and wrong is the origin of wisdom. The presence of these four elements in man is as natural to him as the posses-sion of his four limbs. Having these four elements within him, the man who says he is powerless to act as he should is doing a grave injury to himself. And the man who says the same of his prince is likewise doing him a grave injury. Let a man but know how to expand and develop these four ele-ments existing in the soul, and his progress becomes as irresistible as a newly kindled fire or a spring that has just burst from the ground. If they can be fully developed, these virtues are strong enough to safeguard all within the Four Seas; if allowed to remain undeveloped, they will not suf-fice for the service due to one's parents.

The philosopher Kao said: Man's nature may be likened to a willow tree; righteousness, to a cup or bowl. Making a man's nature righteous and good is like making cups and bowls out of the wood of a willow tree.—Mencius replied: Can you make cups and bowls without interfering with the nature of the willow? No, you can only do so by doing vio-lence to its nature. That being the case, would you say that men can only be made righteous and good by doing violence to their nature? Your argument

From Mencius, The Book of Mencius, *trans. by Lionel Giles (London: John Murray Publishers, 1942), pp. 49–50, 91–92, 94–96, and 98–101. Reprinted with permission.*

would then necessarily lead mankind to regard goodness and righteousness as a misfortune!

* * *

The philosopher Kao said: Man's nature is like a current of water: deflected in an easterly direction, it will flow to the east; deflected in a westerly direction, it will flow to the west. And just as water has no predilection either for east or for west, so man's nature is not predisposed either to good or to evil.—Mencius replied: It is true that water has no predilection for east or west, but will it flow equally well up or down? Human nature is disposed towards goodness just as water flows downwards. There is no water but flows down, and no men but show this tendency to good. Now, if water is splashed up, it can be made to go right over your head; by forcing it along, it can be made to go uphill. But how can that be termed its natural bent? It is some external force that causes it to do so. And likewise, if men are made to do what is not good, their nature is being distorted in a similar way.

It is in virtue of its innate feelings that human nature may be considered good. That is what I mean in calling it good. If a man's actions are evil, it is not his instincts that are to blame. The feelings of compassion, of shame and repugnance, of moral discrimination, are common to all men. The feeling of compassion—that is benevolence; the feeling of shame and repugnance—that is righteousness; the feeling of reverence—that is propriety; the feeling of discrimination between right and wrong—that is wisdom. Benevolence, righteousness, propriety and wisdom are not instilled into us from without—they are part of our very being. Only we give them no thought. Hence the saying: 'You can have them for the seeking, or lose them through neglect.' Some will have twice as much as others, some five times as much, and some incalculably more, but that is because those others have not been able to develop their natural instincts to the full.

Mencius said: Beautiful once were the trees on Mount Niu: but, standing on the outskirts of a great capital, they were ruthlessly lopped with axe and bill: how could their beauty then endure?

Quickened, however, by the alternation of day and night, and fed by the rains and the dew, some shoots again put forth. But cows and goats came and browsed upon them, and so the mountain became denuded as you see it now; and seeing its denudation, people imagine that no timber ever grew upon it. Yet such was assuredly not its real nature. So with the natural endowment of man: how can it be devoid of the feeling of benevolence or the sense of what is right? But these good feelings are shed in the same way as trees are felled by the axe. If they are cut down day after day, how can the beauty of the mind endure? Though quickened by the alternation of day and night, the moral judgments which are intimately associated with the mind of man tend to grow weaker after the breath of dawn, and as the result of the day's destructive work atrophy sets in. As this atrophy continues, the healing influence of night is insufficient to keep them alive; and this being so, the mind reverts to a state not far removed from that of brute beasts. Seeing this, one is apt to imagine that the right disposition never existed. Yet how can such a state be regarded as the real nature of man? Given proper nourishment, all things will develop; if it is withheld, they will inevitably decay. Confucius said: 'Hold fast, and it will remain; relax your hold, and it will disappear. It comes and goes without regard to time and place.' Was it not the mind of which he spake?

Mencius said: Benevolence is the feeling of man's heart, righteousness is the path for man's following. To stray from the path and leave it untrod, to let the feeling go and not know where to seek it:—this is pitiful indeed! When our dogs and fowls are lost, we know how to find them, but our lost feeling we know not how to find. The end and aim of all learning is nothing but this—to seek and find the feeling we have lost.

The disciple Kung-tu asked, saying: Human nature is common to us all. How is it, then, that some are great men and some are small men?—Mencius replied: Those that follow their higher nature are great men; those that follow their lower nature are small men—Kung-tu said; Seeing that all alike are men, how is it that some follow their higher nature and some their lower nature?—Mencius replied: The function of the eye and the ear is not thought, but is determined by material objects; for when objects impinge on the senses, these cannot but follow wherever they lead. Thought is the function of the mind: by thinking, it achieves; by not thinking, it fails to achieve. These faculties are implanted in us by Nature. If we take our stand from the first on the higher part of our being, the lower part will not be able to rob us of it. It is simply this that constitutes the great man.

Of all seeds, the five kinds of grain are the best; yet if unripe, they are not so good as darnel or tares. The same is true of benevolence: here, too, ripeness is all.

A man of Jên asked the disciple Wu-lu, saying: Which is the more important, food or correct behaviour?—He replied: Correct behavior is the more important—And which is the more important, sexual relations or correct behavior?—Correct behaviour.—If observance of the rules of correct behaviour in regard to food means starving to death, whereas the infringement of them means getting food, must those rules still be observed? If

the necessity of fetching one's bride in person prevents one from getting a wife, whereas the omission of this ceremony would make it possible to get one, is the ceremony still to be regarded as essential?—Wu-lu was unable to answer this, so the next day he went to Tsou and put the case to Mencius. Mencius said: What is the difficulty in answering these questions? Any small piece of wood, if adjusted only at the top and not at the bottom, may be brought up to the height of a lofty gable. When we say that gold is heavier than feathers, do we mean that a single golden button is heavier than a cart-load of feathers? Here you are given a case in which rules of behaviour are of little importance as compared with food or sexual relations; but it might just as well be the other way round. Go and say this to your friend: 'If you can get food from your elder brother by twisting his arm and snatching it from him, but not otherwise, will you twist his arm? If you can only get a wife by leaping over your neighbour's wall and carrying off his virgin daughter, will you carry her off in this way?'

Study Questions

1. What were the common themes of Chinese culture known both to Lao-tzu and Confucius?

2. Do Lao-tzu and Confucius mean the same thing by the concept, the "Way"? Explain.

3. For Confucius, is human nature essentially good or essentially evil?

4. What are the moral principles of jen and shu?

5. Explain why hsiao plays such an important role in Confucian ethics.

Chapter 2

Ancient Greek Philosophers 1: Plato

Introduction

We begin our discussion of what Western philosophers have to say about human nature and its associated topics with the ancient Greek philosophers, Socrates and Plato. As with much of Western culture, Western philosophy began in ancient Greece close to twenty-five hundred years ago. The first philosophers, called **Presocratic** philosophers, were men who lived in and around Greece during the fifth and sixth centuries B.C.E. Their investigations of nature set the stage for what we now call the scientific understanding of the world, and paved the way for the teachings of Socrates, Plato, and Aristotle.

Although he himself wrote nothing, the teachings of **Socrates** (470–399 B.C.E.) are well recorded in the first third or so of the many philosophical dialogues written by his most famous student, **Plato** (427–348 B.C.E). Unlike the Presocratics, Socrates was less concerned with investigating nature, and more concerned with understanding what it means to be a human being and with discovering how life ought to be led. Some aspect of these matters usually serves as the subject matter of Plato's dialogues, in which Socrates is usually the lead character. There we find him engaged in discussion with one or more of his fellow Athenians. Sometimes the person questioned by Socrates is an aristocrat, a member of the wealthy, educated class, who represents the wisdom of the past. More often it is one of the **Sophists,** teachers of the sons of Athenian aristocrats. These men were paid to show their students how to be successful in life. They primarily instructed them in the art of rhetoric, especially in the skills of argumentation and public speaking. These were essential skills for success in Athens, where politics was often the chosen path to fame and fortune for wealthy young men.

The training offered by the Sophists also included moral instruction, much of which was based on the assumption of ethical relativism. **Ethical relativism** is the view that what is right is relative to the conventions of a particular time and place. What is right may vary from time to time, from place to place, and from culture to culture, depending upon what people believe is right. The Sophists taught that the good life, the life of happiness, was to be gained by adopting the pathways to success that are the conventional ones of your society. Socrates was an enemy of ethical relativism and did whatever he could to show it to be false. For him, the correct goals to strive for in life are not determined by the current beliefs of a particular society. Instead, they are something *absolute*, something that is the same for everyone, regardless of time, place, and cultural background.

The Greeks were organized politically into groups called city-states. The two most famous of these were Athens and Sparta. During the last quarter of the fifth century B.C.E. these two city-states were engaged in the Peloponnesian war, which brought great suffering and turmoil to Athens. Because he questioned authority during this time, Socrates was seen by those in power as an enemy of Athens. He was accused by some powerful Athenians of corrupting the youth through his teachings and of being an atheist. Convicted, he was sentenced to death. He could have escaped and lived his life in exile, but because of his love and respect for Athens and for the truth he refused that option. Instead, he died in a prison cell as a result of drinking hemlock, a poison. The account given by Plato in his earliest dialogues of the trial and death of Socrates has inspired many generations of philosophers and others to think more seriously about what beliefs they espouse, and whether or not they would be willing to die for them as Socrates did for his. An account of the death of Socrates may be found at the end of *Reading 4.*

Plato was a member of the aristocratic class in Athens. He is one of the most influential philosophers in all of Western philosophy and also one of its finest writers. His dialogues offer the most complete account of philosophical knowledge of his time, including an account of reality, ethics, psychology, politics, education, and much more. Plato's philosophy was the first true system of Western philosophy of which we have a written record. This system of philosophy was so influential in Western culture that the writings of philosophers after Plato have been described as mere "footnotes" to Plato. He was one of the true giants of philosophy.

When Athens finally fell to the Spartans, Plato and other aristocrats blamed the defeat on the democratic form of government that existed at that time in Athens. This was a government whose decisions were made by people not well trained to govern. They were moved more by greed and emotion than by reason and concern for the good of all. Plato also condemned the ethical relativism at the root of this form of government for taking the life of his beloved teacher, Socrates. In perhaps his most famous dialogue, *The Republic,* he outlined in some detail how an ideal state ought to be formed and governed, and how those who are to rule it should be educated. For Plato, such a state is not ruled by the fleeting interests of the masses, but by those educated few who truly understand human nature and what makes it flourish. Somewhere around 388 B.C.E. he founded the Academy, a school designed to provide just such an education. The Academy was later to become the model for the modern university.

Worldview

For Plato, there is such a thing as human nature, and it is absolutely essential to understand what it is in order to understand how best to live our lives. To understand the reality of human nature fully, however, requires an understanding of reality in general. Since the time of Aristotle, at least, the study of what is real has been called **metaphysics.** In addition to knowing what is real, it is also important to understand what knowledge is itself, especially since so much of what is important about human beings is their ability to know. A study of knowledge is called **epistemology.** So it is to Plato's metaphysical and epistemological assumptions that we first turn. We will take some time investigating these assumptions of Plato, trying our best to make sense of them, especially since they are likely to seem a bit strange at first. If history is a series of footnotes to Plato (and Aristotle, we should add), then a good beginning in philosophy requires that we understand well the original text.

Plato believed that his investigation of these areas led him to insights not available to ordinary men. Since there were no common words to express them, he often described his views by using various literary devices—such as metaphor, analogy, simile, and allegory. Through these devices he could explain his views more simply by comparing them to various sorts of ordinary experiences that everyone understood. The first and perhaps most famous account of reality using such devices that will be discussed here is the **allegory of the cave.** In his most famous dialogue, *The Republic,* Plato has Socrates tell a story of prisoners in a cave. *Reading 1* is this story. In it Socrates asks his listeners to imagine a deep underground cave in which prisoners are located. They are tied tightly in chains, and have a view only of the back wall of the cave. They cannot see behind them, nor can they even see each other. They have been in this state for their entire lives, facing the back wall of the cave.

Imagine further, he asks his listeners, that on this wall passes a constant stream of shadows that the prisoners view. The prisoners do not know what causes these shadows. In fact, they are caused by people carrying what we will call cardboard cut-outs of material objects, people, and all sorts of living and nonliving entities. The people who carry these cardboard cut-outs walk back and forth behind the prisoners. They, in turn, have a light source—a fire, behind them. This light projects shadows of these cut-outs on the back wall of the cave. The people holding the cut-outs are walking in a trench, so that their shadows do not get projected onto the screen, just the shadows of the shapes of trees and rocks and people and other objects. To the prisoners, these shadows are all that exists. For them, the shadows are reality.

Suppose next, Socrates suggests, that one of the prisoners escapes from his chains and begins to turn away from the wall. He first sees people behind him, walking back and forth with their cardboard cut-outs, and realizes that the shadows on the back wall are mere copies of these. He next crawls outside of the cave. It is nighttime. In the moonlight he sees real trees and rocks and people, and realizes that the cardboard cut-outs are themselves copies of these. The next morning, in the sunlight, he sees these objects even more clearly for what they really are, recognizing for the first time what is truly real.

What Plato is suggesting is that all of us might be like these prisoners, trapped in the cave of our commonsense experience and beliefs. What seems to be real, our commonsense world, may be nothing but a world of shadows, or appearances, compared to what really exists on a deeper level. For Plato, the everyday world is real, it is not an experience of illusions or dreams or delusions. However, like the shadows in the cave, the world of our everyday experience is a mere copy of a higher reality. For Plato, corresponding to this distinction between what simply *appears* to be real (our commonsense world) and what *is* real, is a distinction between *sense knowledge* and *intellectual knowledge.* Knowledge through our senses—what we see, hear, taste, touch, and smell—gives us information only of the commonsense world. Knowledge of reality is attainable only by the mind, by intellectual knowledge. Plato trusted the mind alone, or reason, to deliver true knowledge. When used properly, it was capable of penetrating the depths of reality.

But what is this reality, how is it known by the mind, and how does it relate to our commonsense world? These questions were addressed by Plato in the *The Republic*, in the simile of **the divided line.** His account is presented in *Reading 2*. The image of the divided line presents a summary description of Plato's basic metaphysical and epistemological beliefs. An understanding of all of the elements presented in this graphic form that is sketched below will give you a good general idea of his view of reality and how we know it.

The first thing to notice is that the vertical line is divided into four segments by three horizontal lines. These horizontal lines are not all of the same length, because Plato wishes to emphasize that the longest line, the one in the middle, signifies a more significant division than those represented by the shorter lines. Everything below this longest horizontal line belongs to the world of appearances—what Plato refers to as "Becoming." It is known through various types of sensory knowledge, such as perception and imagination. Above this line is the world of reality, of Being. It is known by reason, by the mind. Plato ranks the various "objects" that may be known in importance, from top to bottom. He also ranks in importance the various ways of knowing these objects, thus presenting a view of various *levels* of reality and various ways of know-

THE DIVIDED LINE

TYPES OF KNOWLEDGE
(Epistemology)

OBJECTS KNOWN
(Metaphysics)

Understanding   Forms

KNOWLEDGE   BEING

Reasoning   Mathematical objects

Perception   Material Objects

OPINION   BECOMING

Imagination   Images

ing each level. It will be helpful to examine each item on this list separately, both on the "knowledge" side of the line and on the "objects known" side.

On the *lowest level* of "objects known" are found what Plato calls images. By this term he means various sorts of copies of material objects, such as images within your mind or dreams, or a reflection of a face in the water, or a painting, or a play that depicts life in imaginative ways. These are like the shadows in the cave, and they are the lowest form of reality. By using our imaginations, as artists do, we do not get a "deeper" understanding of truth, but only a poor copy of material objects, a distortion of what they really are. Plato had no fondness for artists and playwrights and they, in turn, lost no love on philosophers.

On the *next level* we find material objects, objects that we are aware of through our senses. Our senses deliver to us information about an object's color, shape, location, scent, texture, sound, and so on. When we put this information together we are said to perceive *objects* that have these properties. Material objects, like their corresponding "cardboard cut-outs" in the cave, are viewed by Plato as more real than their images, because their images are mere copies of them. Plato claims that we cannot *know* the everyday material world that is everywhere around us, but can merely form *opinions* of it. The trouble with opinions is that they are unreliable. They differ from person to person and often are incorrect. But we surely think that we have reliable knowledge of this world, even if there is a higher or deeper reality in addition to it. Why does Plato reserve the term "knowledge" for the world above the line and deny it to the material world?

Knowledge Requires Understanding

Partly this has to do with the character of the material world, and partly with Plato's conception of knowledge. The material world is a world of particular, concrete objects, moving about in space and time. Objects and persons in this everyday commonsense world of ours continually undergo change. In this world of Becoming everything is in flux, nothing is permanent. Each object continually changes its properties. Apples, for example, may change from seeds to buds, to small unripe apples, to larger ripe apples, to (if eaten) flesh, or (if pressed) to juice, or to a meal for bugs. And, as far as my perceptions tell me, no object is the same as any other. Apples all have different colors and sizes and shapes and tastes and odors, for example. In a world such as this, a world of changing, unique, particular objects, everything I perceive is as a completely new, never-before-seen object.

If perception gives me only the constant flow of changing events, and if perception is the way I become aware of material objects, then perception will not by itself produce knowledge. To see why is to understand better Plato's concept of knowledge. As the Sophists had taught that virtue is relative, they had also taught that knowledge based on perception was relative. "Man is the measure of all things," said Protagoras, one of the most famous of the Sophists. Not only does each object of perception differ from every other one, but also how one person experiences the properties of an object may differ dramatically from another person. What tastes too sweet to you may be just right for me; what I see as red you may see as pink; the air that feels warm to me as I enter the house on a winter's day may seem cold to you who have been inside all day. No knowledge is possible in a world where nothing is permanent, where nothing is the same as anything else, and where what is perceived is relative to each perceiver. Here there is to be had merely opinions that differ from person to person.

Plato agreed with the Sophist analysis that perception yields only opinion, but did not agree with them that perception is the only kind of knowledge that we have. As with Socrates before him, Plato despised this sort of thinking. If what is true is merely what individual people say is true, then anything and everything is true, which means that nothing is true, and that no statements describe how things really are. But Plato believed that we do have objective knowledge, knowledge that is true for everyone, at all times and places. Plato accepts it as true that there is such knowledge, that there is more than opinion. Without knowledge, after all, there would be no philosophy, no science, no mathematics, and no rational life to be led. If all that perception delivers is opinion, then there must be something else upon which to base knowledge, something more permanent and stable than the objects to be found in the world of Becoming.

For Plato, true knowledge, even knowledge of the material world, involves more than receiving sensory information. It also requires that we *understand* what is perceived. Understanding is basically a process of classifying things as belonging to certain general types. These general types or classes are called *concepts*. General concepts get expressed in statements such as, "This is an apple." Such a statement says that this particular object that I see before me belongs to the general class of apples. If I say, "Releasing a first degree murderer after five years in prison is unjust," then I am saying that this particular action that I observe belongs to the class of unjust actions.

True knowledge, then, involves classifying perceived objects as objects of certain types. This requires us to possess a system of concepts. But these concepts themselves are not the product of perception. We do not see "appleness" or "injustice," for example. Nevertheless, we do have knowledge of these concepts. If we did not, we could not recognize anything *as* an apple, for example, or *as* an act of injustice. So true knowledge has everything to do with possessing concepts. What concepts are, and how we get them, and why they provide a foundation for knowledge when perception does not, are all questions that await us as we ascend to the next level of the divided line, a level that takes us into the world of Being and Knowledge.

Mathematical Objects

The *third level* of the Divided Line is the level of Being called "mathematical objects." Mathematical objects are entities such as numbers, triangles, circles, and other figures, as well as ratios, points, and lines. These sorts of objects are the things studied by arithmetic and geometry, the two basic mathematical systems of the time. They are not material objects, though material objects possess mathematical properties such as shape and quantity. Instead, they are ideas or concepts. Triangles, for example, are two-dimensional, so they cannot exist in space and time as do material objects. Numbers are also not things, but rather are ideas. But if mathematical objects are merely concepts, why does Plato say that they are more real than material objects? Usually we do not think of an idea of something as more real than the thing of which it is an idea.

There are several reasons for Plato to elevate mathematical objects to a level of reality higher than that of material objects. First, he did not think of mathematical concepts as merely ideas in the minds of those who think them. If that was all they were, they would be as relative as our perceptions. After all, we can all understand the same concept in different ways. If concepts were simply states of our minds, then they would vary from person to person, and from time to time, and from culture to culture. Instead, Plato thinks of concepts as existing apart from any mind that thinks them. They exist separately from minds. They exist on their own or, as philosophers say, they "subsist." They are not dependent upon anything else for their existence. Sometimes the phrase "platonic heaven" is used to make this point. As material objects exist in the material world, so nonmaterial objects such as concepts exist in a nonmaterial world, a platonic heaven. Plato ranks the reality of the nonmaterial world higher than the material world. For this reason, because he believes that ideas are more real than material objects, Plato is called an **idealist** in his metaphysical beliefs.

Another reason why mathematical objects rank higher than material objects, is that material objects may be understood as *copies* of mathematical ones. In fact, mathematical objects are symbolized in Plato's cave analogy by material objects known in the moonlight. In what sense are material objects copies of mathematical objects, as cardboard cut-outs are copies of material objects known by moonlight? For one thing, material objects have shape and size and weight, and other quantifiable properties. So they have mathematical properties. Even today, the language of physics is basically mathematical. That is, the world, in its most basic aspects, is understood as a mathematical universe. We describe it according to mathematical models. It answers to mathematical descriptions.

If we grant that mathematical concepts have a different sort of reality than material objects, and that material objects are copies of mathematical concepts, we might still not be satisfied with Plato ranking the world of Being over the world of Becoming. What else makes him choose the abstract world of ideas over the concrete world of material objects? One reason is that ideas provide a basis for knowledge, while material objects provide only a basis for opinion. Bodies of knowledge called arithmetic and geometry do in fact exist. Moreover, they contain knowledge that is not relative to time, place, and the beliefs of various individuals. "$2 + 2 = 4$" even if you do not happen to believe it, even if no one believes it, even if no one exists to believe it. But what is it about concepts that allows such reliable knowledge?

Mathematical ideas (and Forms, too, as we will see) have properties not shared by material objects. They are radically different, warranting Plato's distinction between the realms of Being and Becoming. First, concepts are not material objects or properties of material objects, but are *ideal* objects. They cannot be seen or heard or felt, only thought. They are not in space, have no weight or color or odor or texture, and so on; and they are not in time, as are all material objects. Unlike material objects, mathematical objects are *unchanging*. The idea "triangle," expressed in the definition of a triangle, never changes. It is always the same. Moreover, concepts are *eternal*. They do not get created or destroyed, do not come into and go out of being, but exist outside of time, eternally. Finally, they are *universal*, not particular. The concept "triangle" is not a concept of one particular triangle but of all triangles. It is not an idea of the differences between particular triangular things, but is the idea of triangles in general. These properties of ideas—that they are universal, unchanging, and eternal—are defining properties of all objects on the level of Being.

In the end, for Plato, mathematical concepts are more real than material objects because Being is more real than Becoming. This was an assumption for many of the Presocratic philosophers, and for the classical Greek philosophers as well. The unchanging, the eternal, the universal world of Being was considered more real than the world of Becoming, because the collection of ideas that make it up form a general *pattern*. Like the architectural plan according to which many houses may be built, this ideal pattern is thought of by Plato as copied by individual material objects in the world of Becoming. This pattern of all things is more real than the particular objects that exhibit it, because it is what is most important about these objects. It is what they truly are underneath all their variations and changes.

The Theory of Forms

The ideal pattern to which material objects conform is not just a mathematical one. In addition to mathematical concepts there is also a realm of concepts that Plato calls the **Forms.** In the nonphysical world of ideas, Forms are understood by Plato to have the highest reality, and this for two reasons. First, they are known according to the highest kind of knowing, which he calls "understanding." Notice that Plato has been operating under an assumption that different forms of knowing require different kinds of objects to be known. Imagining requires images; perception requires material objects; reasoning requires mathematical objects; and understanding requires the Forms. Ultimately, this assumption is what leads him to think of reality as having different levels. Instead of thinking that there is one reality known in four different ways, he thinks that the existence of four different ways of knowing must mean that there are four different sorts of things known.

It is important to understand the difference between "reasoning" and "understanding" if we are to understand the difference between mathematical concepts and Forms. We come to know mathematical objects by a process of reasoning whereby we accept certain axioms as true and deduce conclusions (theorems) from them. This is called "reasoning" by Plato, and he considers it an imperfect type of knowledge. It is imperfect because the axioms themselves upon which the truth of the theorems rest are never proven, but merely accepted as true. If they turn out to be false, then the whole mathematical system which rests upon them will also be false. What Plato considers to be a more perfect kind of knowledge resides on the highest level of the divided line. If this is a more perfect kind of knowledge, then Plato assumes that it must be knowledge of a higher kind of reality. For our purposes, it might be better to describe what the Forms are before trying to say what "understanding" is, by which we come to know them.

Plato's theory of Forms is complex and not always easy to follow, but in broad outline it goes as follows. For Plato, the most basic thing that may be said about any sort of being, other than the fact that it exists, is that it is a certain "kind" of thing. Material objects in the world of Becoming, as well as mathematical concepts and Forms in the world of Being, are all known to us as certain kinds or types of things. This is easy to see for objects on the level of Being, where each concept is itself a unique kind, such as the concept of a rectangle. But it is also true for objects on the level of Becoming, for material objects and images. They are all perceived as certain kinds of things.

It is very important to note that what makes a particular material object a certain kind of thing, similar to other things of the same kind, is not a collection of shared *sensory* properties. Apples are apples whether they are red or yellow or green. One apple may not share any sensory properties at all with other apples, but still be classified as belonging to the same general kind or type—apples. For Plato, if objects have different sensory properties but are still perceived by us as the same kinds of things, it is because they all share the same *intelligible* structure. They are all copies of the same Form and thus share a common essence or essential structure.

The intelligible structure, or essence or Form of something is what makes it the kind of being that it is. It is the "appleness" of the apple, for example, as opposed to its color and shape and taste, and so on. It is not a visible structure, one that is perceived, but is rather a structure that is understood by the mind. This is what Plato means by Form—the true nature of a thing, whether that thing be a material object, a moral virtue, or a Form itself. As a blueprint of a house is the idea of the essential structure of the house, so a Form is a "blueprint" of the essential structure of some thing. The idea of "humanity" is a Form, for example, and all human beings are copies of it. So is the idea of "justice," an idea that is the blueprint for all just actions. As houses of the same type may be understood to be imperfect "copies" of the plan according to which they were built, material objects may be seen as imperfect copies of the Form which defines their type.

Forms are located on the highest level of reality because they share the properties of Being that Plato has identified with reality. They are the universal, unchanging, eternal set of ideas that make up the pattern of nature, morality, and human nature. Collectively, they form a system of ideas that Plato identifies with the highest type of reality. Like the prisoner now outside the cave and viewing the world in the sunlight, once we possess this set of ideas called Forms, we understand the true nature of reality. Reality is enduring, permanent, unchanging pattern that all beings reflect. This is what is most important about anything, its permanent rational structure, its *plan*. Particular beings may come and go, but they do so always according to this plan. They exist always according to this pattern, always as one of these types or Forms. Plato believes that there is an order to the universe and that the set of ideas called mathematical concepts and the Forms *is* this order. Knowledge of the Forms brings the highest degree of wisdom, called "understanding" by Plato. This is objective, absolute knowledge of the unchanging world of Being, of which the commonsense world is a mere copy, a mere shadow, a mere appearance.

Knowledge of the Forms

The question now is how does one acquire knowledge of the Forms? Today we might say that concepts are somehow derived from experience. We see lots of apples and eventually get the general idea of "appleness." Aristotle holds such a view, as we will see later. But Plato rejects this explanation. As with mathematical concepts, Forms are understood, not perceived. But what is this process of understanding to which Plato gives the highest position among all the ways of knowing? Most of us do not believe that just by thinking about the world we can discover something about its nature. We have to examine it, observe it, experience it, and only then can we know what it is like. But Plato, along with some Modern philosophers referred to as " rationalists," believes that the only way to find knowledge that is universal, unchanging, and eternal is through reason.

Reason discovers new truths by deducing them from already known truths; this is "reasoning." This is the kind of knowledge that occurs in mathematics. It is the kind of knowledge that Plato finds wanting, because its conclusions rest on assumptions that are not themselves proven to be true. Reason works in another way, however, a more perfect way according to Plato. The mind can grasp the truth of the Forms by a sort of intuition or insight. For Plato, what this amounts to is similar to a process of recollection or remembering. To understand a Form is to remember it. Unable to understand how ideas could arise from experience, he claimed that they did not arise at all. Instead, we always knew them, had them in our memories. Understanding the Forms is not discovering something new. We already know them, we were born with knowledge of them, they are within us, waiting to be discovered.

True knowledge is found not by having lots of experiences of the world, but by looking within our souls. Plato presents what we today call a theory of innate ideas. **Innate ideas** are ideas that are not learned or acquired in any manner, but are part of us from birth, though it often takes some doing to uncover them. Some contemporary cognitive scientists believe that our brains are pre-wired by nature with a knowledge of universal syntactical rules, for example, rules that show themselves as a "readiness" to learn a particular language early in childhood. This may be the closest thing we have today to a theory of innate ideas. Plato's version was explained not by reference to preprogrammed brains, but by belief in reincarnation. Whether Plato really believed in reincarnation, or merely used it to make his notion of understanding more intelligible is not easy to say. In any case, his explanation of how we come to know the Forms goes like this. Before we were born our souls existed in another world, a world that is our true home, a place of happiness. This is the platonic heaven, the world of pure Forms. Our souls knew the Forms directly then, as our senses know the color red directly now.

For some unspecified reason, probably a punishment of some sort inflicted by the gods, we were born into human form. This is an inferior type of existence because, stuffed in a body as it is, the soul now knows only through the body, only through sensation. And what it knows is not the Forms, but just the very poor copies of them that we call material objects. But when the soul withdraws into itself it is capable of remembering the Forms directly, since they are still present in each of us, in our memory. Seeing many human beings, and then thinking about what might be their essence, their Form, may trigger a recollection of the Form of humanity, for example. True knowledge, knowledge of Being, is a process of understanding. Understanding is having an intuition or insight. Having an intuition is remembering a Form. Forms are present in our memories as innate ideas.

The Demiurge and the Good

As he had used the stories of the cave, the divided line, and reincarnation to illuminate various points, Plato used another story to answer the question of how material objects got to be copies of Forms. He says that the world was formed by a divine being, a sort of powerful architect, a being Plato called the **demiurge.** As a carpenter might build a house according to an architectural plan, and in this way the house gets to be a copy of the plan, so also did the world get formed by the demiurge according to mathematical concepts and Forms, the general plan of the universe. In this way material objects now are copies of these ideas. Forms, in turn, exist both perfectly in an ideal world and imperfectly in material objects, insofar as material objects have been patterned after them. Forms may also exist in the minds of persons, as when a philosopher remembers them. But whether or not they get copied or thought, they are in themselves the subsistent, unchanging, eternal pattern of ideas, knowledge of which is absolute truth. In the Medieval period of philosophy, something very much like the Forms of Plato would end up in the mind of God and be referred to as the plan of creation.

The most elusive idea of Plato is his concept of the **Good.** The Good is the goal of life, that which will make us happy once we possess it. He compares it to the sun in the allegory of the cave. The released prisoner is able to see most clearly in the daytime because the sun lights up the world and makes it more visible than moonlight could do. In the same way, the Good lights up the Forms and makes them intelligible. This indirect language gives us a clue to follow, since the Good seems not to be one of the Forms themselves. Nor does Plato seem to equate the Good with some personal being, such as a god. Instead, the Good seems to be the source of our understanding of the Forms, as the sun is what allows us to see.

Plato seems to have one of two things in mind here, and it is anyone's guess which is correct. On the one hand, the Good may be the "light" of reason. As the sun is the light that allows us to see material objects, the Good may be the power of the mind to intuit truth, the power of the mind that illuminates the Forms and makes them intelligible to us as we nudge them from memory. On the other hand, the Good may be understood as the relationship which holds among the Forms, a sort of unity of Forms. As is the case with a scientific theory, where statements are not just presented as a list but fit together in some sort of ordered way, the Forms constitute an interrelated pattern that makes up a unified system of concepts. This unifying order may be what Plato means by the Good. On either interpretation, and there may be others, the Good, that for which we ought to strive to attain happiness, has all to do with discovering the Forms, the ultimate wisdom.

Human Nature

As well as his views on metaphysics and epistemology, Plato has a great deal to say about psychology, ethics, politics, and education as well. Without exception, what he teaches us about these matters all rests on his views of human nature. In discussing his view of human nature we will examine what he believes to be both the structure of human beings, how we are constructed, and our primary functions, what sorts of things we do by nature. The important thing to say about structure at the very beginning is that Plato is a dualist. He thinks that there are two sorts of stuff that make up the world, two sorts of things that especially come together in human beings. A human being is composed of body and soul. The body is a physical thing, while the soul is a spiritual or nonphysical or immaterial thing. The soul is completely different from the body. The body is physical, the soul is nonphysical; the body dies, the soul lives on forever; the body has size and shape and weight and color, the soul has none of these properties.

The idea of a nonphysical nature of human beings did not originate with Plato, but in his writings we find in Western philosophy the first fully developed idea of a human person being composed of two different sorts of entities. This view, called **dualism,** became so deeply entrenched in the West that we sometimes take it as fact. Following Socrates, Plato thought of human beings as essentially their souls. While we *have* bodies, we *are* souls. The body and its desires are important and must be acknowledged, but matters of the soul are far more important. The innate tendencies that define human nature are especially those of our true self, those of the soul.

The "Parts" of the Soul

For Plato, there are three aspects or "parts" of the soul, each with its own innate tendencies. To describe these parts of the soul and how they work together he employed yet another literary figure. This time it is an analogy, which models the structure and function of a soul after the structure and function of a chariot. In this model, the chariot has two horses and a driver. For Plato, the two horses resemble the two irrational elements of the soul. One horse is calm and relatively easy to control; the other is unruly and dashes off fiercely in all directions. The third element of the chariot is the driver. The driver, who resembles the rational part of the soul, must be in control if the two horses are to work together. The first horse is relatively easy to control, but the second one must be whipped into obedience if the chariot is to proceed in the most efficient manner.

The soul also has three parts, each with their own innate tendencies, their own needs and desires. Just as the chariot will make the best progress toward its goal only if the driver is clearly in command of the two horses, so too, a person will be able to achieve his or her goal of living a full, rich, flourishing life only if *reason* is in command of the two irrational parts of the soul. Reason is the ability to know what is real, the Forms, and to figure out how to use this wisdom to guide behavior. The two irrational parts or aspects of a person's soul are what Plato calls our spirit and our appetites. Our *spirit,* about which Plato was not terribly clear, seems to be composed of what today we call our emotions. If we are governed by our emotions, as noble as they may be, our lives will not be happy. A good education, whose goal is knowledge of the Forms, including moral and political ideals, will easily channel our emotions into moral virtues, in the same way as an easy pull on the reins will guide the first horse along the correct path. Our rashness will become courage; our pride, loyalty; our anger, justice.

Controlling our *appetites,* especially our bodily desires, is not such an easy matter. Our desires conflict more intensely with reason, especially with the knowledge of how we ought to behave, than do our emotions. As the unruly horse may be difficult to control, so too, when our desires are strong and in conflict with what is truly good for us, we often have a difficult time overcoming their pull. A person ruled by desire is truly unhappy in the long run, and is fortunate indeed if he learns to control his appetites. As the unruly horse needs to be whipped into shape, human beings need to be controlled by education, by law, and by their own reason if they are to be happy. An ideal life, like an ideally functioning chariot, is one that is governed by reason, not by emotions or desire. This is because deep down, in the realm of our true selves, we are our reason.

Not all people have these three elements to the same degree. Plato says that the apparently natural differences among various people are caused by differences in the ratios of these parts. Some have a greater abundance of reason, for example, and desire a life of knowledge. Others have an abundance of spirit, fitting them best for military life. Still others have great appetites, and are thus more inclined to pursue material pleasures. While there is one structure to human nature, while everyone has a soul with all three aspects or dimensions, the relative amounts of these different elements produce quite different types of lives. Plato believes that these variations are also responsible for class differences in society, and even for the cultural differences between various sorts of societies.

Consequences

We begin our discussion of the consequences which follow from Plato's view of human nature by examining his description of society as it ought to be.

Society

For Plato, just as reason, spirit, and appetite are part of human nature, so living in groups is also natural. Human beings are naturally social beings. The most refined form of group living is the state, what the Greeks called the *polis*. So the state is a natural entity, like the family, and not simply a matter of convention or convenience, or a way for a few to exert power over the many. The state has many functions. Its laws protect people from each other for one thing, and its armies defend them against hostile outside groups. It also makes life more efficient by providing for a division of labor. In a state, not everyone has to provide for all the necessities of life, since there are those who specialize in different trades, crafts, agriculture, and the like. Most importantly, the state for Plato is also a *moral entity*. It is concerned not only with the survival of its members, but also with shaping their lives for their own good. The state civilizes people; it makes them better persons; it allows them to live fuller, richer lives than they would if they were not members of a state. As the good family grows its children into virtuous adults, the good state grows its subjects into the best sorts of people that they can be. For Plato, the state is primarily a moral entity, charged with directing the lives of its subjects onto the road to the good life.

For Plato, the structure of the state grows out of human nature. Because of this, the way that the state should operate to create fuller, richer lives for its subjects is similar to the way that the life of an individual should be lived if that life is to be an excellent one. To see how the state is modeled on human nature it is important to note first that the state has various classes, just as the soul has various parts. In *The Republic* Plato argued that the parts of the soul are like the various classes of society. This argument is presented in *Reading 3*. There are different classes in society because there are different amounts of desire, spirit, and reason that abide in the souls of individuals. Not all human beings have the same balance between spirit, desire, and reason. Some have more of one than another.

In an ideal society, people would be arranged into the classes that reflect their psychological differences. One class would be the working class and consist of people who are motivated especially by their appetites, especially by the desire to accumulate material goods. Next is the military class, which consists of people with an abundance of emotion. Finally there are the rulers who govern the other classes. Ideally, rulers have a greater abundance of reason, a greater ability to understand how things really are and what sorts of policies will achieve the highest good for all. For an ideal society, one that is the happiest, it is imperative that those from the working class or the military class do not rule, just as it is imperative that the charioteer control the chariot. Otherwise, unwise policies will govern political and social life, policies based on desire or emotion, not reason.

The best society for Plato is defined as the harmonious working together of all classes. Just as the desires, emotions, and reason of an individual each have their own role and their proper relationship to one another, so each of three classes that compose a society has its own role and its proper relationship to the other classes. The working class creates the material goods of society, the military class protects it against other states and protects subjects from each other, and the ruling class sets policies and laws that provide for the harmonious relationship among classes. Each of these three functions are good and necessary for a happy society, a society that grows each of its subjects to the level of excellence of which his or her nature is capable.

This conception of the ideal society excludes the notion of treating people equally, and allows for some forms of discrimination. It would not be wise to treat all classes equally for Plato, because that would ignore the natural differences among people. It would not be wise, for example, to allow those from the working class to be rulers because, driven as they are primarily by desire, they have neither the talent nor the training to lead wisely. This is the problem with democracy, for Plato. As rule by the majority, it is rule by those in the more heavily populated lower classes, and thus rule by greed and self-interest. It is not rule by reason for the good of all. This is why everyone in the working class must be subordinate to those in the ruling class. While it is possible now and then for someone in the working class to have the intelligence to move up to the ruling class, generally speaking it is from among the wisest and best people that all rulers will come.

Plato believes that in his ideal society the ruler has no limits. The ruler may pass whatever laws he or she believes will result in the common good. Individual freedom is to be sacrificed for the common good. Since they have little knowledge of what is truly good for them, members of the lower classes would simply use their freedom to live lives driven by desire, as is their nature. Members of the ruling class, however, receive an extensive education, culminating in philosophical studies, and thus they do know what it takes to make someone truly happy. They rule by their cognitive authority, by their ability to know what is good for themselves and for others. No one knows better than they what it takes to live a full and rich life. These rulers Plato refers to as **philosopher-kings,** and he claims that the best type of society will exist only when they rule and rule with absolute power.

There is little incentive in Plato's ideal society for rulers to become corrupt. For one thing, they are not allowed to own property, and thus their temptation to rule for their own advantage will be eliminated. For another, while they are allowed and even encouraged to have children in order to produce more human beings with noble natures, they are not allowed to raise or even to know their own children. There are no exclusive sexual relationships among members of the ruling class in Plato's ideal state, and thus no family structure. Only members of the working classes raise their own children. Any children that rulers have with other members of the ruling class are raised communally by the state. This reduces the temptation of the rulers to rule for the advantage of their families. So, instead of seeking advantages for themselves or their families, rulers will be guided by knowledge to seek the good for all.

Plato extended the model of the tripartite soul to explain not only the differences between classes in any particular society, but also the differences between cultures and races as well. The differences between Athens, the birthplace of so much science and art, and Sparta, a military Greek society, is explained by claiming that Athenians have more "reason" and Spartans more "spirit." Those who were not Greek were dismissed as barbarians and thought of as driven only by desire. So there are natural differences among cultures because the people in some are born with an abundance of reason, while others have less fortunate natures, being easily driven about by their emotions or desires. An ideal society, such as Plato hoped Athens might one day become, is possible because it would contain many more people who have an abundance of reason than are to be found in less noble cultures.

Freedom

One of the big problems in philosophy today is the question of **freedom and determinism.** Partly as a result of the success of science in discovering many of the causes of human behavior, the question has arisen as to whether or not all human behavior is determined by antecedent conditions. At least one Presocratic philosopher, Democritus, seems to have thought that it was. Since his time many philosophers and scientists have defended one form or another of determinism. This is a serious problem, and one to be discussed in some detail in future chapters. For now it is enough to say that most ancient Greek philosophers did not so much argue for the existence of human **free choice,** as they assumed its existence. It was a required assumption for them, especially in order to explain how it is possible to *choose* one way of living over another. The view of human nature defended by Plato assumes that we are most fully free when we are self-governed, that is, when we are governed by our reason.

Although he did not have much to say about freedom of choice, Plato had lots to say about **freedom of action**—the ability to do what we want to do. In a political setting this is often referred to as "liberty." When threatened by others, this is the sort of freedom that people are willing to fight and die for. Plato's ideal state would restrict the liberty of an individual far more dramatically than is the case in the United States today. Just as a parent does not allow her children to do things that may be harmful to them, so Plato would have the rulers pass laws that prevent members of all classes from harming themselves physically, psychologically, and morally. For him, the job of the state is not just to protect us from each other and then leave us alone to live as we please. Instead, its job is to grow us into the best persons that we can be. By its laws it shapes our behavior to good ends and away from evil ones. So Plato would allow state censorship, for example, and any number of other restrictions to be placed on subjects for their own good. Plato's ideal ruler, the philosopher king, is a dictator, though a benevolent one. The view that it is a legitimate function of the state to force its subjects to act for their own good, as a parent does for his or her child, is called **paternalism.**

Ethics

The three parts of the soul comprise the basic elements of human nature, as the three classes are the constituent parts of a state. This is how Plato describes the essential elements of our individual and social natures. There is much more to be said about human nature than this, however. Indeed, the most important question of all is not simply the question of what sorts of beings we are, but the question of what sorts of beings we could be. Since not everyone is blessed with the same proportion of reason, spirit, and appetite, this question is answered by Plato differently for those placed by their natures into the different classes of society. For us, the focus shall be on what Plato considers to be the most noble human beings, those with the greatest amount of reason. As elitist as it sounds, Plato claims that only they can be fully happy. Before turning to his vision of the good life, much of which we have already seen, it will be helpful to discuss briefly the subject of ethics.

As was said in the previous chapter, ethics is about two central areas. One concerns how to tell right from wrong, while the other is about discovering what is the good life, the life of happiness. Perhaps the most important practical idea that followed from Plato's view of human nature was his conception of the good life, the life of happiness. Discovering what the good life is and living it to the fullest is what Plato and Socrates before him understood to be the point of philosophy. They were deeply concerned with what human nature could be when a human being lived a truly excellent life.

Plato's view of what such a life could be like was the one that he had Socrates describe to some of his followers as he was about to die. In the dialogue called the *Phaedo,* just before Socrates drank the poisonous hemlock and died, he described why philosophers should not fear death. What he says there may be found in *Reading 4.* Through the words of Socrates, Plato claims that death, the separation of the soul from the body, is what philosophers strive for throughout their lives. A philosopher is someone trying to understand the Forms, not someone engaged in the pursuit of material gain and physical pleasures. At death, their soul returns to its proper home, the intellectual world of the Forms. The true interests of those who seek happiness are the interests of the soul, especially the interests of reason. Since death frees the soul from the body and allows it to pursue its interests free from its physical confinement, then death may be seen as the goal of a philosophical life.

Philosophers are seekers, even lovers, of wisdom. This is what Plato counts as valuable in itself—wisdom. Wisdom is an understanding of how all things really are (theoretical knowledge), and the use of this knowledge to guide action (practical knowledge). This is what is truly important to human beings, given our natures as rational beings. This is what will really make us happy—not fame or fortune. The pleasures of the soul, not those of the body are what our higher natures are built for. What the soul desires most is wisdom. When reason rules the soul as the charioteer rules the horses, and when reason dictates behavior as the philosopher king rules the city, then we will find our true happiness. Therein lies the secret of a truly excellent life, therein lies life's meaning and purpose.

Even those who by their nature are not capable of becoming wise, those of the working and military classes, may become happy in their limited fashion if they follow the rule of reason as well. It may not be *their* reason that they follow, driven as they are by appetite and emotion. But if they follow the reason of the philosopher king, the one who knows the various types of human nature and what is good for each of them, the one who creates the policies and laws that govern the ideal state, then their lives will be in better balance because of it. The excellent life for Plato, the life that truly nourishes what we really are, is just this life where all the conflicting parts of ourselves are brought into balance by reason. This is his vision of the healthy, flourishing, happy life; this is what it means to be an excellent human being.

God and Immortality

Plato's writings are filled with references to the soul surviving the death of the body and even preexisting the body. The story he tells is that the natural home of our souls is in the world of the Forms. For some unexplained reason, our souls were punished. The punishment was for them to be removed from the world of the Forms and coupled with our bodies. At birth our true selves, our souls, become imprisoned in the cage of our bodies. For those who realize this, the job is to get back home, to escape the body by living the life of the soul. If we succeed, we will return to the Forms and be happy; if we fail, we will have to try again in a new, reincarnated body. So Plato offers us a form of reincarnation, a doctrine accepted by some of the Presocratics, to explain what happens at the time of death and beyond. There is some question as to whether he actually believed in reincarnation. Many believe that he simply used it as another of his literary figures.

What Plato believed about a divine being, if anything, is unclear. It seems fairly clear that he did not accept seriously the polytheism (many gods) of his times. Even though he has Socrates speak respectfully of the official gods of the state, for Plato these were merely what we would call mythological beings today. The demiurge was not thought of as a God for Plato either, but was simply another myth that he used to explain how the Forms could be realized in material objects. As to the Good, while some later Christian writers identified the Good with the personal God of the Bible, there is little reason to believe that

Plato thought of it as a personal being. Instead, for Plato the Good is best understood as the rational order of all things, the unchanging pattern of reality. It is not a personal God, but rather the highest embodiment of reason itself.

Gender

Ancient Greek society was just as sexist as their Asian counterparts, generally relegating women solely to domestic roles. Plato's idea of human nature as consisting of three parts seemed to allow him to maintain this tradition. Since he believed that the three parts of the soul are present in people in different degrees, it would have been easy enough for him to say that women had more "spirit" or more "appetite" than men, and less reason.

Plato, however, as did the Buddha before him, swam against this traditional tide and affirmed that women ought to be allowed to become members of the ruling class in his ideal society. This is because he believed that the best women are different from the best men only biologically—in their inferior strength and their ability to give birth. In all other senses they are naturally on a par with men. Given the proper education and training, these women could exhibit rational ability that is the equal to the best men, and thus could serve as rulers and live lives as full and as rich as men are capable of living.

Readings

1. The Cave

AND NOW, I SAID, LET me show in a figure how far our nature is enlightened or unenlightened:— Behold! human beings living in an underground den, which has a mouth open toward the light and reaching all along the den; here they have been from their childhood, and have their legs and necks chained so that they cannot move, and can only see before them, being prevented by the chains from turning round their heads. Above and behind them a fire is blazing at a distance, and between the fire and the prisoners there is a raised way; and you will see, if you look, a low wall built along the way, like the screen which marionette players have in front of them, over which they show the puppets.

I see.

And do you see, I said, men passing along the wall carrying all sorts of vessels, and statues and figures of animals made of wood and stone and various materials, which appear over the wall? Some of them are talking, others silent.

You have shown me a strange image, and they are strange prisoners.

Like ourselves, I replied; and they see only their own shadows, or the shadows of one another, which the fire throws on the opposite wall of the cave?

True, he said; how could they see anything but the shadows if they were never allowed to move their heads?

And of the objects which are being carried in like manner they would only see the shadows?

Yes, he said.

And if they were able to converse with one another, would they not suppose that they were naming what was actually before them?

From Plato, "The Republic," in The Dialogues of Plato, *trans. by B. Jowett (1937), pp. 773–777. Reprinted with permission from Oxford University Press.*

Very true.

And suppose further that the prison had an echo which came from the other side, would they not be sure to fancy when one of the passers-by spoke that the voice which they heard came from the passing shadow?

No question, he replied.

To them, I said, the truth would be literally nothing but the shadows of the images.

That is certain.

And now look again, and see what will naturally follow if the prisoners are released and disabused of their error. At first, when any of them is liberated and compelled suddenly to stand up and turn his neck round and walk and look toward the light, he will suffer sharp pains; the glare will distress him, and he will be unable to see the realities of which in his former state he had seen the shadows; and then conceive some one saying to him, that what he saw before was an illusion, but that now, when he is approaching nearer to being and his eye is turned toward more real existence, he has a clearer vision,—what will be his reply? And you may further imagine that his instructor is pointing to the objects as they pass and requiring him to name them,—will he not be perplexed? Will he not fancy that the shadows which he formerly saw are truer than the objects which are now shown to him?

Far truer.

And if he is compelled to look straight at the light, will he not have a pain in his eyes which will make him turn away to take refuge in the objects of vision which he can see, and which he will conceive to be in reality clearer than the things which are now being shown to him?

True, he said.

And suppose once more, that he is reluctantly dragged up a steep and rugged ascent, and held fast until he is forced into the presence of the sun himself, is he not likely to be pained and irritated? When he approaches the light his eyes will be dazzled, and he will not be able to see anything at all of what are now called realities.

Not all in a moment, he said.

He will require to grow accustomed to the sight of the upper world. And first he will see the shadows best, next the reflections of men and other objects in the water, and then the objects themselves; then he will gaze upon the light of the moon and the stars and the spangled heaven; and he will see the sky and the stars by night better than the sun or the light of the sun by day?

Certainly.

Last of all he will be able to see the sun, and not mere reflections of him in the water, but he will see him in his own proper place, and not in another; and he will contemplate him as he is.

Certainly.

He will then proceed to argue that this is he who gives the season and the years, and is the guardian of all that is in the visible world, and in a certain way the cause of all things which he and his fellows have been accustomed to behold?

Clearly, he said, he would first see the sun and then reason about him.

And when he remembered his old habitation, and the wisdom of the den and his fellow-prisoners, do you not suppose that he would felicitate himself on the change, and pity them?

Certainly, he would.

And if they were in the habit of conferring honors among themselves on those who were quickest to observe the passing shadows and to remark which of them went before, and which followed after, and which were together; and who were therefore best able to draw conclusions as to the future, do you think that he would care for such honors and glories, or envy the possessors of them? Would he not say with Homer,

'Better to be the poor servant of a poor master,'

and to endure anything, rather than think as they do and live after their manner?

Yes, he said, I think that he would rather suffer anything than entertain these false notions and live in this miserable manner.

Imagine once more, I said, such an one coming suddenly out of the sun to be replaced in his old situation; would he not be certain to have his eyes full of darkness?

To be sure, he said.

And if there were a contest, and he had to compete in measuring the shadows with the prisoners who had never moved out of the den, while his sight was still weak, and before his eyes had become steady (and the time which would be needed to acquire this new habit of sight might be very considerable), would he not be ridiculous? Men would say of him that up he went and down he came without his eyes; and that it was better not even to think of ascending; and if any one tried to loose another and lead him up to the light, let them only catch the offender, and they would put him to death.

No question, he said.

This entire allegory, I said, you may now append, dear Glaucon, to the previous argument; the prison-house is the world of sight, the light of the fire is the sun, and you will not misapprehend me if you interpret the journey upward to be the ascent of the soul into the intellectual world according to my poor belief, which, at your desire, I have expressed—whether rightly or wrongly God knows. But, whether true or false, my opinion is that in the world of knowledge the idea of good appears last of all, and is seen only with an effort; and, when seen, is also inferred to be the universal author of all things beautiful and right, parent of light and of the lord of light in this visible world, and the immediate source of reason and truth in the intellectual; and that this is the power upon which he who would act rationally either in public or private life must have his eye fixed.

I agree, he said, as far as I am able to understand you.

Moreover, I said, you must not wonder that those who attain to this beatific vision are unwilling to descend to human affairs; for their souls are ever hastening into the upper world where they desire to dwell; which desire of theirs is very natural, if our allegory may be trusted.

Yes, very natural.

And is there anything surprising in one who passes from divine contemplations to the evil state of man, misbehaving himself in a ridiculous manner; if, while his eyes are blinking and before he has become accustomed to the surrounding darkness, he is compelled to fight in courts of law, or in other places, about the images or the shadows of images of justice, and is endeavoring to meet the conceptions of those who have never yet seen absolute justice?

Anything but surprising, he replied.

Any one who has common sense will remember that the bewilderments of the eyes are of two kinds, and arise from two causes, either from coming out of the light or from going into the light, which is true of the mind's eye, quite as much as of the bodily eye; and he who remembers this when he sees any one whose vision is perplexed and weak, will not be too ready to laugh; he will first ask whether that soul of man has come out of the brighter life, and is unable to see because unaccustomed to the dark, or having turned from darkness to the day is dazzled by excess of light. And he will count the one happy in his condition and state of being, and he will pity the other; or, if he have a mind to laugh at the soul which comes from below into the light, there will be more reason in this than in the laugh which greets him who returns from above out of the light into the den.

2. The Divided Line

YOU HAVE TO IMAGINE, THEN, that there are two ruling powers, and that one of them is set over the intellectual world, the other over the visible. I do not say heaven, lest you should fancy that I am playing upon the name (οὐρανός, ὁρατός). May I suppose that you have this distinction of the visible and intelligible fixed in your mind?

I have.

From Plato, "The Republic," in The Dialogues of Plato, *trans. by B. Jowett (1937), pp. 771–773. Reprinted with permission from Oxford University Press.*

Now take a line which has been cut into two unequal parts, and divide each of them again in the same proportion, and suppose the two main divisions to answer, one to the visible and the other to the intelligible, and then compare the subdivisions in respect of their clearness and want of clearness, and you will find that the first section in the sphere of the visible consists of images. And by images I mean, in the first place, shadows, and in the second place, reflections in water and in solid, smooth and polished bodies and the like: Do you understand?

Yes, I understand.

Imagine, now, the other section, of which this is only the resemblance, to include the animals which we see, and everything that grows or is made.

Very good.

Would you not admit that both the sections of this division have different degrees of truth, and that the copy is to the original as the sphere of opinion is to the sphere of knowledge?

Most undoubtedly.

Next proceed to consider the manner in which the sphere of the intellectual is to be divided.

In what manner?

Thus:—There are two subdivisions, in the lower of which the soul uses the figures given by the former division as images; the inquiry can only be hypothetical, and instead of going upward to a principle descends to the other end; in the higher of the two, the soul passes out of hypotheses, and goes up to a principle which is above hypotheses, making no use of images as in the former case, but proceeding only in and through the ideas themselves.

I do not quite understand your meaning, he said.

Then I will try again; you will understand me better when I have made some preliminary remarks. You are aware that students of geometry, arithmetic, and the kindred sciences assume the odd and the even and the figures and three kinds of angles and the like in their several branches of science; these are their hypotheses, which they and every body are supposed to know, and therefore they do not deign to give any account of them either to themselves or others; but they begin with them, and go on until they arrive at last, and in a consistent manner, at their conclusion?

Yes, he said, I know.

And do you not know also that although they make use of the visible forms and reason about them, they are thinking not of these, but of the ideals which they resemble; not of the figures which they draw, but of the absolute square and the absolute diameter, and so on—the forms which they draw or make, and which have shadows and reflections in water of their own, are converted by them into images, but they are really seeking to behold the things themselves, which can only be seen with the eye of the mind?

That is true.

And of this kind I spoke as the intelligible, although in the search after it the soul is compelled to use hypotheses; not ascending to a first principle, because she is unable to rise above the region of hypothesis, but employing the objects of which the shadows below are resemblances in their turn as images, they having in relation to the shadows and reflections of them a greater distinctness, and therefore a higher value.

I understand, he said, that you are speaking of the province of geometry and the sister arts.

And when I speak of the other division of the intelligible, you will understand me to speak of that other sort of knowledge which reason herself attains by the power of dialectic, using the hypotheses not as first principles, but only as hypotheses—that is to say, as steps and points of departure into a world which is above hypotheses, in order that she may soar beyond them to the first principle of the whole; and clinging to this and then to that which depends on this, by successive steps she descends again without the aid of any sensible object, from ideas, through ideas, and in ideas she ends.

I understand you, he replied; not perfectly, for you seem to me to be describing a task which is really tremendous; but, at any rate, I understand you to say that knowledge and being, which the science of dialectic contemplates, are clearer than the notions of the arts, as they are termed, which proceed from hypotheses only: these are also contemplated by the understanding, and not by the senses: yet, because they start from hypotheses and do not ascend to a principle, those who contemplate them appear to you not to exercise the higher reason upon them, although when a first principle is added to them they are cognizable by the higher reason. And the habit which is concerned with geometry and the cognate sciences I suppose that you would term understanding and not reason, as being intermediate between opinion and reason.

You have quite conceived my meaning, I said; and now, corresponding to these four divisions, let there be four faculties in the soul—reason answering to the highest, understanding to the second, faith (or conviction) to the third, and perception of shadows to the last—and let there be a scale of them, and let us suppose that the several faculties have clearness in the same degree that their objects have truth.

I understand, he replied, and give my assent, and accept your arrangement.

3. The Individual and the State

THINK, NOW, AND SAY WHETHER you agree with me or not. Suppose a carpenter to be doing the business of a cobbler, or a cobbler of a carpenter; and suppose them to exchange their implements or their duties, or the same person to be doing the work of both, or whatever be the change; do you think that any great harm would result to the State?

Not much.

But when the cobbler or any other man whom nature designed to be a trader, having his heart lifted up by wealth or strength or the number of his followers, or any like advantage, attempts to force his way into the class of warriors, or a warrior into that of legislators and guardians, for which he is unfitted, and either to take the implements or the duties of the other; or when one man is trader, legislator, and warrior all in one, then I think you will agree with me in saying that this interchange and this meddling of one with another is the ruin of the State.

Most true.

Seeing then, I said, that there are three distinct classes, any meddling of one with another, or the change of one into another, is the greatest harm to the State, and may be most justly termed evil-doing?

Precisely.

And the greatest degree of evil-doing to one's own city would be termed by you injustice?

Certainly.

This then is injustice; and on the other hand when the trader, the auxiliary, and the guardian each do their own business, that is justice, and will make the city just.

I agree with you.

We will not, I said, be over-positive as yet; but if, on trial, this conception of justice be verified in the individual as well as in the State, there will be no longer any room for doubt; if it be not verified, we must have a fresh inquiry. First let us complete the old investigation, which we began, as you remember, under the impression that, if we could previously examine justice on the larger scale, there would be less difficulty in discerning her in the individual. That larger example appeared to be the State, and accordingly we constructed as good a one as we could, knowing well that in the good State justice would be found. Let the discovery which we made be now applied to the individual—if they agree, we shall be satisfied; or, if there be a difference in the individual, we will come back to the State and have another trial of the theory. The friction of the two when rubbed together may possibly strike a light in which justice will shine forth, and the vision which is then revealed we will fix in our souls.

That will be in regular course; let us do as you say.

From Plato, "The Republic," in The Dialogues of Plato, *trans. by B. Jowett (1937), pp. 697–698 and 703–709. Reprinted with permission of Oxford University Press.*

I proceeded to ask: When two things, a greater and less, are called by the same name, are they like or unlike in so far as they are called the same?

Like, he replied.

The just man then, if we regard the idea of justice only, will be like the just State?

He will.

And a State was thought by us to be just when the three classes in the State severally did their own business; and also thought to be temperate and valiant and wise by reason of certain other affections and qualities of these same classes?

True, he said.

And so of the individual; we may assume that he has the same three principles in his own soul which are found in the State; and he may be rightly described in the same terms, because he is affected in the same manner?

Certainly, he said.

Once more then, O my friend, we have alighted upon an easy question—whether the soul has these three principles or not?

The same thing cannot at the same time with the same part of itself act in contrary ways about the same.

Impossible.

No more than you can say that the hands of the archer push and pull the bow at the same time, but what you say is that one hand pushes and the other pulls.

Exactly so, he replied.

And might a man be thirsty, and yet unwilling to drink?

Yes, he said, it constantly happens.

And in such a case what is one to say? Would you not say that there was something in the soul bidding a man to drink, and something else forbidding him, which is other and stronger than the principle which bids him?

I should say so.

And the forbidding principle is derived from reason, and that which bids and attracts proceeds from passion and disease?

Clearly.

Then we may fairly assume that they are two, and that they differ from one another; the one with which a man reasons, we may call the rational

principle of the soul, the other, with which he loves and hungers and thirsts and feels the flutterings of any other desire, may be termed the irrational or appetitive, the ally of sundry pleasures and satisfactions?

Yes, he said, we may fairly assume them to be different.

Then let us finally determine that there are two principles existing in the soul. And what of passion, or spirit? Is it a third, or akin to one of the preceding?

I should be inclined to say—akin to desire.

Well, I said, there is a story which I remember to have heard, and in which I put faith. The story is, that Leontius, the son of Aglaion, coming up one day from the Piraeus, under the north wall on the outside, observed some dead bodies lying on the ground at the place of execution. He felt a desire to see them, and also a dread and abhorrence of them; for a time he struggled and covered his eyes, but at length the desire got the better of him; and forcing them open, he ran up to the dead bodies, saying, Look, ye wretches, take your fill of the fair sight.

I have heard the story myself, he said.

The moral of the tale is, that anger at times goes to war with desire, as though they were two distinct things.

Yes; that is the meaning, he said.

And are there not many other cases in which we observe that when a man's desires violently prevail over his reason, he reviles himself, and is angry at the violence within him, and that in this struggle, which is like the struggle of factions in a State, his spirit is on the side of his reason;—but for the passionate or spirited element to take part with the desires when reason decides that she should not be opposed, is a sort of thing which I believe that you never observed occurring in yourself, nor, as I should imagine, in any one else?

Certainly not.

Suppose that a man thinks he has done a wrong to another, the nobler he is the less able is he to feel indignant at any suffering, such as hunger, or cold, or any other pain which the injured person may inflict upon him—these he deems to be just, and, as I say, his anger refuses to be excited by them.

True, he said.

But when he thinks that he is the sufferer of the wrong, then he boils and chafes, and is on the side of what he believes to be justice; and because he suffers hunger or cold or other pain he is only the more determined to persevere and conquer. His noble spirit will not be quelled until he either slays or is slain; or until he hears the voice of the shepherd, that is, reason, bidding his dog bark no more.

The illustration is perfect, he replied; and in our State, as we were saying, the auxiliaries were to be dogs, and to hear the voice of the rulers, who are their shepherds.

I perceive, I said, that you quite understand me; there is, however, a further point which I wish you to consider.

What point?

You remember that passion or spirit appeared at first sight to be a kind of desire, but now we should say quite the contrary; for in the conflict of the soul spirit is arrayed on the side of the rational principle.

Most assuredly.

But a further question arises: Is passion different from reason also, or only a kind of reason; in which latter case, instead of three principles in the soul, there will only be two, the rational and the concupiscent; or rather, as the State was composed of three classes, traders, auxiliaries, counselors, so may there not be in the individual soul a third element which is passion or spirit, and when not corrupted by bad education is the natural auxiliary of reason?

Yes, he said, there must be a third.

Yes, I replied, if passion, which has already been shown to be different from desire, turn out also to be different from reason.

But that is easily proved:—We may observe even in young children that they are full of spirit almost as soon as they are born, whereas some of them never seem to attain to the use of reason, and most of them late enough.

Excellent, I said, and you may see passion equally in brute animals, which is a further proof of the truth of what you are saying. And we may once more appeal to the words of Homer, which have been already quoted by us,

'He smote his breast, and thus rebuked his soul;'

for in this verse Homer has clearly supposed the power which reasons about the better and worse to be different from the unreasoning anger which is rebuked by it.

Very true, he said.

And so, after much tossing, we have reached land, and are fairly agreed that the same principles which exist in the State exist also in the individual, and that they are three in number.

Exactly.

Must we not then infer that the individual is wise in the same way, and in virtue of the same quality which makes the State wise?

Certainly.

Also that the same quality which constitutes courage in the State constitutes courage in the individual, and that both the State and the individual bear the same relation to all the other virtues?

Assuredly.

And the individual will be acknowledged by us to be just in the same way in which the State is just?

That follows of course.

We cannot but remember that the justice of the State consisted in each of the three classes doing the work of its own class?

We are not very likely to have forgotten, he said.

We must recollect that the individual in whom the several qualities of his nature do their own work will be just, and will do his own work?

Yes, he said, we must remember that too.

And ought not the rational principle, which is wise, and has the care of the whole soul, to rule, and the passionate or spirited principle to be the subject and ally?

Certainly.

And, as we were saying, the united influence of music and gymnastic will bring them into accord, nerving and sustaining the reason with noble words and lessons, and moderating and soothing and civilizing the wildness of passion by harmony and rhythm?

Quite true, he said.

And these two, thus nurtured and educated, and having learned truly to know their own functions, will rule over the concupiscent, which in each of us is the largest part of the soul and by nature most insatiable of gain; over this they will keep guard, lest, waxing great and strong with the fullness of bodily pleasures, as they are termed, the concupiscent soul, no longer confined to her own sphere, should attempt to enslave and rule those who are not her natural-born subjects, and overturn the whole life of man?

Very true, he said.

Both together will they not be the best defenders of the whole soul and the whole body against attacks from without; the one counselling, and the other fighting under his leader, and courageously executing his commands and counsels?

True.

And he is to be deemed courageous whose spirit retains in pleasure and in pain the commands of reason about what he ought or ought not to fear?

Right, he replied.

And him we call wise who has in him that little part which rules, and which proclaims these commands; that part too being supposed to have a knowledge of what is for the interest of each of the three parts and of the whole?

Assuredly.

And would you not say that he is temperate who has these same elements in friendly harmony, in whom the one ruling principle of reason, and the two subject ones of spirit and desire are equally agreed that reason ought to rule, and do not rebel?

Certainly, he said, that is the true account of temperance whether in the State or individual.

And surely, I said, we have explained again and again, how and by virtue of what quality a man will be just.

That is very certain.

And is justice dimmer in the individual, and is her form different, or is she the same which we found her to be in the State?

There is no difference in my opinion, he said.

Because, if any doubt is still lingering in our minds, a few commonplace instances will satisfy us of the truth of what I am saying.

What sort of instances do you mean?

If the case is put to us, must we not admit that the just State, or the man who is trained in the principles of such a State, will be less likely than the unjust to make away with a deposit of gold or silver? Would any one deny this?

No one, he replied.

Will the just man or citizen ever be guilty of sacrilege or theft, or treachery either to his friends or to his country?

Never.

Neither will he ever break faith where there have been oaths or agreements?

Impossible.

No one will be less likely to commit adultery, or to dishonor his father and mother, or to fail in his religious duties?

No one.

And the reason is that each part of him is doing its own business, whether in ruling or being ruled?

Exactly so.

Are you satisfied then that the quality which makes such men and such states is justice, or do you hope to discover some other?

Not I, indeed.

Then our dream has been realized; and the suspicion which we entertained at the beginning of our work of construction, that some divine power must have conducted us to a primary form of justice, has now been verified?

Yes, certainly.

And the division of labour which required the carpenter and the shoemaker and the rest of the citizens to be doing each his own business, and not another's, was a shadow of justice, and for that reason it was of use?

Clearly.

But in reality justice was such as we were describing, being concerned however, not with the outward man, but with the inward, which is the true self and concernment of man: for the just man does not permit the several elements within him to interfere with one another, or any of them to do the work of others,—he sets in order his own inner life, and is his own master and his own law, and at peace with himself; and when he has bound together the three principles within him, which may be compared to the higher, lower, and middle notes of the scale, and the intermediate intervals—when he has bound all these together, and is no longer many, but has become one entirely temperate and perfectly adjusted nature, then he proceeds to act, if he has to act, whether in a matter of property, or in the treatment of the body, or in some affair of politics or private business; always thinking and calling that which preserves and co-operates with this harmonious condition, just and good action, and the knowledge which presides over it, wisdom, and that which at any time impairs this condition, he will call unjust action, and the opinion which presides over it ignorance.

You have said the exact truth, Socrates.

Very good; and if we were to affirm that we had discovered the just man and the just State, and the nature of justice in each of them, we should not be telling a falsehood?

Most certainly not.

May we say so, then?

Let us say so.

And now, I said, injustice has to be considered.

Clearly.

Must not injustice be a strife which arises among the three principles—a meddlesomeness, and interference, and rising up of a part of the soul against the whole, an assertion of unlawful authority, which is made by a rebellious subject against a true prince, of whom he is the natural vassal,—what is all this confusion and delusion but injustice, and intemperance and cowardice and ignorance, and every form of vice?

Exactly so.

And if the nature of justice and injustice be known, then the meaning of acting unjustly and being unjust, or, again, of acting justly, will also be perfectly clear?

What do you mean? he said.

Why, I said, they are like disease and health; being in the soul just what disease and health are in the body.

How so? he said.

Why, I said, that which is healthy causes health, and that which is unhealthy causes disease.

Yes.

And just actions cause justice, and unjust actions cause injustice?

That is certain.

And the creation of health is the institution of a natural order and government of one by another in the parts of the body; and the creation of disease is the production of a state of things at variance with this natural order?

True.

And is not the creation of justice the institution of a natural order and government of one by another in the parts of the soul, and the creation of injustice the production of a state of things at variance with the natural order?

Exactly so, he said.

Then virtue is the health and beauty and well-being of the soul, and vice the disease and weakness and deformity of the same?

True.

And do not good practices lead to virtue, and evil practices to vice?

Assuredly.

Still our old question of the comparative advantage of justice and injustice has not been answered: Which is the more profitable, to be just and act justly and practice virtue, whether seen or unseen of gods and men, or to be unjust and act unjustly, if only unpunished and unreformed?

In my judgment, Socrates, the question has now become ridiculous. We know that, when the bodily constitution is gone, life is no longer endurable, though pampered with all kinds of meats and drinks, and having all wealth and all power; and shall we be told that when the very essence of the vital principle is undermined and corrupted, life is still worth having to a man, if only he be allowed to do whatever he likes with the single exception that he is not to acquire justice and virtue, or to escape from injustice and vice; assuming them both to be such as we have described?

Yes, I said, the question is, as you say, ridiculous.

4. The Immortality of the Soul

To be sure, replied Simmias.

Is it not the separation of soul and body? And to be dead is the completion of this; when the soul exists in herself, and is released from the body and the body is released from the soul, what is this but death?

Just so, he replied.

There is another question, which will probably throw light on our present inquiry if you and I can agree about it:—Ought the philosopher to care about the pleasures—if they are to be called pleasures—of eating and drinking?

Certainly not, answered Simmias.

And what about the pleasures of love—should he care for them?

By no means.

And will he think much of the other ways of indulging the body, for example, the acquisition of costly raiment, or sandals, or other adornments of the body? Instead of caring about them, does he not rather despise anything more than nature needs? What do you say?

I should say that the true philosopher would despise them.

Would you not say that he is entirely concerned with the soul and not with the body? He would like, as far as he can, to get away from the body and to turn to the soul.

Quite true.

In matters of this sort philosophers, above all other men, may be observed in every sort of way to dissever the soul from the communion of the body.

Very true.

Whereas, Simmias, the rest of the world are of opinion that to him who has no sense of pleasure and no part in bodily pleasure, life is not worth having; and that he who is indifferent about them is as good as dead.

That is also true.

What again shall we say of the actual acquirement of knowledge?—is the body, if invited to share in the inquiry, a hinderer or a helper? I mean to say, have sight and hearing any truth in them? Are they not, as the poets are always telling us, inaccurate witnesses? and yet, if even they are inaccurate and indistinct, what is to be said of the other senses?—for you will allow that they are the best of them?

Certainly, he replied.

Then when does the soul attain truth?—for in attempting to consider anything in company with the body she is obviously deceived.

True.

Then must not true existence be revealed to her in thought, if at all?

Yes.

And thought is best when the mind is gathered into herself and none of these things trouble her—neither sounds nor sights nor pain nor any pleasure,—when she takes leave of the body, and has as little as possible to do with it, when she has no bodily sense or desire, but is aspiring after true being?

Certainly.

And in this the philosopher dishonors the body; his soul runs away from his body and desires to be alone and by herself?

That is true.

Well, but there is another thing, Simmias: Is there or is there not an absolute justice?

Assuredly there is.

And an absolute beauty and absolute good?

Of course.

But did you ever behold any of them, with your eyes?

Certainly not.

From Plato, "The Phaedo," in The Dialogues of Plato, *trans. by B. Jowett (1937), pp. 447–466 and 500–501. Reprinted with permission from Oxford University Press.*

Or did you ever reach them with any other bodily sense?—and I speak not of these alone, but of absolute greatness, and health, and strength, and of the essence or true nature of everything. Has the reality of them ever been perceived by you through the bodily organs? or rather, is not the nearest approach to the knowledge of their several natures made by him who so orders his intellectual vision as to have the most exact conception of the essence of each thing which he considers?

Certainly.

And he attains to the purest knowledge of them who goes to each with the mind alone, not introducing or intruding in the act of thought sight or any other sense together with reason, but with the very light of the mind in her own clearness searches into the very truth of each; he who has got rid, as far as he can, of eyes and ears and, so to speak, of the whole body, these being in his opinion distracting elements which when they infect the soul hinder her from acquiring truth and knowledge—who, if not he, is likely to attain to the knowledge of true being?

What you say has a wonderful truth in it, Socrates, replied Simmias.

And when real philosophers consider all these things, will they not be led to make a reflection which they will express in words something like the following? 'Have we not found,' they will say, 'a path of thought which seems to bring us and our argument to the conclusion, that while we are in the body, and while the soul is infected with the evils of the body, our desire will not be satisfied? and our desire is of the truth. For the body is a source of endless trouble to us by reason of the mere requirement of food; and is liable also to diseases which overtake and impede us in the search after true being: it fills us full of loves, and lusts, and fears, and fancies of all kinds, and endless foolery, and in fact, as men say, takes away from us the power of thinking at all. Whence come wars, and fightings, and factions? whence but from the body and the lusts of the body? Wars are occasioned by the love of money, and money has to be acquired for the sake and in the service of

the body; and by reason of all these impediments we have no time to give to philosophy; and, last and worst of all, even if we are at leisure and betake ourselves to some speculation, the body is always breaking in upon us, causing turmoil and confusion in our inquiries, and so amazing us that we are prevented from seeing the truth. It has been proved to us by experience that if we would have pure knowledge of anything we must be quit of the body—the soul in herself must behold things in themselves: and then we shall attain the wisdom which we desire, and of which we say that we are lovers; not while we live, but after death; for if while in company with the body, the soul cannot have pure knowledge, one of two things follows—either knowledge is not to be attained at all, or, if at all, after death. For then, and not till then, the soul will be parted from the body and exist in herself alone. In this present life, I reckon that we make the nearest approach to knowledge when we have the least possible intercourse or communion with the body, and are not surfeited with the bodily nature, but keep ourselves pure until the hour when God himself is pleased to release us. And thus having got rid of the foolishness of the body we shall be pure and hold converse with the pure, and know of ourselves the clear light everywhere, which is no other than the light of truth.' For the impure are not permitted to approach the pure. These are the sort of words, Simmias, which the true lovers of knowledge cannot help saying to one another, and thinking. You would agree; would you not?

Undoubtedly, Socrates.

But, O my friend, if this be true, there is great reason to hope that, going whither I go, when I have come to the end of my journey, I shall attain that which has been the pursuit of my life. And therefore I go on my way rejoicing, and not I only, but every other man who believes that his mind has been made ready and that he is in a manner purified.

Certainly, replied Simmias.

And what is purification but the separation of the soul from the body, as I was saying before; the habit of the soul gathering and I collecting herself into herself from all sides out of the body; the dwelling in her own place alone, as in another life, so also in this, as far as she can;—the release of the soul from the chains of the body?

Very true, he said.

And this separation and release of the soul from the body is termed death?

To be sure, he said.

And the true philosophers, and they only, are ever seeking to release the soul. Is not the separation and release of the soul from the body their especial study?

That is true.

And, as I was saying at first, there would be a ridiculous contradiction in men studying to live as nearly as they can in a state of death, and yet repining when it comes upon them.

Clearly.

And the true philosophers, Simmias, are always occupied in the practice of dying, wherefore also to them least of all men is death terrible. Look at the matter thus:—if they have been in every way the enemies of the body, and are wanting to be alone with the soul, when this desire of theirs is granted, how inconsistent would they be if they trembled and repined, instead of rejoicing at their departure to that place where, when they arrive, they hope to gain that which in life they desired—and this was wisdom—and at the same time to be rid of the company of their enemy. Many a man has been willing to go to the world below animated by the hope of seeing there an earthly love, or wife, or son, and conversing with them. And will he who is a true lover of wisdom, and is strongly persuaded in like manner that only in the world below he can worthily enjoy her, still repine at death? Will he not depart with joy? Surely he will, O my friend, if he be a true philosopher. For he will have a firm conviction that there, and there only, he can find wisdom in her purity. And if this be true, he would be very absurd, as I was saying, if he were afraid of death.

He would indeed, replied Simmias.

And when you see a man who is repining at the approach of death, is not his reluctance a sufficient proof that he is not a lover of wisdom, but a lover of the body, and probably at the same time a lover of either money or power, or both?

Quite so, he replied.

And is not courage, Simmias, a quality which is specially characteristic of the philosopher?

Certainly.

There is temperance again, which even by the vulgar is supposed to consist in the control and regulation of the passions, and in the sense of superiority to them—is not temperance a virtue belonging to those only who despise the body, and who pass their lives in philosophy?

Most assuredly.

For the courage and temperance of other men, if you will consider them, are really a contradiction.

How so?

Well, he said, you are aware that death is regarded by men in general as a great evil.

Very true, he said.

And do not courageous men face death because they are afraid of yet greater evils?

That is quite true.

Then all but the philosophers are courageous only from fear, and because they are afraid; and yet that a man should be courageous from fear, and because he is a coward, is surely a strange thing.

Very true.

And are not the temperate exactly in the same case? They are temperate because they are intemperate—which might seem to be a contradiction, but is nevertheless the sort of thing which happens with this foolish temperance. For there are pleasures which they are afraid of losing; and in their desire to keep them, they abstain from some pleasures, because they are overcome by others; and although to be conquered by pleasure is called by men intemperance, to them the conquest of pleasure consists in being conquered by pleasure. And that is what I mean by saying that, in a sense, they are made temperate through intemperance.

Such appears to be the case.

Yet the exchange of one fear or pleasure or pain for another fear or pleasure or pain, and of the greater for the less, as if they were coins, is not the exchange of virtue. O my blessed Simmias, is there not one true coin for which all things ought to be exchanged?—and that is wisdom; and only in exchange for this, and in company with this, is anything truly bought or sold, whether courage or temperance or justice. And is not all true virtue, the companion of wisdom, no matter what fears or pleasures or other similar goods or evils may or may not attend her? But the virtue which is made up of these goods, when they are severed from wisdom and exchanged with one another, is a shadow of virtue only, nor is there any freedom or health or truth in her; but in the true exchange there is a purging away of all these things, and temperance, and justice, and courage, and wisdom herself are the purgation of them. The founders of the mysteries would appear to have had a real meaning, and were not talking nonsense when they intimated in a figure long ago that he who passes unsanctified and uninitiated into the world below will lie in a slough, but that he who arrives there after initiation and purification will dwell with the gods. For 'many,' as they say in the mysteries, 'are the thyrsus-bearers, but few are the mystics,'—meaning, as I interpret the words, 'the true philosophers.' In the number of whom, during my whole life, I have been seeking, according to my ability, to find a place;—whether I have sought in a right way or not, and whether I have succeeded or not, I shall truly know in a little while, if God will, when I myself arrive in the other world—such is my belief. And therefore I maintain that I am right, Simmias and Cebes, in not grieving or repining at parting from you and my masters in this world, for I believe that I shall equally find good masters and friends in another world. But most men do not believe this saying; if then I succeed in convincing you by my defense better than I did the Athenian judges, it will be well.

Cebes answered: I agree, Socrates, in the greater part of what you say. But in what concerns the soul, men are apt to be incredulous; they fear that when she has left the body her place may be nowhere, and that on the very day of death she may perish and come to an end—immediately on her release from the body, issuing forth dispersed like smoke or air and in her flight vanishing away into nothingness. If she could only be collected into herself after she has obtained release from the evils of which you were speaking, there would be good reason to hope, Socrates, that what you say is true. But surely it requires a great deal of argument and many proofs to show that when the man is dead his soul yet exists, and has any force or intelligence.

True, Cebes, said Socrates; and shall I suggest that we converse a little of the probabilities of these things?

I am sure, said Cebes, that I should greatly like to know your opinion about them.

I reckon, said Socrates, that no one who heard me now, not even if he were one of my old enemies, the Comic poets, could accuse me of idle talking about matters in which I have no concern:—If you please, then, we will proceed with the enquiry.

Suppose we consider the question whether the souls of men after death are or are not in the world below. There comes into my mind an ancient doctrine which affirms that they go from hence into the other world, and returning hither, are born again from the dead. Now if it be true that the living come from the dead, then our souls must exist in the other world, for if not, how could they have been born again? And this would be conclusive, if there were any real evidence that the living are only born from the dead; but if this is not so, then other arguments will have to be adduced.

Very true, replied Cebes.

Then let us consider the whole question, not in relation to man only, but in relation to animals generally, and to plants, and to everything of which there is generation, and the proof will be easier. Are not all things which have opposites generated out of their opposites? I mean such things as good and evil, just and unjust—and there are innumerable other opposites which are generated out of opposites. And I want to show that in all opposites there is of necessity a similar alternation; I mean to say, for example, that anything which becomes greater must become greater after being less.

True.

And that which becomes less must have been once greater and then have become less.

Yes.

And the weaker is generated from the stronger, and the swifter from the slower.

Very true.

And the worse is from the better, and the more just is from the more unjust.

Of course.

And is this true of all opposites? and are we convinced that all of them are generated out of opposites?

Yes.

And in this universal opposition of all things, are there not also two intermediate processes which are ever going on, from one to the other opposite, and back again; where there is a greater and a less there is also an intermediate process of increase and diminution, and that which grows is said to wax, and that which decays to wane?

Yes, he said.

And there are many other processes, such as division and composition, cooling and heating, which equally involve a passage into and out of one another. And this necessarily holds of all opposites, even though not always expressed in words—they are really generated out of one another, and there is a passing or process from one to the other of them?

Very true, he replied.

Well, and is there not an opposite of life, as sleep is the opposite of waking?

True, he said.

And what is it?

Death, he answered.

And these, if they are opposites, are generated the one from the other, and have their two intermediate processes also?

Of course.

Now, said Socrates, I will analyze one of the two pairs of opposites which I have mentioned to you, and also its intermediate processes, and you shall analyze the other to me. One of them I term sleep, the other waking. The state of sleep is opposed to the state of waking, and out of sleeping waking is generated, and out of waking, sleeping; and the process of generation is in the one case falling asleep, and in the other waking up. Do you agree?

I entirely agree.

Then, suppose that you analyze life and death to me in the same manner. Is not death opposed to life?

Yes.

And they are generated one from the other?

Yes.

What is generated from the living?

The dead.

And what from the dead?

I can only say in answer—the living.

Then the living, whether things or persons, Cebes, are generated from the dead?

That is clear, he replied.

Then the inference is that our souls exist in the world below?

That is true.

And one of the two processes or generations is visible—for surely the act of dying is visible?

Surely, he said.

What then is to be the result? Shall we exclude the opposite process? and shall we suppose nature to walk on one leg only? Must we not rather assign to death some corresponding process of generation?

Certainly, he replied.

And what is that process?

Return to life.

And return to life, if there be such a thing, is the birth of the dead into the world of the living?

Quite true.

Then here is a new way by which we arrive at the conclusion that the living come from the dead, just as the dead come from the living; and this, if true, affords a most certain proof that the souls of the dead exist in some place out of which they come again.

Yes, Socrates, he said; the conclusion seems to flow necessarily out of our previous admissions.

And that these admissions were not unfair, Cebes, he said; may be shown, I think, as follows: If generation were in a straight line only, and there were no compensation or circle in nature, no turn or return of elements into their opposites, then you know that all things would at last have the same form and pass into the same state, and there would be no more generation of them.

What do you mean? he said.

A simple thing enough, which I will illustrate by the case of sleep, he replied. You know that if there were no alternation of sleeping and waking, the tale of the sleeping Endymion would in the end have no meaning, because all other things would be asleep too, and he would not be distinguishable from the rest. Or if there were composition only, and no division of substances, then the chaos of Anaxagoras would come again. And in like manner, my dear Cebes, if all things which partook of life were to die, and after they were dead remained in the form of death, and did not come to life again, all would at last die, and nothing would be alive—what other result could there be? For if the living spring from any other things, and they too die, must not all things at last be swallowed up in death?

There is no escape, Socrates, said Cebes; and to me your argument seems to be absolutely true.

Yes, he said, Cebes, it is and must be so, in my opinion; and we have not been deluded in making these admissions; but I am confident that there truly is such a thing as living again, and that the living spring from the dead, and that the souls of the dead are in existence, and that the good souls have a better portion than the evil.

Cebes added: Your favorite doctrine, Socrates, that knowledge is simply recollection, if true, also necessarily implies a previous time in which we have learned that which we now recollect. But this would be impossible unless our soul had been in some place before existing in the form of man; here then is another proof of the soul's immortality.

But tell me, Cebes, said Simmias, interposing, what arguments are urged in favor of this doctrine of recollection. I am not very sure at the moment that I remember them.

One excellent proof, said Cebes, is afforded by questions. If you put a question to a person in a right way, he will give a true answer of himself, but how could he do this unless there were knowledge and right reason already in him? And this is most clearly shown when he is taken to a diagram or to anything of that sort.

But if, said Socrates, you are still incredulous, Simmias, I would ask you whether you may not agree with me when you look at the matter in another way;—I mean, if you are still incredulous as to whether knowledge is recollection?

Incredulous I am not, said Simmias; but I want to have this doctrine of recollection brought to my own recollection, and, from what Cebes has said, I am beginning to recollect and be convinced: but I should still like to hear what you were going to say.

This is what I would say, he replied:—We should agree, if I am not mistaken, that what a man recollects he must have known at some previous time.

Very true.

And what is the nature of this knowledge or recollection? I mean to ask, Whether a person who, having seen or heard or in any way perceived anything, knows not only that, but has a conception of something else which is the subject, not of the same but of some other kind of knowledge, may not be fairly said to recollect that of which he has the conception?

What do you mean?

I mean what I may illustrate by the following instance:—The knowledge of a lyre is not the same as the knowledge of a man?

True.

And yet what is the feeling of lovers when they recognize a lyre, or a garment, or anything else which the beloved has been in the habit of using? Do not they, from knowing the lyre, form in the mind's eye an image of the youth to whom the lyre belongs? And this is recollection. In like manner any one who sees Simmias may remember Cebes; and there are endless examples of the same thing.

Endless, indeed, replied Simmias.

And recollection is most commonly a process of recovering that which has been already forgotten through time and inattention.

Very true, he said.

Well; and may you not also from seeing the picture of a house or a lyre remember a man? and from the picture of Simmias, you may be led to remember Cebes;

True.

Or you may also be led to the recollection of Simmias himself?

Quite so.

And in all these cases, the recollection may be derived from things either like or unlike?

It may be.

And when the recollection is derived from like things, then another consideration is sure to arise, which is—whether the likeness in any degree falls short or not of that which is recollected?

Very true, he said.

And shall we proceed a step further, and affirm that there is such a thing as equality, not of one piece of wood or stone with another, but that, over and above this, there is absolute equality? Shall we say so?

Say so, yes, replied Simmias, and swear to it, with all the confidence in life.

And do we know the nature of this absolute essence?

To be sure, be said.

And whence did we obtain our knowledge? Did we not see equalities of material things, such as pieces of wood and stones, and gather from them the idea of an equality which is different from them? For you will acknowledge that there is a difference. Or look at the matter in another way:—Do not the same pieces of wood or stone appear at one time equal, and at another time unequal?

That is certain.

But are real equals ever equal? or is the idea of equality the same as of inequality?

Impossible, Socrates.

Then these (so-called) equals are not the same with the idea of equality?

I should say, clearly not, Socrates.

And yet from these equals, although differing from the idea of equality, you conceived and attained that idea?

Very true, he said.

Which might be like, or might be unlike them?

Yes.

But that makes no difference: whenever from seeing one thing you conceived another, whether like or unlike, there must surely have been an act of recollection?

Very true.

But what would you say of equal portions of wood and stone, or other material equals? and what is the impression produced by them? Are they equals in the same sense in which absolute equality is equal? or do they fall short of this perfect equality in a measure?

Yes, he said, in a very great measure too.

And must we not allow, that when I or any one, looking at any object, observes that the thing which he sees aims at being some other thing, but falls short of, and cannot be, that other thing, but is inferior, he who makes this observation must have had a previous knowledge of that to which the other, although similar, was inferior.

Certainly.

And has not this been our own case in the matter of equals and of absolute equality?

Precisely.

Then we must have known equality previously to the time when we first saw the material equals, and reflected that all these apparent equals strive to attain absolute equality, but fall short of it?

Very true.

And we recognize also that this absolute equality has only been known, and can only be known, through the medium of sight or touch, or of some other of the senses, which are all alike in this respect?

Yes, Socrates, as far as the argument is concerned, one of them is the same as the other.

From the senses then is derived the knowledge that all sensible things aim at an absolute equality of which they fall short?

Yes.

Then before we began to see or hear or perceive in any way, we must have had a knowledge of absolute equality, or we could not have referred to that standard the equals which are derived from the senses?—for to that they all aspire, and of that they fall short.

No other inference can be drawn from the previous statements.

And did we not see and hear and have the use of our other senses as soon as we were born?

Certainly.

Then we must have acquired the knowledge of equality at some previous time?

Yes.

That is to say, before we were born, I suppose?

True.

And if we acquired this knowledge before we were born, and were born having the use of it, then we also knew before we were born and at the instant of birth not only the equal or the greater or the less, but all other ideas; for we are not speaking only of equality, but of beauty, goodness, justice, holiness, and of all which we stamp with the name of essence in the dialectical process, both when we ask and when we answer questions. Of all this we may certainly affirm that we acquired the knowledge before birth.

We may.

But if, after having acquired, we have not forgotten what in each case we acquired, then we must always have come into life having knowledge, and shall always continue to know as long as life lasts—for knowing is the acquiring and retaining knowledge and not forgetting. Is not forgetting, Simmias, just the losing of knowledge?

Quite true, Socrates.

But if the knowledge which we acquired before birth was lost by us at birth, and if afterwards by the use of the senses we recovered what we previously knew, will not the process which we call learning be a recovering of the knowledge which is natural to us, and may not this be rightly termed recollection?

Very true.

So much is clear—that when we perceive something, either by the help of sight, or hearing, or some other sense, from that perception we are able to obtain a notion of some other thing like or unlike which is associated with it but has been forgotten. Whence, as I was saying, one of two alternatives follows:—either we had this knowledge at birth, and continued to know through life; or, after birth, those who are said to learn only remember, and learning is simply recollection.

Yes, that is quite true, Socrates.

And which alternative, Simmias, do you prefer? Had we the knowledge at our birth, or did we recollect the things which we knew previously to our birth?

I cannot decide at the moment.

At any rate you can decide whether he who has knowledge will or will not be able to render an account of his knowledge? What do you say?

Certainly, he will.

But do you think that every man is able to give an account of these very matters about which we are speaking?

Would that they could, Socrates, but I rather fear that tomorrow, at this time, there will no longer be any one alive who is able to give an account of them such as ought to be given.

Then you are not of opinion, Simmias, that all men know these things?

Certainly not.

They are in process of recollecting that which they learned before?

Certainly.

But when did our souls acquire this knowledge?—not since we were born as men?

Certainly not.

And therefore, previously?

Yes.

Then, Simmias, our souls must also have existed without bodies before they were in the form of man, and must have had intelligence.

Unless indeed you suppose, Socrates, that these notions are given us at the very moment of birth; for this is the only time which remains.

Yes, my friend, but if so, when do we lose them? for they are not in us when we are born—that is admitted. Do we lose them at the moment of receiving them, or if not at what other time?

No, Socrates, I perceive that I was unconsciously talking nonsense.

Then may we not say, Simmias, that if, as we are always repeating, there is an absolute beauty, and goodness, and an absolute essence of all things; and if to this, which is now discovered to have existed in our former state, we refer all our sensations, and with this compare them, finding these ideas to be pre-existent and our inborn possession—then our souls must have had a prior existence, but if not, there would be no force in the argument? There is the same proof that these ideas must have existed before we were born, as that our souls existed before we were born; and if not the ideas, then not the souls.

Yes, Socrates; I am convinced that there is precisely the same necessity for the one as for the other; and the argument retreats successfully to the position that the existence of the soul before birth cannot be separated from the existence of the essence of which you speak. For there is nothing which to my mind is so patent as that beauty, goodness, and the other notions of which you were just now speaking, have a most real and absolute existence; and I am satisfied with the proof.

Well, but is Cebes equally satisfied? for I must convince him too.

I think, said Simmias, that Cebes is satisfied: although he is the most incredulous of mortals, yet I believe that he is sufficiently convinced of the existence of the soul before birth. But that after death the soul will continue to exist is not yet proven even to my own satisfaction. I cannot get rid of the feeling of the many to which Cebes was referring—the feeling that when the man dies the soul will be dispersed, and that this may be the extinction of her. For admitting that she may have been born elsewhere, and framed out of other elements, and was in existence before entering the human body, why after having entered in and gone out again may she not herself be destroyed and come to an end?

Very true, Simmias, said Cebes; about half of what was required has been proven; to wit, that our souls existed before we were born—that the soul will exist after death as well as before birth is the other half of which the proof is still wanting, and has to be supplied; when that is given the demonstration will be complete.

But that proof, Simmias and Cebes, has been already given, said Socrates, if you put the two arguments together—I mean this and the former one, in which we admitted that everything living is born of the dead. For if the soul exists before birth, and in coming to life and being born can be born only from death and dying, must she not after death continue to exist, since she has to be born

again?—Surely the proof which you desire has been already furnished. Still I suspect that you and Simmias would be glad to probe the argument further. Like children, you are haunted with a fear that when the soul leaves the body, the wind may really blow her away and scatter her; especially if a man should happen to die in a great storm and not when the sky is calm.

Cebes answered with a smile: Then, Socrates, you must argue us out of our fears—and yet, strictly speaking, they are not our fears, but there is a child within us to whom death is a sort of hobgoblin: him too we must persuade not to be afraid when he is alone in the dark.

Socrates said: Let the voice of the charmer be applied daily until you have charmed away the fear.

And where shall we find a good charmer of our fears, Socrates, when you are gone?

Hellas, he replied, is a large place, Cebes, and has many good men, and there are barbarous races not a few: seek for him among them all, far and wide, sparing neither pains nor money; for there is no better way of spending your money. And you must seek among yourselves too; for you will not find others better able to make the search.

The search, replied Cebes, shall certainly be made. And now, if you please, let us return to the point of the argument at which we digressed.

By all means, replied Socrates; what else should I please?

Very good.

Must we not, said Socrates, ask ourselves what that is which, as we imagine, is liable to be scattered, and about which we fear? and what again is that about which we have no fear? And then we may proceed further to inquire whether that which suffers dispersion is or is not of the nature of soul—our hopes and fears as to our own souls will turn upon the answers to these questions.

Very true, he said.

Now the compound or composite may be supposed to be naturally capable, as of being compounded, so also of being dissolved; but that which is uncompounded, and that only must be, if anything is, indissoluble.

Yes; I should imagine so, said Cebes.

And the uncompounded may be assumed to be the same and unchanging, whereas the compound is always changing and never the same.

I agree, he said.

Then now let us return to the previous discussion. Is that idea or essence, which in the dialectical process we define as essence or true existence—whether essence of equality, beauty, or anything else—are these essences, I say, liable at times to some degree of change? or are they each of them always what they are, having the same simple self-existent and unchanging forms, not admitting of variation at all, or in any way, or at any time?

They must be always the same, Socrates, replied Cebes.

And what would you say of the many beautiful—whether men or horses or garments or any other things which are named by the same names and may be called equal or beautiful,—are they all unchanging and the same always, or quite the reverse? May they not rather be described as almost always changing and hardly ever the same, either with themselves or with one another?

The latter, replied Cebes; they are always in a state of change.

And these you can touch and see and perceive with the senses, but the unchanging things you can only perceive with the mind—they are invisible and are not seen?

That is very true, he said.

Well then, added Socrates, let us suppose that there are two sorts of existences—one seen, the other unseen.

Let us suppose them.

The seen is the changing, and the unseen is the unchanging?

That may be also supposed.

And, further, is not one part of us body, another part soul?

To be sure.

And to which class is the body more alike and akin?

Clearly to the seen—no one can doubt that.

And is the soul seen or not seen?

Not by man, Socrates.

And what we mean by 'seen' and 'not seen' is that which is or is not visible to the eye of man?

Yes, to the eye of man.

And is the soul seen or not seen?

Not seen.

Unseen then?

Yes.

Then the soul is more like to the unseen, and the body to the seen?

That follows necessarily, Socrates.

And were we not saying long ago that the soul when using the body as an instrument of perception, that is to say, when using the sense of sight or hearing or some other sense (for the meaning of perceiving through the body is perceiving through the senses)—were we not saying that the soul too is then dragged by the body into the region of the changeable, and wanders and is confused; the world spins round her, and she is like a drunkard, when she touches change?

Very true.

But when returning into herself she reflects, then she passes into the other world, the region of purity, and eternity, and immortality, and unchangeableness, which are her kindred, and with them she ever lives, when she is by herself and is not let or hindered; then she ceases from her erring ways, and being in communion with the unchanging is unchanging. And this state of the soul is called wisdom?

That is well and truly said, Socrates, he replied.

And to which class is the soul more nearly alike and akin, as far as may be inferred from this argument, as well as from the preceding one?

I think, Socrates, that, in the opinion of every one who follows the argument, the soul will be infinitely more like the unchangeable—even the most stupid person will not deny that:

And the body is more like the changing?

Yes.

Yet once more consider the matter in another light: When the soul and the body are united, then nature orders the soul to rule and govern, and the body to obey and serve. Now which of these two functions is akin to the divine? and which to the mortal? Does not the divine appear to you to be that which naturally orders and rules, and the mortal to be that which is subject and servant?

True.

And which does the soul resemble?

The soul resembles the divine, and the body the mortal—there can be no doubt of that, Socrates.

Then reflect, Cebes: of all which has been said is not this the conclusion?—that the soul is in the very likeness of the divine, and immortal, and intellectual, and uniform, and indissoluble, and unchangeable; and that the body is in the very likeness of the human, and mortal, and unintellectual, and multiform, and dissoluble, and changeable. Can this, my dear Cebes, be denied?

It cannot.

But if it be true, then is not the body liable to speedy dissolution? and is not the soul almost or altogether indissoluble?

Certainly.

And do you further observe, that after a man is dead, the body, or visible part of him, which is lying in the visible world, and is called a corpse, and would naturally be dissolved and decomposed and dissipated, is not dissolved or decomposed at once, but may remain for some time, nay even for a long time, if the constitution be sound at the time of death, and the season of the year favorable? For the body when shrunk and embalmed, as the manner is in Egypt, may remain almost entire through infinite ages; and even in decay, there are still some portions, such as the bones and ligaments, which are practically indestructible:—Do you agree?

Yes.

And is it likely that the soul, which is invisible, in passing to the place of the true Hades, which like her is invisible, and pure, and noble, and on her way to the good and wise God, whither, if God will, my soul is also soon to go,—that the soul, I repeat, if this be her nature and origin, will be blown away and destroyed immediately on quitting the body, as the many say? That can never be, my dear Simmias and Cebes. The truth rather is, that the soul which is pure at departing and draws after her no bodily taint, having never voluntarily during life had connection with the body, which she is ever avoiding, herself gathered into

herself;—and making such abstraction her perpetual study—which means that she has been a true disciple of philosophy; and therefore has in fact been always engaged in the practice of dying? For is not philosophy the study of death?—

Certainly—

That soul, I say, herself invisible, departs to the invisible world to the divine and immortal and rational; thither arriving, she is secure of bliss and is released from the error and folly of men, their fears and wild passions and all other human ills, and for ever dwells, as they say of the initiated, in company with the gods. Is not this true, Cebes?

Yes, said Cebes, beyond a doubt.

THE PRISON GUARD SPEAKS:—To you, Socrates, whom I know to be the noblest and gentlest and best of all who ever came to this place, I will not impute the angry feelings of other men, who rage and swear at me, when in obedience to the authorities, I bid them drink the poison—indeed, I am sure that you will not be angry with me; for others, as you are aware, and not I, are to blame. And so fare you well, and try to bear lightly what must needs be—you know my errand. Then bursting into tears he turned away and went out.

Socrates looked at him and said: I return your good wishes, and will do as you bid. Then turning to us, he said, How charming the man is: since I have been in prison he has always been coming to see me, and at times he would talk to me, and was as good to me as could be, and now see how generously he sorrows on my account. We must do as he says, Crito; and therefore let the cup be brought, if the poison is prepared: if not, let the attendant prepare some.

Yet, said Crito, the sun is still upon the hill-tops, and I know that many a one has taken the draught late, and after the announcement has been made to him, he has eaten and drunk, and enjoyed the society of his beloved; do not hurry—there is time enough.

SOCRATES SAID: Yes, Crito, and they of whom you speak are right in so acting, for they think that they will be gainers by the delay; but I am right in not following their example, for I do not think that I should gain anything by drinking the poison a little later; I should only be ridiculous in my own eyes for sparing and saving a life which is already forfeit. Please then to do as I say, and not to refuse me.

Crito made a sign to the servant, who was standing by; and he went out, and having been absent for some time, returned with the jailer carrying the cup of poison. Socrates said: You, my good friend, who are experienced in these matters, shall give me directions how I am to proceed. The man answered: You have only to walk about until your legs are heavy, and then to lie down, and the poison will act. At the same time he handed the cup to Socrates, who in the easiest and gentlest manner, without the least fear or change of color or feature, looking at the man with all his eyes, Echecrates, as his manner was, took the cup and said: What do you say about making a libation out of this cup to any god? May I, or not? The man answered: We only prepare, Socrates, just so much as we deem enough. I understand, he said: but I may and must ask the gods to prosper my journey from this to the other world—even so—and so be it according to my prayer. Then raising the cup to his lips, quite readily and cheerfully he drank off the poison. And hitherto most of us had been able to control our sorrow; but now when we saw him drinking, and saw too that he had finished the draught, we could no longer forbear, and in spite of myself my own tears were flowing fast; so that I covered my face and wept, not for him, but at the thought of my own calamity in

having to part from such a friend. Nor was I the first; for Crito, when he found himself unable to restrain his tears, had got up, and I followed; and at that moment, Apollodorus, who had been weeping all the time, broke out in a loud and passionate cry which made cowards of us all. Socrates alone retained his calmness: What is this strange outcry? he said. I sent away the women mainly in order that they might not misbehave in this way, for I have been told that a man should die in peace. Be quiet then, and have patience. When we heard his words we were ashamed, and refrained our tears; and he walked about until, as he said, his legs began to fail, and then he lay on his back, according to the directions, and the man who gave him the poison now and then looked at his feet and legs; and after a while he pressed his foot hard, and asked him if he could feel; and he said, No; and then his leg, and so upward and upward, and showed us that he was cold and stiff. And he felt them himself, and said: When the poison reaches the heart, that will be the end. He was beginning to grow cold about the groin, when he uncovered his face, for he had covered himself up, and said—they were his last words—he said: Crito, I owe a cock to Asclepius; will you remember to pay the debt? The debt shall be paid, said Crito; is there anything else? There was no answer to this question; but in a minute or two a movement was heard, and the attendants uncovered him; his eyes were set, and Crito closed his eyes and mouth. Such was the end, Echecrates, of our friend; concerning whom I may truly say, that of all the men of his time whom I have known, he was the wisest and justest and best.

Study Questions

1. What is ethical relativism and why did Socrates so despise it?

2. What is the difference between metaphysics and epistemology?

3. What is the major lesson to be learned from Plato's allegory of the cave?

4. What is Plato's analogy of the divided line designed to show?

5. Why does Plato consider mathematical concepts to be more real than material objects?

6. What are Forms, and why are they the highest level of reality?

7. How are the Forms known by us?

8. Use the "charioteer" analogy to describe the three "parts" of the soul.

9. How are the three parts of the soul ideally related to produce the good life?

10. How are the three parts of the soul related to the three classes in society?

Chapter 3

Ancient Greek Philosophers 2: Aristotle

Introduction

Aristotle (384–322 B.C.E) wrote an immense amount and wrote about every theoretical discipline of his day. He created a system of interrelated theories covering all branches of philosophy and most of the known sciences of his time. When Aquinas and other medieval theologians and philosophers referred to the writings of Aristotle, some sixteen hundred years later, they simply called him "the Philosopher," as though nothing more needed to be said. It is safe to say that the writings of Aristotle, along with those of his famous teacher, Plato, constituted the most significant bodies of philosophical wisdom in Western culture for almost two thousand years after their deaths.

If Plato's life and writings were influenced by the Peloponnesian War, those of Aristotle were influenced especially by Macedonian conquests. Though Aristotle spent most of his twenties and thirties studying with Plato in Athens, he was born in Stagira, a town in Macedonia. Macedonia was a large Greek country to the north of the Greek city-states. It was ruled by King Philip II, and later by his son—Alexander the Great. When he was in his early forties, Aristotle became the young Alexander's tutor, relinquishing that job when the nineteen-year-old Alexander became king. He returned to Athens at the age of forty-nine to open his own school, the Lyceum, which competed with the school that had been founded by Plato, the Academy. Because Aristotle and other teachers at the Lyceum often walked on a pathway as they lectured, known in Greek as the *peripatos*, Aristotle and his followers were referred to as the **Peripatetic** philosophers.

Aristotle believed with Plato that the good life was the life of wisdom and virtue—the life of the philosopher. But he differed with his mentor considerably about the nature of wisdom and virtue. Where Plato found wisdom by recollecting the universal, eternal, unchanging Forms, Aristotle found it by observing the everyday world of particular, temporal, changing material objects. Where Plato thought that virtue was created by understanding what is truly good for us, the Good, Aristotle thought that virtue was the result of training and habit. The "otherworldliness" of Plato's thought was rejected by Aristotle in favor of the study of this world, especially the world of living things. Plato understood the world more as a mathematician might, constructing his theories apart from experience. Aristotle, on the other hand, approached the study of all things more from the perspective of a biologist. His theories were based on careful observations and the reasonable truths that could be inferred from them.

Worldview

The Science of Metaphysics

We begin by examining Aristotle's theories of reality and knowledge. A good place to look for Aristotle's views on reality is in his book, which others later named the *Metaphysics*. In Greek, *meta* means after, or beyond. So this book is about what is beyond the physical, what cannot be observed by the senses. While Aristotle thought that the everyday, commonsense world is real, and not merely a copy of reality as Plato would have it, it is the deeper structure of this world that interested him most. This structure cannot be observed directly, but must be inferred from what can be observed. Much as a scientist constructs hypotheses today to explain what can be observed, so for Aristotle it is through studying the observable that the underlying, unobservable features of reality are to be discovered.

The first sentence of Aristotle's *Metaphysics* is, "All men by nature desire to know."[1] This deep desire within all human beings is not a desire simply to perceive the world around us, to store up memories, and to make our way in life according to what our experience teaches us. Nor is it to be identified with acquiring skills—a profession for example. All this amounts to is *practical* knowledge, a knowledge of how to do something. Most of us need to become competent in a trade, or a profession, or acquire some skill that is marketable, so that we can earn a living. But human beings desire more than survival. They deeply desire what Aristotle calls *scientific* knowledge, the kind of knowledge that explains what things are, how they work, and what is their purpose. So we may *need* the kind of knowledge that allows us to make a living, but we *desire* the kind of knowledge that allows us to understand the world and our place in it.

Practical and Scientific Knowledge

It is important to understand the difference between practical knowledge and scientific knowledge. Many of us today value practical knowledge over scientific knowledge, what Aristotle calls wisdom. For the ancient Greek philosophers, however, only wisdom satisfies our deepest desire. Only its possession will make us truly happy. Practical knowledge is based on perception and experience. On this level we perceive particular objects, houses for example, as individual and as different from each other. One is gray, one is red, another is brown. On the level of practical knowledge, moreover, we are interested in knowing particular objects not so much to examine the general features that they share with other objects, but for purposes of satisfying our needs. Houses are understood to be places of shelter and comfort and protection, not so much instances of a general plan. Especially important on the level of practical knowledge is knowledge of *how* to do something, in this case how to build houses. Practical knowledge is good *for* something. Its value is in its usefulness to produce things that help to satisfy our desires and meet our needs.

Scientific knowledge is not practical. It is not good *for* anything. For Aristotle, far from making it less valuable, this makes it more valuable than practical knowledge. Scientific knowledge has intrinsic value, that is, it is good for its own sake. It is more valuable than practical knowledge because it satisfies our deepest desire, our desire to understand this world as we pass through it. Such knowledge is truly liberating. In understanding our lives and the world around us, we free ourselves from the narrow confines of current opinions, and base our beliefs about the important things of life on knowledge of what truly is. Philosophers call this sort of knowledge wisdom. It is in the highest science, metaphysics, that wisdom is especially to be found.

Wisdom is to be found not in sense experience and in the practical knowledge that rests upon it. We do not become wise just by living and experiencing life as it flows by in our daily lives. Instead, wisdom is to be found in the understanding mind that grasps a deeper reality than that available to common experience. The truly wise person understands the deeper pattern of nature and of life, and is not confined to what personal experience has taught. For Aristotle, wisdom may be divided into many sciences, but the central science is that of metaphysics. Metaphysical science, the most basic science, Aristotle referred to as the study of "being *qua* being," that is, the study of the universal properties and causes possessed by all things that exist, by all being.

When Aristotle talks about scientific knowledge he is not talking about science as we know it today—physics, chemistry, biology, and so on. Science as we know it today would not begin to make its appearance in Western thought for another two thousand years or so. Aristotle's conception of scientific knowledge is like contemporary science in at least one respect, however. Both construct theories to describe and explain things in a general way. The main difference between them is that for the science of today, any beliefs included in a theory must be confirmed by observation. Although Aristotle also placed great importance on observation, much of what he had to say would be thought of today as a set of brilliant but unconfirmed hypotheses. Many of his conclusions were based on reason more than on facts, on speculation more than on experiment, on theorizing more than on observation. What he means by "science" is more like what we mean today by "philosophy." In particular, scientific knowledge has the following properties.

Abstract, Universal, Causal Knowledge

First, scientific knowledge is *abstract* knowledge. It is less concerned with the unique features of particular objects, and more concerned with the general properties that all objects have in common with others. Such understanding is abstract, insofar as it seeks to "abstract" general properties from the particular differences that exist between individual objects. For example, whenever you think about shapes such as rectangles you think abstractly. You ignore the differences between rectangular material objects, such as their color and texture and so on, and focus only on their shared property of being rectangular. To use another example of abstract thinking, several houses constructed according to the same architectural plan all have the same general structure. They may be understood as all exhibiting these common properties, despite their specific differences such as their color, or location, or the type of siding used in their construction. Knowledge of the plan is more abstract than knowledge of the individual houses. Science is not concerned with the concrete, unique features of objects. Instead, it focuses its attention on the general features of objects, the ones that they share with other objects, the ones that are known abstractly.

Besides being abstract, science is also *universal.* That is, scientific knowledge is true of "all" individuals of the type in question. If all houses that ever existed and ever will exist were built according to the same blueprint, then knowledge of that plan would be both an abstract and a universal understanding of the general structure of all houses. A person who had this abstract, universal knowledge would understand what is essential not only to those particular houses that have been experienced so far, but would also understand, once and for all, what is essential to any and all houses. Such an understanding or concept of a particular thing could be expressed in a definition which expresses what a thing is essentially.

In addition to being abstract and universal, scientific knowledge is knowledge of *causes.* When what is truly essential to being a thing of a certain type is understood, when we know its essence, Aristotle says we have knowledge of the **formal cause** of things of that type. That is, we have an idea or a concept of what it means to be a certain kind of thing. Although this sounds very much like what Plato said when he spoke of understanding the Forms, there are dramatic differences between his notion of Form and Aristotle's notion of formal cause. These differences will be discussed later, but for now the two notions should be seen as similar. That is, just as wisdom for Plato is an understanding of universal, abstract, unchanging concepts, so wisdom for Aristotle, science, requires such an understanding as well.

In addition to understanding what something is, however, complete scientific knowledge of something also requires that we know how such things come to be. What produces something Aristotle calls their **efficient cause.** This is usually what we refer to today in science when we talk about the cause of something. We refer to the antecedent conditions that made the thing or event occur. The eight ball went into the pocket because it was struck by the cue-ball which, in turn, was struck by the cue-stick, and so on. Plato had little to say about efficient causes, since he was more concerned with the general pattern of nature and not with how particular things behave. The identification of efficient causes requires much observation of things in "this" world, something that Plato held in low esteem. He wanted especially to know what things are, not where they came from.

In addition to knowing the formal and efficient causes of things, wisdom requires that we also know their **final cause.** Aristotle saw nature as an interrelated system of objects that behave as they do for a purpose. He believed that just as human beings behave for purposes or goals, so do natural objects. There is a purpose for everything, even inanimate objects. The purpose of rain, for example, is to grow plants. Plants exist to feed animals, which in turn exist for the many purposes of human beings. In addition to being part of a system of related purposes, each living thing has as its own built-in specific purpose to grow and develop as fully as possible into the kind of being that it is. An acorn has as its purpose to become an oak tree, for example, while a human embryo strives to grow into a fully developed human being. Only human beings are capable of being conscious of their purposes or goals. Lesser beings are simply driven to achieve them by something within. Since the Greek word for "purpose" is "telos," Aristotle's conception of nature as a system of objects behaving with mutually compatible purposes is called **teleology.**

Even though a teleological theory of nature is no longer accepted, the idea of acting for a purpose is alive and well in the arena of human behavior. We explain human behavior in this manner especially in daily life. We go to the store to buy some food, for example. That is our purpose or reason. That is *why* we go. It makes little sense to explain our behavior in terms of its efficient causes most of the time. What would we say, that we went to the store because our brains made our muscles and tendons contract, which made our legs move in a certain manner? Though we now explain rainfall by its efficient causes, as a process of condensation and not as a goal-seeking activity, we nevertheless still explain human behavior as purpose oriented. This is important, because Aristotle's concept of human nature will especially be concerned with identifying the ultimate goals of human beings.

The main point for now is that for Aristotle, to fully understand something we need to know not only what kind of a thing it is, as Plato thought, but also how it was created and why it exists. For example, what is essential to being a human being is that we are living, physical beings with reason. Because reason is what is unique to human animals, Aristotle defines human beings as rational animals. That is our formal cause, the type of beings that we are. We were produced by other human beings, our parents (our efficient causes), and as we will see later, our ultimate goal (final cause) is to achieve happiness by acquiring wisdom and virtue.

Aristotle on Forms

Although he was a student of Plato, Aristotle differed sharply from his mentor on many points. In the area of metaphysics, the most dramatic of these differences is Aristotle's denial of the independent existence of the Forms. Like Plato, Aristotle believed that knowledge involved more than having sense experience. It also involved understanding that experience, classifying it according to general concepts. He believed with Plato that there are such general ideas that are universal and unchanging and eternal, ideas that mirror the true nature of reality. Aristotle also agrees with his mentor that the goal of life is to discover this set of ideas, to possess wisdom. However, he does not think of these ideas as having a separate existence, independent of the minds that think them and the particular material objects that embody them. For Aristotle, there are no independently existing Forms. Because he believed that there were forms, but that they had a different status than Plato held, we will use the lower case "f" when referring to Aristotle's theory of forms, and the upper case "F" for Plato's version.

It was a puzzle for Aristotle to understand how a particular material object could be a certain kind of thing because of its form, as Plato believed, if its form existed in another world of reality. If forms were to be located in the ideal, transcendent world of Being, a world beyond the space-time world that was home to material objects and persons, then how could they be used to explain how material objects were "copies" of them? The "demiurge" explanation would not do for Aristotle. That was simply a myth. He agreed that there were forms, to be sure. Knowledge of them, after all, is what constitutes science, and science exists. But these forms were to be located right in particular things themselves, not in some separate world of Being. For Aristotle, forms are important because they are the essential, underlying reality of concrete, particular things. They are what make things be certain sorts of things. For this to be so, forms must be "in" the things for our knowledge of them to be knowledge of the essence of things. But how are forms in things, as well as in the minds of those who understand them?

For Aristotle, particular material objects have material components, but that is not all there is to a material object. In addition to its material components, material objects have a deeper structure that it is the job of metaphysics to discover. For example, in addition to its matter, there is an *organization* of the material components of each thing. The matter of an apple is organized or structured in one way, while that of a stone is structured in another. Different kinds of things may each be composed of similar material components, but each different kind of thing has these components "put together," or structured in different ways. This is what accounts for the differences among objects—they have different structures. This is what Aristotle means by "form," the organization of matter. Having a particular organization, or structure, accounts for the sameness among things of the same kind. Apples are all apples because they have the same form—their material components have the same kind of organization. It is not because they are each copies of the same Form that material objects of the same type are alike, but because within each resides the same principle of organization, the same form. This form is the essence of the object, and can be known by the human mind.

Aristotle introduced several concepts to explain other things about the deeper structure of material objects. For example, he referred to material objects as various types of "substances," where a **substance** is the enduring thing itself which possesses various sorts of properties. These properties, such as the color, size, shape, location, and so on of objects, are called **accidents.** The apple is the substance, while its redness, roundness, and sweetness are some of its accidents. This accounts for the fact that there are "things" and "properties" of things. What makes a substance a particular *kind* of substance is its form, as we have already seen. What makes it a *material* substance is its matter. If there are things that are not material things, such as souls, Gods and the like, they would be spiritual substances. They would be forms only, existing apart from matter.

If Aristotle explained the structural features of substances in terms of their matter and form, he explained how they could change by using the categories of act and **potency.** The current form of any material substance is what makes it the sort of thing that it *actually* is. All such forms also contain the *potential* for the object to become something else. This potential, this inner *telos*, is part of the form of each living, changing thing. An apple is an apple (has the form appleness), but also could become part of your body, if you ate it. A pile of wood is potentially a pile of ashes plus heat energy, once someone sets it on fire. In both of these cases a certain kind of thing becomes another kind of thing. This is called a "substantial change" by Aristotle. There can also be accidental changes, as when a thing changes one of its properties but still remains the kind of thing it is. An apple may change its color, for example. The way that substantial changes are explained is to say that a form which is potentially present in a substance becomes actualized, replacing the previous actually existing form.

Knowledge of the Forms

The assumption that led Plato to insist on the separate reality of the Forms was that *for every type of knowing there must be a different type of object known.* This assumption led Plato to think of Forms as separate from material objects because of a process of reasoning that went something like this. Forms are different kinds of objects than material objects, because science is different from perceptual knowledge. Perception produces only opinion, because the things perceived (material objects) change continually. Understanding produced science, because the things understood (the Forms) are objects that are unchanging, eternal, and universal. If they have those properties, then they could not be physical objects. And thus the Forms were not to be located in the world of Becoming, but rather in the world of Being. So philosophy, as the love of wisdom, is knowledge of a nonphysical world, the only sort of world which could possess the requisite properties of Being.

Aristotle denied this argument and the assumption upon which it was built. Instead he held that there was just one type of being, not four, but that it could be known in four different ways. Plato could not see how knowledge of the Forms could arise from seeing, hearing, tasting, touching and smelling the ever changing world of particular material objects. After all, there is nothing in these sensations that appears to contain ideas. We see particular people, not "humanity"; particular acts of justice, not "justice" itself. If knowledge of the Forms is not derived from perception, then they must be innately known, by a process of remembering or recollection. For Plato, you cannot get mathematical and philosophical knowledge from the senses. No matter how many apples you might see, you never see their "appleness." This sort of knowledge arises only from reason, a reason working quite independently of the senses.

So the job facing Aristotle, if he is to undermine the assumption of Plato, and thus the need for an independent world of Forms, is to show how knowledge of these universal, unchanging, eternal ideas could arise from observing the particular, changing, temporal world of material objects and persons. Since he rejects Plato's doctrine of innate ideas, he has to show how knowledge that begins with the observation of particular, unique, changing objects can result in the possession of universal, unchanging ideas—science. He has to show how observing many individual objects of the same type gives rise to a general idea, which reflects the form of things of the same type. This is an important task, because much of what is held to be important to human happiness has to do with the type of knowledge of which we are capable. If to be happy requires that we be wise, and if to be wise is to know these forms, then it is extremely important to understand how scientific knowledge is possible.

Genus and Species

Aristotle was never very clear about how such knowledge was possible, so we have to guess a bit to make sense of his view. He seems to have thought of such knowledge as arising from a process of generalization. You see a lot of apples, for example, and then the general idea of what an apple is gets formed. As we observe many apples, we learn to discount their nonessential features and to focus on the general properties that all apples share. The universal idea, the idea that defines the form shared by all objects of the same type, arises from an examination of the common features present in several observations of individual objects of that type. The idea is that careful observation will reveal the pattern or form of each type of object, and then the recognized pattern may be generalized as true of all objects of that type.

For Aristotle, these general features are primarily captured in the set of classifications which express the *genus* and the *species* of which the thing in question is a member. It is helpful to think of Aristotle's classification system as similar to that of a biologist today, who classifies animals and plants as belonging to various types. The genus is the most general classification, the one that places an object in an abstract category such as "plant" or "animal." The species, or specific difference, is the category that distinguishes the object from others in that genus. It allows us to distinguish between various sorts of plants, or animals, for example.

So concept formation requires us to discover the genus and species of an object. From seeing many apples I am able to classify them as members of the genus "plants" and the species "fruit." From observing many human beings, I may classify them as members of the genus "animal" and the species "rational." Expressing its genus and species defines an object, as we define a human being as a "rational animal." These sorts of definitions express universal concepts, which capture the form of all objects of that type. Apples may be further classified in more specific ways as well, as we do when we classify apples into further types such as "Delicious" or "Macintosh" or "Granny Smith" apples, for example.

Unfortunately, explaining knowledge of the forms by appealing to knowledge of genus and species does not get us very far. If the form of an object can be reduced to its genus and species it is still left unexplained how the general concepts of genus and species can arise from observation. One can almost hear Plato asking at this point how the general idea of "appleness," which is the idea of the essential features or form of all apples, "comes along with" the sensory data. The sensory data, after all, include only the color and shape and size and odor and taste and texture and sound and scent of the object. These vary from particular to particular. They are not essential features. Knowledge of them provides no more knowledge of the form of an apple, then seeing the color of a house provides knowledge of its architectural plan. The essential features of objects, their "intelligible" structure, their form, cannot be observed at all. An apple is something that "has" color and odor and taste, and so on—not something that "is" a collection of these properties. What seems simple enough and true enough at first glance, that our general ideas arise from observing many instances of something, begins now to look very puzzling indeed.

Abstraction

Later commentators on the writings of Aristotle, especially Thomas Aquinas,[2] referred to his discussion of the process of concept formation as a special type of inductive inference called **abstraction**. According to this interpretation of Aristotle, we form our idea of what an apple is by taking a look at a lot of apples and abstracting, or "removing" from consideration, all the *different* properties that exist between them. In this way we end up with the features that are the *same* in all apples. This is what is essential to being an apple, its form. Here is an example of how abstraction is supposed to work. If we remove the differences among groups of three oranges, three computers, and three cars, the shared feature that remains is "three." That is what they have in common. In the same way, in forming the general concept of appleness, the mind separates the properties of apples into those that differ from apple to apple, and those that are shared by all apples. It then removes from consideration (abstracts) all of the former, retaining only what is essential—the form apple. It is this form that makes the object the particular type of object that it is, and it is this form that is represented in the general idea "apple."

Here is how abstraction is supposed to work in forming the concept of an apple. The mind leaves out of its idea of an apple all the properties that are not shared by all apples. For example, the concept of an apple does not include the property of color, since this can vary from apple to apple. An apple is still an apple if it is red, or green, or yellow, or rotting brown. It is not essential to being an apple that it be a particular color, though it may be essential to being a particular type of apple. So right away we can abstract (remove) color from the list of essential properties of what an apple truly is. The same may be said for taste. Apples may be sour or sweet, for example, or something in between, so it cannot be essential to being an apple that it be sweet or sour, or taste in any one particular way.

What about properties known through the other senses? Do they reveal essential properties? Do apples have to feel or smell a certain way, or make certain sorts of sounds when we bite into them or drop them? It appears not. It appears that these are all properties that are not part of the idea apple. But now we are in a curious position indeed. All we know through the senses about particular apples are their "removable" features—their color, odor, taste, touch, and sound. None of these are part of the idea of what it means to be an apple. If our general concept of an apple is to be formed by observing lots of apples and abstracting their differences, then we have a problem. It seems that *everything* we observe, everything that we see, hear, taste, touch, and smell, about particular apples, varies from apple to apple. If this is so, then there are *no* common features left to be the concept of an apple.

The lesson to be learned from all of this is that an idea of apples in general cannot be merely the sensory data common to all experiences of apples. This is because there is nothing that we observe through the senses that is common to all apples. General ideas are ideas of the forms of objects, their intelligible structure. Forms are not observed by the senses. But if Aristotle's claim that forms are "in" material objects is to be accepted, and if he rejects innate ideas, then he "must" show how the form of an object may be known "through" its sensory properties. Somehow, he must show how general ideas may be formed on the basis of sensory experience without being reducible to these experiences. It seems that abstraction requires us to discover something more in the data of sensation than what the senses themselves deliver.

Aquinas claimed that Aristotle should have explained abstraction in the following way. The information received about an apple through each of the five senses arrives separately within the theater of the mind. Once there, somehow these separate seeings, and hearings, and tastings, and so on, get recombined to form a sensory image of an apple, an internal representation of the apple's sensory properties. From this sensory image, the mind then forms a concept that corresponds to the form found in apples. The power of the mind to form such a concept is called the **agent intellect** by Aristotle. It is the power of the mind to *understand* the universal form within the particular sensory image. As the form, or intelligible structure, of an apple that exists in the world is within the apple, so too, the concept that corresponds to the form of the apple is present "in" the internal sensory image of the apple. Aristotle discusses some of the powers of the mind in *Reading 1*.

But, once again, how does the mind "understand" or form such concepts from the sensory data? Concept formation is thought of by Aristotle by analogy with the processes of conception and the subsequent birth of a living thing. For an idea to be *conceived* by the mind, is for the mind to give birth to something new, something not found in the sensory data. In the case of apples, this is an idea of appleness, an idea that mirrors the form of apples found in things. Once these universal ideas are conceived they can be stored in the mind and retained as knowledge of the reality of things, their forms. The power of the mind to possess this knowledge is called the **passive intellect,** since it passively receives the ideas activity conceived by the agent or active intellect. Aristotle thinks of this passive mind as a receiver of forms. In this way do our minds mirror reality. In a sense, they even "become" reality itself. It is the system of these ideas that constitutes philosophical wisdom.

While this account of concept formation as abstraction is in need of further clarification, it is similar to some contemporary accounts of concept formation. Today we might say that our concepts, our systems of classifying nature, persons, mathematical objects, moral values, societies, and so on, are all literally created by us. They are created by communities of people who share the same language which embodies these concepts. Our systems of concepts and beliefs, even those of common sense and science, are all man-made products. They are tools that we use or not depending on how well they do in describing and explaining our experience.

This would not be Aristotle's view, however. He would not admit that concepts are created, since it would then disconnect general concepts from the very items they are supposed to represent, from the intelligible structure of forms of things themselves. One thing is clear—explaining how concepts are acquired, how they are used to classify experience, and how they come to represent objects in the world is an extremely complex and difficult task. It is an important task, however, since understanding human nature has a great deal to do with understanding ourselves as knowers.

Human Nature

To understand the nature of any living being is to understand its structure and its function. In Aristotle's teleological universe, every living being has a natural function. Every living being strives naturally to become excellent within its species, to develop as fully as possible into the kind of thing that it is. This is its purpose; this is its goal; a goal over which it has no control. If left to themselves, for example, acorns that are planted and have sufficient nutrients will grow into oak trees. External conditions may hinder this development. Fires, floods, and animals may destroy the process of development at any stage. But the internal conditions of the acorn, determined by its form, force it to attempt to grow fully in its species.

Human beings act for purposes as well, purposes of which we are often conscious and able to control. We train in order to run a race; we study to pass exams; we shop to buy food; we drive our cars in order to get somewhere. These are goals of our own making which we choose to pursue or not. In addition to acting for these sorts of purposes, however, we, like every other living thing, have natural goals as well. Just as surely as any creature in nature has the goal to be a fully developed particular kind of thing, so human beings have as their natural purpose to become fully developed or "self-actualized" as human beings.

This goal appears to all of us as a general desire for happiness. Because we can choose to pursue happiness in any number of ways, however, and because some of these ways run contrary to our true interests, it is important for us to know just what it is that will really make us happy. In order to understand this, we must understand first just what sorts of beings we are. We must understand just what is our structure. For Aristotle, as for Plato before him, this means understanding the nature of our true selves, our souls. When we discover that, and we understand the function of the soul, then we will have discovered the purpose or *telos* of our lives.

In *Reading 2* Aristotle discusses the nature of the soul. The first thing to say about Aristotle's notion of the soul is that Aristotle rejected Plato's dualism. He does not understand the soul to be a nonphysical substance somehow connected to a physical substance, such as a body. Instead, *the soul is the form of the body.* As the shape of an apple cannot exist apart from the apple, so the soul of a living being cannot exist apart from that being. Souls exist together with matter to provide the structure and function of all living beings. All living beings have souls, though different sorts of souls. Today we might say that living beings differ from one another because they have different genes. These genes grow the organism one way or another. That is, they organize matter into one sort of being or another. For Aristotle, souls play this same explanatory role. Living beings differ from one another not because they are made of different material components. Matter is the same sort of thing in all beings. Instead, it is because they have different sorts of souls.

Plants, for example, have *nutritive* souls, forms that allow them to be alive, especially to provide for nutrition and reproduction. Animals have souls that provide these functions as well, but also allow them to be conscious on a *sensory* level. They can experience their surroundings and remember these experiences, as well as feel and have desires. In addition to these nonrational functions, the souls of human beings provide for even richer, more complex functions. Besides being the source of life and sensation, human souls are also the source of *reason*. So the soul of a human being has three dimensions, or "faculties," as Aristotle calls them. It is the source of life, the source of sensory consciousness, and the source of reason. Aristotle believed that reason is unique to human beings. Its very uniqueness for him defines what is most important about us, what is most human about us. It is here that is to be found our *human* nature. While we have natural biological functions and natural sensory functions, our specifically human natural function is the exercise of our reason.

Reason may be exercised in two ways. First, there is *theoretical reason,* which is the mind seeking truth. This is the quest for a scientific understanding of reality, the quest for wisdom. Next, *practical reason* seeks to use this knowledge and our experience of living to guide our behavior. Practical reason is especially important in the areas of ethics and politics, where we strive to figure out how to live well. Reason may also be exercised well or poorly. To live an excellent life requires that reason be exercised well. Aristotle refers to the excellent use of reason as its "virtuous" use. When we are thinking and understanding well it is because our reason conforms to intellectual standards called **intellectual virtues;** when we are leading good and rational lives it is because our reason conforms to moral standards called **moral virtues.** These are important concepts to understand if we are to understand not only what human nature is, but also what it could be when it is fully developed. In the end, happiness for Aristotle comes to one who has a fully developed human nature. This is a person whose life is led in accordance with the intellectual and moral virtues.

Consequences

Freedom

Before discussing the intellectual and moral virtues it is important to see what Aristotle says about freedom, especially **freedom of choice.** As with Plato, Aristotle assumed that we can freely choose one course of action over another. He assumes this because it is a necessary condition for moral responsibility. Since we do hold people responsible for their actions, praising them for their good choices and blaming them for their evil ones, they must be assumed to be free to choose good over evil. Some of our behavior, however, is not the result of free choice. Some of it is forced upon us or lies beyond our control. So it was not the existence of free choice that troubled Aristotle, but rather the explanation of the conditions required for its existence. If these conditions exist then the person is to be held responsible for his or her action; if not, then they have a lesser responsibility or even no responsibility at all.

Aristotle addressed this question in Book III of the *Nicomachean Ethics.* There he first distinguished between actions that are voluntary and those that are involuntary. *Involuntary* actions are those that "take place under compulsion or owing to ignorance."[3] If we are forced to perform actions at the end of a gun, for example, our actions are not voluntary. Instead they are compulsory. They are compulsory whenever "the cause is in the external circumstances and the agent contributes nothing."[4] Also, if we act out of ignorance of the true facts, if we do not know what we are doing, we are not acting voluntarily. For example, if we give someone poison when we believe it is simply an ordinary drink, we are not responsible for the consequences. By contrast, *voluntary* actions are those that are caused by something in the agent himself, either by irrational elements such as emotion or desire, or by rational elements, such as intentions or decisions.

Though at first glance acting by choice seems to be the same as acting voluntarily, for Aristotle it is not. In addition to being voluntary, actions that are chosen involve reason. If voluntary actions are those that are caused by something within me, nevertheless, some causes internal to me are not rational. Though I ought to be held responsible for my actions that stem from passion or emotion, for example, such actions are often not chosen by me, even though they result from something within me. Instead, to choose between one action and another requires **deliberation.** It requires the rational consideration of the consequences of the various actions available to me under the current circumstances. I weigh the pros and cons of my options and only then choose which action to perform among those available. So a person is truly free only if his or her actions are voluntary and chosen as a result of rational deliberation. For Aristotle, we are most free when we follow the guidance of reason. Since we are our reason, such choices are truly choices of ourselves.

Ethics

For Aristotle, ethics is not so much concerned with following rules that determine right from wrong. While it may include such considerations it is primarily concerned, as it had been for Plato, with discovering how we ought to live if we are to be happy. It is concerned, that is, with an understanding of the good life. Since what is good for any living being is to fulfill its nature, then ethics is concerned with what human nature *ought to be.* As we have seen, all living things of the same type share a common structure or form which results in common, natural behavior. While our form, or soul, includes our biological and sensory dimensions, special emphasis is placed by Aristotle on the development of what is distinctively human in us—our *rational* abilities. While we are animals, and thus must satisfy our animal desires to be happy, we are also uniquely rational, and thus it is most important that we satisfy the desires of reason.

A full, rich, happy life requires that reason be used well, or virtuously. This includes using reason in accordance with intellectual virtue, using reason to acquire that theoretical knowledge called wisdom. A happy life also requires that we then use this wisdom to direct our lives. Aristotle discusses this theme in *Reading 3.* The virtuous use of practical reason to direct our lives occurs when we use reason in accordance with moral virtue. If what is truly good for us is to know and follow our natural goals, and if this requires us to acquire the intellectual and moral virtues, then it is important for us to know what these virtues are. We will begin with moral virtue and with the recognition that happiness requires that we be morally good persons, that we develop a morally good character. To have a good moral character is to acquire habits of action that are morally virtuous. But how do we tell which habits are moral virtues and which are vices, and thus what counts as a good moral character?

Moral Virtue

We can tell what is good for us in several ways. The way that most of us develop our moral character is through moral *training.* Our parents, teachers, peers and so on, tell us what is morally good behavior. They also tell us what counts as appropriate feelings and attitudes and motives for acting. So we can learn what is good for us by training, by others telling us what is good for us. We can also learn from our own *personal experience* which sorts of behaviors are good and which are not good for us. Most of us do not need to experience too many nights of drunkenness, followed by the inevitable morning hangover, for example, to quickly learn that drinking to excess is not good for us.

We can also tell what a good life is by observing the lives of those we admire, says Aristotle. We learn *by example* what is a virtue and a vice. We have examples of moral heroes and ordinary good people, whom we admire and wish to be like. These examples are used as a template by society and by individuals to shape the moral ideals they wish to emulate. Finally, we can also learn what counts as virtuous behavior by *figuring it out for ourselves*, by a process of practical reasoning that Aristotle calls **phronesis,** or prudential reasoning. Aristotle gives us perhaps the most famous example of such reasoning in his discussion of what has been called the golden mean, a discussion to be found in *Reading 4*.

The Golden Mean

Prudential reasoning is a way of figuring out what is good in particular situations. In general, it begins with the assumption that morally good persons, persons who lead good lives, are those who live a life of *moderation* in all things. To live a life of moderation is to choose the "mean" between extreme types of actions. For example, *courage* is a virtue, because it is the mean between the extremes of cowardice, on the one hand, and recklessness, on the other. A coward has too little courage, while a reckless person, someone who takes excessive risks, may have too much for his own good. Another example of a virtue for Aristotle is *temperance*. To be temperate is to regulate your actions in matters of pleasure—avoiding the excesses of self-indulgence, on the one hand, and the deficiencies of abstinence, on the other. The happy life should contain pleasure, but not be driven by its pursuit. *Generosity* is another virtue, because it lies between the extremes of stinginess, on the one hand, and being overly generous, on the other.

For Aristotle, moderation, or choosing the mean between extremes, is the way for reason to control the excesses of the emotions and passions. Each extreme is either a deficiency of character or an excess of it—a vice, in other words. Extreme types of behavior are motivated by desire or feeling, without the benefit of thinking through the consequences of such action. A life of moderation is not a life of safety or boredom, but is a life where reason is in control. Such a life enables one to live fully, to live as closely to the ideal of a good life as possible. A life of moderation does not ignore our feelings and desires, but channels them to their proper function, and thus controls them for the well-being of the person.

The life of moderation, one that avoids the excesses and the deficiencies of behavior, is a life governed by reason, not a life directed by uncontrollable passions and desires. Without a life of choosing the mean, desires will rule your life, and you will be cut off from fulfilling many of your natural functions. You will not realize your full potential as a human being. You will not lead a good life. You will not be happy. In the end, what is important is that one live as fully humanly as possible, that one live as he or she was meant to live, that one live a life that is directed by reason toward the well-being of the individual. Such a life is a truly good life.

Intellectual Virtue

While for Aristotle a happy life requires more than a good life—such as a bit of luck, some material wealth, talent and even, curiously enough, good looks—it is his notion of the good life that concerns us most. We have already seen that such a life requires a morally good character. The best life, however, which is not available to everyone, is the life of the mind, the possession of wisdom. In the *Nicomachean Ethics*, Aristotle defines the good life as "activity of soul in accordance with virtue, and if there are more than one virtue, in accordance with the best and most complete" (see *Reading 5*). The best and most complete virtue or excellence is to be found in what he calls the intellectual virtues. Some of these virtues involve the shaping of native talent into good intellectual habits, such as the ability to understand, to deliberate wisely, and to make wise judgments.

Along with having a good moral character, these intellectual habits of mind place us in a position to acquire scientific and philosophical wisdom. This is knowledge of the forms found in things, the plan of nature itself; the efficient causes of things, how nature works; and the final causes of things, an understanding of the purpose of everything. For Aristotle, this is the central intellectual virtue, discovering the truth about how things really are. It is not enough for him simply to *strive* for the truth. The good life, the highest life, requires that we actually possess it. More than that, however, it requires that we contemplate these truths, that we hold them in our minds and reflect upon them. This is reason working apart from the body and its senses and desires. This, **contemplation** of the deepest truths, is what brings us closest to the divine. For Aristotle, this is the activity of God, and we could do no better than to emulate it. In *Reading 5* Aristotle says: "the activity of God, which surpasses all others in blessedness, must be contemplative; and of human activities, therefore, that which is most akin to this must be most of the nature of happiness." Not surprisingly, it is the life of the philosopher that comes closest to exhibiting the intellectual virtues, and thus such a life has the greatest chance to achieve happiness. For the fortunate few who have the talent, luck, and opportunity to develop their human nature fully, the possession of the moral and especially the intellectual virtues is the meaning of life itself.

Society

Unlike Plato, Aristotle did not compose any works on what a good society, especially an ideal state, ought to be like. Instead, he spent considerable time gathering data on what states *are* like, so that he could discover just what the goals of political societies really are. Aristotle agreed with Plato that various types of society, and especially political societies—states—are necessary to civilize people. A life apart from the group produces nothing but an instinctive life. This is not good life, because our instincts are irrational. Such a life produces human beings whose rational nature is ignored in favor of their animal nature. The natural state for human beings is rather a social one, especially a political one. Human beings are political animals by nature. The state itself is a natural entity, whose laws, policies, and incentives direct people to live according to their higher natures.

Aristotle believed that a wide variety of morally good states are acceptable. For example, rule by a single person, a small group, or by many could all be acceptable ways of governing if two conditions were met. First, the rulers must rule for the benefit of their subjects, not themselves. Second, whatever the form of government, the rule of law must be upheld. Rulers cannot rule by whim, or allow some of their subjects to escape the rule of law while holding others to it. Aristotle did not believe that people were equal by nature. As had Plato before him, Aristotle believed that some people have more noble natures than others, and should therefore assume roles in society befitting their natures. Even if people are not naturally equal, however, they are nevertheless to be treated as equal under the law. Justice, or equality under the law, is more important than the form of government that administers the law. The law, along with other social institutions, such as the family and educational institutions, is what civilizes us, what channels our behavior into habits of character which produce good human beings.

While many forms of government may be acceptable, some forms are best for some, while others are best for others. One reason Aristotle rejected a democratic form of government for Athens is that there such a government created mob rule, not the rule of law. Instead, he seemed to recommend for Athens what he called a **polity.** This is similar to a democracy insofar as it is rule by the many, but unlike a democracy since "many" does not include all. Instead, it includes only citizens, and citizens include only those in the upper and middle classes. These are people who own property and have a stake in running the state in as stable and beneficial a way as possible. For Aristotle, this form of government is especially good when a majority of citizens are aristocrats. Aristocrats are those with noble natures, good educations, and sufficient wealth not to be moved by self-interest.

God and Immortality

Though he did not really believe that the mythological "gods" of society existed, Aristotle did believe that a *God* existed. While this God was a person in the sense that it had a mind, it was not a personal God. This God had no contact with or even any knowledge of individual human beings. It would be a waste of time to pray to such a God. Nor did this God create the universe, which Aristotle believed to be eternal. Instead, God was simply a self-contemplating mind. God contemplated his own mind because therein was to be found the forms in their most perfect state, and thus contemplating them was the most perfect activity. It was as though the Forms of Plato had found a home in the mind of Aristotle's God.

While God did not create the world, however, he did control its movements. He did this by being its final cause, its goal or purpose. In striving to fulfill themselves within their species, all living things were really striving to become like God, at least like the idea of their species as contained in the mind of God. As the final cause, God acts like a magnet, attracting all creatures to their natural goals. Human beings, too, in attempting to fulfill their natures through exercising their practical and theoretical reason, are also striving to become like God. Even the planets move as they do because they are attracted to God. God, as the ultimate cause, moves all while remaining unchanged himself. In fact, Aristotle calls God the "unmoved mover." He is thus the ultimate explanation for why things change as they do. He is especially the explanation for why the possession and contemplation of wisdom is the highest form of life for human beings. Such wisdom is the reflection of the mind of God, and its contemplation is God-like activity.

There is some disagreement about Aristotle's view of *immortality*. Because the soul cannot perform most of its activities without a body, it seemed to Aristotle to make little sense that it could exist apart from the body. Such a soul would be unable to see, hear, taste, touch, and smell, for example. Nor could it have feelings or emotions or engage in practical reasoning. So while mankind may live as a species forever, and in that sense is immortal, it made more sense for Aristotle to think of individual human beings as perishing completely at their deaths.

However, Aristotle did acknowledge that at least some of the time the soul seemed to work apart from the body. This occurs both when the agent intellect forms new concepts and when the philosopher is engaged in pure contemplation. In the former case, the mind seems to go beyond the sensory data provided by the bodily senses; in the latter case, the soul seems to drift beyond the moorings of the body and ascend to the divine. Aristotle never worked through the possibility that the purely rational soul might exist apart from the body. It was left to later writers, most notably the medieval theologian, Thomas Aquinas, to explain how this might be so.

Gender

Aristotle is perhaps the most sexist of all Western philosophers. Although he prided himself on his careful observations and on the meticulous reasoning based upon these observations, and although he was quite conscious of everything that he said, he still upheld the traditional beliefs about women and slaves which were widely accepted during his lifetime. This tradition claimed that women, like slaves, had inferior natures, and thus were best suited to inferior roles in the family and in society. Women were inferior both biologically and rationally. Aristotle believed that they were inferior biologically because their bodies produce only the matter of a fetus, while the male's semen produces its form, its soul. Rationally, they are inferior as well. They have less reason than men and are much more creatures of emotion and desire.

Aristotle believed that even if their reason was equal to a man's in theory, they have reason "without the power to be effective," as he says in his *Politics*.[5] They can think, but not do much with their thoughts, not even rule themselves by their own reason. Women, then, are inferior not simply by social standing, but by nature itself. They are ruled by desire and emotion, while men are ruled by reason. Therefore, since reason should rule the emotions and appetites in order to produce a happy life, males who have greater reason should rule females. Here is to be found the argument for male superiority which reigned supreme in Western thought for more than two more millennia.

Readings

1. The Mind

BOOK III

TURNING NOW TO THE PART of the soul with which the soul knows and thinks (whether this is separable from the others in definition only, or spatially as well) we have to inquire (1) what differentiates this part, and (2) how thinking can take place.

If thinking is like perceiving, it must be either a process in which the soul is acted upon by what is capable of being thought, or a process different from but analogous to that. The thinking part of the soul must therefore be, while impassible, capable of receiving the form of an object; that is, must be potentially identical in character with its object without being the object. Mind must be related to what is thinkable, as sense is to what is sensible.

Therefore, since everything is a possible object of thought, mind in order, as Anaxagoras says, to dominate, that is, to know, must be pure from all admixture; for the co-presence of what is alien to its nature is a hindrance and a block: it follows that it too, like the sensitive part, can have no nature of its own, other than that of having a certain capacity. Thus that in the soul which is called mind (by mind I mean that whereby the soul thinks and judges) is, before it thinks, not actually any real thing. For this reason it cannot reasonably be regarded as blended with the body: if so, it would acquire some quality, e.g. warmth or cold, or even have an organ like the sensitive faculty: as it is, it has none. It was a good idea to call the soul 'the place of forms', though (1) this description holds only of the intellective soul, and (2) even this is the forms only potentially, not actually.

Observation of the sense-organs and their employment reveals a distinction between the impassibility of the sensitive and that of the intellective faculty. After strong stimulation of a sense we are less able to exercise it than before, as e.g. in the case of a loud sound we cannot hear easily immediately after, or in the case of a bright colour or a powerful odour we cannot see or smell, but in the case of mind, thought about an object that is highly intelligible renders it more and not less able afterwards to think objects that are less intelligible: the reason is that while the faculty of sensation is dependent upon the body, mind is separable from it.

Once the mind has become each set of its possible objects, as a man of science has, when this phrase is used of one who is actually a man of science (this happens when he is now able to exercise the power on his own initiative), its condition is still one of potentiality, but in a different sense from the potentiality which preceded the acquisition of knowledge by learning or discovery: the mind too is then able to think *itself*.

Since we can distinguish between a spatial magnitude and what it is to be such, and between water and what it is to be water, and so in many other cases (though not in all; for in certain cases the thing and its form are identical), flesh and what it is to be flesh are discriminated either by different faculties, or by the same faculty in two different states: for flesh necessarily involves matter and is like what is snub-nosed, a *this* in a *this*. Now it is by means of the sensitive faculty that we discriminate the hot and the cold, i.e. the factors which combined in a certain ratio constitute flesh: the essential character of flesh is apprehended by something different either wholly separate from the sensitive faculty or related to it as a bent line to the same line when it has been straightened out.

Again in the case of abstract objects what is straight is analogous to what is snub-nosed; for it necessarily implies a continuum as its matter: its

From Aristotle, "De Anima," in The Oxford Translation of Aristotle, Vol. 3, The Soul, *ed. W. D. Ross (1931), pp. 589–596. Reprinted with permission from Oxford University Press.*

constitutive essence is different, if we may distinguish between straightness and what is straight: let us take it to be two-ness. It must be apprehended, therefore, by a different power or by the same power in a different state. To sum up, in so far as the realities it knows are capable of being separated from their matter, so it is also with the powers of mind.

The problem might be suggested: If thinking is a passive affection, then if mind is simple and impassible and has nothing in common with anything else, as Anaxagoras says, how can it come to think at all? For interaction between two factors is held to require a precedent community of nature between the factors. Again it might be asked, is mind a possible object of thought to itself? For if mind is thinkable *per se* and what is thinkable is in kind one and the same, then either (*a*) mind will belong to everything, or (*b*) mind will contain some element common to it with all other realities which makes them all thinkable.

(1) Have not we already disposed of the difficulty about interaction involving a common element, when we said that mind is in a sense potentially whatever is thinkable, though actually it is nothing until it has thought? What it thinks must be in it just as characters may be said to be on a writing-tablet on which as yet nothing actually stands written: this is exactly what happens with mind.

(2) Mind is itself thinkable in exactly the same way as its objects are. For (*a*) in the case of objects which involve no matter, what thinks and what is thought are identical; for speculative knowledge and its object are identical. (Why mind is not always thinking we must consider later.) (*b*) In the case of those which contain matter each of the objects of thought is only potentially present. It follows that while *they* will not have mind in them (for mind is a potentiality of them only in so far as they are capable of being disengaged from matter) mind may yet be thinkable.

Since in every class of things, as in nature as a whole, we find two factors involved, (1) a matter which is potentially all the particulars included in the class, (2) a cause which is productive in the sense that it makes them all (the latter standing to the former, as e.g. an art to its material), these distinct elements must likewise be found within the soul.

And in fact mind as we have described it is what it is by virtue of becoming all things, while there is another which is what it is by virtue of making all things: this is a sort of positive state like light; for in a sense light makes potential colours into actual colours.

Mind in this sense of it is separable, impassible, unmixed, since it is in its essential nature activity (for always the active is superior to the passive factor, the originating force to the matter which it forms).

Actual knowledge is identical with its object: in the individual, potential knowledge is in time prior to actual knowledge, but in the universe as a whole it is not prior even in time. Mind is not at one time knowing and at another not. When mind is set free from its present conditions it appears as just what it is and nothing more: this alone is immortal and eternal (we do not, however, remember its former activity because, while mind in this sense is impassible, mind as passive is destructible), and without it nothing thinks.

Actual knowledge is identical with its object: potential knowledge in the individual is in time prior to actual knowledge but in the universe it has no priority even in time; for all things that come into being arise from what actually is. In the case of sense clearly the sensitive faculty already was potentially what the object makes it to be actually; the faculty is not affected or altered. This must therefore be a different kind from movement; for movement is, as we saw, an activity of what is imperfect, activity in the unqualified sense, i.e. that of what has been perfected, is different from movement.

To perceive then is like bare asserting or knowing; but when the object is pleasant or painful, the soul makes a quasi-affirmation or negation, and pursues or avoids the object. To feel pleasure or pain is to act with the sensitive mean towards what is good or bad as such. Both avoidance and appetite when actual are identical with this: the faculty of appetite and avoidance are not different, either from one another or from the faculty of sense-perception; but their being *is* different.

To the thinking soul images serve as if they were contents of perception (and when it asserts or denies them to be good or bad it avoids or pursues them). That is why the soul never thinks without an image. The process is like that in which the air modifies the pupil in this or that way and the pupil transmits the modification to some third thing (and similarly in hearing), while the ultimate point of arrival is one, a single mean, with different manners of being.

With what part of itself the soul discriminates sweet from hot I have explained before and must now describe again as follows: That with which it does so is a sort of unity, but in the way just mentioned, i.e. as a connecting term. And the two faculties it connects, being one by analogy and numerically, are each to each as the qualities discerned are to one another (for what difference does it make whether we raise the problem of discrimination between disparates or between contraries, e.g., white and black?). Let then *C* be to *D* as *A* is to *B*: it follows *alternando* that *C:A::D:B*. If then *C* and *D* belong to one subject, the case will be the same with them as with *A* and *B*; *A* and *B* form a single identity with different modes of being; so too will the former pair. The same reasoning holds if *A* be sweet and *B* white.

The faculty of thinking then thinks the forms in the images, and as in the former case what is to be pursued or avoided is marked out for it, so where there is no sensation and it is engaged upon the images it is moved to pursuit or avoidance. E.g. perceiving by sense that the beacon is fire, it recognizes in virtue of the general faculty of sense that it signifies an enemy, because it sees it moving; but sometimes by means of the images or thoughts which are within the soul, just as if it were seeing, it calculates and deliberates what is to come by reference to what is present; and when it makes a pronouncement, as in the case of sensation it pronounces the object to be pleasant or painful, in this case it avoids or pursues; and so generally in cases of action.

That too which involves no action, i.e. that which is true or false, is in the same province with what is good or bad: yet they differ in this, that the one set imply and the other do not a reference to a particular person.

The so-called abstract objects the mind thinks just as, if one had thought of the snub-nosed not as snub-nosed but as hollow, one would have thought of an actuality without the flesh in which it is embodied: it is thus that the mind when it is thinking the objects of Mathematics thinks as separate, elements which do not exist separate. In every case the mind which is actively thinking is the objects which it thinks. Whether it is possible for it while not existing separate from spatial conditions to think anything that is separate, or not, we must consider later.

Let us now summarize our results about soul, and repeat that the soul is in a way all existing things; for existing things are either sensible or thinkable, and knowledge is in a way what is knowable, and sensation is in a way what is sensible: in *what* way we must inquire.

Knowledge and sensation are divided to correspond with the realities, potential knowledge and sensation answering to potentialities, actual knowledge and sensation to actualities. Within the soul the faculties of knowledge and sensation are *potentially* these objects, the one what is knowable, the other what is sensible. They must be either the things themselves or their forms. The former alternative is of course impossible: it is not the stone which is present in the soul but its form.

It follows that the soul is analogous to the hand; for as the hand is a tool of tools, so the mind is the form of forms and sense the form of sensible things.

Since according to common agreement there is nothing outside and separate in existence from sensible spatial magnitudes, the objects of thought are in the sensible forms, viz, both the abstract objects and all the states and affections of sensible things. Hence (1) no one can learn or understand anything in the absence of sense, and (2) when the mind is actively aware of anything it is necessarily aware of it along with an image; for images are like sensuous contents except in that they contain no matter.

Imagination is different from assertion and denial; for what is true or false involves a synthesis of concepts. In what will the primary concepts differ from images? Must we not say that neither these nor even our other concepts are images, though they necessarily involve them?

2. The Soul

BOOK II

LET THE FOREGOING SUFFICE AS our account of the views concerning the soul which have been handed on by our predecessors; let us now dismiss them and make as it were a completely fresh start, endeavouring to give a precise answer to the question, What is soul? i.e. to formulate the most general possible definition of it.

We are in the habit of recognizing, as one determinate kind of what is, substance, and that in several senses, (*a*) in the sense of matter or that which in itself is not 'a this', and (*b*) in the sense of form or essence, which is that precisely in virtue of which a thing is called 'a this', and thirdly (*c*) in the sense of that which is compounded of both (*a*) and (*b*). Now matter is potentiality, form actuality; of the latter there are two grades related to one another as e.g. knowledge to the exercise of knowledge.

Among substances are by general consent reckoned bodies and especially natural bodies; for they are the principles of all other bodies. Of natural bodies some have life in them, others not; by life we mean self-nutrition and growth (with its correlative decay). It follows that every natural body which has life in it is a substance in the sense of a composite.

But since it is also a *body* of such and such a kind, viz. having life, the *body* cannot be soul; the body is the subject or matter, not what is attributed to it. Hence the soul must be a substance in the sense of the form of a natural body having life potentially within it. But substance is actuality, and thus soul is the actuality of a body as above characterized. Now the word actuality has two senses corresponding respectively to the possession of knowledge and the actual exercise of knowledge. It is obvious that the soul is actuality in the first sense, viz. that of knowledge as possessed, for both sleeping and waking presuppose the existence of soul, and of these waking corresponds to actual knowing, sleeping to knowledge possessed but not employed, and, in the history of the individual, knowledge comes before its employment or exercise.

That is why the soul is the first grade of actuality of a natural body having life potentially in it. The body so described is a body which is organized. The parts of plants in spite of their extreme simplicity are 'organs'; e.g. the leaf serves to shelter the pericarp, the pericarp to shelter the fruit, while the roots of plants are analogous to the mouth of animals, both serving for the absorption of food. If, then, we have to give a general formula applicable to all kinds of soul, we must describe it as the first grade of actuality of a natural organized body. That is why we can wholly dismiss as unnecessary the question whether the soul and the body are one: it is as meaningless as to ask whether the wax and the shape given to it by the stamp are one, or generally the matter of a thing and that of which it is the matter. Unity has many senses (as many as 'is' has), but the most proper and fundamental sense of both is the relation of an actuality to that of which it is the actuality.

We have now given an answer to the question, What is soul?—an answer which applies to it in its full extent. It is substance in the sense which corresponds to the definitive formula of a thing's essence. That means that it is 'the essential whatness' of a body of the character just assigned. Suppose that what is literally an 'organ', like an axe, were a *natural* body, its 'essential whatness', would have been its essence, and so its soul; if this disappeared from it, it would have ceased to be an axe, except in name. As it is, it is just an axe; it wants the character which is required to make its whatness or formulable essence a soul; for that, it would have had to be a *natural* body of a particular kind, viz. one having *in itself* the power of setting itself in movement and arresting itself. Next, apply this doctrine in the case of the 'parts' of the

From Aristotle, "De Anima," in The Oxford Translation of Aristotle, Vol. 3, The Soul, *ed. W. D. Ross (1931), pp. 554–560. Reprinted with permission from Oxford University Press.*

living body. Suppose that the eye were an animal—sight would have been its soul, for sight is the substance or essence of the eye which corresponds to the formula, the eye being merely the matter of seeing; when seeing is removed the eye is no longer an eye, except in name—it is no more a real eye than the eye of a statue or of a painted figure. We must now extend our consideration from the 'parts' to the whole living body; for what the departmental sense is to the bodily part which is its organ, that the whole faculty of sense is to the whole sensitive body as such.

We must not understand by that which is 'potentially capable of living' what has lost the soul it had, but only what still retains it; but seeds and fruits are bodies which possess the qualification. Consequently, while waking is actuality in a sense corresponding to the cutting and the seeing, the soul is actuality in the sense corresponding to the power of sight and the power in the tool; the body corresponds to what exists in potentiality; as the pupil *plus* the power of sight constitutes the eye, so the soul *plus* the body constitutes the animal.

From this it indubitably follows that the soul is inseparable from its body, or at any rate that certain parts of it are (if it has parts)—for the actuality of some of them is nothing but the actualities of their bodily parts. Yet some may be separable because they are not the actualities of any body at all. Further, we have no light on the problem whether the soul may not be the actuality of its body in the sense in which the sailor is the actuality of the ship.

This must suffice as our sketch or outline determination of the nature of soul.

Since what is clear or logically more evident emerges from what in itself is confused but more observable by us, we must reconsider our results from this point of view. For it is not enough for a definitive formula to express as most now do the mere fact; it must include and exhibit the ground also. At present definitions are given in a form analogous to the conclusion of a syllogism; e.g. What is squaring? The construction of an equilateral rectangle equal to a given oblong rectangle. Such a definition is in form equivalent to a conclusion. One that tells us that squaring is the discovery of a line which is a mean proportional between the two unequal sides of the given rectangle discloses the ground of what is defined.

We resume our inquiry from a fresh starting-point by calling attention to the fact that what has soul in it differs from what has not in that the former displays life. Now this word has more than one sense, and provided any one alone of these is found in a thing we say that thing is living. Living, that is, may mean thinking or perception or local movement and rest, or movement in the sense of nutrition, decay and growth. Hence we think of plants also as living, for they are observed to possess in themselves an originative power through which they increase or decrease in all spatial directions; they grow up *and* down, and everything that grows increases its bulk alike in both directions or indeed in all, and continues to live so long as it can absorb nutriment.

This power of self-nutrition can be isolated from the other powers mentioned, but not they from it—in mortal beings at least. The fact is obvious in plants; for it is the only psychic power they possess.

This is the originative power the possession of which leads us to speak of things as *living* at all, but it is the possession of sensation that leads us for the first time to speak of living things as animals; for even those beings which possess no power of local movement but do possess the power of sensation we call animals and not merely living things.

The primary form of sense is touch, which belongs to all animals. Just as the power of self-nutrition can be isolated from touch and sensation generally, so touch can be isolated from all other forms of sense. (By the power of self-nutrition we mean that departmental power of the soul which is common to plants and animals: all animals whatsoever are observed to have the sense of touch.) What the explanation of these two facts is, we must discuss later. At present we must confine ourselves to saying that soul is the source of these phenomena and is characterized by them, viz. by the powers of self-nutrition, sensation, thinking, and motivity.

Is each of these a soul or a part of a soul? And if a part, a part in what sense? A part merely distinguishable by definition or a part distinct in local situation as well? In the case of certain of these powers, the answers to these questions are easy, in the case of others we are puzzled what to say. Just as in the case of plants which when divided are observed to continue to live though removed to a distance from one another (thus showing that in *their* case the soul of each individual plant before division was actually one, potentially many), so we notice a similar result in other varieties of soul, i.e. in insects which have been cut in two; each of the segments possesses both sensation and local movement; and if sensation, necessarily also imagination and appetition; for, where there is sensation, there is also pleasure and pain, and, where these, necessarily also desire.

We have no evidence as yet about mind or the power to think; it seems to be a widely different kind of soul, differing as what is eternal from what is perishable; it alone is capable of existence in isolation from all other psychic powers. All the other parts of soul, it is evident from what we have said, are, in spite of certain statements to the contrary, incapable of separate existence though, of course, distinguishable by definition. If opining is distinct from perceiving, to be capable of opining and to be capable of perceiving must be distinct, and so with all the other forms of living above enumerated. Further, some animals possess all these parts of soul, some certain of them only, others one only (this is what enables us to classify animals); the cause must be considered later. A similar arrangement is found also within the field of the senses; some classes of animals have all the senses, some only certain of them, others only one, the most indispensable, touch.

Since the expression 'that whereby we live and perceive' has two meanings, just like the expression 'that whereby we know'—that may mean either (*a*) knowledge or (*b*) the soul, for we can speak of knowing *by* or *with* either, and similarly that whereby we are in health, may be either (*a*) health or (*b*) the body or some part of the body; and since of the two terms thus contrasted knowledge or health is the name of a form, essence, or ratio, or if we so express it an actuality of a recipient matter—knowledge of what is capable of knowing, health of what is capable of being made healthy (for the operation of that which is capable of originating change terminates and has its seat in what is changed or altered); further, since it is the soul by or with which primarily we live, perceive, and think:—it follows that the soul must be a ratio or formulable essence, not a matter or subject. For, as we said, the word substance has three meanings—form, matter, and the complex of both—and of these three what is called matter is potentiality, what is called form actuality. Since then the complex here is the living thing, the body cannot be the actuality of the soul; it is the soul which is the actuality of a certain kind of body. Hence the rightness of the view that the soul cannot be without a body, while it cannot *be* a body; it is not a body but something relative to a body. That is why it is *in* a body, and a body of a definite kind. It was a mistake, therefore, to do as former thinkers did, merely to fit it into a body without adding a definite specification of the kind or character of that body. Reflection confirms the observed fact; the actuality of any given thing can only be realized in what is already potentially that thing, i.e. in a matter of its own appropriate to it. From all this it follows that soul is an actuality or formulable essence of something that possesses a potentiality of being besouled.

Of the psychic powers above enumerated some kinds of living things, as we have said, possess all, some less than all, others one only. Those we have mentioned are the nutritive, the appetitive, the sensory, the locomotive, and the power of thinking. Plants have none but the first, the nutritive, while another order of living things has this *plus* the sensory. If any order of living things has the sensory, it must also have the appetitive; for appetite is the genus of which desire, passion, and wish are the species; now all animals have one sense at least, viz. touch, and whatever has a sense has the capacity for pleasure and pain and therefore has pleasant and painful objects present to it, and wherever these are present, there is desire, for desire is just appetition of what is pleasant. Further, all animals have the sense for food (for touch is the sense for food); the food of all living things consists of what is dry, moist, hot, cold, and these are the qualities apprehended by touch; all other sensible qualities are apprehended by touch only indirectly. Sounds, colours, and odours contribute nothing to nutriment; flavours fall within the field of tangible qualities. Hunger and thirst are forms of desire, hunger a desire for what is dry and hot, thirst a desire for what is cold and moist; flavour is a sort of seasoning added to both. We must later clear up these points, but at present it may be enough to say that all animals that possess the sense of touch have also appetition. The case of imagination is obscure; we must examine it later. Certain kinds of animals possess in addition the power of locomotion, and still another order of animate beings, i.e. man and possibly another order like man or superior to him, the power of thinking, i.e. mind. It is now evident that a single definition can be given of soul only in the same sense as one can be given of figure. For, as in that case there is no figure distinguishable and apart from triangle, &c., so here there is no soul apart from the forms of soul just enumerated. It is true that a highly general definition can be given for figure which will fit all figures without expressing the peculiar nature of any figure. So here in the case of soul and its specific forms. Hence it is absurd in this and similar cases to demand an absolutely general definition, which will fail to express the peculiar nature of anything that *is*, or again, omitting this, to look for separate definitions corresponding to each *infima species*. The cases of figure and soul are exactly parallel; for the particulars subsumed under the common name in both cases—figures and living beings—constitute a series, each successive term of which potentially contains its predecessor, e.g. the square the triangle, the sensory power the self-nutritive. Hence we must ask in the case of each order of living things, What is its soul, i.e. What is the soul of plant, animal, man? Why the terms are related in this serial way must form the subject of later examination. But the facts are that the power of perception is never found apart from the power of self-nutrition, while—in plants—the latter is found isolated from the former. Again, no sense is found apart from that of touch, while touch *is* found by itself; many animals have neither sight, hearing, nor smell. Again, among living things that possess sense some have the power of locomotion, some not. Lastly, certain living beings—a small minority—possess calculation and thought, for (among mortal beings) those which possess calculation have all the other powers above mentioned, while the converse does not hold—indeed some live by imagination alone, while others have not even imagination. The mind that knows with immediate intuition presents a different problem.

It is evident that the way to give the most adequate definition of soul is to seek in the case of *each* of its forms for the most appropriate definition.

3. The Good

BOOK I

EVERY ART AND EVERY INQUIRY, and similarly every action and pursuit, is thought to aim at some good; and for this reason the good has rightly been declared to be that at which all things aim. But a certain difference is found among ends; some are activities, others are products apart from the activities that produce them. Where there are ends apart from the actions, it is the nature of the products to be better than the activities. Now, as there are many actions, arts, and sciences, their ends also are many; the end of the medical art is health, that of

From Aristotle, "Ethics Nicomachea," in The Oxford Translation of Aristotle, Vol. 9, Ethics, *ed. W. D. Ross (1925), pp. 935–936, 941–943, 950–952. Reprinted with permission from Oxford University Press.*

shipbuilding a vessel, that of strategy victory, that of economics wealth. But where such arts fall under a single capacity—as bridle-making and the other arts concerned with the equipment of horses fall under the art of riding, and this and every military action under strategy, in the same way other arts fall under yet others—in all of these the ends of the master arts are to he preferred to all the subordinate ends; for it is for the sake of the former that the latter are pursued. It makes no difference whether the activities themselves are the ends of the actions, or something else apart from the activities, as in the case of the sciences just mentioned.

If, then, there is some end of the things we do, which we desire for its own sake (everything else being desired for the sake of this), and if we do not choose everything for the sake of something else (for at that rate the process would go on to infinity, so that our desire would be empty and vain), clearly this must be the good and the chief good. Will not the knowledge of it, then, have a great influence on life? Shall we not, like archers who have a mark to aim at, be more likely to hit upon what is right? If so, we must try, in outline at least to determine what it is, and of which of the sciences or capacities it is the object. It would seem to belong to the most authoritative art and that which is most truly the master art. And politics appears to be of this nature; for it is this that ordains which of the sciences should be studied in a state, and which each class of citizens should learn and up to what point they should learn them; and we see even the most highly esteemed of capacities to fall under this, e.g. strategy, economics, rhetoric; now, since politics uses the rest of the sciences, and since, again, it legislates as to what we are to do and what we are to abstain from, the end of this science must include those of the others, so that this end must be the good for man. For even if the end is the same for a single man and for a state, that of the state seems at all events something greater and more complete whether to attain or to preserve; though it is worth while to attain the end merely for one man, it is finer and more godlike to attain it for a nation or for city-states. These, then, are the ends at which our inquiry aims, since it is political science, in one sense of that term.

Our discussion will be adequate if it has as much clearness as the subject-matter admits of, for precision is not to be sought for alike in all discussions, any more than in all the products of the crafts. Now fine and just actions, which political science investigates, admit of much variety and fluctuation of opinion, so that they may be thought to exist only by convention, and not by nature. And goods also give rise to a similar fluctuation because they bring harm to many people; for before now men have been undone by reason of their wealth, and others by reason of their courage. We must be content, then, in speaking of such subjects and with such premises to indicate the truth roughly and in outline, and in speaking about things which are only for the most part true and with premises of the same kind to reach conclusions that are no better. In the same spirit, therefore, should each type of statement be *received*; for it is the mark of an educated man to look for precision in each class of things just so far as the nature of the subject admits; it is evidently equally foolish to accept probable reasoning from a mathematician and to demand from a rhetorician scientific proofs.

Now each man judges well the things he knows, and of these he is a good judge. And so the man who has been educated in a subject is a good judge of that subject, and the man who has received an all-round education is a good judge in general. Hence a young man is not a proper hearer of lectures on political science; for he is inexperienced in the actions that occur in life, but its discussions start from these and are about these; and, further, since he tends to follow his passions having this as a sort of pattern we shall know better the goods that are good for us, and if we know them shall attain them. This argument has some plausibility, but seems to clash with the procedure of the sciences; for all of these, though they aim at some good and seek to supply the deficiency of it, leave on one side the knowledge of *the* good. Yet that all the exponents of the arts should be ignorant of, and should not even seek, so great an aid is not probable. It is hard, too, to see how a weaver or a carpenter will be benefited in regard to his own craft by knowing this 'good itself', or how the man who has viewed the Idea itself will be a better doctor or general thereby. For a doctor seems not even to study health in this way, but the health of man, or perhaps rather the health of a particular man; it is individuals that he is healing. But enough of these topics.

Let us again return to the good we are seeking, and ask what it can be. It seems different in different actions and arts; it is different in medicine, in strategy, and in the other arts likewise. What then is the good of each? Surely that for whose sake everything else is done. In medicine this is health, in strategy victory, in architecture a house, in any other sphere something else, and in every action and pursuit the end; for it is for the sake of this that all men do whatever else they do. Therefore, if there is an end for all that we do, this will be the good achievable by action, and if there are more than one, these will be the goods achievable by action.

So the argument has by a different course reached the same point; but we must try to state this even more clearly. Since there are evidently more than one end, and we choose some of these (e.g. wealth, flutes, and in general instruments) for the sake of something else, clearly not all ends are final ends; but the chief good is evidently something final. Therefore, if there is only one final end, this will be what we are seeking, and if there are more than one, the most final of these will be what we are seeking. Now we call that which is in itself worthy of pursuit more final than that which is worthy of pursuit for the sake of something else, and that which is never desirable for the sake of something else more final than the things that are desirable both in themselves and for the sake of that other thing, and therefore we call final without qualification that which is always desirable in itself and never for the sake of something else.

Now such a thing happiness, above all else, is held to be; for this we choose always for itself and never for the sake of something else, but honour, pleasure, reason, and every virtue we choose indeed for themselves (for if nothing resulted from them we should still choose each of them), but we choose them also for the sake of happiness, judging that by means of them we shall be happy. Happiness, on the other hand, no one chooses for the sake of these, nor, in general, for anything other than itself.

From the point of view of self-sufficiency the same result seems to follow; for the final good is thought to be self-sufficient. Now by self-sufficient we do not mean that which is sufficient for a man by himself, for one who lives a solitary life, but also for parents, children, wife, and in general for his friends and fellow citizens, since man is born for citizenship. But some limit must be set to this; for if we extend our requirement to ancestors and descendants and friends' friends we are in for an infinite series. Let us examine this question, however, on another occasion; the self-sufficient we now define as that which when isolated makes life desirable and lacking in nothing; and such we think happiness to be; and further we think it most desirable of all things, without being counted as one good thing among others—if it were so counted it would clearly be made more desirable by the addition of even the least of goods; for that which is added becomes an excess of goods, and of goods the greater is always more desirable. Happiness, then, is something final and self-sufficient, and is the end of action.

Presumably, however, to say that happiness is the chief good seems a platitude, and a clearer account of what it is is still desired. This might perhaps be given, if we could first ascertain the function of man. For just as for a flute-player, a sculptor, or any artist, and, in general, for all things that have a function or activity, the good and the 'well' is thought to reside in the function, so would it seem to be for man, if he has a function. Have the carpenter, then, and the tanner certain functions or activities, and has man none? Is he born without a function? Or as eye, hand, foot, and in general each of the parts evidently has a function, may one lay it down that man similarly has a function apart from all these? What then can this be? Life seems to be common even to plants, but we are seeking what is peculiar to man. Let us exclude, therefore, the life of nutrition and growth. Next there would be a life of perception, but it also seems to be common even to the horse, the ox, and every animal. There remains, then, an active life of the element that has a rational principle; of this, one part has such a principle in the sense of being obedient to one, the other in the sense of possessing one and exercising thought. And, as 'life of the rational element' also has two meanings, we must state that life in the sense of activity is what we mean; for this seems to be the more proper sense of the term. Now if the function of man is an activity of soul which follows or implies a rational principle, and if we say 'a so-and-so' and 'a good so-and-so' have a function which is the same in kind, e.g. a lyre-player and a good lyre-player, and so without qualification in all cases, eminence in respect of goodness being added to the name of the function (for the function of a lyre-player is to play the lyre, and that of a good lyre-player is to do so well): if this is the case, [and we state the function of man to be a certain kind of life, and this to be an activity or actions of the soul implying a rational principle, and the function of a good man to be the good and noble performance of these, and if any action is well performed when it is performed in accordance with the appropriate excellence: if this is the case,] human good turns out to be activity of soul in accordance with virtue, and if there are more than one virtue, in accordance with the best and most complete.

But we must add 'in a complete life'. For one swallow does not make a summer, nor does one day; and so too one day, or a short time, does not make a man blessed and happy.

Let this serve as an outline of the good; for we must presumably first sketch it roughly, and then later fill in the details.

Since happiness is an activity of soul in accordance with perfect virtue, we must consider the nature of virtue; for perhaps we shall thus see better the nature of happiness. The true student of politics, too, is thought to have studied virtue above all things; for he wishes to make his fellow citizens good and obedient to the laws. As an example of this we have the lawgivers of the Cretans and the Spartans, and any others of the kind that there may have been. And if this inquiry belongs to political science, clearly the pursuit of it will be in accordance with our original plan. But clearly the virtue we must study is human virtue; for the good we were seeking was human good and the happiness human happiness. By human virtue we mean not that of the body but that of the soul; and happiness also we call an activity of soul.

But if this is so, clearly the student of politics must know somehow the facts about soul, as the man who is to heal the eyes or the body as a whole must know about the eyes or the body; and all the more since politics is more prized and better than medicine; but even among doctors the best educated spend much labour on acquiring knowledge of the body. The student of politics, then, must study the soul, and must study it with these objects in view, and do so just to the extent which is sufficient for the questions we are discussing; for further precision is perhaps something more laborious than our purposes require.

Some things are said about it, adequately enough, even in the discussions outside our school, and we must use these; e.g. that one element in the soul is irrational and one has a rational principle. Whether these are separated as the parts of the body or of anything divisible are, or are distinct by definition but by nature inseparable, like convex and concave in the circumference of a circle, does not affect the present question.

Of the irrational element one division seems to be widely distributed, and vegetative in its nature, I mean that which causes nutrition and growth; for it is this kind of power of the soul that one must assign to all nurslings and to embryos, and this same power to full-grown creatures; this is more reasonable than to assign some different power to them. Now the excellence of this seems to be common to all species and not specifically human; for this part or faculty seems to function most in sleep, while goodness and badness are least manifest in sleep (whence comes the saying that the happy are no better off than the wretched for half their lives; and this happens naturally enough, since sleep is an inactivity of the soul in that respect in which it is called good or bad), unless perhaps to a small extent some of the movements actually penetrate to the soul, and in this respect the dreams of good men are better than those of ordinary people. Enough of this subject, however; let us leave the nutritive faculty alone, since it has by its nature no share in human excellence.

There seems to be also another irrational element in the soul—one which in a sense, however, shares in a rational principle. For we praise the rational principle of the continent man and of the incontinent, and the part of their soul that has such a principle, since it urges them aright and towards the best objects; but there is found in them also another element naturally opposed to the rational principle, which fights against and resists that principle. For exactly as paralysed limbs when we intend to move them to the right turn on the contrary to the left, so is it with the soul; the impulses of incontinent people move in contrary directions. But while in the body we see that which moves astray, in the soul we do not. No doubt, however, we must none the less suppose that in the soul too there is something contrary to the rational principle, resisting and opposing it. In what sense it is distinct from the other elements does not concern us. Now even this seems to have a share in a rational principle, as we said; at any rate in the continent man it obeys the rational principle—and presumably in the temperate and brave man it is still more obedient; for in him it speaks, on all matters, with the same voice as the rational principle.

Therefore the irrational element also appears to be twofold. For the vegetative element in no way shares in a rational principle, but the appetitive, and in general the desiring element in a sense shares in it, in so far as it listens to and obeys it; this is the sense in which we speak of 'taking account' of one's father or one's friends, not that in which we speak of 'accounting' for a mathematical property. That the irrational element is in some sense persuaded by a rational principle is indicated also by the giving of advice and by all reproof and exhortation. And if this element also must be said to have a rational principle, that which has a rational principle (as well as that which has not) will be twofold, one subdivision having it in the strict sense and in itself, and the other having a tendency to obey as one does one's father.

Virtue too is distinguished into kinds in accordance with this difference; for we say that some of the virtues are intellectual and others moral, philosophic wisdom and understanding and practical wisdom being intellectual, liberality and temperance moral. For in speaking about a man's character we do not say that he is wise or has understanding but that he is good-tempered or temperate; yet we praise the wise man also with respect to his state of mind; and of states of mind we call those which merit praise virtues.

4. Moral Virtue

BOOK II

VIRTUE, THEN, BEING OF TWO kinds, intellectual and moral, intellectual virtue in the main owes both its birth and its growth to teaching (for which reason it requires experience and time), while moral virtue comes about as a result of habit, whence also its *ethike* is one that is formed by a slight variation from the word *ethos* (habit). From this it is also plain that none of the moral virtues arises in us by nature; for nothing that exists by nature can form a habit contrary to its nature. For instance the stone which by nature moves downwards cannot be habituated to move upwards, not even if one tries to train it by throwing it up ten thousand times; nor can fire be habituated to move downwards, nor can anything else that by nature behaves in one way be trained to behave in another. Neither by nature, then, nor contrary to nature do the virtues arise in us; rather we are adapted by nature to receive them, and are made perfect by habit.

Again, of all the things that come to us by nature we first acquire the potentiality and later

From Aristotle, "Ethics Nicomachea," in The Oxford Translation of Aristotle, Vol. 9, Ethics, *ed. W. D. Ross (1925), pp. 952–953, 956–962. Reprinted with permission from Oxford University Press.*

exhibit the activity (this is plain in the case of the senses; for it was not by often seeing or often hearing that we got these senses, but on the contrary we had them before we used them, and did not come to have them by using them); but the virtues we get by first exercising them, as also happens in the case of the arts as well. For the things we have to learn before we can do them, we learn by doing them, e.g. men become builders by building and lyre-players by playing the lyre; so too we become just by doing just acts, temperate by doing temperate acts, brave by doing brave acts.

This is confirmed by what happens in states; for legislators make the citizens good by forming habits in them, and this is the wish of every legislator, and those who do not effect it miss their mark, and it is in this that a good constitution differs from a bad one.

Again, it is from the same causes and by the same means that every virtue is both produced and destroyed, and similarly every art; for it is from playing the lyre that both good and bad lyre-players are produced. And the corresponding statement is true of builders and of all the rest; men will be good or bad builders as a result of building well or badly. For if this were not so there would have been no need of a teacher, but all men would have been born good or bad at their craft. This, then, is the case with the virtues also; by doing the acts that we do in our transactions with other men we become just or unjust, and by doing the acts that we do in the presence of danger, and being habituated to feel fear or confidence, we become brave or cowardly. The same is true of appetites and feelings of anger; some men become temperate and good-tempered, others self-indulgent and irascible, by behaving in one way or the other in the appropriate circumstances. Thus, in one word, states of character arise out of like activities. This is why the activities we exhibit must be of a certain kind; it is because the states of character correspond to the differences between these. It makes no small difference, then, whether we form habits of one kind or of another from our very youth; it makes a very great difference, or rather *all* the difference.

Next we must consider what virtue is. Since things that are found in the soul are of three kinds—passions, faculties, states of character, virtue must be one of these. By passions I mean appetite, anger, fear, confidence, envy, joy, friendly feeling, hatred, longing, emulation, pity, and in general the feelings that are accompanied by pleasure or pain; by faculties the things in virtue of which we are said to be capable of feeling these, e.g. of becoming angry or being pained or feeling pity; by states of character the things in virtue of which we stand well or badly with reference to the passions, e.g. with reference to anger we stand badly if we feel it violently or too weakly, and well if we feel it moderately; and similarly with reference to the other passions.

Now neither the virtues nor the vices are *passions*, because we are not called good or bad on the ground of our passions, but are so called on the ground of our virtues and our vices, and because we are neither praised nor blamed for our passions (for the man who feels fear or anger is not praised, nor is the man who simply feels anger blamed, but the man who feels it in a certain way), but for our virtues and our vices we *are* praised or blamed.

Again, we feel anger and fear without choice, but the virtues are modes of choice or involve choice. Further, in respect of the passions we are said to be moved, but in respect of the virtues and the vices we are said not to be moved but to be disposed in a particular way.

For these reasons also they are not *faculties*; for we are neither called good nor bad, nor praised nor blamed, for the simple capacity of feeling the passions; again, we have the faculties by nature, but we are not made good or bad by nature; we have spoken of this before.

If, then, the virtues are neither passions nor faculties, all that remains is that they should be *states of character*.

Thus we have stated what virtue is in respect of its genus.

We must, however, not only describe virtue as a state of character, but also say what sort of state it is. We may remark, then, that every virtue or excellence both brings into good condition the thing of which it is the excellence and makes the work of that thing be done well; e.g. the excellence of the eye makes both the eye and its work good; for it is by the excellence of the eye that we see well. Similarly the excellence of the horse makes a horse both good in itself and good at running and at carrying its rider and at awaiting the attack of the enemy. Therefore, if this is true in every case, the virtue of man also will be the state of character which makes a man good and which makes him do his own work well.

How this is to happen we have stated already, but it will be made plain also by the following consideration of the specific nature of virtue. In everything that is continuous and divisible it is possible to take more, less, or an equal amount, and that either in terms of the thing itself or relatively to us; and the equal is an intermediate between excess and defect. By the intermediate in the object I mean that which is equidistant from each of the extremes, which is one and the same for all men; by the intermediate relatively to us that which is neither too much nor too little—and this is not one, nor the same for all. For instance, if ten is many and two is few, six is the intermediate, taken in terms of the object; for it exceeds and is exceeded by an equal amount; this is intermediate according to arithmetical proportion. But the intermediate relatively to us is not to be taken so; if ten pounds are too much for a particular person to eat and two too little, it does not follow that the trainer will order six pounds; for this also is perhaps too much for the person who is to take it, or too little—too little for Milo, too much for the beginner in athletic exercises. The same is true of running and wrestling. Thus a master of any art avoids excess and defect, but seeks the intermediate and chooses this—the intermediate not in the object but relatively to us.

If it is thus, then, that every art does its work well—by looking to the intermediate and judging its works by this standard (so that we often say of good works of art that it is not possible either to take away or to add anything, implying that excess and defect destroy the goodness of works of art, while the mean preserves it; and good artists, as we say, look to this in their work), and if, further, virtue is more exact and better than any art, as nature also is, then virtue must have the quality of aiming at the intermediate. I mean moral virtue; for it is this that is concerned with passions and actions, and in these there is excess, defect, and the intermediate. For instance, both fear and confidence and appetite and anger and pity and in general pleasure and pain may be felt both too much and too little, and in both cases not well; but to feel them at the right times, with reference to the right objects, towards the right people, with the right motive, and in the right way, is what is both intermediate and best, and this is characteristic of virtue. Similarly with regard to actions also there is excess, defect, and the intermediate. Now virtue is concerned with passions and actions, in which excess is a form of failure, and so is defect, while the intermediate is praised and is a form of success; and being praised and being successful are both characteristics of virtue. Therefore virtue is a kind of mean, since, as we have seen, it aims at what is intermediate.

Again, it is possible to fail in many ways (for evil belongs to the class of the unlimited, as the Pythagoreans conjectured, and good to that of the limited), while to succeed is possible only in one way (for which reason also one is easy and the other difficult—to miss the mark easy, to hit it difficult); for these reasons also, then, excess and defect are characteristic of vice, and the mean of virtue;

For men are good in but one way, but bad in many.

Virtue, then, is a state of character concerned with choice, lying in a mean, i.e. the mean relative to us, this being determined by a rational principle, and by that principle by which the man of practical wisdom would determine it. Now it is a mean between two vices, that which depends on excess and that which depends on defect; and again it is a mean because the vices respectively fall short of or exceed what is right in both passions and actions, while virtue both finds and chooses that which is intermediate. Hence in respect of its substance and the definition which states its essence virtue is a mean, with regard to what is best and right an extreme.

But not every action nor every passion admits of a mean; for some have names that already imply badness, e.g. spite, shamelessness, envy, and in the case of actions adultery, theft, murder; for all of these and suchlike things imply by their names that they are themselves bad, and not the excesses or deficiencies of them. It is not possible, then, ever to be right with regard to them; one must always be wrong. Nor does goodness or badness with regard to such things depend on committing adultery with the right woman, at the right time, and in the right way, but simply to do any of them is to go wrong. It would be equally absurd, then, to expect that in unjust, cowardly, and voluptuous action there should be a mean, an excess, and a deficiency; for at that rate there would be a mean of excess and of deficiency, an excess of excess, and a deficiency of deficiency. But as there is no excess and deficiency of temperance and courage because what is intermediate is in a sense an extreme, so too of the actions we have mentioned there is no mean nor any excess and deficiency, but however they are done they are wrong; for in general there is neither a mean of excess and deficiency, nor excess and deficiency of a mean.

We must, however, not only make this general statement, but also apply it to the individual facts. For among statements about conduct those which are general apply more widely, but those which are particular are more genuine, since conduct has to do with individual cases, and our statements must harmonize with the facts in these cases. We may take these cases from our table. With regard to feelings of fear and confidence courage is the mean; of the people who exceed, he who exceeds in fearlessness has no name (many of the states have no name), while the man who exceeds in confidence is rash, and he who exceeds in fear and falls short in confidence is a coward. With regard to pleasures and pains—not all of them, and not so much with regard to the pains—the mean is temperance, the excess self-indulgence. Persons deficient with regard to the pleasures are not often found; hence such persons also have received no name. But let us call them 'insensible'.

With regard to giving and taking of money the mean is liberality, the excess and the defect prodigality and meanness. In these actions people exceed and fall short in contrary ways; the prodigal exceeds in spending and falls short in taking, while the mean man exceeds in taking and falls short in spending. (At present we are giving a mere outline or summary, and are satisfied with this; later these states will be more exactly determined. With regard to money there are also other dispositions—a mean, magnificence (for the magnificent man differs from the liberal man; the former deals with large sums, the latter with small ones), an excess, tastelessness and vulgarity, and a deficiency, niggardliness; these differ from the states opposed to liberality, and the mode of their difference will be stated later.

With regard to honour and dishonour the mean is proper pride, the excess is known as a sort of 'empty vanity', and the deficiency is undue humility; and as we said liberality was related to magnificence, differing from it by dealing with small sums, so there is a state similarly related to proper pride, being concerned with small honours while that is concerned with great. For it is possible to desire honour as one ought, and more than one ought, and less, and the man who exceeds in his desires is called ambitious, the man who falls short unambitious, while the intermediate person has no name. The dispositions also are nameless, except that that of the ambitious man is called ambition. Hence the people who are at the extremes lay claim to the middle place; and we ourselves sometimes call the intermediate person ambitious and sometimes unambitious, and sometimes praise the ambitious man and sometimes the unambitious. The reason of our doing this will be stated in what follows; but now let us speak of the remaining states according to the method which has been indicated.

With regard to anger also there is an excess, a deficiency, and a mean. Although they can scarcely be said to have names, yet since we call the intermediate person good-tempered let us call the mean good temper; of the persons at the extremes let the one who exceeds be called irascible, and his vice irascibility, and the man who falls short an inirascible sort of person, and the deficiency inirascibility.

There are also three other means, which have a certain likeness to one another, but differ from one another: for they are all concerned with intercourse in words and actions, but differ in that one is concerned with truth in this sphere, the other two with pleasantness; and of this one kind is exhibited in giving amusement, the other in all the circumstances of life. We must therefore speak of these too, that we may the better see that in all things the mean is praiseworthy, and the extremes neither praiseworthy nor right, but worthy of blame. Now most of these states also have no names, but we must try, as in the other cases, to invent names ourselves so that we may be clear and easy to follow. With regard to truth, then, the intermediate is a truthful sort of person and the mean may be called truthfulness, while the pretence which exaggerates is boastfulness and the person characterized by it a boaster, and that which understates is mock modesty and the person characterized by it mock-modest. With regard to pleasantness in the giving of amusement the intermediate person is ready-witted and the disposition ready wit, the excess is buffoonery and the person characterized by it a buffoon, while the man who falls short is a sort of boor and his state is boorishness. With regard to the remaining kind of pleasantness, that which is exhibited in life in general, the man who is pleasant in the right way is friendly and the mean is friendliness, while the man who exceeds is an obsequious person if he has no end in view, a flatterer if he is aiming at his own advantage, and the man who falls short and is

unpleasant in all circumstances is a quarrelsome and surly sort of person.

There are also means in the passions and concerned with the passions; since shame is not a virtue, and yet praise is extended to the modest man. For even in these matters one man is said to be intermediate, and another to exceed, as for instance the bashful man who is ashamed of everything; while he who falls short or is not ashamed of anything at all is shameless, and the intermediate person is modest. Righteous indignation is a mean between envy and spite, and these states are concerned with the pain and pleasures that are felt at the fortunes of our neighbours; the man who is characterized by righteous indignation is pained at undeserved good fortune, the envious man, going beyond him, is pained at all good fortune, and the spiteful man falls so far short of being pained that he even rejoices. But these states there will be an opportunity of describing elsewhere; with regard to justice, since it has not one simple meaning, we shall, after describing the other states, distinguish its two kinds and say how each of them is a mean; and similarly we shall treat also of the rational virtues.

5. Contemplation

BOOK X

NOW THAT WE HAVE SPOKEN of the virtues, the forms of friendship, and the varieties of pleasure, what remains is to discuss in outline the nature of happiness, since this is what we state the end of human nature to be. Our discussion will be the more concise if we first sum up what we have said already. We said, then, that it is not a disposition; for if it were it might belong to some one who was asleep throughout his life, living the life of a plant, or, again, to some one who was suffering the greatest misfortunes. If these implications are unacceptable,

and we must rather class happiness as an activity, as we have said before, and if some activities are necessary, and desirable for the sake of something else, while others are so in themselves, evidently happiness must be placed among those desirable in themselves, not among those desirable for the sake of something else; for happiness does not lack anything, but is self-sufficient. Now those activities are desirable in themselves from which nothing is sought beyond the activity. And of this nature virtuous actions are thought to be; for to do noble and good deeds is a thing desirable for its own sake.

From Aristotle, "Ethics Nicomachea," in The Oxford Translation of Aristotle, Vol. 9, Ethics, *ed. W. D. Ross (1925), pp. 1102–1107. Reprinted with permission from Oxford University Press.*

Pleasant amusements also are thought to be of this nature; we choose them not for the sake of other things; for we are injured rather than benefited by them, since we are led to neglect our bodies and our property. But most of the people who are deemed happy take refuge in such pastimes, which is the reason why those who are ready-witted at them are highly esteemed at the courts of tyrants; they make themselves pleasant companions in the tyrants' favourite pursuits, and that is the sort of man they want. Now these things are thought to be of the nature of happiness because people in despotic positions spend their leisure in them, but perhaps such people prove nothing; for virtue and reason, from which good activities flow, do not depend on despotic position; nor, if these people, who have never tasted pure and generous pleasure, take refuge in the bodily pleasures, should these for that reason be thought more desirable; for boys, too, think the things that are valued among themselves are the best. It is to be expected, then, that, as different things seem valuable to boys and to men, so they should to bad men and to good. Now, as we have often maintained, those things are both valuable and pleasant which are such to the good man; and to each man the activity in accordance with his own disposition is most desirable, and, therefore, to the good man that which is in accordance with virtue. Happiness, therefore, does not lie in amusement; it would, indeed, be strange if the end were amusement, and one were to take trouble and suffer hardship all one's life in order to amuse oneself. For, in a word, everything that we choose we choose for the sake of something else—except happiness, which is an end. Now to exert oneself and work for the sake of amusement seems silly and utterly childish. But to amuse oneself in order that one may exert oneself, as Anacharsis puts it, seems right; for amusement is a sort of relaxation, and we need relaxation because we cannot work continuously. Relaxation, then, is not an end; for it is taken for the sake of activity.

The happy life is thought to be virtuous; now a virtuous life requires exertion, and does not consist in amusement. And we say that serious things are better than laughable things and those connected with amusement, and that the activity of the better

of any two things—whether it be two elements of our being or two men—is the more serious; but the activity of the better is *ipso facto* superior and more of the nature of happiness. And any chance person—even a slave—can enjoy the bodily pleasures no less than the best man; but no one assigns to a slave a share in happiness—unless he assigns to him also a share in human life. For happiness does not lie in such occupations, but, as we have said before, in virtuous activities.

If happiness is activity in accordance with virtue, it is reasonable that it should be in accordance with the highest virtue; and this will be that of the best thing in us. Whether it be reason or something else that is this element which is thought to be our natural ruler and guide and to take thought of things noble and divine, whether it be itself also divine or only the most divine element in us, the activity of this in accordance with its proper virtue will be perfect happiness. That this activity is contemplative we have already said.

Now this would seem to be in agreement both with what we said before and with the truth. For, firstly, this activity is the best (since not only is reason the best thing in us, but the objects of reason are the best of knowable objects); and, secondly, it is the most continuous, since we can contemplate truth more continuously than we can *do* anything. And we think happiness has pleasure mingled with it, but the activity of philosophic wisdom is admittedly the pleasantest of virtuous activities; at all events the pursuit of it is thought to offer pleasures marvellous for their purity and their enduringness, and it is to be expected that those who know will pass their time more pleasantly than those who inquire. And the self-sufficiency that is spoken of must belong most to the contemplative activity. For while a philosopher, as well as a just man or one possessing any other virtue, needs the necessaries of life, when they are sufficiently equipped with things of that sort the just man needs people towards whom and with whom he shall act justly, and the temperate man, the brave man, and each of the others is in the same case, but the philosopher, even when by himself, can contemplate truth, and the better the wiser he is; he can perhaps do so better if he has fellow-workers, but still he is the most self-sufficient. And this activity alone would seem to be loved for its own sake; for nothing arises from it apart from the contemplating, while from practical activities we gain more or less apart from the action. And happiness is thought to depend on leisure; for we are busy that we may have leisure, and make war that we may live in peace. Now the activity of the practical virtues is exhibited in political or military affairs, but the actions concerned with these seem to be unleisurely. Warlike actions are completely so (for no one chooses to be at war, or provokes war, for the sake of being at war; any one would seem absolutely murderous if he were to make enemies of his friends in order to bring about battle and slaughter); but the action of the statesman is also unleisurely, and— apart from the political action itself—aims at despotic power and honours, or at all events happiness, for him and his fellow citizens—a happiness different from political action, and evidently sought as being different. So if among virtuous actions political and military actions are distinguished by nobility and greatness, and these are unleisurely and aim at an end and are not desirable for their own sake, but the activity of reason, which is contemplative, seems both to be superior in serious worth and to aim at no end beyond itself, and to have its pleasure proper to itself (and this augments the activity), and the self-sufficiency, leisureliness, unweariedness (so far as this is possible for man), and all the other attributes ascribed to the supremely happy man are evidently those connected with this activity, it follows that this will be the complete happiness of man, if it be allowed a complete term of life (for none of the attributes of happiness is *in*complete).

But such a life would be too high for man; for it is not in so far as he is man that he will live so, but in so far as something divine is present in him; and by so much as this is superior to our composite nature is its activity superior to that which is the exercise of the other kind of virtue. If reason is divine, then, in comparison with man, the life according to it is divine in comparison with human life. But we must not follow those who advise us, being men, to think of human things, and, being mortal, of mortal things, but must, so far as we can, make ourselves immortal, and strain every nerve to live in accordance with the best thing in us; for even

if it be small in bulk, much more does it in power and worth surpass everything. This would seem, too, to be each man himself, since it is the authoritative and better part of him. It would be strange, then, if he were to choose not the life of his self but that of something else. And what we said before will apply now; that which is proper to each thing is by nature best and most pleasant for each thing; for man, therefore, the life according to reason is best and pleasantest, since reason more than anything else *is* man. This life therefore is also the happiest.

But in a secondary degree the life in accordance with the other kind of virtue is happy; for the activities in accordance with this befit our human estate. Just and brave acts, and other virtuous acts, we do in relation to each other, observing our respective duties with regard to contracts and services and all manner of actions and with regard to passions; and all of these seem to be typically human. Some of them seem even to arise from the body, and virtue of character to be in many ways bound up with the passions. Practical wisdom too, is linked to virtue of character, and this to practical wisdom, since the principles of practical wisdom are in accordance with the moral virtues and rightness in morals is in accordance with practical wisdom. Being connected with the passions also, the moral virtues must belong to our composite nature; and the virtues of our composite nature are human; so, therefore, are the life and the happiness which correspond to these. The excellence of the reason is a thing apart; we must be content to say this much about it, for to describe it precisely is a task greater than our purpose requires. It would seem, however, also to need external equipment but little, or less than moral virtue does. Grant that both need the necessaries, and do so equally, even if the statesman's work is the more concerned with the body and things of that sort; for there will be little difference there; but in what they need for the exercise of their activities there will be much difference. The liberal man will need money for the doing of his liberal deeds, and the just man too will need it for the returning of services (for wishes are hard to discern, and even people who are not just pretend to wish to act justly); and the brave man will need power if he is to accomplish any of the acts that correspond to his virtue, and the temperate man will need opportunity; for how else is either he or any of the others to be recognized? It is debated, too, whether the will or the deed is more essential to virtue, which is assumed to involve both; it is surely clear that its perfection involves both; but for deeds many things are needed, and more, the greater and nobler the deeds are. But the man who is contemplating the truth needs no such thing, at least with a view to the exercise of his activity; indeed they are, one may say, even hindrances, at all events to his contemplation; but in so far as he is a man and lives with a number of people, he chooses to do virtuous acts; he will therefore need such aids to living a human life.

But that perfect happiness is a contemplative activity will appear from the following consideration as well. We assume the gods to be above all other beings blessed and happy; but what sort of actions must we assign to them? Acts of justice? Will not the gods seem absurd if they make contracts and return deposits, and so on? Acts of a brave man, then, confronting dangers and running risks because it is noble to do so? Or liberal acts? To whom will they give? It will be strange if they are really to have money or anything of the kind. And what would their temperate acts be? Is not such praise tasteless, since they have no bad appetites? If we were to run through them all, the circumstances of action would be found trivial and unworthy of gods. Still, every one supposes that they *live* and therefore that they are active; we cannot suppose them to sleep like Endymion. Now if you take away from a living being action, and still more production, what is left but contemplation? Therefore the activity of God, which surpasses all others in blessedness, must be contemplative; and of human activities, therefore, that which is most akin to this must be most of the nature of happiness.

This is indicated, too, by the fact that the other animals have no share in happiness, being completely deprived of such activity. For while the whole life of the gods is blessed, and that of men too in so far as some likeness of such activity belongs to them, none of the other animals is happy, since they in no way share in contemplation. Happiness extends, then, just so far as contemplation does, and those to whom contemplation more fully belongs are more truly happy, not as a mere concomitant but in virtue of the contemplation; for this is in itself precious. Happiness, therefore, must be some form of contemplation.

Study Questions

1. What are the characteristics of scientific knowledge?

2. Explain the difference between formal, efficient and final causes.

3. What is a teleological system?

4. How does Aristotle's concept of the forms differ from Plato's?

5. Explain how the forms are known.

6. What does Aristotle mean by the soul?

7. What is the golden mean and how is it used?

8. What is intellectual virtue?

9. What sort of a God does Aristotle believe in?

10. Why is contemplation considered to be the highest form of human activity?

Chapter 4

Medieval Theologians: Augustine and Aquinas

Introduction

After the death of Aristotle, Greek philosophy entered the five-hundred-year **Hellenistic** period. The mighty Greek empire was divided up after the death of Alexander the Great, never again to regain its power and glory. The next empire to emerge would be that of Rome, during the first century B.C.E. Though Rome contributed a great deal to Western civilization, it contributed very little to philosophical thought. Instead, during the Hellenistic period various smaller schools of philosophy carried on the cause of philosophical thinking. Among these was **Stoicism,** whose adherents were materialists and determinists. They believed that the universe unfolded according to a divine plan that nothing could alter. The secret of life was not to acquire the things that you desire, since they are beyond your control, but rather to accept things as they are. We have no control over external forces, only our own reactions to them. Herein is found happiness, in accepting to the way that things are, in having a "stoical" attitude.

Another school was called **Epicureanism,** after its founder, Epicurus. Its main teaching was that the good life is solely the life of pleasure, especially the "higher" pleasures, and most importantly, the absence of pain, especially psychological pain. Both the Stoics and the Epicureans placed the focus of philosophy on developing the interior life, a theme that was to influence Augustine significantly. Another powerful influence on Augustine from the later Hellenistic period was **Neoplatonism,** a philosophy influenced by the writings of Plato and developed especially by Plotinus (205–270 C.E.). Because of the devastation caused by many wars and the subsequent lack of support for learning, many of the writings of Plato and most of those of Aristotle were lost to the West for hundreds of years. The writings of Aristotle would not appear in Europe, for example, until the twelfth century, where they greatly influenced the thought of Thomas Aquinas. Augustine was more influenced by Plato than Aristotle, and especially by the platonic themes that were developed by Plotinus. Among these themes two are most important for Augustine. One concerns the manner by which the universe was created, while the other is the idea of Plato, resurrected by Plotinus, that the soul is immaterial.

In addition to Hellenistic philosophy, the other great influence on the mind of Augustine was Christianity. Soon after the death of Jesus, Christianity began to spread beyond its origins in and around Jerusalem. The missionary zeal of its followers, especially that of St. Paul, soon brought Christianity to the city of Rome itself. While Rome was fairly tolerant of many varieties of religion, Christianity was seen by many to be an enemy of the empire. Its followers had allegiance to

God, seen by many as a rival to Caesar, and for some three hundred years were the victims of Roman persecution. It was not until a Roman emperor, Constantine the Great, was himself converted to Christianity, that Rome and Christianity were united. The Christian religion became the official religion of Rome and quickly spread throughout the empire. Even after the fall of the Roman Empire Christianity remained entrenched in the Western world.

St. Augustine

Introduction

Aurelius Augustinus, later known as St. Augustine, Bishop of Hippo, was born in 354 C.E. in Tagaste, a small town in North Africa. In his late teens he traveled to Carthage, the leading city in North Africa at the time, in order to receive a proper education. In one of his most famous works, *The Confessions*, perhaps the first autobiography in Western civilization, he recounts his early days in Carthage as filled with two loves—one for sensual pleasure and one for knowledge. He was very bright, and trained to be a teacher of rhetoric. What he was especially interested in, however, was understanding why there was evil in the world in the presence of a supposedly good God. His mother, Monica, later to be canonized a saint herself, had exposed Augustine to the teachings of Christianity. But he found it to be rather shallow intellectually, especially on the subject of evil. Instead he became a Manichaean.

The Manichaeans were a heretical Christian sect. They believed that there were two gods—one good and one evil. The goodness found in the world came from the good god, while evil was produced by the evil god. It was only later, when he traveled to Rome (383) and the following year to Milan to teach rhetoric, that Augustine gave up his adherence to Manichaeanism and turned to Christianity for his answers. In Milan he met St. Ambrose, a very famous bishop, who exposed him to the intellectual side of Christianity and eventually converted him in 387. In 391 he became a priest and returned to his home in Tagaste. Augustine himself became a bishop, of the North African city of Hippo, in 395 and remained in that post until his death in 440. At the time of his death the Roman Empire was about to fall. Hippo itself was under attack by the Vandals. So much respect did the invaders have for this man, the most important thinker in the West for nearly a thousand years, the man whose writings mark the beginning of the Medieval period of philosophy, that they waited for his death before laying waste to the city.

Worldview

Augustine's worldview was formed by combining elements from Christianity, Neoplatonic, and Stoic philosophy, and his own philosophical insights.

The Influence of Christianity

For Augustine, the teachings of Christianity are to be taken as true because they are the word of God. This does not mean that everything in the Bible must be viewed as literally true. Sometimes things are said in a metaphorical sense and must be interpreted as such. The essential point, however, is that the word of

God, sometimes called revelation, as found in both the Old Testament and the New Testament, always takes priority over the word of man, which is based on mere human reason. Augustine was fond of saying that in matters of importance, belief was required for understanding. Questions of ultimate concern, such as the existence of God, the nature of the soul, the possibility of life after death, the nature of the good life, and even the nature of reality and knowledge, cannot be answered by human wisdom alone. Philosophy alone cannot acquire this kind knowledge. These answers may only be discovered through revelation, and in fact they already exist.

The job of philosophy (human wisdom) is not to discover wisdom, but rather to clarify what is already known through faith. For example, the Bible tells us that human beings are made in the image of God, but what that means is something for philosophy to explain. We learn from reading the word of God that the universe was created in time, and not eternal as thought by the Greeks. For the Greeks it made no sense for a perfect God to create the universe in time. They thought that a perfect God could not change. Creating the universe would be an act, and thus a change. If it is, then it is a change to the more or the less perfect. If this is so, in turn, it means that God either was not perfect or is not now perfect.

For Augustine, however, we know from the scriptures that God is perfect and that the universe was created. This is not to be doubted. The problem is to explain how this can be so, again a job for philosophy. If **theology** is the study of the revealed word of God, philosophy is the "handmaiden" of theology. It is used by theologians to make sense of what they accept as true on the basis of faith. In that role philosophy is very useful, and reason can be very powerful, even though it is not powerful enough to discover wisdom on its own. Augustine is very skeptical that reason has such power. If it did, the fine minds of the Greek philosophers would have come up with the same answers as each other, and the same answers as are found in scripture. So it is in the revealed word of God that we find our answers to the important questions of life, where we find wisdom.

Revelation tells us that the elements of the Christian worldview that are most relevant to the question of human nature are expressed in the following concepts: God, creation, the fall, redemption, salvation, and the kingdom of God. First and most importantly, the Christian view of life claims that there is a God, who is the highest reality. This God is a personal God, a God who knows us and responds to our needs. God created the universe and everything in it. He made some creatures higher than human beings. These are nonphysical beings, commonly called "angels," but more accurately referred to as spiritual substances. At the center of earthly creation, however, are human beings. As we are told in *Genesis,* God created them *in his image.* Our original human nature reflects the nature of God, and thus is very good indeed. All other creatures are good as well, but are lesser beings than humans, and exist for the use of mankind. Plants, animals, and all nonliving things may be used by us as we will, for we are the rulers of creation.

Second, although human nature was created good, it became corrupted by the first humans, Adam and Eve, who freely chose to sin. To sin is to violate the law of God. In this case, again as we learn from *Genesis,* our earthly parents ate the apple from the one tree from which they were forbidden to do so. With food aplenty in the Garden of Eden, they yet had to taste the fruit from the tree of knowledge. This sin, called *original sin,* was motivated by pride, the desire to be above any laws or controls, the desire to be totally free from any constraints, the desire to become like God. For this they, and all of their descendants were punished. They were banished from the Garden, introduced to suffering and misery, denied eternal life, and burdened with a human nature now inclined more to evil than to good. We all share that fate today. We are born with a fallen human nature. If left to ourselves, our lives surely would be miserable.

Third, we are told in the New Testament gospels that God still loved us after our fall from grace. So much did he love us, in fact, that he sent his son to save us from our fate. His "son" was Jesus, the incarnation of God himself. Jesus was God in human form, God existing among his creatures. The Jews had long awaited a messiah (savior) to rescue them from the throes of this world. Jesus, a Jew, was not accepted by them as this savior. He was not seen as the Christ, the anointed one. Followers of Christ, however, believed that he was a savior sent to save us from the misery of this world and to direct us to the next world as well. The Christian teaching is that there is a life after death. After the Fall this was not available to us. In redeeming us from our original sin by his death and resurrection from death, Jesus redeemed us from original sin, restored our relationship with God, and made it possible for us once again to live eternally with God in the life hereafter.

Fourth, in addition to allowing us to attain eternal salvation, Christ also showed us how to live fully in this life. To live fully in this world and the next is to be a member of the *kingdom of heaven.* We attain membership in the kingdom of heaven by freely choosing to love God and each other, and to submit to his will. After the death and resurrection of Christ it became possible for our fallen human natures to choose the good once again, to love properly once again. If we act from love, we can choose to live our lives as we were meant to live them, and we can be happy with God and each other in this world and the next. Happiness is available to all people, not just an elite few. The kingdom of heaven is democratic, entrance is available to all who love God and their neighbor. Because life is eternal, it is important to gain entrance to this kingdom. Because entrance determines our eternal fate, life is serious business indeed. If we conform our actions to the will of God we shall be saved; otherwise there waits for us eternal damnation.

The Influence of Neoplatonism

In the process of clarifying this Christian conception of the origin, purpose, and meaning of life, Augustine blended philosophical notions of his own with those of others. In explaining *reality,* for example, he adopted from the Neoplatonists the dualism that they had found in Plato. St. Paul, the person most responsible for clarifying the teachings of Christianity before the time of Augustine, had claimed that life after death took the form of the resurrection of the *body.* This was not the physical body, of course, which lay rotting in the grave, but some sort of "spiritual body"—if that phrase makes any sense. Augustine thought it better to speak of human beings as composed of bodies and souls, as had Plato before him. At one's death, it was the soul which enjoyed eternal salvation or suffered eternal damnation, while the body was left behind to return to the dust from which it was created.

The next Neoplatonic idea that influenced Augustine was a bit more complex. Plotinus had argued that all the various sorts of beings to be found in creation emanated from the One, the source of all being itself. While "emanation" was a metaphor, evoking an image of a series of waterfalls stacked one upon another, it did lead to two ideas which Augustine adopted. One idea was that emanation was an explanation of how the Forms were copied in the material world, something that Plato failed to provide. Augustine identified the One of Plotinus with God and located the Forms in the mind of God. As the architect builds according to a blueprint, God created the world according to a plan, the Forms. This plan is the pattern of nature, and is found exemplified in nature and especially in our human nature.

The second idea concerns the fullness and goodness of creation. Augustine saw creation as the goodness of God overflowing to create levels of being of every conceivable sort. Each level has its own level of goodness based upon its complexity. Living things are more valuable than nonliving things, for example. Some living things, such as animals, are more valuable than other living things, such as plants. At the top of this "great chain of being" is the human species, with only spiritual substances higher than they. In this way does God create the world as full of goodness as is possible, by creating all possible levels of beings. We will return to Augustine's account of creation later, especially when the problem of evil and the concept of time are discussed.

For Augustine, as for Plato, there are two main divisions of reality, the physical and the nonphysical. In the nonphysical realm are souls, spiritual substances, God, and Forms in the mind of God. In the physical world are images, material objects, space, and time. Augustine would be content to accept Plato's divided line as an accurate description of reality as long as the Good was identified with God and as long as the Forms were placed in the mind of God, and not thought of as existing on their own. In this way Augustine fit Plato's notion of reality to the demands of Christian belief. In this way he used reason to clarify what revelation had taught him about reality.

Augustine's view of *knowledge,* at least some forms of knowledge, was also developed against the background of platonic themes. Before discussing knowledge it should be noted that a recurring theme with Augustine is that anything good or noble about human nature should be attributed to God, while anything evil or weak is the responsibility of human beings. For Augustine, the highest good is God. Without a relationship with God we will not be happy. We can form this relationship through two paths, through love and through knowledge. More will be said about what it means to love God later when we discuss the "will." For now we will concentrate on the journey to God through the intellect's ability to know God. As we have seen, for Augustine scripture reveals the answers to the big questions. Herein is found true wisdom based on faith.

However, the answers found in scripture must be understood further to be clear. This is a job for philosophy, which is human wisdom based on reason. Such human wisdom, especially knowledge of the true nature of the soul and God, as well as an understanding of reality, gets us closer to God because the ideas that we form of such things are most perfectly found in the mind of God. Because our knowledge of the world and ourselves is a reflection of the ideas found in the mind of God, human wisdom is a kind of knowledge of God. In fact, Augustine says that "Truth," a knowledge of all that is, is itself God.

Like Plato before him, Augustine was interested especially in certain knowledge. Augustine also wanted to understand the source of the certainty found in our knowledge of mathematics and the universal, eternal, necessary truths found in the Forms. Again following Plato, Augustine believed that the truth is found from within, through a process of illumination, and not by observing the world of nature. It had been Plato's view that such knowledge arose from a process of remembering the Forms from a past existence, which was made possible by the Good illuminating the mind to remember. Augustine builds upon these Platonic ideas but alters them dramatically.

For Augustine, while reason is too weak to discover answers to the big questions on its own, it is nevertheless very powerful. In fact, reason is divine. Augustine explains what he means by this claim in the process of analyzing his version of the doctrine of illumination. Before examining this explanation, however, it is important to exclude alternative explanations of certainty. To do this it is necessary to examine his notion of teaching. For Augustine, if knowledge, certain knowledge, comes from an external source, then it most likely comes in the form of teaching. After all, most who understand the truth do not discover it for themselves, but have it taught to them by others. However, it is Augustine's belief that such teaching is impossible; that wisdom must be discovered from within and not from without.

His argument that wisdom cannot be taught starts with his theory of language, what he calls "signs." For Augustine, the meaning of a word is the thought with which it is associated. The word "dog" stands for the concept "dog," for example. Without the idea, the word would be meaningless. If I say, for example, "Grass is blunk," you will not understand me. This is because you have no idea of blunk. In the same way, the explanations of someone who knows the truth about reality would not be understood by others unless they already had in mind the ideas being referred to. Since learning is acquiring ideas, and ideas cannot be acquired through words, the usual way to teach another, no one really ever teaches anything to anyone else. At best, a teacher can guide students to discover things for themselves.

In fact, this is how human wisdom is attained, through Christ, the divine teacher, illuminating our minds. To "illuminate" our minds means to create ideas. As Aristotle had used abstraction to explain how seeing many men gave rise to the idea "man," and Plato had said it was a process of remembering what we already knew in a previous life, Augustine says that general concepts are formed by the intervention of Christ. Whenever we understand what is true about ourselves, about God, or about the world, it is because our insight, our formation of an idea, is caused by the activity of Christ. This is why reason is divine, because understanding is made possible by the "light of Christ," and thus is a gift from God.

Human Nature

For Augustine, the three most important things to know about human nature may be summarized under the following headings: dualism, a desire for God, and sin. Following Plato, Augustine adopted *dualism,* the belief that human beings are composed of two substances, bodies and souls. Our souls are what is most important about us. They are not something that we have, they are something that we are. We are spiritual beings at the core of our nature. Our soul is the seat of our intellect or reason, our emotions and our desires, as Plato had taught. Our desires urge us on to live our lives in the ways that we do, and our deepest desires define what sorts of beings we are and what sorts of beings we can be. For Plato, our deepest desire was a desire for wisdom; for Augustine it was a *desire for God.*

Within the first few lines of his *Confessions,* Augustine tells us what is perhaps the most important thing we need to know about human nature: "Thou madest us for Thyself, and our heart is restless, until it repose in Thee."[1] Our deepest desire is for God. A close relationship with God is what we really want, even though we may not be aware of this. The truth about human nature is that God is what we were made for, and only a close relationship with God will make us happy. Wisdom is part of this relationship, since one way to get close to God is through knowledge, Love is even more essential, however, since it is our desire for God, our longing for God, and finally our willing or choosing to live close to God, that really bonds us to him. More will be said later about the satisfaction of this desire for God, about what human nature *could be* when we choose to live as we ought to. Here we focus instead on what human nature *is,* and for Augustine it is not something very noble at all.

For Augustine, as for Plato, reason must control desire if a person is to be happy. We must use our reason especially to understand our true selves and God and to guide our lives according to the laws of God. Unfortunately, for Augustine, reason does not naturally control desire, as Plato thought. Instead, our human natures are weak; they allow desire to rule reason. Though we were made in the image of God and thus originally had a strong and noble nature, nevertheless human beings have fallen from God's grace through original sin. In doing so we have lost our inclination to live well-ordered, harmonious lives. Instead, we are ruled by our emotions, our passions, our desires. Left to ourselves, we would all be sinners, as was Augustine himself in his youth. What he confesses in the *Confessions* are the wayward ways of his youth. It is not that he was evil, but more that he loved the wrong things for the wrong reason. This is the problem with being ruled by desire; this is the nature of sin. We desire what we should not and shun what we should desire.

Augustine recounts one story where he and some comrades stole some pears from a pear tree. They did not need the pears for food. There was no other reason to steal them. So why did they do it? Just because it was wrong, says Augustine. Doing something wrong, in violating well-established moral and legal rules gave him a feeling of freedom, of being beyond any external restrictions. Like Adam in the Garden of Eden, he was motivated by pride to go beyond the rules, to become like God, the creator of morality. Augustine saw in himself what human nature had become as a result of the fall. It was prideful, and sinful. Augustine searched for the deeper causes of sin that were embedded in human nature. The main cause of sin is not so much an evil nature as a disordered one. It is not so much that we hate, but rather that we love the wrong things and expect them to give us what they cannot. Human nature as it is, is ruled by this "disordered love" and the false expectations it produces.

The real cause of our unhappiness is that we expect too much from the satisfaction of desire by transient things. For example, we expect from things only what we can get from people and personal relationships. Having lots of money, fancy cars, and vacation homes in itself does not make us happy. When we expect them to we are loving them as we ought to love people. It requires someone to share these things with, someone to love, to give these things their proper meaning. But even good personal relationships, while they will help, will not of themselves make us happy. For someone else to make you happy requires that they know what you want, and what you should want, and that they get it for you. This is not possible. Most of us do not even know ourselves what we want. Expecting others to make us happy, finding the "right" husband or wife, for example, is another instance of disordered love. We expect from people what we can get only from God.

So at its root, sin is a type of ignorance, as Plato believed. It is ignorance of what is really good for us, and human nature is shot through and through with it. It is only when, with God's help (grace), we learn what is the highest good for ourselves, and we acquire, again with God's grace, the ability to point our lives in its direction, that we have a chance to order our love properly. It is only then that human nature can be turned from sin to desire what it ought to desire for its own good.

Consequences

Freedom

Many of the authors we have seen so far have spoken of freedom as freedom from certain obstacles. Others have talked about freedom of action, the freedom to do what we want to. Aristotle spoke of freedom as the ability to choose our actions, and said that we are responsible for the actions that stem from our choices. For Aristotle our choices are free when they are caused by us and not some external force. We are especially responsible for the actions we perform as a result of conscious deliberation. These choices are *our* choices in the sense that they are caused by us, by the sorts of persons we are, by our character. However, our character itself is the product of external forces. We are the sorts of persons we are because we were brought up in certain ways, have certain parents, live in certain places at certain times, and so on. So even while my choices may be my own, the "me" which produces them is the product of external forces. In this sense my choice in any particular situation, what I want most, is determined by something outside of me.

For Augustine these types of freedom, freedom from obstacles, freedom to act, and freedom to choose, simply will not do. There is another dimension of freedom of which human beings are capable, and that is freedom of choice itself. Free choice Augustine especially discusses in his *On Free Choice of the Will*, selections of which are included in *Reading 1*. One of the central points of this work is that we have something called **free will**. The will is our ability to choose, just as our intellect is our ability to know. The *free* will has the ability not only to to choose to act on its desires, but also to choose among its desires which one to follow.

For Augustine, while our actions may follow from our choices, to say that our choices are the result of our character is to deny freedom in the highest sense. This is because our character, and thus our choices, are produced by forces beyond our control. We are determined to choose one desire rather than another because of our character. For him, our will is free when our choices are not caused either by external forces or internal conditions, our desires which follow from our character. Our will is free when it is not caused by anything at all. Augustine's vision of human freedom is that the soul can soar above the influences of the world, can stand aloof from the natural and psychological forces which shape our character, and choose to do whatever it wills. This is true freedom; not simply the freedom to do what we want, but the freedom to choose what we want as well.

But how are we capable of such majestic feats if our nature is fallen and crushed by sin? Augustine worked out his notion of freedom in contrast to the Welsh monk, Pelagius. Pelagius had claimed that freedom of the will was part of human nature and capable always of choosing the good. Augustine argued vehemently against this optimistic attitude. According to his theme of glorifying God and subjugating human beings, he claimed instead that the will is free only if its choices are supported by the grace of God. Just as the light of Christ was required to produce human wisdom, the grace of God is required to enable us to choose the good. For the will to be free it must be able to have chosen other than it did. If we are inclined to sin, we must nevertheless be able to choose not to sin, if in fact the will is free. We must have a real choice between actually achievable alternatives. Augustine taught that we are free to choose the good; in fact doing so is a requirement for salvation, for admission into the kingdom of heaven. However, we are not capable of doing so by nature, but only by grace. Only because God intervenes and inclines us toward the good are we able to break the bonds of desire and order our loves properly. If God does not intervene we choose sin; if God does, we choose the good.

But if God's intervention is necessary to steer us from sin to the good, does that not mean that God determines the will, that God's intervention makes us choose the way that we do? Are we not like puppets, doing what we do either because desire rules us or, when he chooses to intervene, because God's grace pulls the strings? On the contrary, for Augustine, God's grace and our freedom are not incompatible. God's grace, or intervention, simply removes the obstacles to our choosing the good that were placed in our path by original sin. Since we have been redeemed, we are now capable of choosing not to sin, of choosing to follow God's will. We may not do so; we may still choose to sin. But at least now we have the freedom to choose. But we do not have the choice by nature, as Pelagius had claimed. We are not capable of choosing the good on our own. Rather, we need the grace of God to raise our fallen natures if we are to rise above sin. So we are free, but only by the grace of God.

For Augustine, the fact that we have free will is the key to solving the **problem of evil** that so plagued him in his youth. The problem of evil may be formulated as follows: if God is all good, all powerful, all knowing and the creator of all, then how can there be evil in the world? Augustine says that *moral evil*, the evil caused by the sins of humankind, is caused by us. God created us good and now, through his grace, allows us always to choose the good. Sometimes we do not, sometimes we sin. This is the source of most of the evil in the world, human free will. But is not God responsible for evil because he made us free? No, because our freedom is a good. If God made us as robots, incapable of sin, we would be less good, lower beings on the great chain of being. The existence of evil is the price to pay for the glory of free will, along with reason our most magnificent attribute. When we use it properly it admits us into the kingdom of heaven.

But what about the evil that is caused by nature itself, such as earthquakes, fires, floods, and sickness—*natural evil*? Is not God the cause of this? The Neoplatonic notion of creation as the fullness of being is, for Augustine, the key to solving the problem of natural evil. God made everything good. Evil is just the absence of good. For some reason, God holds back some good on occasion. This absence of the good that is supposed to be there Augustine calls *privation*. Natural evil is therefore not some*thing* itself, but rather is the absence of something. Sickness is the absence of health, earthquakes are the absence of calm, blindness is the absence of sight, and so on. So God is not the creator of evil, because there is no evil. Thus, there is no problem of how he could exist if evil exists. Natural evil does not exist, it is not something. Moral evil is also the absence of something, a good will. Even if it does exist, however, it is caused by us, not by God.

Ethics

For Augustine, right and wrong is not so much a matter of following rules as it is a matter of properly ordering our desires. Plato had said that happiness comes from reason ruling desire and emotion. Augustine agrees that desire and emotion must be ruled, only now it is not reason that rules but will, and in particular our will to love God. If we love God we follow his will. If we follow his will, our desires will be properly ordered. God reveals his will to us through scripture. He tells us there what habits of character, or virtues, he wants us to develop. This is demonstrated by the paradigm case of a good life, the life of Christ. This is our best example of a life of virtue, especially a life of the highest virtue, love. How to love God and one's fellow human beings is what is shown in the life of Christ. Not surpassingly, then, Augustine follows a religious ethic, which claims that what is right is what God says is right, and what is good, the highest good, is God himself.

In addition to giving us scripture as a guide, God also has written into our nature how he wants us to live. The message we read there is that the good life is a life of fulfilling human nature, a life of making ourselves what we can be when we are at our best. This message, called the *natural law,* is a reflection of the *eternal law,* the law or order of nature as it is found in the mind of God. Once the natural law is recognized by us, with the help of God's moral illumination, it is seen as the general moral plan that God wills for us. As such, it is a plan for ordering our desires in accordance with their proper value.

From the Neoplatonists Augustine had come to believe that the most valuable thing to desire is the permanent, the unchanging, the eternal. With the Stoics he placed little value on the transient things of life over which we have little control. These things, like pleasure, wealth, health, youth, and fame, come and go, and constantly disappoint us when we pursue them as the highest goods. It is only when we have our sights set on loving God that they assume their true value.

Pleasures of the body, for example, are not evil in themselves. Like all creation they are good, but their goodness comes from God, their creator, as a gift to us. They are here for us to enjoy, to use, but not to get attached to. We should rank higher than the pleasures of the body the goods of the soul, and rank as the highest the goods of divine love. We should desire everything only as its relates to the permanent, the unchanging, the eternal God.

While part of the natural law tells us that we should not murder, lie, cheat, break promises, and violate other well-accepted moral rules, and another part includes an understanding that the motives for our actions should always be love, still another and perhaps the most important part demands that we submit our will to the will of God. The natural law is present in us as a law higher than any created by man, and and it demands that to it our wills must submit. If the root of unhappiness is prideful action, then the root of happiness is acquiescence in the will of God, the source of morality and our guide to happiness.

For Augustine, as paradoxical as it may sound, the highest freedom is a form of submission. If we believe that God is the highest object of our love, and that one of the things it means to love God is to conform to the will of God, then we will believe that our happiness consists in having our will in harmony with the will of God. The highest freedom is thus to voluntarily give up our freedom to choose what *we* desire, and instead to submit ourselves to what God desires for us. What God wills for us is especially that we love him, and that we value everything in life as a gift from him, and value it relative to him. This is how we order our loves, in relation to God as the highest good. God made us with an immense desire for him. God is what we long for. Even though we do not always recognize it ourselves, God is what human nature has been made to pursue. By submitting to his will we are free to be ourselves, to fulfill our true natures. By submitting to his will, he who is the life of our souls, we find our true selves, and thus our peace, and thus our rest, and thus our home.

God and Immortality

Augustine believed in life after death. Even though St. Paul, the man who did the most to clarify Christianity prior to Augustine, did not think that we needed souls in order to survive our deaths, it made more sense to Augustine to teach the Neoplatonic doctrine that it was our nonphysical souls that survive the death of our bodies. These souls, our true selves, live eternally either with God in blissful happiness, or in hell in eternal damnation. There are many problems with the idea of hell as eternal punishment, and many of Augustine's contemporaries rejected this notion. There are also many problems with just what a disembodied soul's nature and type of existence might be like. It is enough to say for now, however, that Augustine was committed to the view that we are our souls, and our souls are what live on after we die.

Enough has already been said about God to understand how Augustine conceived of him and the role he played in creating and redeeming human nature. Here will be mentioned briefly only one further point of interest, the manner in which God created the world. Augustine rejected the Neoplatonic doctrine of emanation as the explanation of creation, because he believed that God did not create from necessity, as the doctrine of emanation held, but rather his creation was an act of his will. He simply willed the universe into existence from nothing, or *ex nihilo*. He could have chosen not to create the universe, but instead he chose to create it. At first glance this act of the will seems to require that God changed. If his act of will alone caused the world to exist, then as soon as he willed it the universe would exist. Since the universe is not eternal, but created in time, then it seems that God's willing it is a change on his part—from not willing to willing creation. If it is a change, then God, the perfect being, either became more or less perfect. In either case, creation is a denial of God's perfection.

This is why the Greeks denied creation in time, because it would require a denial of God's perfection. But this argument presupposes that for God to perform an action, and thus to change, requires that he be "in" time when he willed creation. If God is "out" of time, however, then his action can be seen as an act of the will to create the universe at a certain time that was an action from eternity, which is consistent with God's permanence. If God's decision to create is not in time it does not require a change. If creation does not require a change, then God can be understood as both perfect and the creator of the universe in time.

For Augustine, another benefit of seeing God as an atemporal being is that it solves the problem of *divine foreknowledge and free will*. The problem may be stated as follows. If God knows everything, then he knows the future. If he knows the future, then he knows what we will do in the future. If God already knows which actions we will perform, then how can we be said to be free? If he knows what is going to happen, is not the future as fixed and frozen as the past, and thus not open to free choice?

One possible solution to this problem is to say that God does not know the future, but then God would not be perfect. The solution which Augustine accepts, is to say that there is no incompatibility between free choice and divine foreknowledge, because God simply knows what we will freely choose to do. This is more clearly understood when we realize that for the atemporal God, the future is as the present is for us. God sees all—past, present and future, as though it were an eternal "now." Just as you can observe what happens in the present, because he is atemporal, God can observe what happens in the future, which to him is as our present.

If time itself is a creation of God, what sort of a creature might it be? It seems to be something that exists in the world, since it seems to be dependent upon the relative motion of bodies. If there was no movement, if everything was "freeze framed," there would be no time. Or would there? Would our thoughts and memories and feelings and other conscious states not continue to flow through time? So time could also be a property of the mind, of consciousness. It might be that our perception of the world causes time, causes sequences of before, now, and after. Being in time is like seeing a movie one frame at a time, while being atemporal is like seeing it all at once. So perhaps human minds create time in the process of experiencing the world around them. After all, there is no past except what resides in our present memories; and there is no future except what resides in our anticipation of things to come. There is only the elusive present, ever poised on the edge of the recent past and anticipated future. Augustine discusses the concept of time in the *Confessions,* selections from which appear in *Reading 2.* Notice how strikingly modern this discussion appears to be.

Society

Another area where time is important to Augustine is in his construction of a philosophy of history. Before his time most of the few attempts to make sense of the flow of historical events assumed a cyclical pattern of history. If the world is eternal, as most believed before Augustine, then it made sense to think of historical patterns as repeating themselves. But Augustine wrote a linear philosophy of history. The earth and our time on it began with creation, was highlighted with the incarnation of Christ, and will be over at the end of time with the day of judgment. In between, individuals work out their salvation by attempting to conform to God's will. Those who succeed will be rewarded with the kingdom of heaven; those who fail will be cursed with a terrible fate.

Since this is the heart of life, the daily drama of constructing a noble soul, there is little concern in Augustine for things of this world. In particular, he was not very much concerned with reforming social conditions to create a better life on earth. One of Augustine's major works was called the *City of God*. While it was designed as an argument to persuade people that the Christians were not responsible for the fall of the Roman Empire, it especially made the point that earthly societies were not terribly important. It was important that they were just, that they enabled people to survive and lead their lives as they saw fit. However, Augustine believed that several types of government were compatible with this aim. Democracies might be better suited under some circumstances, while benevolent dictatorships could work as well under others. The "city of God" was more important than any of the "cities of man," however, since it was there, in the communities of religious belief, that the important decisions of how to live for eternity were made. Since we are spiritual and eternal beings, since this life is merely a place where we pass through on our way to our true homes, any society which allows us to pursue these interests may be acceptable.

Gender

Much of Augustine's vast amount of writing was informed not only by Christianity, Stoicism, and Neoplatonic philosophy, but also by his own personal experiences. Augustine was very attached to his mother, who exerted considerable influence over his conversion to Christianity. As a canonized saint herself, St. Monica, she was a living lesson to her son about the joys of loving God. The Christian teaching was that it required only love of God, not philosophical knowledge, to be happy. For Augustine, women were just as capable as men of such love. Even if human wisdom contributed to a greater happiness, because it provided a greater understanding of God, women were just as capable as men of reaching this more exalted state. St. Augustine seemed to believe that women were just as capable as men of acquiring human wisdom. So the kingdom of heaven is open equally to men and women, for Augustine. Happiness knows no gender boundaries, especially in the next life.

In this life, however, Augustine seems to have thought the less of women. Some of this had to do with what he read in scripture, especially the *Genesis* account of creation which had God creating Adam first, in his image, and Eve second, from Adam's rib, as a helpmate to Adam. Eve, then, seemed to be a second-class citizen in the kingdom of heaven. Some of his belief that women are inferior to men came from his own experience, especially from what he learned during the period of his youthful sexual licentiousness. He saw women as sexual beings, with much of their nature grounded firmly in the role of lovers and mothers. Because he saw their natures incorporating more of their physical selves, and because things of the flesh are less valued by Augustine than things of the spirit, women were seen as created less in the image of God, the "father," than men. Unfortunately, this theme that women are inferior because of their sexuality, and that they have only secondary roles to play both in establishing the kingdom of God, and in holding positions of power and influence in this world, was to remain the accepted view of women throughout not only the Medieval period, but also into the Modern and Contemporary historical periods as well.

Readings

1. Free Will

Editor's Note: On the Free Choice of the Will *is an early work by Augustine, which contains more philosophy than most of his later works. It was very influential all through the Medieval period, often quoted and commented upon by later writers. In it he discusses many of his innovative concepts, such as free will, the problem of evil, the fallen and the redeemed nature of human beings, faith and reason, the divine and the human law, and many other themes. Augustine did not write in a systematic fashion. He would often address one issue only to leave it for awhile while he pursued other related ones. The following selections discuss the nature, function, causes, and consequences of the most important and distinctive element of human nature in addition to the intellect—the free will.*

BOOK ONE

EVODIUS: Please tell me: isn't God the Cause of evil?

AUGUSTINE: I will tell you once you have made clear what kind of evil you are asking about. For we use the word 'evil' in two senses: first, when we say that someone has *done* evil;

and second, when we say that someone has *suffered* evil.

EVODIUS: I want to know about both.

AUGUSTINE: But if you know or believe that God is good—and it is not right to believe otherwise—then he does no evil. On the other hand, if we acknowledge that God is just—and it is impious to deny it—then he rewards the good and punishes the wicked. Those punishments are certainly evils for those who suffer them. Therefore, if no one is punished unjustly—and we must believe this, since we believe that this universe is governed by divine providence—it follows that God is a cause of the second kind of evil, but in no way causes the first kind.

EVODIUS: Then is there some other cause of the evil that God does not cause?

AUGUSTINE: There certainly is. Such evil could not occur unless someone caused it. But if you ask who that someone is, it is impossible to say. For there is no single cause of evil; rather, everyone who does evil is the cause of his own evildoing. If you doubt this, recall what I said earlier: Evil

From Augustine, On the Free Choice of the Will, *trans. by Thomas Williams (Cambridge: Hackett, 1993), pp. 1, 3–6, 17—21; 30, 68–69; 74–77, 103–105. Reprinted by permission of Hackett Publishing Company, Inc. All rights reserved.*

deeds are punished by the justice of God. They would not be punished justly if they had not been performed voluntarily.

EVODIUS: . . . please explain to me what *is* the source of our evildoing.

AUGUSTINE: You have hit upon the very question that worried me greatly when I was still young, a question that wore me out, drove me into the company of heretics, and knocked me flat on my face. I was so hurt by this fall, buried under a mountain of silly fairy tales, that if my love of finding the truth had not secured divine help, I would not have been able to get out from under them to breathe freely and begin to seek the truth. And since such pains were taken to free me from this difficulty, I will lead you on the same path that I followed in making my escape. God will be with us, and he will make us understand what we have believed. For we are well aware that we are at the stage described by the prophet, who says, "Unless you believe, you will not understand." We believe that everything that exists comes from the one God, and yet we believe that God is not the cause of sins. What is troubling is that if you admit that sins come from the souls that God created, and those souls come from God, pretty soon you'll be tracing those sins back to God.

EVODIUS: You have stated plainly what bothers me in thinking about this question. That is the problem that has compelled me and drawn me into this inquiry.

AUGUSTINE: Be courageous, and go on believing what you believe . There is no better belief, even if you do not yet see the explanation for why it is true. The truest beginning of piety is to think as highly of God as possible; and doing so means that one must believe that he is omnipotent, and not changeable in the smallest respect; that he is the creator of all good things, but is himself more excellent than all of them; that he is the supremely just ruler of everything that he created; and that he was not aided in creating by any other being, as if he were not sufficiently powerful by himself. It follows that he created all things from nothing. He did not create from

himself, but generated one who is equal to himself, whom we call the only Son of God. In trying to describe the Son more clearly we call him "the Power of God and the Wisdom of God," through whom God made all the things that were made from nothing. On that basis let us try, with God's help, to achieve an understanding of the problem you have raised.

You want to know the source of our evildoing. So we must first discuss what evildoing *is*. State your view on the matter. If you cannot explain the whole thing at once in a few words, you can at least show me your view by naming particular evil deeds.

EVODIUS: Adultery, murder, and sacrilege, not to mention others that time and memory do not permit me to enumerate. Who could fail to recognize these as evil deeds?

AUGUSTINE: Tell me first, why do you think adultery is evil? Because the law forbids it?

EVODIUS: On the contrary. Clearly, it is not evil because the law forbids it: rather, the law forbids it because it is evil.

AUGUSTINE: But suppose someone were to make things difficult for us by extolling the pleasures of adultery and asking why we think adultery evil and deserving of condemnation. Surely you do not think that people who want to understand, and not merely to believe, would have to take refuge in an appeal to the authority of the law? Now like you I do believe, and believe most firmly, and cry out that all peoples and nations should believe, that adultery is evil. But now we are attempting to know and hold firmly by understanding what we have already accepted by faith. So think this over as carefully as you can, and tell me what reason you have by which you know that adultery is evil.

EVODIUS: I know that it is evil because I would not tolerate it if someone tried to commit adultery with my own wife. Anyone who does to another what he does not want done to himself does evil.

AUGUSTINE: What if someone's lust is so great that he offers his wife to another and willingly allows him to commit adultery with her, and is eager to enjoy the same freedom with the other man's wife? Do you think that this man has done nothing evil?

EVODIUS: Far from it!

AUGUSTINE: But by your rule he does not sin, since he is not doing anything that he is unwilling to have done to himself. You must therefore look for some other argument to show that adultery is evil.

EVODIUS: The reason that I think it is evil is that I have often seen people condemned for this crime.

AUGUSTINE: But haven't people often been condemned for good deeds? Not to refer you to any other books, recall the story that is superior to all others by virtue of its divine authority. There you will find that we must think very poorly of the apostles and martyrs if we intend to make condemnation a sure sign of wrongdoing. All of them were judged worthy of condemnation because of their confession of faith. It follows that if everything that is condemned is evil, it was evil in those days to believe in Christ and to confess that faith. But if not everything that is condemned is evil, find some other way to show why adultery is evil.

EVODIUS: I can't think how to respond.

AUGUSTINE: Then perhaps what makes adultery evil is inordinate desire, whereas so long as you look for the evil in the external, visible act, you are bound to encounter difficulties. In order to understand that inordinate desire is what makes adultery evil, consider this: if a man is unable to sleep with someone else's wife, but it is somehow clear that he would like to, and would do so if he had the chance, he is no less guilty than if he were caught in the act.

EVODIUS: Nothing could be clearer. Now I see that there is no need for a long discussion to persuade me that this is the case with murder and sacrilege and every sin whatsoever. For it is clear now that inordinate desire is what drives every kind of evildoing.

AUGUSTINE: Do you know that inordinate desire is also called 'cupidity'?

AUGUSTINE: The conclusions that we have reached thus far indicate that a mind that is in control, one that possesses virtue, cannot be made a slave to inordinate desire by anything equal or superior to it, because such a thing would be just, or by anything inferior to it, because such a thing would be too weak. Just one possibility remains: only its own will and free choice can make the mind a companion of cupidity.

EVODIUS: I can't see any other alternative.

AUGUSTINE: Then you must also think that the mind justly suffers punishment for so great a sin.

EVODIUS: I cannot deny it.

AUGUSTINE: Surely the very fact that inordinate desire rules the mind is itself no small punishment. Stripped by opposing forces of the splendid wealth of virtue, the mind is dragged by inordinate desire into ruin and poverty; now taking false things for true, and even defending those falsehoods repeatedly; now repudiating what it had once believed and nonetheless rushing headlong into still other falsehoods; now withholding assent and often shying away from clear arguments; now despairing completely of finding the truth and lingering in the shadows of folly; now trying to enter the light of understanding but reeling back in exhaustion.

In the meantime cupidity carries out a reign of terror, buffeting the whole human soul and life with storms coming from every direction. Fear attacks from one side and desire from the other; from one side, anxiety; from the other, an empty and deceptive happiness; from one side, the agony of losing what one loved; from the other, the passion to acquire what one did not have; from one side, the pain of an injury received; from the other, the burning desire to avenge it. Wherever you turn, avarice can pinch, extravagance squander, ambition destroy, pride swell, envy torment, apathy crush, obstinacy incite, oppression chafe, and countless other evils crowd the realm of inordinate desire and run riot. In short, can we consider this punishment trivial—a punishment that, as you realize, all who do not cleave to wisdom must suffer?

EVODIUS: What is a good will?

AUGUSTINE: It is a will by which we desire to live upright and honorable lives and to attain the highest wisdom. So just ask yourself: Do you desire an upright and honorable life and fervently will to be wise? And is it indisputable that when we will these things, we have a good will?

EVODIUS: My answer to both questions is yes. I now admit that I have not just a will, but a good will.

AUGUSTINE: How highly do you value this will? You surely do not think it should be compared with wealth or honors or physical pleasures, or even all of these together.

EVODIUS: God forbid such wicked madness!

AUGUSTINE: Then should we not rejoice a little that we have something in our souls—this very thing that I call a good will—in comparison with which those things we mentioned are utterly worthless, things that a great many human beings will spare no effort and shirk no danger to obtain?

EVODIUS: Indeed, we should rejoice greatly.

AUGUSTINE: Then do you think that those who do not attain such joy suffer a small loss by missing so great a good?

EVODIUS: It is a great loss.

AUGUSTINE: Then I believe you realize that it is up to our will whether we enjoy or lack such a great and true good. For what is so much in the power of the will as the will itself? To have a good will is to have something far more valuable than all earthly kingdoms and pleasures; to lack it is to lack something that only the will itself can give, something that is better than all the goods that are not in our power. Some people consider themselves utterly miserable if they do not achieve a splendid reputation, great wealth, and various goods of the body. But don't you consider them utterly miserable, even if they have all these things, when they cleave to things that they can quite easily lose, things that they do not have simply in virtue of willing them, while they lack a good will, which is incomparably better than those things and yet, even though it is such a great good, can be theirs if only they will to have it?

EVODIUS: I certainly do.

AUGUSTINE: Then fools, even if they were never wise (which is a doubtful and obscure issue), are justly and deservedly afflicted with such misery.

EVODIUS: I agree.

AUGUSTINE: Now do you think that prudence is the knowledge of what is to be desired and what is to be avoided?

EVODIUS: Yes.

AUGUSTINE: And isn't fortitude the disposition of the soul by which we have no fear of misfortune or of the loss of things that are not in our power?

EVODIUS: It is.

AUGUSTINE: And temperance is the disposition that checks and restrains the desire for things that it is wicked to desire. Don't you agree?

EVODIUS: Yes, I do.

AUGUSTINE: And justice, finally, is the virtue by which all people are given their due.

EVODIUS: That is exactly my conception of justice.

AUGUSTINE: Then consider those who have this good will whose excellence we have been discussing for so long now. They lovingly embrace this one unsurpassable good and delight in its presence. They enjoy it to the full and rejoice when they consider that so great a good is theirs and cannot be stolen or taken away from them against their will. Can we doubt that they will resist everything that is inimical to this one good?

EVODIUS: Indeed they must resist such things.

AUGUSTINE: Then they are surely endowed with prudence, since they realize that the good is to be desired and everything inimical to it is to be avoided.

EVODIUS: I don't think anyone could realize that unless he had prudence.

AUGUSTINE: Exactly. And how can we not attribute fortitude to them as well? For they neither love nor value things that are not in our power. Such things are loved by an evil will, which they must resist as an enemy of their own most beloved good. And since they do not love such things, they consider them utterly worthless and are not pained by losing them. And this, as we said earlier, is the role of fortitude.

EVODIUS: Then we must attribute fortitude to them. For I can't imagine anyone who deserves to be called strong. If not those who patiently and calmly bear the absence of those things that it is not in our power to obtain or to keep, as we have found that those who have a good will must necessarily do.

AUGUSTINE: Now consider whether we can deny them temperance, which is the virtue that restrains inordinate desires. For what is more harmful to a good will than inordinate desire? So you may conclude that those who love their own good will resist and oppose inordinate desires in every way they can, and so they are rightly called temperate.

EVODIUS: I agree. Please continue.

AUGUSTINE: Finally comes justice. I don't see how they could lack justice, since those who have and cherish a good will, and resist whatever is inimical to that will, as we have said, cannot wish anyone ill. Therefore they harm no one, which in turn implies that they give all people their due. And I believe you remember agreeing when I said that this is the role of justice.

EVODIUS: I do remember, and I acknowledge that all four virtues that you just described, with my agreement, are present in those who love their own good will and value it highly.

AUGUSTINE: What is to keep us from saying that the lives of such people are praiseworthy?

EVODIUS: Nothing at all. Indeed, all of these considerations urge us, even compel us, to say so.

BOOK TWO

AUGUSTINE: If all of this is true, the question you posed has clearly been answered. If human beings are good things, and they cannot do right unless they so will, then they ought to have a free will, without which they cannot do right. True, they can also use free will to sin, but we should not therefore believe that God gave

them free will so that they would be able to sin. The fact that human beings could not live rightly without it was sufficient reason for God to give it. The very fact that anyone who uses free will to sin is divinely punished shows that free will was given to enable human beings to live rightly, for such punishment would be unjust if free will had been given both for living rightly and for sinning. After all, how could someone justly be punished for using the will for the very purpose for which it was given? When God punishes a sinner, don't you think he is saying, "Why didn't you use your free will for the purpose for which I gave it to you?"—that is, for living rightly?

And as for the goodness that we so admired in God's justice—his punishing sins and rewarding good deeds—how could it even exist if human beings lacked the free choice of the will? No action would be either a sin or a good deed if it were not performed by the will, and so both punishment and reward would be unjust if human beings had no free will. But it was right for there to be justice in both reward and punishment, since this is one of the goods that come from God. Therefore, it was right for God to give free will to human beings.

Therefore, when the will cleaves to the common and unchangeable good, it attains the great and foremost goods for human beings, even though the will itself is only an intermediate good. But when the will turns away from the unchangeable and common good toward its own private good, or toward external or inferior things, it sins. It turns toward its own private good when it wants to be under its own control; it turns toward external things when it is keen on things that belong to others or have nothing to do with itself; it turns toward inferior things when it takes delight in physical pleasure. In this way one becomes proud, meddlesome, and lustful; one is caught up into a life that, by comparison with the higher life, is death. But even that life is governed by divine providence, which places all things in their proper order and gives everyone what he deserves.

Hence, the goods that are pursued by sinners are in no way evil things, and neither is free will itself, which we found is to be counted among the intermediate goods. What is evil is the turning of the will away from the unchangeable good and toward changeable goods. And since this turning is not coerced, but voluntary, it is justly and deservedly punished with misery.

But perhaps you are going to ask what is the source of this movement by which the will turns away from the unchangeable good toward a changeable good. This movement is certainly evil, even though free will itself is to be counted among good things, since no one can live rightly without it. For if that movement, that turning away from the Lord God, is undoubtedly sin, surely we cannot say that God is the cause of sin. So that movement is not from God. But then where does it come from? If I told you that I don't know, you might be disappointed; but that would be the truth. For one cannot know that which is nothing.

You must simply hold with unshaken faith that every good thing that you perceive or understand or in any way know is from God. For any nature you come across is from God. So if you see anything at all that has measure, number, and order, do not hesitate to attribute it to God as craftsman. If you take away all measure, number, and order, there is absolutely nothing left. Even if the rudiments of a form remain, in which you find neither measure nor number nor order—since wherever those things are there is a complete form—you must take that away too, for it seems to be like the material on which the craftsman works. For if the completion of form is a good, then the rudiments of a form are themselves not without goodness. So if you take away everything that is good, you will have absolutely nothing left. But every good thing comes from God, so there is no nature that does not come from God. On the other hand, every defect comes from nothing, and that movement of turning away, which we admit is sin, is a defective movement. So you see where that movement comes from; you may be sure that it does not come from God.

BOOK THREE

AUGUSTINE: Surely this is the problem that is disturbing and puzzling you. How is it that these two propositions are not contradictory and inconsistent: (1) God has foreknowledge of everything in the future; and (2) We sin by the will, not by necessity? For, you say, if God foreknows that someone is going to sin, then it is necessary that he sin. But if it is necessary, the will has no choice about whether to sin; there is an inescapable and fixed necessity. And so you fear that this argument forces us into one of two positions: either we draw the heretical conclusion that God does not foreknow everything in the future; or, if we cannot accept this conclusion, we must admit that sin happens by necessity and not by will. Isn't that what is bothering you?

EVODIUS: That's it exactly.

AUGUSTINE: So you think that anything that God foreknows happens by necessity and not by will.

EVODIUS: Precisely.

AUGUSTINE: Now pay close attention. Look inside yourself for a little while, and tell me, if you can, what sort of will you are going to have tomorrow: a will to do right or a will to sin?

EVODIUS: I don't know.

AUGUSTINE: Do you think that God doesn't know either?

EVODIUS: Not at all—God certainly does know.

AUGUSTINE: Well then, if God knows what you are going to will tomorrow, and foresees the future wills of every human being, both those who exist now and those who will exist in the future, he surely foresees how he is going to treat the just and the irreligious.

EVODIUS: Clearly, if I say that God foreknows all of my actions, I can much more confidently say that he foreknows his own actions and foresees with absolute certainty what he is going to do.

AUGUSTINE: Then aren't you worried that someone might object that God himself will act out of necessity rather than by his will in everything that he is going to do? After all, you said that whatever God foreknows happens by necessity, not by will.

EVODIUS: When I said that, I was thinking only of what happens in his creation and not of what happens within himself. For those things do not come into being; they are eternal.

AUGUSTINE: So God does nothing in his creation.

EVODIUS: He has already established, once for all, the ways in which the universe that he created is to be governed; he does not administer anything by a new act of will.

AUGUSTINE: Doesn't he make anyone happy?

EVODIUS: Of course he does.

AUGUSTINE: And he does this when that person is made happy.

EVODIUS: Right.

AUGUSTINE: Then suppose, for example, that you are going to be happy a year from now. That means that a year from now God is going to make you happy.

EVODIUS: That's right too.

AUGUSTINE: And God knows today what he is going to do a year from now.

EVODIUS: He has always foreknown this, so I admit that he foreknows it now, if indeed it is really going to happen.

AUGUSTINE: Then surely you are not God's creature, or else your happiness does not take place in you.

EVODIUS: But I am God's creature, and my happiness does take place in me.

AUGUSTINE: Then the happiness that God gives you takes place by necessity and not by will.

EVODIUS: His will *is* my necessity.

AUGUSTINE: And so you will be happy against your will.

EVODIUS: If I had the power to be happy I would be happy right now. Even now I will to be happy, but I'm not, since it is God who makes me happy. I cannot do it for myself.

AUGUSTINE: How clearly the truth speaks through you! You could not help thinking that the only thing that is within our power is that which we do when we will it. Therefore, nothing is so much within our power as the will itself, for it is near at hand the very moment that we will. So

we can rightly say, "We grow old by necessity, not by will"; or "We become feeble by necessity, not by will"; or "We die by necessity, not by will," and other such things. But who would be crazy enough to say "We do not will by the will"? Therefore, although God foreknows what we are going to will in the future, it does not follow that we do not will by the will.

When you said that you cannot make yourself happy, you said it as if I had denied it. Not at all; I am merely saying that when you do become happy, it will be in accordance with your will, not against your will. Simply because God foreknows your future happiness—and nothing can happen except as God foreknows it, since otherwise it would not be foreknowledge—it does not follow that you will be happy against your will. That would be completely absurd and far from the truth. So God's foreknowledge, which is certain even today of your future happiness, does not take away your will for happiness once you have begun to be happy; and in the same way, your blameworthy will (if indeed you are going to have such a will) does not cease to be a will simply because God foreknows that you are going to have it.

Just notice how imperceptive someone would have to be to argue thus: "If God has foreknown my future will, it is necessary that I will what he has foreknown, since nothing can happen otherwise than as he has foreknown it. But if it is necessary, then one must concede that I will it by necessity and not by will." What extraordinary foolishness! If God foreknew a future will that turned out not to be a will at all, things would indeed happen otherwise than as God foreknew them. And I will overlook this objector's equally monstrous statement that "it is necessary that I will," for by assuming necessity he tries to abolish will. For if his willing is necessary, how does he will, since there is no will?

Suppose he expressed it in another way and said that, since his willing is necessary, his will is not in his own power. This would run up against the same problem that you had when I asked whether you were going to be happy against your will. You replied that you would already be happy if you had the power; you said that you have the will but not the power. I answered that the truth had spoken through you. For we can deny that something is in our power only if it is not present even when we will it; but if we will, and yet the will remains absent, then we are not really willing at all. Now if it is impossible for us not to will when we are willing, then the will is present to those who will; and if something is present when we will it, then it is in our power. So our will would not be a will if it were not in our power. And since it is in our power, we are free with respect to it. But we are not free with respect to anything that we do not have in our power, and anything that we have cannot be nothing.

Thus, we believe both that God has fore-knowledge of everything in the future and that nonetheless we will whatever we will. Since God foreknows our will, the very will that he foreknows will be what comes about. Therefore, it will be a will, since it is a will that he fore-knows. And it could not be a will unless it were in our power. Therefore, he also foreknows this power. It follows, then, that his foreknowledge does not take away my power; in fact, it is all the more certain that I will have that power, since he whose foreknowledge never errs fore-knows that I will have it.

EVODIUS: But I would like to know, if possible, *why* that nature did not sin which God foreknew would not sin, and *why* that nature sinned which God foresaw would sin. For I no longer think that it was God's foreknowledge itself that compelled the one to sin and the other not to sin. But if there were no cause at all, rational creatures would not be divided into those that never sin, those that persevere in sin, and the intermediate group of those that sometimes sin and sometimes act rightly. What is the cause of this division into three groups? Don't just say, "The will," because I'm looking for the cause of the will itself. All these creatures are of the same kind, so there must be something that causes some of them never to will to sin, some of them always to will to sin, and others to will it sometimes but not other times. I am certain

only that there must be some cause of this threefold will among rational creatures, but I don't know what this cause is.

AUGUSTINE: The will is the cause of sin, but you are asking about the cause of the will itself. Suppose that I could find this cause. Wouldn't we then have to look for the cause of this cause? What limit will there be on this search? Where will our questions and discussions end?

You should not search any further than the root of the issue. Take care that you believe in the unsurpassable truth of the saying that the root of all evils is greed, that is, willing to have more than enough. Enough means whatever is necessary to preserve a nature according to its kind. But greed, which in Greek is called 'phi-larguria,' does not merely have to do with the silver or coins from which the word is derived (for it used to be that coins were made of silver or had some silver mixed in). Rather, it should be understood to apply to any object of immoderate desire, in any case where someone wills to have more than enough. Such greed is cupidity, and cupidity is a perverse will.

Therefore, a perverse will is the cause of all evils. If such a will were in accordance with nature, it would preserve that nature and not harm it, and so it would not be perverse. Thus we can conclude that the root of all evils is not in accordance with nature, and this fact gives us all we need to answer those who want to blame natures. But if you are asking for the cause of this root, how can it be the root of all evils? Its cause would then turn out to be the root of all evils. And as I said, once you have found that, you will have to search for *its* cause, and there will be no limit to your searching.

And besides, what could be the cause of the will before the will itself? Either it is the will itself, in which case the root of all evils is still the will, or else it is not the will, in which case there is no sin. So either the will is the first cause of sin, or no sin is the first cause of sin. And you cannot rightly assign responsibility for a sin to anyone but the sinner; therefore, you cannot rightly assign responsibility except to someone who wills it—but I don't know why you would want to look any further.

2. The Nature of Time

See, I answer him that asketh, "What did God before He made heaven and earth?" I answer not as one is said to have done merrily (eluding the pressure of the question), "He was preparing hell (saith he) for prayers into mysteries." It is one thing to answer enquiries, another to make sport of enquirers. So I answer not; for rather had I answer, "I know not," what I know not, than so as to raise a laugh at him who asketh deep things and gain praise for one who answereth false things. But I say that Thou, our God, art the Creator of every creature: and if by the name "heaven and earth," every creature be understood; I boldly say, "that before God made heaven and earth, He did not make any thing." For if He made, what did He make but a creature? And would I knew whatsoever I desire to know to my profit, as I know, that no creature was made, before there was made any creature.

For what is time? Who can readily and briefly explain this? Who can even in thought comprehend it, so as to utter a word about it? But what in discourse do we mention more familiarly and knowingly, than time? And, we understand, when we speak of it; we understand also, when we hear it spoken of by another. What then is time? If no one asks me, I know: if I wish to explain it to one that asketh, I know not: yet I say boldly that I know, that if nothing passed away, time past were not; and if nothing were coming, a time to come were not; and if nothing were, time present were not. Those two times then, past and to come, how are they, seeing the past now is not, and that to come is not yet? But the present, should it always be present, and never pass into time past, verily it should not be time, but eternity. If time present (if it is to be time) only cometh into existence, because it passeth into time past, how can we say that either this is, whose cause of being is, that it shall not be; so, namely, that we cannot truly say that time is, but because it is tending not to be?

"Who will tell me that there are not three times (as we learned when boys, and taught boys), past, present, and future; but present only, because those two are not? Or are they also; and when from future it becometh present, doth it come out of some secret place; and so, when retiring, from present it becometh past? For where did they, who foretold things to come, see them, if as yet they be not? For that which is not, cannot be seen. And they who relate things past, could not relate them, if in mind they did not discern them, and if they were not, they could no way be discerned. Things then past and to come, are."

Permit me, Lord, to seek further. O my hope, let not my purpose be confounded. For if times past and to come be, I would know where they be. Which yet if I cannot, yet I know, wherever they be, they are not there as future, or past, but present. For if there also they be future, they are not yet there; if there also they be past, they are no longer there. Wheresoever then is whatsoever is, it is only as present. Although when past facts are related, there are drawn out of the memory, not the things themselves which are past, but words which, conceived by the images of the things, they, in passing, have through the senses left as traces in the mind. Thus my childhood, which now is not, is in time past, which now is not: but now when I recall its image, and tell of it, I behold it in the present, because it is still in my memory. Whether there be a like cause of foretelling things to come also; that of things which as yet are not, the images may be perceived before, already existing, I confess, O my God, I know not. This indeed I know, that we generally think before on our future actions, and that forethinking is present, but the action whereof we forethink is not yet, because it is to come. Which, when we have set upon, and have begun to do what we were fore-thinking, then shall that action be; because then it is no longer future, but present.

Which way soever then this secret fore-perceiving of things to come be; that only can be seen, which is. But what now is, is not future, but present. When then things to come are said to be seen, it is not themselves which as yet are not (that is, which are to be), but their causes perchance or signs are seen, which already are.

What now is clear and plain is, that neither things to come nor past are. Nor is it properly said, "there be three times, past, present, and to come": yet perchance it might be properly said, "there be three times; a present of things past, a present of things present, and a present of things future." For these three do exist in some sort, in the soul, but otherwise do I not see them; present of things past, memory; present of things present, sight; present of things future, expectation.

I said then even now, we measure times as they pass, in order to be able to say, this time is twice so much as that one; or, this is just so much as that; and so of any other parts of time, which be measurable. Wherefore, as I said, we measure times as they pass. And if any should ask me, "How knowest thou?" I might answer, "I know, that we do measure, nor can we measure things that are not; and things past and to come, are not." But time present how do we measure, seeing it hath no space? It is measured while passing, but when it shall have passed, it is not measured; for there will be nothing to be measured. But whence, by what way, and whither passes it while it is a measuring? whence, but from the future? Which way, but through the present? whither, but into the past? From that therefore, which is not yet, through that, which hath no space, into that, which now is not. Yet what do we measure, if not time in some space? For we do not say, single, and double, and triple, and equal, or any other like way that we speak of time, except of spaces of times. In what space then do we measure time passing? In the future, whence it passeth through? But what is not yet, we measure not. Or in the present, by which it passes? but no space, we do not measure: or in the

past, to which it passes? But neither do we measure that, which now is not.

Seeing therefore the motion of a body is one thing, that by which we measure how long it is, another; who sees not, which of tie two is rather to be called time? For and if a body be sometimes moved, sometimes stands still, then we measure, not his motion only, but his standing still too by time; and we say, "it stood still, as much as it moved"; or "it stood still twice or thrice so long as it moved"; or any other space which our measuring hath either ascertained, or guessed; more or less, as we use to say. Time then is not the motion of a body.

It is in thee, my mind, that I measure times. Interrupt me not, that is, interrupt not thyself with the tumults of thy impressions. In thee I measure times; the impression, which things as they pass by cause in thee, remains even when they are gone; this it is which still present, I measure, not the things which pass by to make this impression. This I measure, when I measure times. Either then this is time, or I do not measure times. What when we measure silence, and say that this silence hath held as long time as did that voice? do we not stretch out our thought to the measure of a voice, as if it sounded, that so we may be able to report of the intervals of silence in a given space of time? For though both voice and tongue be still, yet in thought we go over poems, and verses, and any other discourse, or dimensions of motions, and report as to the spaces of times, how much this is in respect of that, no otherwise than if vocally we did pronounce them. If a man would utter a lengthened sound, and had settled in thought how long it should be, he hath in silence already gone through a space of time, and committing it to memory, begins to utter that speech, which sounds on, until it be brought unto the end proposed. Yea it hath sounded, and will sound; for so much of it as is finished, hath sounded already, and the rest will sound. And thus passeth it on, until the present intent conveys over the future into the past; the past increasing by the diminution of the future, until by the consumption of the future, all is past.

But how is that future diminished or consumed, which as yet is not? or how that past increased, which is now no longer, save that in the mind which enacteth this, there be three things done? For it expects, it considers, it remembers; that so that which it expecteth, through that which it considereth, passeth into that which it remembereth. Who therefore denieth, that things to come are not as yet? and yet, there is in the mind an expectation of things to come. And who denies past things to be now no longer? and yet is there still in the mind a memory of things past. And who denieth the present time hath no space, because it passeth away in a moment? and yet our consideration continueth, through which that which shall be present proceedeth to become absent. It is not then future time, that is long, for as yet it is not: but a long future, is "a long expectation of the future," nor is it time past, which now is not, that is long; but a long past, is "a long memory of the past."

And now will I stand, and become firm in Thee, in my mould, Thy truth; nor will I endure the questions of men, who by a penal disease thirst for more than they can contain, and say, "what did God before He made heaven and earth?" Or, "How came it into His mind to make any thing, having never before made any thing?" Give them, O Lord, well to bethink themselves what they say, and to find, that "never" cannot be predicated, when "time" is not. This then that He is said "never to have made"; what else is it to say, than "in 'no time' to have made?" Let them see therefore, that time cannot be without created being, and cease to speak that vanity. May they also be extended towards those things which are before; and understand Thee before all times, the eternal Creator of all times, and that no times be coeternal with Thee, nor any creature, even if there be any creature before all times.

Study Questions

1. Why does Augustine say that it is necessary first to believe in order to understand?

2. What does it mean for the Christian view to say that human nature was created good, then became corrupt, and now is redeemed and again capable of being good?

3. What does Augustine mean by "disordered love"? Give an example of such love.

4. For Augustine, how can we be free if we need God's grace to choose the good?

5. How does Augustine explain the existence of evil in the world?

St. Thomas Aquinas

Introduction

After the death of Augustine the Medieval period of Western philosophy was to produce little more of philosophical value for the next several hundred years. This period of time is often referred to as the Dark Ages, because there was so little learning and so many wars. The clergy maintained some libraries, copied and preserved books, but the great centers of learning were gone. The later period of medieval philosophy, the period from the eleventh to the sixteenth century, by contrast, was filled with intellectual vigor, both in the Christian West and in the Muslim world. Here we will focus on one representative of this period, St. Thomas Aquinas. The influence of Aquinas was eventually to surpass even that of Augustine as the leading theologian of the Medieval period and beyond.

Thomas Aquinas, universally regarded as the greatest of the medieval theologians, was born into a wealthy Italian family in 1225. He studied at the University in Naples and, despite his family's objections, became a Dominican monk in 1244. He studied at the University of Paris with Albert the Great, an advocate of the newly rediscovered ideas of Aristotle. Aristotle's writings had been lost to the West, but preserved especially by Islamic philosophers, several of whom, such as Avicenna (80–1037), Al-Ghazali (1058–1111), and Averroes (1126–1198), had written lengthy commentaries on many of them. Aquinas became heir to the most complete and thorough system of human wisdom ever produced in the West, and quickly learned to respect it. He had so much respect for Aristotle, in fact, that he referred to him in his writings simply as "the Philosopher."

Unfortunately, many of the ideas of Aristotle seemed to be incompatible with Christian teaching. For example, Aristotle believed that the universe is eternal and that the human soul perishes with the body. He also believed that God knew only his own mind, and had no knowledge of individuals. This was not the Christian personal God who created the world, received our immortal souls into heavenly bliss, and knew and loved each of his creatures here on earth. In addition, Aristotle did not seem to have a doctrine of freedom sufficient to support the belief that people earn admission to the kingdom of heaven through their free choices. In these and other areas Aquinas was faced with the daunting task of reinterpreting Aristotle to fit the Christian worldview. This project was to constitute much of his life's work.

The most famous works of Aquinas are his *Summa Theologica* and the *Summa Contra Gentiles*. The latter work was written as a guide to be used by missionaries, while the former work is a collection of Aquinas' answers to various **disputed questions.** A debate format was used for answering such questions, both in his written and oral teachings. Oral debates were a common way to teach in medieval universities at the time. They were dramatic public debates and were usually well attended by students and other professors. They would begin with a question, then proceed to give answers that the professor considered to be inadequate, called *objections.* These were often the opinions of other theologians or philosophers. Following these came the *sed contra,* where he claimed that his own view was correct, and the *respondeo,* where he spelled out what this view amounted to. Finally he would reply to all of the objections, taking what was true from them and discarding the error. The readings included in this chapter from Aquinas all have this format.

Because of his reliance upon Aristotle's ideas, three years after his early death in 1274, many of the works of Aquinas were banned by the Bishop of Paris. The ban was not to remain in effect for too long, however, and in 1323 Aquinas was canonized. In 1879, Pope Leo XII proclaimed him to be the most enlightened theologian ever produced by the Catholic Church.

Worldview

As did all medieval theologians, Aquinas accepted the Christian worldview as a given.

The Influence of Christianity

According to this worldview, everything important about life has been revealed in the scriptures—The Old and New Testaments. There we especially discover that the universe was created by a personal God who knows and loves us, and has provided us with the opportunity to gain eternal salvation. In order to understand this message, however, opposing interpretations of how best to understand each of its many elements have to be clarified, defended, and evaluated. So while faith in the revealed word of God is required to know what is true, we must also have reason (philosophy) to help us to understand what we believe. Up to this point Aquinas agrees with Augustine. Aquinas has more faith in reason's power than does Augustine, however, and believes that reason on its own can discover many truths that have been revealed.

While some truths are beyond reason, such as the belief that God is three persons in one nature, many are within its grasp. It can discover the nature of nature, or science, for example, as Aristotle claimed. It can also discover, though only with great effort, some of the truths that have been revealed. Reason can know that God exists, for example, and it can discover some of God's properties. It can also discover that the soul can exist apart from the body and is immortal, as well as discover wherein lies the true happiness of human beings. Reason and faith can often discover the same truths by separate methods. They are both gifts from God and in harmony with one another. The mind well trained in philosophy can not only believe but also know, and to know is to reach a deeper understanding than faith alone can provide. Aquinas was not afraid that reason might lead people astray from God's truth, but rather welcomed it as another avenue to God. If God is truth, in the sense of having the perfect ideas of all creation in his mind, then knowing these truths got one ever closer to God.

The Influence of Aristotle

For Aquinas, reason was most adequately reflected in the ideas of Aristotle. To use these ideas to clarify the teachings of Christianity, however, required that Aquinas add to some of them and correct others. The first addition had to do with the nature of *reality*. Aquinas claims that Aristotle fell short of identifying what is ultimately real. For Aristotle, the most basic thing that may be said about anything is that it is a certain *kind* of thing. This is explained by its form or essence. Different kinds of things are different because they have different forms. But things can have a certain kind of form and not exist. For example, pizza is a certain kind of thing, but there surely was a time during which it did not exist, and there may be a time in the future when it ceases to exist. That it happens to exist or not, and especially that it does not have to exist, were not ideas considered by Aristotle.

For Aquinas, there is something more basic to be said about a thing beyond what kind of thing it is. Whether a thing *exists* or not is the most fundamental thing that can be said about it. Aquinas calls its existence its *being* (*esse*, in Latin). He thinks of things as not simply a combination of form and matter, but also of essence (form and matter) and existence. The importance of this insight is that the entire universe may now be viewed as contingent, as not having to exist. Unlike the Greeks who thought that the universe was necessary (it has to be as it is),

Christianity thinks that it is contingent, it does not have to be at all. It is, but only because it was created by God.

For Aquinas, God as a perfect being is pure *esse*. He is not a certain kind of thing, with a certain type of form, since this would limit his perfection. Moreover, when God created the world he created it with every possible level of being, as Augustine had said. The levels of perfection of various beings are determined by the levels of being (*esse*) they possess. The vision of Aquinas is this: that a being exists at all is determined by God, and the kind of being a thing is is determined by its amount of *esse* given it by God. Things are just various finite levels of *esse*. Their being reflects the being of God on various levels of gradation. It is as though variously shaped buckets scooped out water, and then the buckets were removed and the shaped water remained. In the same way, a thing is the sort of thing it is, has the form it does, because it shares more or less in the being of God. All creatures are dependent upon God, then, both for the type of being that they are and the fact that they exist at all.

Aquinas also introduced some of his own ideas about *knowledge* to fit the requirements of Christianity. Perhaps the most important of these changes concerned the knowledge that we have of God and that he has of us. Aquinas followed the lead of Aristotle and first argued for the *existence* of God. He presented five arguments for God's existence, borrowing some from the Philosopher, and adding some of his own. Especially important is the third argument of Aquinas, which is based on the need for a necessary being to exist in order to account for the contingency of the universe. This argument drew upon the distinction between essence and existence just discussed. These arguments will not be analyzed here, since that task would consume the rest of the chapter, and it is not essential to do so in order to understand the views of Aquinas on human nature. Instead, the arguments are presented in *Reading 1*.

More important for our understanding of human nature is an explanation of how we can know the *nature* of God. Some of the things that we know about God come from revelation, some come from reason, and some from both sources. From revelation, for example, we know that God is the almighty and everlasting being. From reason we know that God is the designer of the universe, and from both we know that God is its creator. If to know something is to have ideas about that thing, and if the meaning of words comes from the ideas that they express, then we may ask about our knowledge of God by asking for the meaning of the words which we use to describe him. But what meaning do the words have that we use to describe God when we say that God is eternal, omniscient, omnipotent, all good, the creator of the universe, and so on?

These terms cannot mean simply what they do when we predicate them of human beings. Surely God's power and might, his creativity and wisdom, his goodness and perfection, and his many other properties surpass anything possessed by humans. To refer to God with words that have the same meaning that they do when applied to humans, sometimes called the **positive way** of speaking of God, is to talk about God as though he were a super human being. This is sometimes called *anthropomorphism*, understanding God's properties to be like those of a human being. Many of the Greek and Roman gods were thought of in this way, as more powerful versions of human beings. We sometimes speak of

God in this way, as well, as when we speak of him as our heavenly "father" and picture him as a man with a beard.

The truth, however, seems to be that such human predicates have only a negative meaning when we apply them to God, that we can use them to speak of God only in a **negative way.** That is, we use them only to say what God is not. To say that God is eternal, for example, is to say that God is not in time. To say that God is all powerful is to say that God lacks no power. To say that God is perfect is to say that God lacks no perfection. This negative way of understanding is helpful sometimes. For example, suppose that we could not see inside a fruit bowl, but we knew that four types of fruit had been placed in the bowl—an apple, an orange, a banana, and a peach. Suppose further we knew that three people had taken one piece of fruit each from the bowl. Now if we asked what fruit was left and someone told us that it was not an apple, not a peach, and not a banana, then we would know it was an orange. Sometimes in ordinary life and in scientific experiments we arrive at the truth in this manner, by a process of elimination.

The problem with this way of speaking about God, however, is that it leaves us with no knowledge whatsoever. We have to know what the alternatives are like and how many there are in order to know something by eliminating all the others. However, we have no idea what it means for God to be wise, for example. God does not observe through his senses, then form concepts and make judgments—as humans do. Nor do we have a concept of what it is like to be eternal, to be a being "out" of time, or to create "from nothing" as God did, and so on. If the positive way of thinking and speaking of God gives us a human-like God, the negative way tells us that God is a complete mystery, totally different from us, totally unintelligible to us.

For Aquinas, there is a third way of understanding God, called the **way of analogy.** An analogy is a comparison of two things which are partly the same and partly different. The words that we use to express our knowledge of God mean partly what they do when we say them of humans, as the positive way claims, and partly not, as the negative way claims. When we call God "wise" for example, we are talking about a kind of knowledge. We are not saying nothing, as we would if we called God "garaga," for example. God's wisdom is in the same general category as human wisdom. This should be no surprise, since we were made in his image to begin with. This is the part of understanding God where the word "wisdom" means something like what it means when we use it to describe human beings. But God's knowledge is vastly superior to that of humans. It has none of the obstacles or other limitations of human knowledge, such as requiring a body with sense organs, or being restricted to a particular time and place. So when we say that God is wise we mean partly what we do when we say that human beings are wise, but also we add that his knowledge is different from human knowledge, insofar as it is free of limitations.

In discussing *God's knowledge of his creatures,* Aquinas was required not simply to add to the ideas of Aristotle, but to correct them. Aristotle's God was an impersonal being who knew only its own mind and the universal ideas that were found there. Such a God had no knowledge of individual creatures. The Christian God, on the other hand, was a personal God who knew each and every one of us, right down to our secret thoughts and future actions. The problem was, how could such knowledge be possible for a perfect God? To be perfect requires that God does not change, and thus that he be out of time, or atemporal, reflecting only upon the contents of his own mind. To know creatures, however, seems to require that God be seeped in time, like the rest of us, and to know the mundane, the less than perfect. So how can God know us in time, as individuals, and still be atemporal? The answer of Aquinas, briefly, is that while God is atemporal and knows primarily his own mind, he knows his creatures individually by knowing, from eternity, the causes of everything. He knows himself as creator, the ultimate cause of all, and thus knows the details of whatever he causes. In this way, by reflecting atemporally on his own essence, God knows the details of each and every one of his creatures.

Human Nature

In discussing human nature as it is, the focus is placed on discovering the innate tendencies and structures shared by all human beings. Aquinas accepts that the most important innate tendencies include our shared desires, such as those highlighted by Aristotle, especially the desire to know, and those mentioned by Augustine, especially our desire for God. Other innate tendencies follow from our shared structures, from the kinds of beings that we are. Aquinas accepts Aristotle's belief about the structure shared by all human beings. Whereas Augustine had followed Plato and defined human beings as a combination of two separate things, bodies and souls, Aquinas followed Aristotle and defined human beings as one thing made up of two components—matter and form. As with every creature, "matter" refers to material components, while "form" refers to how these components are organized. The same matter, say carbon compounds, may be found in various types of living things. Their types, their kind of being, is determined by how these material components are put together, their form. Today we might say that this is determined by genes, but there was no conception of genes at that time. In any case, Aquinas accepted the view that the distinguishing feature of all creatures is their form, since this is what makes them to be the sort of creatures that they are. In human beings the form is called the **soul.**

For Aquinas, as for Aristotle, the soul of each human being produces innate tendencies, or functions, on three levels. There are not three souls, but three basic types of function of the one soul. First, we have vegetative souls, the principle of biological life. Its energy is the source of nutrition, growth, and reproduction. We also have sentient or sensitive souls, which enable us to see, hear, taste, touch, and smell; to form images; have feelings and desires; and to learn from experience. The highest functions of the soul are our rational abilities, our reasoning abilities, such as figuring out the solution to mathematical equations or how to get something that we want, and especially our power to know abstract universal ideas. This is what Aristotle called science and Plato called wisdom. Our reason is primarily what separates us from other animals; it is where our humanness really lies.

For Aquinas, our ability to know universal ideas is explained by the doctrine of **abstraction,** which we have examined briefly in the previous chapter. We briefly review this doctrine here and in *Reading 2*. Knowledge of the world begins with the sensory experience of particular objects. Through the various senses we get to know a particular apple, for example. The information from the various senses is delivered through various sensory organs and combined in our imagination into an image of that apple. This image is called a **phantasm** by Aquinas. To know, however, is to do more than sense something and to create an internal image of it. It is also to understand what we sense. We understand by classifying experience as belonging to certain types. These types are universal ideas. Once we form these ideas, we store them in our minds and continue to use them to recognize and sort out various types of incoming sensory information. But where do we get our ideas in the first place?

Plato says that they are innate; Augustine says that they are given to us by the illumination of Christ. Aristotle says that they are generalizations from many experiences. We see lots of apples and eventually form the idea of an apple. Aquinas follows Aristotle and tries to explain how such generalizations occur. He begins by pointing out that the rational mind or intellect may be understood to have two dimensions—the passive or potential intellect, and the active or agent intellect. The **passive intellect** may be thought of as that part of the mind (soul) where the ideas that we form get deposited and stored. The **active intellect,** on the other hand, is what forms the universal concepts that are stored in the passive intellect. It is what "gets" or "understands" the idea. It does this by reflecting upon the data which is present in the phantasm. As the form of an apple, any apple, is present in each and every apple, so it is present in each and every experience (phantasm) of an apple. It has to be "dug out" of, or *abstracted* from, the phantasm, however, by the rational power of the active intellect. Once formed, these universal ideas may be deposited in the passive intellect where, as science or wisdom, they reflect the permanent pattern of nature and the unchanging mind of God.

Perhaps the most difficult challenge that the teachings of Aristotle bequeathed to Aquinas was the Philosopher's apparent denial of the immortality of individual souls. It seemed easy for Augustine to explain how the soul could live on after the death of the body. If the soul and body are two separate substances united in a human being, then at death the body could disintegrate while the soul continued to exist. For Aquinas, however, if the soul is the form of the body, the way that our material components are organized, then it seems that the soul will disappear when we die. Just as the shape of a table disappears when the table is broken up and burned, so it seems impossible that our soul lives on after us if it is simply the form of the body.

The explanation by Aquinas for how such a soul may indeed survive the body is found in the "God and Immortality" section. Briefly, we will see there that his explanation of immortality depends upon his analysis of abstraction and the role that the active intellect plays in this process. Universal ideas are not themselves composed of matter and form, but are pure forms. The power to understand them, the active intellect, also seems to function apart from matter when it understands or "conceives"—almost literally "gives birth to"—these ideas. It is here, in the active intellect, that the soul seems to escape its chains to the body; and it is here in this escape that lies the key to understanding the soul's immortality.

Consequences

Freedom

Another important area of difference between Aquinas and Aristotle was on the subject of free will. On this matter Aquinas accepted much of what Aristotle said, but was forced to go beyond the Philosopher. While Aristotle had a concept of freedom, he did not have a concept of free will. Christianity seemed to demand that we are free to choose which actions to perform. Since our eternal salvation is determined by our actions in this life, it seems that we must be responsible for them. Responsibility seems to make sense only if we have free will. But what is a will, and what makes it free?

For Augustine, having free will was a requirement of responsibility, which was a requirement of salvation. If revelation talked about earning salvation, then we must have free will. He thought of the will as different from the intellect, just as the imagination or the memory is different from our ability to know. The will had the power to choose freely among competing desires, and also had the power to create and act upon new desires—and all this despite the circumstances of time and place and character. For Aristotle, on the other hand, it was enough to hold a person responsible for his actions if they were caused by something within him, and not by some external force. This was especially true for those actions that were produced as a result of conscious and thoughtful deliberation, where reason was most in control of desire.

Augustine's view was too unrestricted for Aquinas. Human beings are not capable of doing just anything at any time, but are restricted in the choices that are available to them. Aristotle's view, on the other hand, did not allow for enough freedom to attribute to people sufficient responsibility for their actions. This is because our reasons for acting stem from our character, the kinds of persons that we are, which in turn have been produced by external forces. The job for Aquinas is to reinterpret Aristotle's view so that it could include a sufficient amount of free will to make our actions bear the weight of responsibility, while limiting freedom to choices that are compatible with our character. The view arrived at by Aquinas is complex, but seems to be the following (see *Reading 3*).

First, Aquinas agrees with Aristotle that there is no freedom and no responsibility when our choices are caused by external factors, or when we are ignorant of the consequences of our actions. If someone puts a gun to our head and demands that we remain silent or die, we are not responsible for remaining silent when we otherwise may not have. There is no reasonable alternative to remaining silent; we are forced to do so. For all practical purposes the decision to remain silent is necessary, not free. In addition, if we unknowingly give someone poisonous food and they become ill, we did not freely make them ill. If external compulsion and ignorance rule out freedom, then it would appear that to be free we must understand the nature and consequences of our actions, and they must stem from internal states of ours, such as our intentions, motives, and decisions.

The next point is that even the choices that arise knowingly and from ourselves are always restricted. The internal forces that restrict our choices are the innate tendencies of our own human nature. We are built in such a way that we cannot help but choose what we think will help to make us happy. We are created by God always to choose what we perceive to be good for us. We all have some general conception of what it is that will make us happy, and we choose those things in particular situations that we believe will bring us closer and closer to this goal. No one chooses, at any time, to do what they believe will cause them unhappiness. We can be mistaken about what we view as happiness, and also about whether or not what we desire in particular situations will get us to this goal, but it is always toward the good that our choices are inclined.

In this sense, the will is restricted. It is caused, even determined, to choose what it believes to be good for it, what will make us happy. It does this necessarily; it is not free to do otherwise. This is how Aquinas reigns in Augustine's too free will, by restricting it to choices between what it perceives to be competing goods. Through reason and revelation we may some day come to see what is truly good for us—knowledge and love of God. When we have this knowledge, this wisdom, this secret of life, we will be pointed in the direction of true happiness. But even in ignorance of our true good, our desire for what we think is good still lures us to what we think will make us happy. If I equate happiness with fame and fortune, for example, or physical pleasure, then the will necessarily seeks these goods. But if we *have to* choose what we think of as good, if we have no choice in the matter, why does this not rob us of our freedom?

It does not eliminate freedom because even if what we ultimately desire is determined by human nature, the various *means* that we use to satisfy our desire are within our control. While the ultimate good, happiness, determines the will, we are still able freely to choose among the concrete goods that we believe will lead us to happiness. What we ultimately desire may not be freely chosen, but the means to achieve this end are. This freedom is possible because the means are chosen by reason. Reason is free when it deliberates among alternative courses of action and makes a judgment as to the best path to take. Because we can think in abstract concepts, we can consider possible courses of action, not only the ones immediately before us. So in deliberating about these possible courses of action, reason is free to decide whether or not one path is to be preferred over another. Once this judgment is made, the preferred action is then chosen, or willed. The will is just the decision to act upon the final judgment of the intellect.

Aristotle was correct to see that freedom requires choice and deliberation. He fell short, however, in not recognizing that reason itself is free to choose the best course of action among those that it presents to itself. Augustine was correct in thinking that we do indeed have free will, but incorrect to think of it as an irrational force that may be guided by reason or not. Instead, in presenting to itself possibilities for more than one course of action, reason presents itself with a variety of choices from which it may then select what it believes to be best in the circumstances. Such a free choice is called free will. Free will is not an ability outside of reason; it is just the intellect itself—the noblest, most human part of us—freely deciding or judging what to do. It is when we are guided by such rational deliberation that we are most in control of our actions, and thus most free.

Ethics

Aquinas learned from Aristotle and Plato that the highest good a person can find in this life is to be found in the contemplation of the forms. He learned from his faith, however, that we are destined for a life beyond this one where an even richer happiness awaits. There we will find not only the most perfect knowledge of the forms in the mind of God, but also a loving connection with God for which our hearts are hungry. True wisdom tells us that the good life is to be found in the knowledge and the love of the ultimate good, God, the only being that will make us truly happy. In harmony with Aristotle, Aquinas believed that human nature is fully itself and most happy in this life when it contemplates the forms; in harmony with Augustine and his own faith, Aquinas believed that human nature can become even more perfected in the next life, when the deepest desires of the soul to know and love God are most fully satisfied. Near the time of his death, Aquinas had a mystical experience in which he felt bonded to God through love and the deepest kind of knowledge of God that he thought possible. He never wrote another word after that experience, proclaiming that all of his writings were "as straw" by comparison.

Aquinas also followed Aristotle in his discussion of moral virtue, at least part of the way. He took it as true, for example, that morally correct actions were those that helped human nature to flourish, and that bad actions, or sin, amounted to actions and intentions that violated human nature. He further developed Aristotle's notion of what is compatible or not with human nature by working out much more elaborately than had Augustine the notion of a natural law. This concept was used to build a system of ethics where doing what is right is doing what fulfills our nature, and doing wrong is what violates our natural tendencies. This approach to determining right from wrong is called **natural law ethics** and is discussed by Aquinas in *Reading 4.* The basic idea of natural law ethics is that when God created us he implanted in us natural inclinations that, guided by the proper use of reason, can and should be used to determine right from wrong. In this way will we help human nature flourish and grow into what it could be, by following moral rules that enhance its own innate tendencies toward goodness.

The most basic principle of natural law ethics commands that we "Do good and avoid evil." Good is what makes human nature flourish, and evil is whatever violates our natural tendencies. Our entire nature is geared in the direction of the good, from our urges to survive to our quest for the highest good. From this general principle, through observation and reason, we can arrive at more concrete rules. What we *observe* are universal human tendencies, which we think of as natural tendencies. We all have the urge to survive, to reproduce, and to satisfy many other biological desires, for example. In addition, we are social beings by nature and thus need to live in society to be happy. We have rational desires as well, desires to know and love the highest good. What we *reason to* from these observations, guided by our basic principle, are the rules that ensure the best use of these natural urges for our happiness.

For example, since sex is primarily for reproduction, and our offspring require many years of care, sex is best restricted to the confines of marriage. Truth is a requirement of the natural law as well, since society would not last long if lying was the norm. Nor would it be good for society to allow the breaking of promises, stealing, and unjustified confinement. In addition, murder is wrong because it violates our natural urge to life. We have a right to life, given to us by nature, as well as a right to be told the truth, to have promises kept, to own property, and to be free. These and other natural laws follow from what makes our natural tendencies flourish, and thus bind us to perform or refrain from certain actions. In this way the ethics of right and wrong may be seen as God-given, since it outlines the plan of God for our lives, a plan embedded within our divinely created human nature. Right and wrong is not relative to time and place, but is the same for all at all times and in all places. Since it grows from God's plan for human beings, since it is our natural way to be when we are at our best, it is part of the universe itself. It is not merely the law of this or that or any man; it is the moral law of the universe; it is the law of God.

Society

For Aquinas as for Aristotle, political society is a natural outcome of the social nature of human beings. It is not a tool for the rich to exploit the poor, or simply a way for all to be protected from all. Its chief function is to help us to develop fully as human beings, and thus its job is especially to find ways through its human laws to more concretely realize the natural law. There are four kinds of law for Aquinas. **Divine law** is the moral law of God as revealed in scripture. It is the way that God has told us directly that he wants us to act. **Eternal law** is the law of God as revealed throughout creation. It is the plan of creation in the mind of God, a plan that is reflected in the structures and behaviors of all creatures. **Natural law** is part of this plan, the moral law which resides in all human beings and governs how their free actions ought to be performed. **Human law** is the law created by various societies to govern the behavior of citizens.

In his analysis of society, Aquinas is especially concerned with providing a criterion by which human laws may be judged as morally acceptable or not. As with Augustine, Aquinas was not so much concerned with the type of government which ruled society, but rather with the degree of justice that it allowed, especially in its laws. What he says is that any law passed by human governments must not violate God's law, especially as it appears in natural law. Any law that violates natural law may be subject to moral criticism, dissent, and even civil disobedience. If a government passes enough laws and follows enough policies that violate natural rights, it may be justifiably overthrown—even by bloody revolution.

Natural laws specify what today are called natural rights. Sometimes these are called human rights, since they are supposed to be shared by all human beings, whatever their country of origin. In the U.S. Constitution there are many references to natural rights. In the Declaration of Independence the term "unalienable rights" appears. "Unalienable" ("inalienable" today) refers to something that cannot be taken away. These are rights that no government can deny its citizens because they are beyond any government to give to its citizens in the first place. They are given to all of us by God as part of what we need to be happy. The

American revolution was founded upon a doctrine of natural rights. Also, the prosecution of Nazi war criminals was based on this idea as well, that there is a higher law than human law, a God-given law that must be obeyed by all. These war criminals were prosecuted *for* obeying the laws of their country, because these laws were a violation of this higher law that we all are supposed to follow. In the UN Charter there is found a Declaration of Human Rights, listing more than forty human rights that all people ought to have. For Aquinas, no society is just if its fails to conform its laws to the natural law that God has written into the hearts of all persons.

God and Immortality

Since we have already spoken at length about the views of Aquinas on God, this section will focus on the beliefs of Aquinas concerning the immortality of the soul. Once again we find Aquinas reinterpreting Aristotle to meet the demands of faith. For Aristotle, the soul is not a thing in itself, what philosophers call a "substance." Instead, it is the form of the body. As such, it seems that it would simply disappear at death, as the shape of a banana disappears when it is eaten. This, in fact, seems to be what Aristotle believed, that the soul cannot exist apart from the body, and thus that there is no personal immortality. The task for Aquinas is to explain how the soul can be both the form of the person and exist on its own, or "subsist," after death. He discusses this issue in *Reading 5.*

The key for Aquinas is to notice that at least some of the functions of the soul are spiritual or nonphysical in nature. This is not true for the nutritive or sensitive soul, but is for the rational part of the soul, which we might call the intellect or the mind. That the mind is not physical may be observed from its cognitive function. In particular, the action of the agent intellect seems to occur apart from the body itself. While it needs the senses to form an image of particular objects, and it needs an image as a basis for forming ideas, the forming of ideas itself seems to be an act of creating something that is not physical—a universal, necessary, eternal idea. In addition to forming ideas, or understanding, we can use reason to plan, to think logically and to contemplate—all functions that seem to be independent of the body. Only a spiritual being could produce such spiritual objects as universal ideas and think with them in ways that appear to be independent of the body. So the rational soul, the mind or intellect, is itself spiritual. Since the soul is one, however, this means that the entire soul itself is a spiritual substance. It may both be intertwined with material components to form a person, and exist on its own in a spiritual state.

The next step for Aquinas is to argue that spiritual substances have no parts. There are no spiritual "atoms," for example. Now to cease to exist means to be broken up into parts. When a dog dies, for example, its body is broken down into chemical components. Anything with parts may be destroyed by breaking it up into parts, and anything without parts is indestructible. If the soul is spiritual, if it has no parts, it will survive forever. It is indestructible and thus immortal. The only question remaining is what such a soul is like apart from the human person it once "informed." That is, what is a disembodied soul like?

For Aquinas, being in a disembodied state is not the natural condition of the soul. Its natural condition is to be the form of a body. Unlike Augustine, Aquinas follows the interpretation of St. Paul that life after death requires the resurrection of the body. So for Aquinas, the disembodied state of the soul is only temporary. It will remain in that state until it is somehow rejoined with some sort of components, in some way to be determined by God, in order to once again form a person. In this temporary state, without a body, the soul is deaf, dumb, blind, mute, and so on. Without the body none of these functions are possible. Instead, the soul knows only spiritual objects and substances—much as Plato had said a millennium and a half before. In this state beyond nature it can know and love God, its true "super"-natural goal. But my soul is not the true me until it is once again united with my body. How this is supposed to happen appears to be more a matter of faith than reason.

Gender

The view of Aquinas on the status of women, unfortunately, appears to be closely allied to that of Aristotle. With Augustine and Christianity in general, Aquinas believed that women are equal to men in their worthiness for salvation. From the perspective of human wisdom, however, he agreed with Aristotle that their natures are inferior to those of men. In particular, their rational abilities are not the equal of men, and thus the road to God through philosophical knowledge is not open to them. Their lives instead are ruled by passion and emotion. Aquinas goes so far as to agree with Aristotle that women are "misbegotten males."[2] Women are by nature created not to live the full human lives of males, but especially to procreate. Even here they are inferior to men, since men are active contributors to the process of procreation, while women are simply the passive recipients of male sperm.

In addition, women are inferior because they are occasions of sin for man, tempting him with her feminine charms to act against his rational nature. All this leads to the conclusion that women should always be subject to the rule of men. Since men have more reason than women, being ruled by men is the only way that the appetites and emotions of women may be brought under the control of reason. If women have inferior rational natures, they also have inferior biological natures. Being created after Adam, from Adam's rib, they are not fully created in the image of God. They are second-class human beings. Their biological natures, especially their sexuality, suits them well for their roles as wives and mothers. Because of their strong physical urges, however, and their low cognitive capacities, they should not occupy positions of power and influence in society, positions that require the rule of reason.

Aquinas thought that the role of women was to be found exclusively within their families. They are to be helpmates to men in the process of creating and nurturing families, and have little role outside of that context. It goes without saying that this sexist attitude by one of the leading theologians of the then very powerful Catholic Church only solidified the view for centuries more that women were significantly inferior to men.

Readings

1. The Existence of God

Third Article

Whether God Exists?

We Proceed Thus to the Third Article:—

Objection 1. It seems that God does not exist; because if one of two contraries be infinite, the other would be altogether destroyed. But the word "God" means that He is infinite goodness. If, therefore, God existed, there would be no evil discoverable; but there is evil in the world. Therefore God does not exist.

Obj. 2. Further, it is superfluous to suppose that what can be accounted for by a few principles has been produced by many. But it seems that everything we see in the world can be accounted for by other principles, supposing God did not exist. For all natural things can be reduced to one principle, which is nature; and all voluntary things can be reduced to one principle, which is human reason, or will. Therefore there is no need to suppose God's existence.

On the contrary, It is said in the person of God: *I am Who am* (Exod. iii. 14).

I answer that, The existence of God can be proved in five ways.

The first and more manifest way is the argument from motion. It is certain, and evident to our senses, that in the world some things are in motion. Now whatever is in motion is put in motion by another, for nothing can be in motion except it is in potentiality to that towards which it is in motion; whereas a thing moves inasmuch as it is in act. For motion is nothing else than the reduction of something from potentiality to actuality. But nothing can be reduced from potentiality to actuality, except by something in a state of actuality. Thus that which is

actually hot, as fire, makes wood, which is potentially hot, to be actually hot, and thereby moves and changes it. Now it is not possible that the same thing should be at once in actuality and potentiality in the same respect, but only in different respects. For what is actually hot cannot simultaneously be potentially hot; but it is simultaneously potentially cold. It is therefore impossible that in the same respect and in the same way a thing should be both mover and moved, *i.e.,* that it should move itself. Therefore, whatever is in motion must be put in motion by another. If that by which it is put in motion be itself put in motion, then this also must needs be put in motion by another, and that by another again. But this cannot go on to infinity, because then there would be no first mover, and, consequently, no other mover; seeing that subsequent movers move only inasmuch as they are put in motion by the first mover; as the staff moves only because it is put in motion by the hand. Therefore it is necessary to arrive at a first mover, put in motion by no other; and this everyone understands to be God.

The second way is from the nature of the efficient cause. In the world of sense we find there is an order of efficient causes. There is no case known (neither is it, indeed, possible) in which a thing is found to be the efficient cause of itself; for so it would be prior to itself, which is impossible. Now in efficient causes it is not possible to go on to infinity, because in all efficient causes following in order, the first is the cause of the intermediate cause, and the intermediate is the cause of the ultimate cause, whether the intermediate cause be several, or one only. Now to take away the cause is to take away the effect. Therefore if there be no first

From *St. Thomas Aquinas,* Summa Theologica, *trans. by the Fathers of the English Dominican Province (New York: Benziger Bros., 1947), pp. 348–350, 376–380, 389–391, 397–404, 361–362. Reprinted with permission. All of the following five readings are taken from this text.*

cause among efficient causes, there will be no ultimate, nor any intermediate cause. But if in efficient causes it is possible to go on to infinity, there will be no first efficient cause, neither will there be an ultimate effect, nor any intermediate efficient causes; all of which is plainly false. Therefore it is necessary to admit a first efficient cause, to which everyone gives the name of God.

The third way is taken from possibility and necessity, and runs thus. We find in nature things that are possible to be and not to be, since they are found to be generated, and to corrupt, and consequently, they are possible to be and not to be. But it is impossible for these always to exist, for that which is possible not to be at some time is not. Therefore, if everything is possible not to be, then at one time there could have been nothing in existence. Now if this were true, even now there would be nothing in existence, because that which does not exist only begins to exist by something already existing. Therefore, if at one time nothing was in existence, it would have been impossible for anything to have begun to exist; and thus even now nothing would be in existence—which is absurd. Therefore, not all beings are merely possible, but there must exist something the existence of which is necessary. But every necessary thing either has its necessity caused by another, or not. Now it is impossible to go on to infinity in necessary things which have their necessity caused by another, as has been already proved in regard to efficient causes. Therefore we cannot but postulate the existence of some being having of itself its own necessity, and not receiving it from another, but rather causing in others their necessity. This all men speak of as God.

The fourth way is taken from the gradation to be found in things. Among beings there are some more and some less good, true, noble, and the like. But "more" and "less" are predicated of different things, according as they resemble in their different ways something which is the maximum, as a

thing is said to be hotter according as it more nearly resembles that which is hottest; so that there is something which is truest, something best, something noblest, and, consequently, something which is uttermost being; for those things that are greatest in truth are greatest in being, as it is written in *Metaph.* ii. Now the maximum in any genus is the cause of all in that genus; as fire, which is the maximum of heat, is the cause of all hot things. Therefore there must also be something which is to all beings the cause of their being, goodness, and every other perfection; and this we call God.

The fifth way is taken from the governance of the world. We see that things which lack intelligence, such as natural bodies, act for an end, and this is evident from their acting always, or nearly always, in the same way, so as to obtain the best result. Hence it is plain that not fortuitously, but designedly, do they achieve their end. Now whatever lacks intelligence cannot move towards an end, unless it be directed by some being endowed with knowledge and intelligence; as the arrow is shot to its mark by the archer. Therefore some intelligent being exists by whom all natural things are directed to their end; and this being we call God.

Reply Obj. 1. As Augustine says (*Enchir.* xi): *Since God is the highest good, He would not allow any evil to exist in His works, unless His omnipotence and goodness were such as to bring good even out of evil.* This is part of the infinite goodness of God, that He should allow evil to exist, and out of it produce good.

Reply Obj. 2. Since nature works for a determinate end under the direction of a higher agent, whatever is done by nature must needs be traced back to God, as to its first cause. So also whatever is done voluntarily must also be traced back to some higher cause other than human reason or will, since these can change and fail; for all things that are changeable and capable of defect must be traced back to an immovable and self-necessary first principle, as was shown in the body of the *Article.*

2. The Active Intellect

QUESTION 85: OF THE MODE AND ORDER OF UNDERSTANDING

First Article

Whether Our Intellect Understands Corporeal and Material Things by Abstraction from Phantasms?

We Proceed Thus to the First Article:—

Objection 1. It would seem that our intellect does not understand corporeal and material things by abstraction from the phantasms. For the intellect is false if it understands an object otherwise than as it really is. Now the forms of material things do not exist as abstracted from the particular things represented by the phantasms. Therefore, if we understand material things by abstraction of the species from the phantasm, there will be error in the intellect.

Obj. 2. Further, material things are those natural things which include matter in their definition. But nothing can be understood apart from that which enters into its definition. Therefore material things cannot be understood apart from matter. Now matter is the principle of individualization. Therefore material things cannot be understood by abstraction of the universal from the particular, which is the process whereby the intelligible species is abstracted from the phantasm.

Obj. 3. Further, the Philosopher says (*De Anima* iii. 7) that the phantasm is to the intellectual soul what color is to the sight. But seeing is not caused by abstraction of species from color, but by color impressing itself on the sight. Therefore neither does the act of understanding take place by abstraction of something from the phantasm, but by the phantasm impressing itself on the intellect.

Obj. 4. Further, the Philosopher says (*De Anima* iii. 5) there are two things in the intellectual soul—the passive intellect and the active intellect. But it does not belong to the passive intellect to abstract the intelligible species from the phantasm, but to receive them when abstracted. Neither does it seem to be the function of the active intellect which is related to the phantasm, as light is to color; since light does not abstract anything from color, but rather streams on to it. Therefore in no way do we understand by abstraction from phantasms.

Obj. 5. Further, the Philosopher (*De Anima* iii. 7) says that *the intellect understands the species in the phantasm*; and not, therefore, by abstraction.

On the contrary, The Philosopher says (*De Anima* iii. 4) that *things are intelligible in proportion as they are separable from matter.* Therefore material things must needs be understood according as they are abstracted from matter and from material images, namely, phantasms.

I answer that As stated above (Q. 84, A. 7), the object of knowledge is proportionate to the power of knowledge. Now there are three grades of the cognitive powers. For one cognitive power, namely, the sense, is the act of a corporeal organ. And therefore the object of every sensitive power is a form as existing in corporeal matter. And since such matter is the principle of individuality, therefore every power of the sensitive part can only have knowledge of the individual. There is another grade of cognitive power which is neither the act of a corporeal organ, nor in any way connected with corporeal matter; such is the angelic intellect, the object of whose cognitive power is therefore a form existing apart from matter: for though angels know material things, yet they do not know them save in something immaterial, namely, either in themselves or in God. But the human intellect holds a middle place: for it is not the act of an organ; yet it is a power of the soul which is the form of the body, as is clear from what we have said above (Q. 76, A. 1). And therefore it is proper to it to know a form existing individually in corporeal matter, but not as existing in this individual matter. But to know what is in individual matter, not as existing in such matter, is to abstract the form from individual matter which is represented by the phantasms. Therefore we must needs say that our intellect understands material things by abstracting from the phantasms; and through material things thus considered we acquire some knowledge of immaterial things, just as, on the contrary, angels know material things through the immaterial.

But Plato, considering only the immateriality of the human intellect, and not its being in a way united to the body, held that the objects of the intellect are separate ideas; and that we understand not by abstraction, but by participating things abstract, as stated above (Q. 84, A. 1).

Reply Obj. 1. Abstraction may occur in two ways: First, by way of composition and division; thus we may understand that one thing does not exist in some other, or that it is separate therefrom. Secondly, by way of simple and absolute consideration; thus we understand one thing without considering the other. Thus for the intellect to abstract one from another things which are not really abstract from one another, does, in the first mode of abstraction, imply falsehood. But, in the second mode of abstraction, for the intellect to abstract things which are not really abstract from one another, does not involve falsehood, as clearly appears in the case of the senses. For if we understood or said that color is not in a colored body, or that it is separate from it, there would be error in this opinion or assertion. But if we consider color and its properties, without reference to the apple which is colored; or if we express in word what we thus understand, there is no error in such an opinion or assertion, because an apple is not essential to color, and therefore color can be understood independently of the apple. Likewise, the things which belong to the species of a material thing, such as a stone, or a man, or a horse, can be thought of apart from the individualizing principles which do not belong to the notion of the species. This is what we mean by abstracting the universal from the particular, or the intelligible species from phantasm; that is, by considering the nature of the species apart from its individual qualities represented by the phantasms. If, therefore, the intellect is said to be false when it understands a thing otherwise than as it is, that is so, if the word *otherwise* refers to the thing understood;

for the intellect is false when it understands a thing otherwise than as it is; and so the intellect would be false if it abstracted the species of a stone from its matter in such a way as to regard the species as not existing in matter, as Plato held. But it is not so, if the word *otherwise* be taken as referring to the one who understands. For it is quite true that the mode of understanding, in one who understands, is not the same as the mode of a thing in existing: since the thing understood is immaterially in the one who understands, according to the mode of the intellect, and not materially, according to the mode of a material thing.

Reply Obj. 2. Some have thought that the species of a natural thing is a form only, and that matter is not part of the species. If that were so, matter would not enter into the definition of natural things. Therefore it must be said otherwise, that matter is twofold, common, and *signate* or individual; common, such as flesh and bone; and individual, as this flesh and these bones. The intellect therefore abstracts the species of a natural thing from the individual sensible matter, but not from the common sensible matter; for example, it abstracts the species of man from *this flesh and these bones,* which do not belong to the species as such, but to the individual (*Metaph.* vii, Did. vi. 10), and need not be considered in the species: whereas the species of man cannot be abstracted by the intellect from *flesh and bones.*

Mathematical species, however, can be abstracted by the intellect from sensible matter, not only from individual, but also from common matter; not from common intelligible matter, but only from individual matter. For sensible matter is corporeal matter as subject to sensible qualities, such as being cold or hot, hard or soft, and the like: while intelligible matter is substance as subject to quantity, Now it is manifest that quantity is in substance before other sensible qualities are. Hence quantities, such as number, dimension, and figures, which are the terminations of quantity, can be considered apart from sensible qualities; and this is to abstract them from sensible matter; but they cannot be considered without understanding the substance which is subject to the quantity; for that would be to abstract them from common intelligible matter. Yet they can be considered apart from this or that substance; for that is to abstract them from individual intelligible matter. But some things can be abstracted even from common intelligible matter, such as *being unity, power, act,* and the like; all these can exist without matter, as is plain regarding immaterial things. Because Plato failed to consider the twofold kind of abstraction, as above explained (*ad* 1), he held that all those things which we have stated to be abstracted by the intellect are abstract in reality.

Reply Obj. 3. Colors, as being in individual corporeal matter, have the same mode of existence as the power of sight: and therefore they can impress their own image on the eye. But phantasms, since they are images of individuals, and exist in corporeal organs, have not the same mode of existence as the human intellect, and therefore have not the power of themselves to make an impression on the passive intellect. This is done by the power of the active intellect which by turning towards the phantasm produces in the passive intellect a certain likeness which represents, as to its specific conditions only, the thing reflected in the phantasm. It is thus that the intelligible species is said to be abstracted from the phantasm; not that the identical form which previously was in the phantasm is subsequently in the passive intellect, as a body transferred from one place to another.

Reply Obj. 4. Not only does the active intellect throw light on the phantasm: it does more; by its own power it abstracts the intelligible species from the phantasm. It throws light on the phantasm, because, just as the sensitive part acquires a greater power by its conjunction with the intellectual part, so by the power of the active intellect the phantasms are made more fit for the abstraction therefrom of intelligible intentions. Furthermore, the active intellect abstracts the intelligible species from the phantasm, forasmuch as by the power of the active intellect we are able to disregard the conditions of individuality, and to take into our consideration the specific nature, the image of which informs the passive intellect.

Reply Obj. 5. Our intellect both abstracts the intelligible species from the phantasms, inasmuch as it considers the natures of things in universal,

and, nevertheless, understands these natures in the phantasms, since it cannot understand even the things of which it abstracts the species, without turning to the phantasm, as we have said above (Q. 84, A. 7).

Second Article

Whether the Intelligible Species Abstracted from the Phantasm Is Related to Our Intellect as That Which Is Understood?

We Proceed Thus to the Second Article:—

Objection 1. It would seem that the intelligible species abstracted from the phantasm is related to our intellect as that which is understood. For the understood in act is in the one who understands: since the understood in act is the intellect itself in act. But nothing of what is understood is in the intellect actually understanding, save the abstracted intelligible species. Therefore this species is what is actually understood.

Obj. 2. Further, what is actually understood must be in something; else it would be nothing. But it is not in something outside the soul: for, since what is outside the soul is material, nothing therein can be actually understood. Therefore what is actually understood is in the intellect. Consequently it can be nothing else than the aforesaid intelligible species.

Obj. 3. Further, the Philosopher says (1 *Peri Herm.* i) that *words are signs of the passions in the soul.* But words signify the things understood, for we express by word what we understand. Therefore these passions of the soul, viz., the intelligible species, are what is actually understood.

On the contrary, The intelligible species is to the intellect what the sensible image is to the sense. But the sensible image is not what is perceived, but rather that by which sense perceives, Therefore the intelligible species is not what is actually understood, but that by which the intellect understands.

I answer that, Some have asserted that our intellectual faculties know only the impression made on them; as, for example, that sense is cognizant only of the impression made on its own organ. According to this theory, the intellect understands only its own impression namely, the intelligible species which it has received, so that this species is what is understood.

This is, however, manifestly false for two reasons. First, because the things we understand are the objects of science; therefore if what we understand is merely the intelligible species in the soul, it would follow that every science would not be concerned with objects outside the soul, but only with the intelligible species within the soul; thus, according to the teaching of the Platonists all science is about ideas, which they held to be actually understood. Secondly, it is untrue, because it would lead to the opinion of the ancients who maintained that *whatever seems, is true,* and that consequently contradictories are true simultaneously. For if the faculty knows its own impression only, it can judge of that only. Now a thing seems, according to the impression made on the cognitive faculty. Consequently the cognitive faculty will always judge of its own impression as such; and so every judgment will be true: for instance, if taste perceived only its own impression, when anyone with a healthy taste perceives that honey is sweet, he would judge truly; and if anyone with a corrupt taste perceives that honey is bitter, this would be equally true; for each would judge according to the impression on his taste. Thus every opinion would be equally true; in fact, every sort of apprehension.

Therefore it must be said that the intelligible species is related to the intellect as that by which it understands: which is proved thus. There is a twofold action (*Metaph.* ix, Did. viii. 8), one which remains in the agent; for instance, to see and to understand; and another which passes into an external object; for instance, to heat and to cut; and each of these actions proceeds in virtue of some form. And as the form from which proceeds an act tending to something external is the likeness of the object of the action, as heat in the heater is a likeness of the thing heated; so the form from which proceeds an action remaining in the agent is the likeness of the object. Hence that by which the sight sees is the likeness of the visible thing; and the likeness of the thing understood, that is, the intelligible species, is the form by which the intellect understands. But since the intellect reflects upon itself, by such reflection it understands both its own act of intelligence, and the species by which it understands. Thus the intelligible species is that which is understood secondarily; but that which is primarily understood is the object, of which the species is the likeness. This also appears from the opinion of the ancient philosophers, who said that *like is known by like.* For they said that the soul knows the earth outside itself, by the earth within itself; and so of the rest. If, therefore, we take the species of the earth instead of the earth, according to Aristotle (*De Anima* iii. 8), who says *that a stone is not in the soul, but only the likeness of the stone;* it follows that the soul knows external things by means of its intelligible species.

Reply Obj. 1. The thing understood is in the intellect by its own likeness; and it is in this sense that we say that the thing actually understood is the intellect in act, because the likeness of the thing understood is the form of the intellect, as the likeness of a sensible thing is the form of the sense in act. Hence it does not follow that the intelligible species abstracted is what is actually understood; but rather that it is the likeness thereof.

Reply Obj. 2. In these words *the thing actually understood* there is a double implication:—the thing which is understood, and the fact that it is understood. In like manner the words *abstract universal* imply two things, the nature of a thing and its abstraction or universality, Therefore the nature itself to which it occurs to be understood, abstracted or considered as universal is only in individuals; but that it is understood, abstracted or considered as universal is in the intellect. We see something similar to this in the senses. For the sight sees the color of the apple apart from its smell. If therefore it be asked where is the color which is seen apart from the smell, it is quite clear that the color which is seen is only in the apple: but that it be perceived apart from the smell, this is owing to the sight, forasmuch as the faculty of sight receives the likeness of color and not of smell. In like manner humanity understood is only in this or that man; but that humanity be apprehended without conditions of individuality, that is, that it be abstracted and consequently considered as universal, occurs to humanity inasmuch as it is brought under the consideration of the intellect, in which there is a likeness of the specific nature, but not of the principles of individuality.

Reply Obj. 3. There are two operations in the sensitive part. One, in regard of impression only, and thus the operation of the senses takes place by the senses being impressed by the sensible. The other is formation, inasmuch as the imagination forms for itself an image of an absent thing, or even of something never seen. Both of these operations are found in the intellect. For in the first place there is the passion of the passive intellect as informed by the intelligible species; and then the passive intellect thus informed forms a definition, or a division, or a composition, expressed by a word. Wherefore the concept conveyed by a word is its definition; and a proposition conveys the intellect's division or composition. Words do not therefore signify the intelligible species themselves; but that which the intellect forms for itself for the purpose of judging of external things.

3. Free Will

QUESTION 10: OF THE MANNER IN WHICH THE WILL IS MOVED

Second Article

Whether the Will Is Moved, of Necessity, by Its Object?

We Proceed Thus to the Second Article:—

Objection 1. It seems that the will is moved, of necessity, by its object. For the object of the will is compared to the will as mover to movable, as stated in *De Anima* iii. 10. But a mover, if it be sufficient, moves the movable of necessity. Therefore the will can be moved of necessity by its object.

Obj. 2. Further, just as the will is an immaterial power, so is the intellect: and both powers are ordained to a universal object, as stated above (A. 1 *ad* 3). But the intellect is moved, of necessity, by its object: therefore the will also, by its object.

Obj. 3. Further, whatever one wills, is either the end, or something ordained to an end. But, seemingly, one wills an end necessarily: because it is like the principle in speculative matters, to which principle one assents of necessity. Now the end is the reason for willing the means; and so it seems that we will the means also necessarily. Therefore the will is moved of necessity by its object.

On the contrary, The rational powers, according to the Philosopher (*Metaph.* ix. 2) are directed to opposites. But the will is a rational power, since it is in the reason, as stated in *De Anima* iii. 9. Therefore the will is directed to opposites. Therefore it is not moved, of necessity, to either of the opposites.

I answer that, The will is moved in two ways: first, as to the exercise of its act; secondly, as to the specification of its act, derived from the object. As to the first way, no object moves the will necessarily, for no matter what the object be, it is in man's power not to think of it, and consequently not to will it actually. But as to the second manner of motion, the will is moved by one object necessarily, by another not. For in the movement of a power by its object, we must consider under what aspect the object moves the power. For the visible moves the sight, under the aspect of color actually visible. Wherefore if color be offered to the sight, it moves the sight necessarily: unless one turns one's eyes away; which belongs to the exercise of the act. But if the sight were confronted with something not in all respects colored actually, but only so in some respects, and in other respects not, the sight would not of necessity see such an object: for it might look at that part of the object which is not actually colored, and thus it would not see it. Now just as the actually colored is the object of sight, so is good the object of the will. Wherefore if the will be offered an object which is good universally and from every point of view, the will tends to it of necessity, if it wills anything at all; since it cannot will the opposite. If, on the other hand, the will is offered an object that is not good from every point of view, it will not tend to it of necessity. And since lack of any good whatever, is a non-good, consequently, that good alone which is perfect and lacking in nothing, is such a good that the will cannot not-will it: and this is Happiness. Whereas any other particular goods, in so far as they are lacking in some good, can be regarded as non-goods: and from this point of view, they can be set aside or approved by the will, which can tend to one and the same thing from various points of view.

Reply Obj. 1. The sufficient mover of a power is none but that object that in every respect presents the aspect of the mover of that power. If, on the other hand, it is lacking in any respect, it will not move of necessity, as stated above.

Reply Obj. 2. The intellect is moved, of necessity, by an object, which is such as to be always and necessarily true: but not by that which may be either true or false—viz., by that which is contingent: as we have said of the good.

Reply Obj. 3. The last end moves the will necessarily, because it is the perfect good. In like manner whatever is ordained to that end, and without which the end cannot be attained, such as *to be* and *to live*, and the like. But other things without which the end can be gained, are not necessarily willed by one who wills the end: just as he who assents to the principle, does not necessarily assent to the conclusions, without which the principles can still be true.

QUESTION 13: OF CHOICE, WHICH IS AN ACT OF THE WILL WITH REGARD TO THE MEANS

Sixth Article

Whether Man Chooses of Necessity or Freely?

We Proceed Thus to the Sixth Article:—

Objection 1. It would seem that man chooses of necessity. For the end stands in relation to the object of choice, as the principle of that which

follows from the principles, as declared in *Ethic.* vii. 8. But conclusions follow of necessity from their principles. Therefore man is moved of necessity from (willing) the end to the choice (of the means).

Obj. 2. Further, as stated above (A. 1 *ad* 2), choice follows the reason's judgment of what is to be done. But reason judges of necessity about some things: on account of the necessity of the premises. Therefore it seems that choice also follows of necessity.

Obj. 3. Further, if two things are absolutely equal, man is not moved to one more than to the other; thus if a hungry man, as Plato says (cf. *De Cælo* ii. 13), be confronted on either side with two portions of food equally appetizing and at an equal distance, he is not moved towards one more than to the other; and he finds the reason of this in the immobility of the earth in the middle of the world. Now, if that which is equally (eligible) with something else cannot be chosen, much less can that be chosen which appears as less (eligible). Therefore if two or more things are available, of which one appears to be more (eligible), it is impossible to choose any of the others. Therefore that which appears to hold the first place is chosen of necessity. But every act of choosing is in regard to something that seems in some way better. Therefore every choice is made necessarily.

On the contrary, Choice is an act of a rational power; which according to the Philosopher (*Metaph.* ix. 2) stands in relation to opposites.

I answer that, Man does not choose of necessity. And this is because that which is possible not to be, is not of necessity. Now the reason why it is possible not to choose, or to choose, may be gathered from a twofold power in man. For man can will and not will, act and not act; again, he can will this or that, and do this or that. The reason of this is seated in the very power of the reason. For the will can tend to whatever the reason can apprehend as good. Now the reason can apprehend as good, not only this, viz., *to will or to act,* but also this, viz., *not to will* or *not to act.* Again, in all particular goods, the reason can consider an aspect of some good, and the lack of some good, which has the aspect of evil: and in this respect, it can apprehend any single one of such goods as to be chosen or to be avoided. The perfect good alone, which is Happiness, cannot be apprehended by the reason as an evil, or as lacking in any way. Consequently man wills Happiness of necessity, nor can he will not to be happy, or to be unhappy. Now since choice is not of the end, but of the means, as stated above (A. 3); it is not of the perfect good, which is Happiness, but of other particular goods. Therefore man chooses not of necessity, but freely.

Reply Obj. 1. The conclusion does not always of necessity follow from the principles, but only when the principles cannot be true if the conclusion is not true. In like manner, the end does not always necessitate in man the choosing of the means, because the means are not always such

that the end cannot be gained without them; or, if they be such, they are not always considered in that light.

Reply Obj. 2. The reason's decision or judgment of what is to be done is about things that are contingent and possible to us. In such matters the conclusions do not follow of necessity from principles that are absolutely necessary but from such as are so conditionally; as, for instance, *If he runs, he is in motion.*

Reply Obj. 3. If two things be proposed as equal under one aspect, nothing hinders us from considering in one of them some particular point of superiority, so that the will has a bent towards that one rather than towards the other.

4. The Natural Law

QUESTION 94: OF THE NATURAL LAW

Second Article

Whether the Natural Law Contains Several Precepts, or One Only?

We Proceed Thus to the Second Article:—

Objection 1. It would seem that the natural law contains, not several precepts, but one only. For law is a kind of precept, as stated above (Q. 92, A. 2). If therefore there were many precepts of the natural law, it would follow that there are also many natural laws.

Obj. 2. Further, the natural law is consequent to human nature. But human nature, as a whole, is one; though, as to its parts, it is manifold. Therefore, either there is but one precept of the law of nature, on account of the unity of nature as a whole; or there are many, by reason of the number of parts of human nature. The result would be that even things relating to the inclination of the concupiscible faculty belong to the natural law.

Obj. 3. Further, law is something pertaining to reason, as stated above (Q. 90, A. 1). Now reason is

but one in man. Therefore there is only one precept of the natural law.

On the contrary, The precepts of the natural law in man stand in relation to practical matters, as the first principles to matters of demonstration. But there are several first indemonstrable principles. Therefore there are also several precepts of the natural law.

I answer that, As stated above (Q. 91, A. 3), the precepts of the natural law are to the practical reason, what the first principles of demonstrations are to the speculative reason; because both are self-evident principles. Now a thing is said to be self-evident in two ways: first, in itself; secondly, in relation to us. Any proposition is said to be selfevident in itself, its predicate is contained in the notion of the subject: although, to one who knows not the definition of the subject, it happens that such a proposition is not self-evident. For instance, this proposition, *Man is a rational being,* is, in its very nature, self-evident, since who says *man,* says a *rational being:* and yet to one who knows not what a man is, this proposition is not self-evident. Hence it is that, as Boethius says (*De Hebdom.*), certain axioms or propositions are universally self-evident to all; and such are those propositions whose terms are known to all, as, *Every whole is greater than its part,* and, *Things equal to one and the same are equal to one another.* But some propositions are self-evident only to the wise, who understand the meaning of the terms of such propositions: thus to one who understands that an angel is not a body, it is self-evident that an angel is not circumscriptively in a place: but this is not evident to the unlearned, for they cannot grasp it.

Now a certain order is to be found in those things that are apprehended universally. For that which, before aught else, falls under apprehension, is *being,* the notion of which is included in all things whatsoever a man apprehends. Wherefore the first indemonstrable principle is that *the same thing cannot be affirmed and denied at the same time,* which is based on the notion of being and not-being: and on this principle all others are based, as is stated in *Metaph.* iv, text. 9. Now as being is the first thing that falls under the apprehension simply, so *good* is the first thing that falls under the apprehension of the practical reason, which is directed to action: since every agent acts for an end under the aspect of good. Consequently the first principle in the practical reason is one founded on the notion of good, viz., that *good is that which all things seek after.* Hence this is the first precept of law, that *good is to be done and pursued, and evil is to be avoided.* All other precepts of the natural law are based upon this: so that whatever the practical reason naturally apprehends as man's good (or evil) belongs to the precepts of the natural law as something to be done or avoided.

Since, however, good has the nature of an end, and evil, the nature of a contrary, hence it is that all those things to which man has a natural inclination, are naturally apprehended by reason as being good, and consequently as objects of pursuit, and their contraries as evil, and objects of avoidance. Wherefore according to the order of natural inclinations, is the order of the precepts of the natural law. Because in man there is first of all an inclination to good in accordance with the nature which he has in common with all substances: inasmuch as every substance seeks the preservation of its own being, according to its nature: and by reason of this inclination, whatever is a means of preserving human life, and of warding off its obstacles, belongs to the natural law. Secondly, there is in man an inclination to things that pertain to him more specially, according to that nature which he has in common with other animals: and in virtue of this inclination, those things are said to belong to the natural law, *which nature has taught to all animals,* such as sexual intercourse, education of offspring and so forth. Thirdly, there is in man an inclination to good, according to the nature of his reason, which nature is proper to him: thus man has a natural inclination to know the truth about God, and to live in society: and in this respect, whatever pertains to this inclination belongs to the natural law; for instance, to shun ignorance, to avoid offending those among whom one has to live, and other such things regarding the above inclination.

Reply Obj. 1. All these precepts of the law of nature have the character of one natural law, inasmuch as they flow from one first precept.

Reply Obj. 2. All the inclinations of any parts whatsoever of human nature, *e.g.,* of the concupiscible and irascible parts, in so far as they are ruled by reason, belong to the natural law, and are reduced to one first precept, as stated above: so that the precepts of the natural law are many in themselves, but are based on one common foundation.

Reply Obj. 3. Although reason is one in itself, yet it directs all things regarding man; so that whatever can be ruled by reason, is contained under the law of reason.

Fourth Article

Whether the Natural Law Is the Same in All Men?

We Proceed Thus to the Fourth Article:—

Objection 1. It would seem that the natural law is not the same in all. For it is stated in the Decretals (*Dist.* i) that *the natural law is that which is contained in the Law and the Gospel.* But this is not common to all men: because, as it is written (Rom. x, 16), *all do not obey the gospel.* Therefore the natural law is not the same in all men.

Obj. 2. Further, *Things which are accordingly to the law are said to be just,* as stated in *Ethic.* v. But it is stated in the same book that nothing is so universally just as not to be subject to change in regard to some men. Therefore even the natural law is not the same in all men.

Obj. 3. Further, as stated above (AA. 2, 3), to the natural law belongs everything to which a man is inclined according to his nature. Now different men are naturally inclined to different things; some to the desire of pleasures, others to the desire of honors, and other men to other things. Therefore there is not one natural law for all.

On the contrary, Isidore says (*Etym.* v. 4): *The natural law is common to all nations.*

I answer that, As stated above (AA. 2, 3), to the natural law belongs those things to which a man is inclined naturally: and among these it is proper to man to be inclined to act according to reason. Now the process of reason is from the common to the proper, as stated in *Phys.* i. The speculative reason, however, is differently situated in this matter, from the practical reason. For, since the speculative reason is busied chiefly with necessary things, which cannot be otherwise than they are, its proper conclusions, like the universal principles, contain the truth without fail. The practical reason, on the other hand, is busied with contingent matters, about which human actions are concerned: and consequently, although there is necessity in the general principles, the more we descend to matters of detail, the more frequently we encounter defects. Accordingly then in speculative matters truth is the same in all men, both as to principles and as to conclusions: although the truth is not known to all as regards the conclusions, but only as regards the principles which are called *common notions.* But in matters of action, truth or practical rectitude is not the same for all, as to matters of detail, but only as to the general principles: and where there is the same rectitude in matters of detail, it is not equally known to all.

It is therefore evident that, as regards the general principles whether of speculative or of practical reason, truth or rectitude is the same for all, and is equally known by all. As to the proper conclusions of the speculative reason, the truth is the same for all, but is not equally known to all: thus it is true for all that the three angles of a triangle are together equal to two right angles, although it is not known to all. But as to the proper conclusions of the practical reason, neither is the truth or rectitude the same for all, nor, where it is the same, is it equally known by all. Thus it is right and true for all to act according to reason: and from this principle it follows as a proper conclusion, that goods entrusted to another should be restored to their owner. Now this is true for the majority of cases: but it may happen in a particular case that it would be injurious, and therefore unreasonable, to restore goods held in trust; for instance if they are claimed for the purpose of fighting against one's country. And this principle will be found to fail the more, according as we descend further into detail, e.g., if one were to say that goods held in trust should be restored with such and such a guarantee, or in such and such a way; because the greater the number of conditions added, the greater the number of ways in which the principle may fail, so that it be not right to restore or not to restore.

Consequently we must say that the natural law, as to general principles, is the same for all, both as to rectitude and as to knowledge. But as to certain matters of detail, which are conclusions, as it were, of those general principles, it is the same for all in the majority of cases, both as to rectitude and as to knowledge; and yet in some few cases it may fail, both as to rectitude, by reason of certain obstacles (just as natures subject to generation and corruption fail in some few cases on account of some obstacle), and as to knowledge, since in some the reason is perverted by passion, or evil habit, or an evil disposition of nature; thus formerly, theft, although it is expressly contrary to the natural law, was not considered wrong among the Germans, as Julius Caesar relates (*De Bello Gall.* vi).

Reply Obj. 1. The meaning of the sentence quoted is not that whatever is contained in the Law and the Gospel belongs to the natural law, since they contain many things that are above nature; but that whatever belongs to the natural law is fully contained in them. Wherefore Gratian, after saying that *the natural law is what is contained in the Law and the Gospel,* adds at once, by way of example, *by which everyone is commanded to do to others as he would be done by.*

Reply Obj. 2. The saying of the Philosopher is to be understood of things that are naturally just, not as general principles, but as conclusions drawn from them, having rectitude in the majority of cases, but failing in a few.

Reply Obj. 3. As, in man, reason rules and commands the other powers, so all the natural inclinations belonging to the other powers must needs be directed according to reason. Wherefore it is universally right for all men, that all their inclinations should be directed according to reason.

Fifth Article

Whether the Natural Law Can Be Changed?

We Proceed Thus to the Fifth Article:—

Objection 1. It would seem that the natural law can be changed. Because on Ecclus. xvii. 9, *He gave them instructions, and the law of life,* the gloss says: *He wished the law of the letter to be written, in order to correct the law of nature.* But that which is corrected is changed. Therefore the natural law can be changed.

Obj. 2. Further, the slaying of the innocent, adultery, and theft are against the natural law. But we find these things changed by God: as when God commanded Abraham to slay his innocent son (Gen. xxii. 2); and when he ordered the Jews to borrow and purloin the vessels of the Egyptians (Exod. xii. 35); and when He commanded Osee to take to himself *a wife of fornications* (Osee i. 2). Therefore the natural law can be changed.

Obj. 3. Further, Isidore says (*Etym.* v. 4) that *the possession of all things in common, and universal freedom, are matters of natural law.* But these things are seen to be changed by human laws. Therefore it seems that the natural law is subject to change.

On the contrary, It is said in the Decretals (*Dist.* v): *The natural law dates from the creation of the rational creature. It does not vary according to time, but remains unchangeable.*

I answer that, A change in the natural law may be understood in two ways. First, by way of addition. In this sense nothing hinders the natural law from being changed; since many things for the benefit of human life have been added over and above the natural law, both by the Divine law and by human laws.

Secondly, a change in the natural law may be understood by way of subtraction, so that what previously was according to the natural law, ceases to be so. In this sense, the natural law is altogether unchangeable in its first principles: but in its secondary principles, which, as we have said (A. 4), are certain detailed proximate conclusions drawn from the first principles, the natural law is not changed so that what it prescribes be not right in most cases. But it may be changed in some particular cases of rare occurrence, through some special causes hindering the observance of such precepts, as stated above (A. 4).

Reply Obj. 1. The written law is said to be given for the correction of the natural law, either because it supplies what was wanting to the natural law; or because the natural law was perverted in the hearts of some men, as to certain matters, so that they esteemed those things good which are naturally evil; which perversion stood in need of correction.

Reply Obj. 2. All men alike, both guilty and innocent, die the death of nature: which death of nature is inflicted by the power of God on account of original sin, according to 1 Kings ii. 6: *The Lord killeth and maketh alive.* Consequently, by the command of God, death can be inflicted on any man, guilty or innocent, without any injustice whatever.—In like manner adultery is intercourse with another's wife; who is allotted to him by the law emanating from God. Consequently intercourse with any woman, by the command of God, is neither adultery nor fornication.—The same applies to theft, which is the taking of another's property. For whatever is taken by the command of God, to Whom all things belong, is not taken against the will of its owner, whereas it is in this that theft consists.—Nor is it only in human things, that whatever is commanded by God is right; but also in natural things, whatever is done by God, is, in some way, natural, as stated in the First Part (Q. 105, A. 6 *ad* 1).

Reply Obj. 3. A thing is said to belong to the natural law in two ways. First, because nature inclines thereto: *e.g.,* that one should not do harm to another. Secondly, because nature did not bring in the contrary: thus we might say that for man to be naked is of the natural law, because nature did not give him clothes, but art invented them. In this sense, *the possession of all things in common and universal freedom* are said to be of the natural law, because, to wit, the distinction of possessions and slavery were not brought in by nature, but devised by human reason for the benefit of human life. Accordingly the law of nature was not changed in this respect, except by addition.

QUESTION 95: OF HUMAN LAW

First Article

Whether It Was Useful for Laws to Be Framed by Men?

We Proceed Thus to the First Article:—

Objection 1. It would seem that it was not useful for laws to be framed by men. Because the purpose of every law is that man be made good thereby, as stated above (Q. 92, A.1), But men are more to be induced to be good willingly by means of admonitions, than against their will, by means of laws. Therefore there was no need to frame laws.

Obj. 2. Further, as the Philosopher says (*Ethic.* v. 4), *men have recourse to a judge as to animate justice.* But animate justice is better than inanimate justice, which is contained in laws. Therefore it would have been better for the execution of justice to be entrusted to the decision of judges, than to frame laws in addition.

Obj. 3. Further, every law is framed for the direction of human actions, as is evident from what has been stated above (Q. 90, AA. 1, 2). But since human actions are about singulars, which are infinite in number, matters pertaining to the direction of human actions cannot be taken into sufficient consideration except by a wise man, who looks into each one of them. Therefore it would have been better for human acts to be directed by the judgment of wise men, than by the framing of laws. Therefore there was no need of human laws.

On the contrary, Isidore says (*Etym.* v. 20): *Laws were made that in fear thereof human audacity might be held in check, that innocence might be safeguarded in*

the midst of wickedness, and that the dread of punishment might prevent the wicked from doing harm. But these things are most necessary to mankind. Therefore it was necessary that human laws should be made.

I answer that, As stated above (Q. 63, A. 1; Q. 94, A. 3), man has a natural aptitude for virtue; but the perfection of virtue must be acquired by man by means of some kind of training. Thus we observe that man is helped by industry in his necessities, for instance, in food and clothing. Certain beginnings of these he has from nature, viz., his reason and his hands; but he has not the full complement, as other animals have, to whom nature has given sufficiency of clothing and food. Now it is difficult to see how man could suffice for himself in the matter of this training: since the perfection of virtue consists chiefly in withdrawing man from undue pleasures, to which above all man is inclined, and especially the young, who are more capable of being trained. Consequently a man needs to receive this training from another, whereby to arrive at the perfection of virtue. And as to those young people who are inclined to acts of virtue, by their good natural disposition, or by custom, or rather by the gift of God, paternal training suffices, which is by admonitions. But since some are found to be depraved, and prone to vice, and not easily amenable to words, it was necessary for such to be restrained from evil by force and fear, in order that, at least, they might desist from evil-doing, and leave others in peace, and that they themselves, by being habituated in this way, might be brought to do willingly what hitherto they did from fear, and thus become virtuous. Now this kind of training, which compels through fear of punishment, is the discipline of laws. Therefore, in order that man might have peace and virtue, it was necessary for laws to be framed: for, as the Philosopher says (Polit. i. 2), *as man is the most noble of animals if he be perfect in virtue, so is he the lowest of all, if he be severed from law and righteousness;* because man can use his reason to devise means of satisfying his lusts and evil passions, which other animals are unable to do.

Reply Obj. 1. Men who are well disposed are led willingly to virtue by being admonished better than by coercion: but men who are evilly disposed are not led to virtue unless they are compelled.

Reply Obj. 2. As the Philosopher says (*Rhet.* i. 1), *it is better that all things be regulated by law, than left to be decided by judges: and this for three reasons. First, because it is easier to find a few wise men competent to frame right laws, than to find the many who would be necessary to judge aright of each single case.—Secondly, because those who make laws consider long beforehand what laws to make; whereas judgment on each single case has to be pronounced as soon as it arises:* and it is easier for man to see what is right, by taking many instances into consideration, than by considering one solitary fact.—Thirdly, because lawgivers judge in the abstract and of future events; whereas whose who sit in judgment judge of things present, towards which they are affected by love, hatred, or some kind of cupidity; wherefore their judgment is perverted.

Since then the animated justice of the judge is not found in every man, and since it can be deflected, therefore it was necessary, whenever possible, for the law to determine how to judge, and for very few matters to be left to the decision of men.

Reply Obj. 3. Certain individual facts which cannot be covered by the law *have necessarily to be committed to judges,* as the Philosopher says in the same passage: for instance, *concerning something that has happened or not happened,* and the like.

Second Article

Whether Every Human Law Is Derived from the Natural Law?

We Proceed Thus to the Second Article:—

Objection 1. It would seem that not every human law is derived from the natural law. For the Philosopher says (*Ethic.* v. 7) that *the legal just is that which originally was a matter of indifference.* But those things which arise from the natural law are not matters of indifference. Therefore the enactments of human laws are not all derived from the natural law.

Obj. 2. Further, positive law is contrasted with natural law, as stated by Isidore (*Etym.* v. 4) and

the Philosopher (*Ethic.* v, *loc. cit.*). But those things which flow as conclusion from the general principles of the natural law belong to the natural law, as stated above (Q. 94, A. 4). Therefore that which is established by human law does not belong to the natural law.

Obj. 3. Further, the law of nature is the same for all; since the Philosopher says (*Ethic.* v. 7) *that the natural just is that which is equally valid everywhere,* If therefore human laws were derived from the natural law, it would follow that they too are the same for all: which is clearly false.

Obj. 4. Further, it is possible to give a reason for things which are derived from the natural law. But *it is not possible to give the reason for all the legal enactments of the lawgivers,* as the jurist says. Therefore not all human laws are derived from the natural law.

On the contrary, Tully says (*Rhetor.* ii): *Things which emanated from nature and were approved by custom, were sanctioned by fear and reverence for the laws.*

I answer that, As Augustine says (*De Lib. Arb.* i. 5), *that which is not just seems to be no law at all: wherefore the force of a law depends on the extent of its justice. Now in human affairs a thing is said to be just, from being right, according to the rule of reason. But the first rule of reason is the law of nature, as is clear from what has been stated above* (Q. 91, A. 2 *ad* 2). Consequently every human law has just so much of the nature of law, as it is derived from the law of nature. But if in any point it deflects from the law of nature, it is no longer a law but a perversion of law.

But it must be noted that something may be derived from the natural law in two ways: first, as a conclusion from premises, secondly, by way of determination of certain generalities. The first way is like to that by which, in sciences, demonstrated conclusions are drawn from the principles: while the second mode is likened to that whereby, in the arts, general forms are particularized as to details: thus the craftsman needs to determine the general form of a house to some particular shape. Some things are therefore derived from the general principles of the natural law, by way of conclusions; *e.g.,* that *one must not kill* may be derived as a conclusion from the principle that one should do harm to no man: while some are derived therefrom by way of determination; *e.g.,* the law of nature has it that the evil-doer should be punished; but that he be punished in this or that way, is a determination of the law of nature.

Accordingly both modes of derivation are found in the human law. But those things which are derived in the first way, are contained in human law not as emanating therefrom exclusively, but have some force from the natural law also. But those things which are derived in the second way, have no other force than that of human law.

Reply Obj. 1. The Philosopher is speaking of those enactments which are by way of determination or specification of the precepts of the natural law.

Reply Obj. 2. This argument avails for those things that are derived from the natural law, by way of conclusions.

Reply Obj. 3. The general principles of the natural law cannot be applied to all men in the same way on account of the great variety of human affairs: and hence arises the diversity of positive laws among various people.

Reply Obj. 4. These words of the Jurist are to be understood as referring to decisions of rulers in determining particular points of the natural law: on which determinations the judgment of expert and prudent men is based as on its principles; in so far, to wit, as they see at once what is the best thing to decide.

Hence the Philosopher says (*Ethic.* vi. 11) that in such matters, *we ought to pay as much attention to the undemonstrated sayings and opinions of persons who surpass us in experience, age and prudence, as to their demonstrations.*

5. The Nature of the Soul

Second Article

Whether the Human Soul Is Something Subsistent?

We Proceed Thus to the Second Article:—

Objection 1. It would seem that the human soul is not something subsistent. For that which subsists is said to be *this particular thing.* Now *this particular thing* is said not of the soul, but of that which is composed of soul and body. Therefore the soul is not something subsistent.

Obj. 2. Further, everything subsistent operates. But the soul does not operate; for, as the Philosopher says (*De Anima* i. 4), *to say that the soul feels or understands is like saying that the soul weaves or builds.* Therefore the soul is not subsistent.

Obj. 3. Further, if the soul were subsistent, it would have some operation apart from the body. But it has no operation apart from the body, not even that of understanding: for the act of understanding does not take place without a phantasm, which cannot exist apart from the body. Therefore the human soul is not something subsistent.

On the contrary, Augustine says (*de Trin.* x. 7): *Whoever understands that the nature of the soul is that of a substance and not that of a body, will see that those who maintain the corporeal nature of the soul, are led astray through associating with the soul those things without which they are unable to think of any nature— i.e., imaginary pictures of the corporal things.* Therefore the nature of the human intellect is not only incorporeal, but it is also a substance, that is, something subsistent.

I answer that, It must necessarily be allowed that the principle of intellectual operation which we call the soul, is a principle both incorporeal and subsistent. For it is clear that by means of the intellect man can have knowledge of all corporeal things. Now whatever knows certain things cannot have any of them in its own nature; because that which is in it naturally would impede the knowledge of anything else. Thus we observe that a sick man's tongue being vitiated by a feverish and bitter humor, is insensible to anything sweet and everything seems bitter to it. Therefore if the intellectual principle contained the nature of a body it would be unable to know all bodies. Now every body has its own determinate nature. Therefore it is impossible for the intellectual principle to be a body. It is likewise impossible for it to understand by means of a bodily organ; since the determinate nature of that organ would impede knowledge of all bodies; as when a certain determinate color is not only in the pupil of the eye, but also in a glass vase, the liquid in the vase seems to be of that same color.

Therefore the intellectual principle which we call the mind or the intellect has the operation *per se* apart from the body. Now only that which subsists can have an operation *per se*. For nothing can operate but what is actual: wherefore a thing operates according as it is; for which reason we do not say that heat imparts heat, but that what is hot gives heat. We must conclude, therefore, that the human soul, which is called the intellect or the mind, is something incorporeal and subsistent.

Reply Obj. 1. *This particular thing* can be taken in two senses. Firstly, for anything subsistent; secondly, for that which subsists, and is complete in a specific nature. The former sense excludes the inherence of an accident or of a material form; the latter excludes also the imperfection of the part, so that a hand can be called *this particular thing* in the first sense, but not in the second. Therefore as the human soul is a part of human nature, it can indeed be called *this particular thing,* in the first sense, as being something subsistent; but not in the

second, for in this sense, what is composed of body and soul is said to *this particular thing.*

Reply Obj. 2 Aristotle wrote those words as expressing not his own opinion, but the opinion of those who said that to understand is to be moved, as is clear from the context. Or we may reply that to operate *per se* belongs to what exists *per se*. But for a thing to exist *per se*, it suffices sometimes that it be not inherent, as an accident or a material form; even though it be part of something. Nevertheless, that is rightly said to subsist *per se* which is neither inherent in the above sense nor part of anything else. In this sense, the eye or the hand cannot be said to subsist *per se;* nor can it for that reason be said to operate *per se*. Hence the operation of the parts is through each part attributed to the whole. For we say that the man sees with the eye, and feels with the hand and, and not in the same sense as when we say that what is hot gives heat by its heat; for heat, strictly speaking, does not give heat. We may therefore say that the soul understands, as the eye sees; but it is more correct to say that man understands through the soul.

Reply Obj. 3. The body is necessary for intellect, not as its origin of action, but on the part of the object; for the phantasm is to the intellect what color is to the sight. Neither does such a dependence on the body prove the intellect to be non-subsistent; otherwise it would follow that an animal is not subsistent, since it requires external objects of the senses in order to perform its act of perception.

Study Questions

1. What change does Aquinas make to the view of reality developed by Aristotle?

2. Explain what Aquinas means when he says that we describe God by analogy with human beings.

3. What is "abstraction," and how does Aquinas use this concept to explain the formation of general ideas?

4. What is the natural law, and how does Aquinas use it as a basis for criticizing human laws?

5. Explain how Aquinas reconciles the apparently contrary beliefs that the soul is the form of the body and the soul is a spiritual substance.

Chapter 5

The Ghost in the Machine: René Descartes

Introduction

The period of modern philosophy dates from around 1600 to 1900. The French philosopher, René Descartes, is often called the "father" of modern philosophy. Just as Plato set the tone for ancient Greek philosophy, Descartes' approach to the subject matter and the method of philosophy was to determine the major problems and strategies of European philosophy for the next three centuries and beyond.

In 1596, Descartes was born in a small town in central France, then called La Haye and now called Descartes. He was educated through his teens at a Jesuit school, where he was exposed to mathematics and medieval philosophy. He later studied law and served in the military, where he spent much of his spare time studying philosophy. After leaving military service, he devoted the rest of his short life to science and philosophy, while living on a small inherited income. Because of his philosophical renown, and because she was interested in philosophy, he was invited to the court of Queen Christina of Sweden, to instruct her. Unfortunately, he died there of pneumonia in the cold Swedish winter of 1650.

Descartes' world was in the process of undergoing great change. Religion and politics witnessed the weakening of the centralized power of the popes, and the establishment of nation-states. Much of the impetus behind this was the Protestant Reformation, led especially by Martin Luther and John Calvin. They had sparked the formation of groups of Christians who separated from the authority of Rome and formed their own denominations, with their own interpretations of scripture and its demands. This led to the Counterreformation of the Catholic Church, and thirty years of war among various countries who were supporters of one Christian denomination or another.

In addition to the unraveling of the centralized political power of Rome and its ensuing chaos, Descartes was also heir to the fruits of the Renaissance period (1450–1600), which included a rebirth of classical Greek and Roman art and architecture, and a new faith in the use of human reason to discover the truths of nature and philosophy. Of particular importance was the emergence of a new way of knowing the world that was neither philosophical nor theological, and depended only upon the twin authorities of observation and reason. This new way of knowing was called science, science as we know it today.

Great discoveries already had been made in what were then the emerging sciences of physics, astronomy, and medicine. Copernicus (1473–1543) and Kepler (1571–1630) led the way in astronomy. Some of their ideas were further developed by Galileo (1564–1642), whose discoveries also established the basis for modern physics, and paved the way for Isaac Newton (1642–1727), who was born in the very year that Galileo died. Others who made significant scientific contributions included William Harvey (1578–1657), who discovered the mechanism of the circulatory system, and Robert Boyle (1627–1691), who would lay the foundations of modern chemistry. By the end of the seventeenth century, knowledge of the world was no longer seen by the enlightened to be the province of philosophers and theologians. Instead, it was seen as something to be discovered by scientists. The scientific method of careful observation, discovery of general laws, and the mathematical description of these laws simply worked. With the discovery of scientific method, Descartes and others of his time believed deeply and enthusiatically that the key to unlocking the secrets of nature at last had been found.

Descartes himself was a scientist. Though he worked in physics, he was primarily a mathematician. His greatest contribution to mathematics was his discovery of analytic geometry (think of "cartesian" coordinates). Though he was dedicated to the emergence of the new sciences, he was also interested in philosophy. He believed that just as science was unlocking the secrets of nature, the use of its method could also unlock the secrets of philosophy. In keeping with the exciting spirit of the times, Descartes believed that especially three of the most elusive philosophical questions could be answered with certitude, once and for all, if only the correct method was used to investigate them. These questions concerned the existence of God, the nature of the self, and the nature of the world.

In discussing and writing about scientific and philosophical matters, however, Descartes had to be careful. The forces of religion were still powerful within the countries in which they were officially adopted, both those of Catholicism and those of Protestantism. Many religious leaders believed that the Christian worldview, even religion itself, was threatened by the new science. The Catholic Church had already suppressed some of the ideas of Galileo and Kepler. In the eyes of religion, the new science appeared to undermine doctrines which, at the time, seemed essential to the Christian view of the world, doctrines such as the view that the Earth was the center of the solar system. How could humans be the center of God's creation, after all, if the Earth was not the geographical center of the universe?

Questions such as these were concrete examples of the clash between religion and science about which Descartes was very conscious. As a Catholic in Catholic France, he was still subject to the authority of the Church. He knew that it had the power to suppress his ideas and even to imprison him. He also knew that the Church was wary of anyone adopting the scientific method to study philosophical issues. One reason for their concern, in addition to the disturbing discoveries of Copernicus, Kepler, and Galileo, was what a British contemporary of Descartes, Thomas Hobbes (1588–1679), had to say. Hobbes, who was not subject to the authority of the Catholic Church, argued on the basis of scientific observation and reason that there is no soul, no free will, and that reality, including human beings, is composed entirely of atoms. In addition, he claimed that nature works as it does solely as a result of mechanical forces, not by any internal teleological urges on the part of natural objects to reach perfection. For Hobbes, the world is a mechanical system, like a watch, where things are rigidly determined to happen as they do because of previous events. Now, if these were the dramatic changes in understanding ourselves and the world that the new science led to, then the Church would surely be interested in what Descartes had to say about the same matters.

Worldview

Any discussion of human nature would be incomplete without a discussion of human *knowledge.* Knowing, after all, is one of the most basic universal traits of all human beings. For modern philosophers, knowledge is important for other reasons as well. While they discussed the whole range of philosophical problems, modern philosophers were especially interested in understanding the origin, nature, extent and justification of knowledge. In the Modern period philosophers began asking such questions as, How do I know that I know?, How much can I know?, and Where does my knowledge come from?

The Influence of Science

One reason for this focus on knowledge is that there were several types of knowledge available; commonsense knowledge, philosophy, theology, and science were all presented as various ways to understand the world around us. Sometimes, however, they gave different accounts of what is real. So it was important to discover which sort of knowledge is most reliable, which way of understanding the world most closely reflects the way that the world really is. For people like Hobbes and Descartes, this was not the most important reason for studying knowledge, since they had already made their minds up and simply assumed that science was the most reliable type of knowledge. Their task was to understand why it worked so well and thus to understand the essence of reliable knowledge itself. However, the task was not that simple, since scientific knowledge has more than one central component, and there were disagreements about which of these was primary.

Think of science less as a list of true statements about the world, and more as a method of knowing. The scientific method has several components. For convenience we may divide these into two, observation and theory. Some say that the heart of science lies in its careful observations. Scientists are much more careful about their observations than we are in our daily lives. From their observations and careful measurements of individual events, scientists form generalizations that are called the laws of science. The law of gravity, for example, which says that "All objects fall at 32'/second squared" (minus air friction), was discovered after carefully observing and measuring individual falling bodies of various sorts. The generalization involved from these individual observations is a process of reasoning called **inductive generalization.** Here it is argued that if all objects observed thus far fall at this rate, then all objects fall at this rate, even the ones not observed thus far. To see scientific method as primarily inductive, is to see it as based on observation and inductive generalization.

Many modern philosophers who saw science as the paradigm case of what it means to know something about the world, did indeed focus on the inductive part of science as its most important part. The secret of the success of science, they believed, was to be found in its careful observations. They then argued that all reliable knowledge of the world must be based on experience and the inferences that we may make on the basis of experience. Some of the most famous of these philosophers of the Modern period were the **British Empiricists.** They included the English philosopher, John Locke (1632–1704), the Irish philosopher and Anglican Bishop, George Berkeley (1685–1753), and the Scottish philosopher, David Hume (1711–1776). Empiricists believe that there is no knowledge of the world that is not based upon sense experience. If we cannot see, hear, taste, touch, or smell something, then we cannot know anything about it.

In contrast to the empiricist philosophers stand the rationalists, among whom we find Descartes. **Rationalists** believe that the part of science which lets us in on the nature of reality is theory, not observation. Theories try to explain why the things that we observe behave as they do. In constructing a theory, scientists often create hypotheses about objects that cannot be observed. For example, to explain why the pressure increases in a fixed volume of gas when the temperature increases, scientists say that gases are composed of molecules that move more rapidly when energy (heat in this case) is added to them, thus increasing the force with which they crash into the walls of the container that holds them. In addition to making assumptions about objects that cannot be observed, scientists use mathematical systems to describe these unobservable objects and their behavior. Mathematics is the language of science, especially of physics. For those who believe that the theories constructed by the mind tell us more about reality than observations do, the mathematics used to describe these theories is what truly mirrors reality.

Plato is often classified as a rationalist, focusing as he does on the power of reason over the senses; while Aristotle is often viewed as an empiricist by contrast. Descartes followed the lead of Plato in many ways in the construction of his views. He agreed with Plato, for example, that human beings are composed of both a spiritual substance (a mind or soul) and a physical substance (a body). He also agreed that we are born with innate ideas which mirror reality much more accurately than the senses do. Finally, Descartes followed Plato in believing that mathematics gave a truer account of reality than observation. That the new sciences were a very successful way to understand the world, Descartes attributed especially to their use of mathematics to describe its workings. He was deeply impressed with the certitude to be found in mathematics, especially when compared to the many disagreements found in philosophy. He wished that philosophers could answer their questions with the same degree of certitude that mathematicians answered theirs. They could, he thought, if only they used the right method.

The Influence of Mathematics

For Descartes, the right method for gaining philosophical knowledge is the one used by the theory construction part of science, especially its use of mathematics. His view of any reliable knowledge, including philosophical knowledge, is modeled on mathematical knowledge. So if we can discover how mathematical knowledge is developed and justified, we will be on our way to discovering what Descartes believed to be the correct philosophical method. The first thing to say is that mathematical systems are constructed by beginning with **axioms.** Axioms are statements that are not proven, but simply taken to be true. They are the starting points of a mathematical system of knowledge. They are not known to be true either by observation or by a process of reasoning. Instead, for Descartes, axioms are known to be true by the light of reason; our minds simply "see" that they are true.

For example, "Parallel lines never meet," or "The whole is greater than or equal to the sum of its parts," are not statements known to be true because we have observed all parallel lines or counted the parts of every whole. Axioms need no evidence to support them. They are "self-evident." Our mind or reason simply understands that they are true and could not possibly be false. We know that axioms are true by reason, by the light of the mind that "sees" that they could not be false, that they are "indubitable." Let us call such a mental act of understanding the truth of self-evident, indubitable axioms, **rational intuition.** At the heart of rationalism lies the belief that at least some truths about the world may be discovered by rational intuition. Rationalists reject entirely the empiricist belief that *all* knowledge arises through observation.

Mathematical systems consist not only of axioms, but also of the **theorems** that follow from these axioms. Think of axioms as premises in valid deductive arguments, and theorems as the conclusions of these arguments. A valid **deductive argument** is a process of reasoning in which the conclusion must be true if the premises are true. For example, if it is true that "All human beings are going to die," and that "Socrates is a human being," then it follows necessarily that "Socrates is going to die," as well. Deductive arguments differ from inductive ones in many ways. For our present purpose of discussing the role of arguments in science, it is best to think of inductive arguments as inferences from many particular observations of an event of a certain type to a conclusion that states something about *all* events of that type. Since it is never certain if our experience of something thus far will remain the same for future cases, conclusions of inductive arguments are given as likely to be true, or as probable. If we conclude that "All swans are white" on the basis of many past experiences of white swans, for example, our conclusion nevertheless could be wrong. In fact, black swans have been discovered in Australia.

The arguments found within mathematics are all deductive. In these arguments the truth of theorems follows with certitude, not probability, from the truths of axioms. After a theorem is proven it may then serve as a premise in additional arguments in order to prove further theorems, until an entire system of mathematical knowledge is constructed. So mathematical systems such as algebra, geometry, calculus, and any number of other systems, develop by reasoning from axioms to further mathematical truths. The important point for us is that every belief in such a system has the same degree of certainty as the axioms from which it began to grow. The key to finding certain knowledge, the kind that Descartes is confident that philosophy can finally acquire, is not to base knowledge on observations which may be incorrect, but rather to find self-evident axioms that will serve as a foundation for the rest. What makes a belief an axiom in mathematics is that its truth is self-evident. The test for its being self-evident is that there is no way to doubt its truth.

Using this criterion of indubitability, Descartes went in search of truths outside of mathematics that were just as immune from doubt as those found in mathematics. His search was for indubitable truths that would serve as axioms in a system of philosophical beliefs. They would be the foundation upon which philosophical knowledge would be built. His method was the **method of doubt,** which required that he accept something as true only if it could not possibly be doubted. If he could find any, even one, then he might be able to reason from its truth to the truth of other beliefs about the world. This was to be the first step in removing from philosophy all of the errors into which it had fallen over the centuries that had preceded him. He would accept nothing as true unless it was true beyond the shadow of a doubt. If there was any way possible to doubt a belief, no matter how unrealistic such a doubt might be, the belief was not to be accepted. With this beginning he opens the discussion about the nature of the mind, of God, and of the world that is found in the readings of this chapter, selections from his *Meditations on First Philosophy.*

The Method of Doubt

As a first step in this quest, he decided to inspect his current beliefs about the world to see if there were any among them that were indubitable. In doubting his beliefs, Descartes first rejected all of what he had learned during his philosophical studies. This was not difficult, especially since the history of philosophy was filled with different opinions, based on unwarranted assumptions and weak reasoning. Next he examined his scientific beliefs. At his time, sciences such as physics and astronomy were still in their developing stages. Because of this their beliefs about the world were not always set on the firmest of foundations and thus could be doubted as well. How about commonsense beliefs? Instead of examining each of his ordinary beliefs about the world individually, Descartes examined the reliability of perceptual experience itself, upon which most commonsense beliefs about the world are based. It was easy enough to convince himself that his beliefs about the past could be mistaken. Memories are often faulty. It was also easy enough to believe that his reasoning about the future could lead to incorrect conclusions as well. Inductive arguments are at best guides to what may happen. So that left him to question his present perceptual experience.

He asked himself how anyone could possibly be mistaken about what they *presently* see, hear, taste, touch, and smell. Is it possible that someone looking right at their hands could be wrong to believe that they have hands? After all, if I see my hands then I have hands, do I not? And how could anyone sitting next to the fireplace and hearing the fire crackle be wrong to believe that there is a fire in the fireplace? After all, if I see the fire and hear it crackle then there is a crackling fire, is there not? These beliefs are based on what I see and hear so plainly, so immediately, so evidently. Yet Descartes concludes that it may indeed be possible that even beliefs based on current perception could be wrong. How is this possible?

Essentially, Descartes argues that everything that we can perceive we also can dream. Just as I see my hands before me and hear the fire crackling, so I may also dream that I see my hands before me and hear the fire crackling. Moreover, there is no way to tell if you are dreaming while you are dreaming. Dreams contain the same sorts of experiences that waking experiences do. It is only when you wake up from your dream that you know that, for example, there really is no tiger chasing you around your room. In the *Meditations* Descartes says,

> How often have I dreamt that I was in these familiar circumstances—that I was dressed and occupied this place by the fire, when I was lying undressed in bed? . . . I have been deceived in sleep by similar illusions; and, attentively considering those cases, I perceive so clearly that there exist no certain marks by which the state of waking can ever be distinguished from sleep, that I feel greatly astonished; and in amazement I almost persuade myself that I am now dreaming.[1]

Descartes suggests that perhaps all of what we think of as ordinary experience is just a dream, a dream in which what is called a waking state is just another form of dreaming. He does not really believe this, of course; it is only a theoretical doubt. But since it *could* be true that what I think of as waking states are really dream states, then there are grounds for doubting the reliability of perceptual experiences. If perceptual states are not reliable, if they may not tell us about what really exists, if they may be dream states that have no corresponding reality, then all the commonsense and scientific beliefs which depend upon perceptual experiences are not reliable either. Just as dream states are not about anything, and just as dreams exist only in the mind, so also when I see my hands there might not be any hands, or when I hear the crackling of fire, there might not be any fire. Perhaps the commonsense world exists only in my mind, as do my dreams. Perhaps all of my beliefs about the world and the persons existing in it are false.

If this **dream doubt** argument is not enough to cast doubt on the certainty of our commonsense beliefs, Descartes asks us to imagine an **evil genius.** This is a sort of evil god, a being so powerful that he has the ability to deceive us into believing all sorts of things that are not true. Perhaps my beliefs about the existence and nature of the world are all false; perhaps even my mathematical beliefs, such as "2+2=4" are false. Perhaps the evil genius somehow tricks me into these beliefs, when in fact all that really exists is myself and this evil genius. Perhaps such an evil genius exists and is the source of my experience. Perhaps he somehow projects experience about the past and present into my mind, as a movie projector casts its images onto a screen. In such a world, all of my experiences about the past and present would be illusions. I may even be deceived about my mathematical beliefs.

Granted the implausibility that such a being really exists, nevertheless it is theoretically possible, and so it is possible that all of my commonsense beliefs and mathematical beliefs are false. Because of the possibility that he is dreaming, or that an evil genius exists, Descartes cannot accept his perceptions of the world as being about the world. There may not be such a world, or any world for that matter. So for now at least he is stuck knowing only the contents of his own mind, the experiences of seeing, hearing, thinking, and so on. He must accept what he experiences as a series of private mental states, as a collection of experiences in the mind, and not as a direct awareness of the world. It is no longer simply to be accepted as true that just because I experience something, that something exists. From this perspective is there anything that can be accepted as true, any belief that is beyond doubt?

I Think, Therefore I Am

It is at this point that Descartes discovers the indubitable truth of at least one belief—the belief that he exists. "I exist" is an indubitable belief, because to doubt it you must exist to perform the act of doubting. To be able to doubt your own existence you must exist, so it is impossible to doubt your own existence without contradiction. It is to say, "I (who exist) do not exist." So it appears that Descartes has succeeded in the first part in his project, to discover an axiom that is beyond doubt, one that is known with absolute certitude. This belief is the bedrock of Descartes' entire philosophy, the starting point upon which everything else is to be built, the foundation of his philosophical mansion. From here the story turns to an examination of what may be deductively inferred from this indubitable philosophical truth. He first turns to a consideration of the nature of this "I" whose existence is known with certitude.

For Descartes, his self is his nonphysical mind, or soul. It does not yet include his body. His body, like any physical object, is known through the senses, and thus might not exist. The dream doubt and evil genius arguments have undermined the reliability of the senses, and thus cast into doubt the reliability of all perceptual beliefs, even beliefs about the existence of his body. Descartes' argument that the self is the mind, not the body, goes something like this:

1. If I exist and my body may not exist, then I am not my body.

2. I exist.

3. My body may not exist. Therefore,

4. I am not my body.

Later he will say that he "has" a body, but he always says that what is essential to being a self is the nonphysical mind, not the body. We will have much more to say about the nature of the mind in the "Human Nature" section.

For Descartes, part of the mind is what is "in" it, the collection of all the contents of the mind. One of the ideas he claims to find in his mind is the idea of "perfection." Descartes believes that the existence of God may be proven from this idea, and offers arguments to support this belief. His claim that we have an idea of perfection is highly dubious, and his arguments that God must exist if this idea exists are not very strong. We will examine his arguments for God's existence later. For now we simply pretend for the sake of pursuing his larger argument that they work. Let us assume, then, that we do indeed have an idea of perfection, and that from this idea we may infer the existence of a perfect being, and then take stock of what Descartes believes he knows for sure at this point. For him, the following four beliefs are known with certainty:

a. I exist.

b. I am my mind.

c. God exists.

d. God is a perfect being.

If we know that there is a nonphysical self and a God, and we know this with certainty, then we are two-thirds of the way along in Descartes' quest to answer the big three philosophical questions. What remains are the *reality* questions, questions about the existence and nature of the world. Previous philosophers had simply taken for granted the existence of the world. Descartes himself acknowledges that belief in the existence of the world is a very strong, very natural belief, perhaps the most basic of all of our assumptions. But he reminds us that we do not *know* with any certainty that it exists. And since it is possible that it does not, then the existence of the material world, including my body which is part of it, must be argued for. Is there any way to infer the existence and nature of the world from statements (a) through (d)?

The Existence of the World

Descartes' argument for the existence of the material world begins with the recognition that he strongly believes that the world exists. If it did not exist—if he were merely dreaming it, or if the evil genius was tricking him into believing it exists when it does not—then God would be allowing him to be deceived. But, since God is a perfect being, he cannot allow this type of deception, a type where I am constantly and inescapably deceived. It would go against God's nature as a perfect being to allow this. Being deceptive, an imperfection, would contradict the very idea of a perfect being. So, for Descartes, we may now conclude that the world exists, as we have always believed in our hearts that it did. We may formulate this argument as follows:

1. If the world does not exist, then God deceives.

2. God cannot deceive. Therefore,

3. The world exists.

The existence of God as a perfect being guarantees that my strong natural belief that the world exists is true. Because God cannot continuously deceive me or allow me to be deceived, then I know that the external world is not an illusion. I am not always dreaming or being deceived by an evil genius. As a perfect being, God could not allow either of these types of universal deception to occur and still be a perfect being.

If God is a perfect being, the question of why there is any human error at all may well arise. Granted that God cannot allow us to be deceived all of the time about the existence of the world, nevertheless he does seem to allow us to be deceived at least some of the time about the nature of the world. Our everyday beliefs, and even our scientific beliefs are often mistaken. But if God is perfect, how can he allow us to be deceived at all? Descartes' answer is formulated especially in another of his works, *Rules for the Direction of the Mind*. In general, he says that God's perfection guarantees only that *some* of our beliefs about the world are accurate, not all of our beliefs. Our errors are our own fault. They are caused by hastily formed beliefs, misperceptions, faulty logic, and beliefs that go beyond the evidence. Just as we can use our freedom to choose either good or evil, so also we can use it to form beliefs that are reliable and those that are not. The most reliable beliefs are those formed on the basis of the best evidence. But what sort of evidence is best, and therefore, what sorts of beliefs does God's perfection guarantee?

The Reliability of Knowledge

It may seem strange to be back to questions of knowledge when we are trying to discover Descartes' belief about the nature of reality. However, for Descartes and other modern philosophers as well, this is not at all strange. This is because most of them accept some sort **representational theory of perception.** That is, they accept the general belief of the science of their day, that to know something through the senses is not to know it directly, as it is in itself, but to be aware of our representation of the object, which representation exists in our minds. To see something, for example, is to have a visual perception of that thing. Light waves from the object stimulate my sense organs and send information along my optic nerve to the brain. Only then do I become conscious of the object—after it has entered the theater of my mind. So I do not experience the world directly, rather I experience only the way that I represent it to myself. If the world as it is in itself is called *reality*, then it is correct to say that I experience only how reality *appears* to me.

It may be that the real world is nothing like my experience of it. My experience may, on the other hand, be an exact copy of reality. But how do I know what is real if I am stuck with only the awareness of how I represent reality? I cannot hover above the world and my mind, examining if my mind accurately represents things or not. I am stuck within the world as I represent it, without being able to compare my representations to how things really are. How do I know that I know? How do I justify my beliefs about the world as reliable, as good representations of what truly exists?

For Descartes, the perfection of God guarantees that I am not constantly in error. However, the only beliefs that we have about the world that are guaranteed by God's perfection as reliable are those that are known with *certitude*. Only these beliefs reflect what the world is really like. No beliefs formed on the basis of experience can be known with certitude; we can always be mistaken about them. Only beliefs known by reason and reasoning are known with certitude, so only they are reliable. Descartes calls such beliefs "clear and distinct" beliefs. As with axioms and theorems in mathematics, we clearly see their truth as beyond doubt and we do not confuse one sort of belief with another. For Descartes, these beliefs that come from reason and reasoning are the most reliable beliefs that we possess. They tell us how things really are, and they are justified not by experience but by reason alone—either as axioms or truths deduced from axioms. The main point is that for Descartes, there is an identifiable class of beliefs that is taken to reflect what exists—self-evident axioms and those truths that are derived from these axioms by valid forms of reasoning. This is the very heart of rationalism, the claim that it is reason and not experience which allows us to tell reliable beliefs from those which are not.

For Descartes, beliefs that are justified by observation are not certain, and thus are not guaranteed by God as reliable. By appealing to the perfection of God, Descartes has eliminated the possibility that when we see something we might be dreaming. He has also eliminated the possibility that there is an evil genius who constantly deceives us. Because of this we can now be sure, once again, that our senses give us information about the *existence* of the world. When we see a tree we can generally be confident that a tree is there to be seen. Even so, while sense experience may be a reliable indicator of existence, it is not a reliable guide to understanding the *nature* of the world. Our senses may tell us that objects exist; they may also tells us where they are located, how fast they appear to be moving, and what sorts of sensory properties they seem to have. But they do not tell us what objects are really like. In general, knowledge based on sense experience provides no reliable information about the true nature of reality. Beliefs based on sense experience are not to be trusted as accurate descriptions of what the world is really like.

Since the senses are not to be trusted, then our commonsense beliefs about reality also are not to be trusted. These beliefs, after all, are based on sense experience. Descartes tells us that all the properties that things seem to have, properties that we perceive them as having—their color, odor, sound, taste, and texture and so on—are not to be taken as properties that they really do have. We have no guarantee, says Descartes, that these properties really exist apart from our perceptions. The perfection of God, the fact that he will not deceive us, extends no further than our rational knowledge of the world. We cannot be certain whether or not it really contains tastes or textures, odors or sounds, or even colors—like the fiery red of a late summer sunset. Because our knowledge of such qualities is based on observation and not reason, such beliefs cannot be known with certitude, and thus are not guaranteed by God's perfection.

While sensory qualities surely exist in our minds, while things *appear* to have colors, odors, sounds, tastes, and so on, Descartes does not believe that such properties exist as *real* properties of things. Following the assumptions of science about the nature and perception of reality, he believes that things have no colors, sounds, odors, and the like. These properties exist *only* in the minds of perceivers. They are simply the way that the real world appears to us through our senses. I experience the colorless flower *as* red, but it is not red in itself. I hear the sweet sound of the violin, but in reality there are just vibrating strings and air waves. I smell the rich aroma of the morning's first coffee, but this aroma exists only in my mind. If this is so, then the picture of reality delivered through the senses is a distortion of how things are, not a true picture at all. This is why the senses are not to be trusted.

Reality According to Reason

It is only knowledge that arises through reason that is to be trusted as reliable. The concept of reality discovered by reason presents a crystal clear picture of how things really are. According to the knowledge which God guarantees to be reliable, certain knowledge, reality in itself consists of a world of material substances (things), which possess only *mathematical* properties. Here is what Descartes says:

> . . . they (material objects) are not perhaps exactly as we perceive by the senses, for their comprehension by the senses is, in many instances, very obscure and confused; but it is at least necessary to admit that all which I clearly and distinctly conceive as in them, that is, generally speaking, all that is comprehended in the object of speculative geometry, really exists external to me.[2]

Let us consider the first part of Descartes' claim first, that reality consists of material substances, or things. We all seem to believe this, and seem to know it on the basis of our senses. We just see that there are things in the world, do we not? So why would he say that this is something known through reason? Descartes' answer is that the senses deliver information about color, odor, size, shape, location, texture, and so on, but they do not inform us about material substances. We do not sense the "thingness" of an object. The mind, or reason, is the only source of knowledge that material substances exist. If it was not for the rational intuition of the mind, the mind understanding that things exist, we would never have an idea of a world filled with things. For all that our senses tell us, the world consists solely of collections of sensory properties, not of things. But for reason, an apple would be thought of as just a collection of redness, roundness, sweetness, and so on, and not as a thing that has these properties.

Descartes gives an example to convince us of his insight that reason alone tells us that reality is composed of things. When the entire list of sensory properties of an object changes, as when a piece of white, sweet, soft, solid wax melts into a clear liquid with no odor, we still know that the liquid is the very same substance as the once firm wax. There is some "thing" that still is the wax, despite our senses telling us that nothing remains the same. There is some thing called "wax" that underlies the changes of all of its sensory properties. Since everything that we sense has changed, then how else do we know it is the same wax except through the mind?

The second part of Descartes' quote claims that in addition to knowing with certitude that material substances exist, we can also know something about their essential properties with certainty. Essential properties are those that something must have if it is to be the kind of thing that it is. For example, a triangle must have three sides to be a triangle. This is one of its essential properties. Now, what are the essential properties of material objects? It is not their colors, odors, or tastes. These can change and the object will remain the same type of thing or substance. A green apple is still an apple if it turns red; it is still an apple if it starts to rot and smell bad; it is still an apple if it tastes sour one day and sweet the next.

From considerations such as these Descartes takes it as true that sensory properties are not essential for being a material object. A material object could have no sensory properties and still be a material object, for Descartes. But there is one property that any material object must have in order to be a material object. If it lost this property it would no longer exist. That property is what Descartes calls its *extension*. The only thing about the wax that remained the same through its change from a solid to a liquid were its properties of shape and size, even though it had a different shape and size as a solid than it did as a liquid. These spatial properties, its extension, are essential to being a material object. Any material object must occupy space and have some sort of shape. Something could not be a material object unless it had three dimensional spatial properties. What would a material object be like that had no size or shape? Even the tiniest points made by a pen on paper have some spatial dimension.

How do we know that material objects really do have extension, however? How do we know that the shape and size of objects, like their color and odor, are not simply in our minds? It is not because we see their size and shape, since sense experience is an unreliable indicator of what really exists. Besides, seeing or touching the size and shape of something does not give us the real size and shape. Sensing shape varies with our location and perspective. The shape of a table top, for example, appears different if I am looking down on it than if I am seeing it from the side. It may look different to you, over there, than it does to me, over here. So it is not because we can see the shapes of things that we know that they have shapes.

Instead, we know that material objects really do have size and shape because we can know their extension with certainty, and anything that we can know for sure is guaranteed by God's perfection to be true of reality. The spatial properties of objects, their size and shape, may be known with certitude through mathematics. The science of shapes is geometry, especially analytical geometry. As Descartes says in the last quote, reality has only those properties that may be known by geometry. For Descartes, the axioms and theorems of analytical geometry are true of the world, and true of what is most real about the world, its mathematical nature. Everything about material substances that may be known through mathematics really exists in material objects themselves.

Since mathematics is the only science of the world that delivers certainty, the only science that provides a priori knowledge of the world, then for Descartes, *reality is what may be described in mathematical systems.* Besides a perfect God and the nonphysical self, this is what is real: material substances with extension. While minds are essentially what Descartes calls *res cogitans,* things that think or are conscious, material objects are essentially *res extensa,* things that occupy space. On this view of things, the world, including my body, is one giant mathematical machine.

The Origin of Knowledge: Innate Ideas

Several things led Descartes to this rather thin conception of reality, a reality consisting of God, minds, and material substances which possess only spatial properties. Chief among them is belief that God guarantees that only those beliefs which are known with certitude "fit" reality. The only beliefs known with certitude are those which arise from reason, not sense experience. Following the model of mathematics, "arise from reason" means either taken as self-evident axioms or inferred from axioms. It is easy enough to see how beliefs arise as conclusions in deductive arguments. This is one source or origin of knowledge. But what does "taken as self-evident axioms" mean? How does the mind just "see" that some axioms are true, without any help from sense experience? What is the source or origin of such axioms which are so important for building Descartes' philosophical system?

Ultimately, as with most rationalists, beliefs of reason that are taken to be true of the world are understood by Descartes to be *innate.* Innate knowledge is knowledge with which we were born. We did not have to acquire it through experience or any type of learning. But how did it get there? Descartes believed that God, the author of all nature, made the material world with a mathematical nature, and also implanted these ideas of mathematics which mirror this nature into our minds. Mathematical systems are the blueprints of reality that were stamped onto our minds by a benevolent creator, a creator who wanted us to be able to know the world as it really is.

So knowledge of the true nature of the world, as well as knowledge of God as a perfect being, and knowledge of ourselves as nonphysical beings, is knowledge implanted in us by God from the time of our birth. It is there within us, waiting for us to have the time and inclination to discover it. The discovery of this knowledge within, knowledge that we acquire through reflection, not observation, is what enables us to find reliable answers to the truly great questions of existence. The details of our knowledge of the world may have to be acquired through experience, but the general ideas about its true nature, as well as the true nature of God and the self, are known innately, by reason inspecting its own treasures. Our minds are powerful. God has seen that they are made for truth, especially when truth is known from within.

Human Nature

Descartes did not develop a full theory of human nature. Instead, he focused on the narrower topic of the nature of the human person. What would have to be added to his view of persons to create a doctrine of human nature is a description of our innate tendencies or functions. While he left this part of the theory of human nature out, he had so much to say about the structure of human beings that he may be forgiven for the omission. This is especially true, since what he does have to say about the nature of persons both provided the basis for a great deal of further philosophical discussion, and established the foundation for the modern concept of the self. With the possible exception of Buddhism, persons have been understood as primarily members of society by all of the theories considered in this text thus far. For them, it is from membership in the group that the meaning and fulfillment of human nature is to be found. The self of Descartes' world, however, will be first and foremost an autonomous individual, one who is free to think and to act, and to create a life according to his or her own experience and reason.

Descartes agreed with Hobbes and modern science that the physical world should be thought of mechanistically, not teleologically. For both material objects are composed of atoms, collections of which formed the larger objects of everyday life. These objects move about in a rigidly determined manner, a manner to be explained solely in terms of what Aristotle had called their "efficient" causes. These causes are just the antecedent conditions that determine how something is to happen. Just as the velocity and the angle of a cue ball striking an eight ball determines where the eight ball is to go and how fast it will travel, so too, the universe runs as it does because current events are caused by previous events.

The same is true of the human body. Descartes agreed with Hobbes that the human body, like anything material, was a kind of machine. This belief was strengthened by Descartes' visits to the French Royal Gardens where mechanical creations in the form of humans and animals were displayed. They were driven by water flowing through hidden tubes which moved wheels and pulleys. They were so intricately designed that they seemed lifelike indeed. Our bodies are like that, Descartes thought, though much more complex. The bodies of animals he also thought of as types of machines. Bodies, whether human or animal, are not themselves capable of thought or free choice, however. Animals are driven solely by instinct, desire, and other forces of nature.

This is called the **mechanistic** conception of nature, the view that nature is like a vast machine whose current movements are caused by previous events. This view of the world was a necessary assumption of the new science, which thought of its business as discovering the causal patterns or laws according to which the machine called nature operated. Descartes wanted to make this view of nature explicit and to argue that the scientific assumption of a mechanistic world correctly represented how nature really is. In his mind, science works so well because its assumptions about what the world is like are correct. It fell to him, as a philosopher, to explain and justify this view of reality that science simply assumed to be correct. His success in clarifying and defending this scientific conception of reality helped to pave the way for the scientific and technological revolution that would soon follow and become a defining characteristic of Western civilization.

Hobbes thought that science forced us to see human beings as immersed in this mechanistic world of nature as well. We are part of nature, and thus entirely material beings who cannot escape the determinism of nature. For Descartes, however, while mechanism is true of nature, it is not true of human persons. Human beings are very different from animals and anything else in nature. We can do lots of things in nonmechanistic ways, such as refuse to act on a strong desire, or move our bodies just by an act of will, or think abstract thoughts, or plan future events and make decisions, and so on. We can do all of these things because we are not entirely physical things; we are also nonphysical things; we have minds. So we are bodies *and* minds. It is the job of science to study bodies, along with the rest of nature; and it is the job of philosophy and even theology to study the mind. Descartes knew that his cherished beliefs about the mechanistic nature of reality would not be accepted by the Church unless he could clearly show that the materialism and determinism that held among physical events did not lead to the denial of the soul, especially to the denial of the soul's immortality and free will. So the task for Descartes was to develop a notion of the human person that avoided these implications. His theory of human persons and their nature is called **dualistic interactionism.**

The Nature of the Mind

We have already seen something of the "dualistic" part of Descartes' view. Human beings are composed of bodies, which are part of nature, and minds, which are not. This dualistic conception of human beings is not new. We have seen it in the teachings of Plato and Augustine. It had become a widely accepted view in religion, philosophy, and everyday life. What was new was the degree to which Descartes emphasized the differences between bodies and our souls—or *minds* as he preferred to call them. In particular, he saw the mind as completely different from the body. They were so different, in fact, that he considered it possible that each could exist separately from the other. Just as animals exist with no minds, so human bodies could exist in a machine-like fashion. Since the mind can be thought of apart from the body, moreover, the mind can surely exist alone, as well. Neither does exist alone in this life, but they could. In fact, for Descartes, the mind could even have experiences of perceptions, bodily desires, and physical pains apart from the body!

Before discussing how minds and bodies differ, it is best to begin with his concept of what the mind is. The first thing to say is that Descartes equates the soul, the mind, and the self. For him, I am my mind. By "mind" he does not simply mean the rational mind or intellect, but rather he means "a thing which thinks." To say that a mind *thinks* means for Descartes more than that it simply exercises rational thought. Instead, he means by "thinks," roughly, "is conscious." To think, then, includes a variety of mental acts, such as to perceive, to feel, to imagine, to reason, to hope, to decide, and so on—all ways of being conscious. So the mind is consciousness itself, a consciousness which produces and is exhibited in various forms of consciousness, called mental acts. The basic point is that for Descartes I am my conscious mind.

The first part of the above definition of mind says that the mind is a thing or, as philosophers say, a *substance.* It is not a collection of mental events, for example, nor is consciousness itself simply a property of something else, such as the brain. Descartes, like Plato and Augustine, is a **substance dualist.** He believes that there are two kinds of *things* in the world, bodies and minds. Bodies make up the physical world and are studied as public objects by science; minds make up the private mental world and escape objective scientific study. Instead, our inner world of consciousness is accessible only to ourselves, only the one who is conscious. I am a private, inner, subjective self, and what goes on within the theater of my mind is known fully by me, and only by me.

The next important thing that Descartes says about minds is that they are completely *different* from material objects. The two substances which make up a human being are nothing at all alike. All material objects, including human bodies, have size and shape, mass and location, and even appear to us as having color and odor, and so on. Minds, as nonmaterial objects, have none of these properties. They have no color, for example. Is your mind red or green or blue? They have no mass either. How much does your mind weigh? Nor do they have shape or size or location. Where is your mind? In your head, your heart, all throughout your body? Minds, and thus our selves, have none of these properties because they are different in kind from bodies.

Though Descartes claims that the mind is totally different from the body, he nevertheless understood the mind as *like* the body as well. The mind and the body are both substances, and they both have events going on within them. As blood flows through my veins, as food gets digested in my stomach, and as skin cells come and go, so also, thoughts flow through my mind, past events get stored in my memory, and feelings come and go from consciousness. Further, as science observes the events in the material world and describes how they are related, so each of us may observe the events in our own private mental world and describe how they are related. We can observe, for example, how one thought leads to another, how it arose from a feeling which, in turn, may have arisen from an image, and so on.

So a human being is a nonphysical mind or consciousness that produces conscious mental states, such as thinking, remembering, perceiving and desiring, imagining, hoping, and so on. Because it is totally distinct from bodies, Descartes can argue that it escapes the materialism of nature; because his model of mind is based on that of bodies, Descartes can see minds as things where events occur which are related to each other. While some of these events may be caused by other events (seeing an ice cream sundae makes me desire it, for example), others are not caused by anything; they are free. The mind has the power simply to will some mental events into existence, because its actions are not determined by the forces of nature. Our minds are not controlled by natural forces because they are not part of nature. The mind, or self, is an autonomous self, a self that is unaffected by physical, social and psychological forces. In its private, inner, subjective mental world, it lies beyond the forces of time, place, and heredity.

Descartes' concept of the human person has many explanatory benefits, even in today's world. It explains, for example, why minds and their *mental states appear to be so different* from states of the body, such as brain states. To those like Hobbes who argue that so-called mental states are simply brain states, Descartes replies that when we look within ourselves and examine the goings on in our minds, they appear to be nothing at all like brain states. If pains are brain states, for example, why don't some brain states throb? If perception is a brain state, visual perception, for example, why is there not a red brain state when I see a red rose? What about feeling angry or falling in love? Are there any brain states that are like these mental events?

In addition, substance dualism also explains the *privacy* of mental states. Mental states are states of a private mind, a mind to which no one else has access. We may express our thoughts and feelings in our behavior, but no one else can know them directly. If they were material events, such as brain events, they could be publicly observed by, for example, the brain scanners of today. Perhaps most importantly, substance dualism also explains the *consciousness* of mental states. Only minds, or consciousness itself, can be conscious. It is difficult to see how brains, for example, can be conscious. They are composed of tissue, after all. Does it make any sense to think of blood, bones, flesh, or even neurons as capable of being conscious?

Substance dualism explains other well-known facts as well, such as the *difference between human beings and animals.* Human beings build bridges and cities, write books, invent computers, send space craft out to explore other parts of the universe, and rule the planet. No animal comes close to us in ability and achievement, but some come close in sharing the physical properties that should allow them to compete with us more effectively. Some of our simian relatives, for example, share close to 99 percent of our genes. These genes direct the building of their bodies, including their brains. Their brains seem to be as large and as complex as ours. With brains so nearly resembling our own, the difference between us should not be as great as it is. Therefore, the difference between us and them has to be explained in ways other than by pointing to our brains as more complex sorts of computers than the ones they possess. A better explanation is that we are different *kinds* of beings, beings who have nonphysical minds as well as bodies.

The Mind-Body Problem

If substance dualism has its benefits, it also has its problems. One problem is that there is no easy explanation for how we can know that other people exist. If a person is his or her mind, and if that can only be known by the person, then it may be possible that no one else exists but myself. This is referred to today as the problem of *other minds*. If Descartes' self runs the risk of being alienated from others, whose existence is uncertain, it also runs the risk of being alienated from nature, which is viewed as completely different from the mind. Many of the problems of Descartes' theory, in fact, are caused by thinking of minds and bodies as completely different from each other. While my body is included in the vast mathematical machine of nature, my mind, my self, is a spiritual being that resides outside of nature. But there is at least one point at which minds and nature must meet, since our minds appear to be intertwined with "our" bodies. The problems that have to do with this connection, the "interactionist" part of Descartes' theory of dualistic interactionism, are among the most serious faced by Descartes. Descartes simply does not do very well at explaining how minds and bodies are related to each other, how they interact.

While there are many ways for two things to be related, the sort of relationship between minds and bodies that is crucial for Descartes is their *causal* relationship: the fact that events that occur in one of them are capable of producing events in the other. At first sight it seems that nothing could be truer than that the mind and the body causally interact. For example, every time that I am conscious of something in my external environment (mental event), it is because the world around me delivers information to my brain, through my sensory receptors. According to substance dualism, the brain delivers this information to my mind, and thus causes a conscious experience of seeing, hearing, smelling, or tasting something in the world. In this way, a brain state produces or "causes" a mental state to come into existence. Other things in the world cause mental states as well, events such as burning my finger with a candle's flame. This causes damage to my skin, which sends a signal to my brain, which causes a feeling of pain. Events within my internal physical environment also cause mental states. The excitation of nerves in my gums causes a toothache; my empty stomach causes the secretion of chemicals, which causes brain states, which cause a feeling of hunger.

In the opposite direction, mental states also cause physical events. The feeling of being burned causes me to hold my finger under cold running water, or my perception of the wonderful taste of the food before me causes me to eat more of it. My decision to get out of bed in the early hours of a cold, dark winter morning is what makes me get out of bed. If I had made a different decision, to stay in bed and skip work that day, for example, I would not move. My plans cause me to act in one way rather than another, as well. If I plan to eat pizza for dinner, a pizza made at the pizza shop, I will do very different things than if I plan to eat a turkey of my own preparation. What I perceive, think, feel, desire, and decide are all nonphysical events according to substance dualism. They cause changes in my brain, which sends signals to my body to act in certain ways.

For many, substance dualism seems to describe how minds and bodies interact just right. When we think seriously about it, however, we can see that this sort of relationship is rather strange in many respects. Though there are several problems that substance dualism has with explaining interaction, it will be helpful to reduce these to the following two questions: How does this two-way interaction happen? and Where does it happen? *How* do brain states, physical processes as they are, create nonphysical mental states? We know how events in our external and internal physical environments cause brain states, and how brain states cause other brain states, but how do states of a nonphysical mind, a different type of being altogether, get created by the brain states? How does a pattern of firing neurons produce a conscious feeling of pain, for example? How does something with electrochemical properties "become" something (the *feeling* of pain) with no physical properties at all? How does something physical become something nonphysical?

The problem gets no less mysterious when we look at interaction in the other direction, when we think about how a mental state could create a brain state. When I decide to call the pizza shop, this decision creates brain activity which causes me to dial the number of the pizza shop. But how can a mental state, which has no location (it is not next to the brain state), no power to move anything (it has no mass, no inertia), no electrochemical properties (it cannot fire neurons), and so on, bring a physical event into existence? Is it like the way a carpenter brings a kitchen cabinet into existence? No, because he just shapes preexisting materials into a new form. The already existing wood is cut, and shaped, and fastened together to make a cabinet. Nonphysical events, however, do not have any physical materials to work with in their production of mental states. Instead, for mental states to bring about changes in the brain seems more like God creating the universe from nothing, than a carpenter making a cabinet. It almost seems as if a miracle occurs every one of the countless times that the mind affects the body.

To the other question, *where* does this interaction occur, Descartes had a now famous response. It happens, he said, in a special gland deep within the brain, a part of the brain we now call the *pineal gland*. This is where minds and bodies meet, the bridge where nonphysical events and physical events continually cross into each other's world. Today, we might picture the way that Descartes envisioned mind-body interactions by analogy with an old-fashioned telephone system. Imagine a telephone operator seated at a switchboard. Incoming calls light up the switchboard, are answered by the operator, and then routed to their proper locations. The operator makes the proper connections by plugging in wires to the incoming call lights, answering the call, and then plugging in the appropriate output wires. In a way similar to that, the pineal gland was somehow supposed to make the proper connections between mind and body. Incoming brain states became mental states after passing through, as did incoming mental states become brain states after passing back over the bridge.

Descartes never explained how a gland in the brain, a physical thing, could create nonphysical events out of physical events. Nor did he explain how a nonphysical being, a substance dualism type of mind, a being without any spatial properties, could be "located" there. He did not explain how the pineal gland made the proper connections, because substance dualism has no good explanation for this. The problem of how minds and bodies could possibly interact could not be solved by showing where it was that they interact. This simply transferred the "how" question to a specific place, and left followers and critics of Descartes asking how it could be that mind-body interaction could take place in the pineal gland. If mental states are thought of as nonphysical events, then our common experience that minds and bodies interact becomes quite difficult, if not impossible, to explain. Problems such as these led one recent writer to refer to the mind-body dualism of Descartes as the theory of the "ghost" (the nonphysical mind) in the "machine" (the body).[3]

Consequences

Freedom

For Descartes, the existence of free will was as self-evident as his own existence. After all, he had been free to doubt, had he not? He had been free to go against his inclinations to believe the truths of common sense, philosophy, and even science, and to imagine all sorts of unlikely things being true as a basis for this doubt. Besides, freedom of the will is a requirement for ethics and responsibility in general. How can a person be held responsible for actions over which he has no control? If it is certain that we have free will, however, it remains to be seen just how this is to be understood. What is it that sets apart human beings from the rest of nature and allows them to escape its rigid determinism? To answer this question it might be helpful first to examine an explanation of how human freedom may be denied.

One reason to question our freedom is that most of us believe that the following claim is true: *Every event has a cause.* This is called the **principle of determinism.** What it says is that nothing happens without a cause. The principle of determinism, or determinism for short, seems to rule out the possibility of freedom. If *every* event has a cause, then so do human choices. To say that an event has a cause means that if the cause exists, then the event which it causes has to occur. If our choices have causes, then they have to be as they are, as do the actions which follow from them. If the cause is present, then only the choice and the action which are its effects are possible. There is no other choice that could have been made, no other action that could have been performed. If a rule programmed into a computer says "Print '2' when the keyboard input is 1 + 1 =", then only "2" can be printed. As the printing of "2" is determined by the rule of the program and the hardware of the computer, so our actions are determined by our environment and heredity. But how does this causation work for human choice?

Our actions are determined by our desires. We act as we do because we want certain things. If we are hungry, we eat. If we are tired, we sleep. If we want to go to the opera, we save our money for a ticket. Our current desires, in turn, are what they are because of the sorts of people we are, our character. If we were raised to love opera, then we save our money in order to buy a ticket. If we live in a society where any excess weight is seen as a curse, we may starve ourselves thin. If we have an inherited propensity for running very fast, we may ignore our fatigue to train our bodies for racing. So nature and nurture make us the kinds of people we are, and this determines what we want to do in certain circumstances, and this determines how we behave. If we have a desire, we act on it; if we have conflicting desires, we act on the strongest one. This, roughly, was the view of Hobbes, and remains the view of various versions of determinism today. It claims that human choices, like everything else in nature, are subject to the rigid determinism of nature.

Descartes, of course, will have none of this. We are not part of nature, we transcend the deterministic flow of natural events, we are free. How do our choices become free? For Descartes, they are free because they are not caused by anything. They are undetermined. This view today is called **indeterminism.** As the name suggests, indeterminism is the opposite of determinism. It claims that it is not true that every event has a cause. In particular, some human choices are not caused by anything at all—they are free. Indeterminism may accept the findings of science about how the powerful forces of nature and society influence our behavior. But indeterminists claim that our desires, caused as they may be by events beyond our control, are themselves under our control. We can choose to eat or gain weight, to run or to sleep, to save or to spend—because our behavior is not determined by our strongest desire. It is determined by our free choice of which desire, if any, to act on. We simply choose the desire that we wish to act upon and the action follows. We can suppress stronger desires in favor of weaker ones, and vice versa, and so can act in one way or another according to our *will.*

According to the indeterminist, a view accepted by Descartes, human free choices, sometimes called voluntary choices, are outside of the flow of events of which nature is composed. If we call the collection of our actual and possible choices our *will,* then the claim of indeterminism is that we have **free will.** We have the power to govern our desires, to suppress some, to release others into action, and to hold some at bay for the moment. This is the source of our dignity, the spark of the divine that dwells in us and raises us above the droning determinism of nature. We are not simply animals, driven by need, instinct, and experience. We are human, and thus free to control which of the forces of nature we shall resist, which we shall bow to, and which we shall ignore. While indeterminism sounds right to many, it is not without its problems. Some of these will be discussed in later chapters, when additional possible solutions to the problem of free will and determinism are introduced.

Ethics

While Descartes did have some things to say about ethics, his remarks were brief, scattered, and never fully developed. Descartes had almost nothing to say in a formal way about the goals of life, the highest virtues or moral rules. Instead, many of his ethical views were concerned with his personal moral beliefs. Some of these were discussed in his *Discourse of Method,* while others were mentioned in passing in his letters. For Descartes, in order to develop a formal system of ethics, more would have to be known about the nature of the soul, its deepest desires, and especially how our reason interacts with the body to control the passions and emotions and to guide behavior. This study he had not yet undertaken, so our brief comments are restricted to his personal moral beliefs.

While it may be assumed that he accepted eternal life with God as the goal of the next life, the goal that he seemed to believe to be the most important one in this life was similar to the Stoic ideal. This included the acceptance of external conditions over which he had no control, and the attempt to bring his own desires in line with these conditions. Instead of trying to acquire things, such as wealth and fame, he tried to not want these things in the first place. This stoical self-control or peaceful resignation was important for Descartes, but it was not his highest goal. Instead it was a necessary means to what he valued the most, the rational life itself. The pursuit of philosophical knowledge and the resolve to live according to the truth were the key elements of his personal ethics, and the goals that he most ardently pursued.

God and Immortality

Descartes argues in the *Meditations* that he could think of his self without thinking of it as having a body. From this he concluded that the self was different from the body. If my body is physical, then my self or my mind is not. From here it should have been open to Descartes to prove that the soul was immortal. The traditional argument, used widely by medieval theologians, says that only things composed of parts can be destroyed. Spiritual entities have no parts; therefore they cannot be destroyed. Descartes stopped short of using this argument, however, and deliberately so. The very long full title of his major philosophy book, usually referred to simply as the *Meditations*, is *Meditations on First Philosophy in Which the Existence of God and the Distinction of the Soul from the Body Are Demonstrated.* In the original title, the phrase "Immortality of the Soul" was used instead of the later "Distinction of the Soul from the Body." Apparently Descartes thought that the traditional argument, or any argument for that matter, was too weak to prove with certainty the soul's immortality. Instead, it was enough for him to show that bodies and souls are distinct, from which it could be inferred that it was at least *likely* that the soul was unaffected by the death of the body. In either case, while there was no certain proof from Descartes that the soul survives the body's demise, it was accepted by him personally as an act of faith, and philosophically as a likely result of the soul's spirituality.

Descartes had several arguments for God's existence, none of them very strong. All were based on the idea of God as the idea of a perfect being. This was an idea that Descartes claimed to have, and one that he assumed all of us had. The arguments then proceeded, each in its own way, to infer that a perfect being, God, must exist as the only explanation of this idea. One argument inferred that God was the cause of this idea, since only a perfect being could cause the idea of perfection, while another claimed that only God could explain my own existence. The third argument Descartes borrowed from St. Anselm, an eleventh-century English monk. It is usually referred to as the **ontological argument.** It has a long history in philosophy, and still claims many supporters, as well as critics. The heart of it is as follows:

> If God is a perfect being, then God lacks nothing that counts as a perfection. A perfection is a property that adds something to the being. To say that God is wise, for example, predicates of God a particular perfection. On the other hand, to say that God is not wise is to deny a perfection to God. Since God is a perfect being, then to deny of him a perfection is to utter a contradiction. To say that God is not wise is really to say that the being who has all perfection (including wisdom) lacks wisdom. In the same way, saying that God does not exist (atheism) is a contradiction as well, since existence is a perfection. A real existing hundred dollars has more "reality" than just the image or thought of the money, for example. To

deny God's existence is every bit as logically impossible as denying his wisdom or denying that triangles have three sides. The definition of "God," which expresses the idea of God, includes existence as one of its parts, just as having three sides is included in the concept of a triangle. So God has to be thought of existing, just as triangles have to be thought of as having three sides. If God cannot be thought of as not existing, then God must exist.

The fact that these arguments are weak is important, since upon the proof of the existence of God rests Descartes' proof that the world exists. If we cannot know that there is a world without first knowing that God exists, all that Descartes is entitled to rescue from his program of systematic doubt is his own existence. Unless he wants to accept the existence of God and world (and other people) simply as a practical matter, and he does not, Descartes seems to be stuck with knowing for certain only that he exists. This view in philosophy is called **solipsism**—the belief that I alone exist. The attempt both to begin philosophizing where Descartes did, within the apparent security of the ego, and to avoid solipsism as well, drove many of his followers to devise other methods of proving the existence of the world. As we shall see later, this proved to be a difficult task indeed.

Gender

It is not easy to determine Descartes' attitude toward women. It seems clear that he did not take the party line of the Church as outlined by Augustine and Aquinas. Descartes, in fact, seems to have had great personal respect for the ability of women to think and to act on a par with men. Of the many contemporary intellectuals with whom he corresponded regularly about philosophical matters were included Princess Elizabeth of Bohemia and Queen Christina of Sweden. He respected their ability to learn and to understand on a par with men, as well as their ability to engage in matters beyond domestic duties, including matters of the state.

If he shows little sign of explicit sexism, however, his concept of the self has come under attack recently as being implicitly sexist.[4] Specifically, it has been seen by some as excluding female qualities as part of our essential selves. Descartes' self, for example is independent, autonomous, rational, dominating, and transcendent. These are traits that men have been socialized to acquire and that society has valued as male traits. They do not include, for example, the qualities of interdependence, community, emotion, sharing, and involvement with daily life, qualities that are usually associated with the way that women have been socialized. Their exclusion from what is essential to being human, both male and female, leaves us with only a male self, not a human self. While ancient and medieval philosophers may not have valued female characteristics such as those just mentioned as highly as those of males, they at least have acknowledged them. In excluding them altogether, Descartes leaves the impression that there is only one way to be human. In doing so he helped to banish female human nature from conscious consideration. If there was only one type of "soul," and that was male, then the voices and concerns of women were destined to remain unheard by those who were to frame the ideals of civilization for the Modern period and beyond.

Readings

1. The Nature of the Mind

MEDITATIONS ON THE FIRST PHILOSOPHY

In Which the Existence of God, and the Real Distinction of Mind and Body, Are Demonstrated

Preface to the Reader

I HAVE ALREADY SLIGHTLY TOUCHED upon the questions respecting the existence of God and the nature of the human soul, in the "Discourse on the Method of Rightly Conducting the Reason, and Seeking Truth in the Sciences," published in French in the year 1637; not, however, with the design of there treating of them fully, but only, as it were, in passing, that I might learn from the judgments of my readers in what way I should afterwards handle them: for these questions appeared to me to be of such moment as to be worthy of being considered more than once, and the path which I follow in discussing them is so little trodden, and so remote from the ordinary route, that I thought it would not be expedient to illustrate it at greater length in French, and in a discourse that might be read by all, lest even the more feeble minds should believe that this path might be entered upon by them.

But, as in the Discourse on Method, I had requested all who might find aught meriting censure in my writings, to do me the favour of pointing it out to me, I may state that no objections worthy of remark have been alleged against what I then said on these questions, except two, to which I will here briefly reply, before undertaking their more detailed discussion.

The first objection is that though, while the human mind reflects on itself, it does not perceive that it is any other than a thinking thing, it does not follow that its nature or essence consists only in its being a thing which thinks; so that the word *only* shall exclude all other things which might also perhaps be said to pertain to the nature of the mind.

To this objection I reply, that it was not my intention in that place to exclude these according to the order of truth in the matter (of which I did not then treat), but only according to the order of thought; so that my meaning was, that I clearly apprehended nothing, so far as I was conscious, as belonging to my essence, except that I was a thinking thing, or a thing possessing in itself the faculty of thinking. But I will show hereafter how, from the consciousness that nothing besides thinking belongs to the essence of the mind, it follows that nothing else does in truth belong to it.

The second objection is that it does not follow, from my possessing the idea of a thing more perfect than I am, that the idea itself is more perfect than myself, and much less that what is represented by the idea exists.

But I reply that in the term *idea* there is here something equivocal; for it may be taken either materially for an act of the understanding, and in this sense it cannot be said to be more perfect than I, or objectively, for the thing represented by that act, which, although it be not supposed to exist out of my understanding, may, nevertheless, be more perfect than myself, by reason of its essence. But in the sequel of this treatise I will show more amply how, from my possessing the idea of a thing more perfect than myself, it follows that this thing really exists.

Besides these two objections, I have seen, indeed, two treatises of sufficient length relating to the present matter. In these, however, my conclusions, much more than my premises, were

Selections from René Descartes, Meditations on First Philosophy, *trans. by John Veitch (New York: Open Court, 1901).*

impugned, and that by arguments borrowed from the commonplaces of the atheists. But, as arguments of this sort can make no impression on the minds of those who shall rightly understand my reasonings, and as the judgments of many are so irrational and weak that they are persuaded rather by the opinions on a subject that are first presented to them, however false and opposed to reason they may be, than by a true and solid, but subsequently received, refutation of them, I am unwilling here to reply to these strictures from a dread of being, in the first instance, obliged to state them.

I will only say, in general, that all which the atheists commonly allege in favour of the non-existence of God, arises continually from one or other of these two things, namely, either the ascription of human affections to Deity, or the undue attribution to our minds of so much vigour and wisdom that we may essay to determine and comprehend both what God can and ought to do; hence all that is alleged by them will occasion us no difficulty, provided only we keep in remembrance that our minds must be considered finite, while Deity is incomprehensible and infinite.

Now that I have once, in some measure, made proof of the opinions of men regarding my work, I again undertake to treat of God and the human soul, and at the same time to discuss the principles of the entire First Philosophy, without, however, expecting any commendation from the crowd for my endeavours, or a wide circle of readers. On the contrary, I would advise none to read this work, unless such as are able and willing to meditate with me in earnest, to detach their minds from commerce with the senses, and likewise to deliver themselves from all prejudice; and individuals of this character are, I well know, remarkably rare. But with regard to those who, without caring to comprehend the order and connection of the reasonings, shall study only detached clauses for the purpose of small but noisy criticism, as is the custom with many, I may say that such persons will not profit greatly by the reading of this treatise; and although perhaps they may find opportunity for cavilling in several places, they will yet hardly start any pressing objections, or such as shall be deserving of reply.

But since, indeed, I do not promise to satisfy others on all these subjects at first sight, nor arrogate so much to myself as to believe that I have been able to foresee all that may be the source of difficulty to each one, I shall expound, first of all, in the *Meditations,* those considerations by which I feel persuaded that I have arrived at a certain and evident knowledge of truth, in order that I may ascertain whether the reasonings which have prevailed with myself will also be effectual in convincing others. I will then reply to the objections of some men, illustrious for their genius and learning, to whom these Meditations were sent for criticism before they were committed to the press; for these objections are so numerous and varied that I venture to anticipate that nothing, at least nothing of any moment, will readily occur to any mind which has not been touched upon in them.

Hence it is that I earnestly entreat my readers not to come to any judgment on the questions raised in the Meditations until they have taken care to read the whole of the Objections, with the relative Replies.

Synopsis of the Six Following Meditations

In the First Meditation I expound the grounds on which we may doubt in general of all things, and especially of material objects, so long, at least, as we have no other foundations for the sciences than those we have hitherto possessed. Now, although the utility of a doubt so general may not be manifest at first sight, it is nevertheless of the greatest, since it delivers us from all prejudice, and affords the easiest pathway by which the mind may withdraw itself from the senses; and, finally, makes it impossible for us to doubt wherever we afterwards discover truth.

In the Second, the mind which, in the exercise of the freedom peculiar to itself, supposes that no object is, of the existence of which it has even the slightest doubt, finds that, meanwhile, it must itself exist. And this point is likewise of the highest moment, for the mind is thus enabled easily to distinguish what pertains to itself, that is, to the intellectual nature, from what is to be referred to the body. But since some, perhaps, will expect, at this stage of our progress, a statement of the reasons which establish the doctrine of the immortality of the soul, I think it proper here to make such aware, that it was my aim to write nothing of which I could not give exact demonstration, and that I therefore felt myself obliged to adopt an order similar to that in use among the geometers, viz., to premise all upon which the proposition in question depends, before coming to any conclusion respecting it. Now, the first and chief prerequisite for the knowledge of the immortality of the soul is our being able to form the clearest possible conception of the soul itself, and such as shall be absolutely distinct from all our notions of body; and how this is to be accomplished is there shown. There is required, besides this, the assurance that all objects which we clearly and distinctly think are true in that very mode in which we think them; and this could not be established previously to the Fourth Meditation. Farther, it is necessary, for the same purpose, that we possess a distinct conception of corporeal nature, which is given partly in the Second and partly in the Fifth and Sixth Meditations. And, finally, on these grounds, we are necessitated to conclude, that all those objects which are clearly and distinctly conceived to be diverse substances, as mind and body, are substances really reciprocally distinct; and this inference is made in the Sixth Meditation. The absolute distinction of mind and body is, besides, confirmed in this Second Meditation, by showing that we cannot conceive body unless as divisible; while, on the other hand, mind cannot be conceived unless as indivisible. For we are not able to conceive the half of a mind, as we can of any body, however small, so that the natures of these two substances are to be held, not only as diverse, but even in some measure as contraries. I have not, however, pursued this discussion further in the present treatise, as well for the reason that these considerations are sufficient to show that the destruction of the mind does not follow from the corruption of the body, and thus to afford to men the hope of a future life, as also because the premises from which it is competent for us to infer the immortality of the soul, involve an explication of the whole principles of Physics: in order to establish, in the first place, that generally all substances, that is, all things which can exist only in consequence of having been created by God, are in their own nature incorruptible, and can

never cease to be, unless God himself, by refusing his concurrence to them, reduce them to nothing; and, in the second place, that body, taken generally, is a substance, and therefore can never perish, but that the human body, in as far as it differs from other bodies, is constituted only by a certain configuration of members, and by other accidents of this sort, while the human mind is not made up of accidents, but is a pure substance. For although all the accidents of the mind be changed—although, for example, it think certain things, will others, and perceive others, the mind itself does not vary with these changes; while, on the contrary, the human body is no longer the same if a change take place in the form of any of its parts: from which it follows that the body may, indeed, without difficulty perish, but that the mind is in its own nature immortal.

In the Third Meditation, I have unfolded at sufficient length, as appears to me, my chief argument for the existence of God. But yet, since I was there desirous to avoid the use of comparisons taken from material objects, that I might withdraw, as far as possible, the minds of my readers from the senses, numerous obscurities perhaps remain, which, however, will, I trust, be afterwards entirely removed in the Replies to the Objections: thus, among other things, it may be difficult to understand how the idea of a being absolutely perfect, which is found in our minds, possesses so much objective reality that it must be held to arise from a cause absolutely perfect. This is illustrated in the Replies by the comparison of a highly perfect machine, the idea of which exists in the mind of some workman; for as the objective perfection of this idea must have some cause, viz., either the science of the workman, or of some other person from whom he has received the idea, in the same way the idea of God, which is found in us, demands God himself for its cause.

In the Fourth, it is shown that all which we clearly and distinctly perceive is true; and, at the same time, is explained wherein consists the nature of error; points that require to be known as well for confirming the preceding truths, as for the better understanding of those that are to follow. But, meanwhile, it must be observed, that I do not at all there treat of Sin, that is, of error committed in the pursuit of good and evil, but of that sort alone which arises in the determination of the true and the false. Nor do I refer to matters of faith, or to the conduct of life, but only to what regards speculative truths, and such as are known by means of the natural light alone.

In the Fifth, besides the illustration of corporeal nature, taken generically, a new demonstration is given of the existence of God, not free, perhaps, any more than the former, from certain difficulties, but of these the solution will be found in the Replies to the Objections. I further show, in what sense it is true that the certitude of geometrical demonstrations themselves is dependent on the knowledge of God.

Finally, in the Sixth, the act of the understanding is distinguished from that of the imagination; the marks of this distinction are described; the human mind is shown to be really distinct from the body, and, nevertheless, to be so closely conjoined therewith, as together to form, as it were, a unity. The whole of the errors which arise from the senses are brought under review, while the means of avoiding them are pointed out; and, finally, all the grounds are adduced from which the existence of material objects may be inferred; not, however, because I deemed them of great utility in establishing what they prove, viz., that there is in reality a world, that men are possessed of bodies, and the like, the truth of which no one of sound mind ever seriously doubted; but because, from a close consideration of them, it is perceived that they are neither so strong nor clear as the reasonings which conduct us to the knowledge of our mind and of God; so that the latter are, of all which come under human knowledge, the most certain and manifest—a conclusion which it was my single aim in these Meditations to establish; on which account I here omit mention of the various other questions which, in the course of the discussion, I had occasion likewise to consider.

Meditation I: Of the Things of Which We May Doubt

Several years have now elapsed since I first became aware that I had accepted, even from my youth, many false opinions for true, and that consequently what I afterwards based on such principles was highly doubtful; and from that time I was convinced of the necessity of undertaking once in my life to rid myself of all the opinions I had adopted, and of commencing anew the work of building from the foundation, if I desired to establish a firm and abiding superstructure in the sciences. But as this enterprise appeared to me to be one of great magnitude, I waited until I had attained an age so mature as to leave me no hope that at any stage of life more advanced I should be better able to execute my design. On this account, I have delayed so long that I should henceforth consider I was doing wrong were I still to consume in deliberation any of the time that now remains for action. To-day, then, since I have opportunely freed my mind from all cares, . . . and since I am in the secure possession of leisure in a peaceable retirement, I will at length apply myself earnestly and freely to the general overthrow of all my former opinions. But, to this end, it will not be necessary for me to show that the whole of these are false—a point, perhaps, which I shall never reach; but as even now my reason convinces me that I ought not the less carefully to withhold belief from what is not entirely certain and indubitable, than from what is manifestly false, it will be sufficient to justify the rejection of the whole if I shall find in each some ground for doubt. Nor for this purpose will it be necessary even to deal with each belief individually, which would be truly an endless labour; but, as the removal from below of the foundation necessarily involves the downfall of the whole edifice, I will at once approach the criticism of the principles on which all my former beliefs rested.

All that I have, up to this moment, accepted as possessed of the highest truth and certainty, I received either from or through the senses. I observed, however, that these sometimes misled us; and it is the part of prudence not to place absolute confidence in that by which we have even once been deceived.

But it may be said, perhaps, that, although the senses occasionally mislead us respecting minute objects, and such as are so far removed from us as to be beyond the reach of close observation, there are yet many other of their informations, of the truth of which it is manifestly impossible to doubt; as for example, that I am in this place, seated by the fire, clothed in a winter dressing-gown, that

I hold in my hands this piece of paper, with other intimations of the same nature. But how could I deny that I possess these hands and this body, and withal escape being classed with persons in a state of insanity, whose brains are so disordered and clouded by dark bilious vapours as to cause them pertinaciously to assert that they are monarchs when they are in the greatest poverty; or clothed [in gold] and purple when destitute of any covering; or that their head is made of clay, their body of glass, or that they are gourds? I should certainly be not less insane than they, were I to regulate my procedure according to examples so extravagant.

Though this be true, I must nevertheless here consider that I am a man, and that, consequently, I am in the habit of sleeping, and representing to myself in dreams those same things, or even sometimes others less probable, which the insane think are presented to them in their waking moments. How often have I dreamt that I was in these familiar circumstances,—that I was dressed, and occupied this place by the fire, when I was lying undressed in bed? At the present moment, however, I certainly look upon this paper with eyes wide awake; the head which I now move is not asleep; I extend this hand consciously and with express purpose, and I perceive it; the occurrences in sleep are not so distinct as all this. But I cannot forget that, at other times, I have been deceived in sleep by similar illusions; and, attentively considering those cases, I perceive so clearly that there exist no certain marks by which the state of waking can ever be distinguished from sleep, that I feel greatly astonished; and in amazement I almost persuade myself that I am now dreaming.

Let us suppose, then, that we are dreaming, and that all these particulars—namely, the opening of the eyes, the motion of the head, the forth-putting of the hands—are merely illusions; and even that we really possess neither an entire body nor hands such as we see. Nevertheless, it must be admitted at least that the objects which appear to us in sleep are, as it were, painted representations which could not have been formed unless in the likeness of realities; and, therefore, that those general objects, at all events,—namely, eyes, a head, hands, and an entire body—are not simply imaginary, but

really existent. For, in truth, painters themselves, even when they study to represent sirens and satyrs by forms the most fantastic and extraordinary, cannot bestow upon them natures absolutely new, but can only make a certain medley of the members of different animals; or if they chance to imagine something so novel that nothing at all similar has ever been seen before, and such as is, therefore, purely fictitious and absolutely false, it is at least certain that the colours of which this is composed are real.

And on the same principle, although these general objects, viz., eyes, a head, hands, and the like, be imaginary, we are nevertheless absolutely necessitated to admit the reality at least of some other objects still more simple and universal than these, of which, just as of certain real colours, all those images of things, whether true and real, or false and fantastic, that are found in our consciousness, are formed.

To this class of objects seem to belong corporeal nature in general and its extension; the figure of extended things, their quantity or magnitude, and their number, as also the place in, and the time during, which they exist, and other things of the same sort. We will not, therefore, perhaps reason illegitimately if we conclude from this that Physics, Astronomy, Medicine, and all the other sciences that have for their end the consideration of composite objects, are indeed of a doubtful character; but that Arithmetic, Geometry, and the other sciences of the same class, which regard merely the simplest and most general objects, and scarcely inquire whether or not these are really existent, contain somewhat that is certain and indubitable: for whether I am awake or dreaming, it remains true that two and three make five, and that a square has but four sides; nor does it seem possible that truths so apparent can ever fall under a suspicion of falsity.

Nevertheless, the belief that there is a God who is all-powerful, and who created me, such as I am, has, for a long time, obtained steady possession of my mind. How, then, do I know that he has not arranged that there should be neither earth, nor sky, nor any extended thing, nor figure, nor magnitude, nor place, providing at the same time, however, for [the rise in me of the perceptions of all these objects, and] the persuasion that these do not exist otherwise than as I perceive them? And further, as I sometimes think that others are in error respecting matters of which they believe themselves to possess a perfect knowledge, how do I know that I am not also deceived each time I add together two and three, or number the sides of a square, or form some judgment still more simple, if more simple indeed can be imagined? But perhaps Deity has not been willing that I should be thus deceived, for He is said to be supremely good. If, however, it were repugnant to the goodness of Deity to have created me subject to constant deception, it would seem likewise to be contrary to his goodness to allow me to be occasionally deceived; and yet it is clear that this is permitted. Some, indeed, might perhaps be found who would be disposed rather to deny the existence of a Being so powerful than to believe that there is nothing certain. But let us for the present refrain from opposing this opinion, and grant that all which is here said of a Deity is fabulous: nevertheless in whatever way it be supposed that I reached the state in which I exist, whether by fate, or chance, or by an endless series of antecedents and consequents, or by any other means, it is clear that the probability of my being so imperfect as to be the constant victim of deception, will be increased exactly in proportion as the power possessed by the cause, to which they assign my origin, is lessened. To these reasonings I have assuredly nothing to reply, but am constrained at last to avow that there is nothing of all that I formerly believed to be true of which it is impossible to doubt, and that not through thoughtlessness or levity, but from cogent and maturely considered reasons; so that henceforward, if I desire to discover anything certain, I ought not the less carefully to refrain from assenting to those same opinions than to what might be shown to be manifestly false.

But it is not sufficient to have made these observations; care must be taken likewise to keep them in remembrance. For those old and customary opinions perpetually recur—long and familiar usage giving them the right of occupying my mind, even almost against my will, and subduing

my belief; nor will I lose the habit of deferring to them and confiding in them so long as I shall consider them to be what in truth they are, viz., opinions to some extent doubtful, as I have already shown, but still highly probable, and such as it is much more reasonable to believe than deny. It is for this reason I am persuaded that I shall not be doing wrong, if, taking an opposite judgment of deliberate design, I become my own deceiver, by supposing, for a time, that all those opinions are entirely false and imaginary, until at length, having thus balanced my old by my new prejudices, my judgment shall no longer be turned aside by perverted usage from the path that may conduct to the perception of truth. For I am assured that, meanwhile, there will arise neither peril nor error from this course, and that I cannot for the present yield too much to distrust, since the end I now seek is not action but knowledge.

I will suppose, then, not that Deity, who is sovereignly good and the fountain of truth, but that some malignant demon, who is at once exceedingly potent and deceitful, has employed all his artifice to deceive me; I will suppose that the sky, the air, the earth, colours, figures, sounds, and all external things, are nothing better than the illusions of dreams, by means of which this being has laid snares for my credulity; I will consider myself as without hands, eyes, flesh, blood, or any of the senses, and as falsely believing that I am possessed of these; I will continue resolutely fixed in this belief, and if indeed by this means it be not in my power to arrive at the knowledge of truth, I shall at least do what is in my power, . . . and guard with settled purpose against giving my assent to what is false, and being imposed upon by this deceiver, whatever be his power and artifice.

But this undertaking is arduous, and a certain indolence insensibly leads me back to my ordinary course of life; and just as the captive, who, perchance, was enjoying in his dreams an imaginary liberty, when he begins to suspect that it is but a vision, dreads awakening, and conspires with the agreeable illusions that the deception may be prolonged; so I, of my own accord, fall back into the train of my former beliefs, and fear to arouse myself from my slumber, lest the time of laborious wakefulness that would succeed this quiet rest, in place of bringing any light of day, should prove inadequate to dispel the darkness that will arise from the difficulties that have now been raised.

Meditation II: Of the Nature of the Human Mind and That It Is More Easily Known Than the Body

The Meditation of yesterday has filled my mind with so many doubts, that it is no longer in my power to forget them. Nor do I see, meanwhile, any principle on which they can be resolved; and, just as if I had fallen all of a sudden into very deep water, I am so greatly disconcerted as to be unable either to plant my feet firmly on the bottom or sustain myself by swimming on the surface. I will, nevertheless, make an effort, and try anew the same path on which I had entered yesterday, that is, proceed by casting aside all that admits of the slightest doubt, not less than if I had discovered it to be absolutely false; and I will continue always in this track until I shall find something that is certain, or at least, if I can do nothing more, until I shall know with certainty that there is nothing certain. Archimedes, that he might transport the entire globe from the place it occupied to another, demanded only a point that was firm and immoveable; so also, I shall be entitled to entertain the highest expectations, if I am fortunate enough to discover only one thing that is certain and indubitable.

I suppose, accordingly, that all the things which I see are false; I believe that none of those objects which my fallacious memory represents ever existed; I suppose that I possess no senses; I believe that body, figure, extension, motion, and place are merely fictions of my mind. What is there, then, that can be esteemed true? Perhaps this only, that there is absolutely nothing certain.

But how do I know that there is not something different altogether from the objects I have now enumerated, of which it is impossible to entertain the slightest doubt? Is there not a God, or some being, by whatever name I may designate him, who causes these thoughts to arise in my mind? But why suppose such a being, for it may be I

myself am capable of producing them? Am I, then, at least not something? But I before denied that I possessed senses or a body; I hesitate, however, for what follows from that? Am I so dependent on the body and the senses that without these I cannot exist? But I had the persuasion that there was absolutely nothing in the world, that there was no sky and no earth, neither minds nor bodies; was I not, therefore, at the same time, persuaded that I did not exist? Far from it; I assuredly existed, since I was persuaded. But there is I know not what being, who is possessed at once of the highest power and the deepest cunning, who is constantly employing all his ingenuity in deceiving me. Doubtless, then, I exist, since I am deceived; and let him deceive me as he may, he can never bring it about that I am nothing, so long as I shall be conscious that I am something. So that it must, in fine, be maintained, all things being maturely and carefully considered, that this proposition I am, I exist, is necessarily true each time it is expressed by me, or conceived in my mind.

But I do not yet know with sufficient clearness what I am, though assured that I am; and hence, in the next place, I must take care, lest perchance I inconsiderately substitute some other object in room of what is properly myself, and thus wander from truth, even in that knowledge which I hold to be of all others the most certain and evident. For this reason, I will now consider anew what I formerly believed myself to be, before I entered on the present train of thought; and of my previous opinion I will retrench all that can in the least be invalidated by the grounds of doubt I have adduced, in order that there may at length remain nothing but what is certain and indubitable. What then did I formerly think I was? Undoubtedly I judged that I was a man. But what is a man? Shall I say a rational animal? Assuredly not; for it would be necessary forthwith to inquire into what is meant by animal, and what by rational, and thus, from a single question, I should insensibly glide into others, and these more difficult than the first; nor do I now possess enough of leisure to warrant me in wasting my time amid subtleties of this sort. I prefer here to attend to the thoughts that sprung up of themselves in my mind, and were inspired by my own nature alone, when I applied myself to the consideration of what I was. In the first place, then, I thought that I possessed a countenance, hands, arms, and all the fabric of members that appears in a corpse, and which I called by the name of body. It further occurred to me that I was nourished, that I walked, perceived, and thought, and all those actions I referred to the soul; but what the soul itself was I either did not stay to consider, or, if I did, I imagined that it was something extremely rare and subtile, like wind, or flame, or ether, spread through my grosser parts. As regarded the body, I did not even doubt of its nature, but thought I distinctly knew it, and if I had wished to describe it according to the notions I then entertained, I should have explained myself in this manner: By body I understand all that can be terminated by a certain figure; that can be comprised in a certain place, and so fill a certain space as therefrom to exclude every other body; that can be perceived either by touch, sight, hearing, taste, or smell; that can be moved in different ways, not indeed of itself, but by something foreign to it by which it is touched; for the power of self-motion, as likewise that of perceiving and thinking, I held as by no means pertaining to the nature of body; on the contrary, I was somewhat astonished to find such faculties existing in some bodies.

But, since I suppose there exists an extremely powerful, and, if I may so speak, malignant being, whose whole endeavours are directed towards deceiving me? Can I affirm that I possess any one of all those attributes of which I have lately spoken as belonging to the nature of body? After attentively considering them in my own mind, I find none of them that can properly be said to belong to myself. To recount them were idle and tedious. Let us pass, then, to the attributes of the soul. The first mentioned were the powers of nutrition and walking; but, if it be true that I have no body, it is true likewise that I am capable neither of walking nor of being nourished. Perception is another attribute of the soul; but perception too is impossible without the body: besides, I have frequently, during sleep, believed that I perceived objects which I afterwards observed I did not in reality perceive. Thinking is another attribute of the soul; and here I

discover what properly belongs to myself. This alone is inseparable from me. I am—I exist: This is certain; but how often? As often as I think; for perhaps it would even happen, if I should wholly cease to think, that I should at the same time altogether cease to be. I now admit nothing that is not necessarily true: I am therefore, precisely speaking, only a thinking thing, that is, a mind, understanding, or reason,—terms whose signification was before unknown to me. I am, however, a real thing, and really existent; but what thing? The answer was, a thinking thing. The question now arises, am I aught besides? I will stimulate my imagination with a view to discover whether I am not still something more than a thinking being. Now it is plain I am not the assemblage of members called the human body; I am not a thin and penetrating air diffused through all these members, or wind, or flame, or vapour, or breath, or any of all the things I can imagine; for I supposed that all these were not, and, without changing the supposition, I find that I still feel assured of my existence.

But it is true, perhaps, that those very things which I suppose to be non-existent, because they are unknown to me, are not in truth different from myself whom I know. This is a point I cannot determine, and do not now enter into any dispute regarding it. I can only judge of things that are known to me: I am conscious that I exist, and I who know that I exist inquire into what I am. It is, however, perfectly certain that the knowledge of my existence, thus precisely taken, is not dependent on things, the existence of which is as yet unknown to me: and consequently it is not dependent on any of the things I can feign in imagination. Moreover, the phrase itself, I frame an image, reminds me of my error; for I should in truth frame one if I were to imagine myself to be anything, since to imagine is nothing more than to contemplate the figure or image of a corporeal thing; but I already know that I exist, and that it is possible at the same time that all those images, and in general all that relates to the nature of body, are merely dreams [or chimeras]. From this I discover that it is not more reasonable to say, I will excite my imagination that I may know more distinctly what I am, than to express myself as follows: I am now awake, and perceive something real; but because my perception is not sufficiently clear, I will of express purpose go to sleep that my dreams may represent to me the object of my perception with more truth and clearness. And, therefore, I know that nothing of all that I can embrace in imagination belongs to the knowledge which I have of myself, and that there is need to recall with the utmost care the mind from this mode of thinking, that it may be able to know its own nature with perfect distinctness.

But what, then, am I? A thinking thing, it has been said. But what is a thinking thing? It is a thing that doubts, understands, affirms, denies, wills, refuses, that imagines also, and perceives. Assuredly it is not little, if all these properties belong to my nature. But why should they not belong to it? Am I not that very being who now doubts of almost everything; who, for all that, understands and conceives certain things; who affirms one alone as true, and denies the others; who desires to know more of them, and does not wish to be deceived; who imagines many things, sometimes even despite his will; and is likewise percipient of many, as if through the medium of the senses. Is there nothing of all this as true as that I am, even although I should be always dreaming, and although he who gave me being employed all his ingenuity to deceive me? Is there also any one of these attributes that can be properly distinguished from my thought, or that can be said to be separate from myself? For it is of itself so evident that it is I who doubt, I who understand, and I who desire, that it is here unnecessary to add anything by way of rendering it more clear. And I am as certainly the same being who imagines; for, although it may be that nothing I imagine is true, still the power of imagination does not cease really to exist in me and to form part of my thought. In fine, I am the same being who perceives, that is, who apprehends certain objects as by the organs of sense, since, in truth, I see light, hear a noise, and feel heat. But it will be said that these presentations are false, and that I am dreaming. Let it be so. At all events it is certain that I seem to see light, hear a noise, and feel heat; this cannot be false, and this is what in me is properly called perceiving, which is

nothing else than thinking. From this I begin to know what I am with somewhat greater clearness and distinctness than heretofore.

But, nevertheless, it still seems to me, and I cannot help believing, that corporeal things, whose images are formed by thought, and are examined by the same, are known with much greater distinctness than that I know not what part of myself which is not imaginable; although, in truth, it may seem strange to say that I know and comprehend with greater distinctness things whose existence appears to me doubtful, that are unknown, and do not belong to me, than others of whose reality I am persuaded, that are known to me, and appertain to my proper nature; in a word, than myself. But I see clearly what is the state of the case. My mind is apt to wander, and will not yet submit to be restrained within the limits of truth. Let us therefore leave the mind to itself once more, and, according to it every kind of liberty, in order that, having afterwards withdrawn it from these gently and opportunely, it may then be the more easily controlled.

Let us now accordingly consider the objects that are commonly thought to be the most distinctly known, viz., the bodies we touch and see; not, indeed, bodies in general, for these general notions are usually somewhat more confused, but one body in particular. Take, for example, this piece of wax; it is quite fresh, having been but recently taken from the beehive; it has not yet lost the sweetness of the honey it contained; it still retains somewhat of the odour of the flowers from which it was gathered; its colour, figure, size, are apparent; it is hard, cold, easily handled; and sounds when struck upon with the finger. In fine, all that contributes to make a body as distinctly known as possible, is found in the one before us. But, while I am speaking, let it be placed near the fire—what remained of the taste exhales, the smell evaporates, the colour changes, its figure is destroyed, its size increases, it becomes liquid, it grows hot, it can hardly be handled, and, although struck upon, it emits no sound. Does the same wax still remain after this change? It must be admitted that it does remain; no one doubts it, or judges otherwise. What, then, was it I knew with so much distinctness in the piece of wax? Assuredly, it could be nothing of all that I observed by means of the senses, since all the things that fell under taste, smell, sight, touch, and hearing are changed, and yet the same wax remains. It was perhaps what I now think, viz., that this wax was neither the sweetness of honey, the pleasant odour of flowers, the whiteness, the figure, nor the sound, but only a body that a little before appeared to me conspicuous under these forms, and which is now perceived under others. But, to speak precisely, what is it that I imagine when I think of it in this way? Let it be attentively considered, and, retrenching all that does not belong to the wax, let us see what remains. There certainly remains nothing, except something extended, flexible, and movable. But what is meant by flexible and movable? Is it not that I imagine that the piece of wax, being round, is capable of becoming square, or of passing from a square into a triangular figure? Assuredly such is not the case, because I conceive that it admits of an infinity of similar changes; and I am, moreover, unable to compass this infinity by imagination, and consequently this conception which I have of the wax is not the product of the faculty of imagination. But what now is this extension? Is it not also unknown? for it becomes greater when the wax is melted, greater when it is boiled, and greater still when the heat increases; and I should not conceive according to truth, the wax as it is, if I did not suppose that the piece we are considering admitted even of a wider variety of extension than I ever imagined. I must, therefore, admit that I cannot even comprehend by imagination what the piece of wax is, and that it is the mind alone which perceives it. I speak of one piece in particular; for, as to wax in general, this is still more evident. But what is the piece of wax that can be perceived only by the mind? It is certainly the same which I see, touch, imagine; and, in fine, it is the same which, from the beginning, I believed it to be. But the perception of it is neither an act of sight, of touch, nor of imagination, and never was either of these, though it might formerly seem so, but is simply an intuition of the mind, which may be imperfect and confused, as it formerly was, or very clear and distinct, as it is at present, according as the attention is more or less directed to the elements which it contains, and of which it is composed.

But, meanwhile, I feel greatly astonished when I observe its proneness to error. For although, without at all giving expression to what I think, I consider all this in my own mind, words yet occasionally impede my progress, and I am almost led into error by the terms of ordinary language. We say, for example, that we see the same wax when it is before us, and not that we judge it to be the same from its retaining the same colour and figure: whence I should forthwith be disposed to conclude that the wax is known by the act of sight, and not by the intuition of the mind alone, were it not for the analogous instance of human beings passing on in the street below, as observed from a window. In this case I do not fail to say that I see the men themselves, just as I say that I see the wax; and yet what do I see from the window beyond hats and cloaks that might cover artificial machines, whose motions might be determined by springs? But I judge that there are human beings from these appearances, and thus I comprehend, by the faculty of judgment alone which is in the mind, what I believed I saw with my eyes.

The man who makes it his aim to rise to knowledge superior to the common, ought to be ashamed to seek occasions of doubting from the vulgar forms of speech: instead, therefore, of doing this, I shall proceed with the matter in hand, and inquire whether I had a clearer and more perfect perception of the piece of wax when I first saw it, and when I thought I knew it by means of the external sense itself, or, at all events, by the common sense as it is called, that is, by the imaginative faculty; or whether I rather apprehend it more clearly at present, after having examined with greater care, both what it is, and in what way it can be known. It would certainly be ridiculous to entertain any doubt on this point. For what, in that first perception, was there distinct? What did I perceive which any animal might not have perceived? But when I distinguish the wax from its exterior forms, and when, as if I had stripped it of its vestments, I consider it quite naked, it is certain, although some error may still be found in my judgment, that I cannot, nevertheless, thus apprehend it without possessing a human mind.

But, finally, what shall I say of the mind itself, that is, of myself? for as yet I do not admit that I am anything but mind. What, then! I who seem to possess so distinct an apprehension of the piece of wax,—do I not know myself, both with greater truth and certitude, and also much more distinctly and clearly? For if I judge that the wax exists because I see it, it assuredly follows, much more evidently, that I myself am or exist, for the same reason: for it is possible that what I see may not in truth be wax, and that I do not even possess eyes with which to see anything; but it cannot be that when I see, or, which comes to the same thing, when I think I see, I myself who think am nothing. So likewise, if I judge that the wax exists because I touch it, it will still also follow that I am; and if I determine that my imagination, or any other cause, whatever it be, persuades me of the existence of the wax, I will still draw the same conclusion. And what is here remarked of the piece of wax, is applicable to all the other things that are external to me. And further, if the perception of wax appeared to me more precise and distinct, after that not only sight and touch, but many other causes besides, rendered it manifest to my apprehension, with how much greater distinctness must I now know myself, since all the reasons that contribute to the knowledge of the nature of wax, or of any body whatever, manifest still better the nature of my mind? And there are besides so many other things in the mind itself that contribute to the illustration of its nature, that those dependent on the body, to which I have here referred, scarcely merit to be taken into account.

But, in conclusion, I find I have insensibly reverted to the point I desired; for, since it is now manifest to me that bodies themselves are not properly perceived by the senses nor by the faculty of imagination, but by the intellect alone; and since they are not perceived because they are seen and touched, but only because they are understood, I readily discover that there is nothing more easily or clearly apprehended than my own mind. But because it is difficult to rid one's self so promptly of an opinion to which one has been long accustomed, it will be desirable to tarry for some time at this stage, that, by long continued meditation, I may more deeply impress upon my memory this new knowledge.

Meditation VI: Of the Existence of Material Things and of the Real Distinction Between the Mind and Body of Man

There now only remains the inquiry as to whether material things exist. With regard to this question, I at least know with certainty that such things may exist, in as far as they constitute the object of the pure mathematics, since, regarding them in this aspect, I can conceive them clearly and distinctly. For there can be no doubt that God possesses the power of producing all the objects I am able distinctly to conceive, and I never considered anything impossible to him, unless when I experienced a contradiction in the attempt to conceive it aright. Further, the faculty of imagination which I possess, and of which I am conscious that I make use when I apply myself to the consideration of material things, is sufficient to persuade me of their existence: for, when I attentively consider what imagination is, I find that it is simply a certain application of the cognitive faculty to a body which is immediately present to it, and which therefore exists.

And to render this quite clear, I remark, in the first place, the difference that subsists between imagination and pure intellection. For example, when I imagine a triangle I not only conceive that it is a figure comprehended by three lines, but at the same time also I look upon these three lines as present by the power and internal application of my mind, and this is what I call imagining. But if I desire to think of a chiliogon, I indeed rightly conceive that it is a figure composed of a thousand sides, as easily as I conceive that a triangle is a figure composed of only three sides; but I cannot imagine the thousand sides of a chiliogon as I do the three sides of a triangle, nor, so to speak, view them as present. And although, in accordance with the habit I have of always imagining something when I think of corporeal things, it may happen that, in conceiving a chiliogon, I confusedly represent some figure to myself, yet it is quite evident that this is not a chiliogon, since it in no wise differs from that which I would represent to myself, if I were to think of a myriogon, or any other figure of many sides; nor would this representation be of any use in discovering and unfolding the properties that constitute the difference between a chiliogon and other polygons. But if the question turns on a pentagon, it is quite true that I can conceive its figure, as well as that of a chiliogon, without the aid of imagination; but I can likewise imagine it by applying the attention of my mind to its five sides, and at the same time to the area which they contain. Thus I observe that a special effort of mind is necessary to the act of imagination, which is not required to conceiving or understanding; and this special exertion of mind clearly shows the difference between imagination and pure intellection. I remark, besides, that this power of imagination which I possess, in as far as it differs from the power of conceiving, is in no way necessary to my essence, that is, to the essence of my mind; for although I did not possess it, I should still remain the same that I now am, from which it seems we may conclude that it depends on something different from the mind. And I easily understand that, if some body exists, with which my mind is so conjoined and united as to be able, as it were, to consider it when it chooses, it may thus imagine corporeal objects; so that this mode of thinking differs from pure intellection only in this respect, that the mind in conceiving turns in some way upon itself, and considers some one of the ideas it possesses within itself; but in imagining it turns towards the body, and contemplates in it some object conformed to the idea which it either of itself conceived or apprehended by sense. I easily understand, I say, that imagination may be thus formed, if it is true that there are bodies; and because I find no other obvious mode of explaining it, I thence, with probability, conjecture that they exist, but only with probability; and although I carefully examine all things, nevertheless I do not find that, from the distinct idea of corporeal nature I have in my imagination, I can necessarily infer the existence of any body.

But I am accustomed to imagine many other objects besides that corporeal nature which is the object of the pure mathematics, as, for example,

colours, sounds, tastes, pain, and the like, although with less distinctness; and, inasmuch as I perceive these objects much better by the senses, through the medium of which and of memory, they seem to have reached the imagination, I believe that, in order the more advantageously to examine them, it is proper I should at the same time examine what sense-perception is, and inquire whether from those ideas that are apprehended by this mode of thinking, I cannot obtain a certain proof of the existence of corporeal objects.

And, in the first place, I will recall to my mind the things I have hitherto held as true, because perceived by the senses, and the foundations upon which my belief in their truth rested; I will, in the second place, examine the reasons that afterwards constrained me to doubt of them; and, finally, I will consider what of them I ought now to believe.

Firstly, then, I perceived that I had a head, hands, feet, and other members composing that body which I considered as part, or perhaps even as a whole, of myself. I perceived further, that that body was placed among many others, by which it was capable of being affected in diverse ways, both beneficial and hurtful; and what was beneficial I remarked by a certain sensation of pleasure, and what was hurtful by a sensation of pain. And, besides this pleasure and pain, I was likewise conscious of hunger, thirst, and other appetites, as well as certain corporeal inclinations towards joy, sadness, anger, and similar passions. And, out of myself, besides the extension, figure, and motions of bodies, I likewise perceived in them hardness, heat, and the other tactile qualities, and, in addition, light, colours, odours, tastes, and sounds, the variety of which gave me the means of distinguishing the sky, the earth, the sea, and generally all the other bodies, from one another. And certainly, considering the ideas of all these qualities, which were presented to my mind, and which alone I properly and immediately perceived, it was not without reason that I thought I perceived certain objects wholly different from my thought, namely, bodies from which those ideas proceeded; for I was conscious that the ideas were presented to me without my consent being required, so that I could not perceive any object, however desirous I might be, unless it were present to the organ of sense; and it was wholly out of my power not to perceive it when it was thus present. And because the ideas I perceived by the senses were much more lively and clear, and even, in their own way, more distinct than any of those I could of myself frame by meditation, or which I found impressed on my memory, it seemed that they could not have proceeded from myself, and must therefore have been caused in me by some other objects; and as of those objects I had no knowledge beyond what the ideas themselves gave me, nothing was so likely to occur to my mind as the supposition that the objects were similar to the ideas which they caused. And because I recollected also that I had formerly trusted to the senses, rather than to reason, and that the ideas which I myself formed were not so clear as those I perceived by sense, and that they were even for the most part composed of parts of the latter, I was readily persuaded that I had no idea in my intellect which had not formerly passed through the senses. Nor was I altogether wrong in likewise believing that that body which, by a special right, I called my own, pertained to me more properly and strictly than any of the others; for in truth, I could never be separated from it as from other bodies: I felt in it and on account of it all my appetites and affections, and in fine I was affected in its parts by pain and the titillation of pleasure, and not in the parts of the other bodies that were separated from it. But when I inquired into the reason why, from this I know not what sensation of pain, sadness of mind should follow, and why from the sensation of pleasure joy should arise, or why this indescribable twitching of the stomach, which I call hunger, should put me in mind of taking food, and the parchedness of the throat of drink, and so in other cases, I was unable to give any explanation, unless that I was so taught by nature; for there is assuredly no affinity, at least none that I am able to comprehend between this irritation of the stomach and the desire of food, any more than between the perception of an object that causes pain and the consciousness of sadness which springs from the perception. And in the same way it seemed to me that all the other judgments I had formed regarding the objects of sense, were dictates of nature; because I remarked that those judgments were formed in me, before I had leisure to weigh and consider the reasons that might constrain me to form them.

But, afterwards, a wide experience by degrees sapped the faith I had reposed in my senses; for I frequently observed that towers, which at a distance seemed round, appeared square when more closely viewed, and that colossal figures, raised on the summits of these towers, looked like small statues, when viewed from the bottom of them; and, in other instances without number, I also discovered error in judgments founded on the external senses; and not only in those founded on the external, but even in those that rested on the internal senses; for is there aught more internal than pain? and yet I have sometimes been informed by parties whose arm or leg had been amputated, that they still occasionally seemed to feel pain in that part of the body which they had lost, —a circumstance that led me to think that I could not be quite certain even that any one of my members was affected when I felt pain in it. And to these grounds of doubt I shortly afterwards also added two others of very wide generality: the first of them was that I believed I never perceived anything when awake which I could not occasionally think I also perceived when asleep, and as I do not believe that the ideas I seem to perceive in my sleep proceed from objects external to me, I did not any more observe any ground for believing this of such as I seem to perceive when awake; the second was that since I was as yet ignorant of the author of my being, or at least supposed myself to be so, I saw nothing to prevent my having been so constituted by nature as that I should be deceived even in matters that appeared to me to possess the greatest truth. And, with respect to the grounds on which I had before been persuaded of the existence of sensible objects, I had no great difficulty in finding suitable answers to them; for as nature seemed to incline me to many things from which reason made me averse, I thought that I ought not to confide much in its teachings. And although the perceptions of the senses were not dependent on my will, I did not think that I ought on that ground to conclude that they proceeded from things different from myself, since perhaps there might be found in me some faculty, though hitherto unknown to me, which produced them.

But now that I begin to know myself better, and to discover more clearly the author of my being, I do not, indeed, think that I ought rashly to admit all which the senses seem to teach, nor, on the other hand, is it my conviction that I ought to doubt in general of their teachings.

And, firstly, because I know that all which I clearly and distinctly conceive can be produced by God exactly as I conceive it, it is sufficient that I am able clearly and distinctly to conceive one thing apart from another, in order to be certain that the one is different from the other, seeing they may at least be made to exist separately, by the omnipotence of God; and it matters not by what power this separation is made, in order to be compelled to judge them different; and, therefore, merely because I know with certitude that I exist, and because, in the meantime, I do not observe that aught necessarily belongs to my nature or essence beyond my being a thinking thing, I rightly conclude that my essence consists only in my being a thinking thing, [or a substance whose whole essence or nature is merely thinking]. And although I may, or rather, as I will shortly say, although I certainly do possess a body with which I am very closely conjoined; nevertheless, because, on the one hand, I have a clear and distinct idea of myself, in as far as I am only a thinking and unextended thing, and as, on the other hand, I possess a distinct idea of body, in as far as it is only an extended and unthinking thing, it is certain that I, [that is, my mind, by which I am what I am], is entirely and truly distinct from my body, and may exist without it.

Moreover, I find in myself diverse faculties of thinking that have each their special mode: for example, I find I possess the faculties of imagining and perceiving, without which I can indeed clearly and distinctly conceive myself as entire, but I cannot reciprocally conceive them without conceiving myself, that is to say, without an intelligent

substance in which they reside, for [in the notion we have of them, or to use the terms of the schools] in their formal concept, they comprise some sort of intellection; whence I perceive that they are distinct from myself as modes are from things. I remark likewise certain other faculties, as the power of changing place, of assuming diverse figures, and the like, that cannot be conceived and cannot therefore exist, any more than the preceding, apart from a substance in which they inhere. It is very evident, however, that these faculties, if they really exist, must belong to some corporeal or extended substance, since in their clear and distinct concept there is contained some sort of extension, but no intellection at all. Farther, I cannot doubt but that there is in me a certain passive faculty of perception, that is, of receiving and taking knowledge of the ideas of sensible things; but this would be useless to me, if there did not also exist in me, or in some other thing, an other active faculty capable of forming and producing those ideas. But this active faculty cannot be in me [in as far as I am but a thinking thing], seeing that it does not presuppose thought, and also that those ideas are frequently produced in my mind without my contributing to it in any way, and even frequently contrary to my will. This faculty must therefore exist in some substance different from me, in which all the objective reality of the ideas that are produced by this faculty, is contained formally or eminently, as I before remarked; and this substance is either a body, that is to say, a corporeal nature in which is contained formally [and in effect] all that is objectively [and by representation] in those ideas; or it is God himself, or some other creature, of a rank superior to body, in which the same is contained eminently. But as God is no deceiver, it is manifest that he does not of himself and immediately communicate those ideas to me, nor even by the intervention of any creature in which their objective reality is not formally, but only eminently, contained. For as he has given me no faculty whereby I can discover this to be the case, but, on the contrary, a very strong inclination to believe that those ideas arise from corporeal objects, I do not see how he could be vindicated from the charge of deceit, if in truth they proceeded from any other source, or were produced by other causes than corporeal things: and accordingly it must be concluded, that corporeal objects exist. Nevertheless they are not perhaps exactly such as we perceive by the senses, for their comprehension by the senses is, in many instances, very obscure and confused; but it is at least necessary to admit that all which I clearly and distinctly conceive as in them, that is, generally speaking, all that is comprehended in the object of speculative geometry, really exists external to me.

But with respect to other things which are either only particular, as, for example, that the sun is of such a size and figure, etc., or are conceived with less clearness and distinctness, as light, sound, pain, and the like, although they are highly dubious and uncertain, nevertheless on the ground alone that God is no deceiver, and that consequently he has permitted no falsity in my opinions which he has not likewise given me a faculty of correcting, I think I may with safety conclude that I possess in myself the means of arriving at the truth. And, in the first place, it cannot be doubted that in each of the dictates of nature there is some truth; for by nature, considered in general, I now understand nothing more than God himself, or the order and disposition established by God in created things; and by my nature in particular I understand the assemblage of all that God has given me.

But there is nothing which that nature teaches me more expressly [or more sensibly] than that I have a body which is ill affected when I feel pain, and stands in need of food and drink when I experience the sensations of hunger and thirst, etc. And therefore I ought not to doubt but that there is some truth in these informations.

Nature likewise teaches me by these sensations of pain, hunger, thirst, etc., that I am not only lodged in my body as a pilot in a vessel, but that I am besides so intimately conjoined, and as it were intermixed with it, that my mind and body compose a certain unity. For if this were not the case, I should not feel pain when my body is hurt, seeing I am merely a thinking thing, but should perceive the wound by the understanding alone, just as a pilot perceives by sight when any part of his vessel is damaged; and when my body has need of food

or drink, I should have a clear knowledge of this, and not be made aware of it by the confused sensations of hunger and thirst; for, in truth, all these sensations of hunger, thirst, pain, etc., are nothing more than certain confused modes of thinking, arising from the union and apparent fusion of mind and body.

Besides this, nature teaches me that my own body is surrounded by many other bodies, some of which I have to seek after, and others to shun. And indeed, as I perceive different sorts of colours, sounds, odours, tastes, heat, hardness, etc., I safely conclude that there are in the bodies from which the diverse perceptions of the senses proceed, certain varieties corresponding to them, although, perhaps, not in reality like them; and since, among these diverse perceptions of the senses, some are agreeable, and others disagreeable, there can be no doubt that my body, or rather my entire self, in as far as I am composed of body and mind, may be variously affected, both beneficially and hurtfully, by surrounding bodies.

But there are many other beliefs which, though seemingly the teaching of nature, are not in reality so, but which obtained a place in my mind through a habit of judging inconsiderately of things. It may thus easily happen that such judgments shall contain error: thus, for example, the opinion I have that all space in which there is nothing to affect my senses is void; that in a hot body there is something in every respect similar to the idea of heat in my mind; that in a white or green body there is the same whiteness or greenness which I perceive; that in a bitter or sweet body there is the same taste, and so in other instances; that the stars, towers, and all distant bodies, are of the same size and figure as they appear to our eyes, etc. But that I may avoid everything like indistinctness of conception, I must accurately define what I properly understand by being taught by nature. For nature is here taken in a narrower sense than when it signifies the sum of all the things which God has given me; seeing that in that meaning the notion comprehends much that belongs only to the mind [to which I am not here to be understood as referring when I use the term nature]; as, for example, the notion I have of the truth, that what is done cannot be undone, and all the other truths I discern by the natural light; and seeing that it comprehends likewise much besides that belongs only to body, and is not here any more contained under the name nature, as the quality of heaviness, and the like, of which I do not speak,—the term being reserved exclusively to designate the things which God has given to me as a being composed of mind and body. But nature, taking the term in the sense explained, teaches me to shun what causes in me the sensation of pain, and to pursue what affords me the sensation of pleasure, and other things of this sort; but I do not discover that it teaches me, in addition to this, from these diverse perceptions of the senses, to draw any conclusions respecting external objects without a previous consideration of them by the mind; for it is, as appears to me, the office of the mind alone, and not of the composite whole of mind and body, to discern the truth in those matters. Thus, although the impression a star makes on my eye is not larger than that from the flame of a candle, I do not, nevertheless, experience any real or positive impulse determining me to believe that the star is not greater than the flame; the true account of the matter being merely that I have so judged from my youth without any rational ground. And, though on approaching the fire I feel heat, and even pain on approaching it too closely, I have, however, from this no ground for holding that something resembling the heat I feel is in the fire, any more than that there is something similar to the pain; all that I have ground for believing is, that there is something in it, whatever it may be, which excites in me those sensations of heat or pain. So also, although there are spaces in which I find nothing to excite and affect my senses, I must not therefore conclude that those spaces contain in them no body; for I see that in this, as in many other similar matters, I have been accustomed to pervert the order of nature, because these perceptions of the senses, although given me by nature merely to signify to my mind what things are beneficial and hurtful to the composite whole of which it is a part, and being sufficiently clear and distinct for that purpose, are nevertheless used by me as infallible rules by which to determine immediately the essence of the bodies that exist

out of me, of which they can of course afford me only the most obscure and confused knowledge.

But I have already sufficiently considered how it happens that, notwithstanding the supreme goodness of God, there is falsity in my judgments. A difficulty, however, here presents itself, respecting the things which I am taught by nature must be pursued or avoided, and also respecting the internal sensations in which I seem to have occasionally detected error: Thus, for example, I may be so deceived by the agreeable taste of some viand with which poison has been mixed, as to be induced to take the poison. In this case, however, nature may be excused, for it simply leads me to desire the viand for its agreeable taste, and not the poison, which is unknown to it; and thus we can infer nothing from this circumstance beyond that our nature is not omniscient; at which there is assuredly no ground for surprise, since, man being of a finite nature, his knowledge must likewise be of limited perfection. But we also not unfrequently err in that to which we are directly impelled by nature, as is the case with invalids who desire drink or food that would be hurtful to them. It will here, perhaps, be alleged that the reason why such persons are deceived is that their nature is corrupted; but this leaves the difficulty untouched, for a sick man is not less really the creature of God than a man who is in full health; and therefore it is as repugnant to the goodness of God that the nature of the former should be deceitful as it is for that of the latter to be so. And, as a clock, composed of wheels and counter weights, observes not the less accurately all the laws of nature when it is ill made, and points out the hours incorrectly, than when it satisfies the desire of the maker in every respect; so likewise if the body of man be considered as a kind of machine, so made up and composed of bones, nerves, muscles, veins, blood, and skin, that although there were in it no mind, it would still exhibit the same motions which it at present manifests involuntarily, and therefore without the aid of the mind. I easily discern that it would also be as natural for such a body, supposing it dropsical, for example, to experience the parchedness of the throat that is usually accompanied in the mind by the sensation of thirst, and to be disposed by this parchedness to move its nerves and its other parts in the way required for drinking, and thus increase its malady and do itself harm, as it is natural for it, when it is not indisposed to be stimulated to drink for its good by a similar cause; and although looking to the use for which a clock was destined by its maker, I may say that it is deflected from its proper nature when it incorrectly indicates the hours, and on the same principle, considering the machine of the human body as having been formed by God for the sake of the motions which it usually manifests, although I may likewise have ground for thinking that it does not follow the order of its nature when the throat is parched and drink does not tend to its preservation, nevertheless I yet plainly discern that this latter acceptation of the term nature is very different from the other; for this is nothing more than a certain denomination, depending entirely on my thought, and hence called extrinsic, by which I compare a sick man and an imperfectly constructed clock with the idea I have of a man in good health and a well made clock; while by the other acceptation of nature is understood something which is truly found in things, and therefore possessed of some truth.

But certainly, although in respect of a dropsical body, it is only by way of exterior denomination that we say its nature is corrupted when, without requiring drink, the throat is parched; yet, in respect of the composite whole, that is, of the mind in its union with the body, it is not a pure denomination, but really an error of nature, for it to feel thirst when drink would be hurtful to it: and, accordingly, it still remains to be considered why it is that the goodness of God does not prevent the nature of man thus taken from being fallacious.

To commence this examination accordingly, I here remark, in the first place, that there is a vast difference between mind and body, in respect that body, from its nature, is always divisible, and that mind is entirely indivisible. For in truth, when I consider the mind, that is, when I consider myself in so far only as I am a thinking thing, I can distinguish in myself no parts, but I very clearly discern that I am somewhat absolutely one and entire; and although the whole mind seems to be united to the

whole body, yet, when a foot, an arm, or any other part is cut off, I am conscious that nothing has been taken from my mind; nor can the faculties of willing, perceiving, conceiving, etc., properly be called its parts, for it is the same mind that is exercised [all entire] in willing, in perceiving, and in conceiving, etc. But quite the opposite holds in corporeal or extended things; for I cannot imagine any one of them [how small soever it may be], which I cannot easily sunder in thought, and which, therefore, I do not know to be divisible. This would be sufficient to teach me that the mind or soul of man is entirely different from the body, if I had not already been apprised of it on other grounds.

I remark, in the next place, that the mind does not immediately receive the impression from all the parts of the body, but only from the brain, or perhaps even from one small part of it, viz., that in which the common sense is said to be, which as often as it is affected in the same way, gives rise to the same perception in the mind, although meanwhile the other parts of the body may be diversely disposed, as is proved by innumerable experiments, which it is unnecessary here to enumerate.

I remark, besides, that the nature of body is such that none of its parts can be moved by another part a little removed from the other, which cannot likewise be moved in the same way by any one of the parts that lie between those two, although the most remote part does not act at all. As, for example, in the cord A, B, C, D, if its last part D, be pulled, the first part A, will not be moved in a different way than it would be were one of the intermediate parts B or C to be pulled, and the last part D meanwhile to remain fixed. And in the same way, when I feel pain in the foot, the science of physics teaches me that this sensation is experienced by means of the nerves dispersed over the foot, which, extending like cords from it to the brain, when they are contracted in the foot, contract at the same time the inmost parts of the brain in which they have their origin, and excite in these parts a certain motion appointed by nature to cause in the mind a sensation of pain, as if existing in the foot: but as these nerves must pass through the tibia, the leg, the loins, the back, and neck, in order to reach the brain, it may happen that although their extremities in the foot are not affected, but only certain of their parts that pass through the loins or neck, the same movements, nevertheless, are excited in the brain by this motion as would have been caused there by a hurt received in the foot, and hence the mind will necessarily feel pain in the foot, just as if it had been hurt; and the same is true of all the other perceptions of our senses.

I remark, finally, that as each of the movements that are made in the part of the brain by which the mind is immediately affected, impresses it with but a single sensation, the most likely supposition in the circumstances is, that this movement causes the mind to experience, among all the sensations which it is capable of impressing upon it, that one which is the best fitted, and generally the most useful for the preservation of the human body when it is in full health. But experience shows us that all the perceptions which nature has given us are of such a kind as I have mentioned; and accordingly, there is nothing found in them that does not manifest the power and goodness of God. Thus, for example, when the nerves of the foot are violently or more than usually shaken, the motion passing through the medulla of the spine to the innermost parts of the brain affords a sign to the mind on which it experiences a sensation, viz., of pain, as if it were in the foot, by which the mind is admonished and excited to do its utmost to remove the cause of it as dangerous and hurtful to the foot. It is true that God could have so constituted the nature of man as that the same motion in the brain would have informed the mind of something altogether different: the motion might, for example, have been the occasion on which the mind became conscious of itself, in so far as it is in the brain, or in so far as it is in some place intermediate between the foot and the brain, or, finally, the occasion on which it perceived some other object quite different; whatever that might be; but nothing of all this would have so well contributed to the preservation of the body as that which the mind actually feels. In the same way, when we stand in need of drink, there arises from this want a certain parchedness in the throat that moves its nerves, and by means of them the internal parts

of the brain; and this movement affects the mind with the sensation of thirst, because there is nothing on that occasion which is more useful for us than to be made aware that we have need of drink for the preservation of our health; and so in other instances.

Whence it is quite manifest that, notwithstanding the sovereign goodness of God, the nature of man, in so far as it is composed of mind and body, cannot but be sometimes fallacious. For, if there is any cause which excites, not in the foot, but in some one of the parts of the nerves that stretch from the foot to the brain, or even in the brain itself, the same movement that is ordinarily created when the foot is ill affected, pain will be felt, as it were, in the foot, and the sense will thus be naturally deceived; for as the same movement in the brain can but impress the mind with the same sensation, and as this sensation is much more frequently excited by a cause which hurts the foot than by one acting in a different quarter, it is reasonable that it should lead the mind to feel pain in the foot rather than in any other part of the body. And if it sometimes happens that the parchedness of the throat does not arise, as is usual, from drink being necessary for the health of the body, but from quite the opposite cause, as is the case with the dropsical, yet it is much better that it should be deceitful in that instance, than if, on the contrary, it were continually fallacious when the body is well-disposed; and the same holds true in other cases.

And certainly this consideration is of great service, not only in enabling me to recognize the errors to which my nature is liable, but likewise in rendering it more easy to avoid or correct them: for, knowing that all my senses more usually indicate to me what is true than what is false, in matters relating in the advantage of the body, and being able almost always to make use of more than a single sense in examining the same object, and besides this, being able to use my memory in connecting present with past knowledge, and my understanding which has already discovered all the causes of my errors, I ought no longer to fear that falsity may be met with in what is daily presented to me by the senses. And I ought to reject all the doubts of those bygone days, as hyperbolical and ridiculous, especially the general uncertainty respecting sleep, which I could not distinguish from the waking state: for I now find a very marked difference between the two states, in respect that our memory can never connect our dreams with each other and with the course of life, in the way it is in the habit of doing with events that occur when we are awake. And, in truth, if some one, when I am awake, appeared to me all of a sudden and as suddenly disappeared, as do the images I see in sleep, so that I could not observe either whence he came or whither he went, I should not without reason esteem it either a spectre or phantom formed in my brain, rather than a real man. But when I perceive objects with regard to which I can distinctly determine both the place whence they come, and that in which they are, and the time at which they appear to me, and when, without interruption, I can connect the perception I have of them with the whole of the other parts of my life, I am perfectly sure that what I thus perceive occurs while I am awake and not during sleep. And I ought not in the least degree to doubt of the truth of those presentations, if, after having called together all my senses, my memory, and my understanding for the purpose of examining them, no deliverance is given by any one of these faculties which is repugnant to that of any other: for since God is no deceiver, it necessarily follows that I am not herein deceived. But because the necessities of action frequently oblige us to come to a determination before we have had leisure for so careful an examination, it must be confessed that the life of man is frequently obnoxious to error with respect to individual objects; and we must, in conclusion, acknowledge the weakness of our nature.

Study Questions

1. Why was it important that Descartes believed that scientific theory was more important than scientific observation?

2. Explain the difference between axioms and theorems in mathematics.

3. What is the "method of doubt" and what is its goal?

4. How can I know for sure that I exist?

5. For Descartes, what is the mind?

6. How does Descartes use God to prove that the world exists?

7. Why does Descartes believe that the world is a mathematical machine?

8. What is the "mind-body" problem, and how does Descartes attempt to solve it?

9. Why is it that the mind escapes the determinism that rules the rest of nature?

10. Does Descartes ever prove that the soul is immortal? Explain.

Chapter 6

Science and Religion: Immanuel Kant

Introduction

There are some who claim that Modern philosophy had two fathers, Descartes and the English philosopher, Francis Bacon (1561–1626). As with Descartes, Bacon applied the method of science to the study of the great philosophical questions. Unlike Descartes, however, the part of science that he considered most valuable was observation, not theory. The British empiricists, Locke (1632–1704), Berkeley (1685–1753) and Hume (1711–1776), followed Bacon's lead and emphasized almost exclusively the importance of factual or empirical evidence to prove their philosophical conclusions. In contrast to the *empiricism* of the English speaking world, continental Europe was inclined toward the *rationalism* of Descartes. Several philosophers, including the Jewish philosopher, Benedict Spinoza (1632–1677), the German philosopher, Gottfried Leibniz (1646–1716), and his disciple, Christian Wolff (1679–1754), deduced elaborate theories of reality from what they considered to be a few self-evident axioms.

The great German philosopher, Immanuel Kant (1724–1804), inherited these two dominant and opposed philosophical traditions. He also was heir to the work of Isaac Newton (1642–1727), whose tremendously influential theories of nature completed the work in physics that had been begun by Galileo. The success of science in understanding the material world led to a growing confidence that similar results could be produced in philosophy. The faith of the time was that with the proper use of human reason and observation, questions about the nature of persons, society, God, right and wrong, and other complex philosophical questions could finally be answered. This confident spirit, especially strong in eighteenth-century Europe, is often called the **Enlightenment.** The Enlightenment is more of an attitude than a set of theories, a confidence in human reason to solve both intellectual and practical problems for the betterment of mankind. This attitude was shared by most progressive thinkers in Europe during the eighteenth century, and certainly was close to the heart of Kant himself.

Kant spent almost all of his life in the Prussian town of his birth, Konigsberg. He was raised by Lutheran parents who instilled in him respect for moral character and good intentions. He was educated at the University in Konigsberg and in 1755 was appointed there first to a position as a lecturer in philosophy, and later to a professorship. He was a scientist as well as a philosopher, and wrote and taught courses in both areas. In philosophy he was a practicing rationalist, a follower of Christian Wolff until his late forties. At that time he changed his philosophical orientation, and soon after became an extremely prolific author. The many books which expressed his new ideas include especially his masterful work on knowledge and reality, the *Critique of Pure Reason* (1781), an introduction to this work called *Prolegomena to any Future Metaphysics* (1783), and his books on ethics, the *Fundamental Principles (or Groundwork) of the Metaphysics of Morals* (1785), and the *Critique of Practical Reason* (1788). In addition, he wrote a third critique called the *Critique of Judgment* (1790), on the imagination and its use in aesthetic creation, and late in his life wrote a book on religion, *Religion Within the Limit of Pure Reason* (1793).

Worldview

The rejection of rationalism by Kant was a rejection of what he called "pure reason," the ability of the mind to know the world independently of experience. Kant did believe at one time that the mind had the power to know reality through rational intuition and deduction alone, but he rejected this belief after reading the works of the great Scottish philosopher David Hume. Kant gave credit to Hume for awakening him from his "dogmatic slumbers," as he called his rationalistic assumptions. Hume convinced him instead that all knowledge of the world is based on experience, and that theories constructed merely by thinking, apart from any experience to back them up, have no claim to be accepted as true. They might be coherent, clever, even beautiful constructs of the imagination; but without experience to verify what they say about the world they are simply elaborate fictions.

Locke and Berkeley

While Kant rejected rationalism because of Hume's critique, and while he did become an empiricist, he did not accept the type of empiricism championed by his British colleagues. In fact, many of Kant's ideas were reactions to those of Hume. A clearer understanding of Kant's worldview will result from first understanding the views of Hume on knowledge and reality. In turn, it is best to understand what Hume said by first examining the views of his own influential predecessors, Locke and Berkeley. We will begin with **John Locke.**

The story of **British empiricism** begins with Locke's claim that all knowledge of the world begins with experience. Some knowledge is not based on experience, such as math and logic, but these systems of beliefs are not knowledge of the world. Instead, the beliefs of logic and math are simply true by definition. To acquire knowledge of the external world requires observation through the senses; what Locke calls *perception*. This is the origin of our knowledge of the world; there is no other source. In particular, there are no innate ideas or rational intuitions which reveal the nature of the world, as rationalists believe. We also have knowledge of ourselves which is based on experience. We know the content of our own minds by what Locke calls *reflection*, and others have called introspection. By observing our minds we can learn about our mental states, such as imagining, thinking, willing, deciding and so on.

Locke and Descartes held very different views on the nature of knowledge, but Locke adopted much from his French mentor about the nature of the mind and the nature of perception. The mind is like a theater for both men, where all of its goings on are conscious and readily accessible to reflection. We know the contents of our minds directly, and as they really are in themselves. Later writers, including Kant, will claim that much of the workings of the mind are not conscious, and that those that are may simply be appearances. If this is so, then knowledge of the mind must be gained indirectly, through a process of reasoning. We will have much more to say about this later.

Locke also adopted a representational theory of perception from Descartes. According to this view, when I see something, I am not aware of what I see directly, but rather I am aware of how I represent or perceive the object. Locke's version of this theory has been called the **copy theory** of knowledge, since our perceptions are understood to be copies of objects in the external world. Since knowledge is based on experience, and since experience (perception) provides no direct awareness of the external world, then to know that the external world exists and to know what it is like, will require a process of reasoning. This is something else that Locke inherited from Descartes, the need to prove that the world exists.

As with Descartes before him, Locke begins with the contents of his conscious mind and proceeds to reason to things beyond. He first presents a *causal* argument for the existence of the world. For Locke, the world exists as the best explanation for why I experience anything. My experience could not come from my self, as do my dreams, because sometimes I experience things beyond my control. My experience is passively received and thus must have an external source. As to the nature of the world, Locke adopts the fairly standard scientific view, the view taken by Descartes, that things have only some of the properties that they appear to have.

In particular, they have only measurable qualities, what Locke calls **primary qualities.** These include size, shape, motion, location, and the like. Their colors, odors, sounds, tastes, and textures, however, called **secondary qualities,** are simply the way that I perceive them. If a tree falls in the forest and there is no one there to hear it, it makes sound waves but no sounds. Secondary qualities are mental states; they exist only in the mind. They are merely reactions of my mind to the information received from the world of primary qualities. By identifying reality with only quantitative features, Locke helps the cause of science. Since science, especially physics, is the study of various quantities, and since the world is composed solely of various quantities, then science can know reality completely.

Unlike Descartes, Locke believed that he had to argue for the existence of the mind. This was required because there was no experience of a mind, only mental states. Once again he used a causal argument. As material objects are the cause of perception, so my mind exists as the cause of my mental states. It made no sense to Locke to think of a mental act apart from something which produces it. How could there be thinking, for example, without a thinker? So there must be some sort of a substance called the mind. But what is this mind itself like? Locke admits that he does not know. Since it is beyond experience through reflection, the mind can only be known as the cause of mental acts. So Locke thought he had proven that the mind exists, but he did not claim to know its true nature. For all he knew, it may be a spiritual substance, as Descartes claimed, or a material substance, as Hobbes claimed.

Locke also presented a causal argument for the existence of God. It was a weak argument and will be ignored here. Instead, we shall turn to the views of **Bishop George Berkeley.** While himself an empiricist, Berkeley was a harsh critic of Locke. For Berkeley, Locke's argument for the existence of the material world, or "material substances," was especially suspect. Locke was correct to believe that experience comes from some external source, but Berkeley thought that he had no right whatsoever to believe that this cause was something material. In the first place, what our experience tells us is that there is no difference in importance to be found between primary and secondary qualities. All of our perceptions contain both equally. I never see something of a certain shape, for example, without also seeing that it has a certain color. To say that primary qualities are more important because they exist in the mind and in material objects is just to state a prejudice for the scientific view of reality. According to experience, wherever one type of quality exists, so does the other.

From this critique, Berkeley did not infer the commonsense conclusion that material objects contain both types of properties. Instead he drew the opposite, and quite startling conclusion that neither type of property exists in material objects. If secondary qualities exist only in our minds, then so do primary qualities. Does that mean that material objects, the entire material world, exists devoid of any type of properties? No, because there are no material objects; there is no material world. We know this because there is no experience of material substances, only properties. We do not experience an apple, for example, only the properties of red, round, juicy, sweet, smooth, and so on. There is no apple, in addition to these properties, something that has these properties. Instead, things are simply collections of properties, all of which exist solely in the mind. This is what my experience tells me—that reality is a collection of mental events. The famous expression used by Berkeley to express this claim is "to be is to be perceived" (*esse est percipi*, in Latin). Only the mind and its contents exist.

At first glance, this seems like we are back in Descartes' dream world. However, Berkeley does argue to the existence of something beyond his mind. Berkeley agrees with Locke that because our experience of the world seems to be passively received it may be inferred that there is some external source of experience. This external source, however, is another mind, not the material world. This powerful mind Berkeley thinks of as God. So what exists is my mind, the minds of others, God as a mind, and the experience within all minds. Acting as a giant movie projector, God projects experience onto the minds of all in roughly the same manner, so we all share the same "world." This view is sometimes referred to as a type of **idealism,** since what is real is to be found solely in our mental lives.

Berkeley was a more rigorous empiricist than Locke. He did not allow Locke to get away with his claim that something beyond experience is knowable. For Berkeley, not only does knowledge begin with experience, it should not go beyond experience either. If a statement about the world cannot be verified by observation, then it is not to be taken as true. "Material objects have only primary qualities," is surely one of these statements that escapes verification. But if Berkeley really believes this principle of empiricism, then how can he claim that God exists? Surely God is no more observable than material objects.

The motive for Berkeley's idealism may have been to avoid what he saw as the materialism of Locke, but his reason for it rests upon his **theory of meaning.** According to this theory, the meaning of a word is the experience for which it stands. The word "dog" has meaning, since it stands for a common experience. The word "larfta," on the other hand, has no meaning. There is no experience to which it corresponds. In the same way, the phrase "material substance" has no meaning, since we do not experience material objects. The word "mind," however, has meaning, claims Berkeley because we can experience our own minds. This is simply something that he assumes to be true. While we cannot experience God, we can think of him by analogy with our finite minds, and thus may speak meaningfully about him as an all powerful mind. Since there are no material causes of experience, and since minds are the only thing left, the existence of a powerful spiritual being may be inferred as their cause.

The Influence of Hume

In his books, *The Treatise of Human Nature* (1738), and *An Enquiry Concerning Human Understanding* (1748), **David Hume** presents his version of empiricism. Hume was an even more devastating critic of his empiricist precursors than was Berkeley. He begins by showing how all knowledge arises from simple sensations. Where Locke had referred to simple sensations as perceptions and reflections, Hume refers to them as *impressions*.[1] Impressions can be "of" the world or "of" the mind. They are mental states such as seeing something in front of you, hearing a sound across the room, or feeling the throbbing pain of a toothache. Though he calls sensations "impressions," Hume does not assume that they are "impressed" upon us by external causes such as material objects that exist outside of our minds. They may have such causes, but they may also have spiritual causes, as Berkeley believed. Or perhaps we create them ourselves or, for all we know, they may have no causes at all. The simple fact of seeing and hearing and so on, does not tell us anything about the causes of our perceptions. I experience only the subjective states of my own mind, not the cause of these states. Subjective impressions are simply the sounds, sights, tastes, odors, desires, feelings, and so on, of which I am conscious.

Hume agreed with Berkeley that we have no experience of material substances. He went further than Berkeley, however, when he pointed out that we have no experience of our minds either. When he looks inside himself, Hume is aware only of his mental activity—activity such as thinking, imagining, remembering, and so on. He is not aware of any "thing" that is doing the thinking and imagining and remembering. He is not aware of a mind, or a mental substance. Hume says that he experiences his self simply as a stream of conscious experiences, not as a single subject that these conscious experiences belong to. Just as the word "material object" refers to nothing but a collection of sensory experiences, so "self" is a word that refers only to a collection of experiences, as well. As a material object is the sum total of all the experiences I have of it through perception, my self is the sum total of all the experiences I have of it through introspection.

I may *believe* that there is an abiding subject that endures through time, the subject who is me, the subject that thinks and hopes and remembers. But such belief is impossible, since I have no impressions of what such a self would be like. Following Berkeley's theory of meaning, Hume says that considering the existence of a self that lies behind the stream of consciousness, a self to which my various mental states belong, is another example of what he calls metaphysical nonsense. When I speak of a self or a mind, my words refer to nothing. To think of a mind as a substance is not even possible. Because I do not experience my self as the subject of my conscious experiences, it makes no sense even to talk about it as a possibility. For all I know, I may be simply a collection or a "bundle" of conscious experiences flowing by in time.

In a similar manner, Hume makes short work of claims to know God. There are no good inductive or deductive inferences for God's existence. This is something that he attempts to show in many places in his writings. We have no experience of God either, and therefore no idea of God, not even an idea by analogy. Because of this, it is just as senseless to talk about the existence and nature of God as it is to talk about the existence and nature of material and spiritual substances. As Berkeley disposed of Locke's material substances, Hume now disposes of Berkeley's spiritual substances, both human minds and divine minds, leaving all claims to know anything about the world, the self, and God to be understood as meaningless noise.

According to Hume, we really cannot know anything about what causes our experience (the world), or about the subject who has such experience (the mind), or about the ultimate cause or creator of existence (God). These are the central questions of metaphysics, the study of reality. Philosophical attempts to gain this sort of knowledge should simply be abandoned as impossible. Systems of metaphysics that make claims to know reality, God, and the mind are merely creations of the imagination, like novels, not a kind of knowledge that goes "deeper" than experience. Books that contain such pretensions to such knowledge should, as Hume says it, be "cast into the flames." Specifically, Hume denies as meaningful all claims made by philosophers to know anything about the three main subjects of metaphysics—God, our own minds, and the world that causes my sensations.

The Unreliability of Science

Kant might have been more accepting of these conclusions of Hume had the Scottish skeptic stopped here. But Hume went on to claim that even the findings of science are unreliable. For Kant, however, if there is any reliable knowledge of the world at all it is the knowledge expressed by Newton in his famous book on physics, the *Principia Mathematica*. In particular, laws like the law of gravity and Newton's three laws of motion express knowledge of how the world really is and works. For Hume, however, if scientific laws are to be counted as reliable knowledge they must originate from experience and be verified by experience. They do seem to originate from experience, since the first step in discovering a law of nature is to make observations of individual events of a certain sort. However, scientific laws do not seem to be *verified* by experience.

To see this, notice that the truth of scientific laws rests on the experiences that we have had about what has happened so far. But scientific laws claim to be true of "all" instances, including ones that have yet to be observed. They make claims about what is true of all experiences of a certain type, not simply claims about the experiences that we have had to this point. Since the experiences upon which the truth of a law rests, however, are only those of the past and present, it follows that it is not possible to confirm scientific laws by reference to experience. Scientific laws are beliefs that go beyond past and present experience to say how things *always* will be, even how they *must* be. They are claims about the future, as well as the past and the present. Taken as such, they are every bit as meaningless as those philosophical statements which make claims about what lies beyond experience. At most, scientific laws are meaningful only as claims about how the world has worked so far, and as a type of faith that it will continue to work that way in the future as well.

Hume's empiricist beliefs that our knowledge of the world arises solely from experience and is justified only by appealing to experience, leads him inescapably to claim that reliable knowledge is limited only to what can be immediately experienced in the present. We can be mistaken about our memories, so knowledge of the past in unreliable. We can be mistaken about our knowledge of the future as well, since our inferences about what will happen in the future are based on the belief that things will continue to work in the future as they have in the past. This is a questionable assumption for Hume. The only reliable knowledge that we possess is based on present experience, what can here-and-now be experienced through the senses and through introspection. It is only beliefs based on my present impressions—what I see, hear, taste, touch, smell, and introspect, that I can count on.

Solipsism

But even beliefs about present experience do not get to be reliable because we know that they correspond to reality. Hume accepts the *cogito* of Descartes, the view that perceptions are not "of" objects in the world, but simply exist in my mind. There is no way to check our perceptions against a world that lies beyond experience, a world that they are supposed to be "of." If Hume is to be consistent with his principles he would be forced to adopt **solipsism.** So far Hume has claimed that nothing can be *known* but my own experience, while solipsism is the view that nothing *exists* beyond my own private, subjective experiences—the contents of my mind. If it is impossible to argue for the existence of anything beyond what I can experience, and if it makes no sense to think or talk about anything but what I can experience, then it would seem to be irrational to believe and to act as if there was anything that *exists* beyond my experience. In particular, it is irrational to think that there is a world, a mind, other persons, and a God—that really exist outside of my own mind.

I can talk about a world, but such talk refers only to the collection of all my experience. I can talk about particular material objects, but such talk refers only to particular bundles of impressions and ideas. I can talk about my self, but such talk refers to no more than the collection of all my thoughts, feelings, hopes, desires, and so on—the "bundle" of experiences I call my self. So what Hume should say is that there is no reality beyond experience or, at the very least, that it is a meaningless question to ask if there is such a reality. As far as we know, all that exists is experience, period. This is what *reality* amounts to for Hume, a bundle of experiences that I call my self. This solipsistic view of reality is the only one that is consistent with Hume's epistemological principles.

Solipsism is a belief avoided by Descartes and Berkeley only because they invoked God as the justification for belief in something other than their own subjective experience. Because Hume rejects such moves, and because he believes that it is not even meaningful to speak of such things that lie beyond experience, his solipsism seems to be entirely unavoidable. In the end, however, Hume was unable or unwilling to follow his epistemological principles consistently to this solipsistic conclusion. Instead, he accepted the existence of the world, which he simply assumed was very much like his present perceptions. He accepted this reality, however, as a matter of *faith,* not as a matter of knowledge. Though there was no evidence for its existence, he accepted the commonsense view of the world as a necessary assumption for living and acting in daily life. After all, how could one possibly live as a solipsist? When he leaves his study, he says, and leaves philosophical thinking behind, he accepts the assumptions of the ordinary person about reality and knowledge.

Solipsism is an admittedly absurd view and Hume was right to reject it. However, if his view of knowledge led invariably to such a view, then it is his view of knowledge, his epistemology, that should be rejected. At the very least his brand of empiricism should be drastically revised. The radical attempt to do just that was undertaken by Kant, whose criticism of Hume we shall next examine.

Kant's Worldview

Until he read Hume, **Immanuel Kant** was a rationalist, accepting the belief that reason could discover truths about reality independently of experience. Reading Hume awakened him from what this famous German philosopher called his "dogmatic slumber," his uncritical acceptance of rationalist epistemological beliefs. Hume's attack on reason as a source of knowledge convinced Kant to accept the empiricist view that all knowledge of the world *begins* with experience, with our simple sensations of sounds, odors, colors, and the like. But Kant did not agree with Hume that knowledge was therefore *limited* to experience, to an awareness of our own subjective mental states. Kant recognized that taking such a view of knowledge led directly to skepticism and solipsism, and thereby spelled the end for both philosophy and science.

Instead, Kant took it as a given that we could have knowledge of the world, and not just knowledge of the contents of our minds, our subjective experience. In fact, he believed that we already do have such knowledge, and he even believed that some of it is known by us with certitude. The laws of motion discovered by the great physicist, Isaac Newton, was the prime example of this type of knowledge. Unlike Hume, Kant understood that the laws of science tell us for sure what the world is really like. Even our commonsense understanding of the world is a way of thinking about the world, not about our subjective mental states. We do not experience collections of sounds and colors and tastes, and so on. Rather, we experience a world of material objects that we think of as existing outside of ourselves, objects that really do have both primary and secondary qualities.

Explaining just how certain knowledge of an objective world is possible, when all knowledge begins with subjective impressions, is the goal of Kant's most famous work, *The Critique of Pure Reason.* This is a monumental work that dramatically changed to this day the way that philosophers think about knowledge and reality. It is also a work that is monumentally difficult to understand. As with so many great works that change our ways of thinking, the time and effort spent wrestling with its key ideas are well worth it.

The "Copernican Revolution"

Prior to Kant, certain knowledge of the world was either denied (by empiricists) or explained by appealing to reason as its source (by rationalists). As the title of his book suggests, Kant denies that reason alone, which he calls "pure reason," can know anything about the world apart from experience. Neither rational intuition nor innate ideas are the source of certain knowledge of the world. In the absence of experience, mere thinking produces no knowledge of the world of any degree of certitude. So how is it possible to have knowledge about the world apart from experience, if reason is not its source? Kant's answer to this question requires us to think of knowledge in an entirely new way. This new way of thinking he calls his "Copernican revolution."

The great astronomer, **Copernicus** (1473–1543) changed our thinking about the solar system. Prior to Copernicus it was thought that the Earth was the center of our solar system, with the Sun revolving around it. Because of the work of Copernicus, however, the Sun replaced the Earth as the center of the solar system, with the Earth moving around it. As it moves, the Earth revolves on its axis, leaving the impression of the Sun rising and setting. Even though the Sun appeared to move, and even though the Earth appeared to be stationary, a change in our thinking about how these two celestial bodies were related led us to believe the reverse.

In a similar manner, Kant says that we should *not* think of acquiring knowledge as the process of our minds conforming to the way that the world is. To know something should not be thought of as having mental representations that correspond to the world as it exists outside of us. Both rationalists and empiricists had thought of knowing in this way, they just differed in which types of representations they considered to be superior. For empiricists, it was sensations that provided the most reliable type of knowledge; for rationalists, it was innate ideas and what could be deduced from them that represented reality.

For Kant, we should abandon the idea of knowledge as the having of conscious representations that conform to the world. We should replace it with a new way of thinking, one that sees knowledge as a process of the world conforming to the way that our minds work. This new way of thinking rejects the idea that our minds are like empty containers that hold sensations and ideas, and replaces it with the idea that they are filled with their own innate, invariable ways of functioning. Minds are active, not passive; they do something to the experience they receive other than simply receive it. Just as shoveling snow is an activity that requires snow to conform to the shape of our shovel, and just as chewing, swallowing, and digesting our food are active mechanisms that make food conform to our bodies, so the various innate mechanisms that constitute our minds force the information which we receive from the world to conform to their requirements. So Kant's dramatic claim is that our minds act on the data that they receive, simple sensations, and construct this data into the world as we know it in our daily lives and in science.

This is the central insight of Kant's *Critique of Pure Reason,* and the major one that has survived to this day: *The mind partially constructs the world that it knows, in the very process of coming to know it.* To know something is not just to have experience, it is to *understand* experience. To understand experience is for the knowing mind to organize and structure the information it receives from the environment. Just as a computer processes the information it receives according to the programs it happens to be running, so the human mind processes the data it receives according to its own "programs." But what are these functions of the mind like, and how do they work?

The Innate Mechanisms of the Mind

Kant's insight about the mind as an active shaper of knowledge is alive and well in cognitive science today, as will be seen later. With revision, it is also accepted as essentially correct by many philosophers today. One difference between his original views and those of contemporary Kantians is that Kant thinks that there is only *one* way to understand the world, a way that we are born with and cannot change. Our minds are similar to a computer that can be programmed in only one way. The "program" that is hard wired into our minds is referred to here as the **innate mechanisms** of the mind. Most philosophers today believe that there are many ways to understand our experience, many "programs" that the mind can run. Just as a computer can run many programs, the human mind can learn to understand the world in many ways. We focus now on what Kant said about the innate mechanisms of the mind and return to these contemporary revisions in a later chapter.

The information which the mind passively receives from the environment is called the "given" element of experience. The given element of knowledge is received by the mind from an outside source. This is information received from the environment in the form of sense impressions. In a manner that Kant leaves unexplained, information from the world produces in our minds the sensory data of colors, odors, sounds, tastes, and textures, and the like. This is what Locke called secondary qualities and Hume thought of as impressions. If this is all that there is to experience, simply our own subjective sensory states, then the world would be experienced as a stream of unconnected sensations, each one different from all the others. It would be a world filled with bits of sights and sounds, odors and tastes, pains and images. Since each sensation is different from all others, nothing of what we experience would resemble anything that went before. Further, sensations would not be experienced as properties of things, since we do not experience things. Instead, if the given element of experience is all that there is to knowledge, the world that we experience would be a stream of unrelated colors, odors, tastes, sounds, and the like. It would be a jumbled, unintelligible mess. Such a world would make no sense to us at all.

Our experience does make sense, however, because what we experience is not our subjective mental states. Instead, we experience a world filled with material objects that are connected to each other in causal relationships. These material objects are experienced as things with properties of their own, and as existing apart from us in a space-time world. We also experience ourselves as the subject of our experiences, and we even experience the existence of other persons as well. We get to such a rich world of experience from the very thin world of sensory data, because the mind builds such a world from these sensations. As a sculptor shapes the clay to form a statue, the innate mechanisms of the mind construct our commonsense world from the given. We are not aware that our minds operate on sensory experience to create the general features of the world that we experience. This is because our minds operate on simple sensations in a preconscious and automatic manner. We are only aware of the results produced by the active mind—our experience of the everyday world. We experience the world that we do only *after* sensations have been constructed by the mind into these patterns that we call the commonsense world. The everyday world is constructed by the innate mechanisms of the mind from the given.

Kant assumes that each of us has roughly the same sort of inborn mechanisms, and therefore that we all organize experience in roughly the same ways. If this is right, then organizing the given according to these innate mechanisms becomes the only way for any human person to have any experience at all. Perhaps other species have different innate mechanisms that allow them to experience the world in their own way, to be conscious of very different sorts of "worlds" from us and each other. But Kant assumes that this sort of relativism does not exist among human persons. The key point now is that these mechanisms leave their mark on all experience, they stamp all experience with certain general features. Once we understand what these mechanisms are like, we can then know something for sure about the general features that all experience will have.

Moreover, the processing of sensations by these mechanisms is *necessary* for the having of any conscious experience. We simply cannot make sense of the world unless sense impressions are organized into the very patterns created by the innate mechanisms of the mind. This is a requirement for experiencing something in a meaningful way. If this sort of organization by the mind is a requirement for any experience, then once we know what these general features are, we can know about the general features of all experience, and know them with certitude. To use an analogy, if only one cookie cutter was used to shape all cookies that ever existed and ever will exist, then once we knew the shape of this cookie cutter we would know something about the shape of all cookies. In a similar manner, if something cannot get to be a conscious experience without having the general features of experience that are contributed by the mind, then we can know something for sure about all experience—past, present, and future—once we understand the nature of the mind's innate activity. Before following Kant's analysis of how the activity of the mind is known, it is important to say something about his concept of reality.

Noumena and Phenomena

In discussing the nature of *reality,* one of the central distinctions made by Kant is that between noumena and phenomena. Simply put, the **noumenal** world is the world as it exists outside of our minds. This is the world as it really is. The **phenomenal** world is the world as it appears to us, as it is experienced by us, as it exists in our minds. Kant's distinction between noumena and phenomena parallels the distinction between reality and appearances that we have referred to several times before. It is the difference between what the world is really like and how it is experienced by us. But if all knowledge begins with experience, and if the noumenal world cannot be experienced, then how do we know what it is like?

Kant claims that we simply do not know what the noumenal world is like. More than that, we can never know the nature of the noumenal world. This is because knowledge of reality is beyond our limited cognitive abilities. Perhaps God knows reality, but humans will always remain ignorant of its true nature. We know that it exists as the source of the given element of experience, but we have not now and never will have any idea of its nature. All we can know is the phenomenal world, the noumenal world as it appears to us. This world of our experience is the commonsense world, the world of persons and material objects in space and time, causally related to each other. For Kant, the commonsense world that most of us equate with reality, exists only in our minds.

For all we know, the noumenal world *may* really be like the commonsense phenomenal world of our experience. On the other hand, the noumenal world may be radically different from the phenomenal world. It may, for example, be like the world as described by contemporary theoretical physics, containing only packets of energy with none of the properties that the material objects of our experience possess. Then again, it may be entirely different from either of these worlds, and from any world that we might possibly imagine. We mere humans know nothing of its nature. We may speculate about the nature of reality, but because our knowledge is limited to what we can experience, we will never be able to know anything about this world which lies forever beyond our experience.

Our experience of the commonsense world is produced as a result of the mind processing information received from the noumenal world through the senses. The noumenal world is thought of by Kant as a "something-I-know-not-what" that is the source of this *given* element of experience. The given provides the content of experience. It is composed of sense data, the data we receive through the senses. These include the colors, odors, sounds, tastes, and textures that we sense. These sensory experiences are not to be understood as accurate representations of the properties of noumena, since noumena may contain none of these qualities as they appear to us.

All of our conscious experience, the phenomenal world in other words, should be understood as a combination of the given element of experience and the structuring of it into the meaningful commonsense world that exists only in our minds. Most of us mistakenly believe that this world, the phenomenal world exists independently of our minds. Most of us identify it with reality. The Copernican revolution of Kant, however, claims that the commonsense world does not exist independently of our experience. Instead, our everyday commonsense world is constructed by the mind as it processes information received from the noumenal world.

The Transcendental Deduction

So what does the mind contribute, what are its innate mechanisms like? It turns out that we cannot observe directly how our minds work on the preconscious level where they operate on the given element of experience. This area of our minds is not open to direct inspection, but remains clothed in a veil of mystery. We can know how our minds function only indirectly, by the results that they produce. Kant calls this indirect method for knowing the innate mechanisms of the mind the **transcendental deduction.** Kant uses this rather imposing name to refer to a process of reasoning. The name is a little misleading, because the process of reasoning involved is actually not a deductive one at all. In fact, it is better thought of as an inference to the best possible explanation. In this type of argument we attempt to infer the existence of something that we cannot observe, in this case the innate mechanisms of the mind, on the basis of some features of experience that we can observe. This is the significance of the "transcendental" part of Kant's name for this process. We are attempting to reason to something that transcends, or lies beyond what may be observed or experienced. We infer its existence as the cause of, or as the best explanation for the existence of what we can observe.

What we can observe, of course, is our experience. Kant is especially interested in particular aspects of experience, the ones that are *universal* (they appear in all experience) and *necessary* (you cannot experience anything without these features). If we want to discover how the mind works to construct the general features exhibited by all of our conscious experiences, then the place to begin is by identifying these features. Just as we might infer the shape of the cookie cutter referred to earlier, even if we had never seen it, by observing many cookies shaped by it, so too we may infer the contribution of the mind to experience by observing the general features shared by all experience.

These general features of experience are not to be found in the sensory *content* of experience, which differs from experience to experience. I see a red apple today and a green one tomorrow; I smell a fragrant rose or rotting fish; I hear the scream of a fire engine or the melodic tones of a great soprano. The changing content of experience is given, it is caused by variations in the noumenal world, not contributed by the mind. Instead, the universal and necessary features of all experience are to be found in what Kant calls the *formal* features of experience. It is in the way in which the content is arranged, in how its various separate elements are associated, that the universal and necessary features of experience are to be found. When we find these features of experience, then we may infer something about how the mind works to organize our sense data into meaningful patterns.

Kant thinks that included among the universal and necessary features of all experience are **space** and **time.** We cannot experience an object unless it has some sort of shape and location, for example. Nor can we have experience unless it is arranged in a temporal sequence. Maybe there is no space and time in the noumenal world, but it is essential for the phenomenal world. What would it be like to see something, for example, with no size, shape, or location? And how could we experience everything "all at once"? So the spatial and temporal properties of experience are contributed by the mind. The mind "makes" space and, as Augustine already had suggested, it makes time as well.

In addition to space and time, we also experience the phenomenal world as consisting of "things," **material objects,** not just collections of properties. So the mind not only arranges experience in space and time, but also combines sense impressions into combinations that we call material objects. What would experience be like if we saw only collections of properties not united into objects? What would it be like to experience a world of colors, sounds, or odors, for example, none of which were properties of things? Such a world would make no sense to us; it could not be experienced.

In addition to constructing a world of material objects in space and time, the mind also connects these objects into **causal relationships.** This is what gives the world its order and regularity, our experience of things happening in the same way, over and over again. Some of the relationships form patterns which may be observed and formulated as scientific laws. If we experienced things being totally unconnected our experience would be meaningless. In addition, if we experienced things as connected differently each time we experienced them, our world would also be meaningless. If one day fire caused smoke and another it caused air, and on another day air caused fire, and so on, there would be no basis for understanding how the world works.

We experience instead a coherent world, a regular and orderly system of things, because they are causally related to each other. When one exists (fire, for example) the other will follow (smoke). So we can be confident that where there is smoke there is fire. The mind constructs this causal connection. This is the basis for the order found in the commonsense world. The commonsense world is also the world studied by science. The laws of science are not merely probabilities, as Hume thought, describing what has been and what might continue to be. Rather, they describe what has to be. Because the mind constructs the general features of the phenomenal world, including the necessary connection between its various elements, its causal relations, the phenomenal world has to be as it is experienced. For Kant, scientific laws describe the way that the world necessarily works, just as Newton thought it did.

Human Nature

We experience the world as a world of material objects causally related in space and time, because that is the way that the mind works to build the phenomenal world. Another universal and necessary feature of experience is **persons.** We experience not only things in our world, but also other persons and our selves. How can it be that the mind constructs experience so as to produce the experience of a person, especially the inner person or the self? Kant's explanation is difficult to follow but, as usual, very much worth the effort. It is best to begin by examining various meanings of the self, or as Kant says, the *ego.*

One way to talk about my self is to refer to the *collection* of all my conscious experiences, all my thoughts and feelings and desires and memories and so on. This Kant calls the **psychological ego.** This is the self of which I am aware, the self that I experience in the phenomenal world of my everyday experience, the self that I think of as "me." There is also the **noumenal self,** the self as it really is, a self about which we know nothing. The psychological self that I experience may be thought of as how the noumenal self is experienced, or how it appears to itself. In addition to these two notions of the self, Kant introduces a third, the **transcendental ego.** This is not a personal self, but is rather what Kant calls the "formal self." It is the collection of all the innate mechanisms of the mind that produce the general features of experience.

In discussing persons, Kant ignores the noumenal self as unknowable. He concentrates instead on the psychological ego and the transcendental ego. He is especially concerned with the following problem. If my personal self, the psychological ego, is merely a collection of ever changing experience, then how is it that I experience myself as a substance, a single subject that has these experiences? After all, I do not think of myself as a *collection* of thoughts, feelings, and so on. Instead, I think of myself as the "me" that has such thoughts and feelings. They are mine, they are states of me. I think of myself as something that thinks and feels and desires, not something that is simply a collection of my thoughts and feelings and desires. As an apple is not simply its collection of properties—red, round, sweet, and so on—so I am not simply my collection of properties, my mental states. Instead, I am the subject that has or produces these mental states.

I experience myself not only as a substance, but also as being the *same* person now as I was before. I experience this abiding sameness despite the continual changes in my mental states. So I am a subject that remains the same throughout time. But, as Hume pointed out, I never experience such a self, only a collection of continuously changing mental events. How is it, then, that I come to understand my psychological ego as the abiding subject which underlies my changing mental states? Kant's answer to this question is brilliant, though we can at best hint at it here. It requires us to switch for a moment from the question of how we can experience a single self, to the question of how we can experience a single world. As it turns out, the reason why we experience ourselves as a subject of experience is closely related to the reason why we experience the world as a single system.

So far we have discussed how the innate mechanisms of the mind must process sense data for us to experience the commonsense world—the world of material objects that are causally related in space and time. But how is it that we think of these separate experiences of material objects as all belonging to one system, as all in the same space and time, as all part of a single web of causal relationships, as all part of one world? Kant's answer is that we experience a single world, and not simply a collection of events, because the innate mechanisms of the mind are themselves united into a single system, a system called the transcendental ego. If each of the innate mechanisms of the mind that make up the transcendental ego were not connected to the others, if they did not work together as a unified system, there would be no experience of individual objects existing in a single system called the world.

This unity of the transcendental ego is also in the background of the unity of my self. While I do not directly experience the unity of this system of innate structures called the transcendental ego, I am aware of it indirectly, by how it is reflected in the experience of the world whose unity it is responsible for constructing. The transcendental ego is revealed in what it does in the process of constructing the world. The sense of a unified self that I possess, this unobservable self that seems always to be in the background, is the sense of the unity of the transcendental ego. This sense of unity emerges out of a growing awareness of the unity of the world whose general features it has constructed. This sense of self serves to connect the separate experiences of my psychological ego into a unified whole, into a set of experiences that are produced by, and belong to the same mind.

So my self is the psychological ego plus a sense of its unity derived from the transcendental ego. Nothing can be known about the metaphysical status of the psychological ego, whether it is a material or a spiritual being. It is not in space as are all other material beings; but there is also no experience of it as a nonmaterial being. If our psychological egos are substances, we do not know at all what type of substances they might be. As far as we *know,* our self is just a collection of experiences, attitudes, desires, and tendencies to behave (character), as Hume claimed.

Kant is an empiricist, so only what is found in our experience can be known. The phenomenal world is the only world that we experience, and is thus all that we can know. The mind cannot discover the real nature of itself or anything else in the noumenal world, since it is a reality that lies beyond what we can experience. The innate mechanisms of the mind, space, time, material substance, causality, and persons are not to be understood as innate ideas that correspond to the true nature of the noumenal world, as rationalists might be tempted to do. Just because we organize sense impressions in these ways does not mean that there really are things, persons, space, time, and causality as features of the noumenal world. We know only the world as we experience it, the phenomenal world, the world as it appears to us.

Limiting our knowledge to the world of appearances is a price that Kant is willing to pay to undermine Hume's skepticism and establish scientific knowledge on a firm foundation. For him, our minds work in such a way that we have to think of the (phenomenal) world as an orderly, coherent whole where all events are connected in a causally determined system. This is why science works, because the deterministic world that it assumes to exist is just the world that our minds construct in the process of experiencing. By his "Copernican revolution," by thinking of knowledge as the conformity of the world to my mind, Kant has rescued science from Hume's critique and reestablished it as a type of reliable knowledge.

Unfortunately, our psychological egos are also within the phenomenal world, and thus also subject to its deterministic laws. His view of human nature seems that it ought to be similar to that of Hobbes, who saw human beings as just another part of the scientific world, to be studied and understood completely by science. This presents a real problem for Kant, since a denial that we are free is totally unacceptable to him. If we are not free, what sense is there to be made of moral responsibility and the basic belief of the religious life that we earn our salvation through our free choices? We certainly act as if we are free when we deliberate among what seems to be a variety of choices. But where do freedom and religion fit in an otherwise deterministic world?

The manner in which Kant resolves the tension between determinism and freedom is the key to understanding his concept of human nature. His basic strategy is to look for freedom not in the psychological ego but in the noumenal self. Our true selves, our true human nature, is to be found here, in our noumenal selves. The psychological ego, the way that the noumenal self appears to itself, is no freer than anything else in the phenomenal world. But if the noumenal self cannot be experienced, how does Kant know that it is free? The answer is that Kant does not *know* that we are free. Our freedom is not something that can be observed. Our freedom lies beyond human experience and explanation.

However, all is not lost. Kant believes that even though we cannot know that we are free, we can reasonably infer that we are from we how act.

Consequences

Freedom

For Hume, it is possible to believe that we are determined and still to make sense of responsibility. This view that freedom and determinism are compatible is sometimes called **soft determinism.** It accepts determinism and claims that like everything else in nature human actions are caused. They are caused by our desires, which are caused by our character, which is caused by the forces of nature and nurture—which lie beyond our control. It nevertheless still makes sense to hold us responsible for our choices, to praise and blame us for them, because doing so will help to shape our character in socially appropriate directions. One of the things that we may desire, for example, is to stay out of prison. This may convince us to avoid stealing money from the liquor store even though we have a strong desire to do so. Our desire to stay out of jail is stronger, and thus causes us to refrain from stealing. So praise and blame of the legal and moral sort is one of the forces that helps to determine what we desire and thus how we behave.

For Hume, we can reconcile responsibility with determinism because holding someone responsible is itself a way to determine their behavior. Kant rejects this resolution of the problem, however, since it allows too weak an idea of responsibility. His idea of responsibility is that praise and blame is an after-the-fact reward or punishment for choosing which desire to follow or reject, not simply the addition of another desire designed to shape our behavior. These two competing notions of responsibility are important ingredients in understanding human nature. Are we really self-governed, autonomous beings who control our own destinies by our free choices, or are we submerged in the causal flow of events that determine our actions for us? Kant sides very strongly with the former view.

For Kant, the type of responsibility championed by Hume is insufficient to explain the moral life. We are more than just free to do what we want. We are also free to control our wants, our desires. This is the only type of freedom worth having for Kant, and the only type of freedom that is compatible with true moral responsibility. This is the type of freedom, the freedom to initial new chains of action, that Kant attributes to the noumenal self. While the noumenal self may not be known to have this type of freedom, its full self-governing freedom may be presupposed as a necessary condition of practical reason. **Practical reason** is the use of reason to guide behavior, especially moral behavior. So freedom is seen by Kant as a necessary condition for moral behavior.

Kant's intense faith in the truth of Newtonian science is matched only by his conviction that morality is real, not an illusion. The "moral law within," the sense of being bound by rules of right and wrong, was for him as real an experience as the "starry skies above," the scientific nature of the physical world. It made no sense to him whatsoever to think of ourselves as moral beings and as determined at the same time. To act as a being who is bound by duty, one who takes personal responsibility for his actions, one who accepts the praise and blame of others for them, one who deliberates about various paths of action, one who resists some desires and cooperates with others, and so on, requires us to think of ourselves as outside of the deterministic universe, and as free to choose one course of action over another. In the readings which follow, selections from Kant's *Fundamental Principles of the Metaphysics of Morals*, he discusses freedom in the context of describing his ethical theory.

Ethics

Hume's moral theory falls loosely into the category of **utilitarianism.** According to this view, the ultimate good is happiness, usually identified with some sort of pleasure and the avoidance of pain. Right actions are those that bring about this sort of good or avoid evil. For Hume, our feelings or sentiments are the best guides of right and wrong, not our reason. Reason does not motivate us to act, where feelings do. Hume even claims that saying that a certain action is right or wrong is simply the expression of a feeling, usually a feeling of approval or disapproval for the action. We generally approve of those actions which lead to a greater good or less evil for ourselves and others. Thus our guide to the moral life is the utilitarian principle that requires us to do good and avoid evil for ourselves and others. Our moral character, especially shaped by our human nature, is a collection of sentiments and the corresponding dispositions to behave according to them. If they are generally productive of the good, we have a good moral character; otherwise, we do not.

The first thing to say about Kant's ethical views is that he rejects Hume's brand of morality in its entirety, and replaces it with one that stresses reason as the source of morality. For Kant, the source of morality is not feeling, and its goal is not happiness. Kant's ethical theory is one of his grandest creations, and one that continues to exert a powerful influence even today. Here there is only time to hint at its main outlines, though *Reading 1* describes it in much greater detail. It will be helpful to understand Kant's theory if we first say a few words about human nature. While we may not know the true nature of our selves, Kant says that we do know three of our central natural tendencies. For one, we are free beings, as we just discussed. For another, we are rational beings. We are capable of understanding mathematics, logic, and science. We can know the phenomenal world and our psychological selves. This is how we exercise our theoretical reason, how we act as cognitive beings. Third, we are also capable of practical reason, the use of reason to figure out how to live.

Reason is the source of morality in two senses, for Kant. First, it is the highest good, and second it alone determines right from wrong. According to Kant's **theory of value,** practical reason, thought of as the will, is the highest good. For Kant, the only thing good in itself is a *good will*. The term "will" is used by Kant to refer to our choices. To say that a person has a good will is to say that he or she makes good choices. For Kant, choice itself is a product of reason, and so will is an exercise in practical reason. To make a good choice in moral matters is to do what is reasonable in practical life. This includes both doing what is right *and* doing it with the correct motive. To choose to perform a morally acceptable action because it might make you look good, for example, is to act from the wrong motive. The only correct motive for moral action is duty. One should do what is right simply because it is his or her duty to do so, simply because it is right. Doing what is right because it leads to something else—pleasure for example, or a good reputation, or avoidance of guilt—is to act from the wrong motive. Having a good will, then, should not be seen as a means to some other good. It is good in itself. It has intrinsic value. We sometimes express this by saying things like "virtue is its own reward." For Kant, there can be no greater life for a person, no higher fulfillment in this life, than developing a good moral character.

Why does Kant say that having a good will, or as we might say today a good moral character, is the *only* thing that has intrinsic value? Why not add knowledge, love, freedom, pleasure, and the like to this list of things that are good in themselves? Kant's answer is that anything else can be turned to evil by an evil will. Knowledge can be used for evil ends, for example. Pleasure can be gotten through an evil means, and even a relationship with God can sometimes look like a pact with the devil. Many dastardly deeds have been performed in the name of God. Love may be twisted, freedom abused, and power corrupted by an evil will. Anything other than a good will that is thought of as good in itself may be transformed to an evil by an evil will.

If we should do what is right just because it is right, the question still remains, how do we determine what is right? A very brief version of Kant's notion of right and wrong, his **theory of obligation,** is as follows. Right and wrong is a matter of following rules, what he calls maxims. These rules are acceptable only if they conform to his highest principle of ethics, the **categorical imperative.** According to this principle doing what is right means following maxims that meet three conditions. First, they must be *universal.* That is, they must be rules that everyone in similar circumstances should follow. "Keep your promises," for example, is a rule that everyone ought to follow. If they did not, if we broke our promises whenever it was in our interest to do so, pretty soon there would be nothing called "promising." So it would be contradictory to have a rule that could be broken whenever it was in someone's interest to do so. It would go against reason.

Next, the maxims that we follow must *not allow persons to be used solely as a means* for the good of others. Persons ought to be respected and not used as things or valued only for their social status. We might learn a lot about cancer by experimenting on human subjects, say old and senile folks in nursing homes, for example. However, such a violation of their intrinsic worth is always immoral. The end (good scientific knowledge) does not justify such an immoral means. Even these people are worthwhile in themselves, because they exhibit (or did exhibit) the capacity to understand—reason. Finally, acceptable moral maxims must allow for autonomy. That is, they must be accepted freely by those who follow them. We may train our children to conform their behavior to morality, but until the moral life is seen as valuable in itself and respected as such, and until its maxims are followed freely, there is no true moral action. In the end, doing the right thing amounts to the free and rational use of practical reason. This is important, because at the heart of human nature lies this truth, *we are our reason and our freedom;* we are free and rational beings. What gives us our dignity and worth is that we can rise above the droning determinism of nature and desire, and govern ourselves by reason as do the gods. We are not creatures of feeling and desire; we are creatures of reason.

God and Immortality

Kant had much to say about society, and even wrote a book recommending the formation of a sort of United Nations to ensure world stability. We will skip Kant's comments on society as beyond our scope, and instead consider briefly his reasons for believing in God and the immortality of the soul. Once again, these beliefs are going to be accepted by Kant on practical grounds. We cannot know that God exists or that the soul is immortal. These are matters that lie beyond experience. However, we can assume their truth in order to make sense of morality. Just as human freedom must be assumed, or postulated, to explain moral responsibility, so the existence of God and an afterlife must be assumed to explain other dimensions of morality. Freedom, God, and immortality are all going to be accepted by Kant as what he calls "postulates of practical reason."

In discussing immortality, it is first important to remind ourselves of the distinction between what human nature is and what it could be. In the earlier section on "Ethics," Kant painted us a picture of what we can be if we follow the dictates of morality. A life of virtue guided by reason and freedom is the most noble of lives. It is a self-governed life of worth and dignity. In his book on religion, *Religion Within the Boundaries of Mere Reason,* Kant speaks of what human nature is and paints a much gloomier picture. He says there that we have a great propensity for moral evil. Most of us simply do not lead lives of virtue, but are rather directed by self interest and especially by the need to satisfy of our own desires.

Though many of us may not attain virtue, however, we all desire happiness. It is a natural desire, deeply embedded in human nature. For Kant, true happiness requires the immortality of the soul, just as moral responsibility requires that we are free. To see this, remember first that the highest good is a good will, or virtue, as Kant has already shown us. This alone is valuable in itself. But it is reasonable to assume that complete or perfect virtue will lead to happiness. Clearly, moral perfection is beyond possibility in this life. Some few people may overcome their natural tendencies to evil and move closer and closer to moral perfection, but no one ever achieves it in this life. If our desire for happiness depends upon achieving moral perfection for its satisfaction, and if moral perfection is not achieved in this life, then for Kant it is reasonable to assume that there must be a life after this one in which happiness is to be found.

If the natural desire for happiness leads to postulating life after death, it also requires that we postulate the existence of God. For in the afterlife is where happiness is to be found. It will be found by the virtuous because they will there find justice. In the afterlife is where justice is finally to be gained by those who have been virtuous in this life. Their just reward is happiness. Those who have not lived according to the dictates of morality will also find their just reward there, but it will not consist of happiness. With God's existence as a further requirement of morality, Kant is now in a position to assert that not only is science compatible with morality, but it is also compatible with religion, the worship of God. Even though we are part of the mechanistic universe of science, we may justifiably live our lives *as though* we are free and immortal beings whose ultimate destiny is to live with the divine.

Gender

One of Kant's greatest contributions to ethics is his claim that human beings are worthwhile in themselves, that each human being is just as worthwhile as any other, and that because of this intrinsic worth no human being should ever be treated simply as "a means to the good of another." People are not things to be bought and sold, deceived or manipulated, coerced or forced, or in any other way to be used by others. Our value stems from our reason and autonomy, the very qualities that set us apart from and above everything else in nature. It is our reason that is especially valuable, since it not only allows us to understand, but it also informs our choices. The principle that forbids people to use others merely as a means to the good of others is sometimes today called the **respect for persons** principle. There is some question as to whether or not Kant believed that women ought to have as much respect as men, since they do not have as much rational ability as men. There is even some evidence that Kant questioned the desirability of women pursuing matters of the mind, even if they are as rational as men. This may take away from their femininity, he thought, and lead to the repression of their emotional behavior, one of their stronger and more benevolent qualities. So once again, this time in Kant, human nature is different for men and women. And once again it is the male nature that is highlighted.

Kant has been criticized for believing this now familiar general theme, one deeply embedded in Western culture until fairly recently. The theme is that women are more creatures of the body than the mind, more emotional and less rational than men—and all this not because of inequalities of opportunity, but by nature. Kant also has been criticized by women for his ethical views. For one thing, his critics claim, the only morally acceptable motive for acting morally is not duty, but also love. A mother who cares for her children because it is her duty to do so is not nearly as admirable to most of us as one who does so because she loves them. More importantly, the whole rule-bound approach to ethics taken by Kant has come under attack fairly recently, as representing only the way that males think about right and wrong.[2] The claim is that women see right and wrong less as a matter of following rules and more as a matter of caring and sharing. An ethics of care concerns relationships more than rights, cooperation more than justice, and love more than duty. This new approach to ethics is supposed to reflect how women understand morality. Kant's approach, on the other hand, ignores the voices, concerns, and contributions of women. While Kant was not a sexist in any explicit way, his critics complain that some of his teachings were sexist, at least implicitly. In the same way that Descartes' self excluded female qualities, Kant's ethics excludes them as well. More will be said in future chapters about which type of ethical theory most accurately reflects the moral nature of women.

Readings

1. The Nature of Ethics

FIRST SECTION

Transition from the Common Rational Knowledge of Morality to the Philosophical

The Good Will

NOTHING CAN POSSIBLY BE CONCEIVED in the world, or even out of it, which can be called good without qualification, except a *good will*. Intelligence, wit, judgment, and the other *talents* of the mind, however they may be named, or courage, resolution, perseverance, as qualities of temperament, are undoubtedly good and desirable in many respects; but these gifts of nature may also become extremely bad and mischievous if the will which is to make use of them, and which, therefore, constitutes what is called *character*, is not good. It is the same with the *gifts of fortune*. Power, riches, honor, even health, and the general well-being and contentment with one's condition which is called *happiness*, inspire pride, and often presumption, if there is not a good will to correct the influence of these on the mind, and with this also to rectify the whole principle of acting, and adapt it to its end. The sight of a being who is not adorned with a single feature of a pure and good will, enjoying unbroken prosperity, can never give pleasure to an impartial rational spectator. Thus a good will appears to constitute the indispensable condition even of being worthy of happiness.

There are even some qualities which are of service to this good will itself, and may facilitate its action, yet which have no intrinsic unconditional value, but always presuppose a good will,

and this qualifies the esteem that we justly have for them, and does not permit us to regard them as absolutely good. Moderation in the affections and passions, self-control, and calm deliberation are not only good in many respects, but even seem to constitute part of the intrinsic worth of the person; but they are far from deserving to be called good without qualification, although they have been so unconditionally praised by the ancients. For without the principles of a good will, they may become extremely bad; and the coolness of a villain not only makes him far more dangerous, but also directly makes him more abominable in our eyes than he would have been without it.

A good will is good not because of what it performs or effects, not by its aptness for the attainment of some proposed end, but simply by virtue of the volition—that is, it is good in itself, and considered by itself is to be esteemed much higher than all that can be brought about by it in favor of any inclination, nay, even of the sum-total of all inclinations. Even if it should happen that, owing to special disfavor of fortune, or the niggardly provision of a step-motherly nature, this will should wholly lack power to accomplish its purpose, if with its greatest efforts it should yet achieve nothing, and there should remain only the good will (not, to be sure, a mere wish, but the summoning of all means in our power), then, like a jewel, it would still shine by its own light, as a thing which has its whole value in itself. Its usefulness or fruitlessness can neither add to nor take away anything from this value. It would be, as it were, only the setting to enable us to handle it the more

Selections from Immanuel Kant, Fundamental Principles of the Metaphysics of Morals *(Indianapolis: Bobbs-Merrill, 1949), pp. 11–21, 30–32, 36–41, 44–56, 63–72. Reprinted with permission.*

conveniently in common commerce, or to attract to it the attention of those who are not yet connoisseurs, but not to recommend it to true connoisseurs, or to determine its value.

There is, however, something so strange in this idea of the absolute value of the mere will, in which no account is taken of its utility, that notwithstanding the thorough assent of even common reason to the idea, yet a suspicion must arise that it may perhaps really be the product of mere high-flown fancy, and that we may have misunderstood the purpose of nature in assigning reason as the governor of our will. Therefore we will examine this idea from this point of view.

In the physical constitution of an organized being, that is, a being adapted suitably to the purposes of life, we assume it as a fundamental principle that no organ for any purpose will be found but what is also the fittest and best adapted for that purpose. Now in a being which has reason and a will, if the proper object of nature were its *conservation*, its *welfare*, in a word, its *happiness*, then nature would have hit upon a very bad arrangement in selecting the reason of the creature to carry out this purpose. For all the actions which the creature has to perform with a view to this purpose, and the whole rule of its conduct, would be far more surely prescribed to it by instinct, and that end would have been attained thereby much more certainly than it ever can be by reason. Should reason have been communicated to this favored creature over and above, it must only have served it to contemplate the happy constitution of its nature, to admire it, to congratulate itself thereon, and to feel thankful for it to the beneficent cause, but not that it should subject its desires to that weak and delusive guidance, and meddle bunglingly with the purpose of nature. In a word, nature would have taken care that reason should not break forth into *practical exercise*, nor have the presumption, with its weak insight, to think out for itself the plan of happiness and of the means of attaining it. Nature would not only have taken on herself the choice of the ends but also of the means, and with wise foresight would have entrusted both to instinct.

And, in fact, we find that the more a cultivated reason applies itself with deliberate purpose to the enjoyment of life and happiness, so much the more does the man fail of true satisfaction. And from this circumstance there arises in many, if they are candid enough to confess it, a certain degree of *misology*, that is, hatred of reason, especially in the case of those who are most experienced in the use of it, because after calculating all the advantages they derive—I do not say from the invention of all the arts of common luxury, but even from the sciences (which seem to them to be after all only a luxury of the understanding)—they find that they have, in fact, only brought more trouble on their shoulders rather than gained in happiness; and they end by envying rather than despising the more common stamp of men who keep closer to the guidance of mere instinct, and do not allow their reason much influence on their conduct. And this we must admit, that the judgment of those who would very much lower the lofty eulogies of the advantages which reason gives us in regard to the happiness and satisfaction of life, or who would even reduce them below zero, is by no means morose or ungrateful to the goodness with which the world is governed, but that there lies at the root of these judgments the idea that our existence has a different and far nobler end, for which, and not for happiness, reason is properly intended, and which must, therefore, be regarded as the supreme condition to which the private ends of man must, for the most part, be postponed.

For as reason is not competent to guide the will with certainty in regard to its objects and the satisfaction of all our wants (which it to some extent even multiplies), this being an end to which an implanted instinct would have led with much greater certainty; and since, nevertheless, reason is imparted to us as a practical faculty, that is, as one which is to have influence on the *will*, therefore, admitting that nature generally in the distribution of her capacities has adapted the means to the end, its true destination must be to produce a *will*, not merely good as a *means* to something else, but *good in itself*, for which reason was absolutely necessary. This will then, though not indeed the sole and complete good, must be the supreme good and the condition of every other, even of the desire of happiness. Under these circumstances, there is nothing inconsistent with the wisdom of nature in the fact that the cultivation of the reason, which is requisite for the first and unconditional purpose, does in many ways interfere, at least in this life, with the attainment of the second, which is always conditional—namely, happiness. Nay, it may even reduce it to nothing, without nature thereby failing of her purpose. For reason recognizes the establishment of a good will as its highest practical destination, and in attaining this purpose is capable only of a satisfaction of its own proper kind, namely, that from the attainment of an end, which end again is determined by reason only, notwithstanding that this may involve many a disappointment to the ends of inclination.

We have then to develop the notion of a will which deserves to be highly esteemed for itself, and is good without a view to anything further, a notion which exists already in the sound natural understanding, requiring rather to be cleared up than to be taught, and which in estimating the value of our actions always takes the first place and constitutes the condition of all the rest. In order to do this, we will take the notion of duty, which includes that of a good will, although implying certain subjective restrictions and hindrances. These, however, far from concealing it or rendering it unrecognizable, rather bring it out by contrast and make it shine forth so much the brighter.

I omit here all actions which are already recognized as inconsistent with duty, although they may be useful for this or that purpose, for with these the question whether they are done *from duty* cannot arise at all, since they even conflict with it. I also set aside those actions which really conform to duty, but to which men have *no* direct *inclination,* performing them because they are impelled thereto by some other inclination. For in this case we can readily distinguish whether the action which agrees with duty is done *from duty* or from a selfish view. It is much harder to make this distinction when the action accords with duty, and the subject has besides a *direct* inclination to it. For example, it is always a matter of duty that a dealer should not overcharge an inexperienced purchaser; and wherever there is much commerce the prudent tradesman does not overcharge, but keeps

a fixed price for everyone, so that a child buys of him as well as any other. Men are thus *honestly* served; but this is not enough to make us believe that the tradesman has so acted from duty and from principles of honesty; his own advantage required it; it is out of the question in this case to suppose that he might besides have a direct inclination in favor of the buyers, so that, as it were, from love he should give no advantage to one over another. Accordingly the action was done neither from duty nor from direct inclination, but merely with a selfish view.

On the other hand, it is a duty to maintain one's life; and, in addition, everyone has also a direct inclination to do so. But on this account the often anxious care which most men take for it has no intrinsic worth, and their maxim has no moral import. They preserve their life *as duty requires*, no doubt, but not *because duty requires.* On the other hand, if adversity and hopeless sorrow have completely taken away the relish for life, if the unfortunate one, strong in mind, indignant at his fate rather than desponding or dejected, wishes for death, and yet preserves his life without loving it—not from inclination or fear, but from duty—then his maxim has a moral worth.

To be beneficent when we can is a duty; and besides this, there are many minds so sympathetically constituted that, without any other motive of vanity or self-interest, they find a pleasure in spreading joy around them, and can take delight in the satisfaction of others so far as it is their own work. But I maintain that in such a case an action of this kind, however proper, however amiable it may be, has nevertheless no true moral worth, but is on a level with other inclinations, for example, the inclination to honor, which, if it is happily directed to that which is in fact of public utility and accordant with duty, and consequently honorable, deserves praise and encouragement, but not esteem. For the maxim lacks the moral import, namely, that such actions be done *from duty,* not from inclination. Put the case that the mind of that philanthropist was clouded by sorrow of his own, extinguishing all sympathy with the lot of others, and that while he still has the power to benefit others in distress, he is not touched by their trouble because he is absorbed with his own; and now suppose that he tears himself out of this dead insensibility and performs the action without any inclination to it, but simply from duty, then first has his action its genuine moral worth. Further still, if nature has put little sympathy in the heart of this or that man, if he, supposed to be an upright man, is by temperament cold and indifferent to the sufferings of others, perhaps because in respect of his own he is provided with the special gift of patience and fortitude, and supposes, or even requires, that others should have the same—and such a man would certainly not be the meanest product of nature—but if nature had not specially framed him for a philanthropist, would he not still find in himself a source from whence to give himself a far higher worth than that of a good-natured temperament could be? Unquestionably. It is just in this that the moral worth of the character is brought out which is incomparably the highest of all, namely, that he is beneficent, not from inclination, but from duty.

To secure one's own happiness is a duty, at least indirectly; for discontent with one's condition, under a pressure of many anxieties and amidst unsatisfied wants, might easily become a great *temptation to transgression of duty*. But here again, without looking to duty, all men have already the strongest and most intimate inclination to happiness, because it is just in this idea that all inclinations are combined in one total. But the precept of happiness is often of such a sort that it greatly interferes with some inclinations, and yet a man cannot form any definite and certain conception of the sum of satisfaction of all of them which is called happiness. It is not then to be wondered at that a single inclination, definite both as to what it promises and as to the time within which it can be gratified, is often able to overcome such a fluctuating idea, and that a gouty patient, for instance, can choose to enjoy what he likes, and to suffer what he may, since, according to his calculation, on this occasion at least, he has [only] not sacrificed the enjoyment of the present moment to a possibly mistaken expectation of a happiness which is supposed to be found in health. But even in this case, if the general desire for happiness did not influence his will, and supposing that in his particular case health was not a necessary element in this calculation, there yet remains in this, as in all other cases, this law—namely, that he should promote his happiness not from inclination but from duty, and by this would his conduct first acquire true moral worth.

It is in this manner, undoubtedly, that we are to understand those passages of Scripture also in which we are commanded to love our neighbor, even our enemy. For love, as an affection, cannot be commanded, but beneficence for duty's sake may, even though we are not impelled to it by any inclination—nay, are even repelled by a natural and unconquerable aversion. This is *practical* love, and not *pathological*—a love which is seated in the will, and not in the propensions of sense—in principles of action and not of tender sympathy; and it is this love alone which can be commanded.

The second proposition is: That an action done from duty derives its moral worth, *not from the purpose* which is to be attained by it, but from the maxim by which it is determined, and therefore does not depend on the realization of the object of the action, but merely on the *principle of volition* by which the action has taken place, without regard to any object of desire. It is clear from what precedes that the purposes which we may have in view in our actions, or their effects regarded as ends and springs of the will, cannot give to actions any unconditional or moral worth. In what, then, can their worth lie if it is not to consist in the will and in reference to its expected effect? It cannot lie anywhere but in the *principle of the will* without regard to the ends which can be attained by the action. For the will stands between its *a priori* principle, which is formal, and its *a posteriori* spring, which is material, as between two roads, and as it must be determined by something, it follows that it must be determined by the formal principle of volition when an action is done from duty, in which case every material principle has been withdrawn from it.

The third proposition, which is a consequence of the two preceding, I would express thus: *Duty is the necessity of acting from respect for the law.* I may have *inclination* for an object as the effect of my proposed action, but I cannot have *respect* for it just for this reason that it is an effect and not an energy of will. Similarly, I cannot have respect for inclination, whether my own or another's; I can at most, if my own, approve it; if another's, sometimes even love it, that is, look on it as favorable to my own interest. It is only what is connected with my will as a principle, by no means as an effect—what does not subserve my inclination, but overpowers it, or at least in case of choice excludes it from its calculation—in other words, simply the law of itself, which can be an object of respect, and hence a command. Now an action done from duty must wholly exclude the influence of inclination, and with it every object of the will, so that nothing remains which can determine the will except objectively the *law,* and subjectively *pure respect* for this practical law, and consequently the maxim that I should follow this law even to the thwarting of all my inclinations.

Thus the moral worth of an action does not lie in the effect expected from it, nor in any principle of action which requires to borrow its motive from this expected effect. For all these effects— agreeableness of one's condition, and even the promotion of the happiness of others—could have been also brought about by other causes, so that for this there would have been no need of the will of a rational being; whereas it is in this alone that the supreme and unconditional good can be found. The pre-eminent good which we call moral can therefore consist in nothing else than *the conception of law* in itself, *which certainly is only possible in a rational being,* in so far as this conception, and not the expected effect, determines the will. This is a good which is already present in the person who acts accordingly, and we have not to wait for it to appear first in the result.

But what sort of law can that be the conception of which must determine the will, even without paying any regard to the effect expected from it, in order that this will may be called good absolutely and without qualification? As I have deprived the will of every impulse which could arise to it from obedience to any law, there remains nothing but the universal conformity of its actions to law in general, which alone is to serve the will as a principle, that is, I am never to act otherwise than so *that*

I could also will that my maxim should become a universal law. Here, now, it is the simple conformity to law in general, without assuming any particular law applicable to certain actions, that serves the will as its principle, and must so serve it if duty is not to be a vain delusion and a chimerical notion. The common reason of men in its practical judgments perfectly coincides with this, and always has in view the principle here suggested. Let the question be, for example: May I when in distress make a promise with the intention not to keep it? I readily distinguish here between the two significations which the question may have: whether it is prudent or whether it is right to make a false promise? The former may undoubtedly often be the case. I see clearly indeed that it is not enough to extricate myself from a present difficulty by means of this subterfuge, but it must be well considered whether there may not hereafter spring from this lie much greater inconvenience than that from which I now free myself, and as, with all my supposed *cunning,* the consequences cannot be so easily foreseen but that credit once lost may be much more injurious to me than any mischief which I seek to avoid at present, it should be considered whether it would not be more *prudent* to act herein according to a universal maxim, and to make it a habit to promise nothing except with the intention of keeping it. But it is soon clear to me that such a maxim will still only be based on the fear of consequences. Now it is a wholly different thing to be truthful from duty, and to be so from apprehension of injurious consequences. In the first case, the very notion of the action already implies a law for me; in the second case, I must first look about elsewhere to see what results may be combined with it which would affect myself. For to deviate from the principle of duty is beyond all doubt wicked; but to be unfaithful to my maxim of prudence may often be very advantageous to me, although to abide by it is certainly safer. The shortest way, however, and an unerring one, to discover the answer to this question whether a lying promise is consistent with duty, is to ask myself, Should I be content that my maxim (to extricate myself from difficulty by a false promise) should hold good as a universal law, for myself as well as for others; and should I be able to say to myself, "Every one may make a deceitful promise when he finds himself in a difficulty from which he cannot otherwise extricate himself"? Then I presently become aware that, while I can will the lie, I can by no means will that lying should be a universal law. For with such a law there would be no promises at all, since it would be in vain to allege my intention in regard to my future actions to those who would not believe this allegation, or if they over-hastily did so, would pay me back in my own coin. Hence my maxim, as soon as it should be made a universal law, would necessarily destroy itself.

I do not, therefore, need any far-reaching penetration to discern what I have to do in order that my will may be morally good. Inexperienced in the course of the world, incapable of being prepared for all its contingencies, I only ask myself: Canst thou also will that thy maxim should be a universal law? If not, then it must be rejected, and that not because of a disadvantage accruing from it to myself or even to others, but because it cannot enter as a principle into a possible universal legislation, and reason extorts from me immediate respect for such legislation. I do not indeed as yet *discern* on what this respect is based (this the philosopher may inquire), but at least I understand this—that it is an estimation of the worth which far outweighs all worth of what is recommended by inclination, and that the necessity of acting from *pure* respect for the practical law is what constitutes duty, to which every other motive must give place because it is the condition of a will being good *in itself*, and the worth of such a will is above everything. . . .

Hypothetical and Categorical Imperatives

Everything in nature works according to laws. Rational beings alone have the faculty of acting according *to the conception* of laws—that is, according to principles, that is, have a *will*. Since the deduction of actions from principles requires *reason*, the will is nothing but practical reason. If reason infallibly determines the will, then the actions of such a being which are recognized as objectively

necessary are subjectively necessary also, that is, the will is a faculty to choose *that only* which reason independent on inclination recognizes as practically necessary, that is, as good. But if reason of itself does not sufficiently determine the will, if the latter is subject also to subjective conditions (particular impulses) which do not always coincide with the objective conditions, in a word, if the will does not *in itself* completely accord with reason (which is actually the case with men), then the actions which objectively are recognized as necessary are subjectively contingent, and the determination of such a will according to objective laws is *obligation*, that is to say, the relation of the objective laws to a will that is not thoroughly good is conceived as the determination of the will of a rational being by principles of reason, but which the will from its nature does not of necessity follow.

The conception of an objective principle, in so far as it is obligatory for a will, is called a command (of reason), and the formula of the command is called an Imperative.

All imperatives are expressed by the word *ought* [or *shall*], and thereby indicate the relation of an objective law of reason to a will which from its subjective constitution is not necessarily determined by it (an obligation). They say that something would be good to do or to forbear, but they say it to a will which does not always do a thing because it is conceived to be good to do it. That is practically *good*, however, which determines the will by means of the conceptions of reason, and consequently not from subjective causes, but objectively, that is, on principles which are valid for every rational being as such. It is distinguished from the *pleasant* as that which influences the will only by means of sensation from merely subjective causes, valid only for the sense of this or that one, and not as a principle of reason which holds for every one.

A perfectly good will would therefore be equally subject to objective laws (viz., laws of good), but could not be conceived as *obliged* thereby to act lawfully, because of itself from its subjective constitution it can only be determined by the conception of good. Therefore no imperatives hold for the Divine will, or in general for a *holy* will; *ought* is here out of place because the volition is already of itself necessarily in unison with the law. Therefore imperatives are only formulae to express the relation of objective laws of all volition to the subjective imperfection of the will of this or that rational being, for example, the human will.

Now all *imperatives* command either *hypothetically* or *categorically*. The former represent the practical necessity of a possible action as means to something else that is willed (or at least which one might possibly will). The categorical imperative would be that which represented an action as necessary of itself without reference to another end, that is, as objectively necessary.

Since every practical law represents a possible action as good, and on this account, for a subject who is practically determinable by reason as necessary, all imperatives are formulae determining an action which is necessary according to the principle of a will good in some respects. If now the action is good only as a means *to something else,* then the imperative is *hypothetical;* if it is conceived as good *in itself* and consequently as being necessarily the principle of a will which of itself conforms to reason, then it is *categorical.*

Thus the imperative declares what action possible by me would be good, and presents the practical rule in relation to a will which does not forthwith perform an action simply because it is good, whether because the subject does not always know that it is good, or because, even if it know this, yet its maxims might be opposed to the objective principles of practical reason. . . .

On the other hand, the question, how the imperative of *morality* is possible, is undoubtedly one, the only one, demanding a solution, as this is not at all hypothetical, and the objective necessity which it presents cannot rest on any hypothesis, as is the case with the hypothetical imperatives. Only here we must never leave out of consideration that we *cannot* make out *by any example,* in other words, empirically, whether there is such an imperative at all; but it is rather to be feared that all those which seem to be categorical may yet at bottom be hypothetical. For instance, when the precept is: Thou shalt not promise deceitfully; and it is assumed that the necessity of this is not a mere counsel to avoid

some other evil, so that it should mean: Thou shalt not make a lying promise, lest if it become known thou shouldst destroy thy credit, but that an action of this kind must be regarded as evil in itself, so that the imperative of the prohibition is categorical; then we cannot show with certainty in any example that the will was determined merely by the law, without any other spring of action, although it may appear to be so. For it is always possible that fear of disgrace, perhaps also obscure dread of other dangers, may have a secret influence on the will. Who can prove by experience the nonexistence of a cause when all that experience tells us is that we do not perceive it? But in such a case the so-called moral imperative, which as such appears to be categorical and unconditional, would in reality be only a pragmatic precept, drawing our attention to our own interests, and merely teaching us to take these into consideration.

We shall therefore have to investigate *a priori* the possibility of a categorical imperative, as we have not in this case the advantage of its reality being given in experience, so that [the elucidation of] its possibility should be requisite only for its explanation, not for its establishment. In the meantime it may be discerned beforehand that the categorical imperative alone has the purport of a practical law; all the rest may indeed be called *principles* of the will but not laws, since whatever is only necessary for the attainment of some arbitrary purpose may be considered as in itself contingent, and we can at any time be free from the precept if we give up the purpose; on the contrary, the unconditional command leaves the will no liberty to choose the opposite, consequently it alone carries with it that necessity which we require in a law.

Secondly, in the case of this categorical imperative or law of morality, the difficulty (of discerning its possibility) is a very profound one. It is an *a priori* synthetical practical proposition; and as there is so much difficulty in discerning the possibility of speculative propositions of this kind, it may readily be supposed that the difficulty will be no less with the practical.

In this problem we will first inquire whether the mere conception of a categorical imperative may not perhaps supply us also with the formula of it, containing the proposition which alone can be a categorical imperative; for even if we know the tenor of such an absolute command, yet how it is possible will require further special and laborious study, which we postpone to the last section.

When I conceive a hypothetical imperative, in general I do not know beforehand what it will contain until I am given the condition. But when I conceive a categorical imperative, I know at once what it contains. For as the imperative contains besides the law only the necessity that the maxims shall conform to this law, while the law contains no conditions restricting it, there remains nothing but the general statement that the maxim of the action should conform to a universal law, and it is this conformity alone that the imperative properly represents as necessary.

There is therefore but one categorical imperative, namely, this: *Act only on that maxim whereby thou canst at the same time will that it should become a universal law.*

Now if all imperatives of duty can be deduced from this one imperative as from their principle, then, although it should remain undecided whether what is called duty is not merely a vain notion, yet at least we shall be able to show what we understand by it and what this notion means.

Since the universality of the law according to which effects are produced constitutes what is properly called *nature* in the most general sense (as to form)—that is, the existence of things so far as it is determined by general laws—the imperative of duty may be expressed thus: *Act as if the maxim of thy action were to become by thy will a universal law of nature.*

We will now enumerate a few duties, adopting the usual division of them into duties to ourselves and to others, and into perfect and imperfect duties.

1. A man reduced to despair by a series of misfortunes feels wearied of life, but is still so far in possession of his reason that he can ask himself whether it would not be contrary to his duty to himself to take his own life. Now he inquires whether the maxim of his action could become a universal law of nature. His maxim is: From self-love I adopt it as a principle to shorten my life when its longer duration is likely to bring more evil than satisfaction. It is asked then simply whether this principle founded on self-love can become a universal law of nature. Now we see at once that a system of nature of which it should be a law to destroy life by means of the very feeling whose special nature it is to impel to the improvement of life would contradict itself, and therefore could not exist as a system of nature; hence that maxim cannot possibly exist as a universal law of nature, and consequently would be wholly inconsistent with the supreme principle of all duty.

2. Another finds himself forced by necessity to borrow money. He knows that he will not be able to repay it, but sees also that nothing will be lent to him unless he promises stoutly to repay it in a definite time. He desires to make this promise, but he has still so much conscience as to ask himself: Is it not unlawful and inconsistent with duty to get out of a difficulty in this way? Suppose, however, that he resolves to do so, then the maxim of his action would be expressed thus: When I think myself in want of money, I will borrow money and promise to repay it, although I know that I never can do so. Now this principle of self-love or of one's own advantage may perhaps be consistent with my whole future welfare; but the question now is, Is it right? I change then the suggestion of self-love into a universal law, and state the question thus: How would it be if my maxim were a universal law? Then I see at once that it could never hold as a universal law of nature, but would necessarily contradict itself. For supposing it to be a universal law that everyone when he thinks himself in a difficulty should be able to promise whatever he pleases, with the purpose of not keeping his promise, the promise itself would become impossible, as well as the end that one might have in view in it, since no one would consider that anything was promised to him, but would ridicule all such statements as vain pretenses.

3. A third finds in himself a talent which with the help of some culture might make him a useful man in many respects. But he finds himself in comfortable circumstances and prefers to indulge in pleasure rather than to take pains in enlarging and improving his happy natural capacities. He asks,

however, whether his maxim of neglect of his natural gifts, besides agreeing with his inclination to indulgence, agrees also with what is called duty. He sees then that a system of nature could indeed subsist with such a universal law, although men (like the South Sea islanders) should let their talents rest and resolve to devote their lives merely to idleness, amusement, and propagation of their species—in a word, to enjoyment; but he cannot possibly *will* that this should be a universal law of nature, or be implanted in us as such by a natural instinct. For, as a rational being, he necessarily wills that his faculties be developed, since they serve him, and have been given him, for all sorts of possible purposes.

4. A fourth, who is in prosperity, while he sees that others have to contend with great wretchedness and that he could help them, thinks: What concern is it of mine? Let everyone be as happy as Heaven pleases, or as he can make himself; I will take nothing from him nor even envy him, only I do not wish to contribute anything to his welfare or to his assistance in distress! Now no doubt, if such a mode of thinking were a universal law, the human race might very well subsist, and doubtless even better than in a state in which everyone talks of sympathy and good-will, or even takes care occasionally to put it into practice, but, on the other side, also cheats when he can, betrays the rights of men, or otherwise violates them. But although it is possible that a universal law of nature might exist in accordance with that maxim, it is impossible to *will* that such a principle should have the universal validity of a law of nature. For a will which resolved this would contradict itself, inasmuch as many cases might occur in which one would have need of the love and sympathy of others, and in which, by such a law of nature, sprung from his own will, he would deprive himself of all hope of the aid he desires. . . .

Respect for Persons, Autonomy and the Kingdom of Ends

The question then is this: Is it a necessary law *for all rational beings* that they should always judge of their actions by maxims of which they can themselves will that they should serve as universal laws? If it is so, then it must be connected (altogether *a priori*) with the very conception of the will of a rational being generally. But in order to discover this connection we must, however reluctantly, take a step into metaphysic, although into a domain of it which is distinct from speculative philosophy—namely, the metaphysic of morals. In a practical philosophy, where it is not the reasons of what *happens* that we have to ascertain, but the laws of what *ought to happen*, even although it never does, that is, objective practical laws, there it is not necessary to inquire into the reasons why anything pleases or displeases, how the pleasure of mere sensation differs from taste, and whether the latter is distinct from a general satisfaction of reason; on what the feeling of pleasure or pain rests, and how from it desires and inclinations arise, and from these again maxims by the cooperation of reason; for all this belongs to an empirical psychology, which would constitute the second part of physics, if we regard physics as the *philosophy* of nature, so far as it is based on *empirical laws*. But here we are concerned with objective practical laws, and consequently with the relation of the will to itself so far as it is determined by reason alone, in which case whatever has reference to anything empirical is necessarily excluded; since if *reason of itself alone* determines the conduct (and it is the possibility of this that we are now investigating), it must necessarily do so *a priori*.

The will is conceived as a faculty of determining oneself to action *in accordance with the conception of certain laws*. And such a faculty can be found only in rational beings. Now that which serves the will as the objective ground of its self-determination is the *end*, and if this is assigned by reason alone, it must hold for all rational beings. On the other hand, that which merely contains the ground of possibility of the action of which the effect is the end, this is called the *means*. The subjective ground of the desire is the *spring*, the objective ground of the volition is the *motive*; hence the distinction between subjective ends which rest on springs, and objective ends which depend on motives valid for every rational being. Practical principles are *formal*, when they abstract from all subjective ends; they are *material* when they assume these, and therefore particular, springs of action. The ends which a rational being proposes to himself at pleasure as *effects* of his actions (material ends) are all only relative, for it is only their relation to the particular desires of the subject that gives them their worth, which therefore cannot furnish principles universal and necessary for all rational beings and for every volition, that is to say, practical laws. Hence all these relative ends can give rise only to hypothetical imperatives.

Supposing, however, that there were something *whose existence* has *in itself* an absolute worth, something which, being *an end in itself*, could be a source of definite laws, then in this and this alone would lie the source of a possible categorical imperative, that is, a practical law.

Now I say: man and generally any rational being *exists* as an end in himself, *not merely as a means* to be arbitrarily used by this or that will, but in all his actions, whether they concern himself or other rational beings, must be always regarded at the same time as an end. All objects of the inclinations have only a conditional worth; for if the inclinations and the wants founded on them did not exist, then their object would be without value. But the inclinations themselves, being sources of want, are so far from having an absolute worth for which they should be desired that, on the contrary, it must be the universal wish of every rational being to be wholly free from them. Thus the worth of any object which is *to be acquired* by our action is always conditional. Beings whose existence depends not on our will but on nature's, have nevertheless, if they are nonrational beings, only a relative value as means, and are therefore called *things*; rational beings, on the contrary, are called *persons*, because their very nature points them out as ends in themselves, that is, as something which must not be used merely as means, and so far therefore restricts freedom of action (and is an object of respect). These, therefore, are not merely subjective ends whose existence has a worth *for us* as an effect of our action, but *objective ends*, that is, things whose existence is an end in itself—an end, moreover, for which no other can be substituted, which they should subserve *merely* as means, for otherwise nothing whatever would possess

absolute worth; but if all worth were conditioned and therefore contingent, then there would be no supreme practical principle of reason whatever.

If then there is a supreme practical principle or, in respect of the human will, a categorical imperative, it must be one which, being drawn from the conception of that which is necessarily an end for everyone because it is *an end in itself*, constitutes an *objective* principle of will, and can therefore serve as a universal practical law. The foundation of this principle is: *rational nature exists as an end in itself.* Man necessarily conceives his own existence as being so; so far then this is a *subjective* principle of human actions. But every other rational being regards its existence similarly, just on the same rational principle that holds for me; so that it is at the same time an objective principle from which as a supreme practical law all laws of the will must be capable of being deduced. Accordingly the practical imperative will be as follows: *So act as to treat humanity, whether in thine own person or in that of any other, in every case as an end withal, never as means only.* We will now inquire whether this can be practically carried out.

To abide by the previous examples:

First, under the head of necessary duty to oneself: He who contemplates suicide should ask himself whether his action can be consistent with the idea of humanity *as an end in itself.* If he destroys himself in order to escape from painful circumstances, he uses a person merely as *a mean* to maintain a tolerable condition up to the end of life. But a man is not a thing, that is to say, something which can be used merely as means, but must in all his actions be always considered as an end in himself. I cannot, therefore, dispose in any way of a man in my own person so as to mutilate him, to damage or kill him. (It belongs to ethics proper to define this principle more precisely, so as to avoid all misunderstanding, for example, as to the amputation of the limbs in order to preserve myself; as to exposing my life to danger with a view to preserve it, etc. This question is therefore omitted here.)

Secondly, as regards necessary duties, or those of strict obligation, towards others: He who is thinking of making a lying promise to others will see at once that he would be using another man *merely as a mean,* without the latter containing at the same time the end in himself. For he whom I propose by such a promise to use for my own purposes cannot possibly assent to my mode of acting towards him, and therefore cannot himself contain the end of this action. This violation of the principle of humanity in other men is more obvious if we take in examples of attacks on the freedom and property of others. For then it is clear that he who transgresses the rights of men intends to use the person of others merely as means, without considering that as rational beings they ought always to be esteemed also as ends, that is, as beings who must be capable of containing in themselves the end of the very same action.

Thirdly, as regards contingent (meritorious) duties to oneself: It is not enough that the action does not violate humanity in our own person as an end in itself, it must also *harmonize with it.* Now there are in humanity capacities of greater perfection which belong to the end that nature has in view in regard to humanity in ourselves as the subject; to neglect these might perhaps be consistent with the *maintenance* of humanity as an end in itself, but not with the *advancement* of this end.

Fourthly, as regards meritorious duties towards others: The natural end which all men have is their own happiness. Now humanity might indeed subsist although no one should contribute anything to the happiness of others, provided he did not intentionally withdraw anything from it; but after all, this would only harmonize negatively, not positively, with *humanity as an end in itself,* if everyone does not also endeavor, as far as in him lies, to forward the ends of others. For the ends of any subject which is an end in himself ought as far as possible to be *my* ends also, if that conception is to have its *full* effect with me.

This principle that humanity and generally every rational nature is *an end in itself* (which is the supreme limiting condition of every man's freedom of action), is not borrowed from experience, *first,* because it is universal, applying as it does to all rational beings whatever, and experience is not capable of determining anything about them; *secondly,* because it does not present humanity as an

end to men (subjectively), that is, as an object which men do of themselves actually adopt as an end; but as an objective end which must as a law constitute the supreme limiting condition of all our subjective ends, let them be what we will; it must therefore spring from pure reason. In fact the objective principle of all practical legislation lies (according to the first principle) in *the rule* and its form of universality which makes it capable of being a law (say, for example, a law of nature); but the *subjective* principle is in the *end;* now by the second principle, the subject of all ends is each rational being inasmuch as it is an end in itself. Hence follows the third practical principle of the will, which is the ultimate condition of its harmony with the universal practical reason, viz., the idea of *the will of every rational being as a universally legislative will.*

On this principle all maxims are rejected which are inconsistent with the will being itself universal legislator. Thus the will is not subject to the law, but so subject that it must be regarded *as itself giving the law,* and on this ground only subject to the law (of which it can regard itself as the author).

In the previous imperatives, namely, that based on the conception of the conformity of actions to general laws, as in a *physical system of nature,* and that based on the universal *prerogative* of rational beings as *ends* in themselves—these imperatives just because they were conceived as categorical excluded from any share in their authority all admixture of any interest as a spring of action; they were, however, only *assumed* to be categorical, because such an assumption was necessary to explain the conception of duty. But we could not prove independently that there are practical propositions which command categorically, nor can it be proved in this section; one thing, however, could be done, namely, to indicate in the imperative itself, by some determinate expression, that in the case of volition from duty all interest is renounced, which is the specific criterion of categorical as distinguished from hypothetical imperatives. This is done in the present (third) formula of the principle, namely, in the idea of the will of every rational being as a *universally legislating will.*

For although a will *which is subject to laws* may be attached to this law by means of an interest, yet a will which is itself a supreme lawgiver, so far as it is such, cannot possibly depend on any interest, since a will so dependent would itself still need another law restricting the interest of its self-love by the condition that it should be valid as universal law.

Thus the *principle* that every human will is *a will which in all its maxims gives universal laws*, provided it be otherwise justified, would be very *well adapted* to be the categorical imperative, in this respect, namely, that just because of the idea of universal legislation it is *not based on any interest*, and therefore it alone among all possible imperatives can be *unconditional*. Or still better, converting the proposition, if there is a categorical imperative (that is, a law for the will of every rational being), it can only command that everything be done from maxims of one's will regarded as a will which could at the same time will that it should itself give universal laws, for in that case only the practical principle and the imperative which it obeys are unconditional, since they cannot be based on any interest.

Looking back now on all previous attempts to discover the principle of morality, we need not wonder why they all failed. It was seen that man was bound to laws by duty, but it was not observed that the laws to which he is subject are *only those of his own giving*, though at the same time they are *universal*, and that he is only bound to act in conformity with his own will—a will, however, which is designed by nature to give universal laws. For when one has conceived man only as subject to a law (no matter what), then this law required some interest, either by way of attraction or constraint, since it did not originate as a law from *his own* will, but this will was according to a law obliged by *something else* to act in a certain manner. Now by this necessary consequence all the labor spent in finding a supreme principle of *duty* was irrevocably lost. For men never elicited duty, but only a necessity of acting from a certain interest. Whether this interest was private or otherwise, in any case the imperative must be conditional, and could not by any means be capable of being a moral command. I will therefore call this the principle of *Autonomy* of

the will, in contrast with every other which I accordingly reckon as *Heteronomy*.

The conception of every rational being as one which must consider itself as giving in all the maxims of its will universal laws, so as to judge itself and its actions from this point of view—this conception leads to another which depends on it and is very fruitful, namely, that of a *kingdom of ends*.

By a "kingdom" I understand the union of different rational beings in a system by common laws. Now since it is by laws that ends are determined as regards their universal validity, hence, if we abstract from the personal differences of rational beings, and likewise from all the content of their private ends, we shall be able to conceive all ends combined in a systematic whole (including both rational beings as ends in themselves, and also the special ends which each may propose to himself), that is to say, we can conceive a kingdom of ends, which on the preceding principles is possible.

For all rational beings come under the *law* that each of them must treat itself and all others *never merely as means*, but in every case *at the same time as ends in themselves*. Hence results a systematic union of rational beings by common objective laws, that is, a kingdom which may be called a kingdom of ends, since what these laws have in view is just the relation of these beings to one another as ends and means. It is certainly only an ideal.

A rational being belongs as a *member* to the kingdom of ends when, although giving universal laws in it, he is also himself subject to these laws. He belongs to it *as sovereign* when, while giving laws, he is not subject to the will of any other.

A rational being must always regard himself as giving laws either as member or as sovereign in a kingdom of ends which is rendered possible by the freedom of will. He cannot, however, maintain the latter position merely by the maxims of his will, but only in case he is a completely independent being without wants and with unrestricted power adequate to his will.

Morality consists then in the reference of all action to the legislation which alone can render a kingdom of ends possible. This legislation must be capable of existing in every rational being, and of emanating from his will, so that the principle of this will is never to act on any maxim which could not without contradiction be also a universal law, and accordingly always so to act *that the will could at the same time regard itself as giving in its maxims universal laws.* If now the maxims of rational beings are not by their own nature coincident with this objective principle, then the necessity of acting on it is called practical necessitation, that is, *duty.* Duty does not apply to the sovereign in the kingdom of ends, but it does to every member of it and to all in the same degree.

The practical necessity of acting on this principle, that is, duty, does not rest at all on feelings, impulses, or inclinations, but solely on the relation of rational beings to one another, a relation in which the will of a rational being must always be regarded as *legislative,* since otherwise it could not be conceived as *an end in itself.* Reason then refers every maxim of the will, regarding it as legislating universally, to every other will and also to every action towards oneself; and this not on account of any other practical motive or any future advantage, but from the idea of the *dignity* of a rational being, obeying no law but that which he himself also gives.

In the kingdom of ends everything has either *value* or *dignity.* Whatever has a value can be replaced by something else which is *equivalent;* whatever, on the other hand, is above all value, and therefore admits of no equivalent, has a dignity.

Whatever has reference to the general inclinations and wants of mankind has a *market value;* whatever, without presupposing a want, corresponds to a certain taste, that is, to a satisfaction in the mere purposeless play of our faculties, has a *fancy value;* but that which constitutes the condition under which alone anything can be an end in itself, this has not merely a relative worth, that is, value, but an intrinsic worth, that is, *dignity.*

Now morality is the condition under which alone a rational being can be an end in himself, since by this alone it is possible that he should be a legislating member in the kingdom of ends. Thus morality, and humanity as capable of it, is that which alone has dignity. Skill and diligence in labor have a market value; wit, lively imagination, and humor have fancy value; on the other hand, fidelity to promises, benevolence from principle (not from instinct), have an intrinsic worth. Neither nature nor art contains anything which in default of these it could put in their place, for their worth consists not in the effects which spring from them, not in the use and advantage which they secure, but in the disposition of mind, that is, the maxims of the will which are ready to manifest themselves in such actions, even though they should not have the desired effect. These actions also need no recommendation from any subjective taste or sentiment, that they may be looked on with immediate favor and satisfaction; they need no immediate propension or feeling for them; they exhibit the will that performs them as an object of an immediate respect, and nothing but reason is required to *impose* them on the will; not to *flatter* it into them, which, in the case of duties, would be a contradiction. This estimation therefore shows that the worth of such a disposition is dignity, and places it infinitely above all value, with which it cannot for a moment be brought into comparison or competition without as it were violating its sanctity.

What then is it which justifies virtue or the morally good disposition, in making such lofty claims? It is nothing less than the privilege it secures to the rational being of participating in the giving of universal laws, by which it qualifies him to be a member of a possible kingdom of ends, a privilege to which he was already destined by his own nature as being an end in himself, and on that account legislating in the kingdom of ends; free as regards all laws of physical nature, and obeying those only which he himself gives, and by which his maxims can belong to a system of universal law to which at the same time he submits himself. For nothing has any worth except what the law assigns it. Now the legislation itself which assigns the worth of everything must for that very reason possess dignity, that is, an unconditional incomparable worth; and the word *respect* alone supplies a becoming expression for the esteem which a rational being must have for it. *Autonomy* then is the basis of the dignity of human and of every rational nature.

The three modes of presenting the principle of morality that have been adduced are at bottom only so many formulae of the very same law, and each of itself involves the other two. There is, however, a difference in them, but it is rather subjectively than objectively practical, intended, namely, to bring an idea of the reason nearer to intuition (by means of a certain analogy), and thereby nearer to feeling. All maxims, in fact, have—

1. A *form*, consisting in universality; and in this view the formula of the moral imperative is expressed thus, that the maxims must be so chosen as if they were to serve as universal laws of nature.

2. A *matter*, namely, an end, and here the formula says that the rational being, as it is an end by its own nature and therefore an end in itself, must in every maxim serve as the condition limiting all merely relative and arbitrary ends.

3. A *complete characterization* of all maxims by means of that formula, namely, that all maxims ought, by their own legislation, to harmonize with a possible kingdom of ends as with a kingdom of nature. There is a progress here in the order of the categories of *unity* of the form of the will (its universality), *plurality* of the matter (the objects, that is, the ends), and *totality* of the system of these. In forming our moral *judgment* of actions it is better to proceed always on the strict method, and start from the general formula of the categorical imperative: *Act according to a maxim which can at the same time make itself a universal law.* If, however, we wish to gain an *entrance* for the moral law, it is very useful to bring one and the same action under the three specified conceptions, and thereby as far as possible to bring it nearer to intuition.

We can now end where we started at the beginning, namely, with the conception of a will unconditionally good. *That will is absolutely good* which cannot be evil—in other words, whose maxim, if made a universal law, could never contradict itself. This principle, then, is its supreme law: *Act always on such a maxim as thou canst at the same time will to be a universal law*; this is the sole condition under which a will can never contradict itself; and such an imperative is categorical. Since the validity of the will as a universal law for possible actions is analogous to the universal connection of the existence of things by general laws, which is the formal notion of nature in general, the categorical imperative can also be expressed thus: *Act on maxims which can at the same time have for their object themselves as universal laws of nature.* Such then is the formula of an absolutely good will.

Rational nature is distinguished from the rest of nature by this that it sets before itself an end. This end would be the matter of every good will. But since in the idea of a will that is absolutely good without being limited by any condition (of attaining this or that end) we must abstract wholly from every end *to be effected* (since this would make every will only relatively good), it follows that in this case the end must be conceived, not as an end to be effected, but as an *independently* existing end. Consequently it is conceived only negatively, that is, as that which we must never act against, and which, therefore, must never be regarded merely as means, but must in every volition be esteemed as an end likewise. Now this end can be nothing but the subject of all possible ends, since this is also the subject of a possible absolutely good will; for such a will cannot without contradiction be postponed to any other object. This principle: So act in regard to every rational being (thyself and others) that he may always have place in thy maxim as an end in himself, is accordingly essentially identical with this other: Act upon a maxim which, at the same time, involves its own universal validity for every rational being. For that in using means for every end I should limit my maxim by the condition of its holding good as a law for every subject, this comes to the same thing as that the fundamental principle of all maxims of action must be that the subject of all ends, that is, the rational being himself, be never employed merely as means, but as the supreme condition restricting the use of all means—that is, in every case as an end likewise.

It follows incontestably that, to whatever laws any rational being may be subject, he being an end in himself must be able to regard himself as also legislating universally in respect of these same laws, since it is just this fitness of his maxims for universal legislation that distinguishes him as an end in himself; also it follows that this implies his dignity (prerogative) above all mere physical beings, that he must always take his maxims from the point of view which regards himself, and likewise every other rational being, as lawgiving beings (on which account they are called persons). In this way a world of rational beings (*mundus intelligibilis*) is possible as a kingdom of ends, and this by virtue of the legislation proper to all persons as members. Therefore, every rational being must so act as if he were by his maxims in every case a legislating member in the universal kingdom of ends. The formal principle of these maxims is: So act as if thy maxim were to serve likewise as the universal law (of all rational beings). A kingdom of ends is thus only possible on the analogy of a kingdom of nature, the former, however, only by maxims—that is, self-imposed rules—the latter only by the laws of efficient causes acting under necessitation from without. Nevertheless, although the system of nature is looked upon as a machine, yet so far as it has reference to rational beings as its ends, it is given on this account the name of a kingdom of nature. Now such a kingdom of ends would be actually realized by means of maxims conforming to the canon which the categorical imperative prescribes to all rational beings, *if they were universally followed*. But although a rational being, even if he punctually follows this maxim himself, cannot reckon upon all others being therefore true to the same, nor expect that the kingdom of nature and its orderly arrangements shall be in harmony with him as a fitting member, so as to form a kingdom of ends to which he himself contributes, that is to say, that it shall favor his expectation of happiness, still that law: Act according to the maxims of a member of a merely possible kingdom of ends legislating in it universally, remains in its full force inasmuch as it commands categorically. And it is just in this that the paradox lies; that the mere dignity of man as a rational creature, without any other end or advantage to be attained thereby, in other words, respect for a mere idea, should yet serve as an inflexible precept of the will, and that it is precisely in this independence of the maxim on all such springs of action that its sublimity consists; and it is this that makes every rational

subject worthy to be a legislative member in the kingdom of ends, for otherwise he would have to be conceived only as subject to the physical law of his wants. And although we should suppose the kingdom of nature and the kingdom of ends to be united under one sovereign, so that the latter kingdom thereby ceased to be a mere idea and acquired true reality, then it would no doubt gain the accession of a strong spring, but by no means any increase of its intrinsic worth. For this sole absolute lawgiver must, notwithstanding this, be always conceived as estimating the worth of rational beings only by their disinterested behavior, as prescribed to themselves from that idea [the dignity of man] alone. The essence of things is not altered by their external relations, and that which, abstracting from these, alone constitutes the absolute worth of man is also that by which he must be judged, whoever the judge may be, and even by the Supreme Being. *Morality*, then, is the relation of actions to the autonomy of the will, that is, to the potential universal legislation by its maxims. An action that is consistent with the autonomy of the will is *permitted*; one that does not agree therewith is *forbidden*. A will whose maxims necessarily coincide with the laws of autonomy is a *holy* will, good absolutely. The dependence of a will not absolutely good on the principle of autonomy (moral necessitation) is obligation. This then, cannot be applied to a holy being. The objective necessity of actions from obligation is called *duty*. . . .

THIRD SECTION

Transition from the Metaphysic of Morals to the Critique of Pure Practical Reason

The Concept of Freedom Is the Key That Explains the Autonomy of the Will

The *will* is a kind of causality belonging to living beings in so far as they are rational, and *freedom* would be this property of such causality that it can be efficient, independently on foreign causes *determining* it; just as *physical necessity* is the property that the causality of all irrational beings has of being determined to activity by the influence of foreign causes.

The preceding definition of freedom is *negative,* and therefore unfruitful for the discovery of its essence; but it leads to a *positive* conception which is so much the more full and fruitful. Since the conception of causality involves that of laws, according to which, by something that we call cause, something else, namely, the effect, must be produced [laid down]; hence, although freedom is not a property of the will depending on physical laws, yet it is not for that reason lawless; on the contrary, it must be a causality acting according to immutable laws, but of a peculiar kind; otherwise a free will would be an absurdity. Physical necessity is a heteronomy of the efficient causes, for every effect is possible only according to this law— that something else determines the efficient cause to exert its causality. What else then can freedom of the will be but autonomy, that is, the property of the will to be a law to itself? But the proposition: The will is in every action a law to itself, only expresses the principle to act on no other maxim than that which can also have as an object itself as a universal law. Now this is precisely the formula of the categorical imperative and is the principle of morality, so that a free will and a will subject to moral laws are one and the same.

On the hypothesis, then, of freedom of the will, morality together with its principle follows from it by mere analysis of the conception. However, the latter is a synthetic proposition, viz., an absolutely good will is that whose maxim can always include itself regarded as a universal law; for this property of its maxim can never be discovered by analyzing the conception of an absolutely good will. Now such synthetic propositions are only possible in this way—that the two cognitions are connected together by their union with a third in which they are both to be found. The *positive* concept of freedom furnishes this third cognition, which cannot, as with physical causes, be the nature of the sensible world (in the concept of which we find conjoined the concept of something in relation as cause to *something else* as effect). We cannot now at once show what this third is to which freedom points us, and of which we have an idea *a priori,* nor can we make intelligible how the concept of freedom is shown to be legitimate from principles of pure practical reason, and with it the possibility of a categorical imperative; but some further preparation is required.

FREEDOM

Must Be Presupposed as a Property of the Will of All Rational Beings

It is not enough to predicate freedom of our own will, from whatever reason, if we have not sufficient grounds for predicating the same of all rational beings. For as morality serves as a law for us only because we are *rational beings,* it must also hold for all rational beings; and as it must be deduced simply from the property of freedom, it must be shown that freedom also is a property of all rational beings. It is not enough, then, to prove it from certain supposed experiences of human nature (which indeed is quite impossible, and it can only be shown *a priori*), but we must show that it belongs to the activity of all rational beings endowed with a will. Now I say every being that cannot act except *under the idea of freedom* is just for that reason in a practical point of view really free, that is, to say, all laws which are inseparably connected with freedom have the same force for him as if his will had been shown to be free in itself by a proof theoretically conclusive. Now I affirm that we must attribute to every rational being which has a will that it has also the idea of freedom and acts entirely under this idea. For in such a being we conceive a reason that is practical, that is, has causality in reference to its objects. Now we cannot possibly conceive a reason consciously receiving a bias from any other quarter with respect to its judgments, for then the subject would ascribe the determination of its judgment not to its own reason, but to an impulse. It must regard itself as the author of its principles independent on foreign influences. Consequently, as practical reason or as the will of a rational being it must regard itself as free, that is to say, the will of such a being cannot be a will of its own except under the idea of freedom. This idea must therefore in a practical point of view be ascribed to every rational being.

Of the Interest Attaching to the Ideas of Morality

We have finally reduced the definite conception of morality to the idea of freedom. This latter, however, we could not prove to be actually a property of ourselves or of human nature; only we saw that it must be presupposed if we would conceive a being as rational and conscious of its causality in respect in its actions, that is, as endowed with a will; and so we find that on just the same grounds we must ascribe to every being endowed with reason and will this attribute of determining itself to action under the idea of its freedom.

Now it resulted also from the presupposition of this idea that we became aware of a law that the subjective principles of action, that is, maxims, must also be so assumed that they can also hold as objective, that is, universal principles, and so serve as universal laws of our own dictation. But why, then, should I subject myself to this principle and that simply as a rational being, thus also subjecting to it all other beings endowed with reason? I will allow that no interest *urges* me to this, for that would not give a categorical imperative, but I must *take* an interest in it and discern how this comes to pass; for this "I ought" is properly an "I would," valid for every rational being, provided only that reason determined his actions without any hindrance. But for beings that are in addition affected as we are by springs of a different kind, namely, sensibility, and in whose case that is not always done which reason alone would do, for these that necessity is expressed only as an "ought," and the subjective necessity is different from the objective.

It seems, then, as if the moral law, that is, the principle of autonomy of the will, were properly speaking only presupposed in the idea of freedom, and as if we could not prove its reality and objective necessity independently. In that case we should still have gained something considerable by at least determining the true principle more exactly than had previously been done; but as regards its validity and the practical necessity of subjecting oneself to it, we should not have advanced a step. For if we were asked why the universal validity of our maxim as a law must be the condition restricting our actions, and on what we ground the worth which we assign to this manner of acting—a worth so great that there cannot be any higher interest—and if we were asked further how it happens that it is by this alone a man believes he feels his own personal worth, in comparison with which that of an agreeable or disagreeable condition is to be regarded as nothing, to these questions we could give no satisfactory answer.

We find indeed sometimes that we can take an interest in a personal quality which does not involve any interest of external condition, provided this quality makes us capable of participating in the condition in case reason were to effect the allotment; that is to say, the mere being worthy of happiness can interest of itself even without the motive of participating in this happiness. This judgment, however, is in fact only the effect of the importance of the moral law which we before presupposed (when by the idea of freedom we detach ourselves from every empirical interest); but that we ought to detach ourselves from these interests, that is, to consider ourselves as free in action and yet as subject to certain laws, so as to find a worth simply in our own person which can compensate us for the loss of everything that gives worth to our condition, this we are not yet able to discern in this way, nor do we see how it is possible so to act—in other words, *whence the moral law derives its obligation.*

It must be freely admitted that there is a sort of circle here from which it seems impossible to escape. In the order of efficient causes we assume ourselves free, in order that in the order of ends we may conceive ourselves as subject to moral laws; and we afterwards conceive ourselves as subject to these laws because we have attributed to ourselves freedom of will; for freedom and self-legislation of will are both autonomy, and therefore are reciprocal conceptions, and for this very reason one must not be used to explain the other or give the reason of it, but at most only for logical purposes to reduce apparently different notions of the same object to one single concept (as we reduce different fractions of the same value to the lowest terms).

One resource remains to us, namely, to inquire whether we do not occupy different points of view when by means of freedom we think ourselves as causes efficient *a priori,* and when we form our conception of ourselves from our actions as effects which we see before our eyes.

It is a remark which needs no subtle reflection to make, but which we may assume that even the commonest understanding can make, although it be after its fashion by an obscure discernment of judgment which it calls feeling, that all the "ideas" that come to us involuntarily (as those of the senses) do not enable us to know objects otherwise than as they affect us; so that what they may be in themselves remains unknown to us, and consequently that as regards "ideas" of this kind even with the closest attention and clearness that the understanding can apply to them, we can by them only attain to the knowledge of *appearances,* never to that of *things in themselves.* As soon as this distinction has once been made (perhaps merely in consequence of the difference observed between the ideas given us from without, and in which we are passive, and those that we produce simply from ourselves, and in which we show our own activity), then it follows of itself that we must admit and assume behind the appearance something else that is not an appearance, namely, the things in themselves; although we must admit that, as they can never be known to us except as they affect us, we can come no nearer to them, nor can we ever know what they are in themselves. This must furnish a distinction, however crude, between a *world of sense* and the *world of understanding,* of which the former may be different according to the difference of the sensuous impressions in various observers, while the second which is its basis always remains the same. Even as to himself, a man cannot pretend to know what he is in himself from the knowledge he has by internal sensation. For as he does not as it were create himself, and does not come by the conception of himself *a priori* but empirically, it naturally follows that he can obtain his knowledge even of himself only by the inner sense, and consequently only through the appearances of his nature

and the way in which his consciousness is affected. At the same time, beyond these characteristics of his own subject, made up of mere appearances, he must necessarily suppose something else as their basis, namely, his *ego,* whatever its characteristics in itself may be. Thus in respect to mere perception and receptivity of sensations he must reckon himself as belonging to the *world of sense;* but in respect of whatever there may be of pure activity in him (that which reaches consciousness immediately and not through affecting the senses), he must reckon himself as belonging to the *intellectual world,* of which, however, he has no further knowledge. To such a conclusion the reflecting man must come with respect to all the things which can be presented to him; it is probably to be met with even in persons of the commonest understanding, who, as is well known, are very much inclined to suppose behind the objects of the senses something else invisible and acting of itself. They spoil it, however, by presently sensualizing this invisible again, that is to say, wanting to make it an object of intuition, so that they do not become a whit the wiser.

Now man really finds in himself a faculty by which he distinguishes himself from everything else, even from himself as affected by objects, and that is *reason.* This being pure spontaneity is even elevated above the *understanding.* For although the latter is a spontaneity and does not, like sense, merely contain intuitions that arise when we are affected by things (and are therefore passive), yet it cannot produce from its activity any other conceptions than those which merely serve *to bring the intuitions of sense under rules,* and thereby to unite them in one consciousness, and without this use of the sensibility it could not think at all; whereas, on the contrary, reason shows so pure a spontaneity in the case of what I call "ideas" [Ideal Conceptions] that it thereby far transcends everything that the sensibility can give it, and exhibits its most important function in distinguishing the world of sense from that of understanding, and thereby prescribing the limits of the understanding itself.

For this reason a rational being must regard himself *qua* intelligence (not from the side of his lower faculties) as belonging not to the world of sense, but to that of understanding; hence he has two points of view from which he can regard himself, and recognize laws of the exercise of his faculties, and consequently of all his actions; *first*, so far as he belongs to the world of sense, he finds himself subject to laws of nature (heteronomy); *secondly*, as belonging to the intelligible world, under laws which, being independent on nature, have their foundation not in experience but in reason alone.

As a reasonable being, and consequently belonging to the intelligible world, man can never conceive the causality of his own will otherwise than on condition of the idea of freedom, for independence on the determining causes of the sensible world (an independence which reason must always ascribe to itself) is freedom. Now the idea of freedom is inseparably connected with the conception of *autonomy*, and this again with the universal principle of morality which is ideally the foundation of all actions *of rational* beings, just as the law of nature is of all phenomena.

Now the suspicion is removed which we raised above, that there was a latent circle involved in our reasoning from freedom to autonomy, and from this to the moral law, viz., that we laid down the idea of freedom because of the moral law only that we might afterwards in turn infer the latter from freedom, and that consequently we could assign no reason at all for this law, but could only [present] it as a *petito principii* which well-disposed minds would gladly concede to us, but which we could never put forward as a provable proposition. For now we see that when we conceive ourselves as free we transfer ourselves into the world of understanding as members of it, and recognize the autonomy of the will with its consequence, morality; whereas, if we conceive ourselves as under obligation, we consider ourselves as belonging to the world of sense, and at the same time to the world of understanding.

How Is a Categorical Imperative Possible?

Every rational being reckons himself *qua* intelligence as belonging to the world of understanding, and it is simply as an efficient cause belonging to that world that he calls his causality a *will*. On the other side, he is also conscious of himself as a part of the world of sense in which his actions, which are mere appearances [phenomena] of that causality, are displayed; we cannot, however, discern how they are possible from this causality which we do not know; but instead of that, these actions as belonging to the sensible world must be viewed as determined by other phenomena, namely, desires and inclinations. If therefore I were only a member of the world of understanding, then all my actions would perfectly conform to the principle of autonomy of the pure will; if I were only a part of the world of sense, they would necessarily be assumed to conform wholly to the natural law of desires and inclinations, in other words, to the heteronomy of nature. (The former would rest on morality as the supreme principle, the latter on happiness.) Since, however, *the world of understanding contains the foundation of the world of sense, and consequently of its laws also,* and accordingly gives the law to my will (which belongs wholly to the world of understanding) directly, and must be conceived as doing so, it follows that, although on the one side I must regard myself as a being belonging to the world of sense, yet, on the other side, I must recognize myself, as an intelligence, as subject to the law of the world of understanding, that is, to reason, which contains this law in the idea of freedom, and therefore as subject to the autonomy of the will; consequently I must regard the laws of the world of understanding as imperatives for me, and the actions which conform to them as duties.

And thus what makes categorical imperatives possible is this—that the idea of freedom makes me a member of an intelligible world, in consequence of which, if I were nothing else, all my actions *would* always conform to the autonomy of the will; but as I at the same time intuit myself as a member of the world of sense, they *ought* so to conform, and this *categorical* "ought" implies a synthetic *a priori* proposition, inasmuch as besides my will as affected by sensible desires there is added further the idea of the same will, but as belonging to the world of the understanding, pure and practical of itself, which contains the supreme condition according to reason of the former will; precisely as to the intuitions of sense there are added concepts of the understanding which of themselves signify nothing but regular form in general, and in this way synthetic *a priori* propositions become possible, on which all knowledge of physical nature rests.

The practical use of common human reason confirms this reasoning. There is no one, not even the most consummate villain, provided only that he is otherwise accustomed to the use of reason, who, when we set before him examples of honesty of purpose, of steadfastness in following good maxims, of sympathy and general benevolence (even combined with great sacrifices of advantages and comfort), does not wish that he might also possess these qualities. Only on account of his inclinations and impulses he cannot attain this in himself, but at the same time he wishes to be free from such inclinations which are burdensome to himself. He proves by this that he transfers himself in thought with a will free from the impulses of the sensibility into an order of things wholly different from that of his desires in the field of the sensibility; since he cannot expect to obtain by that wish any gratification of his desires, nor any position which would satisfy any of his actual or supposable inclinations (for this would destroy the preeminence of the very idea which wrests that wish from him), he can only expect a greater intrinsic worth of his own person. This better person, however, he imagines himself to be when he transfers himself to the point of view of a member of the world of the understanding, to which he is involuntarily forced by the idea of freedom, that is, of independence on *determining* causes of the world of sense; and from this point of view he is conscious of a good will, which by his own confession constitutes the law for the bad will that he possesses as a member of the world of sense—a law whose authority he recognizes while transgressing it. What he morally "ought" is then what he necessarily "would" as a member of the world of the understanding, and is conceived by him as an "ought" only inasmuch as he likewise considers himself as a member of the world of sense.

Study Questions

1. How does Locke prove that the world exists?

2. What is the difference between primary and secondary qualities?

3. What is Berkeley's argument for the denial of the existence of the material world?

4. Why does Hume think that we cannot know our own minds?

5. For Hume, what makes scientific knowledge unreliable?

6. Explain what Kant means by his "Copernican Revolution."

7. What are some of the innate mechanisms of the mind?

8. What is the difference between the noumenal and phenomenal worlds?

9. What are the psychological and transcendental egos?

10. Explain how Kant accepts belief in freedom, immortality, and the existence of God as postulates of practical reason.

Chapter 7

The Social Self: Karl Marx

Introduction

Many of the theories of human nature thus far examined have identified human nature with reason. The goal of theoretical reason is to know, to acquire wisdom; the goal of practical reason is to act reasonably, especially to be virtuous. For many of our authors, to become a wise and virtuous person is not an easy task. People are often uneducated about the merits of pursuing these goals. Even when they know that they should strive for them they are often too selfish, or too weak, or even too depraved to do so on their own. People need help to shape themselves into the persons they should become. This help may come from many sources, such as enlightenment or grace, but most often it comes in the form of training and education.

The most important training and education for creating wise and virtuous persons is the process of acquiring the habits, skills, beliefs, and ideals that society has identified as the most important for our development. However various societies go about shaping their members, the important point is that our character is formed for good or evil by the groups in which we live. It is important for a society to be good if it is to produce good citizens. A good society shapes and molds us into civilized beings with high ideals. This is why, for Confucius, social relationships have to be formed in certain ways rather than others, and it is why, for Plato and Aristotle, politics is considered a branch of ethics. We do not become good human beings by ourselves. We are social animals. Our character, and even our identity is formed by the group. Without the group, Confucius, Plato, and Aristotle all see us as uncivilized brutes, capable of great evil, and destined to lead lives of misery.

Karl Marx (1818–1883), often called the father of modern **communism,** also understood human nature to be the product of society. For Marx, however, society does not steer us in the direction of perfection and happiness. Instead, it is the process of socialization itself that causes misery and suffering. It takes our natural selves, which are essentially good, and in "civilizing" us causes us to be selfish and unhappy human beings. Marx spent most of his career explaining how and why this distortion of our natural selves by society is created, and describing how it might be prevented and how human nature might be restored to its state of goodness.

Marx was born in Germany, at a time of great political, social, and economic unrest. The French Revolution of 1789 had marked the beginning of the end of most European monarchies, and various nations began to establish more democratic forms of government in their place. Marx studied law and philosophy in Germany, and ended up editing a liberal newspaper from which he directed scathing criticism at some of these new forms of government. This was a job that paid little and frequently got him into trouble with the law. In his thirties, for the safety of himself and his family, Marx left Germany and eventually settled in London. There he wrote the books that would establish him as the intellectual founder of communism. He was supported financially during this time by Friedrich Engels (1820–1895), the co-author with Marx of *The Manifesto of the Communist Party* (1848). The first two parts of this work are reprinted here, with all of its original zeal, as *Reading 2.* Because of the support of Engels, Marx was able to work on his monumental *Capital,* the first volume of which was published in 1868. Marx's ideas about the nature of society had a widespread and profound influence on others. For example, they inspired the Russian Revolution of 1917, the Chinese revolution led by Mao Tse-Tung, and the Cuban Revolution, led by Fidel Castro. Less than one hundred years after his death, his theories of society had become the basis for socialist countries containing more than a third of the world's population.

Worldview

The theories of human nature thus far considered have grown out of religious or philosophical frameworks. Even the ideas about human nature developed as a reaction to science by Descartes and Kant are philosophical in origin, not scientific. Many of the theories of human nature to be considered in this and following chapters, however, have their roots in science, not philosophy. Marx, for example, considered himself to be a social scientist. Indeed, he is considered by many to be among the founders of modern day sociology. He thought of his views on human nature and society as the product of observation and theory, confirmable by observation. The same will be true for the views of Freud, Skinner, Darwin, and others, views that will be examined in later chapters. Their innovative concepts of human nature grew and developed within the very sciences that they created.

While a theory of human nature may have its origins in science, its development into a full blown theory often takes its claims beyond what can be confirmed by observation. This is certainly true in the case of Marx. Theories were constructed by Marx on such a grand scale that they included more than a little speculation. A great deal of what Marx has to say cannot be confirmed by experimentation. In particular, in explaining the social, political, and economic forces that shape human nature, Marxism goes far beyond observable facts. Even though Marx thinks of himself as a scientist, and even though he usually begins with facts, it is important to be aware that his theories often go well beyond mere descriptions and explanations of facts. It is important to be aware that many of his theories are as philosophical in nature as those of Plato or Aristotle.

If a worldview consists especially in basic beliefs about reality and knowledge, the worldview of Marx is easy to describe. He was a materialist, an atheist, and considered the scientific method to be the most reliable sort of knowledge that we have. Since the reality that interests him is social reality, however, simply calling him a materialist and an atheist is insufficient to understand his concept of *reality.* Likewise, it is an inadequate account of his *epistemology* to say only that he was an advocate of the scientific method. A fuller account of his theory of knowledge would also include how he applies the scientific method to the study of society, something that Marx largely invented in the process of constructing his theories. In what follows we will have little to say about his concept of social science, and focus instead on his concept of social reality. The important questions for Marx about the nature of social reality concern the nature of society, especially political societies, and the mechanisms of social change. Marx especially wanted to understand what causes the great changes in society, the ones that result in new types of societies being formed. He wanted to know, for example, how a slave society gets to be a feudal society, and how that gets to be a capitalist society. He wanted this knowledge not simply for its own sake, moreover, but for the very practical purpose of learning how consciously and intentionally to change society. For Marx, the point of studying society was to change it, not merely to understand it.

The Influence of Capitalism

Something that strikes many as odd when they first read Marx is how much he talks about work. For Marx this is a central concept, since people are largely defined by their work, and especially by what they produce. The type of work we do is fundamental to our very being, and is basic to understanding the nature of society as well. In fact, Marx believes that the way work is organized in a particular society largely determines everything else about it, even its loftiest philosophical theories. Marx will not focus on our reason, or on our will, or on our virtue, in defining who we are as human beings; instead, he will focus on what we produce. Human beings are by nature makers of things, and in this activity is where our identity and happiness is to be found. Unfortunately, society has managed to corrupt our natural ways of working and producing things, and has harnessed our productive powers for the good of others. This is why Marx wants to change society, to return us to a more natural state of work where our true selves have a chance to develop as they are supposed to.

One of the most influential experiences in the life of Marx was his witnessing firsthand the effects of capitalism in London. At the heart of the economic system called **capitalism** is the doctrine of private property, the right to own businesses, farms, and other means of producing a product. Capitalism not only allows private property, but it also allows people who own this property to use others to create products. These workers are paid very little for their labor, and as a result the owners are able to sell the goods that workers create for a profit. In this way those who own private property are allowed to accumulate wealth. With no restrictions on how much wealth a person may legally acquire, capitalism allows people to use the labor of others to increase their own wealth. If I have enough money, I can buy a factory and hire people to produce a product. Then I can sell that product for more than the cost of the materials and the wages required to produce it. In this way I may make a profit and increase my wealth. Then I can buy more factories, hire more people, and get richer and richer.

With *laissez-faire* (from the French, meaning literally "allow to act") capitalism, the government allows such accumulation of wealth without interference. The major form of interference is taxation, where some of the profits are taken from the owner and used by the government for other purposes. With laissez-faire capitalism, the taxation is minimal. Marx had witnessed the evils of laissez-faire capitalism while he was living in England, during the beginnings of the Industrial Revolution. Among its evils were unsafe working conditions, poverty-level wages, and children working long hours in miserable conditions. Especially painful to see was the ever widening economic gap between the increasingly wealthy capitalists and members of the poor working class, whose wages barely sustained their existence. Much of what Marx wrote and worked for during his lifetime was inspired by this vision of misery, this terrible lot of the majority of mankind. For Marx, the goal ultimately was universal liberation from its burdensome yoke.

The Influence of Hegel

While it was the evils of capitalism that motivated Marx to criticize it in his writings, it was the thought of Hegel that guided the development of his analyses. The German philosopher, Georg Wilhelm Friedrich Hegel (1770–1831), had developed a philosophy of history which claimed that the history of the world, and especially the history of social change, unfolded according to a pattern that moved humankind always toward something progressively better. For Hegel, the underlying pattern of historical development was what he called the **dialectic,** a process of social change that results from prior conflicting elements. Hegel clothed his theories in an idealist metaphysics, where what evolved through history was understood to be not the plain and simple material world of everyday life, but rather a world spirit or a mind of which we are all simply constituent parts. So for him, the conflicting elements are ideas, or systems of ideas called cultures, existing in the mind of God. God himself evolves through history by the evolution of these ideas toward perfection. The conflict of competing cultures creates a new culture, which then eventually conflicts with another, and so on until perfection is reached. This is the dialectic, the resolution of opposing forces to create something new and better.

Marx's philosophy of history follows a similar line, but it is thoroughly materialistic; thus the name **dialectical materialism.** The influence of Ludwig Feuerbach (1804–1872), another German philosopher, persuaded Marx to accept both materialism and atheism. Feurbach argued that God is created by man, in the image of man, and not the other way around. God is merely a personification of all that is best about human beings—their goodness, love, knowledge, power, and creativity. Unfortunately, claimed Feurbach, by idealizing these qualities and thinking of them as belonging to God, humans have abandoned the effort to create for themselves a better world, one which exhibits these properties. The net result is an acceptance of suffering and misery as our natural lot.

Marx agrees with Hegel that social change begins with conflict. However, it is not the clash of ideas that leads to change, rather it is the clash of social classes that does. A class within society is an economic class, for Marx, such as the working class, or the wealthy class. Membership in these various classes is determined by economic similarities. A **class** is simply a group whose members all have the same economic relationships. Among these relationships are what Marx calls the "means of production," the "forces of production," and the "profits." The **means of production** are the natural resources used to create a product, and the **forces**

of production are what are used to create the goods of society, including factories and farms, businesses, and labor. **Profits** are what is gained by selling a product after the costs of labor and other production costs have been met. This is called the **surplus value** of a product.

For Marx, social change occurs because of **class conflict.** Two opposing classes—one weak and large, one small and strong—struggling against each other produce a new set of economic relationships or classes, and thus a new type of society. Struggle occurs because the dominant class exploits the other for their own purposes, and the subordinate class wishes to throw off the yoke of servitude. Slaves may struggle against their masters in a slave society, for example, to escape from their miserable condition and produce a society where slavery is no more. A struggle is required, even though there are many more slaves than masters, because of the role of the **state.** The power of the state is always on the side of the dominant class, and is used by them to maintain the condition of exploitation. The subordinate class has to struggle to overcome the power of the dominant class, exercised mainly through the state.

For Marx, the state is not a natural entity, as it was for Plato. Its job is not to foster the moral goodness of its citizens, or even to administer justice fairly in the process of protecting everyone from everyone else. It may pretend to do this; it may even have grand theories of justice and happiness to explain and describe how it actually plays this role. The reality is, however, that the state is a tool of exploitation. Whenever there is more than one class in a society one of these is the dominant class. Usually it is far outnumbered by the class it exploits. The state, with the power to introduce and enforce laws, protects the interests of the dominant class; it uses its might to maintain the injustices of the exploitation. This is why the major engine for social change is class "struggle," and not merely the majority class subduing the minority with ease; because the force of state sides with the interests of the dominant class.

In addition to the power of the state, another way in which exploitation is maintained by the dominant class is through ideas—political theories, philosophical and religious ideas, images found in art, literature, and so on. These ideas form what Marx calls the "ideology" of a society, the central beliefs of its culture. These are the entities that matter for Hegel, and that most of us think of as quite influential. After all, ideas shape the world, do they not? For Marx, they indeed do not. Ideas are simply shadows of the underlying economic reality. Their function is not so much to reveal truth, but to cover up the reality of exploitation. For example, religion tells us that our suffering comes from God and that we should simply bear it for the sake of our eternal reward. Because it makes our suffering bearable by giving it meaning and purpose, and because this makes us feel better, Marx calls religion the "opium of the people." The reality, however, is that suffering comes from the exploitation of some men by others.

Marx calls the basic cultural beliefs of a society its **ideological superstructure.** Like shadows these ideas are created by a deeper reality that Marx refers to as the **economic substructure.** These are the economic patterns and laws that determine class structures. These economic realities determine all else in society, even the theories of its philosophers, the art of its creative people, the practices and policies of politics, even its concept of human nature. Ideas do not change the world; instead they themselves are the products of **economic determinism.** According to this view, we think the way that we do about ourselves because of the economic forces that exist in society. While most of us believe that our concept of "justice," for example, determines how we distribute the goods of society, exactly the reverse is true. The way that the wealth is distributed determines how we think about what is fair. Our ideologies are the products of underlying economic laws, and never serve to change anything. Instead they serve merely as tools of the dominant class to justify and thus maintain its exploitation.

Armed with these concepts of economic determinism, class conflict and the true role of the state, Marx sets out to explain the evolution of European history from ancient Greece to the present day. Ancient Greece had a *slave society*. The two basic economic classes were slaves and masters. Remember, a class is defined by Marx relative to its ownership of the means and forces of production and the profits. Slaves own none of the means or forces of production, such as farms, tools, money, and even their own labor. They surely do not own any of the profits that might be enjoyed from the sale of the goods which their labor produces. The masters control the means and forces of production as well as the profits.

In the Medieval period, the slave-master society was replaced by the *landlord-tenant society*. The landlord owned the farms and allowed the tenants each to work small portions of it. In return, the tenant had to give to the landlord the majority of what he produced on the land, keeping only enough to support himself and his family. Once again, the landed nobility owned the means of production and the profits, but now the tenants owned at least some of the forces of production, part of their labor, and a bit of the profits. *Capitalist societies* grew out of this landlord-tenant structure. They began during the late Medieval period with the rise of a merchant class, and flourished within the modern nation-states of the nineteenth century. Capitalist societies have two classes—the capitalists (the *bourgeoisie* as Marx calls them) and the working class (the *proletariat*). Their relationship is one of conflict, with the relatively few capitalists controlling most of society's wealth by owning the means and forces of production and the profits. The workers are at least paid for their labor in such a system, but not the true value of their labor. Instead, they live so poorly compared to the capitalists that the power of the state is required to keep them in their place. The inherent evil of capitalism is that the capitalists keep the surplus value of products, and thus acquire great wealth at the expense of the workers. Capitalism creates a tremendous gulf between the rich and the poor. Even in the presence of such wealth, the poor are hardly able to subsist.

Marx thought that capitalistic societies would dissolve simply because competition among capitalists would result in fewer and fewer capitalists. The more successful would buy out the less successful or drive them out of business. These fewer capitalists, driven by greed, would overproduce goods, leading to lower prices and thus an economic depression. This, in turn, would lead to lower wages, layoffs, and, in general, great insecurity for the working class. The mass of workers would finally see their plight for what it is and simply overthrow the capitalists. No government would be strong enough to stop them. Others, such as Engels, thought that a bloody revolution was required to change the system, a revolution such as the Russian Revolution, or the Chinese Revolution which was led by Mao Tse-Tung, or the Cuban Revolution, led by Fidel Castro. Such revolutions would then lead to the formation of new forms of economic relationships, or societies.

The first of these would be *socialism*. In a socialist society there are two classes—the workers and the government. The state owns the means of production and the profits, the workers own only their labor. In completely socialist states, while personal property may be privately owned, the means of production are not privately owned. Simply put, everyone works for the state. The state is like one giant corporation owning all of the factories, farms, banks, and anything else required to make an economy run. It controls what the economy produces and how such products get distributed. The state has absolute power over the workers, controlling where they live, what they do for work, and the level of their wages. The state even decides how and to what degree basic needs are to be met.

Finally, Marx predicted that the best type of society, *communism*, would emerge from socialism as soon as the supervision of the economy by the state was no longer required. In a communist society everyone owns the means and forces of production equally. There is no private property, and thus no need for a state to protect it. In such a society there are no classes and thus no class conflict, and thus there is nothing for the state to do. In a classless society the state simply disappears. There is only one rule needed to guide behavior in such a society, the rule of justice. Marx defines justice in such a society as: *"From each according to his ability, to each according to this needs."* In a communist society, everyone contributes what they can and takes what they need.

For Marx, the power of government is not required when there is justice. Justice is enough, since communism, a classless society, eliminates class exploitation and thus the need for the state. If a society is just, moreover, it will produce the most good for all and will also produce the most freedom. This is because people will be free from the chains of exploitation, free from the demands of excessive labor, free to create products for themselves, and free to live in a more natural way. As an example of this sort of society, think of a community of monks living together, sharing the work and the fruits of their labors. In such a society everyone's basic needs are met and any surplus wealth goes toward the good of the society. There is usually not much surplus wealth, however, since the point of a communist society is to create only that amount of wealth which is necessary for an adequate material existence. This frees up more time from the demands of work and allows workers to live their lives in a more natural, happier fashion.

Human Nature

Although Marx thought of himself as a materialist, he did not develop a materialist theory of the mind. For the most part he ignores the problem of whether conscious states are different or not from brain events, a problem that so plagued Descartes and others. Instead, when he speaks of human nature he is usually not so much concerned with what we are made of, our *structure*. He is more concerned with the social forces, especially the economic forces, that shape who we are and how we live. Marx goes so far as to say that human nature itself varies from society to society, and even from class to class within a society. So powerful is the economic substructure that it determines almost everything about us. It controls how we work, how we think, how we feel, what we desire, and how we act. Since these laws vary from one type of society to another, human nature itself is thus relative to the type of society in which it is found. There is a nature for slaves, for example, and another for aristocrats. Aristotle wrote about their differences in Greek society.

As a social scientist Marx tried to be morally neutral about the various societies and economic classes that he analyzed. However, he clearly thought of communism as the best type of society, and the one in which human nature would most flourish. But what would human nature be like under a communist organization of society? It would not be like modern day socialist societies, which more often than not have produced miserable lives for their citizens. These societies have greatly distorted the views of Marx even as they appeal to his writings as guides. Instead, human nature would be more like it used to be, before it became corrupted by the various types of societies in which it later found itself. In one of his early writings, *The Economic and Philosophical Manuscripts of 1844*, Marx spoke of human nature as it once was, when we lived in much simpler, more cooperative societies. Selections from this work are found in *Reading 1*. In thinking of the human condition as it must have existed in more primitive societies, Marx joined a group of philosophers, sometimes called **social contract** theorists, who had done the same. It will be helpful for understanding Marx's concept of human nature to compare and contrast it with their views.

Several political philosophers of the Modern period have used the model of a contract to explain why some have the right to rule others. Chief among these are Thomas Hobbes and John Locke, whose views on knowledge and reality we examined in Chapter 6, and the French philosopher, Jean-Jacques Rousseau (1712–1778). According to social contract theorists, the best way to understand the nature and purposes and proper limitations of the state is to imagine people forming one for the first time. We are first supposed to imagine them living in the **state of nature.** This is the natural way to live, or living according to human nature. In this condition, there is no state, no rulers, no laws. Then, for reasons that vary from one social contract view to another, they decided it would be best to give up some of their freedom, appoint a ruler, and live according to rules that governed all. The reason why people form political societies is to escape from some evil condition of the state of nature.

Next we are to imagine that the first political societies were based on an agreement, freely entered into. It is to be understood as a type of contract—a social contract, where citizens agree to give up some of their freedom and to have much of their lives ruled by others. In return, they are to receive some benefits, such as protection, from the ruler. When social contract theorists speak of *contracts* they do not mean actual contracts that were agreed to when societies were first formed. Perhaps there never was a time when there was not some sort of society, ruler, and ruled, however primitive it may have been. Instead, by using the model of a contract to understand the origins of the state, social contract theorists hope to understand what any rational person would agree to about the limits of the ruler's authority, and the nature of social justice.

Writing during a war-torn period of English history,[1] Thomas Hobbes had seen firsthand the horrors of war and the vicious things that men do to each other in war. Accordingly, he came to believe that the natural condition of human beings, their state of nature, is a condition of perpetual warfare. What is natural for us, he thought, what are our innate tendencies, is selfishness, greed, and power. This leads to a condition where everyone is in constant fear of death from everyone else. In the state of nature there is no morality, no law, and no security of any sort. These are all the products of the state and the civilization that it produces. Nor in the state of nature is there any chance for effective collaboration. There is no division of labor, for example. Instead, each person or family must provide completely for their own needs.

Hobbes believes that human beings always act from selfish motives. It is our nature to do so. But if human beings are selfish, they are also rational. To escape from the horrors of the state of nature and to serve their long-term interests, they would have agreed to give up acting on some of their selfish desires as long as everyone did the same. The existence of the state is required to ensure that everyone does so, because it alone has the power to punish those who continue to harm others, and thus it alone has the power to deter such actions. According to Hobbes, rational people would see it as in their long-term interests to give up their freedom in return for escaping the horrors of the state of nature. They would form a contract with the ruler, granting the ruler authority over their lives in return for the establishment of peace and order.

The ruler rules by the consent of the people, which is the basis for political authority. This is where the state gets its legitimacy, from the agreement of its citizens to be ruled. In return, the ruler must provide protection for the citizens from each other and from external threats. Today this role of the ruler is accomplished by the government enforcing criminal laws and providing an army for defense from hostile external forces. Hobbes holds the extreme view that *there are no limits to the authority of the ruler.* The ruler has absolute authority over the citizens, who give up *all* rights to govern themselves. Why would people agree to have no say in how their own lives are to be run? Because if citizens had some power to prevent some state actions, then because of our selfish human nature, there would be continual conflict between ruler and ruled. Such conflict would eventually destroy the state and return everyone to the state of nature. Citizens would agree to give up all rights to govern themselves, because anything, even a tyrant, is better than the viciousness of the state of nature.

For Hobbes, if the state is to provide peace and order, then conflict must be eliminated not only between ruler and ruled, but also within the government itself. The best form of government is a monarchy, with all power located in one place, with no separation of powers. If there were several sources of power in a government, such as an executive branch, a legislative branch, and a judiciary, they would be constantly seeking their own advantage against each other, as is the case in the state of nature. Such a government would be ineffective and even dangerous. One ruler with absolute power is the only way to ensure control, and thus the only way to ensure peace and security. It is only through the absolute obedience to the law by all citizens that peace and order will exist, and a return to the horrors of the state of nature will be avoided. The social contract grants to the ruler absolute power to do as he wishes to provide peace and security. If he fails to provide it, then civil disobedience and revolution are morally acceptable—since now he has broken his part of the bargain. Short of that, however, because human nature is so selfish and violent, even the laws of a tyrant who keeps peace and order must be obeyed.

John Locke agreed with Hobbes that the state is formed by the consent of the people. This consent is directly given by those who formed the contract, and tacitly given by those who continue to be born into an already existing political society.[2] He disagreed with Hobbes about many important elements of the contract, however. At the time of his writing, he envisioned the end of the war in England, the restoration of a stable government, and a time of great prosperity. His works reflect the need he felt to protect this prosperity from government interference.

Underlying Locke's disagreements with Hobbes was his very different conception of human nature. For Locke, the state of nature was not as nasty a condition as Hobbes thought it to be. For one thing, there were moral restrictions on behavior in the state of nature. Agreeing with Aquinas, Locke believed that every person possessed a collection of **natural rights** which were recognized by all. Chief among these were the rights to life, liberty, and property. While most people in the state of nature respected these rights, some did not. In the state of nature we have the right to defend our rights, and to punish those who would violate them. Sometimes, however, we may not be strong enough to do so, and therefore are unable to protect our natural rights. Thus arose the need for the existence of the state, with the power to protect all citizens from each other. The job of the state is to protect our lives, our freedom, and our property from those who attempt to take them from us.

For Locke, the state is formed on the basis of a social contract, where all citizens enter into an agreement with each other. The type of rule they would select is not a monarchy, but a democracy. They would agree to be ruled by the will of the majority, and they would insist on a separation of powers. A separation of powers is necessary to prevent too much power being located in the hands of one branch of government. In the best society there is to be a legislative branch to create laws, an executive branch to enforce them, and a judicial branch to adjudicate them. The job of the government is to protect our natural rights by creating and enforcing laws designed to do so. For Hobbes, there was no limit on what the state could do to secure protection. For Locke, however, the state's authority is limited by natural rights. The state must not violate our natural rights in the process of providing protection. If any law or policy enforced by the state violates the natural rights of the citizenry, people have the right to disobey it. Just as in the state of nature people have the right to protect their natural rights, so also in a political society they continue to have that right. Any law that violates natural rights is rightly subject to resistance. If such violations continue to occur, citizens even have the right to overthrow a government which creates them.

In addition to the right to life and the right to liberty, Locke was especially concerned to promote the idea that the state could not take our property. In particular, he insisted that our wealth could not be taken from us through taxation, for example, unless the majority agreed to it. We have the natural right to property, for Locke, because we have the right to keep what our labor takes from the state of nature. In the state of nature all natural resources are available to every-one. We may make them our own by our labor. When we catch a fish, the fish is ours. When we grow crops, the crops are ours. When we shoot an animal, it becomes ours to do with as we please. The only restriction on how much we can own is need. It is wrong to take from nature more than you need, because it is wasteful to own more than you can use. This natural right to property remains when we enter political societies, and it even increases with the introduction of currency. Money, unlike fish or fowl, does not spoil. It may be accumulated. Some people may work harder than others and accumulate more of it, resulting in an unequal distribution of wealth. Inequalities in wealth are acceptable for Locke. Citizens may get as rich as their efforts allow, and they may use their wealth to pursue their own idea of the good life in any lawful manner that they choose. The state has no right to place restrictions on how rich a person may become by his or her own labor, or how they use their wealth as long as they harm no one else.

But what if some become very rich while others become very poor, even unable to sustain their own existence? Should not the rich give from their plenty to the poor, at least in a just society? Locke's idea of social justice does not include the redistribution of wealth. Even though everyone has the rights to life, liberty, and property, the state has no obligation to provide the means for procuring these rights. Natural rights are not positive rights, for Locke; they are merely negative rights. To have such rights simply means that the government cannot take our lives, our liberties, or our property. The government has no obligation to redistribute income in order to provide whatever is required to sustain life, or to provide a higher standard of living to the poor in order to promote their liberty, or to provide property to those of its citizens who have none. In fact, for the government to take property from some and give it to others is itself a violation of natural rights.

For Locke, the best political society has a very minimum government, one whose only job is to protect our lives, our liberties and our property from others. It is then to leave us alone to pursue our lives as we see fit. It owes us all due process, fairness, and the freedom to decide for ourselves what sorts of lives we shall lead. Where Hobbes had stressed order at any cost and favored a government with unlimited power, Locke stresses the freedom of the individual over too much government interference. The government is not to interfere with our lives past the point required to protect us from each other. It is clear that these dramatic differences between Hobbes and Locke may be traced directly to their assumptions about human nature.

Because his view of the role of government stresses individual liberty, Locke has been called a liberal. The term "liberal" has many meanings and we will have to be careful how we use it. In the United States today, for example, the group whose beliefs are closest to Locke's are political conservatives. It is best to refer to Locke's view as "classical liberalism," to distinguish it from contemporary liberal views. Much of what Locke had to say about natural rights, social contracts, civil disobedience, and revolution were very much in the minds of the men who began the American Revolution. In fact, the U.S. Constitution may be understood as a type of Lockean social contract. It claims that certain rights are natural rights ("unalienable"), namely those of "life, liberty and the pursuit of happiness." The pursuit of happiness is usually interpreted to mean the right to property. It also claims that all people possess these natural rights equally, because they were given to them equally by their creator. It also lays down the rules for acceptable civil disobedience and revolution, especially those that give people the right to overthrow any government which attempts to rob them of their natural rights.

Jean-Jacques Rousseau also used a social contract model to develop his beliefs about the nature of a just society.[3] Simply put, if Hobbes considered human nature to be selfish and violent, as had Hsun-tzu, and Locke thought of it as capable of both good and evil, as had Confucius, Rousseau thought that human nature, human beings in the state of nature, were basically good, as did Mencius. In the state of nature we form communities in which we share with others, in which we are compassionate beings. For Rousseau, the evil thoughts, feelings, and deeds of human beings are produced by society. Society teaches us to use others, to be against each other, to calculate our own interests against theirs, to forget compassion, and to act selfishly instead of altruistically.

Rousseau thinks of the state of nature as a utopian condition, where people live in small wandering groups, where only minimal effort is required to take from the bounty of nature goods sufficient to meet their subsistence needs, and where strife and conflict are nearly nonexistent. If life was so wonderful lived in this natural way, however, then why did people change their ways of living and form political societies? Influenced by Locke's theory of labor, Rousseau traces the beginnings of civilization to ownership. Some people claimed sole possession of some of nature's goods, and thus had to protect them from others. Great amounts of private property such as land could be amassed by a few, and soon inequities of wealth arose that did not exist in the state of nature. Power was tied to wealth and corruption to power, so soon enough evil was created and domination of man by man followed.

To escape this situation and restore a level of equality and safety, people formed political societies. In his *The Social Contract*, Rousseau claims that society was established on the basis of a social contract. Unlike Hobbes, the contract did not require relinquishing all of our freedom to an absolute ruler, nor did it even require handing over some freedom, as Locke had claimed. This is because the rulers of the truly democratic society envisaged by Rousseau are the people themselves. For Rousseau, the best society is a society of laws which are not made by representatives of the people, as they are in most contemporary democracies. Instead, in the best society, a true democracy, each law is to be voted on by each individual. In the best sort of government, the sort of self-government that is similar to that found in the state of nature, the people freely choose to accept the laws according to which they agree to be bound.

But in a democracy, the majority rules. So how can someone in the minority on a certain issue, who has to live by the majority's decision, still be said to have freely chosen to abide by such a law? If it is simply imposed by the majority, is this not itself a form of tyranny? To answer this question Rousseau distinguishes between the will of the majority and the **general will**. The will of the majority is simply what the majority of those voting want. It stems from each person's notion of what is in their self-interest, what they believe is good for them. The general will, however, is the view of the majority about what each member *should* want, what will serve the common good. It is the perspective taken by society when each member votes for what is in the common interest, not in his or her individual interest. So if people vote as they should, and you find yourself in the minority, then you should have voted the other way. You should have freely chosen to be governed by the law in question.

Marx's view about the nature of human beings was especially influenced by that of Rousseau. Because human nature was good before becoming "civilized," his view of what human nature is in its natural state is really his view of what it can become if the burdens of exploitive societies are stripped away. This is something that occurs in a communist society, where human nature is expected to return to its natural, Rousseau-like state. We need certain things to be happy, according to Marx, and only socialism, and eventually communism, can supply them. Like Aristotle, Marx thought that happiness comes from fully realizing the distinctively human dimensions of a person. Beyond subsistence needs, we all have other basic needs that must be met if we are to live fully human lives.

Unlike Aristotle, Marx did not identify our basic human needs with understanding for its own sake, but rather thought of them as practical ones. In particular, human beings need creative work that is freely chosen by them. In the process of creating something people change the world around them, leaving their image stamped upon it. For Marx, human beings are naturally creative. Like Rousseau, he believed that before living in political societies they probably lived in small communal societies, where they created items to meet their basic needs and to express their creativity. Human beings are what they make, what their labor produces. We express what we are in our products or projects. This is at the very heart of our humanity, in the things that we make we put some of ourselves, making our creations reflect our identity and the meaning of our lives.

Marx said little more than this about what a future communist society in which our natures would have a chance to fully develop might look like. He seemed to think that living in small communal societies work would vary, and everyone would get to do the whole variety of things that were required to meet their needs and the needs of the group. There would be no division of labor; people would not specialize in a particular task and perform it over and over again. In addition, what the workers produced—their food, shelter, education, art, and so on, would be kept by them or distributed freely to the group. If in what people produce they realize themselves, then by retaining their products for their own use, people would no longer be alienated from their work, from themselves, or from others. Unlike a capitalist system, where what is to be produced by workers is decided by others and then taken away to be sold for a profit, the goods produced in a socialist society are produced by workers to meet their own needs. They decide among themselves what are the rules according to which they work, and express their creativity in their building, farming, art, music, and writing. In these small societies people work together to meet the material and other needs of all. Everyone works to the level of their ability, and everyone receives from the group what they need.

In this type of society there are no haves and have-nots. There are no wages and no individually owned profits. Most importantly, in such a society there is none of the alienation found in modern capitalistic societies, where work is often found to be dehumanizing and hateful. In particular, workers in a communist state are not alienated from each other. Since there are no social or economic classes, there is no exploitation of one class by another. Nor are there the feelings of isolation from members of the same class, a feeling created by the competitive individualism of capitalism. No longer is it everyone for himself, but now we are all in it together.

Consequences

Ethics

For the sake of clarity we will begin our discussion of the consequences of accepting Marx's theory of human nature not with a discussion of freedom, as we usually do, but rather with his notion of ethics, especially his idea of the good life. The good life is the life of fully realizing in our work our natures as producers of goods that meet our basic needs and define us by our projects. Such a life is only attainable in a communist society. This can be seen more clearly by examining the evils of capitalism, which communism will eventually replace. Among the evils of capitalism is that it is inefficient, wasteful, irrational, and unjust. It is *inefficient* and *wasteful* because much of the workforce is not employed at any one time, much of the wealth it creates is spent on advertising and sales instead of on production, much of what it produces are useless luxuries—instead of the necessities of life, and because it places profits ahead of human needs. It is *irrational* because it claims that the only way to benefit the whole of society is to allow the selfish desires of individuals for profits to control the economy, because it ignores the role of conscious planning in determining what goods ought to be produced to meet human needs, and because while espousing humanitarian virtues in daily life it practices ruthless self-interest in business. It is *unjust* because the wealth it creates ends up in the hands of a very few, while frightening insecurity, degrading poverty, and inequality of opportunity are the lot of the large poorer class.[4]

In addition to these problems, capitalism forces people to live in ways that alienate them, ways that make them feel that they are removed from their true condition. It is one of the true evils of capitalism that it denies to people what is required to fulfill their true natures. Our true human nature is one of the goods that gets crushed by capitalism. In capitalist economies there is generally a division of labor, where each person performs a narrow repetitive job that eventually make him or her feel like a mere cog in the economic machine. The real evil of these jobs, and the entire capitalist system itself, is that they **alienate** human beings, they separate or cut people off from their true selves. Capitalism alienates workers from themselves not only by subjecting them to dehumanizing working conditions, but also by taking from them what they produce. If our very selves are reflected in what we make, and if what we make is taken from us and sold to others, then workers cannot express their creativity in their work. People become alienated from their true creative natures; they become mere "things" at the disposal of those who own the means of production. People lose their true selves.

People are not only alienated from themselves, but also from each other and from nature. They are cut off from each other because of the competitive individualism fostered by capitalism. Instead of the unselfish sharing that takes place in a cooperative community, capitalism breeds a selfish "everyone-for-himself" attitude. In addition, capitalism alienates people from nature, their true home. The long hours spent working in shops and factories in subhuman conditions, leaves people hungry to get back to nature in their leisure time. We belong together, cooperatively living in natural settings, working to fulfill our basic needs, to express our creativity and to promote the common good. Capitalism alienates us from these natural goals and in the process dehumanizes us, crushes our very spirit. See *Reading 1* for further analysis by Marx of these various types of alienation.

In addition to alienating people from their work, from each other, and from nature, capitalism **exploits** workers. The basic way that it exploits workers is to pay them a wage that is less than the value of their labor. The capitalist gets rich because he is allowed to sell the goods produced by the workers for a profit, for more than it costs to produce them. Costs include materials and other means of production, but they also include the price of labor. The capitalist's profit is possible only because he pays less for labor than its true value. The product created thus has a *surplus value* which is retained by the capitalist. Capitalism, especially the way it operated in the factories of mid-nineteenth-century London, created great wealth for the *bourgeoisie,* while all the while forcing workers into lives of servitude and domination. It exploited the very soul of workers. This is why Marx rejects it as an evil and looks to its overthrow as a means of liberating the human spirit within a communist society.

Freedom

Marx is a determinist, so his idea of freedom has more to do with freedom of action than free will. Since the type of society in which we live determines our behavior, the question of freedom is the question of which society allows for the greatest freedom of action. Capitalism during the Industrial Revolution may have been oppressive, but capitalist societies today seem to allow the most freedom of any type of society. Capitalist economies today typically produce consumer societies, where the standard of living is relatively high and where there are plenty of goods and services from which to choose. Having such a range of choices is not true freedom for Marx, however, since workers are exploited in the process of producing such goods, on the one hand, and since what is produced is not what people really want, on the other.

To clarify this idea that capitalist economies suppress real freedom, it is helpful to consider the views of Herbert Marcuse (1898–1979), a contemporary Marxist. Marcuse, like Marx, thought that capitalism attacks the very soul of human beings, but in a more subtle manner than Marx was able to observe during his time. His book, *One Dimensional Man,* was very popular in the 1960s, inspiring many young people who had become disenchanted with American culture to "drop out" of society, or to attempt to change it, sometimes through violent means.[5] For Marcuse, the change from capitalism to socialism predicted by Marx was far from inevitable. This was mainly due to the tremendous success of capitalism in creating a consumer society. In a consumer society, people make and buy things that they really do not need, thus fueling the economy to create more and more such goods. New technology has allowed for the dramatically increased production of ever new and enticing products. Cars, electrical appliances, computers, fancy clothes, travel, and so on, are readily accessible to the masses, because they can be cheaply and efficiently produced.

In the midst of this plenty, workers no longer feel exploited by capitalism. Instead, they have become a willing part of the system itself. Workers feel secure that their needs will be met within such a system, and that they will be able to live happy lives. The trouble with this, for Marcuse, is that the workers have come to identify themselves with the products that meet only one dimension of their nature. The materialism that results from the success of capitalism may supply workers with food and clothing, toys and entertainment, and so on, but it leaves the worker's truly essential needs unmet. Workers are controlled by the advertising media to strive for material goods that do not meet their true needs. In a capitalist society, people are not free because they are driven to lead the lives they do by social forces, not by their own choices. Workers identify themselves with the consumer items that they possess. They come to value their worth by their ability to possess more and more of them, and especially to "keep up with the Jones."

But these items are not the result of the creative impulses within the worker, items freely produced according to his or her choices, items that defined a person as unique, items that flowed from his or her very being. Instead, what is produced is determined by others—the capitalists. The workers are brainwashed by advertising and the media to believe that they really need such items to be happy, all the while putting more and more money into the hands of those who own the means and forces of production. Once again, workers are exploited by the system, only now they do not even know it, let alone resent it. Once again, the evils of capitalism have robbed workers of their very soul, only now they do not even recognize its absence. So while capitalism may allow for more choices, it does not allow for true freedom.

Society

The best type of society is one that avoids the twin evils of alienation and exploitation. It is also one that returns human beings to the working conditions similar to those that exist in the state of nature as envisaged by Rousseau. For Marx this type of society is **communism.** In a communist society there is no private ownership of the means of production. Everyone owns everything communally. This is the key change from capitalism, since it is private property that led to the formation of the state in the first place. There are no classes in a communist society. There is no dominant class that exploits a subordinate one, for example, since everyone has the same relationship to the means of production as everyone else. With no exploitation there is no using the labor of others for a profit and thus no alienation. With the disappearance of these twin evils there is no need for the existence of the state.

In a communist society, there is work, to be sure. Creative, fulfilling work is necessary for happiness. But there is less time spent at work, because the goal of work is no longer to produce and consume unnecessary goods. Instead, work is performed to meet subsistence needs, to aid the common good, and to provide creative outlets for human nature. There is a much greater degree of autonomy in a communist society because the driving force of work is to create goods that truly benefit all. In such a society people will have more free time, because less work will be required to meet their goals. The means and forces of production will not be used to create consumer goods, only goods that meet basic needs, and thus people will be more free to be their true selves.

As was mentioned earlier in this chapter, Marx thought that capitalism would simply die of its own excesses. As businesses become larger and capitalists fewer, the plight of workers will worsen. As the number of workers increase and the power of the state becomes insufficient to contain them, workers will take over the means and powers of production from the capitalists and form a new society. This society will at first be **socialism,** in which the state owns the means of production. This is necessary to prevent workers from acting on the selfish impulses that they developed within capitalistic societies. After a couple of generations people will see that there is no need for the state. Human nature will have grown closer to its original condition, everyone's basic needs will be met, and people will be treated fairly. Because of this everyone will be ready to work unselfishly for the common good. When all of these conditions have been met, the socialist government will dissolve, political power will no longer be necessary, and all people will simply live cooperatively by the general principle of justice—from each according to his ability; to each according to his need.

Engels thought that communism was not inevitable, and that it would take a bloody revolution to bring it about. Marxist states that were created from the misery of these revolutions, such as Russia, China, and Cuba, did adopt various versions of socialism. Unfortunately, communism did not emerge from socialism as Marx expected. Instead, since socialist governments had so much control of their citizens, socialism more often than not evolved into various types of totalitarianism. Socialist economies have not fared well either. There was more equality in socialist societies than capitalist ones, as Marx had predicted. But this often meant that everyone was treated poorly. Beyond what was required for subsistence needs, little else was produced in most socialist economies. Most of them have been abandoned today, as has been especially witnessed in the fall of the Soviet Union. This does not mean that Marx was wrong about the benefits of communism, only that those who tried to put his ideas into practice, Marxists, did not follow his advice. But what would his advice be today to the capitalist economies of large industrialized nations and multinational corporations?

First he would probably point out to rich countries and multinational corporations alike that capitalism continues to exploit workers. Even though the horrific sweat shops of mid-nineteenth-century England are gone, there still exists today consumerism, alienation, and exploitation within wealthy nations. Today a middle class has arisen which owns much of the stock of corporations, so it may be said that the workers themselves have become the capitalists. However, capitalism still creates a poor working class, and the differences between the masses who are its members and the rich classes is often staggering. In addition, *global* exploitation has increased in recent decades. Today we see rich countries and incredibly large multinational companies exploiting poor nations. So if Marx could examine the situation today, he would most likely proclaim once again that the workers of the world have to unite to overthrow the exploitive forces of capitalism.

On the other hand, it is difficult to imagine how large industrialized nations could exist if they adopted the idealized scheme of communal living proposed by Marx. Technological advances have connected everyone within a nation more firmly than ever. Our economic systems are national, not local. In fact, they are international, as are our monetary systems and our systems of communication, transportation, trade, and so on. A turn to socialism today could not be a turn to this simple, communal form of living. But what, then, would it be like, to adopt socialism today—with a view that communism would be its replacement in the near future?

Types of Socialism

In a capitalist economic system, which products are created and which services are offered is determined by the free choice of the people. Any product or service will flourish as long as enough people are willing to pay for it. If they are not, the person who makes such products or offers such services is soon out of business. In a socialist system, however, these economic decisions are not made by individuals. Instead, they are made by the choices and plans of various groups. Such plans control the entire economy by determining which products are to be produced, what they will cost, what the wages are that will be paid for various types of work, and so on.

So socialist states may be divided into various types, depending on the level at which the economy is planned. One type of socialist state may be called **central planning socialism.** A central planning socialist society is one in which the economic lives of citizens are controlled by a central government. In such a state, no private ownership of the means of production is allowed. No citizen may own a factory or farm, for example. There are no private corporations or small businesses of any sort allowed in such a state. The capitalist system of free enterprise is banned. You cannot produce and sell something as you desire, retaining the profits for your own personal wealth. You may own personal property, such as a house or car or clothing, and so on, but no one may own the means or forces of production or the profits. In this sense, no private property is permitted. Instead, in central planning socialist states, the state owns all the means and forces of production.

Most of the former Soviet Union, including Russia and its Eastern European allies, were central planning socialist states. In these states, the governments were not democratically elected in any real sense. The result was that in addition to controlling the economies of their countries, they also controlled the political and social lives of their citizens. In such states, the people had only as much freedom as was granted by the government. As Marx envisioned it, the socialist state was supposed to be the representative of the people. In truth, however, these totalitarian socialist states controlled the lives of the people, often to their significant misfortune.

There are few who would defend totalitarian versions of socialism as the best type of society. A better option is a central planning socialist state with a *democratic* form of government, one which allows political and social freedoms comparable to capitalist societies. Such socialist states may be democratic in a second sense, as well. Not only may their governments be elected democratically, but their economic planning also may be democratic. This second type of socialism is called **democratic socialism.** As a form of socialism, democratic socialism does not allow the means of production to be privately owned any more than central planning socialism does. However, what it does allow for is a more democratic process of planning the economy. In such a socialist system, the economy is controlled on the local level, by various groups of workers, as Marx had originally envisioned it. Those who work in a particular factory, for example, may collectively decide what to produce and how to distribute the resulting income.

Some socialist systems combine a mix of democratic and central planning, planning their economies partially at the central level and partially at the local level. At whatever level the economy is planned, socialists insist on one important point: goods produced must be distributed according to need. Since everyone's needs are roughly equal, there will be much greater economic equality in a socialist state than a capitalist one. Economic equality would be valued in such a state much more highly than economic freedom. In a socialized democratic state, after everyone's subsistence needs are met, any surplus wealth remaining is distributed for the common good of the workers in a manner to be determined by the workers or their government representatives. Salaries are to be regulated not by the laws of supply and demand, as they are in the free marketplace of capitalism, but by the people themselves—either on the local or national level.

There would be differences in salaries, but significantly less difference than in capitalist economies. Skilled workers would be paid more than unskilled workers, for example, as would those who are more productive than others. But even here there is less inequality than in capitalism, since everyone would get an equal chance to become a skilled worker and to be more productive. Many capitalist states today, in a quest for greater social equality, are partly socialized societies. Parts of their economies are planned and regulated by the government, such as medicine, transportation, and the arts. For example, we have argued for some time now in the United States about the value of "socialized medicine." If we were to implement such a system, it would be funded by taxation, allowing us to remain a capitalist economy in other economic areas.

Such partially socialized states would help to make the transition from capitalism to socialism. Such a transition today would probably involve several steps. First would be the creation of a welfare state, where the subsistence needs of all citizens who could not work would be met. Next, various areas of the economy would be socialized, or "nationalized." No longer would some areas, such as the health care system, for example, be privately owned and run for a profit. Instead, it would be controlled by the people, through their government, for the good of all citizens. Many capitalist democracies have already taken these first two steps. A third step would be to move from central planning to local control of some of the means and forces of production. For example, factories, farms, educational systems, and others might come under the control of local workers and their local government representatives. This type of "industrial democracy" would give control of what was produced directly to the workers, instead of some central planning agency, coming closer to the spirit of a community of workers that Marx had envisioned. In this way, socialism might be seen as even more democratic than capitalism, because it democratizes not only political life, but also economic life as well. A final step would be to eliminate all private ownership of the means of production, resulting in a completely socialized economy.

For Marx, socialist economies may not be as productive as capitalist ones, but they do a better job at producing meaningful work that satisfies all the basic needs of their citizens. Capitalist economies thrive because they produce goods beyond those required for the necessities of life, and because they convince people that they need them. People work harder and harder to acquire these goods, all the while putting more profits in the hands of the capitalists and alienating themselves more and more from their work, from other people, and even from themselves. For Marx, socialist economies may not be as powerful as capitalist ones, but they produce a happier society. Not only are the subsistence needs of everyone met—no one goes without education, health care, food and shelter, and the like, but—their other basic needs are also equally met. Everyone works who can, and everyone, not just the rich, has access to the arts, entertainment, transportation, health care, education, and the like. While there may be differences in salaries, reflecting the different levels of skills and effort required by various jobs, these differences are not as extreme as they are in capitalist societies. In a socialist state, there are no untalented rock stars and mediocre athletes and greedy CEOs making enormous salaries, while millions of children go hungry. Instead, there is much greater equality, and thus there is true justice.

Unlike a capitalist system, where what is produced by workers is decided by others and then taken away to be sold for a profit, the goods produced in a socialist society, and especially in a communist society to which it eventually will lead, are produced by workers to meet their own needs. The closest model of this communist way of life that I have witnessed is that of a group of Trappist monks. They live communally, decide among themselves what are the rules according to which they work, sell products to others to support themselves and improve their living conditions, and express their creativity in their building, farming, art, music, writing, praying, chanting, and meditating. There is a leader, an abbot, and sometimes decisions are made by central planning instead of by the entire group, but it is essentially a democratic society which works together to meet the material and spiritual needs of all. Everyone works to the level of their ability, and everyone receives from the group what they need.

In this type of society there are no haves and have-nots. There are no wages and no individually owned profits. Products made and sold to others in such a communist society may bring a profit, but these are returned to the group which decides for itself how they are to be used for the benefit of all. Most importantly, in such a society there is none of the *alienation* found in modern capitalistic societies, where work is often found to be dehumanizing and hateful. In particular, workers in a communist state are not alienated from each other. Since there are no social and economic classes, there is no exploitation of one class by another. Nor are there the feelings of isolation from members of the same class, a feeling created by the competitive individualism of capitalism. No longer is it everyone for himself, but now we are all in it together.

God and Immortality

It is clear that Marx, a materialist and an atheist, believed neither in the existence of God nor the immortality of the soul. God was merely an invention of the human race, a belief sustained even in the absence of evidence, because of its role in explaining suffering. God allows evil in the world to test our worthiness for eternal salvation. With God and the blissful afterlife as its explanation, the true economic cause of evil could be concealed. Even though Marx was not a theist, however, his theory of human nature was strikingly religious in tone. The comparison of Marxism to Christianity, for example, shows many parallels. Where Christianity talks about the Garden of Eden, for example, Marx talks about the goodness of the natural human condition. Then there is the Christian fall from grace and the Marxist concept of alienation. Sin for the Christian is like exploitation for the Marxist, and a heavenly state of bliss becomes the heaven on earth of a communist society. Christianity and Marxism also share a concept of history that gives a serious and dramatic meaning to life. The Christian message is to accept God's grace, turn from sin, love God and your fellow human beings, and be saved. The message of Marxism is directed primarily to the current exploited class, the proletariat, and urges them to unite, overthrow the forces of oppression, form a true communist society, and be saved.

Gender

For Marx, in a communist society men and women are to be equals in most respects. Women are considered to be just as competent as men intellectually, just as able to overcome their emotions and desires by reason, and thus just as capable of holding positions of power and influence in a socialist state. In socialist and communist societies, all people, not just males, will be liberated. The real oppressors of women are not men, but capitalist economies and the social roles into which their ideologies force both men and women. Women's freedom will be an inevitable outcome, once the last vestiges of capitalism have disappeared. Marx was especially opposed to marriage as it existed in capitalist societies, since its patriarchal basis provided a legally acceptable way for men to dominate women. Communism would not include marriage, but rather have other, more natural ways for men and women to relate.

While opposed to marriage, Marx did not grant equal family roles to men and women. While women could work effectively outside of the home and family, Marx followed Rousseau in believing that child rearing was primarily their responsibility. With this possible exception, Marx was not a sexist. Unfortunately, Marxism often was. Very often the culture which existed in a nation before it accepted the ideas of Marx determined the prevailing ways of treating women. In China under Mao Tse-Tung, for example, while men and women were considered equal for some purposes, women were still generally considered to be second-class citizens.

Readings

1. The Human Condition

ESTRANGED LABOR

WE HAVE PROCEEDED FROM THE premises of political economy. We have accepted its language and its laws. We presupposed private property, the separation of labor, capital and land, and of wages, profit of capital and rent of land—likewise division of labor, competition, the concept of exchange-value, etc. On the basis of political economy itself, in its own words, we have shown that the worker sinks to the level of a commodity and becomes indeed the most wretched of commodities; that the wretchedness of the worker is in inverse proportion to the power and magnitude of his production; that the necessary result of competition is the accumulation of capital in a few hands, and thus the restoration of monopoly in a more terrible form; and that finally the distinction between capitalist and land rentier, like that between the tiller of the soil and the factory worker, disappears and that the whole of society must fall apart into the two classes—the property *owners* and the propertyless *workers*.

Political economy starts with the fact of private property, but it does not explain it to us. It expresses in general, abstract formulas the *material* process through which private property actually passes, and these formulas it then takes for *laws*. It does not *comprehend* these laws, i.e., it does not demonstrate how they arise from the very nature of private property. Political economy does not disclose the source of the division between labor and capital, and between capital and land. When, for example, it defines the relationship of wages to profit, it takes the interest of the capitalists to be the ultimate cause, i.e., it takes for granted what it is supposed to explain. Similarly, competition comes in everywhere. It is explained from external circumstances. As to how far these external and apparently accidental circumstances are but the expression of a necessary course of development, political economy teaches us nothing. We have seen how exchange itself appears to it as an accidental fact. The only wheels which political economy sets in motion are *greed* and the war *amongst the greedy—competition.*

Precisely because political economy does not grasp the way the movement is connected, it was possible to oppose, for instance, the doctrine of competition to the doctrine of the guild, the doctrine of the division of landed property to the doctrine of the big estate—for competition, freedom of the crafts, and the division of landed property were explained and comprehended only as accidental, premeditated, and violent consequences of monopoly, of the guild system, and of feudal property, not as their necessary, inevitable, and natural consequences.

Now, therefore, we have to grasp the essential connection between private property, greed, and the separation of labor, capital and landed property; between exchange and competition, value and the devaluation of men, monopoly and competition, etc.—the connection between this whole estrangement and the *money* system.

Do not let us go back to a fictitious primordial condition as the political economist does, when he tries to explain. Such a primordial condition explains nothing; it merely pushes the question away into a gray nebulous distance. It assumes in the form of a fact, of an event, what the economist is supposed to deduce—namely, the necessary relationship between two things—between, for

From Karl Marx, Economic and Philosophic Manuscripts of 1844, *trans. by Dirk J. Struik (New York: International Publishers, 1971), pp. 226–235. Reprinted with permission.*

example, division of labor and exchange. Theology in the same way explains the origin of evil by the fall of man; that is, it assumes as a fact, in historical form, what has to be explained.

We proceed from an economic fact *of the present.*

The worker becomes all the poorer the more wealth he produces, the more his production increases in power and size. The worker becomes an ever cheaper commodity the more commodities he creates. With the *increasing value* of the world of things proceeds in direct proportion the *devaluation* of the world of men. Labor produces not only commodities: it produces itself and the worker as a *commodity*—and this in the same general proportion in which it produces commodities.

This fact expresses merely that the object which labor produces—labor's product—confronts it as *something alien*, as a *power independent* of the producer. The product of labor is labor which has been embodied in an object, which has become material: it is the *objectification* of labor. Labor's realization is its objectification. In the sphere of political economy this realization of labor appears as *loss of realization* for the workers; objectification as *loss of the object* and *bondage to it*; appropriation as *estrangement*, as *alienation.*

So much does labor's realization appear as loss of realization that the worker loses realization to the point of starving to death. So much does objectification appear as loss of the object that the worker is robbed of the objects most necessary not only for his life but for his work. Indeed, labor itself becomes an object which he can obtain only with the greatest effort and with the most irregular interruptions. So much does the appropriation of the object appear as estrangement that the more objects the worker produces, the less he can possess and the more he falls under the sway of his product, capital.

All these consequences result from the fact that the worker is related to the *product of his labor* as to an *alien* object. For on this premise it is clear that the more the worker spends himself, the more powerful becomes the alien world of objects which he creates over and against himself, the poorer he himself—his inner world—becomes, the less belongs to him as his own. It is the same

in religion. The more man puts into God, the less he retains in himself. The worker puts his life into the object; but now his life no longer belongs to him but to the object. Hence, the greater this activity, the greater is the worker's lack of objects. Whatever the product of his labor is, he is not. Therefore the greater this product, the less is he himself. The *alienation* of the worker in his product means not only that his labor becomes an object, an *external* existence, but that it exists *outside him*, independently, as something alien to him, and that it becomes a power on its own confronting him. It means that the life which he has conferred on the object confronts him as something hostile and alien.

Let us now look more closely at the *objectification*, at the production of the worker; and in it at the *estrangement*, the loss of the object, of his product.

The worker can create nothing without *nature*, without the *sensuous external world*. It is the material on which his labor is realized, in which it is active, from which and by means of which it produces.

But just as nature provides labor with the *means of life* in the sense that labor cannot *live* without objects on which to operate, on the other hand, it also provides the *means of life* in the more restricted sense, i.e., the means for the physical subsistence of the *worker* himself.

Thus the more the worker by his labor *appropriates* the external world, hence sensuous nature, the more he deprives himself of *means of life* in a double manner: first, in that the sensuous external world more and more ceases to be an object belonging to his labor—to be his labor's *means of life*; and secondly, in that it more and more ceases to be *means of life* in the immediate sense, means for the physical subsistence of the worker.

In both respects, therefore, the worker becomes a slave of his object, first, in that he receives an *object of labor*, i.e., in that he receives *work*; and secondly, in that he receives *means of subsistence*. Therefore, it enables him to exist, first, as a *worker*; and secondly as a *physical subject*. The height of this bondage is that it is only as a *worker* that he continues to maintain himself as a *physical subject*, and that it is only as a *physical subject* that he is a *worker*.

(The laws of political economy express the estrangement of the worker in his object thus: the more the worker produces, the less he has to consume; the more values he creates, the more valueless, the more unworthy he becomes; the better formed his product, the more deformed becomes the worker; the more civilized his object, the more barbarous becomes the worker; the more powerful labor becomes, the more powerless becomes the worker; the more ingenious labor becomes, the less ingenious becomes the worker and the more he becomes nature's bondsman.)

Political economy conceals the estrangement inherent in the nature of labor by not considering the direct relationship between the worker (labor) *and production.* It is true that labor produces for the rich wonderful things—but for the worker it produces privation. It produces palaces—but for the worker, hovels. It produces beauty—but for the worker, deformity. It replaces labor by machines, but it throws a section of the workers back to a barbarous type of labor, and it turns the other workers into machines. It produces intelligence—but for the worker stupidity, cretinism.

The direct relationship of labor to its products is the relationship the worker to the objects of his production. The relationship of the man of means to the objects of production and to production itself is only a *consequence* of this first relationship—and confirms it. We shall consider this other aspect later.

When we ask, then, what is the essential relationship of labor, we are asking about the relationship of the *worker* to production.

Till now we have been considering the estrangement, the alienation, of the worker only in one of its aspects, i.e., the worker's *relationship to the products of his labor.* But the estrangement is manifested not only in the result but in the *act of production,* within the *producing activity* itself. How could the worker come to face the product of his activity as a stranger, were it not that in the very act of production he was estranging himself from himself? The product is after all but the summary of the activity, of production. If then the product of labor is alienation, production itself must be active alienation, the alienation of activity, the activity of alienation. In the estrangement of the object of

labor is merely summarized the estrangement, the alienation, in the activity of labor itself.

What, then, constitutes the alienation of labor?

First, the fact that labor is *external* to the worker, i.e., it does not belong to his essential being; that in his work, therefore, he does not affirm himself but denies himself, does not feel content but unhappy, does not develop freely his physical and mental energy but mortifies his body and ruins his mind. The worker therefore only feels himself outside his work, and in his work feels outside himself. He is at home when he is not working, and when he is working he is not at home. His labor is therefore not voluntary, but coerced; it is *forced labor.* It is therefore not the satisfaction of a need; it is merely a *means* to satisfy needs external to it. Its alien character emerges clearly in the fact that as soon as no physical or other compulsion exists, labor is shunned like the plague. External labor, labor in which man alienates himself, is a labor of self-sacrifice, of mortification. Lastly, the external character of labor for the worker appears in the fact that it is not his own, but someone else's, that it does not belong to him, that in it he belongs, not to himself, but to another. Just as in religion the spontaneous activity of the human imagination, of the human brain and the human heart, operates independently of the individual—that is, operates on him as an alien, divine or diabolical activity—so is the worker's activity not his spontaneous activity. It belongs to another; it is the loss of his self.

As a result, therefore, man (the worker) only feels himself freely active in his animal functions—eating, drinking, procreating, or at most in his dwelling and in dressing-up, etc.; and in his human functions he no longer feels himself to be anything but an animal. What is animal becomes human and what is human becomes animal.

Certainly eating, drinking, procreating, etc., are also genuinely human functions. But abstractly taken, separated from the sphere of all other human activity and turned into sole and ultimate ends, they are animal functions.

We have considered the act of estranging practical human activity, labor, in two of its aspects. (1) The relation of the worker to the *product of labor* as an alien object exercising power over him. This relation is at the same time the relation to the sensuous external world, to the objects of nature, as an alien world inimically opposed to him. (2) The relation of labor to the *act of production* within the *labor* process. This relation is the relation of the worker to his own activity as an alien activity not belonging to him; it is activity as suffering, strength as weakness, begetting as emasculating, the worker's *own* physical and mental energy, his personal life—indeed, what is life but activity?—as an activity which is turned against him, independent of him and not belonging to him. Here we have *self-estrangement,* as previously we had the estrangement of the *thing.*

We have still a third aspect of *estranged labor* to deduce from the two already considered.

Man is a species being, not only because in practice and in theory he adopts the species as his object (his own as well as those of other things), but—and this is only another way of expressing it—also because he treats himself as the actual, living species; because he treats himself as a *universal* and therefore a free being.

The life of the species, both in man and in animals, consists physically in the fact that man (like the animal) lives on inorganic nature; and the more universal man is compared with an animal, the more universal is the sphere of inorganic nature on which he lives. Just as plants, animals, stones, air, light, etc., constitute theoretically a part of human consciousness, partly as objects of natural science, partly as objects of art—his spiritual inorganic nature, spiritual nourishment which he must first prepare to make palatable and digestible—so also in the realm of practice they constitute a part of human life and human activity. Physically man lives only on these products of nature, whether they appear in the form of food, heating, clothes, a dwelling, etc. The universality of man appears in practice precisely in the universality which makes all nature his *inorganic* body—both inasmuch as nature is (1) his direct means of life, and (2) the material, the object, and the instrument of his life activity. Nature is man's *inorganic body*—nature, that is, in so far as it is not itself the human body. Man *lives* on nature—means that nature is his *body,* with which he must remain in continuous interchange if he is not to die.

That man's physical and spiritual life is linked to nature means simply that nature is linked to itself, for man is part of nature.

In estranging from man (1) nature, and (2) himself, his own active functions, his life activity, estranged labor estranges the *species* from man. It changes for him the *life of the species* into a means of individual life. First it estranges the life of the species and individual life, and secondly it makes individual life in its abstract form the purpose of the life of the species, likewise in its abstract and estranged form.

Indeed, labor, *life-activity, productive life* itself, appears in the first place merely as a *means* of satisfying a need—the need to maintain physical existence. Yet the productive life is the life of the species. It is life-engendering life. The whole character of a species—its species character—is contained in the character of its life activity; and free, conscious activity is man's species character. Life itself appears only as a *means to life.*

The animal is immediately one with its life activity. It does not distinguish itself from it. It is *its life activity.* Man makes his life activity itself the object of his will and of his consciousness. He has conscious life activity. It is not a determination with which he directly merges. Conscious life activity distinguishes man immediately from animal life activity. It is just because of this that he is a species being. Or rather, it is only because he is a species being that he is a conscious being, i.e., that his own life is an object for him. Only because of that is his activity free activity. Estranged labor reverses this relationship, so that it is just because man is a conscious being that he makes his life activity, his *essential* being, a mere means to his *existence.*

In creating a *world of objects* by his practical activity, in *his work upon* inorganic nature, man proves himself a conscious species being, i.e., as a being that treats the species as its own essential being, or that treats itself as a species being. Admittedly animals also produce. They build themselves nests, dwellings, like the bees, beavers, ants, etc. But an animal only produces what it immediately needs for itself or its young. It produces one-sidedly, whilst man produces universally. It produces only under the dominion of immediate physical need, whilst man produces even when he is free from physical need and only truly produces in freedom therefrom. An animal produces only itself, whilst man reproduces the whole of nature. An animal's product belongs immediately to its physical body, whilst man freely confronts his product. An animal forms things in accordance with the standard and the need of the species to which it belongs, whilst man knows how to produce in accordance with the standard of every species, and knows how to apply everywhere the inherent standard to the object. Man therefore also forms things in accordance with the laws of beauty.

It is just in his work upon the objective world, therefore, that man first really proves himself to be a *species being.* This production is his active species life. Through and because of this production, nature appears as *his* work and his reality. The object of labor is, therefore, the *objectification of man's species life:* for he duplicates himself not only, as in consciousness, intellectually, but also actively, in reality, and therefore he contemplates himself in a world that he has created. In tearing away from man the object of his production, therefore, estranged labor tears from him his *species life,* his real objectivity as a member of the species, and transforms his advantage over animals into the disadvantage that his inorganic body, nature, is taken away from him.

Similarly, in degrading spontaneous, free activity, to a means, estranged labor makes man's species life a means to his physical existence.

The consciousness which man has of his species is thus transformed by estrangement in such a way that species life becomes for him a means.

Estranged labor turns thus:

(3) *Man's species being,* both nature and his spiritual species property, into a being *alien* to him, into a *means* to his *individual existence.* It estranges from man his own body, as well as external nature and his spiritual essence, his *human* being.

(4) An immediate consequence of the fact that man is estranged from the product of his labor, from his life activity, from his species being, is the *estrangement of man* from *man.* When man confronts himself, he confronts the *other* man. What applies to a man's relation to his work, to the product of his labor and to himself, also holds of a man's relation to the other man, and to the other man's labor and object of labor.

In fact, the proposition that man's species nature is estranged from him means that one man is estranged from the other, as each of them is from man's essential nature.

The estrangement of man, and in fact every relationship in which man stands to himself, is first realized and expressed in the relationship in which a man stands to other men.

Hence within the relationship of estranged labor each man views the other in accordance with the standard and the relationship in which he finds himself as a worker.

We took our departure from a fact of political economy—the estrangement of the worker and his production. We have formulated this fact in conceptual terms as *estranged, alienated* labor. We have analyzed this concept—hence analyzing merely a fact of political economy.

Let us now see, further, how the concept of estranged, alienated labor must express and present itself in real life.

If the product of labor is alien to me, if it confronts me as an alien power, to whom, then, does it belong?

If my own activity does not belong to me, if it is an alien, a coerced activity, to whom, then, does it belong?

To a being *other* than myself.

Who is this being?

The *gods?* To be sure, in the earliest times the principal production (for example, the building of temples, etc., in Egypt, India, and Mexico) appears to be in the service of the gods, and the product belongs to the gods. However, the gods on their own were never the lords of labor. No more was *nature.* And what a contradiction it would be if, the more man subjugated nature by his labor and the more the miracles of the gods were rendered superfluous by the miracles of industry, the more man were to renounce the joy of production and the enjoyment of the product in favor of these powers.

The *alien* being, to whom labor and the product of labor belongs, in whose service labor is done and for whose benefit the product of labor is provided, can only be *man* himself.

If the product of labor does not belong to the worker, if it confronts him as an alien power, then this can only be because it belongs to some *man other than the worker*. If the worker's activity is a torment to him, to another it must be *delight* and his life's joy. Not the gods, not nature, but only man himself can be this alien power over man.

We must bear in mind the previous proposition that man's relation to himself only becomes for him *objective* and *actual* through his relation to the other man. Thus, if the product of his labor, his labor *objectified*, is for him an *alien*, hostile, powerful object independent of him, then his position towards it is such that someone else is master of this object, someone who is alien, hostile, powerful, and independent of him. If his own activity is to him related as an unfree activity, then he is related to it as an activity performed in the service, under the dominion, the coercion, and the yoke of another man.

Every self-estrangement of man, from himself and from nature, appears in the relation in which he places himself and nature to men other than and differentiated from himself. For this reason religious self-estrangement necessarily appears in the relationship of the layman to the priest, or again to a mediator, etc., since we are here dealing with the intellectual world. In the real practical world, self-estrangement can only become manifest through the real practical relationship to other men. The medium through which estrangement takes place is itself *practical*. Thus through estranged labor man not only creates his relationship to the object and to the act of production as to men that are alien and hostile to him; he also creates the relationship in which other men stand to his production and to his product, and the relationship in which he stands to these other men. Just as he creates his own production as the loss of his reality, as his punishment; his own product as a loss, as a product not belonging to him; so he creates the domination of the person who does not produce over production and over the product. Just as he estranges his own activity from himself, so he confers to the stranger an activity which is not his own.

We have until now only considered this relationship from the standpoint of the worker and later we shall be considering it also from the standpoint of the non-worker.

Through *estranged, alienated labor*, then, the worker produces the relationship to this labor of a man alien to labor and standing outside it. The relationship of the worker to labor creates the relation to it of the capitalist (or whatever one chooses to call the master of labor). *Private property* is thus the product, the result, the necessary consequence, of *alienated labor*, of the external relation of the worker to nature and to himself.

Private property thus results by analysis from the concept of *alienated labor*, i.e., of *alienated man*, of estranged labor, of estranged life, of *estranged* man.

True, it is as a result of the *movement of private property* that we have obtained the concept of *alienated labor (of alienated life)* from political economy. But on analysis of this concept it becomes clear that though private property appears to be the source, the cause of alienated labor, it is rather its consequence, just as the gods are *originally* not the cause but the effect of man's intellectual confusion. Later this relationship becomes reciprocal.

Only at the last culmination of the development of private property does this, its secret, appear again, namely, that on the one hand it is the *product* of alienated labor, and that on the other it is the *means* by which labor alienates itself, the *realization of this alienation*.

This exposition immediately sheds light on various hitherto unsolved conflicts.

(1) Political economy starts from labor as the real soul of production; yet to labor it gives nothing, and to private property everything. Confronting this contradiction, Proudhon has decided in favor of labor against private property. We understand however, that this apparent contradiction is the contradiction of *estranged labor* with itself, and that political economy has merely formulated the laws of estranged labor.

We also understand, therefore, that *wages* and *private property* are identical: since the product, as the object of labor pays for labor itself, therefore the wage is but a necessary consequence of labor's estrangement. After all, in the wage of labor, labor does not appear as an end in itself but as the servant of the wage. We shall develop this point later, and meanwhile will only derive some conclusions.

An enforced increase of wages (disregarding all other difficulties, including the fact that it would only be by force, too, that higher wages, being an anomaly, could be maintained) would therefore be nothing but *better payment for the slave,* and would not win either for the worker or for labor their human status and dignity.

Indeed, even the *equality of wages* demanded by Proudhon only transforms the relationship of the present-day worker to his labor into the relationship of all men to labor. Society is then conceived as an abstract capitalist.

Wages are a direct consequence of estranged labor, and estranged labor is the direct cause of private property. The downfall of the one must involve the downfall of the other.

(2) From the relationship of estranged labor to private property it follows further that the emancipation of society from private property, etc., from servitude, is expressed in the *political* form of the *emancipation of the workers*; not that *their* emancipation alone is at stake, but because the emancipation of the workers contains universal human emancipation—and it contains this, because the whole of human servitude is involved in the relation of the worker to production, and every relation of servitude is but a modification and consequence of this relation.

Just as we have derived the concept of *private property* from the concept of *estranged, alienated labor* by *analysis* so we can develop every *category* of political economy with the help of these two factors; and we shall find again in each category, e.g., trade, competition, capital, money, only a *definite* and *developed expression* of these first elements.

Before considering this aspect, however, let us try to solve two problems.

(1) To define the general *nature of private property,* as it has arisen as a result of estranged labor, in its relation to *truly human* and *social property.*

(2) We have accepted the *estrangement of labor,* its *alienation,* as a fact, and we have analyzed this fact. How, we now ask, does *man* come to *alienate,* to estrange, *his labor?* How is this estrangement rooted

in the nature of human development? We have already gone a long way to the solution of this problem by *transforming* the question of the *origin of private property* into the question of the relation of *alienated labor* to the course of humanity's development. For when one speaks of *private property,* one thinks of dealing with something external to man. When one speaks of labor, one is directly dealing with man himself. This new formulation of the question already contains its solution.

As to (1): The general nature of private property and its relation to truly human property.

Alienated labor has resolved itself for us into two elements which mutually condition one another, or which are but different expressions of one and the same relationship. *Appropriation* appears as *estrangement,* as *alienation;* and *alienation* appears as *appropriation, estrangement* as true introduction into society.

We have considered the one side—*alienated* labor in relation to the *worker* himself, i.e., the *relation of alienated labor to itself.* The *property relation of the non-worker to the worker and to labor* we have found as the product, the necessary outcome of this relationship. *Private property,* as the material, summary expression of alienated labor, embraces both relations—the *relation of the worker to work and to the product of his labor and to the non-worker,* and the relation of the *non-worker to the worker and to the product of his labor.*

Having seen that in relation to the worker who *appropriates* nature by means of his labor, this appropriation appears as estrangement, his own spontaneous activity as activity for another and as activity of another, vitality as a sacrifice of life, production of the object as loss of the object to an alien power, to an *alien* person—we shall now consider the relation to the worker, to labor and its object of this person who is *alien* to labor and the worker.

First it has to be noted that everything which appears in the worker as an *activity of alienation, of estrangement,* appears in the non-worker as a *state of alienation, of estrangement.*

Secondly, that the worker's *real, practical attitude* in production and to the product (as a state of mind) appears in the non-worker confronting him as a *theoretical* attitude.

Thirdly, the non-worker does everything against the worker which the worker does against himself; but he does not do against himself what he does against the worker.

Let us look more closely at these three relations.

[*At this point the first manuscript breaks off unfinished.*]

2. The Inevitability of Communism

THE COMMUNIST MANIFESTO

A spectre is haunting Europe—the spectre of Communism. All the Powers of old Europe have entered into a holy alliance to exorcise this spectre: Pope and Tsar, Metternich and Guizot, French Radicals and German police-spies.

Where is the party in opposition that has not been decried as Communistic by its opponents in power? Where the Opposition that has not hurled back the branding reproach of Communism, against the more advanced opposition parties, as well as against its reactionary adversaries?

Two things result from this fact.

I. Communism is already acknowledged by all European Powers to be itself a Power.

II. It is high time that Communists should openly, in the face of the whole world, publish their views, their aims, their tendencies, and meet this nursery tale of the Spectre of Communism with a Manifesto of the party itself.

To this end, Communists of various nationalities have assembled in London, and sketched the following Manifesto, to be published in the English, French, German, Italian, Flemish, and Danish languages.

I

Bourgeois and Proletarians

The history of all hitherto existing society is the history of class struggles.

Freeman and slave, patrician and plebeian, lord and serf, guild-master and journeyman—in a word, oppressor and oppressed, stood in constant opposition to one another, carried on an uninterrupted, now hidden, now open fight, a fight that each time ended either in a revolutionary re-constitution of society at large or in the common ruin of the contending classes.

In the earlier epochs of history, we find almost everywhere a complicated arrangement of society into various orders, a manifold gradation of social rank. In ancient Rome we have patricians, knights, plebeians, slaves; in the Middle Ages, feudal lords, vassals, guild-masters, journeymen, apprentices, serfs; in almost all of these classes, again, subordinate gradations.

The modern bourgeois society that has sprouted from the ruins of feudal society has not done away with class antagonisms. It has but established new classes, new conditions of oppression, new forms of struggle in place of the old ones.

Our epoch, the epoch of the bourgeoisie, possesses, however, this distinctive feature: it has simplified the class antagonisms. Society as a whole is more and more splitting up into two great hostile camps, into two great classes directly facing each other: Bourgeoisie and Proletariat.

From the serfs of the Middle Ages sprang the chartered burghers of the earliest towns. From these burgesses the first elements of the bourgeoisie were developed.

From "The Communist Manifesto," in Marx and Engels Collected Works, Vol. 6 *(Lawrence & Wishart, 1976). Reprinted with permission.*

The discovery of America, the rounding of the Cape, opened up fresh ground for the rising bourgeoisie. The East Indian and Chinese markets, the colonization of America, trade with the colonies, the increase in the means of exchange and in commodities generally, gave to commerce, to navigation, to industry, an impulse never before known, and thereby, to the revolutionary element in the tottering feudal society, a rapid development.

The feudal system of industry, under which industrial production was monopolized by closed guilds, now no longer sufficed for the growing wants of the new markets. The manufacturing system took its place. The guild-masters were pushed on one side by the manufacturing middle class; division of labour between the different corporate guilds vanished in the face of division of labour in each single workshop.

Meantime the markets kept ever growing, the demand ever rising. Even manufacture no longer sufficed. Thereupon, steam and machinery revolutionized industrial production. The place of manufacture was taken by the giant, Modern Industry, the place of the industrial middle class, by industrial millionaires, the leaders of whole industrial armies, the modern bourgeois.

Modern industry has established the world-market, for which the discovery of America paved the way. This market has given an immense development to commerce, to navigation, to communication by land. This development has, in its turn, reacted on the extension of industry; and in proportion as industry, commerce, navigation, railways extended, in the same proportion the bourgeoisie developed, increased its capital, and pushed into the background every class handed down from the Middle Ages.

We see, therefore, how the modern bourgeoisie is itself the product of a long course of development, of a series of revolutions in the modes of production and of exchange.

Each step in the development of the bourgeoisie was accompanied by a corresponding political advance of that class. An oppressed class under the sway of the feudal nobility, an armed and self-governing association in the medieval commune; here independent urban republic (as in Italy and Germany), there taxable 'third estate' of the monarchy (as in France), afterwards, in the period of manufacture proper, serving either the semi-feudal or the absolute monarchy as a counterpoise against the nobility, and, in fact, corner-stone of the great monarchies in general, the bourgeoisie has at last, since the establishment of Modern Industry and of the world market, conquered for itself, in the modern representative State, exclusive political sway. The executive of the modern State is but a committee for managing the common affairs of the whole bourgeoisie.

The bourgeoisie, historically, has played a most revolutionary part.

The bourgeoisie, wherever it has got the upper hand, has put an end to all feudal, patriarchal, idyllic relations. It has pitilessly torn asunder the motley feudal ties that bound man to his 'natural superiors', and has left remaining no other nexus between man and man than naked self-interest, than callous 'cash payment'. It has drowned the most heavenly ecstasies of religious fervour, of chivalrous enthusiasm, of philistine sentimentalism, in the icy water of egotistical calculation. It has resolved personal worth into exchange value, and in place of the numberless indefeasible chartered freedoms, has set up that single, unconscionable freedom—Free Trade. In one word, for exploitation, veiled by religious and political illusions, it has substituted naked, shameless, direct, brutal exploitation.

The bourgeoisie has stripped of its halo every occupation hitherto honoured and looked up to with reverent awe. It has converted the physician, the lawyer, the priest, the poet, the man of science into its paid wage-labourers.

The bourgeoisie has torn away from the family its sentimental veil, and has reduced the family relation to a mere money relation.

The bourgeoisie has disclosed how it came to pass that the brutal display of vigour in the Middle Ages, which Reactionists so much admire, found its fitting complement in the most slothful indolence. It has been the first to show what man's activity can bring about. It has accomplished wonders far surpassing Egyptian pyramids, Roman aqueducts, and Gothic cathedrals; it has conducted expeditions that put in the shade all former Exoduses of nations and crusades.

The bourgeoisie cannot exist without constantly revolutionizing the instruments of production, and thereby the relations of production, and with them the whole relations of society. Conservation of the old modes of production in unaltered form, was, on the contrary, the first condition of existence for all earlier industrial classes. Constant revolutionizing of production, uninterrupted disturbance of all social conditions, everlasting uncertainty and agitation distinguish the bourgeois epoch from all earlier ones. All fixed, fast-frozen relations, with their train of ancient and venerable prejudices and opinions, are swept away, all new-formed ones become antiquated before they can ossify. All that is solid melts into air, all that is holy is profaned, and man is at last compelled to face with sober senses, his real conditions of life, and his relations with his kind.

The need of a constantly expanding market for its products chases the bourgeoisie over the whole surface of the globe. It must nestle everywhere, settle everywhere, establish connections everywhere.

The bourgeoisie has through its exploitation of the world-market given a cosmopolitan character to production and consumption in every country. To the great chagrin of Reactionists, it has drawn from under the feet of industry the national ground on which it stood. All old-established national industries have been destroyed or are daily being destroyed. They are dislodged by new industries, whose introduction becomes a life-and-death question for all civilized nations, by industries that no longer work up indigenous raw material, but raw material drawn from the remotest zones; industries whose products are consumed, not only at home, but in every quarter of the globe. In place of the old wants, satisfied by the productions of the country, we find new wants, requiring for their satisfaction the products of distant lands and climes. In place of the old local and national seclusion and self-sufficiency, we have intercourse in every direction, universal interdependence of nations. And as in material, so also in intellectual production. The intellectual creations of individual nations become common property. National

one-sidedness and narrow-mindedness become more and more impossible, and from the numerous national and local literatures, there arises a world literature.

The bourgeoisie, by the rapid improvement of all instruments of production, by the immensely facilitated means of communication, draws all, even the most barbarian, nations into civilization. The cheap prices of its commodities are the heavy artillery with which it batters down all Chinese walls, with which it forces the barbarians' intensely obstinate hatred of foreigners to capitulate. It compels all nations, on pain of extinction, to adopt the bourgeois mode of production; it compels them to introduce what it calls civilization into their midst, i.e., to become bourgeois themselves. In one word, it creates a world after its own image.

The bourgeoisie has subjected the country to the rule of the towns. It has created enormous cities, has greatly increased the urban population as compared with the rural, and has thus rescued a considerable part of the population from the idiocy of rural life. Just as it has made the country dependent on the towns, so it has made barbarian and semi-barbarian countries dependent on the civilized ones, nations of peasants on nations of bourgeois, the East on the West.

The bourgeoisie keeps more and more doing away with the scattered state of the population, of the means of production, and of property. It has agglomerated population, centralized means of production, and has concentrated property in a few hands. The necessary consequence of this was political centralization. Independent or but loosely connected provinces, with separate interests, laws, governments, and systems of taxation, became lumped together into one nation, with one government, one code of laws, one national class-interest, one frontier, and one customs-tariff.

The bourgeoisie, during its rule of scarcely one hundred years, has created more massive and more colossal productive forces than have all preceding generations together. Subjection of Nature's forces to man, machinery, application of chemistry to industry and agriculture, steam-navigation, railways, electric telegraphs, clearing of whole continents for cultivation, canalization of rivers, whole populations conjured out of the ground—what earlier century had even a presentiment that such productive forces slumbered in the lap of social labour?

We see then that the means of production and of exchange, on whose foundation the bourgeoisie built itself up, were generated in feudal society. At a certain stage in the development of these means of production and of exchange, the conditions under which feudal society produced and exchanged, the feudal organization of agriculture and manufacturing industry, in one word, the feudal relations of property become no longer compatible with the already developed productive forces; they became so many fetters. They had to be burst asunder; they were burst asunder.

Into their place stepped free competition, accompanied by a social and political constitution adapted to it, and by the economical and political sway of the bourgeois class.

A similar movement is going on before our own eyes. Modern bourgeois society with its relations of production, of exchange and of property, a society that has conjured up such gigantic means of production and of exchange, is like the sorcerer, who is no longer able to control the powers of the nether world which he has called up by his spells. The history of industry and commerce for many a decade past is but the history of the revolt of modern productive forces against modern conditions of production, against the property relations that are the conditions for the existence of the bourgeoisie and of its rule. It is enough to mention the commercial crises that by their periodical return put on trial, each time more threateningly, the existence of the entire bourgeois society. In these crises a great part not only of the existing products, but also of the previously created productive forces, are periodically destroyed. In these crises there breaks out an epidemic that, in all earlier epochs, would have seemed an absurdity—the epidemic of over production. Society suddenly finds itself put back into a state of momentary barbarism; it appears as if a famine, a universal war of devastation, has cut off the supply of every means of subsistence; industry and commerce seem to be destroyed; and why?

Because there is too much civilization, too much means of subsistence, too much industry, too much commerce. The productive forces at the disposal of society no longer tend to further the development of the conditions of bourgeois property; on the contrary, they have become too powerful for these conditions, by which they are fettered, and so soon as they overcome these fetters, they bring disorder into the whole of bourgeois society, endanger the existence of bourgeois property. The conditions of bourgeois society are too narrow to comprise the wealth created by them. And how does the bourgeoisie get over these crises? On the one hand by enforced destruction of a mass of productive forces; on the other, by the conquest of new markets, and by the more thorough exploitation of the old ones. That is to say, by paving the way for more extensive and more destructive crises, and by diminishing the means whereby crises are prevented.

The weapons with which the bourgeoisie felled feudalism to the ground are now turned against the bourgeoisie itself.

But not only has the bourgeoisie forged the weapons that bring death to itself; it has also called into existence the men who are to wield those weapons—the modern working class—the proletarians.

In proportion as the bourgeoisie, i.e., capital, is developed, in the same proportion is the proletariat, the modern working class, developed—a class of labourers, who live only so long as they find work, and who find work only so long as their labour increases capital. These labourers, who must sell themselves piecemeal, are a commodity, like every other article of commerce, and are consequently exposed to all the vicissitudes of competition, to all the fluctuations of the market.

Owing to the extensive use of machinery and to division of labour, the work of the proletarians has lost all individual character, and, consequently, all charm for the workman. He becomes an appendage of the machine, and it is only the most simple, most monotonous, and most easily acquired knack, that is required of him. Hence, the cost of production of a workman is restricted, almost entirely, to the means of subsistence that he requires for his maintenance, and for the propagation of his race. But the price of a commodity, and therefore also of labour, is equal to its cost of production. In proportion, therefore, as the repulsiveness of the work increases, the wage decreases. Nay more, in proportion as the use of machinery and division of labour increases, in the same proportion the burden of toil also increases, whether by prolongation of the working hours, by increase of the work exacted in a given time or by increased speed of the machinery, etc.

Modern industry has converted the little workshop of the patriarchal master into the great factory of the industrial capitalist. Masses of labourers, crowded into the factory, are organized like soldiers. As privates of the industrial army they are placed under the command of a perfect hierarchy of officers and sergeants. Not only are they slaves of the bourgeois class, and of the bourgeois State; they are daily and hourly enslaved by the machine, by the overlooker, and, above all, by the individual bourgeois manufacturer himself. The more openly this despotism proclaims gain to be its end and aim, the more petty, the more hateful, and the more embittering it is.

The less the skill and exertion of strength implied in manual labour, in other words, the more modern industry becomes developed, the more is the labour of men superseded by that of women. Differences of age and sex have no longer any distinctive social validity for the working class. All are instruments of labour, more or less expensive to use, according to their age and sex.

No sooner is the exploitation of the labourer by the manufacturer, so far, at an end, and he receives his wages in cash, than he is set upon by the other portions of the bourgeoisie, the landlord, the shopkeeper, the pawnbroker, etc.

The lower strata of the middle class—the small tradespeople, shopkeepers, and retired tradesmen generally, the handicraftsmen and peasants—all these sink gradually into the proletariat, partly because their diminutive capital does not suffice for the scale on which Modern Industry is carried on, and is swamped in the competition with the large capitalists, partly because their specialized skill is rendered worthless by new methods of production. Thus the proletariat is recruited from all classes of the population.

The proletariat goes through various stages of development. With its birth begins its struggle with the bourgeoisie. At first the contest is carried on by individual labourers, then by the workpeople of a factory, then by the operatives of one trade, in one locality, against the individual bourgeois who directly exploits them. They direct their attacks not against the bourgeois conditions of production, but against the instruments of production themselves; they destroy imported wares that compete with their labour, they smash to pieces machinery, they set factories ablaze, they seek to restore by force the vanished status of the workman of the Middle Ages.

At this stage the labourers still form an incoherent mass scattered over the whole country, and broken up by their mutual competition. If anywhere they unite to form more compact bodies, this is not yet the consequence of their own active union, but of the union of the bourgeoisie, which class, in order to attain its own political ends, is compelled to set the whole proletariat in motion, and is moreover yet, for a time, able to do so. At this stage, therefore, the proletarians do not fight their enemies, but the enemies of their enemies, the remnants of absolute monarchy, the landowners, the non-industrial bourgeois, the petty bourgeoisie. Thus the whole historical movement is concentrated in the hands of the bourgeoisie; every victory so obtained is a victory for the bourgeoisie.

But with the development of industry the proletariat not only increases in number; it becomes concentrated in greater masses, its strength grows, and it feels that strength more. The various interests and conditions of life within the ranks of the proletariat are more and more equalized, in proportion as machinery obliterates all distinctions of labour, and nearly everywhere reduces wages to the same low level. The growing competition among the bourgeois, and the resulting commercial crises, make the wages of the workers ever more fluctuating. The unceasing improvement of machinery, ever more rapidly developing, makes their livelihood more and more precarious; the collisions between individual workmen and individual bourgeois take more and more the character of collisions between two classes. Thereupon the workers begin to form combinations (Trades' Unions) against the bourgeois; they club together in order to keep up the rate of wages; they found permanent associations in order to make provision beforehand for these occasional revolts. Here and there the contest breaks out into riots.

Now and then the workers are victorious, but only for a time. The real fruit of their battles lies, not in the immediate result, but in the ever-expanding union of the workers. This union is helped on by the improved means of communication that are created by modern industry and that place the workers of different localities in contact with one another. It was just this contact that was needed to centralize the numerous local struggles, all of the same character, into one national struggle between classes. But every class struggle is a political struggle. And that union, to attain which the burghers of the Middle Ages, with their miserable highways, required centuries, the modern proletarians, thanks to railways, achieve in a few years.

This organization of the proletarians into a class, and consequently into a political party, is continually being upset again by the competition between the workers themselves. But it ever rises up again, stronger, firmer, mightier. It compels legislative recognition of particular interests of the workers, by taking advantage of the divisions among the bourgeoisie itself. Thus the ten-hours' bill in England was carried.

Altogether, collisions between the classes of the old society further in many ways the course of development of the proletariat. The bourgeoisie finds itself involved in a constant battle. At first with the aristocracy; later on, with those portions of the bourgeoisie itself whose interests have become antagonistic to the progress of industry; at all times, with the bourgeoisie of foreign countries. In all these battles it sees itself compelled to appeal to the proletariat, to ask for its help, and thus to drag it into the political arena. The bourgeoisie

itself, therefore, supplies the proletariat with its own elements of political and general education, in other words, it furnishes the proletariat with weapons for fighting the bourgeoisie.

Further, as we have already seen, entire sections of the ruling classes are, by the advance of industry, precipitated into the proletariat, or are at least threatened in their conditions of existence. These also supply the proletariat with fresh elements of enlightenment and progress.

Finally, in times when the class struggle nears the decisive hour, the process of dissolution going on within the ruling class, in fact within the whole range of old society, assumes such a violent, glaring character, that a small section of the ruling class cuts itself adrift, and joins the revolutionary class, the class that holds the future in its hands. Just as, therefore, at an earlier period, a section of the nobility went over to the bourgeoisie, so now a portion of the bourgeoisie goes over to the proletariat, and in particular, a portion of the bourgeois ideologists, who have raised themselves to the level of comprehending theoretically the historical movement as a whole.

Of all the classes that stand face to face with the bourgeoisie today, the proletariat alone is a really revolutionary class. The other classes decay and finally disappear in the face of Modern Industry; the proletariat is its special and essential product.

The lower middle class, the small manufacturer, the shopkeeper, the artisan, the peasant, all these fight against the bourgeoisie, to save from extinction their existence as fractions of the middle class. They are therefore not revolutionary, but conservative. Nay more, they are reactionary, for they try to roll back the wheel of history. If by chance they are revolutionary, they are so only in view of their impending transfer into the proletariat; they thus defend not their present, but their future interests, they desert their own standpoint to place themselves at that of the proletariat.

The 'dangerous class', the social scum, that passively rotting mass thrown off by the lowest layers of old society, may, here and there, be swept into the movement by a proletarian revolution; its conditions of life, however, prepare it far more for the part of a bribed tool of reactionary intrigue.

In the conditions of the proletariat, those of old society at large are already virtually swamped. The proletarian is without property; his relation to his wife and children has no longer anything in common with the bourgeois family relations; modern industrial labour, modern subjection to capital, the same in England as in France, in America as in Germany, has stripped him of every trace of national character. Law, morality, religion are to him so many bourgeois prejudices, behind which lurk in ambush just as many bourgeois interests.

All the preceding classes that got the upper hand, sought to fortify their already acquired status by subjecting society at large to their conditions of appropriation. The proletarians cannot become masters of the productive forces of society, except by abolishing their own previous mode of appropriation, and thereby also every other previous mode of appropriation. They have nothing of their own to secure and to fortify; their mission is to destroy all previous securities for, and insurances of, individual property.

All previous historical movements were movements of minorities, or in the interests of minorities. The proletarian movement is the self-conscious, independent movement of the immense majority, in the interests of the immense majority. The proletariat, the lowest stratum of our present society, cannot stir, cannot raise itself up, without the whole superincumbent strata of official society being sprung into the air.

Though not in substance, yet in form, the struggle of the proletariat with the bourgeoisie is at first a national struggle. The proletariat of each country must, of course, first of all settle matters with its own bourgeoisie.

In depicting the most general phases of the development of the proletariat, we traced the more or less veiled civil war, raging within existing society, up to the point where that war breaks out into open revolution, and where the violent overthrow of the bourgeoisie lays the foundation for the sway of the proletariat.

Hitherto, every form of society has been based, as we have already seen, on the antagonism of oppressing and oppressed classes. But in order to oppress a class, certain conditions must be assured to it under which it can, at least, continue its slavish existence. The serf, in the period of serfdom, raised himself to membership in the commune, just as the petty bourgeois, under the yoke of feudal absolutism, managed to develop into a bourgeois. The modern labourer, on the contrary, instead of rising with the progress of industry, sinks deeper and deeper below the conditions of existence of his own class. He becomes a pauper, and pauperism develops more rapidly than population and wealth. And here it becomes evident, that the bourgeoisie is unfit any longer to be the ruling class in society, and to impose its conditions of existence upon society as an overriding law. It is unfit to rule because it is incompetent to assure an existence to its slave within his slavery, because it cannot help letting him sink into such a state, that it has to feed him, instead of being fed by him. Society can no longer live under this bourgeoisie, in other words, its existence is no longer compatible with society.

The essential condition for the existence, and for the sway of the bourgeois class, is the formation and augmentation of capital; the condition for capital is wage-labour. Wage-labour rests exclusively on competition between the labourers. The advance of industry, whose involuntary promoter is the bourgeoisie, replaces the isolation of the labourers, due to competition, by their revolutionary combination, due to association. The development of Modern Industry, therefore, cuts from under its feet the very foundation on which the bourgeoisie produces and appropriates products. What the bourgeoisie, therefore, produces, above all, is its own grave-diggers. Its fall and the victory of the proletariat are equally inevitable.

II

Proletarians and Communists

In what relation do the Communists stand to the proletarians as a whole?

The Communists do not form a separate party opposed to other working-class parties.

They have no interests separate and apart from those of the proletariat as a whole.

They do not set up any sectarian principles of their own, by which to shape and mould the proletarian movement.

The Communists are distinguished from the other working-class parties by this only: 1. In the national struggles of the proletarians of the different countries, they point out and bring to the front the common interests of the entire proletariat, independently of all nationality. 2. In the various stages of development which the struggle of the working class against the bourgeoisie has to pass through, they always and everywhere represent the interests of the movement as a whole.

The Communists, therefore, are on the one hand, practically, the most advanced and resolute section of the working-class parties of every country, that section which pushes forward all others; on the other hand, theoretically, they have over the great mass of the proletariat the advantage of clearly understanding the line of march, the conditions, and the ultimate general results of the proletarian movement.

The immediate aim of the Communists is the same as that of all the other proletarian parties: formation of the proletariat into a class, overthrow of the bourgeois supremacy, conquest of political power by the proletariat.

The theoretical conclusions of the Communists are in no way based on ideas or principles that have been invented, or discovered, by this or that would-be universal reformer.

They merely express, in general terms, actual relations springing from an existing class struggle, from a historical movement going on under our very eyes. The abolition of existing property relations is not at all a distinctive feature of Communism.

All property relations in the past have continually been subject to historical change consequent upon the change in historical conditions.

The French Revolution, for example, abolished feudal property in favour of bourgeois property.

The distinguishing feature of Communism is not the abolition of property generally, but the abolition of bourgeois property. But modern bourgeois private property is the final and most complete expression of the system of producing and appropriating products, that is based on class antagonisms, on the exploitation of the many by the few.

In this sense, the theory of the Communists may be summed up in the single sentence: Abolition of private property.

We Communists have been reproached with the desire of abolishing the right of personally acquiring property as the fruit of a man's own labour, which property is alleged to be the groundwork of all personal freedom, activity, and independence.

Hard-won, self-acquired, self-earned property! Do you mean the property of the petty artisan and of the small peasant, a form of property that preceded the bourgeois form? There is no need to abolish that; the development of industry has to a great extent already destroyed it, and is still destroying it daily.

Or do you mean modern bourgeois private property?

But does wage-labour create any property for the labourer? Not a bit. It creates capital, i.e., that kind of property which exploits wage-labour, and which cannot increase except upon condition of begetting a new supply of wage-labour for fresh exploitation. Property, in its present form, is based on the antagonism of capital and wage-labour. Let us examine both sides of this antagonism.

To be a capitalist, is to have not only a purely personal, but a social, status in production. Capital is a collective product, and only by the united action of many members, nay, in the last resort, only by the united action of all members of society, can it be set in motion.

Capital is, therefore, not a personal, it is a social power.

When, therefore, capital is converted into common property, into the property of all members of society, personal property is not thereby transformed into social property. It is only the social character of the property that is changed. It loses its class-character.

Let us now take wage-labour.

The average price of wage-labour is the minimum wage, i.e., that quantum of the means of subsistence which is absolutely requisite to keep the labourer in bare existence as a labourer. What, therefore, the wage-labourer appropriates by means of his labour merely suffices to prolong and reproduce a bare existence. We by no means intend to abolish this personal appropriation of the products of labour, an appropriation that is made for the maintenance and reproduction of human life, and that leaves no surplus wherewith to command the labour of others. All that we want to do away with is the miserable character of this appropriation, under which the labourer lives merely to increase capital, and is allowed to live only in so far as the interest of the ruling class requires it.

In bourgeois society, living labour is but a means to increase accumulated labour. In Communist society, accumulated labour is but a means to widen, to enrich, to promote the existence of the labourer.

In bourgeois society, therefore, the past dominates the present; in Communist society, the present dominates the past. In bourgeois society capital is independent and has individuality, while the living person is dependent and has no individuality.

And the abolition of this state of things is called by the bourgeois abolition of individuality and freedom! And rightly so. The abolition of bourgeois individuality, bourgeois independence, and bourgeois freedom is undoubtedly aimed at.

By freedom is meant, under the present bourgeois conditions of production, free trade, free selling and buying.

But if selling and buying disappears, free selling and buying disappears also. This talk about free selling and buying, and all the other 'brave words' of our bourgeoisie about freedom in general, have a meaning, if any, only in contrast with restricted selling and buying, with the fettered traders of the Middle Ages, but have no meaning when opposed to the Communistic abolition of buying and selling, of the bourgeois conditions of production, and of the bourgeoisie itself.

You are horrified at our intending to do away with private property. But in your existing society, private property is already done away with for nine-tenths of the population; its existence for the few is solely due to its nonexistence in the hands of those nine-tenths. You reproach us, therefore, with intending to do away with a form of property, the necessary condition for whose existence is the non-existence of any property for the immense majority of society.

In one word, you reproach us with intending to do away with your property. Precisely so; that is just what we intend.

From the moment when labour can no longer be converted into capital, money, or rent, into a social power capable of being monopolized, i.e., from the moment when individual property can no longer be transformed into bourgeois property, into capital, from that moment, you say, individuality vanishes.

You must, therefore, confess that by 'individual' you mean no other person than the bourgeois, than the middle-class owner of property. This person must, indeed, be swept out of the way, and made impossible.

Communism deprives no man of the power to appropriate the products of society; all that it does is to deprive him of the power to subjugate the labour of others by means of such appropriation.

It has been objected that upon the abolition of private property all work will cease, and universal laziness will overtake us.

According to this, bourgeois society ought long ago to have gone to the dogs through sheer idleness; for those of its members who work acquire nothing, and those who acquire anything do not work. The whole of this objection is but another expression of the tautology: that there can no longer by any wage-labour when there is no longer any capital.

All objections urged against the Communistic mode of producing and appropriating material products have, in the same way, been urged against the Communistic modes of producing and appropriating intellectual products. Just as, to the bourgeois, the disappearance of class property is the disappearance of production itself, so the disappearance of class culture is to him identical with the disappearance of all culture.

That culture, the loss of which he laments, is, for the enormous majority, a mere training to act as a machine.

But don't wrangle with us so long as you apply, to our intended abolition of bourgeois property, the standard of your bourgeois notions of freedom, culture, law, etc. Your very ideas are but the outgrowth of the conditions of your bourgeois production and bourgeois property, just as your jurisprudence is but the will of your class made into a law for all, a will whose essential character and direction are determined by the economical conditions of existence of your class.

The selfish misconception that induces you to transform into eternal laws of nature and of reason the social forms springing from your present mode of production and form of property—historical relations that rise and disappear in the progress of production—this misconception you share with every ruling class that has preceded you. What you see clearly in the case of ancient property, what you admit in the case of feudal property, you are of course forbidden to admit in the case of your own bourgeois form of property.

Abolition of the family! Even the most radical flare up at this infamous proposal of the Communists.

On what foundation is the present family, the bourgeois family, based? On capital, on private gain. In its completely developed form this family exists only among the bourgeoisie. But this state of things finds its complement in the practical absence of the family among the proletarians, and in public prostitution.

The bourgeois family will vanish as a matter of course when its complement vanishes, and both will vanish with the vanishing of capital.

Do you charge us with wanting to stop the exploitation of children by their parents? To this crime we plead guilty.

But, you will say, we destroy the most hallowed of relations, when we replace home education by social.

And your education! Is not that also social, and determined by the social conditions under which you educate, by the intervention, direct or indirect, of society, by means of schools, etc.? The Communists have not invented the intervention of society in education; they do but seek to alter the character

of that intervention, and to rescue education from the influence of the ruling class.

The bourgeois clap-trap about the family and education, about the hallowed co-relation of parent and child, becomes all the more disgusting, the more, by the action of Modern Industry, all family ties among the proletarians are torn asunder, and their children transformed into simple articles of commerce and instruments of labour.

But you Communists would introduce community of women, screams the whole bourgeoisie in chorus.

The bourgeois sees in his wife a mere instrument of production. He hears that the instruments of production are to be exploited in common, and, naturally, can come to no other conclusion than that the lot of being common to all will likewise fall to the women.

He has not even a suspicion that the real point aimed at is to do away with the status of women as mere instruments of production.

For the rest, nothing is more ridiculous than the virtuous indignation of our bourgeois at the community of women which, they pretend, is to be openly and officially established by the Communists. The Communists have no need to introduce community of women; it has existed almost from time immemorial.

Our bourgeois, not content with having the wives and daughters of their proletarians at their disposal, not to speak of common prostitutes, take the greatest pleasure in seducing each other's wives.

Bourgeois marriage is in reality a system of wives in common and thus, at the most, what the Communists might possibly be reproached with, is that they desire to introduce, in substitution for a hypocritically concealed, an openly legalized, community of women. For the rest, it is self-evident that the abolition of the present system of production must bring with it the abolition of the community of women springing from that system, i.e., of prostitution both public and private.

The Communists are further reproached with desiring to abolish countries and nationality.

The working men have no country. We cannot take from them what they have not got. Since the proletariat must first of all acquire political supremacy, must rise to be the leading class of the nation, must constitute itself *the* nation, it is, so far, itself national, though not in the bourgeois sense of the world.

National differences and antagonisms between peoples are daily more and more vanishing, owing to the development of the bourgeoisie, to freedom of commerce, to the world-market, to uniformity in the mode of production and in the conditions of life corresponding thereto.

The supremacy of the proletariat will cause them to vanish still faster. United action, of the leading civilized countries at least, is one of the first conditions for the emancipation of the proletariat.

In proportion as the exploitation of one individual by another is put an end to, the exploitation of one nation by another will also be put an end to. In proportion as the antagonism between classes within the nation vanishes, the hostility of one nation to another will come to an end.

The charges against Communism made from a religious, a philosophical, and, generally, from an ideological standpoint are not deserving of serious examination.

Does it require deep intuition to comprehend that man's ideas, views, and conceptions, in one word, man's consciousness, changes with every change in the conditions of his material existence, in his social relation, and in his social life?

What else does the history of ideas prove, than that intellectual production changes its character in proportion as material production is changed? The ruling ideas of each age have ever been the ideas of its ruling class.

When people speak of ideas that revolutionize society, they do but express the fact, that within the old society, the elements of a new one have been created, and that the dissolution of the old ideas keeps even pace with the dissolution of the old conditions of existence.

When the ancient world was in its last throes, the ancient religions were overcome by Christianity. When Christian ideas succumbed in the eighteenth century to rationalist ideas, feudal society fought its death battle with the then revolutionary bourgeoisie. The ideas of religious liberty and freedom of conscience merely gave expression to the sway of free competition within the domain of knowledge.

'Undoubtedly,' it will be said, 'religious, moral, philosophical, and juridical ideas have been modified in the course of historical development. But religion, morality, philosophy, political science, and law constantly survived this change.'

'There are, besides, eternal truths, such as Freedom, Justice, etc., that are common to all states of society. But Communism abolishes eternal truths, it abolishes all religion and all morality, instead of constituting them on a new basis; it therefore acts in contradiction to all past historical experience.'

What does this accusation reduce itself to? The history of all past society has consisted in the development of class antagonisms, antagonisms that assumed different forms at different epochs.

But whatever form they may have taken, one fact is common to all past ages, viz., the exploitation of one part of society by the other. No wonder, then, that the social consciousness of past ages, despite all the multiplicity and variety it displays, moves within certain common forms, or general ideas, which cannot completely vanish except with the total disappearance of class antagonisms.

The Communist revolution is the most radical rupture with traditional property relations; no wonder that its development involves the most radical rupture with traditional ideas.

But let us have done with the bourgeois objections to Communism.

We have seen above, that the first step in the revolution by the working class is to raise the proletariat to the position of ruling class, to win the battle of democracy.

The proletariat will use its political supremacy to wrest, by degrees, all capital from the bourgeoisie, to centralize all instruments of production in the hands of the State, i.e., of the proletariat organized as the ruling class; and to increase the total of productive forces as rapidly as possible.

Of course, in the beginning this cannot be effected except by means of despotic inroads on the rights of property, and on the conditions of bourgeois production; by means of measures, therefore, which appear economically insufficient and untenable, but which, in the course of the movement, outstrip themselves, necessitate further inroads upon the old social order, and are unavoidable as a means of entirely revolutionizing the mode of production.

These measures will of course be different in different countries.

Nevertheless, in the most advanced countries, the following will be pretty generally applicable.

1. Abolition of property in land and application of all rents of land to public purposes.

2. A heavy progressive or graduated income tax.

3. Abolition of all right of inheritance.

4. Confiscation of the property of all emigrants and rebels.

5. Centralization of credit in the hands of the State, by means of a national bank with State capital and an exclusive monopoly.

6. Centralization of the means of communication and transport in the hands of the State.

7. Extension of factories and instruments of production owned by the State; the bringing into cultivation of wastelands, and the improvement of the soil generally in accordance with a common plan.

8. Equal liability of all to labour. Establishment of industrial armies, especially for agriculture.

9. Combination of agriculture with manufacturing industries; gradual abolition of the distinction between town and country, by a more equable distribution of the population over the country.

10. Free education for all children in public schools. Abolition of children's factory labour in its present form. Combination of education with industrial production, etc., etc.

When, in the course of development, class distinctions have disappeared, and all production has been concentrated in the hands of associated individuals, the public power will lose its political character. Political power, properly so called, is merely the organized power of one class for oppressing another. If the proletariat during its contest with the bourgeoisie is compelled, by the force of circumstances, to organize itself as a class, if, by means of a revolution, it makes itself the ruling class, and, as such, sweeps away by force the old conditions of production, then it will, along with these conditions, have swept away the conditions for the existence of class antagonisms and of classes generally, and will thereby have abolished its own supremacy as a class.

In place of the old bourgeois society, with its classes and class antagonisms, we shall have an association, in which the free development of each is the condition for the free development of all.

Study Questions

1. What were the ideas of Hegel and Feuerbach that especially influenced Marx?

2. For Marx, what is the purpose of the state?

3. Explain the difference between the economic substructure and the ideological superstructure. Which has the most important influence on defining human nature?

4. How will capitalism inevitably lead to socialism, and socialism to communism?

5. What ideas did Marx take from Rousseau in formulating his concept of human nature?

6. Marx claims that capitalism causes three types of alienation. What are they and how does capitalism produce them?

7. What does it mean to say that capitalism exploits the working class?

8. According to Marcuse, how does the more worker friendly form of capitalism today continue to exploit the working class?

9. Explain the difference between central planning socialism and democratic socialism.

10. What is the difference between socialism and communism?

Chapter 8

Existentialism: Jean-Paul Sartre

Introduction

The term "existentialism" was first introduced by the twentieth-century French philosopher, Jean-Paul Sartre. His succinct definition for this now well-known term is that "existence precedes essence." What this means for Sartre is that human beings have no fixed nature or essence. We are not born into this world with a certain way to be. Instead we are pure potential (existence) for becoming whatever we choose to become. Instead of thinking of ourselves as possessing a shared human nature, and thus as being alike in our basic tendencies to behave, we should think of ourselves and our lives as starting with a blank canvas. We become the particular kind of person we end up being because the brush strokes of our choices in life create who we are. There is no common human nature. The only thing that we share in common beyond our biological structures is the freedom to create through what we do the very sorts of persons we are to become.

While this may be the general meaning that the term has for existential philosophers, it also has a much broader meaning that allows poets, novelists, artists, and others to be called existentialists as well. According to this meaning, existentialism is an *attitude,* a way of viewing and describing life, as much as it is a set of shared philosophical doctrines. As such, it focuses upon concrete, unique experiences instead of abstract theories. It is concerned with the individual and his or her situation in life, not with general scientific or philosophical definitions. It is more likely to discuss the irrational, the emotional, the passionate side of life, than it is to discuss the grand achievements of reason. Existentialism as an attitude is just as often found expressed in novels, plays, poems, and art as it is in philosophical texts. As an attitude, it has been present in all cultures since their very beginnings, found in religious myths, art, poems and plays, and in their grandest literary achievements. Existentialism as an attitude is often found running parallel with, and contrary to, abstract philosophical theories about rational nature.

It is not uncommon for novelists to be referred to as existentialists. For example, Dostoyevski, Camus, Unamuno, and Ortega y Gasset are often thought of as existentialist novelists. James Joyce and Ernest Hemingway have been included in this category as well. The same is true for playwrights such as Samuel Beckett, and artists such as Picasso. Many religious writers have also been thought of as expressing existentialist themes, including Augustine, Pacal, Martin Buber, Gabriel Marcel, and Meister Eckhart. These and many others that could be added to this list all have written on themes about the deepest, the most passionate, and often the most secret elements of human existence.[1] They write in concrete ways about the unique, often emotional experiences of individuals which have shaped their lives for better or for worse.

In this chapter the views of three existential philosophers will be considered. The first of these is the Danish philosopher and religious writer Soren Kierkegaard (1813–1855). Kierkegaard was every bit as much an eccentric as was Socrates. He roamed the streets of Copenhagen in the wee hours of the morning, his black cape flowing in his wake. His bent and pale body was an object of ridicule by the street youth, and his rebellious writings were vehemently rejected by the religious conservatives of his time. In one of the most dramatic decisions of his life, he broke off his engagement to his beloved Regina Olsen, sacrificing his much desired life as a conventional family man for his greater desire to devote his every waking moment to his newly found mission. As had Socrates before him, he came to see that his life's work was to be a critic of society in order to reform it. He would explain to people why their lives, especially their religious lives, were bankrupt. He would do this not simply to point out what was wrong, but also to show them the true path to fulfillment.

As it was in the Germany of Karl Marx, the intellectual climate of Kierkegaard's Copenhagen was dominated by the philosophical theories of Hegel. For Kierkegaard, this was especially damaging to religious belief. People began to identify God with Hegel's notion of an "absolute mind," thus substituting for a personal, passionate relationship with God a purely intellectual one. Kierkegaard made it his mission during his tragically short life to show his fellow European Christians how to be true Christians again, first by rejecting the intellectualization of God, and next by showing them how to develop a personal relationship with God. For Kierkegaard, developing this personal relationship was important because nothing short of it was required for happiness. Without it we would never be as fully human as we might be, because we would never be as fully free as we might be.

For Friedrich Nietzsche (1844–1900), on the other hand, religion is the enemy of the truly fulfilled life. As long as God is in his heaven, human beings will be constrained by his laws. If there is no God, on the other hand, and no necessity for accepting Christian values as absolute, then human freedom may be released from bondage and be allowed to set itself upon any number of courses. Nietzsche is every bit as much an atheist as Kierkegaard is a theist. This is one of the reasons why existentialism cannot be defined by pointing to shared conclusions among its adherents; sometimes there are more differences than similarities. Beyond this major difference in doctrine, however, Kierkegaard and Nietzsche share much in common, especially their focus on the uniqueness of the individual. Although he never read or knew about Kierkegaard, Nietzsche follows the Dane, for example, in rejecting reason as the core of human nature. Our desire for knowledge is not our strongest desire. Instead, at the very root of human beings is our desire for power, our desire to exercise our freedom as we will, our desire to create our own lives according to our own wishes. There is no preestablished human nature, only freedom to be whatever we choose to be.

These very personal beliefs of Nietzsche grew out of his early training in classical studies. Although he was raised a Lutheran, he soon grew to believe that the Greek aristocrats exemplified a more honest, more human set of values than his fellow European Christians. For Nietzsche, the Christian values expressed in the sermon on the mount were values of weakness. Turning the other cheek and valuing the poor and the meek were the choices of a suppressed people. The Greeks for him had it right—value strength and domination and pride, be the master of your own fate wherever that took you, and whomever that displeased. When such an attitude was expressed in his writings it earned Nietzsche, then the youngest ever professor at the University of Leipzig, nothing but criticism and ostricization. His poor health contributed to his isolation, keeping him on the fringes of society and maintaining him as a critic of the status quo until he finally became insane in his mid-fifties. Nietzsche spent the last eleven years of his life in a mental institution.

In the following section we will see much more clearly how both Kierkegaard and Nietzsche, each in their own way, reject the Western ideal of "rational man" and instead identify human nature with freedom. These themes were appropriated and developed more fully and in more technical ways by the central figure of this chapter, Jean-Paul Sartre (1905–1980). Sartre had observed and been a part of World War II as a member of the French Resistance, where he witnessed the brutality of war and the collapse of Western morality. The Western ideal of human nature, especially the Christian ideal of the wise and virtuous person who longed for a close relationship with a loving God, simply lost its credibility for Sartre. Sartre adopted the atheism of Nietzsche, and followed the lead of both Kierkegaard and Nietzsche in locating freedom at the core of human existence. We may use reason, but we are not our reason. Instead, we are what we make ourselves by our free choices. We are always and everywhere free to act and to be in whatever ways that we choose to be.

Worldview

In this section we first discuss some of the ideas about knowledge and reality that have been adopted by most existential philosophers. Next, we consider the unique elements of existentialism found in the writings of Kierkegaard and Nietzsche, especially those aspects which later influenced the worldview of Sartre. Finally, we consider Sartre's own beliefs about knowledge and reality, especially those aspects which form the basis of his concept of human nature.

The first common theme of existentialism, one that has especially to do with *knowledge,* is its denial of the supremacy of reason as the defining characteristic of human beings. Reason is no longer the key to understand human nature, either in philosophy, science, ethics, or religion. In **philosophy,** for example, both Kierkegaard and Nietzsche reject not only the idea of "rational man," but also the belief that knowledge comes primarily through reason, a belief known as rationalism. This is the view that reason is the best source of knowledge and that all reality, including human beings, can be understood through the theories constructed by philosophical reasoning. Nietzsche was especially concerned with attacking the rationalism of the ancient Greek philosophers, especially that of Plato, while Kierkegaard leveled his attack on the nineteenth century and the rationalism of Hegel.

Existential philosophers attack the abstract theories of human nature found in **science** as well, especially the materialistic conceptions of human beings that reduce them to a collection of material components. For existentialists, a scientific explanation of who we are leaves what is most important about us completely unexplained. It leaves our selves, our subjectivity, our own personal, unique conscious experience out of the real world. As we will soon see, for existentialists this subjective domain of being, what they call *human existence,* is what is most real and what must be at the center of any adequate account of human nature. Our biological selves may be adequately explained by the laws of science, but our subjective selves remain forever beyond its ability to explain.

If the theories of philosophers and scientists fail to capture the core of the reality of human beings, ethical theories fail to capture the essence of **morality.** Our moral lives are not the stuff of reason any more than our subjective selves are the stuff of abstract scientific and philosophical theories. The heart of morality is not simply to follow common rules that either come from religion or can be derived by reason from rationally accepted principles. Instead, existentialists tell us that true morality lies beyond commonly accepted religious and philosophical rules and values. True morality involves choices to live according to your own freely chosen values and ideas about right and wrong. These choices are not based upon what others tell us we ought to do or how we ought to live, but rather flow from the desires and emotions that lie at the core of our unique subjective being. We may rationalize what we do by appealing to rules and principles, but the power and direction behind true moral choice lies deep within our nonrational hearts.

Finally, the role of reason in **religion** is also rejected by existentialists. This is true both for atheistic existentialists such as Sartre and Nietzsche, and also for existentialists who are theists, such as Kierkegaard. The rejection of reason means several things. First, reason cannot prove that God exists. The traditional arguments for God's existence are rejected by existentialists. Next, the nature of God cannot be known by reason. God is not to be understood as an abstract object of thought, like an unmoved mover, a necessary being, or an absolute mind, for example. For theistic existentialists, God is not an object at all, but rather something to be experienced within, in the quiet of one's soul. It is not the external, formal trappings of religion or its intellectualization that is important. It is the spiritual development of the individual. As choosing a lover is not a matter of reason or reasoning, so is relating to God more a matter of passion and emotion than a matter of reason or reasoning.

In addition to their shared negative theme of limiting the importance of reason and theoretical knowledge in general for understanding the nature of human beings, existentialists also share at least one positive theme that defines what they consider to be the most important reality of all—**subjectivity.** For existentialists, the focus is always on the individual. Moreover, it is on what is unique about the individual, our subjectivity. While we all possess common physical, biological, and even behavioral characteristics, our true selves are to be found only in our individual, unique, subjective conscious states. This is the self that must be experienced directly to be known; it cannot be captured in an abstract concept or theory. Perhaps our public features can be described in general terms and understood in scientific theories, but our private world is known only by experience. As each song differs from all others and must be heard to be appreciated, so our subjective lives all differ and must be experienced as they are to be known.

One of the things that we experience about ourselves, perhaps the most important of all for existentialists, is our **freedom.** Existentialists focus on freedom as the chief aspect of ourselves. We experience our freedom as absolute, as not conditioned by the time or the place in which we live, or by social, economic, psychological, or even genetic forces. Most existentialists hold some form of libertarian view of freedom. They claim that we are not only free to act, but that we are free to feel and to think and to desire and even to be whatever we choose. This is the opposite of determinism, especially as it is found in science. So central an idea is freedom to an existential understanding of human nature that it may be more accurate to say that we *are* our freedom, than to say that we merely *have* it. We are free to choose our lives, even our selves. If we fail to do so, if we give up our freedom to do so, then we lead what most existentialists refer to as an *inauthentic* existence. This is a life chosen for us by other individuals and by society in general.

The Influence of Kierkegaard

While many writers and artists prior to his time possessed an existential attitude, Kierkegaard is thought by most to be the first existential philosopher. Although his philosophical writings were developed largely in the context of his religious thinking, a great deal of what he has to say is separable from his religious agenda and stands as true or false on its own. Much of what Kierkegaard has written about choice, about subjectivity, and especially about the emotions, has been highly influential for later existential philosophers, and for psychologists, as well as for religious writers. Even his discussion of our journey to God may be read as a journey to our own deeper selves. Whatever the perspective through which he is read, all of what Kierkegaard writes is framed by what he saw as his mission in life—to show apparent Christians how to be real Christians. In this sense he was like Socrates, whose mission was to question the current moral beliefs of his time, and whose attitude toward philosophy was to see it as a quest for the meaning and purpose of life.

This was an important mission for Kierkegaard because he believed that what we desire more than anything else is a close personal relationship with God. We may not be conscious of this longing, but it is within us as surely as night follows day. If we do not satisfy this desire we will never be happy. Even if we have great riches and many friends, without God in our lives we will always be restless, we will always be searching for something more to life. This is not a terribly new message; it was always part of Christian morality, for example, and surely part of the Lutheran upbringing of Kierkegaard. However, the message had been lost to many of those contemporaries of Kierkegaard who professed to be Christians. He thought that this was due primarily to their concentration on the external expressions of religion, and especially to their intellectualizing the concept of God. Following Hegel, it became fashionable to think of God as less a person and more an abstract philosophical concept. For Kierkegaard, there can be no personal relationship with a philosophical concept. His mission was to be a critic of religion, how it was thought of and how it was lived, in order to show those who thought of themselves as Christians how to be real Christians once again.

Kierkegaard is often referred to as a **fideist,** someone who believes that reason plays no role in religion, and that all is based on faith. In fact, Kierkegaard thinks that it is even a blessing that we cannot know that God exists and cannot demonstrate what his properties are through reason alone. If we could, then God would be for us an object, like a mathematical equation or a scientific law. We cannot have disinterested, objective knowledge of God if we are to have a personal, subjective connection with him. To know God on the basis of faith, on the other hand, allows for such a relationship, since it means to take what it says in scripture as true about God. It may be false, however; the New Testament may not be divinely inspired; it may just be a big hoax after all. To believe that it is not, even in the absence of evidence, is to have faith. This is faith in a personal God, the God of the Bible, not a philosophical God, the God of reason. The uncertainty associated with basing our lives on faith allows us to have passion in our relationship with God. God is not an object of knowledge, but a person, and thus an object of love.

A fulfilling relationship with God can be freely chosen by us or not. In the absence of evidence for God, we may choose to live our lives as though no God exists just as we may choose to live as though God is real. For Kierkegaard, the decision is not initially faced this starkly by most of us. Instead, as the years go by we make all sorts of choices about how to live our lives, or we allow others to do so for us, and only then work our way to God by feeling the inadequacy of these ways of living. Kierkegaard discovered what he thought of as a pattern of choosing various ways of living that most of us follow in some form or another throughout our lives. "Life's journey" was thought of by him as a struggle along this path from one point to another. He wanted to provide "signposts" along the way so that we could understand where we were in life and orient ourselves correctly. These signposts are descriptions of various "stages" of life, or "levels of existence," and include an examination of the emotions which accompany them. The journey of life is an arrational one, for Kierkegaard, and emotions are to be our primary guide.

Levels of Existence

The idea that life has stages or levels is a conceptual device that Kierkegaard uses to make sense of the variety of emotions that we encounter at different times in our lives. He does not mean that we move from one level or type of existence to another always in a forward direction. We may move back and forth between levels just as well. Nor does it mean that we exist only on one level at a time. Sometimes we can have one foot in each level, so to speak. Levels are merely abstractions to help us think more clearly about life's journey, but they are helpful abstractions. The main point is that there is more than one way to live our lives and that we can always choose to adopt any of them. We are free to be as we decide to be. However, some ways of living are more fulfilling, given our nature, than others.

We begin by observing that we all find ourselves at some point of our lives living on what Kierkegaard calls the **aesthetic** level of existence. This is the state into which we are born and in which many of us remain for our entire lives. It is marked by hedonism and self-gratification. On this level of existence we seek the momentary gratification of either gross or sophisticated pleasures. The trouble with this type of existence, however enticing it may first appear, is that even if you had all the money in the world, so that you could fly here and there and buy whatever you wanted, this constant pursuit of pleasure eventually leads to *boredom*. This is the first emotional signpost along life's way. The bored "jet-set" metaphor captures the meaning of this deep, persistent boredom, as well as its corresponding truth that the pursuit of pleasure is eventually felt as an empty pursuit. There is no meaning to such a life and there is very little freedom; it is a life of bondage to desire.

Along with the feeling of boredom comes the realization that we can choose another way to live. We now become aware of our freedom to choose how to live our lives, not just to drift along following our desires wherever they lead. We see that we can live another way and become something else. When this realization is accompanied by an awareness of our finiteness, our limited time on this earth to make up our minds, it is then that spiritual growth begins. We can recognize the beginning of this growth, which Kierkegaard identifies with personal growth, because it is accompanied by *anxiety* (*angst* in German). Anxiety is like fear, but it is fear without an object. It is felt as a fear of nothing in particular. A fear of something, like a tiger, vanishes once the object of fear is removed. Angst, however, is not so easy to eliminate, especially because it is the fear of human freedom itself.

This is a crucial insight for Kierkegaard and existentialism in general. Freedom seems to be something we value, after all. So why should it cause us anxiety? It is because freedom carries with it responsibility. If we can think of our lives as governed by others, if we allow them to make the choice for how we are to live, then we do not have to take responsibility for how we turn out. If we act out our lives in the social roles defined by others—a good girl, a good daughter, a good wife, a good nurse, a good mother, and so on, then we do not have to blame ourselves if we turn out to be unhappy, unfulfilled, unrealized. On the other hand, if we take responsibility for who we are, if we accept our freedom, then we also have to accept the responsibility for how our lives go. Because of this, angst is usually accompanied by *guilt*, the third emotional signpost, because guilt signifies the acceptance by us of our freedom. Guilt is often seen as a negative emotion, as is anxiety. But Kierkegaard tells us that both are positive ones, signs that personal development has begun—there has been a consciousness of the aesthetic mode of existence and a willingness to change and grow and become a person, an individual.

Unfortunately, such powerful emotions as anxiety and guilt drive many back to the security of the aesthetic level of existence and to the roles defined by society. Kierkegaard's works, *Fear and Trembling* and *Sickness Unto Death*, describe this return and the feelings which accompany it. The main emotion is *despair*, since we have seen our freedom and have abandoned it through fear. We know now, where once we did not, that our lives can be different and better if we have the courage to make them so. But when we flee from freedom we abandon courage; we choose instead to live an *inauthentic* existence, an existence defined by the choices of others.

If, on the other hand, we accept our freedom, the next level of existence is the **ethical** stage. On this level we choose not to be driven by desire or the expectations of others or society in general, but by a sense of duty to ourselves and to others. Here we live according to moral principles which we have chosen to accept. We freely adopt a set of rules to govern our actions and to live our lives in the way that we think that they ought to be lived. Because we have chosen our life, we now begin to become a self, to accept responsibility for who we are and what we are to become. We enter into relationships with others, such as marriage and family, and become concerned for the good of others as well as ourselves. We live the life of virtue and responsibility.

Unfortunately, while the life of virtue represents an advance over the aesthetic life, and while it is a sufficient goal for which to strive for many who write about human nature, it is an inadequate life for Kierkegaard This is because we all fail to do what we ought to do. We are just too weak to live up to our duties on our own. Since we are not capable of perfecting ourselves by our own powers, the ethical stage will always fail to fulfill us. For Kierkegaard, we may continue to try and remain steadfast in the ethical stage, with more failure and more guilt to look forward to in our future, or we may move ahead to the next level of existence where our true happiness lies.

As noble an advance as the ethical stage is over the aesthetic, it nevertheless represents for Kierkegaard merely a temporary transition to the highest level of being, the **religious** level. We reach this level of existence when we admit our weaknesses and our readiness to sin, and give ourselves over to God completely. Kierkegaard uses the biblical story of Abraham and his beloved son Isaac to illustrate this point. When God commands Abraham to kill his son as a sacrifice to him, Abraham eventually becomes willing to go beyond the demand of ethics not to kill, in order to show his complete obedience and subservience to God. In his willingness to go beyond the demands of society and even reason, in his willingness to do something that is irrational, immoral, and even absurd from the human standpoint, Abraham freely transforms himself into a creature of God. Here is the recognition that only in a personal relationship with God, one based on trust in his word, can fulfillment be found.

And so it is for us, says Kierkegaard. First we must admit our powerlessness to escape desire and to live up to the demands of duty. Next we must bind ourselves to God through faith. If we do so, then our consciousness will be rid of boredom, anxiety, despair, and guilt, and we will be truly free to be ourselves. This is because our true selves are made for a relationship with God. We are beings who are finite, yet have a longing for the infinite; we are temporal, but desire to be eternal; we are conditioned by external forces, but long to be free. A relationship with God now allows the pleasure that we seek on the aesthetic level to be achieved in its proper and meaningful perspective, as a gift from God. It also allows for the fulfilling pursuit of virtue that we sought on the ethical level, since God's forgiveness will free us from our inevitable failure to be perfect. We are partly animal and partly divine, and a full rich relationship with God allows both aspects of our nature to blossom. On the religious level of existence, we are free to live in the most fully human way, for Kierkegaard because:

> the disparate paradoxes of one's character are united into a meaningful whole. One can feel secure in one's finitude if one relates to a God who is infinite and ultimately

caring. One can accept responsibility for one's social conditioning if one has the power, granted by God, to overcome one's conditioning and to freely carve one's character in terms of one's calling. One can avoid paralysis due to one's sinful nature if there is forgiveness. One can affirm one's bodily nature, if it is ruled by one's spirit since the spirit sees to the proper satisfaction of all of one's desires. One can feel unchained from the necessities of time, if the eternal breaks into the temporal and redeems our wasted time and misspent lives. Finite and infinite, necessity and freedom, sinner and saint, body and spirit, temporal and eternal, all are kept in creative tension by faith in God.[2]

The Influence of Nietzsche

Nietzsche and Kierkegaard share many beliefs in common, such as the rejection of reason, the focus on human existence, and the need to understand human beings as creators of their own lives. Despite these common elements, there are many areas of disagreement as well, not the least of which is the atheism of Nietzsche. Before discussing why Nietzsche chose to be an atheist and what role this belief plays in his thinking, it is important to begin with an analysis of Nietzsche's moral beliefs, especially his ideas about which moral virtues ought to be pursued. Nietzsche concentrated much of his scholarly research energy on a study of Greek and Roman society, and came to admire the moral character of aristocrats. He used them as a model for understanding one type of moral character, contrasting it with the typical character of the slaves which they rule. He labeled these two types of morality, respectively, master or aristocratic morality, and slave morality.

Slave morality is the morality of the weak. It values obedience, submission, and conformity. Greek and Roman slaves hardly had a choice in the matter, of course, but Nietzsche also thought of his own German culture and all of Christian Europe as locked into a form of slave morality. Although the newly emerging nation-states often conspired to reduce all persons to the moral character of slaves, Christianity was the main source of slave morality. Christianity, for Nietzsche, is a religion of the weak. It asks us to turn the other cheek, to be meek, to be poor in spirit, to be kind to others, and to sacrifice our own interests for their good. Above all, it requires us to be obedient to the word of God, our father and supreme ruler, and to devalue things of importance in this life for the greater goods of the next life. Conformity to Christian morality was the order of the day in Nietzsche's Lutheran Germany. Those of the flock who dared to march to their own drummer were quickly labeled as evil, and their behavior was summarily suppressed.

Aristocratic morality, on the other hand, modeled on the Homeric warrior king, is the morality of the independent person, not the morality of the herd. It values this life over the next, values self-assertion over conformity, values strength over weakness, self-interest over sacrificing for others, and power over obedience. It is the morality of the future, for Nietzsche, as well as the morality of the distant past. The persons who adopt this morality in the future will be the leading warriors, statesmen, scientists, artists, and philosophers of their age, the ones who will rise above the expectations currently held for the average human being. These are people who choose to rise above the herd, the crowd, the slaves, and who choose to live life dangerously. Nietzsche calls this sort of person an **overman,** or a superman. The herd morality may serve the masses well enough, and even may be required for stability in society, but for Nietzsche there must be room for the overman to emerge as well. This is the person who creates his or her own values, who defines a new way of life that breaks from the masses and creates a new system of values that they and their followers come to adopt.

An overman was conceived of by Nietzsche as the next step in the evolution of mankind. History shows examples of such superior men, such as Alexander the Great, Napoleon, Galileo, Goethe, and Darwin, who very much influenced Nietzsche, and many others. Christ was also an overman, because he created a new way of life; he required us to love each other. Christians are mere followers of this way of life, as sheep follow the shepherd. In politics, law, the military, science, and art there needs to be room for the overman to emerge, for people to create new forms of living and experiment with them to see if they are adaptive or not. Just as nature produces variations of animals and plants and allows the fittest to survive, so allowing for the master morality would produce various new ways of life and thought, and create various ways of living, on our march of the evolution of mankind to the overman.

Unfortunately, for Nietzsche, the overman cannot emerge in the midst of Christianity. This is why Nietzsche is an atheist. If God exists and has defined the one true set of moral values, then variations from this are not allowed. As long as God is in his heaven, there is no chance for the human race to escape his domination. He is the ruler, we are the herd. We have no freedom to be as we please; only the freedom to conform to what God has decided is good or the freedom not to and thus to choose evil. Nietzsche wants to go beyond the idea of good and evil found in Christian morality. If there is no God, then Christian morality is just a man-made set of rules that may be ignored or replaced. This is why Nietzsche announces the **death of God**—to liberate the human race from the bondage of slave morality.

Nietzsche did not arrive at atheism by a process of reasoning. Although he was raised a Christian and at one time considered the ministry, he came to believe that God is simply an idea created by human beings. This idea is no longer really taken as true, Nietzsche believed, because in an age of scientific explanations for the universe, for life, and for mankind, there is no longer a need for God. The Judeo-Christian God should simply be allowed to go the way of other dead gods such as Zeus and Athena. The idea of an eternal life of bliss as payment for obedience should also be abandoned, according to Nietzsche, because there is no such life that awaits us. To help us accept this last point Nietzsche introduces a concept that is really more of a metaphor than a scientific hypothesis, his idea of the **eternal return.**

Imagine, says Nietzsche that time is infinite and various things and behaviors are finite. If this is true, then it is theoretically possible for the same situations to recur over and over again. That is, the life that you now lead you will lead again and again, eternally. Nietzsche did not so much take this concept to be true as use it to get his readers to feel that this is the only life that there is. There is no supernatural world of bliss, only this life—forever. The idea of God being in his heaven ready to accept us if we do his bidding here on earth is entirely bankrupt and should be discarded. Only this life matters, for only this life exists. If we accept the death of God and give up the belief in an afterlife, if we came to realize that God is not in his heaven, then the startling conclusions that follow are that Christian morality may now be seen as an outdated and harmful set of values and, more importantly, that human beings are now free to create themselves as they choose. Now, with the death of God, *anything goes!*

The notion that "anything goes" has been taken by many to signify that Nietzsche is a moral nihilist. **Moral nihilism** is the belief that there are no values. Just as animals have no values, so a moral nihilist believes that human beings have no values, only different ways to live, none any better or worse than another. It seems clear, however, that Nietzsche was not a moral nihilist, since he did believe that there are some moral systems such as Christianity and aristocratic morality. What he really wants to deny when he says that anything goes is **moral absolutism,** the belief that there is one set of values for all people at all times. This would be a set of values not created by human beings but rather created by God or nature and found branded into human nature itself. There is no such system of values for Nietzsche. There is no one way to live. There is no one purpose or meaning to life. In this sense, life is absurd; it is devoid of meaning; there is no "the" meaning of life. If this is so, then how can any set of values be more worthwhile and meaningful and not just different from any other?

At the heart of human nature, for Nietzsche, is not a desire to be close to God or to acquire abstract philosophical knowledge, or even to be loved or to have pleasure or meaning. Instead, deep within us is the one desire that must be fulfilled, even if it makes us unhappy to do so. This desire, this drive, this urge, Nietzsche calls the **will to power.** Nietzsche answers the question of the value of life not by identifying one particular system of values as superior to all others, but rather by identifying the creating of values itself, the mark of the overman, as the superior form of life. This is because self-creation is life itself. There is a creative life force within us all, but most strongly in the overman, that cries out for the "dangerous" life, creating the meaning and value of our own lives. It is dangerous because creating and living by new value systems means going against the crowd; and it means destroying other value systems; and it means dominating and controlling and exploiting others who follow the lead of the overman.

The will to power is the desire to create ourselves, to make our lives mean what we choose them to mean. It is the desire to take control of our own lives, to become our own masters, to be the overman for our own lives. This is our source of life, of strength, of meaning and value. If we accept this power, we throw off the yoke of living according to the values of others and begin to create ourselves as we desire. It is then that we begin to be like the gods.

The Influence of Husserl

The positive popular reception of Sartre's early writings, especially his novels and plays, was widespread and immediate. His image was of a man writing late into the night in cafes, spewing out such phrases as "man is a useless passion," "we are condemned to be free," and "human reality must be what it is not, and not be what it is," and inspiring especially the young to rebel against traditional Western conceptions of value and society. Some philosophers at first thought of his work as just an overreaction to the horrors of war and the Nazi occupation of France. Sartre, however, was a professional philosopher himself, with a highly successful academic career and a thorough knowledge of the philosophical systems in Europe which preceded him. His earlier philosophical works, *Imagination* (1936) and *The Transcendence of the Ego* (1937) sketched some of the basic ideas later to be found in his massive *Being and Nothingness* (1943), written while he was a prisoner of war. These and other works demonstrated his knowledge and acceptance of the method of doing philosophy developed by the German philosopher, Edmond Husserl. This method is called **phenomenology.** Because of his acceptance of it, at least in his revised form, Sartre is often referred to as a **phenomenological existentialist.**

It is impossible to give an accurate description of something as complex as Husserl's phenomenological method in a few sentences. However, we can get an idea of what it amounts to by considering the following points. First, Husserl accepts the starting point for philosophizing introduced by Descartes—the conscious experience of the subject, the *cogito*. He has a different notion of consciousness, however, than that of Descartes (see Chapter 5). For Husserl, consciousness is not isolated from the world, as it was for Descartes, but since every conscious act is a consciousness "of" something, it is already in the world. The term used to refer to the fact that conscious states such as perceiving, thinking, desiring, and so on are always about something beyond themselves is **intentionality.** To say that consciousness is intentional means that every *act* of conscious experience contains an *object* of experience as well. I never just think, I always think about something; I never just see, I see something; I never just desire or imagine or hope; I desire something, imagine something, and hope for something.

The things that conscious states are about should not be thought of as part of an independently existing world, but rather should be understood collectively as the phenomena of experience. This is what the phenomenologist studies, something like the phenomenal world of Kant (see Chapter 6), before it is organized by concepts. What about the source of experience? Is there something like Locke's material substances or Kant's noumenal world that causes experience? Phenomenologists ignore this question, they "bracket" it off from discussion, and instead focus on very careful descriptions of phenomena or experience itself. The source of experience, whatever that might be, cannot be experienced. Because it is the very careful descriptions of what can be experienced that is the business of phenomenology, the philosophical question of the nature of some reality external to experience is ignored.

In addition to avoiding questions about "reality," phenomenological descriptions are supposed to capture only how the world is directly experienced, not how it is understood through concepts or theories. Because of this, phenomenology does not really give us an epistemological theory, a theory of *knowledge.* This is because knowledge involves concepts, theories, and explanations, not just experience. Husserl wants to get beneath scientific and philosophical knowledge, which is always a rational reconstruction of experience, and thus a distortion of experience, to pure experience itself. This pure experience then may become the basis for a more accurate sort of knowledge, one which often requires the formation of new ideas to express what experience reveals to us.

In his later writings Husserl went beyond advocating pure description and attempted to explain the origin of experience by reference to an expanded notion of Kant's transcendental ego. Sartre, who accepted the phenomenological method of Husserl's as his own way of doing philosophy, refused to follow him in this venture and remained true to pure description. In fact, Sartre not only brackets questions of reality as the earlier Husserl had done, but comes to consider them to be meaningless. For Sartre, the only reality that it makes any sense to talk about is the reality of experience itself. What is real about any being that I experience are the common features or pattern of all the actual and possible experiences that I may have of that being.

Following the lead of Kierkegaard and Nietzsche, Sartre believes that the most important *reality* to investigate through the phenomenological method is human existence itself. What Sartre uncovers about human existence is quite different from that discovered before him by Descartes. While Sartre retains a distinction between conscious and nonconscious beings, he rejects Descartes' concept of consciousness as a mental substance. Along with this, he rejects the notion that reality is divided into two separate spheres—*res cogitans* and *res extensa*—two worlds that were forever separated for Descartes. Instead, since consciousness is intentional, it already contains the world within itself, at least the world of experience, the only world that it makes any sense to talk about for Sartre. It is not necessary to prove that the world exists through a process of reasoning, as Descartes and many of his followers attempted to do, because the world, my world, is already present in experience. If we are to take what experience says as the criterion of reality, then it tells us that wherever our consciousness is, there too is the world.

The intentionality of consciousness is one of the keys to understanding Sartre, and it bears further comment. Think of consciousness as like a magnet, with two opposing poles. These magnetic poles are just two opposing aspects of the same thing, the magnet. In the same way, an act of consciousness has two opposing poles, a subjective and an objective pole. The subjective aspect of consciousness Sartre calls Being-for-itself (*l'etre pour-soi*), while the objective aspect of consciousness is called Being-in-itself (*l'etre en-soi*). When we *think* about being conscious, when we use concepts to raise the experiential level of consciousness to the conceptual level, we separate these two aspects into self and world. When someone asks us what we are feeling, for example, we think about our feeling as an object and our selves as distinct from it as a subject. This level of consciousness Sartre calls the **reflexive** level, where we are aware of our conscious states and discuss them and our consciousness in general as objects. This is what Descartes did, and it led to the separation of self and world as two distinct sorts of substances.

On the **prereflexive** level, where I am conscious but not reflecting on being conscious, there is no distinction between self and world, and thus no need to worry about how they relate. They are never apart, so they do not have to be joined. For example, if I am thinking about going to Paris on the prereflexive level I am not aware of my "self" as doing the thinking and what I am thinking about as an object. The two are part of the same conscious experience. If my attention is drawn to my thinking, however, if someone asks me what I am thinking about, for example, then I become aware of my thoughts and my thinking as objects.

While Descartes was concerned with reflexive consciousness, Sartre is concerned only with prereflexive consciousness and what experience is like on this level. What he finds is that in prereflexive experience there is no self and no objects, just two aspects of experience that do not exist separately. On this level, consciousness is impersonal. There is no "I" that is conscious, only consciousness.

In the next section we discuss Being-for-itself, what Sartre calls "Nothingness," the main topic for our understanding of human nature. Here we say a few words about the other pole of conscious reality, **Being-in-itself.** Being-in-itself is nonconscious being. If we think of the term "absurd" as meaning "meaningless," or "without reason or purpose," Being-in-itsef is absurd. It has no meaning. It is just a block of frozen, static "thereness" with no reason or sense or intelligibility. It contains no relations, such as space and time, and has no causal origin. It is just *there.* It is not divided into types of things, nor is it invested with our general concepts, our feelings and emotions, or our desires and needs. As pure actuality, it is only what it is, not what it could be. It is static, like a block of frozen marble waiting to be carved into meaningful bits by our experience of it. This is what a careful phenomenological description reveals to us about Being-in-itself, one pole of consciousness considered apart from our experience of it.

To say that the description of Being-in-itself offered in *Being and Nothingness* is vague is an understatement. It seems that Sartre wants to posit some "blob" of matter as the stuff that our consciousness molds into our world. As such it is similar to the Kantian noumenal world. But Sartre also says that Being-in-itself is not different from the phenomena found in experience. It is perhaps best to think of it as what is discovered in our experience minus what we have placed into experience in the very process of being conscious. This, of course, makes Being-in-itself impossible to describe literally because in so doing we give it intelligibility, and thus make it an object of experience. Perhaps a better way for Sartre to describe Being-in-itself is found in his novel, *Nausea.* The hero, Roquentin, becomes nauseous when he intuits Being-in-itself one day, as he stares at a tree in the park. The dramatic description of this experience by Sartre is intended to get the reader to *feel* the presence of Being-in-itself, more than to understand what it is. Roquentin says:[3]

> Existence everywhere, infinitely, in excess, for ever and everywhere; existence—
> which is limited only by existence. I sank down on the bench, stupefied stunned by
> this profusion of beings without origin: everywhere blossomings, hatchings out, my
> ears buzzed with existence, my very flesh throbbed and opened, abandoned itself to
> the universal burgeoning. It was repugnant. But why, I thought, why so many
> existences. . . . That abundance did not give the effect of generosity, just the opposite.
> It was dismal, ailing, embarrassed at itself. . . . Every existing thing is born without a
> reason, prolongs itself out of weakness and dies by chance. I leaned back and closed
> my eyes. But the images, forewarned, immediately leaped up and filled my closed
> eyes with existences: existence is a fullness which man can never abandon.

The final element of the worldview of Sartre discussed here is his atheism. Following Nietzsche, Sartre accepts atheism and then explores what life is like without God in the world. In fact, in his popular essay on existentialism, *Existentialism is a Humanism* (1946), he says that existentialism is simply "an attempt to draw the full conclusions from a consistently atheistic position." One of the most crucial of these conclusions is, as it was for Nietzsche, that if there is no God, then man is free. For Nietzsche we are free to create ourselves according to our choices; for Sartre this is also true but even more radically—we are our freedom right down to the very center of our being.

Human Nature

In discussing the *structure* of human nature, Sartre agrees with everyone else that there is a physical and biological structure shared by human beings. He does not agree that human nature is reducible to a Cartesian self, however. Descartes identified consciousness with this self and called it a mind, a thing which thinks. Sartre agrees that there is such a thing, but that this "thing" is a product of our reflexive consciousness. It is our consciousness or mind considered as an object of thought. It is consciousness as it thinks about itself, and thus makes an object of itself. Sartre finds the structure of human nature on a deeper level of consciousness than this, on the level of prereflexive consciousness, where there is no distinction in experience between self and world. On this level there is just an impersonal consciousness of things, not an "I" that is conscious of objects. In fact, on the prereflexive level of consciousness there is no self at all.

The Cartesian self for Sartre is not where our true nature is to be found because it is not the true human subject. Our true subjectivity, and the main area of interest for existentialists, is rather to be found on the prereflexive level of consciousness. In fact, Sartre believes that our Cartesian self, our self as we think of it and identify with "I" or "me," is constructed by us mainly to cover up this true nature. How and why we do this requires some explanation. First, "constructed" here means "thought of" or made into an object. Just as I can think of the "average man" as a convenient way to refer to a collection of statistical data about lots of individuals, so I can think of my self as the unity of a collection of conscious states—the being that thinks, imagines, desires, hopes, and so on. In so doing I objectify my self, I think of my self as a mental *substance*, something with permanence and stability that abides through all the changes that my consciousness goes through. But why would I and everyone else who believes in a self do this? Why would we need to deceive ourselves, to cover up the truth about ourselves? The answer lies in Sartre's explanation of our true subjectivity, Being-for-itself, and the fear that we have of facing this reality. This is what the concept of a "self" helps us to avoid.

To understand Sartre's concept of **Being-for-itself** it is helpful to recall his definition of human existence: *existence precedes essence*. Most things that we experience are things, they are certain types of being, they have an essence. A triangle, for example, is a certain kind of thing. Its essence is to have three sides and three angles. Triangles exist only as three sided and three angled figures. What they are, like the past, is fixed and frozen. Triangles cannot become something other than they are, they cannot become something else. They just are what they are. If God exists, and if God created individuals according to a set of ideas of which individual essences are a reflection, then all beings are certain kinds of beings. If God exists, even human beings are certain kinds of beings. We have a certain nature with a specific structure and inborn desires to achieve an ideal version of that essence.

In the absence of God, however, and with no plan of creation to conform to, human beings may be viewed as beings whose existence precedes their essence. This means that we find ourselves existing first and then become certain sorts of things. Apart from our physical and biological type, we are not born a certain sort of something. We are instead, as Nietzsche said earlier, only the *possibility* of becoming something. As pure possibility, we are freedom itself. In fact, for Sartre there is no human nature, no way for all human beings to be. There is only the human condition—which is pure freedom. We literally start out as nothing. We become what we do, from all the limitless possibilities that exist, by our own choices. This is why we create a stable self, an ego, a fixed essence of ourselves; to cover up the emptiness, the nothingness, the dread, the anxiety and insecurity that Kierkegaard said we will encounter once we recognize ourselves as we truly are.

"Being-for-itself" names the human condition of nothingness. The human condition is that we are no-thing (no particular sort of thing), and we are nothing-ers, and that we are pure freedom. Each of these meanings of "nothing" requires further elaboration. First, to say that we are *no-thing* means that our subjectivity is not any particular sort of object, such as a stable, abiding self. Instead, it is one pole of the impersonal consciousness found on the prereflexive level. Next, the function of subjectivity, and thus the root of the human condition, is to "nothing" Being-in-itself, and thus makes it the objective pole of consciousness, collectively referred to as my world of experience. To be a "nothinger," for Sartre thus means something positive. It means that I create the meaning and structure of my world of experience. Meaning is created by dividing up the static *en-soi* into substances with properties and relationships such as space, time, and causality—much as Kant had said. It is this separation of Being into meaningful parts, each now different from the other, that Sartre refers to as the "nothing-ing" function of the *pour-soi*. It is the insertion of emptiness and divisions and otherness into the absurd solid block of Being-in-itself, thereby making it meaningful. Being-for-itself also separates Being-in-itself from consciousness, becoming aware of its own subjectivity and its own ego by contrast with the world of objects.

In addition to creating a world of intelligible objects and a self, human subjectivity also inserts into Being its own wants, needs, and emotions. If I see a piece of pie and want it because I am hungry, it takes on a different meaning for me than it would have if I was an artist who wanted to paint it, or if it reminded me of my dear departed mother's pie and made me feel sad. Our whole world of experience is colored by our desires and emotions and needs. These also are a nothing-ing of Being, since the perspective we take rules out all other possible ones. It is important to note that for Sartre our emotions and the way we respond to needs and wants are not inevitable. Contrary to popular belief, we can help feeling what we do and can control our wants and needs. This is because nothing determines how we are in the world and how we react to it, except ourselves. There is no determinism for Sartre, only freedom so radical that it applies even to our feelings and desires.

Freedom is the third meaning of "nothing," and the one which brings us to the center of the human condition. To say that we are free, for Sartre, is not merely to adopt some theory of the will, such as libertarianism. Freedom is deeper than that; freedom is something that we are. Human beings are "condemned to be free," says Sartre. There is no escaping freedom because we are freedom. Our past may be defined, as an object is defined. We may be a certain sort of being with a certain type of character thus far in life. But at every instant of the present and future we are nothing but pure possibility. There is always a choice in every situation to become something quite different from how we have been in the past. There is always a choice in how to see or how to understand or how to act. There is never an excuse that I could or could not do something because of how I was raised, or because of my genetic background, or because I was depressed or sad or otherwise psychologically impaired, or because of my character, for example. I can always resist the pressure of external forces. I *always* have a choice to do or to feel or to desire something else, or to take another perspective, or to accept another interpretation of the facts before me. Like a blank slate, I am capable of becoming any number of things, taking on any number of projects, living in any number of ways. Even in the direst of circumstances, when all choice seems absent, I always retain the choice to end my life. We cannot escape our freedom because it is the human condition.

Consequences

Ethics

In discussing the consequences of Sartre's views on human nature we will skip a discussion of freedom and God, since these topics have been addressed sufficiently already. Instead we will concentrate first on ethical matters. Sartre developed no ethical system as such. He had no general principles or moral rules to determine right from wrong, and he rejected the view that there is one best way to live. Like Nietzsche, he thought that there were many systems of value that may be freely adopted, and thus many ways to live. Unlike Nietzsche, however, Sartre believed that everyone, not just the overman, may, even must, choose their own ways of living, their own projects. While this seems to mean that Sartre believed that any way of living is as good as any other, and he surely has been accused of this type of relativism, the matter is not as simple as this. For Sartre, though there is not any one correct way to live, there are qualities of living that are to be admired and encouraged. Chief among these is **authenticity.**

The problem with absolute freedom, as Kierkegaard pointed out so forcefully, lies with our unwillingness to accept the responsibility for our lives that falls squarely on our own shoulders. We cannot take refuge in determinisms of various sorts, saying that someone or something or some circumstances made us live our lives as we do. Responsibility often frightens us beyond our ability to bear it, producing anxiety, as Kierkegaard says it, and **anguish** as Sartre says it. Anguish is not our constant companion, but it does show itself when we have to make important decisions about how to be or what to do. It is at times like these that we are most conscious of our freedom. In these kinds of circumstances, such as changing careers or ending important relationships, for example, we often recognize that we are much freer than we usually think. This is when anguish shows itself and often produces attempts on our part to escape the responsibility for our freedom. To do this, to abandon our freedom, is to live in **bad faith**—a form of self-deception. Someone living in bad faith attempts to pass off the responsibility for their choices and their lives on others.

They might simply adopt a way of life that others expect of them, for example, acting out the social roles of a good son, a loyal husband, an efficient waiter, and so on, as if that is essentially what they are. There is security in this, in being a some-thing, an essence. It is more comfortable than being a pure possibility. We all long for being some thing, some specific type. But only objects can be specific sorts of things, so that being some *thing* means that you are no longer conscious. Since we do not want to lose our consciousness, this means that what we really want is to be a thing, to have the fullness and security of being, and still be a subject. In other words, we want to be Being-in-itself-for-itself, a conscious being who contains all reality. For Sartre, this is clearly a contradiction. It is also a good definition of God, which is why he believes that the idea of God is a contradiction. Because we have this desire, nonetheless, is why Sartre says that "man is a useless passion."

In the end the identification of yourself with being, especially with roles defined by others, is itself a choice. Freedom and the responsibility for one's life cannot be avoided. We are "condemned to be free," as he puts it. Living in good faith, or authentically, is deliberately choosing who you are going to become and accepting the responsibility for these choices with no excuses. As with most existentialists, Sartre believes that the point of philosophy is to make a difference in our lives. The main difference that his teachings make is that they encourage us to accept our freedom in every area of thought and deed. If Sartre favors any ideal way of living it is this one: whatever it is that you choose to make of your life, live it authentically. These themes are discussed by Sartre in *Reading 1.*

Society

Sartre spent most of his time and energy discussing the individual, not society. When he did discuss society in his later years, the central issue for him was still freedom. Now it was how the freedom of an individual was to be balanced against the freedom of other individuals and against the authority of the state. Much of what he had to say was an adaptation of Marxist theory, and focused on disclosing the hidden social and economic sources or obstacles to freedom.

Perhaps one of the more interesting and innovative things that Sartre had to say about how the individual relates to others had to do not so much with social structures themselves, but rather with a more fundamental issue, how we know that others exist at all. This was a problem Sartre inherited from Descartes, which he never really solved. For Descartes the issue was that we could see the bodies of others but not their minds. If we cannot experience their minds, neither can we infer that they have minds on the basis of their behavior. For all we know, others might be like robots with no inner conscious life. Sartre's method restricted him to the data of prereflexive experience. This shows the existence of his own subjectivity and of the objects of experience. It even shows the existence of other humans as objects. But where does it show the existence of others as *subjects*? How do we experience them as subjects, and thus know that others exist at all?

Sartre discusses this issue in part three of *Being and Nothingness,* called "Being-for-others" (see *Reading 2*). His view, briefly stated, is that we become aware of the subjectivity of others when we experience ourselves as an object under their gaze. For example, if someone sees us doing something that we are ashamed of, this feeling of shame is an experience of ourselves as an object. We can only be an object in the presence of another subject. If I was spying on someone, peeking in their window while they undressed, for example, I would not feel ashamed if a bird or a tree or a rock were present. These are objects; they are part of my world; they have no power to alter my subjectivity. If another person sees me, however, I am ashamed. By their "look" I am objectified, made an object in their world of experience. Thus when I experience myself as an object I am aware of the subjectivity of the other. In this way do I know that other subjects exist.

Gender

For some fifty years of his life, Sartre was friend, companion, and lover of Simone de Beauvoir (1908–1986). Beauvoir was an existential philosopher of some note herself, adopting many of the theories of Sartre, some of which she no doubt inspired. More importantly, however, was her contribution to feminism and the liberation of women. The impact of her famous work, *The Second Sex* (1949), a selection from which is reprinted here (see *Reading 3*), was widespread and profound. In it she demonstrated that gender differences, and especially the feelings of inferiority that many women have, were learned attitudes, not inherited. Adopting the existential view that we have no nature but are what we choose to become, she argued against the prevailing view that women could not fill social and political roles on a par with men. Beauvoir would surely not have been a close companion of Sartre's if he was a sexist, and there is no evidence in his writings that he was anything but a believer in the equality of males and females.

Readings

1. The Authentic Life

FREEDOM AND ANGUISH

. . . MAN DOES NOT EXIST FIRST in order to be free *subsequently*; there is no difference between the being of man and his *being-free*. . . .

If freedom is the being of consciousness, consciousness ought to exist as a consciousness of freedom. What form does this consciousness of freedom assume? In freedom the human being is his own past (as also his own future) in the form of nihilation. If our analysis has not led us astray, there ought to exist for the human being, in so far as he is conscious of being, a certain mode of standing opposite his past and his future, as being both this past and this future and as not being them. We shall be able to furnish an immediate reply to this question; it is in anguish that man gets the consciousness of his freedom, or if you prefer, anguish is the mode of being of freedom as consciousness of being; it is in anguish that freedom is, in its being, in question for itself.

From parts 1 and 2 of Jean-Paul Sartre, Being and Nothingness, *trans. by Hazel Barnes (New York: Washington Square Press, 1966), pp. 272–289. Reprinted with permission from Philosophical Library, New York.*

Kierkegaard describing anguish in the face of what one lacks characterizes it as anguish in the face of freedom. But Heidegger, whom we know to have been greatly influenced by Kierkegaard, considers anguish instead as the apprehension of nothingness. These two descriptions of anguish do not appear to us contradictory; on the contrary the one implies the other.

First we must acknowledge that Kierkegaard is right; anguish is distinguished from fear in that fear is fear of beings in the world whereas anguish is anguish before myself. Vertigo is anguish to the extent that I am afraid not of falling over the precipice, but of throwing myself over. A situation provokes fear if there is a possibility of my life being changed from without; my being provokes anguish to the extent that I distrust myself and my own reactions in that situation. The artillery preparation which precedes the attack can provoke fear in the soldier who undergoes the bombardment, but anguish is born in him when he tries to foresee the conduct with which he will face the bombardment, when he asks himself if he is going to be able to "hold up." Similarly the recruit who reports for active duty at the beginning of the war can in some instances be afraid of death but more often he is "afraid of being afraid"; that is, he is filled with anguish before himself. Most of the time dangerous or threatening situations present themselves in facets; they will be apprehended through a feeling of fear or anguish according to whether we envisage the situation as acting on the man or the man as acting on the situation. The man who has just received a hard blow—for example, losing a great part of his wealth in a crash—can have the fear of threatening poverty. He will experience anguish a moment later when nervously wringing his hands (a symbolic reaction to the action which is imposed but which remains still wholly undetermined), he exclaims to himself; "What am I going to do? But what am I going to do?" In this sense fear and anguish are exclusive of one another since fear is unreflective apprehension of the transcendent and anguish is reflective apprehension of the self; the one is born in the destruction of the other. The normal process in the case which I have just cited is a constant transition from the one to the other. But

there exist also situations where anguish appears pure; that is, without ever being preceded or followed by fear. If, for example, I have been raised to a new dignity and charged with a delicate and flattering mission, I can feel anguish at the thought that I will not be capable perhaps of fulfilling it, and yet I will not have the least fear in the world of the consequences of my possible failure.

What is the meaning of anguish in the various examples which I have just given? Let us take up again the example of vertigo. Vertigo announces itself through fear: I am on a narrow path—without a guard-rail—which goes along a precipice. The precipice presents itself to me as *to be avoided*; it represents a danger of death. At the same time I conceive of a certain number of causes, originating in universal determinism, which can transform that threat of death into reality; I can slip on a stone and fall into the abyss; the crumbling earth of the path can give way under my steps. Through these various anticipations, I am given to myself as a thing; I am passive in relation to these possibilities; they come to me from without; in so far as I am also an object in the world, subject to gravitation, they are my possibilities. At this moment *fear* appears, which in terms of the situation is the apprehension of myself as a destructible transcendent in the midst of transcendents, as an object which does not contain in itself the origin of its future disappearance. My reaction will be of the reflective order: I will pay attention to the stones in the road; I will keep myself as far as possible from the edge of the path. I realize myself as pushing away the threatening situation with all my strength, and I project before myself a certain number of future conducts destined to keep the threats of the world at a distance from me. These conducts are *my* possibilities. I escape fear by the very fact that I am placing myself on a plane where *my own* possibilities are substituted for the transcendent probabilities where human action had no place.

But these conducts, precisely because they are my possibilities, do not appear to me as determined by foreign causes. Not only is it not strictly certain that they will be effective; in particular it is not strictly certain that they will be adopted, for they do not have existence sufficient in itself. We could say, varying the expression of Berkeley, that their "being is a sustained-being" and that their "possibility of being is only an ought-to-be-sustained." Due to this fact their possibility has as a necessary condition the possibility of negative conduct (*not* to pay attention to the stones in the road, to run, to think of something else) and the possibility of the opposite conduct (to throw myself over the precipice). The possibility which I make *my* concrete possibility can appear as my possibility only by raising itself on the basis of the totality of the logical possibilities which the situation allows. But these rejected possibles in turn have no other being then their "sustained-being"; it is I who sustain them in being, and inversely, their present non-being is an "ought-not-to-be-sustained." No external cause will remove them. I alone am the permanent source of their non-being, I engage myself in them; in order to cause *my* possibility to appear, I posit the other possibilities so as to nihilate them. This would not produce anguish if I could apprehend myself in my relations with these possibles as a cause of producing its effects. In this case the effect defined as my possibility *would be strictly* determined. But then it would cease to be *possible;* it would become simply "about-to-happen." If then I wished to avoid anguish and vertigo, it would be enough if I were to consider the motives (instinct of self-preservation, prior fear, etc.), which make me reject the situation envisaged, as *determining* my prior activity in the same way that the presence at a determined point of one given mass determines the courses followed by other masses; it would be necessary, in other words, that I apprehend in myself a strict psychological determinism. But I am in anguish precisely because any conduct on my part is only *possible,* and this means that while constituting a totality of motives *for* pushing away that situation, I at the same moment apprehend these motives as not sufficiently effective. At the very moment when I apprehend my being as *horror* of the precipice, I am conscious of that horror as *not determinant* in relation to my possible conduct. In one sense that horror calls for prudent conduct, and it is in itself a pre-outline of that conduct; in another sense, it posits the final developments of that conduct only

as possible, precisely because I do not apprehend it as the cause of these final developments but as need, appeal, etc.

Now as we have seen, consciousness of being is the being of consciousness. There is no question here of a contemplation which I could make after the event, of an horror already constituted; it is the very being of horror to appear to itself as "not being the cause" of the conduct it calls for. In short, to avoid fear, which reveals to me a transcendent future strictly determined, I take refuge in reflection, but the latter has only an undetermined future to offer. This means that in establishing a certain conduct as a possibility and precisely because it is *my* possibility, I am aware that *nothing* can compel me to adopt that conduct. Yet I am indeed already there in the future; it is for the sake of that being which I will be there at the turning of the path that I now exert all my strength, and in this sense there is already a relation between my future being and my present being. But a nothingness has slipped into the heart of this relation; I *am* not the self which I will be. First I am not that self because time separates me from it. Secondly, I am not that self because what I am is not the foundation of what I will be. Finally I am not that self because no actual existent can determine strictly what I am going to be. Yet as I am already what I will be (otherwise I would not be interested in any one being more than another), *I am the self which I will be, in the mode of not being it.* It is through my horror that I am carried toward the future, and the horror nihilates itself in that it constitutes the future as possible. Anguish is precisely my consciousness of being my own future, in the mode of not-being. To be exact, the nihilation of horror as a *motive,* which has the effect of reinforcing horror as a *state,* has as its positive counterpart the appearance of other forms of conduct (in particular that which consists in throwing myself over the precipice) as *my* possible *possibilities.* If *nothing* compels me to save my life, *nothing* prevents me from precipitating myself into the abyss. The decisive conduct will emanate from a self which I am not yet. Thus the self which I am depends on the self which I am not yet to the exact extent that the self which I am not yet does not depend on the self which I am. Vertigo appears as the apprehension of this dependence. I approach the precipice, and my scrutiny is searching for myself in my very depths. In terms of this moment, I play with my possibilities. My eyes, running over the abyss from top to bottom, imitate the possible fall and realize it symbolically; at the same time suicide, from the fact that it becomes a *possibility* possible for *me*, now causes to appear possible motives for adopting it (suicide would cause anguish to cease). Fortunately these motives in their turn, from the sole fact that they are motives of a possibility, present themselves as ineffective, as non-determinant; they can no more *produce* the suicide than my horror of the fall can *determine me* to avoid it. It is this counter-anguish which generally puts an end to anguish by transmuting it into indecision. Indecision in its turn, calls for decision. I abruptly put myself at a distance from the edge of the precipice and resume my way.

The example which we have just analyzed has shown us what we could call "anguish in the face of the future." There exists another: anguish in the face of the past. It is that of the gambler who has freely and sincerely decided not to gamble any more and who when he approaches the gaming table, suddenly sees all his resolutions melt away. This phenomenon has often been described as if the sight of the gaming table reawakened in us a tendency which entered into conflict with our former resolution and ended by drawing us in spite of this. Aside from the fact that such a description is done in materialistic terms and peoples the mind with opposing forces (there is, for example, the moralists' famous "struggle of reason with the passions"), it does not account for the facts. In reality—the letters of Dostoevsky bear witness—there is nothing in us which resembles an inner debate as if we had to weigh motives and incentives before deciding. The earlier resolution of "not playing anymore" is always there, and in the majority of cases the gambler when in the presence of the gaming table, turns toward it as if to ask it for help; for he does not wish to play, or rather having taken his resolution the day before, he thinks of himself still as not wanting to play anymore; he believes in the effectiveness of this

resolution. But what he apprehends then in anguish is precisely the total inefficacy of the past resolution. It is there doubtless but fixed, ineffectual, surpassed by the very fact that I am conscious of it. The resolution is still *me* to the extent that I realize constantly my identity with myself across the temporal flux, but it is no longer me—due to the fact that it has become an object for my consciousness. I am not subject to it, it fails in the mission which I have given it. The resolution is there still, I am it in the mode of not-being. What the gambler apprehends at this instant is again the permanent rupture in determinism; it is nothingness which separates him from himself; I should have liked so much not to gamble anymore; yesterday I even had a synthetic apprehension of the situation (threatening ruin, disappointment of my relatives) as *forbidding me* to play. It seemed to me that I had established a *real barrier* between gambling and myself, and now I suddenly perceive that my former understanding of the situation is no more than a memory of an idea, a memory of a feeling. In order for it to come to my aid once more, I must remake it *ex nihilo* and freely. The not-gambling is only one of my possibilities, as the fact of gambling is another of them, neither more nor less. I *must rediscover* the fear of financial ruin or of disappointing my family, etc., I must re-create it as experienced fear. It stands behind me like a boneless phantom. It depends on me alone to lend it flesh. I am alone and naked before temptation as I was the day before. After having patiently built up barriers and walls, after enclosing myself in the magic circle of a resolution, I perceive with anguish that *nothing* prevents me from gambling. The anguish *is me* since by the very fact of taking my position in existence as consciousness of being I make myself *not to be* the past good resolutions which *I am*.

It would be in vain to object that the sole condition of this anguish is ignorance of the underlying psychological determinism. According to such a view my anxiety would come from lack of knowing the real and effective incentives which in the darkness of the unconscious determine my action. In reply we shall point out first that anguish has not appeared to us as a *proof* of human freedom;

the latter was given to us as the necessary condition for the question. We wished only to show that there exists a specific consciousness of freedom, and we wished to show that this consciousness is anguish. This means that we wished to established anguish in its essential structure as consciousness of freedom. Now from this point of view the existence of a psychological determinism could not invalidate the results of our description. Either indeed anguish is actually an unrealized ignorance of this determinism—and than anguish apprehends itself in fact as freedom—or else one may claim that anguish is consciousness of being ignorant of the real causes of our acts. In the latter case anguish would come from that of which we have a presentiment, a screen deep within ourselves for monstrous motives which would suddenly release guilty acts. But in this case we should be to ourselves as *things in the world;* we should be to ourselves our own transcendent situation. Then anguish would disappear to give away to *fear,* for fear is a synthetic apprehension of the transcendent as dreadful. . . .

FREEDOM AND VALUES

Now at each instant we are thrust into the world and engaged there. This means that we act before positing our possibilities and that these possibilities which are disclosed as realized or in process of being realized refer to meanings which necessitate special acts in order to be put into question. The alarm which rings in the morning refers to the possibility of my going to work, which is *my* possibility. But to apprehend the summons of the alarm as a summons is to get up. Therefore the very act of getting up is reassuring, for it eludes the question, "Is work *my* possibility?" Consequently it does not put me in a position to apprehend the possibility of quietism, of refusing to work, and finally the possibility of refusing the world and the possibility of death. In short, to the extent that I apprehend the meaning of the ringing, I am already up at its summons; this apprehension guarantees me against the anguished intuition that it is I who confer on the alarm clock its exigency—I and I alone.

In the same way, what we might call everyday morality is exclusive of ethical anguish. There is ethical anguish when I consider myself in my original relation to values. Values in actuality are demands which lay claim to a foundation. But this foundation can in no way be *being,* for every value which would base its ideal nature on its being would thereby cease even to be a value and would realize the heteronomy of my will. Value derives its being from its exigency and not its exigency from its being. It does not deliver itself to a contemplative intuition which would apprehend it as *being* value and thereby would remove from it its right over my freedom. On the contrary, it can be revealed only to an active freedom which makes it exist as value by the sole fact of recognizing it as such. It follows that my freedom is the unique foundation of values and that *nothing,* absolutely nothing, justifies me in adopting this or that particular value, this or that particular scale of values. As a being by whom values exist, I am unjustifiable. My freedom is anguished at being the foundation of values while itself without foundation. It is anguished in addition because values, due to the fact that they are essentially revealed to a freedom, can not disclose themselves without being at the same time "put into question," for the possibility of overturning the scale of values appears complementarily as *my* possibility. It is anguish before values which is the recognition of the ideality of values.

Ordinarily, however, my attitude with respect to values is eminently reassuring. In fact I am engaged in a world of values. The anguished apperception of values as sustained in being by my freedom is a secondary and mediated phenomenon. The immediate is the world with its urgency; and in this world where I engage myself, my acts cause values to spring up like partridges. My indignation has given to me the negative value "baseness," my admiration has given the positive value "grandeur." Above all my obedience to a multitude of tabus, which is real, reveals these tabus to me as existing in fact. The bourgeois who call themselves "respectable citizens" do not become respectable as the result of contemplating moral values. Rather from the moment of their arising in the world they are thrown into a pattern of behavior the meaning of which is respectability. Thus respectability acquires a being; it is not put into question. Values are sown on my path as thousands of little real demands, like the signs which order us to keep off the grass.

Thus in what we shall call the world of the immediate, which delivers itself to our unreflective consciousness, we do not first appear to ourselves, to be thrown subsequently into enterprises. Our being is immediately "in situation"; that is, it arises in enterprises and knows itself first in so far as it is reflected in those enterprises. We discover ourselves then in a world peopled with demands, in the heart of projects "in the course of realization." I write. I am going to smoke. I have an appointment this evening with Pierre. I must not forget to reply to Simon. I do not have the right to conceal the truth any longer from Claude. All these trivial passive expectations of the real, all these commonplace, everyday values, derive their meaning from an original projection of myself which stands as my choice of myself in the world. But to be exact, this projection of myself toward an original possibility, which causes the existence of values, appeals, expectations, and in general a world, appears to me only beyond the world as the meaning and the abstract, logical signification of my enterprises. For the rest, there exist concretely alarm clocks, signboards, tax forms, policemen, so many guard rails against anguish. But as soon as the enterprise is held at a distance from me, as soon as I am referred to myself because I must await myself in the future, then I discover myself suddenly as the one who gives its meaning to the alarm clock, the one who by a signboard forbids himself to walk on a flower bed or on the lawn, the one from whom the boss's order borrows its urgency, the one who decides the interest of the book which he is writing, the one finally who makes the values exist in order to determine his action by their demands. I emerge alone and in anguish confronting the unique and original project which constitutes my being; all the barriers, all the guard rails collapse, nihilated by the consciousness of my freedom. I do not have nor can I have recourse to any value against the fact that it is I who sustain values in being. Nothing can ensure me against myself, cut off from the world and from my essence by this nothingness which I am. I have to realize the meaning of the world and the essence; I make my decision concerning them—without justification and without excuse. . . .

BAD FAITH: THE DENIAL OF FREEDOM

The human being is not only the being by whom *négatités* are disclosed in the world; he is also the one who can take negative attitudes with respect to himself. We defined consciousness as "a being such that in its being, its being is in question in so far as this being implies a being other than itself." But now that we have examined the meaning of "the question," we can at present also write the formula thus: "Consciousness is a being, the nature of which is to be conscious of the nothingness of its being." In a prohibition or a veto, for example, the human being denies a future transcendence. But his negation is not explicative. My consciousness is not restricted to *envisioning a négatité*. It constitutes itself in its own flesh as the nihilation of a possibility which another human reality projects as its possibility. For that reason it must arise in the world as a *Not*; it is as a Not that the slave first apprehends the master, or that the prisoner who is trying to escape sees the guard who is watching him. There are even men (for example, caretakers, overseers, gaolers,) whose social reality is uniquely that of the Not, who will live and die, having forever been only a Not upon the earth. Others so as to make the Not a part of their very subjectivity, establish their human personality as a perpetual negation. This is the meaning and function of what Scheler calls "the man of resentment"—in reality, the Not. But there exist more subtle behaviors, the description of which will lead us further into the inwardness of consciousness. Irony is one of these. In irony a man annihilates what he posits within one and the same act; he leads us to believe in order not to be believed; he affirms to deny and denies to affirm; he creates a positive object but it has no being other than its nothingness. Thus attitudes of negation toward the self permit us to raise a new question: What are we to say is the being of man who has the possibility of denying himself? But it is out of the question to discuss the attitude of "self-negation" in its universality. The kinds of behavior which can be ranked under this heading are too diverse; we risk retaining only the abstract form of them. It is best to choose and to examine one determined attitude which is essential to human reality and which is such that consciousness instead of directing its negation outward turns it toward itself. This attitude, it seems to me, is *bad faith (mauvaise foi)*.

Frequently this is identified with falsehood. We say indifferently of a person that he shows signs of bad faith or that he lies to himself. We shall willingly grant that bad faith is a lie to oneself, on condition that we distinguish the lie to oneself from lying in general. Lying is a negative attitude, we will agree to that. But this negation does not bear on consciousness itself; it aims only at the transcendent. The essence of the lie implies in fact that the liar actually is in complete possession of the truth which he is hiding. A man does not lie about what he is ignorant of; he does not lie when he spreads an error of which he himself is the dupe; he does not lie when he is mistaken. . . .

The situation can not be the same for bad faith if this, as we have said, is indeed a lie to oneself. To be sure, the one who practices bad faith is hiding a displeasing truth or presenting as truth a pleasing untruth. Bad faith then has in appearance the structure of falsehood. Only what changes everything is the fact that in bad faith it is from myself that I am hiding the truth. Thus the duality of the deceiver and the deceived does not exist here. Bad faith on the contrary implies in essence the unity of a single consciousness. . . .

Take the example of a woman who has consented to go out with a particular man for the first time. She knows very well the intentions which the man who is speaking to her cherishes regarding her. She knows also that it will be necessary sooner or later for her to make a decision. But she does not want to realize the urgency; she concerns herself only with what is respectful and discreet in the attitude of her companion. She does not apprehend this conduct as an attempt to achieve what

we call "the first approach"; that is, she does not want to see possibilities of temporal development which his conduct presents. She restricts this behavior to what is in the present; she does not wish to read in the phrases which he addresses to her anything other than their explicit meaning. If he says to her, "I find you so attractive!" she disarms this phrase of its sexual background; she attaches to the conversation and to the behavior of the speaker, the immediate meanings, which she imagines as objective qualities. The man who is speaking to her appears to her sincere and respectful as the table is round or square, as the wall coloring is blue or gray. The qualities thus attached to the person she is listening to are in this way fixed in a permanence like that of things, which is no other than the projection of the strict present of the qualities into the temporal flux. This is because she does not quite know what she wants. She is profoundly aware of the desire which she inspires, but the desire cruel and naked would humiliate and horrify her. Yet she would find no charm in a respect which would be only respect. In order to satisfy her, there must be a feeling which is addressed wholly to her *personality*—that is, to her full freedom—and which would be a recognition of her freedom. But at the same time this feeling must be wholly desire; that is, it must address itself to her body as object. This time then she refuses to apprehend the desire for what it is; she does not even give it a name; she recognizes it only to the extent that it transcends itself toward admiration, esteem, respect and that it is wholly absorbed in the more refined forms which it produces, to the extent of no longer figuring anymore as a sort of warmth and density. But then suppose he takes her hand. This act of her companion risks changing the situation by calling for an immediate decision. To leave the hand there is to consent in herself to flirt, to engage herself. To withdraw it is to break the troubled and unstable harmony which gives the hour its charm. The aim is to postpone the moment of decision as long as possible. We know what happens next; the young woman leaves her hand there, but she *does not notice* that she is leaving it. She does not notice because it happens by chance that she is at this moment all intellect. She draws her companion up to the most lofty regions of sentimental speculation; she speaks of Life, of her life, she shows herself in her essential aspect—a personality, a consciousness. And during this time the divorce of the body from the soul is accomplished; the hand rests inert between the warm hands of her companion—neither consenting nor resisting—a thing.

We shall say that this woman is in bad faith. But we see immediately that she uses various procedures in order to maintain herself in this bad faith. She has disarmed the actions of her companion by reducing them to being only what they are; that is, to existing in the mode of the in-itself. But she permits herself to enjoy his desire, to the extent that she will apprehend it as not being what it is, will recognize its transcendence. Finally while sensing profoundly the presence of her own body—to the degree of being disturbed perhaps— she realizes herself as *not being* her own body, and she contemplates it as though from above as a passive object to which events can *happen* but which can neither provoke them nor avoid them because all its possibilities are outside of it. What unity do we find in these various aspects of bad faith? It is a certain art of forming contradictory concepts which unite in themselves both an idea and the negation of that idea. . . .

. . . The basic concept which is thus engendered, utilizes the double property of the human being, who is at once a *facticity* and a *transcendence*. These two aspects of human reality are and ought to be capable of a valid coordination. But bad faith does not wish either to coordinate them nor to surmount them in a synthesis. Bad faith seeks to affirm their identity while preserving their difference. It must affirm facticity as *being* transcendence and transcendence as *being* facticity, in such a way that at the instant when a person apprehends the one he can find himself abruptly faced with the other. . . .

. . . If man is what he is, bad faith is forever impossible and candor ceases to be his ideal and becomes instead his being. But is man what he is? And more generally, how can he *be* what he is when he exists as consciousness of being? If candor or sincerity is a universal value, it is evident that

the maxim "one must be what one is" does not serve solely as a regulating principle for judgments and concepts by which I express what I am. It posits not merely an ideal of knowing but an ideal of *being*; it proposes for us an absolute equivalence of being with itself as a prototype of being. In this sense it is necessary that we *make ourselves* what we are. But what *are we* then if we have the constant obligation to make ourselves what we are, if our mode of being is having the obligation to be what we are?

Let us consider this waiter in the café. His movement is quick and forward, a little too precise, a little too rapid. He comes toward the patrons with a step a little too quick. He bends forward a little too eagerly; his voice, his eyes express an interest a little too solicitous for the order of the customer. Finally there he returns, trying to imitate in his walk the inflexible stiffness of some kind of automaton while carrying his tray with the recklessness of a tight-rope-walker by putting it in a perpetually unstable, perpetually broken equilibrium which he perpetually re-establishes by a light movement of the arm and hand. All his behavior seems to us a game. He applies himself to chaining his movements as if they were mechanisms, the one regulating the other; his gestures and even his voice seem to be mechanisms; he gives himself the quickness and pitiless rapidity of things. He is playing, he is amusing himself. But what is he playing? We need not watch long before we can explain it: he is playing at *being* a waiter in a café. There is nothing there to surprise us. The game is a kind of marking out and investigation. The child plays with his body in order to explore it, to take inventory of it; the waiter in the café plays with his condition in order to *realize* it. This obligation is not different from that which is imposed on all tradesmen. This condition is wholly one of ceremony. The public demands of them that they realize it as a ceremony; there is the dance of the grocer, of the tailor, of the auctioneer, by which they endeavor to persuade their clientele that they are nothing but a grocer, an auctioneer, a tailor. A grocer who dreams is offensive to the buyer, because such a grocer is not wholly a grocer. Society demands that he limit himself to his function as a grocer, just as the soldier at attention makes himself into a soldier-thing with a direct regard which does not see at all, which is no longer meant to see, since it is the rule and not the interest of the moment which determines the point he must fix his eyes on (the sight "fixed at ten paces"). There are indeed many precautions to imprison a man in what he is, as if we lived in perpetual fear that he might escape from it, that he might break away and suddenly elude his condition.

In a parallel situation, from within, the waiter in the café can not be immediately a café waiter in the sense that this inkwell *is* an inkwell, or the glass is a glass. It is by no means that he can not form reflective judgments or concepts concerning his condition. He knows well what it "means"; the obligation of getting up at five o'clock, of sweeping the floor of the shop before the restaurant opens, of starting the coffee pot going, *etc.* He knows the rights which it allows: the right to the tips, the right to belong to a union, *etc.* But all these concepts, all these judgments refer to the transcendent. It is a matter of abstract possibilities, of rights and duties conferred on a "person possessing rights." And it is precisely this person *who I have to be* (if I am the waiter in question) and who I am not. It is not that I do not wish to be this person or that I want this person to be different. But rather there is no common measure between his being and mine. It is a "representation" for others and for myself, which means that I can be he only in *representation*. But if I represent myself as him, I am not he; I am separated from him as the object from the subject, separated *by nothing*, but this nothing isolates me from him. I can not be he, I can only play *at being* him; that is, imagine to myself that I am he. And thereby I affect him with nothingness. In vain do I fulfill the functions of a café waiter. I can be he only in the neutralized mode, as the actor is Hamlet, by mechanically making the *typical gestures* of my state and by aiming at myself as an imaginary café waiter through those gestures taken as an "analogue." What I attempt to realize is a being-in-itself of the café waiter, as if it were not just in my power to confer their value and their urgency upon my duties and the rights of my position, as if it were not my free choice to get up each morning at five o'clock or to remain in bed, even though it meant getting fired. As if from the very fact that I sustain this role in existence I did not transcend it on every side, as if I did not constitute myself as one *beyond* my condition. Yet there is no doubt that I *am* in a sense a café waiter—otherwise could I not just as well call myself a diplomat or a reporter? But if I am one, this can not be in the mode of being in-itself. I am a waiter in the mode of *being what I am not.* . . .

2. The Look

THIS WOMAN WHOM I SEE coming toward me, this man who is passing by in the street, this beggar whom I hear calling before my window, all are for me *objects*—that there is no doubt. Thus it is true that at least one of the modalities of the Other's presence to me is *object-ness*. But we have seen that if this relation of object-ness is the fundamental relation between the Other and myself, then the Other's existence remains purely conjectural. Now it is not only conjectural but *probable* that this voice which I hear is that of a man and not a song on a phonograph; it is infinitely *probable* that the passerby whom I see is a man and not a perfected robot. This means that without going beyond the limits of probability and indeed because of this very probability, my apprehension of the Other as

From part 3 of Jean-Paul Sartre, Being and Nothingness, *trans. by Hazel Barnes (New York: Washington Square Press, 1966), pp. 310–329. Reprinted with permission from Philosophical Library, New York.*

an object essentially refers me to a fundamental apprehension of the Other in which he will not be revealed to me as an object but as a "presence in person." In short, if the Other is to be a probable object and not a dream of an object, then his object-ness must of necessity refer not to an original solitude beyond my reach, but to a fundamental connection in which the Other is manifested in some way other than through the knowledge which I have of him. The classical theories are right in considering that every perceived human organism *refers* to something and that this to which it refers is the foundation and guarantee of its probability. Their mistake lies in believing that this reference indicates a separate existence, a consciousness which would be behind its perceptible manifestations as the noumenon is behind the Kantian *Empfindung*. Whether or not this consciousness exists in a separate state, the face which I see does not refer to it; it is not this consciousness which is the *truth* of the probable object which I perceive. In actual fact the reference to a twin upsurge in which the Other is presence for me is to a "being-in-a-pair-with-the-Other," and this is given outside of knowledge proper even if the latter be conceived as an obscure and unexpressible form on the order of intuition. In other words, the problem of Others has generally been treated as if the primary relation by which the Other is discovered is object-ness; that is, as if the Other were first revealed—directly or indirectly—to our perception. But since this perception by its very nature *refers* to something other than to itself and since it can refer neither to an infinite series of appearances of the same type—as in idealism the perception of the table or of the chair does—nor to an isolated entity located on principle outside my reach, its essence must be to refer to a primary relation between my consciousness and the Other's. This relation, in which the Other must be given to me directly as a subject although in connection with me, is the fundamental relation, the very type of my being-for-others.

Nevertheless the reference here cannot be to any mystic or ineffable experience. It is in the reality of everyday life that the Other appears to us, and his probability refers to everyday reality. The problem is precisely this: there is in everyday reality an original relation to the Other which can be constantly pointed to and which consequently can be revealed to me outside all reference to a religious or mystic unknowable. In order to understand it I must question more exactly this ordinary appearance of the Other in the field of my perception; since this appearance refers to that fundamental relation, the appearance must be capable of revealing to us, at least as a reality aimed at, the relation to which it refers.

I am in a public park. Not far away there is a lawn and along the edge of that lawn there are benches. A man passes by those benches. I see this man; I apprehend him as an object and at the same time as a man. What does this signify? What do I mean when I assert that this object *is a man*?

If I were to think of him as being only a puppet, I should apply to him the categories which I ordinarily use to group temporal-spatial "things." That is, I should apprehend him as being "beside" the benches, two yards and twenty inches from the lawn, as exercising a certain pressure on the ground, *etc.* His relation with other objects would be of the purely additive type; this means that I could have him disappear without the relations of the other objects around him being perceptibly *changed*. In short, no new relation would appear *through him* between those things in my universe: grouped and synthesized *from my point of view* into instrumental complexes, they would *from his* disintegrate into multiplicities of indifferent relations. Perceiving him as a *man*, on the other hand, is not to apprehend an additive relation between the chair and him; it is to register an organization *without distance* of the things in my universe around that privileged object. To be sure, the lawn remains two yards and twenty inches away from him, but it is also *as a lawn* bound to him in a relation which at once both transcends distance and contains it. Instead of the two terms of the distance being indifferent, interchangeable, and in a reciprocal relation, the distance *is unfolded starting from* the man whom I see and *extending up to* the lawn as the synthetic upsurge of a univocal relation. We are dealing with a relation which is without *parts*, given at one stroke, inside of which there unfolds a spatiality which is not *my* spatiality; for instead of a grouping *toward me* of the objects, there is now an orientation *which flees from me*.

Of course this relation without distance and without parts is in no way that original relation of the Other to me which I am seeking. In the first place, it concerns only the man and the things in the world. In addition it is still an object of knowledge; I shall express it, for example, by saying that this man sees the lawn, or that in spite of the prohibiting sign he is preparing to walk on the grass, *etc.* Finally it still retains a pure character of probability: First, it is *probable* that this object is a man. Second, even granted that he is a man, it remains only probable that he sees the lawn at the moment that I perceive him; it is possible that he is dreaming of some project without exactly being aware of what is around him, or that he is blind, *etc., etc.* Nevertheless this new relation of the object-man to the object-lawn has a particular character; it is simultaneously given to me as a whole, since it is there in the world as an object which I can know (it is, in fact, an objective relation which I express by saying: Pierre has glanced at this watch, Jean has looked out the window, *etc.*), and at the same time it entirely escapes me. To the extent that the man-as-object is the fundamental term of this relation, to the extent that the relation *reaches toward him*, it escapes me. I can not put myself at the center of it. The distance which unfolds between the lawn and the man across the synthetic upsurge of this primary relation is a negation of the distance which I establish—as a pure type of external negation—between these two objects. The distance appears as a pure *disintegration* of the relations which I apprehend between the objects of my universe. It is not I who realize this disintegration; it appears to me as a relation which I aim at emptily across the distances which I originally established between things. It stands as a background of things, a background which on principle escapes me and which is conferred on them from without. Thus the appearance among the objects of *my* universe of an element of disintegration in that universe is what I mean by the appearance of a man in my universe.

The Other is first the permanent flight of things toward a goal which I apprehend as an object at a certain distance from me but which escapes me

inasmuch as it unfolds about itself its own distances. Moreover this disintegration grows by degrees; if there exists between the lawn and the Other a relation which is without distance and which creates distance, then there exists necessarily a relation between the Other and the statue which stands on a pedestal *in the middle of* the lawn, and a relation between the Other and the big chestnut trees which border the walk; there is a total space which is grouped around the Other, and this space is made *with my space;* there is a regrouping in which I take part but which escapes me, a regrouping of all the objects which people my universe. This regrouping does not stop there. The grass is something qualified; it is *this* green grass which exists for the Other; in this sense the very quality of the object, its deep, raw green is in direct relation to this man. This green turns toward the Other a face which escapes me. I apprehend the relation of the green to the Other as an objective relation, but I can not apprehend the green *as* it appears to the Other. Thus suddenly an object has appeared which has stolen the world from me. Everything is in place; everything still exists for me; but everything is traversed by an invisible flight and fixed in the direction of a new object. The appearance of the Other in the world corresponds therefore to a fixed sliding of the whole universe, to a decentralization of the world which undermines the centralization which I am simultaneously effecting.

But *the Other,* is still an object *for me.* He belongs to *my distances;* the man is there, twenty paces from me, he is turning his back on me. As such he is again two yards, twenty inches from the lawn, six yards from the statue; hence the disintegration of my universe is contained within the limits of this same universe; we are not dealing here with a flight of the world toward nothingness or outside itself. Rather it appears that the world has a kind of drain hole in the middle of its being and that it is perpetually flowing off through this hole. The universe, the flow, and the drain hole are all once again recovered, reapprehended, and fixed as an object. All this is there *for me* as a partial structure of the world, even though the total disintegration of the universe is involved. Moreover these disintegrations may often be contained within more narrow limits. There, for example, is a man who is reading while he walks. The disintegration of the universe which he represents is purely virtual; he has ears which do not hear, eyes which see nothing except his book. Between his book and him I apprehend an undeniable relation without distance of the same type as that which earlier connected the walker with the grass. But this time the form has closed in on itself. There is a full object for me to grasp. In the midst of the world I can say "man-reading" as I could say "cold stone," "fine rain." I apprehend a closed "Gestalt" in which the *reading* forms the essential quality; for the rest, it remains blind and mute, lets itself be known and perceived as a pure and simple temporal-spatial thing, and seems to be related to the rest of the world by a purely indifferent externality. The quality "man-reading" as the relation of the man to the book is simply a little particular crack in my universe. At the heart of this solid, visible form he makes himself a particular emptying. The form is massive only in appearance; its peculiar meaning is to be—in the midst of my universe, at ten paces from me, at the heart of that massivity—a closely consolidated and localized flight.

None of this enables us to leave the level on which the Other is an *object*. At most we are dealing with a particular type of objectivity akin to that which Husserl designated by the term *absence* without, however, his noting that the Other is defined not as the absence of a consciousness in relation to the body which I see but by the absence of the world which I perceive, an absence discovered at the very heart of my perception of this world. On this level the Other is an object in the world, an object which can be defined by the world. But this relation of flight and of absence on the part of the world in relation to me is only probable. If it is this which defines the objectivity of the Other, then to what original presence of the Other does it refer? At present we can give this answer: if the Other-as-object is defined in connection with the world as the object which sees what I see, then my fundamental connection with the Other-as-subject must be able to be referred back to my permanent possibility of *being seen* by the Other. It is

in and through the revelation of my being-as-object for the Other that I must be able to apprehend the presence of his being-as-subject. For just as the Other is a probable object for me-as-subject, so I can discover myself in the process of becoming a probable object for only a certain subject. This revelation can not derive from the fact that *my universe is an object for the Other-as-object*, as if the Other's look after having wandered over the lawn and the surrounding objects came following a definite path to place itself on me. I have observed that I can not be an object for an object. A radical conversion of the Other is necessary if he is to escape objectivity. Therefore I can not consider the look which the Other directs on me as one of the possible manifestations of his objective being; the Other can not look at *me* as he looks at the grass. Furthermore my objectivity can not itself derive *for me* from the objectivity of the world since I am precisely the one by whom *there is* a world; that is, the one who on principle can not be an object for himself.

Thus this relation which I call "being-seen-by-another," far from being merely one of the relations signified by the word *man*, represents an irreducible fact which can not be deduced either from the essence of the Other-as-object, or from my being-as-subject. On the contrary, if the concept of the Other-as-object is to have any meaning, this can be only as the result of the conversion and the degradation of that original relation. In a word, my apprehension of the Other in the world as *probably being* a man refers to my permanent possibility of *being-seen-by-him*; that is, to the permanent possibility that a subject who sees me may be substituted for the object seen by me. "Being-seen-by-the-Other" is the *truth of* "seeing-the-Other." Thus the notion of the Other can not under any circumstances aim at a solitary, extra-mundane consciousness which I can not even think. The man is defined by his relation to the world and by his relation to myself. He is that object in the world which determines an internal flow of the universe, an internal hemorrhage. He is the subject who is revealed to me in that flight of myself toward objectivation. But the original relation of myself to the Other is not only an absent truth aimed at across the concrete presence of an object in my universe; it is also a concrete, daily relation which at each instant I experience. At each instant the Other *is looking at me.* It is easy therefore for us to attempt with concrete examples to describe this fundamental connection which must form the basis of any theory concerning the Other. If the Other is on principle the *one who looks at me,* then we must be able to explain the meaning of the Other's look.

Every look directed toward me is manifested in connection with the appearance of a sensible form in our perceptive field, but contrary to what might be expected, it is not connected with any determined form. Of course what *most often* manifests a look is the convergence of two ocular globes in my direction. But the look will be given just as well on occasion when there is a rustling of branches, or the sound of a footstep followed by silence, or the slight opening of a shutter, or a light movement of a curtain. During an attack men who are crawling through the brush apprehend as a *look to be avoided,* not two eyes, but a white farmhouse which is outlined against the sky at the top of a little hill. It is obvious that the object thus constituted still manifests the look as being probable. It is only probable that behind the bush which has just moved there is someone hiding who is watching me. But this probability need not detain us for the moment; we shall return to this point later. What is important first is to define the look in itself. Now the bush, the farmhouse are not the look; they only represent the *eye,* for the eye is not at first apprehended as a sensible organ of vision but as the support for the look. They never refer therefore to the actual eye of the watcher hidden behind the curtain, behind a window in the farmhouse. In themselves they are already eyes. On the other hand neither is the look one quality among others of the object which functions as an eye, nor is it the total form of that object, nor a "worldly" relation which is established between that object and me. On the contrary, far from perceiving the look *on* the objects which manifest it, my apprehension of a look turned toward me appears on the ground of the destruction of the eyes which "look at me." If I apprehend the look, I cease to perceive the eyes; they are there, they remain in the field of my

perception as pure *presentations,* but I do not make any use of them; they are neutralized, put out of play; they are no longer the object of a thesis but remain in that state of "disconnection" in which the world is put by a consciousness practicing the phenomenological reduction prescribed by Husserl. It is never when eyes are looking at you that you can find them beautiful or ugly, that you can remark on their color. The Other's look hides his eyes; he seems to go *in front of them.* This illusion stems from the fact that eyes as objects of my perception remain at a precise distance which unfolds from me to them (in a word, I am present to the eyes without distance, but they are distant from the place where I "find myself") whereas the look is upon me without distance while at the same time it holds me at a distance—that is, its immediate presence to me unfolds a distance which removes me from it. I can not therefore direct my attention on the look without at the same stroke causing my perception to decompose and pass into the background. There is produced here something analogous to what I attempted to show elsewhere in connection with the subject of the imagination. We can not, I said then, perceive and imagine simultaneously; it must be either one or the other. I should willingly say here: we can not perceive the world and at the same time apprehend a look fastened upon us; it must be either one or the other. This is because to perceive is to *look at,* and to apprehend a look is not to apprehend a look-as-object in the world (unless the look is not directed upon us); it is to be conscious of *being looked at.* The look which the *eyes* manifest, no matter what kind of eyes they are is a pure reference to myself. What I apprehend immediately when I hear the branches crackling behind me is not that *there is someone there;* it is that I am vulnerable, that I have a body which can be hurt, that I occupy a place and that I can not in any case escape from the space in which I am without defense—in short, that I *am* seen. Thus the look is first an intermediary which refers from me to myself. What is the nature of this intermediary? What does *being seen* mean for me?

Let us imagine that moved by jealousy, curiosity, or vice I have just glued my ear to the door and looked through a keyhole. I am alone and on the level of a non-thetic self-consciousness. This means first of all that there is no self to inhabit my consciousness, nothing therefore to which I can refer my acts in order to qualify them. They are in no way *known*; I *am my acts* and hence they carry in themselves their whole justification. I am a pure consciousness *of* things, and things, caught up in the circuit of my selfness, offer to me their potentialities as the proof of my non-thetic consciousness (of) my own possibilities. This means that behind that door a spectacle is presented as "to be seen," a conversation as "to be heard." The door, the keyhole are at once both instruments and obstacles; they are presented as "to be handled with care"; the keyhole is given as "to be looked through close by and a little to one side," *etc.* Hence from this moment "I do what I have to do." No transcending view comes to confer upon my acts the character of a *given* on which a judgment can be brought to bear. My consciousness sticks to my acts, it *is* my acts; and my acts are commanded only by the ends to be attained and by the instruments to be employed. My attitude, for example, has no "outside"; it is a pure process of relating the instrument (the keyhole) to the end to be attained (the spectacle to be seen), a pure mode of losing myself in the world, of causing myself to be drunk in by things as ink is by a blotter in order that an instrumental-complex oriented toward an end may be synthetically detached on the ground of the world. The order is the reverse of causal order. It is the end to be attained which organizes all the moments which precede it. The end justifies the means; the means do not exist for themselves and outside the end.

Moreover the ensemble exists only in relation to a free project of my possibilities. Jealousy, as the possibility which I *am*, organizes this instrumental complex by transcending it toward itself. But I *am* this jealousy; I do not *know* it. If I contemplated it instead of making it, then only the worldly complex in instrumentality could teach it to me. This ensemble in the world with its double and inverted determination (there is a spectacle to be seen behind the door only because I am jealous, but my jealousy is nothing except the simple objec-

tive fact that *there is* a sight *to be seen* behind the door)—this we shall call *situation.* This situation reflects to me at once both my facticity and my freedom; on the occasion of a certain objective structure of the world which surrounds me, it refers my freedom to me in the form of tasks to be freely done. There is no constraint here since my freedom eats into my possibles and since correlatively the potentialities of the world indicate and offer only themselves. Moreover I can not truly define myself as *being* in a situation: first because I am not a positional consciousness of myself; second because I am my own nothingness. In this sense—and since I am what I am not and since I am not what I am—I can not even define myself as truly *being* in the process of listening at doors. I escape this provisional definition of myself by means of all my transcendence. There as we have seen is the origin of bad faith. Thus not only am I unable to *know* myself, but my very being escapes—although I *am* that very escape from my being—and I am absolutely nothing. There is nothing *there* but a pure nothingness encircling a certain objective ensemble and throwing it into relief outlined upon the world, but this ensemble is a real system, a disposition of means in view of an end.

But all of a sudden I hear footsteps in the hall. Someone is looking at me! What does this mean? It means that I am suddenly affected in my being and that essential modifications appear in my structure—modifications which I can apprehend and fix conceptually by means of the reflective *cogito.*

First of all, I now exist as *myself* for my unreflective consciousness. It is this irruption of the self which has been most often described: I see *myself* because *somebody* sees me—as it is usually expressed. This way of putting it is not wholly exact. But let us look more carefully. So long as we considered the for-itself in its isolation, we were able to maintain that the unreflective consciousness can not be inhabited by a self; the self was given in the form of an object and only for the reflective consciousness. But here the self comes to haunt the unreflective consciousness. Now the unreflective consciousness is a consciousness *of* the world. Therefore for the unreflective consciousness the self exists on the level of objects in the world;

this role which devolved only on the reflective consciousness—the making-present of the self—belongs now to the unreflective consciousness. Only the reflective consciousness has the self directly for an object. The unreflective consciousness does not apprehend the *person* directly or as *its* object; the person is presented to consciousness *in so far as the person is an object for the Other.* This means that *all* of a sudden I am conscious of myself as escaping myself, not in that I am the foundation of my own nothingness but in that I have my foundation outside myself. I am for myself only as I am a pure reference to the Other.

Nevertheless we must not conclude here that the object is the Other and that the *Ego* present to my consciousness is a secondary structure or a meaning of the Other-as-object; the Other is not an object here and can not be an object, as we have shown, unless by the same stroke *my* self ceases to be an object-for-the-Other and vanishes. Thus I do not aim at the Other as an object nor at my *Ego* as an object for myself; I do not even direct an empty intention toward that *Ego* as toward an object presently out of my reach. In fact it is separated from me by a nothingness which I can not fill since I apprehend it *as not being for me* and since on principle it exists for the Other. Therefore I do not aim at it as if it could someday be given to me but on the contrary in so far as it on principle flees from me and will never belong to me. Nevertheless I *am that Ego;* I do not reject it as a strange image, but it is present to me as a self which I *am* without *knowing* it; for I discover it in shame and, in other instances, in pride. It is shame or pride which reveals to me the Other's look and myself at the end of that look. It is the shame or pride which makes me *live,* not *know* the situation of being looked at.

Now, shame, as we noted at the beginning of this chapter, is shame of *self;* it is the *recognition* of the fact that I *am* indeed that object which the Other is looking at and judging. I can be ashamed only as my freedom escapes me in order to become a *given* object. Thus originally the bond between my unreflective consciousness and my *Ego,* which is being looked at, is a bond not of knowing but of being. Beyond any knowledge which I can have, I am this self which another knows. And this self

which I am—this I am in a world which the Other has made alien to me, for the Other's look embraces my being and correlatively the walls, the door, the keyhole, All these instrumental-things in the midst of which I am, now turn toward the Other a face which on principle escapes me. Thus I am my *Ego* for the Other in the midst of a world which flows toward the Other. Earlier we were able to call this internal hemorrhage the flow of *my* world toward the Other-as-object. This was because the flow of blood was trapped and localized by the very fact that I fixed as an object in my world that Other toward which this world was bleeding. Thus not a drop of blood was lost; all was recovered, surrounded, localized although in a being which I could not penetrate. Here on the contrary the flight is without limit; it is lost externally; the world flows out of the world and I flow outside myself. The Other's look makes me be beyond my being in this world and puts me in the midst of the world which is at once *this world* and beyond this world. What sort of relations can I enter into with this being which I am and which shame reveals to me?

In the first place there is a relation of being. I *am* this being. I do not for an instant think of denying it; my shame is a confession. I shall be able later to use bad faith so as to hide it from myself, but bad faith is also a confession since it is an effort to flee the being which I am. But I am this being, neither in the mode of "having to be" nor in that of "was"; I do not found it in its being; I can not produce it directly. But neither is it the indirect, strict effect of my acts as when my shadow on the ground or my reflection in the mirror is moved in correlation with the gestures which I make. This being which I am preserves a certain indetermination, a certain unpredictability. And these new characteristics do not come only from the fact that I can not *know* the Other; they stem also and especially from the fact that the Other is free. Or to be exact and to reverse the terms, the Other's freedom is revealed to me across the uneasy indetermination of the being which I am for him. Thus this being is not my possible; it is not always in question at the heart of my freedom. On the contrary, it is the limit of my freedom, its "backstage" in the sense that we speak of "behind the scenes." It is given to me as a burden which I carry without ever being able to turn back to know it, without even being able to realize its weight. If it is comparable to my shadow, it is like a shadow which is projected on a moving and unpredictable material such that no table of reference can be provided for calculating the distortions resulting from these movements. Yet we still have to do with *my* being and not with an image of my being. We are dealing with my being as it is written in and by the Other's freedom. Everything takes place as if I had a dimension of being from which I was separated by a radical nothingness; and this nothingness is the Other's freedom. The Other has to make my being-for-him *be* in so far as he has to be his being. Thus each of my free conducts engages me in a new environment where the very stuff of my being is the unpredictable freedom of another. Yet by my very shame I claim as mine that freedom of another. I affirm a profound unity of consciousnesses, not that harmony of monads which has sometimes been taken as a guarantee of objectivity but a unity of being; for I accept and wish that others should confer upon me a being which I recognize.

Shame reveals to me that I *am* this being, not in the mode of "was" or of "having to be" but *in-itself*. When I am alone, I can not realize my "being-seated"; at most it can be said that I simultaneously both am it and am not it. But in order for me to be what I am, it suffices merely that the Other look at me. It is not for myself, to be sure; I myself shall never succeed at realizing this being-seated which I grasp in the Other's look. I shall remain forever a consciousness. But it is for the Other. Once more the nihilating escape of the for-itself is fixed, once more the in-itself closes in upon the for-itself. But once more this metamorphosis is effected *at a distance*. For the Other *I am seated* as this inkwell *is on* the table; for the Other, *I am leaning over* the keyhole as this tree *is bent* by the wind. Thus for the Other I have stripped myself of transcendence. This is because my transcendence becomes for whoever makes himself a witness of it (*i.e.*, determines himself *as not being* my transcendence) a purely established transcendence, a given-transcendence; that is, it acquires a nature by the sole fact that the *Other* confers on it an outside. This is accomplished, not by any distortion or by a refraction which the Other would impose on my transcendence through his categories, but by his very being. If there is an Other, whatever or whoever he may be, whatever may be his relations with me, and without his acting upon me in any way except by the pure upsurge of his being—then I have an outside, I have a *nature*. My original fall is the existence of the Other. Shame—like pride—is the apprehension of myself as a nature although that very nature escapes me and is unknowable as such. Strictly speaking, it is not that I perceive myself losing my freedom in order to become a *thing*, but my nature is—over there, outside my lived freedom—as a given attribute of this being which I am for the Other.

I grasp the Other's look at the very center of my *act* as the solidification and alienation of my own possibilities. In fear or in anxious or prudent anticipation, I perceive that these possibilities which I *am* and which are the condition of my transcendence are given also to another, given as about to be transcended in turn by his own possibilities. The Other as a look is only that—my transcendence transcended. Of course I still *am* my possibilities in the mode of non-thetic consciousness (of) these possibilities. But at the same time the look alienates them from me. Hitherto I grasped these possibilities thetically on the world and in the world in the form of the potentialities of instruments: the dark corner in the hallway referred to me the possibility of hiding—as a simple potential quality of its shadow, as the invitation of its darkness. This quality or instrumentality of the object belonged to it alone and was given as an objective, ideal property marking its real belonging to that complex which we have called *situation*. But with the Other's look a new organization of complexes comes to superimpose itself on the first. To apprehend myself as seen is, in fact, to apprehend myself as seen *in the world* and from the standpoint of the world. The look does not carve me out in the universe; it comes to search for me at the heart of my situation and grasps me only in irresolvable relations with instruments. If I am seen as seated, I must be seen as "seated-on-a-chair," if I am grasped as bent over, it is as "bent-over-the-keyhole," *etc.* But suddenly the alienation of myself, which is the act of being-looked-at, involves the alienation of the world which I organize. I am seen as seated on this chair with the result that I do not see it at all, that it is impossible for me to see it, that it escapes me so as to organize itself into a new and differently oriented complex—with other relations and other distances in the midst of other objects which similarly have for me a secret face.

Thus I, who in so far as I am my possibles, am what I am not and am not what I am—behold now I *am* somebody! And the one who I am—and who on principle escapes me—I am he *in the midst of the world* in so far as he escapes me. Due to this fact my relation to an object or the potentiality of an object decomposes under the Other's look and appears to me in the world as my possibility of utilizing the object, but only as this possibility on principle escapes me; that is, in so far as it is surpassed by the Other toward his own possibilities. For example, the potentiality of the dark corner becomes a given possibility of hiding in the corner by the sole fact that the Other can pass beyond it toward his possibility of illuminating the corner with his flashlight. This possibility is there, and I apprehend it but as absent, as *in the Other*; I apprehend it through my anguish and through my decision to give up that hiding place which is *"too risky."* Thus my possibilities are present to my unreflective consciousness in so far as the Other *is watching me.* If I see him ready for anything, his hand in his pocket where he has a weapon, his finger placed on the electric bell and ready "at the slightest movement on my part" to call the police, I apprehend my possibilities from outside and through him at the same time that I *am* my possibilities, somewhat as we objectively apprehend four thought through language at the same time that we think it *in order to* express it in language. This inclination to run away, which dominates me and carries me along and which I *am*—this I read in the Other's watchful look and in that other look—the gun pointed at me. The Other apprehends this inclination in me in so far as he has anticipated it and is already prepared for it. He apprehends it in me in so far as he surpasses it and disarms it. But I do not grasp the actual surpassing;

I grasp simply the death of my possibility. A subtle death: for my possibility of hiding still remains *my* possibility; inasmuch as I *am* it, it still lives; and the dark corner does not cease to signal me, to refer its potentiality to me. But if instrumentality is defined as the fact of "being able to be surpassed toward _____," then my very possibility becomes an instrumentality. My possibility of biding in the corner becomes the fact that the Other can surpass it toward his possibility of pulling me out of concealment, of identifying me, of arresting me. *For the Other* my possibility is at once an obstacle and a means as all instruments are. It is an obstacle, for it will compel him to certain new acts (to advance toward me, to turn on his flashlight). It is a means, for once I am discovered in this cul-de-sac, I "am caught." In other words every act performed against the Other can on principle be for the Other an instrument which will serve him against me. And I grasp the Other not in the clear vision of what he can make out of my act but in a fear which *lives* all my possibilities as ambivalent. The Other is the hidden death of my possibilities in so far as I live that death as hidden in the midst of the world. The connection between my possibility and the instrument is no more than between two instruments which are adjusted to each other outside in view of an end which escapes me. *Both* the obscurity of the dark corner and my possibility of hiding there are surpassed by the Other when, before I have been able to make a move to take refuge there, he throws the light on the corner. Thus in the shock which seizes me when I apprehend the Other's look, this happens—that suddenly I experience a subtle alienation of all my possibilities, which are now associated with objects of the world, far from me in the midst of the world. . . .

. . . To be looked at is to apprehend oneself as the unknown object of unknowable appraisals—in particular, of value judgments. But at the same time that in shame or pride I recognize the justice of these appraisals, I do not cease to take them for what they are—a free surpassing of the given toward possibilities. A judgment is the transcendental act of a free being. Thus being-seen constitutes me as a defenseless being for a freedom which is not my freedom. It is in this sense that we can consider ourselves as "slaves" in so far as we appear to the Other. But this slavery is not a historical result—capable of being surmounted—of a *life* in the abstract form of consciousness. I am a slave to the degree that my being is dependent at the center of a freedom which is not mine and which is the very condition of my being. In so far as I am the object of values which come to qualify me without my being able to act on this qualification or even to know it, I am enslaved. By the same token in so far as I am the instrument of possibilities which are not my possibilities, whose pure presence beyond my being I can not even glimpse, and which deny my transcendence in order to constitute me as a means to ends of which I am ignorant—I am *in danger*. This danger is not an accident but the permanent structure of my being-for-others. . . .

3. The Causes of Gender Inequality

. . . To state the question (What is a woman?) is, to me, to suggest, at once, a preliminary answer. The fact that I ask it is in itself significant. A man would never get the notion of writing a book on the peculiar situation of the human male. But if I wish to define myself, I must first of all say: "I am a woman"; on this truth must be based all further discussion. A man never begins by presenting himself as an individual of a certain sex; it goes without saying that he is a man. The terms *masculine* and *feminine* are used symmetrically only as a matter of form, as on legal papers. In actuality the relation of the two sexes is not quite like that of two electrical poles, for man represents both the positive and the neutral, as is indicated by the common use of *man* to designate human beings in general; whereas woman represents only the negative, defined by limiting criteria, without reciprocity. In the midst of an abstract discussion it is vexing to hear a man say: "You think thus and so because you are a woman"; but I know that my only defense is to reply: "I think thus and so because it is true," thereby removing my subjective self from the argument. It would be out of the question to reply: "And you think the contrary because you are a man," for it is understood that the fact of being a man is no peculiarity. A man is in the right in being a man; it is the woman who is in the wrong. It amounts to this: just as for the ancients there was an absolute vertical with reference to which the oblique was defined, so there is an absolute human type, the masculine. Woman has ovaries, a uterus; these peculiarities imprison her in her subjectivity, circumscribe her within the limits of her own nature. It is often said that she thinks with her glands. Man superbly ignores the fact that his anatomy also includes glands, such as the testicles, and that they secrete hormones. He thinks of his body as a direct and normal connection with the world, which he believes he apprehends objectively, whereas he regards the body of woman as a hindrance, a prison, weighed down by everything peculiar to it. "The female is a female by virtue of a certain *lack* of qualities," said Aristotle; "we should regard the female nature as afflicted with a natural defectiveness." And St. Thomas for his part pronounced woman to be an "imperfect man," an "incidental" being. This is symbolized in Genesis where Eve is depicted as made from what Bossuet called "a supernumerary bone" of Adam.

Thus humanity is male and man defines woman not in herself but as relative to him; she is not regarded as an autonomous being. Michelet writes: "Woman, the relative being. . . ." And Benda is most positive in his *Rapport d' Uriel:* "The body of man makes sense in itself quite apart from that of woman, whereas the latter seems wanting in significance by itself. . . . Man can think of himself without woman. She cannot think of herself without man." And she is simply what man decrees; thus she is called "the sex," by which is meant that she appears essentially to the male as a sexual being. For him she is sex—absolute sex, no less. She is defined and differentiated with reference to man and not he with reference to her; she is the incidental, the inessential as opposed to the essential. He is the Subject, he is the Absolute—she is the Other.

The category of the *Other* is as primordial as consciousness itself. In the most primitive societies, in the most ancient mythologies, one finds the expression of a duality—that of the Self and the Other. This duality was not originally attached to the division of the sexes; it was not dependent upon any empirical facts. It is revealed in such works as that of Granet on Chinese thought and those of Dumézil on the East Indies and Rome. The feminine element was at first no more involved in such pairs as Varuna-Mitra, Uranus-Zeus, Sun-Moon, and Day-Night than it was in the contrasts between Good and Evil, lucky and unlucky auspices, right and left, God and Lucifer. Otherness is a fundamental category of human thought.

Thus it is that no group ever sets itself up as the One without at once setting up the Other over against itself. If three travelers chance to occupy the same compartment, that is enough to make vaguely hostile "others" out of all the rest of the passengers on the train. In small-town eyes all persons not belonging to the village are "strangers" and suspect; to the native of a country all who inhabit other countries are "foreigners"; Jews are "different" for the anti-Semite, Negroes are "inferior" for American racists, aborigines are "natives" for colonists, proletarians are the "lower class" for the privileged.

. . . These phenomena would be incomprehensible if in fact human society were simply a *Mitsein* or fellowship based on solidarity and friendliness. Things become clear, on the contrary, if, following Hegel, we find in consciousness itself a fundamental hostility toward every other consciousness; the subject can be posed only in being opposed—he sets himself up as the essential, as opposed to the other, the inessential, the object.

But the other consciousness, the other ego, sets up a reciprocal claim. The native traveling abroad is shocked to find himself in turn regarded as a "stranger" by the natives of neighboring countries. As a matter of fact, wars, festivals, trading, treaties, and contests among tribes, nations, and classes tend to deprive the concept *Other* of its absolute sense and to make manifest its relativity; willy-nilly, individuals and groups are forced to realize the reciprocity of their relations. How is it, then, that this reciprocity has not been recognized between the sexes, that one of the contrasting terms is set up as the sole essential, denying any relativity in regard to its correlative and defining the latter as pure otherness? Why is it that women do not dispute male sovereignty? No subject will readily volunteer to become the object, the inessential; it is not the Other who, in defining himself as the Other, establishes the One. The Other is posed as such by the One in defining himself as the One. But if the Other is not to regain the status of being the One, he must be submissive enough to accept this alien point of view. Whence comes this submission in the case of woman? . . .

The reason for this is that women lack concrete means for organizing themselves into a unit which can stand face to face with the correlative unit. They have no past, no history, no religion of their own; and they have no such solidarity of work and interest as that of the proletariat. . . . They live dispersed among the males, attached through residence, housework, economic condition, and social standing to certain men—fathers or husbands—more firmly than they are to other women. If they belong to the bourgeoisie, they feel solidarity with men of that class, not with proletarian women; if they are white, their allegiance is to white men, not to Negro women. The proletariat can propose to massacre the ruling class, and a sufficiently fanatical Jew or Negro might dream of getting sole possession of the atomic bomb and making humanity wholly Jewish or black; but woman cannot even dream of exterminating the males. The bond that unites her to her oppressors is not comparable to any other. The division of the sexes is a biological fact, not an event in human history. Male and female stand opposed within a primordial *Mitsein,* and woman has not broken it. The couple is a fundamental unity with its two halves riveted together, and the cleavage of society along the line of sex is impossible. Here is to be found the basic trait of woman: she is the Other in a totality of which the two components are necessary to one another. . . .

Master and slave, also, are united by a reciprocal need, in this case economic, which does not liberate the slave. In the relation of master to slave the master does not make a point of the need that he has for the other; he has in his grasp the power of satisfying this need through his own action; whereas the slave, in his dependent condition, his hope and fear, is quite conscious of the need he has for his master. Even if the need is at bottom equally urgent for both, it always works in favor of the oppressor and against the oppressed. That is why the liberation of the working class, for example, has been slow.

Now, woman has always been man's dependent, if not his slave; the two sexes have never shared the world in equality. And even today woman is heavily handicapped, though her situation is beginning to change. Almost nowhere is her legal status the same as man's, and frequently it is much to her disadvantage. Even when her rights are legally recognized in the abstract, longstanding custom prevents their full expression in the mores. In the economic sphere men and women can almost be said to make up two castes; other things being equal, the former hold the better jobs, get higher wages, and have more opportunity for success than their new competitors. In industry and politics men have a great many more positions and they monopolize the most important posts. In addition to all this, they enjoy a traditional prestige that the education of children tends in every way to support, for the present enshrines the past—and in the past all history has been made by men. At the present time, when women are beginning to take part in the affairs of the world, it is still a world that belongs to men—they have no doubt of it at all and women have scarcely any. To decline to be the Other, to refuse to be a party to the deal—this would be for women to renounce all the advantages conferred upon them by their alliance with the superior caste. Man-the-sovereign will provide woman-the-liege with material protection and will undertake the moral justification of her existence; thus she can evade at once both economic risk and the metaphysical risk of a liberty in which ends and aims must be contrived without assistance. Indeed, along with the ethical urge of each individual to affirm his subjective existence, there is also the temptation to forgo liberty and become a thing. This is an inauspicious road, for he who takes it—passive, lost, ruined—becomes henceforth the creature of another's will, frustrated in his transcendence and deprived of every value. But it is an easy road; on it one avoids the strain involved in undertaking an authentic existence. When man makes of woman the *Other,* he may, then, expect her to manifest deep-seated tendencies toward complicity. Thus, woman may fail to lay claim to the status of subject because she lacks definite resources, because she feels the necessary bond that ties her to man regardless of reciprocity, and because she is often very well pleased with her role as the *Other.*

But it will be asked at once: how did all this begin? It is easy to see that the duality of the sexes, like any duality, gives rise to conflict. And doubtless the winner will assume the status of absolute. But why should man have won from the start? It seems possible that women could have won the victory; or that the outcome of the conflict might never have been decided. How is it that this world has always belonged to the men and that things have begun to change only recently? Is this change a good thing? Will it bring about an equal sharing of the world between men and women?

These questions are not new, and they have often been answered. But the very fact that woman *is the Other* tends to cast suspicion upon all the justifications that men have ever been able to provide for it. These have all too evidently been dictated by men's interest. . . . But the males could not enjoy this privilege fully unless they believed it to be founded on the absolute and the eternal; they sought to make the fact of their supremacy into a right. . . .

In proving woman's inferiority, the antifeminists then began to draw not only upon religion, philosophy, and theology, as before, but also upon science—biology, experimental psychology, etc. At most they were willing to grant "equality in difference" to the *other* sex. . . .

So it is that many men will affirm as if in good faith that women *are* the equals of man and that they have nothing to clamor for, while *at the same time* they will say that women can never be the equals of man and that their demands are in vain. It is, in point of fact, a difficult matter for man to realize the extreme importance of social discriminations which seem outwardly insignificant but which produce in woman moral and intellectual effects so profound that they appear to spring from her original nature. The most sympathetic of men never fully comprehend woman's concrete situation. And there is no reason to put much trust in the men when they rush to the defense of privileges whose full extent they can hardly measure. . . .

. . . Every subject plays his part as such specifically through exploits or projects that serve as a mode of transcendence; he achieves liberty only through a continual reaching out toward other liberties. There is no justification for present existence other than its expansion into an indefinitely open future. Every time transcendence falls back into immanence, stagnation, there is a degradation of existence into the *"en-soi"*—the brutish life of subjection to given conditions—and of liberty into constraint and contingence. This downfall represents a moral fault if the subject consents to it; if it is inflicted upon him, it spells frustration and oppression. In both cases it is an absolute evil. Every individual concerned to justify his existence feels that his existence involves an undefined need to transcend himself, to engage in freely chosen projects.

Now, what peculiarly signalizes the situation of woman is that she—a free and autonomous being like all human creatures—nevertheless finds herself living in a world where men compel her to assume the status of the Other. They propose to stabilize her as object and to doom her to immanence since her transcendence is to be overshadowed and forever transcended by another ego (*conscience*) which is essential and sovereign. The drama of woman lies in this conflict between the fundamental aspirations of every subject (ego)—who always regards the self as the essential—and the compulsions of a situation in which she is the inessential. How can a human being in woman's situation attain fulfillment? What roads are open to her? Which are blocked? How can independence be recovered in a state of dependency? What circumstances limit woman's liberty and how can they be overcome? These are the fundamental questions on which I would fain throw some light. This means that I am interested in the fortunes of the individual as defined not in terms of happiness but in terms of liberty. . . .

Study Questions

1. What does "existentialism" mean for existential philosophers, and how does this differ from its meaning as an attitude toward life and literature?

2. What are some of the themes of knowledge and reality shared by most existentialists?

3. Why does Kierkegaard think that it would not be a good thing for us to know that God exists?

4. Explain what Kierkegaard means by the aesthetic, the ethical, and the religious levels of existence.

5. For Nietzsche, what is the difference between slave or herd morality, and aristocratic or master morality?

6. Why for Nietzsche is the death of God necessary for emergence of the overman?

7. What does it mean to say that consciousness is intentional?

8. Explain the difference between Being-in-itself and Being-for-itself.

9. Explain the difference between authentic existence and living in bad faith.

10. How does Sartre know that other people exist?

Chapter 9

Psychoanalysis: Sigmund Freud

Introduction

Very often when a field of study is first developed it contains at its heart a new theory of human nature. This has been true not only of philosophical and theological theories, many of which we have already seen, but also of the sciences developed to study human beings. This was surely true of dialectical materialism, as we have seen in Chapter 7, and is strikingly true of Darwin's theory of evolution, as we will see in the next chapter. Nowhere, however, is this more true than in the psychological theories constructed by Freud to explain human personality, and in their associated method of treatment—the method of psychoanalysis. This may not be surprising, since one of the central subjects of psychology is the *psyche,* which is Greek for the "soul." If psychology focuses on an understanding of the structure and function of the psyche, if its primary concern is human nature, it would follow that a new psychology would have a new concept of human nature at its core. And what a new and comprehensive theory it was! After Freud, we would never again be able to understand ourselves as we did before.

With the exception of the first and last few years, Sigmund Freud (1856–1939) lived his entire life in Vienna, Austria. At the time Freud moved there as a young child, Vienna was at the center of the political, economic, and intellectual life of Europe. Unfortunately for Freud, a Jew, it also was home to intense anti-Semitic attitudes. Freud blossomed in Vienna as a student, but his career choices were limited by prejudice against Jews to business, the law, and medicine. He chose medical research and trained as a neurologist. Since research paid so little and since he wanted to marry and raise a family, he soon turned to the clinical practice of neurology and began to treat patients with psychological disorders. Gradually he evolved the innovative treatment methods that became known as **psychoanalysis.**

Some of the assumptions of this method, especially those about infantile sexuality, brought him ridicule and rejection by the medical community. This was most unfortunate for Freud, since he suffered greatly in the absence of acceptance and respect. His biographer, Ernest Jones,[1] recounts an important episode in Freud's youth which created the basis of this need. While walking in the streets of Vienna, his father was confronted by some anti-Semitic men who knocked his new expensive hat from his head into a puddle of mud. When the young Freud asked his father what he did in response, his father answered that he did nothing, simply picked up his hat and went along his way. This perceived weakness of his father was to drive Freud, at least for the first half of his career, to seek a strong male mentor. This was especially an important need for someone developing new and controversial ideas in isolation from most of his peers. As he matured and his theories became more widely accepted, Freud was able to become a strong father to himself, needing less and less the support of others.

This internal strength also allowed him to endure stoically the thirteen years of pain that he suffered because of mouth cancer, a disease that finally killed him in London in 1939, where he had escaped to avoid the horrors of Nazism.

Freud's career developed through five phases.[2] The first phase was that of a medical researcher. For two years before he received his medical diploma in neurology (1881), until 1885, he worked in the laboratory of his first mentor, Ernst Brucke, the leading physiologist of his time. Brucke's main project was to apply the methods of the natural sciences to the study of living organisms. There Freud learned the scientific method, especially developing his ability to make careful observations. But the work paid little and he needed money to marry, so he moved into the second phase of his career, his early days in clinical psychiatry, and began to practice medicine. A very common type of patient for Freud and others at that time were people, usually women, who suffered from *hysteria*. The symptoms of this condition were irrational and uncontrollable expressions of emotion, diminished will power, occasional fits, sometimes paralysis of limbs, experiences of fantasy, and the like. There is no such category of mental illness today. Such symptoms now would be classified instead as one or another type of neurosis. The standard treatments for hysteria at the time were electrotherapy, hydrotherapy, and massage—all of which were relatively ineffective.

During this time (1886) Freud traveled to Paris on a fellowship and studied for several months with the famous French neurologist, Jean-Martin Charcot. Charcot developed a new method for treating hysteria that involved *hypnosis.* More than that, however, he introduced several techniques and concepts that had an immense influence on Freud and the development of psychoanalysis. Charcot listened to the history of his patients and their families, especially their descriptions of childhood behavior and the emotional traumas that they may have experienced. He developed the notion that such traumatic events may be forgotten and later become the cause of the symptoms of hysteria. In addition, he believed that these forgotten experiences can be relived in dreams and while under hypnosis. He claimed even further, that once the trauma and its associated emotion is relived, or made conscious, it no longer produces the symptoms of hysteria—the patient is cured.

When Freud returned to Vienna he joined forces with a man with a flourishing practice that already included the use of hypnosis, Josef Breuer. Breuer soon became Freud's new mentor, and for the next three years he and Freud applied the method of hypnosis to their patients. One of the main things that Freud learned from Breuer was revealed in the famous case of Anna O., an earlier patient of Breuer's who suffered from hysteria. Freud was especially impressed with the fact that Anna fell in love with Breuer, as had many of his patients. This led Freud to his idea of *transference,* the shifting of the patient's feelings that she has for someone else to the therapist. Freud tried to convince Breuer that this was a normal part of therapy, but Breuer would have none of it. At the same time, Freud began to develop his ideas of infant sexuality, which Breuer also rejected. These theoretical differences, along with the fact that hypnosis seemed to offer patients only brief periods of relief, drove Freud away from Breuer and toward the development of his own ideas.

In his third phase of intellectual development, Freud came to understand that hypnosis was less than effective because the patient was not in control of her conscious states when she remembered the traumatic experience and its associated emotions. A new method would have to be discovered to dig into the unconscious while the patient was in control of her conscious states so that the remembered events could become part of her personality. It is during this time (1889–1920) that Freud developed the method of **psychoanalysis,** the analysis of deeply repressed psychological events. For him, the way into the unconscious was no longer to be hypnosis, but rather the "talking" therapy.

As with Charcot and Breuer, this method involved formulating case histories of patients, since Freud believed that their problems stemmed from their life experiences. But it also involved what Freud called *free association.* This allowed patients to say whatever came to mind while the therapist would listen and remain passive. The idea was that by interpreting what the patient said when his or her mind was not required to be logical, information about important unconscious beliefs and emotions would be revealed. The second avenue to the unconscious for Freud was the interpretation of dreams. Freud thought that dreams were symbolic representations of the unconscious, and that a skilled interpreter could read their messages. He gave many examples of dream interpretation in what may be the most important of his many works, *The Interpretation of Dreams* (1900).

The fourth phase is Freud's theoretical phase. From 1920 until his death he began to construct theories to explain what he had observed in his patients. It is during this time that he wrote such works as *Beyond the Pleasure Principle* (1920), *The Ego and the Id* (1923), and *New Introductory Lectures on Psychoanalysis* (1933). In these and other writings he speculated about the underlying mechanisms of the mind, its structure, and its dynamic functioning, the effects of which he had carefully observed for so many years. Here Freud is writing more as a philosopher, interpreting and explaining experience in terms of theoretical entities that cannot themselves be observed. It is here that he appeals to such concepts as the id, the ego, and the superego, which will be discussed later. It is here that he categorizes our basic desires as the death (*thanatos*) wish and the life wish (*eros*). It is here that he developed his full, mature theory of personality, one that applies not only to the neurotic and even the psychotic mind, but also to the structure and function of the normal mind.

The fifth and final stage of Freud's career was devoted not so much to the study of individual personality, but rather to the psychological analysis of society itself. An early work on this topic was his *Totem and Taboo* (1913), in which he locates the origin of society in the Oedipus complex. His major work on society is *Civilization and Its Discontents* (1927), in which he discusses the role of repression that is played by society's demands.

As Freud and his theories grew and developed to maturity he attracted many followers, such as Carl Jung and Alfred Adler. As early as 1910 a group was formed called the *International Psychoanalytic Association.* Freud's fame and the influence of psychoanalysis soon grew and spread not only throughout Europe but also in the United States, and even to India and South America. Societies were formed, periodicals established, and training institutions founded to promote his ideas and methods. By the end of World War II psychoanalysis was firmly established as a leading psychiatric method and as a penetrating type of self-knowledge. Although many of its teachings have been challenged and even abandoned since that time, much of what Freud had to say about the teeming world of the unconscious not only shapes the perspective of popular culture today, but still significantly guides current psychological research. Freud outlines many of his views in *Reading 1* of this chapter.

Worldview

The natural sciences were so well established by Freud's time that the *reality* of the world of nature was simply taken to be what science said it was. Unlike the existentialists, Freud thought that the methods of the natural sciences could also be applied to the study of the mind. Given his training in neurology, it is not surprising that he identified the mind with the brain. For him, there was no soul or nonphysical mind to study. Freud was a **materialist.** Everything that existed was composed of matter, including the human mind. It was one of Freud's early goals to be able to explain the mind and the psychological phenomena that he observed in terms of the brain and its neurological functions.

The most important reality for Freud was the *unconscious* mind. Others had referred to unconscious mental events before Freud, but Freud was the first to carve out this realm of reality for detailed study. It may even be said that he invented the unconscious as an object of study. It was as if he pointed out a new continent or new planet or something else that no one had ever really noticed before. A whole new world was opened to us by Freud, the world of the secret, hidden self. The conscious self might be completely open to view, but it is simply a small part of the mind, for Freud. The self that he discovered was the self buried deeply below the conscious surface. It was here, for Freud, that the structure and function of human nature was to be found.

Freud was careful to distinguish the unconscious from the *preconscious.* Preconscious mental events are those that may be recalled to consciousness, through memory, for example. Not everything that you know and feel and want and so on can be conscious at the same time. That would be like having everything that exists on the hard drive of your computer displayed on your computer screen all at once. Instead, we store most of what is in our minds on the preconscious level for recall when necessary. Unconscious events, on the other hand, cannot be made conscious without using special techniques, such as the methods of psychoanalysis. This is Freud's world and the area of reality that concerns him the most—the unconscious world of the human mind.

In the area of *knowledge,* while Freud was a materialist he was not a reductionist. A **reductionist** is someone who wants to explain his or her subject matter by reducing it to explanations of another type of subject matter. For example, some want to reduce sociology to psychology, because they believe that group behavior may be explained as the sum of individual behaviors. Some want to reduce psychology to biology, because they believe that most important behaviors are genetically determined. Still others want to reduce biology to chemistry, since we are just a collection of cells made up of molecules; and others want to take the further trip of reducing chemistry to physics, since molecules are nothing but collections of atoms. According to the reductionist, we should be able to explain group behavior in terms of the movements of atoms.

Such minute, detailed explanations are hardly likely, however. What would it take to explain a football game, for example, by reference to all the atoms involved? And what would it mean to plot the movements of the atoms involved even if that could be done? Would anyone understand such movement *as* football? While it may be the case that groups and individuals and cells and molecules are nothing but atoms, it is not possible to study and explain groups and individuals, or even cells and molecules for that matter, only by reference to what we know about atoms. Instead, various sciences have various methods aimed at various levels of complexity. Although he believed that mental events were nothing but brain events, Freud did not study the brain to explain either mental illness or ordinary personality. Too little was known about the brain to do this effectively. Instead of neurological explanations he offered psychological ones, ones that saw mental events such as beliefs, desires, and emotions as events within a person trying to live a life in the world.

The innovative belief that Freud had about the study of psychological phenomena was that his psychological explanations could be just as scientific as neurological explanations. Instead of philosophical speculations about human nature, he would develop what he believed to be scientific ones. Just as knowledge of the natural world is gained through the scientific method, so for Freud, knowledge of the mind, even the unconscious mind, is to be gained through the scientific method. The scientific method may be understood as having three levels. First is the level of observation. Freud was very good at this task as his carefully documented case reports show. What he observed were the symptoms of his patients, their descriptions of dreams and fantasies, and the results of their free associations.

The second level of science is the level of empirical generalization. Here general laws are formed on the basis of observation. If we see object after object fall without exception at $32'/\text{sec}^2$ (minus air friction), then we are entitled to say that "All objects fall at $32'/\text{sec}^2$." Just as we are justified in inferring the law of gravity and other scientific laws from many observations, so also Freud believed, generalizations could be established about the relationships between unconscious mental events and their conscious, usually symbolic, manifestations. It may take a skilled interpreter to read dreams and free association utterances as signs of unconscious events, but the lawlike connections were there to be found.

The third level of scientific explanation is the theoretical level. Very often in science, especially in the natural sciences, unobservable entities are postulated to explain observable behavior. The existence of electrons, for example, which cannot be observed, explain such things as electricity and the photo-electric effect. Black holes in space, which cannot be observed, explain the whirling motion of galaxies, and so on. In the same way, the unconscious mind, which is not directly observable, is required to explain many observable psychological phenomena, such as the repression of the conflict that exists between our bubbling, boiling desires, and the restrictions that attempt to prevent us from acting upon them. As we have seen briefly in the previous section, Freud resisted hypothesizing about such unobservable entities for many decades, preferring instead to focus on observation and description instead of explanation. Fortunately, however, in the last couple of decades of his life, he wrote a great deal about the structure and function of the unconscious and of human nature in general.

Human Nature

The Structure of Human Nature

Freud describes the *structure* of human personality in the following way. The first thing to note is that the mind is not simply a place where thoughts and desires, memories and emotions, and other types of mental states reside. It is not passive. Instead, as Kant believed (see Chapter 6), it consists of active mechanisms that churn away beneath the surface in order to keep us adapted to the world in which we must live. Into this mind is introduced a variety of issues each day, issues about which it makes compromises and decisions, all for the purpose of adjusting our behavior and feelings to our world and preventing normal activity from breaking down. What makes normal activity break down and result in the psychopathological symptoms of neurosis or psychosis is unresolvable conflict.

It is one of Freud's great insights that at the heart of the human condition lies **conflict.** Conflict usually involves a clash between what I want and what society will allow. Often natural desires have to be suppressed for the sake of living together in society. I may wish to sleep with my neighbor's wife, to kill my tax accountant, or to steal my colleague's new car. None of these actions are permitted by society, however. So I must either violate social restrictions and pay the consequences for doing so, channel these desires into more acceptable avenues, or deny them altogether. In normal life I may resolve conflicts fairly easily. I can sleep with my own wife, merely shout at my tax accountant, and buy my own car. Sometimes conflicts do not have such easy resolutions, however, even in normal life.

In these cases my aggressive and sexual desires, for example, may have to be channeled into other avenues. Freud claims that acts of creation found in such things as art, poetry, and music are substitutions for sex, and that they help to relieve sexual tension. In the same way, sports are a substitute for aggression. He calls it **sublimation** when we use these types of outlets to resolve conflicts. Sometimes the conflict cannot be resolved or sublimated, however. This happens especially when the conflict itself is between what appear to be irreconcilable emotions. It is here especially that the conflict results in emotional injury or trauma that may later lead to symptoms of mental illness. For example, a young girl who witnesses sexual relations between the father she loves and respects and another woman whom she otherwise admires, may feel hate, jealousy, and disgust. There is a conflict between these feelings, on the one hand, and her love for her father and admiration for his lover, on the other.

In order to go on living in the family the girl must resolve this conflict, but there is no socially acceptable way of doing so. Instead, she represses her memory of the incident and the associated feelings, stuffs them way down into her unconscious mind, and goes on with her life. This type of conflict resolution Freud calls **repression.** The trouble with it is that the memory and the associated feelings still exist in the unconscious mind, where she has no longer any control over them. Here they play themselves out, perhaps years later, in her dreams and very often in neurotic or psychotic symptoms. The only way for her to escape these symptoms is to bring the conflict back to consciousness long enough to resolve it by means other than repression and neurosis.

More will be said later about mental illness and its treatment. The point for now, as we attempt to understand the structure of human nature, is that behind both our ordinary and our pathological behaviors lies a mind that is constantly in conflict by its very nature. If it is in conflict, then it must be composed of conflicting elements, it must have a structure that consists of various elements in conflict. This was an insight that Plato had many centuries earlier. His conflicting elements were reason, spirit, and appetite. For Freud, they are the id, the ego, and the superego.

The **id** is for Freud a collection of all of our basic desires, what he calls our *instinctual drives.* He discusses these drives in *Reading 1.* These instincts are not learned but part of our biology. They are our desires for such things as sex, self-preservation, love, and aggression. The id is unconscious, but shows itself in specific ways as urges of one sort or another, such as lust, hunger, and anger. Later, Freud would reduce the basic drives of the id to two fundamental ones, the drive for life (*eros*), which includes the desires for sex, love, and self-preservation, and the desire for death (*thanatos*), which includes our aggressive desires.

The id operates under what Freud calls the **pleasure principle.** Satisfying our desires gives us pleasure, and in our natural state we want that and we want it right now. We do not care about the effects that the immediate satisfaction of our desires will have either on ourselves or on others. The id is a principle of individual happiness, and it is also where all of our psychic energy lies. What makes us get up in the morning and seek out goals of one sort or another during the day is that we want things. Plato said that we are driven by reason, one of whose jobs is to control desire; Freud says that we are driven by desire, and that reason is one of its slaves. When the desires of the id cannot be satisfied through one channel or another, therein lies the beginning of psychological problems.

The foil of the id is the **superego.** The superego is why basic drives sometimes cannot immediately be satisfied in the manner desired, or even satisfied at all. The id needs a foil or else we would live in a Hobbesean world of social conflict where life would be "nasty, brutish and short." If we all went around satisfying our basic desires at will, with no consideration for others or the harmony of our own lives, there would be no peace and order in society or in our individual lives. Such a life would not be worth living. The superego is the set of rules that society invents to keep our drives in check. These rules we assimilate ordinarily through our parents. They are rules which civilize us and make us fit for cooperative living. The superego is thus a set of habits that represents the attitudes, beliefs, and directives of our parents; it is our parents as internalized by us. Like our actual parents, it molds our egotistical id into socially acceptable channels of behavior. When we disobey the dictates of the superego, often expressed as the laws and moral rules of society, we trigger off feelings of *guilt.* Guilt is the sign that our natural ways of being have not submitted to the forces of civilization.

It is the job of the **ego** to determine what the acceptable channels of behavior are going to be. Freud called the ego, the conscious self, the *reality principle,* since its function is to determine how our desires are to be expressed in socially acceptable ways. So the human personality is the result of a balance struck by the ego between the need to satisfy basic desires and the need to live in society. When the ego faces what appears to be an unresolvable conflict, the result is a feeling of *anxiety.* Both guilt and anxiety, then, are understood by Freud as reactions of different parts of our personality to conflict. Guilt arises from the id crashing through the barriers of the superego, and anxiety from the ego's inability to strike a balance between id and superego. The ego is a dynamic self, always striking deals, always settling for compromises, and always somewhat unhappy with life. If happiness comes from getting what we want, then we will be unhappy to the degree that we cannot get what our basic drives crave. We will be unhappy to the degree that the ego allows the superego to control the id. In fact, Freud once said that the goal of psychoanalysis is to return seriously unhappy people to ordinary unhappiness.

This structure of the human personality is not full blown at birth but develops through various stages during childhood. It is one of Freud's lasting legacies that he identified these stages which, with revision, continue to influence psychologists and the popular culture even today. He describes most of these in *Reading 2*. Before identifying these stages a few background comments are in order. First, each stage is associated with various forms of sexuality. Even infants, for Freud, have sexual desires, though very early on they do not have genital sexual desires. The word "sex," for Freud, often means something like "sensual pleasure gained through various body parts." So to talk about infants having sexual desires is to talk about them wanting various types of oral, anal, and genital sensual pleasure. This general desire for sensual pleasure he called the **libido.** Freud discovered the stages of the development of personality by a process of self-analysis. Much of the product of these analyses he revealed in his many letters to his friend and new mentor, Wilhelm Fliess, a fellow physician. Nowhere is Freud's honesty and objectivity more evident than in his reports of these self-explorations.

The first stage of development, from birth to eighteen months, is called the **oral** stage. Pleasure comes mainly through the mouth to the infant, through sucking and chewing and swallowing food. Here there is complete dependence upon the mother for the satisfaction of the infant's desires. If his desires are not met, he or she becomes frustrated and aggressive. The next stage, from eighteen months to about three years, is called the **anal** stage. Pleasure comes to the child not only orally but also through retaining and expelling feces. Toilet training is introduced during this period and interferes with this pleasure. The child cannot eliminate where and when it chooses, but now is being controlled by the parents. It is during this period that emotions such as envy and possessiveness, along with aggression, dominate the child's personality.

The next phase goes from about three years to six years and is called the **phallic** stage. Pleasure comes not only from oral and anal sources now, but also from genital stimulation. Sexual curiosity is high during this period. Especially important is what Freud calls the **Oedipus complex.** Freud named this discovery, one of his most controversial, after the ancient Greek tragedy, *Oedipus Rex.* In this play a son sleeps with his mother and kills his father. In the same way, says Freud, children during the phallic period have a desire to acquire the unconditional love and affection of the parent of the opposite sex. Freud had more to say about the development of boys than girls during this period. Boys want to possess their mothers exclusively, and to eliminate their rival fathers from the picture. If all goes well, the father asserts his claim to the mother as a sexual mate and the child represses his sexual and aggressive drives, and now is prepared to move on with the process of maturation.

After six years the child enters the **latent** period, where much of his sexual curiosity is replaced by other things, such as curiosity about his now wider environment. It is only with the onset of puberty that the interest of the now adolescent returns to sexual matters. This **genital** phase begins with insecurity and an egoistic quest for independence, and sometimes even a return to the Oedipus complex. If all goes well, it ends with a mature individual who is capable of seeking pleasure, sexual and otherwise, in a world wider than self and family. Here the child now identifies, or becomes like, the parent of the same sex and moves into the world to find a mate and a life of his or her own. While both parental models are within the maturing child, playing the role of his or her superego, as the child matures and becomes an adult he or she will move "beyond" them and the desire to live within their restrictions. The well-adjusted ego will become a parent to itself and guide itself along the path of life. In this way, through these phases of conflict and resolution, is the particular, unique personality formed.

The Function of Human Nature

For Freud, the structure of the conscious and unconscious mind developed in order to adapt our selfish, aggressive, pleasure seeking selves to cooperative social life. Left to ourselves each of us would be concerned only with the satisfaction of our basic desires. There would be no law, no order, no ethics, no economic cooperation, no society, no art, no science—nothing that requires human cooperation. Later Freud's ideas about society will be examined, but for now it is enough to say that the general function of the various aspects of human nature is to shape us from the egoistic beings we are at birth to the civilized beings we eventually become.

At our very core lies the id. Some have likened it to the "black horse" of Plato's charioteer analogy (see Chapter 2). To do so is misleading, however, since there is no corresponding role in Freud of Plato's powerful reason. Reason guides and controls the appetites for Plato, your own reason or someone else's. For Kant as well, reason is what we are. If we only follow its theoretical and practical dictates we may become perfected in wisdom and virtue. Freud will have none of this optimism, however. He is more like Augustine, who believes that we are born with original sin, and thus a propensity for the evil that living according to desire inevitably produces. For Freud, it is not sin but the id that we must battle. This is our original evil, which is not to be eliminated by the saving grace of God or a powerful Platonic reason.

It is the superego, the cultural forces which we have absorbed through the teachings and prohibitions of our parents, that alone puts the brakes on the id. Reason by itself cannot control desire. Reason, in fact, is used by the id to satisfy its desires. Reason, the rational ego for Freud, figures out how to get what the id wants in acceptable and nondestructive ways. It is also used to rationalize away our true, often seamy, motives. All of our goals are set by the id. This is the powerful, irrational engine that drives us. Reason merely carries out its wishes in one way or another. For Freud, heavily influenced by Darwin's theory of evolution (see Chapter 10), we are not creatures of reason, likened to the gods; we are creatures of desire, likened to the animal world from which we came. The main task of anyone in life is not to contemplate eternal forms, or to develop a good moral character, or even to get close to God. Instead, it is to satisfy basic natural desires in socially acceptable ways. This is how we are built by nature; this is what life is all about.

How human nature works in more detail is perhaps best seen by examining Freud's notion of mental illness; its nature, causes, and cures. Much of what he says about the functioning of people who are ill also applies to those who are not. However, by placing the emphasis on defective personalities we can see what is normal by contrast. Generally speaking, the seeds of mental illness are sown when a conflict between the id and the superego seems too difficult or even impossible for the ego to resolve. Conflicts are usually between a wish for something (the id) and its social prohibition (the superego). Attached to these conflicting elements are strong emotions, often experienced as unbearable. If the conflict cannot be resolved, the emotions and the memory of the traumatic event which caused them must be repressed. The trouble is, since the emotion has not been discharged it still remains strong and continually searches for other ways to be expressed—including symptoms of the various sorts of neuroses and psychoses which Freud treated. These symptoms are just so many attempts of the unconscious to discharge the repressed emotion.

Quite often repression of emotions originates in childhood and has to do with the sexual (sensual) or aggressive wishes that the child has for its parents. Trauma experienced during any of the developmental stages can lead to symptoms that Freud calls *fixation* and *regression*. We never let go (fixation) or wish to return (regression) to the patterns of behavior that served us well in the past. Adults who are fixated in the oral stage, for example, show symptoms associated with oral pleasure, while those fixated in the anal stage are typically orderly and clean to a fault. Treating symptoms like these requires that the emotion and its original cause be brought to consciousness and seen now for what it is. In so doing, the emotion is discharged and loses it power to create symptoms. The patient is thus cured by becoming conscious of the causes of his or her symptoms.

Removing symptoms such as anxiety, guilt, paralysis, various sorts of phobias, and a whole spectrum of other inappropriate behavioral and emotional responses is no easy task. This is because they have unconscious causes and a variety of **defense mechanisms** to protect them from detection. These defense mechanisms block patients from knowing the causes of their symptoms, and sometimes even to deny that they have symptoms at all. In addition to *repression*, Freud lists among our defense mechanisms *projection* (attributing unacceptable thoughts and feelings to others), *reaction formation* (overcompensating for a defect of character by developing the opposite type of behavior), and *displacement* (transferring feelings for inappropriate things or persons to another), among others. A man who has incestuous thoughts and feelings about his mother, for example, may deny them by repressing them, projecting them on to others (a brother, for example), begin to act as though he hated his mother, or transfer these feelings and thoughts to another woman.

Defense mechanisms may be viewed as an attempt by patients to cure themselves. Such attempts to rid the personality of conflict by denying that it exists always fail. Instead, it takes a skilled therapist to search for and root out the trauma. To do this the psychoanalyst first learns as much as he or she can about the history of the patient and his family. The therapist then uses the techniques of free association and dream interpretation to discover the symbolic expressions of the unconscious, and to trace them back to the original trauma. Finally, he must get the patient to relive the repressed experience and to discharge the associated emotions. In this way the cause of the psychopathological symptoms, the original emotional conflict that was too much to bear, is brought to consciousness and becomes capable of resolution. Once the conflict is resolved, the patient can then function normally in the world.

It is the human condition—not just the lot of the neurotic and psychotic but all of us—to adapt our desires to the demands of civilization. This is the function of human nature, to resolve the inevitable conflicts between the id and superego. The only difference between normal and abnormal behavior is a matter of the degree of success or failure at such resolutions. Normal behavior may seem conflict free on the surface, but this is because we are not conscious of most of the conflict resolution going on beneath the surface. What we are conscious of is merely the tip of the iceberg of the mind. It is only when the unconscious erupts into consciousness, usually in symbolic or other ways, that we become conscious of our subterranean selves in conflict.

For example, we all dream. According to Freud, dreams are symbolic expressions of the unconscious, especially of conflicts yet to be fully resolved. In addition, even such apparently harmless and seemingly accidental errors such as slips of the tongue and memory lapses can be shown by clever and informed interpretation not to be accidents at all. Instead they are external clues to attempts of the unconscious mind to resolve conflicts. A person may say to an artist to whom he is sexually attracted something like, "I very much lust your work." This is not an accident, for Freud. Rather, such "Freudian slips" reveal our true desires, though now in socially acceptable ways, especially since we can act as though they were accidental.

Memory lapse is another way to avoid conflict. A man opposed to abortion, for example, may have a wife who has had one. To resolve the conflict and its attendant guilt, he may forget that she did. No matter how often she reminds him he always forgets. This is his way of resolving the conflict within him, to deny it by a memory lapse. Once again, dreams are probably the most common way to deal with conflict, by representing unconscious conflict in symbolic ways. For Freud, dreams mean something; they reveal forgotten and avoided and otherwise unresolved conflicts, both in normal and abnormal people. Freudian slips, memory lapses, dreams—in these and other ways all of us attempt to resolve conflicts that have no easy solution on the conscious level. When we fail to resolve our conflicts between desire and social necessities, as we often do in ordinary life, we must either live with the anxiety of the conflict on the conscious level, or live with the repression of the conflict on the unconscious level, where repressed desires persistently burst forth symbolically in conscious experience and behavior. When we cannot live with the conflict or its repression, it produces mental illness, escape from which requires the help of others.

Consequences

Freedom

Freud accepted the principle of **determinism** in both theory and practice. He, along with most of the scientists of his time, accepted the belief that all the material events of nature were causally determined by prior material events. Unlike Descartes and Kant, who allowed the mind to escape the determinism of nature, Freud accepted that ultimately the mind is the brain, a part of nature that operated in a manner that was just as determined as the rest of nature. Even though he explained the mind and human behavior in psychological terms, by referring to mental events and not to neurological events, he assumed that mental events were neurological events, and thus just as determined as the events occurring in the rest of the physical world.

Freud's denial of free will is especially evident in his search for the causes of behavior. For Freud, free choice is never the cause of behavior. All of our behavior results ultimately from instinctual drives and the attempt by the ego to resolve them with the demands of the superego. If a cause of behavior is not evident, or if the one we point to is not sufficient to explain it, it is because the real causes of behavior are mostly hidden from view. Causes for all behavior are always there in the unconscious. They spring from the desires of the id and the demands of the superego for restraint. These are the energies which the ego channels into physical and psychological outcomes of one sort or another. Whenever a human choice appears to be uncaused, it is simply because we are ignorant of its cause, not because it has no cause. For Freud, psychological determinism is every bit as much a reality as the determinism of physics and chemistry. Our personalities, which have been molded early in our lives, shape who we are and what we do. Even apparently meaningless everyday activity stems from our personal psychic lives, as his analysis of Freudian slips and memory lapses has shown.

And yet, we are free in a sense, even while we are determined by past events. For Freud, the type of freedom we may possess arises from self-knowledge. Through psychoanalysis, the deepest form of self-knowledge, a person may bring his or her unconscious causal mechanisms to light and learn about what it is that drives his or her behavior and emotions. Human beings are not rigid machines or unalterable computer programs. We are plastic, moldable entities. We may behave differently in the future than we have in the past. Once we gain self-knowledge, once we understand our personality for what it is, once we learn about the factors which lie in the id and the superego which make us behave as we do, we then may become free. We are free not in the sense that our actions have no causes, but in the sense that we now understand that our actions are caused by ourselves. Once we understand what makes us act as we do, we may take some measure of control over our behavior. We may even change some of it if we desire strongly enough to do so. Once I understand why I behave as I do, therein lies the possibility of self-mastery. My desire to change may now be a stronger cause than my previously unconscious desires, and thus direct my action. It is not an easy journey to change my personality, and it usually fails, but it is possible.

Ethics

Psychoanalysis has often been accused of replacing the idea of right and wrong with the idea of normality. It has even been accused of ignoring ethics altogether, of denying that there is a difference between right and wrong, and of attempting to replace ethics with unrepressed and guilt free sexual behavior. This is not the view of Freud. He did believe that rules about right and wrong are simply social inventions, without either divine or natural origin. Despite this, moral rules play an important role in the process of civilizing human beings. Like the law, they are important ways that society exerts its influence on the individual. They are important ways to form his or her superego, to deny some of his or her tendencies to behave in ways that society finds unacceptable. The superego plays such a powerful role in life that to ignore its important ethical dimension entirely in favor of the pleasure principle would be to court disaster.

In discussing ethics Freud does not offer a rigid set of moral rules or principles, nor does he recommend one particular way to live as best. Instead, in addition to talking about the role that morality plays in shaping our personality, he warns us that this role can be quite destructive. This is because some forms of morality require so much denial of our basic desires that they can act as agents of repression and even destruction of the personality. A great deal of harm has been done to a great number of people in the name of right, according to Freud, both from religious and secular ethics, and especially as they are wielded in the hands of misguided parents. It is important for Freud that moral systems be suitably adapted to the needs of the id as well as the demands of the superego, in order to avoid the creation of unnecessary repression, guilt, and anxiety.

Society

Some of the most dramatic consequences of Freud's view of human nature are especially evident in his description of how and why society was first developed. On this matter Freud was deeply influenced again by Charles Darwin. Freud believed Darwin's theory of evolution by natural selection was one of three great contributions from science that forever changed the way that we think about ourselves. The first insight came from Copernicus, who taught us that our planet is not the center of the universe, but instead one among many. The second important discovery Freud, not very modestly, took credit for himself. He taught us, he believed, that there is an unconscious mind, and that it, not our conscious mind, controls our behavior. What Darwin taught us is that we came from animals, and not from a special act of creation by a divine being.

It was Darwin's emphasis on the evolution of the human species from lower forms of life, resulting in our inheritance of what is essentially an animal nature, that especially influenced Freud. Because we are animals, the basic instinctual drives found in our natural state leave us especially unfit for social existence. We are not born good, altruistic, and cooperative beings, as Rousseau believed. Instead we are selfish and aggressive seekers of our own pleasure, ready to possess our neighbor's goods and even to torture and kill him, just because we have such desires to do so. If this is so, then what needs to be explained is how we ever came to form societies and civilizations in the first place and, more importantly, how they remain intact in the face of the inborn evilness of human nature.

Like Thomas Hobbes before him (see Chapter 7), Freud believes that human beings are extremely aggressive in the state of nature. They must be forced by a powerful ruler with absolute authority to give up satisfying some of their desires for the benefits of cooperative living. The difference for Freud is that this tyrant is not an external monarch, but rather is internal to each person in the form of their superego. In his *Totem and Taboo* (1913), Freud follows Darwin further in speculating about the origin of society. It was Darwin's view that primitive societies were small and consisted of packs of brothers and sisters who were ruled by an all-powerful father. Following the forces of the Oedipus complex, the sons killed the father and ended up becoming a group of brothers with no leader. But human nature requires a leader, someone like their father whom they loved and respected as well as hated. So they erected a totem, a symbol of the dead father's authority. Sometimes this was thought of as an animal, and sometimes as a type of god. In all cases it was a symbol of a strong, stable leader. Freud describes this theory in the following passage:[3]

> . . . the tumultuous mob of brothers were filled with the same contradictory feelings which we can see at work in the ambivalent father-complexes of our children and our neurotic patients. They hated their father, who presented such a formidable obstacle for their craving for power and their sexual desires; but they loved and admired him too. After they got rid of him, had satisfied their hatred and had put into effect their wish to identify themselves with him, the affection which had all this time been pushed under was bound to make itself felt. It did so in the form of remorse. A sense of guilt made its appearance, which in this instance coincided with the remorse felt by the whole group. The dead father became stronger than the living one had been—for events took the course we so often see them follow in human affairs to this day. What had up to then been prevented by his actual existence was thenceforward prevented by the sons themselves, in accordance with the psychological procedure so familiar to us in psycho-analyses under the name of "deferred obedience." They revoked their deed by forbidding the killing of the totem, the substitute of their father; and they renounced its fruits by resigning their claim to the women who had now been set free. They thus created out of their filial sense of guilt the two fundamental taboos of totemism, which for that very reason inevitably corresponded to the two repressed wishes of the Oedipus complex.

One of the things that was forbidden in society as a result of this patricide, one of its taboos, was incest. Freud claims that, in addition to the slaying of the father, the taboo against incest is also the result of the psychological demands of the Oedipus complex. If he develops normally, the mature male does not get to sleep with his mother or other closely related females. Instead, he must mate with females from other families. In this way families join other families, resulting in larger groups being formed, such as clans and tribes and eventually entire nations. So for Freud, it is the Oedipus complex that not only forms individual personalities, but also is behind the formation of society itself. It is not society that shapes the individual, as Marx believed, but rather the individual that shapes society.

In *Civilization and Its Discontents* (1930), Freud took up the task of explaining how society, once formed, shapes and civilizes its members. An essential requirement of civilization is that people harness their instinctual drives, especially their aggressive ones. In particular, it is essential for the individual to repress the destructive impulse to slay the father, carried out by primitive societies and relived by each male through the Oedipus complex. It is also essential for society to reinforce this repression. It does so with strong laws and moral systems, whose functions are to prevent murderous acts and other crimes, and to shape the superego of each individual.

Despite its benefits, which Freud highly endorsed, civilization also produces in each of us a certain degree of "discontent." This stems both from the strictness of the superego in suppressing our instinctual drives, and the guilt we feel when we nevertheless wish to act on them. In some societies more than others, and in some families more than others, the superego suppresses too ruthlessly. Victorian sexual mores, for example, do not allow for the free expression of our libido, even when such expression is healthy and nondestructive. Freud says:[4]

> Present-day civilization makes it plain that it will only permit sexual relationships on the basis of a solitary, indissoluble bond between one man and one woman, and that it does not like sexuality as a source of pleasure in its own right and is only prepared to tolerate it because there is so far no substitute for it as a means of propagating the human race.

More importantly, for Freud, there is no outlet for aggression in society, short of war itself. We are by nature, he says, "not gentle creatures who want to be loved," but rather "creatures among whose instinctual endowments is to be reckoned a powerful share of aggressiveness." The primitive man within is suffocated and constantly banging on the doors of the superego to express this aggression. From the prison of the superego there can be no release, however, if society is to survive. So we must suppress our aggressive drives or be punished by authorities. Even when we do not act upon them, however, or when we do and do not get caught, we end up being punished. We suffer the pangs of guilt. Freud says:[5]

> . . . we know of two origins of the sense of guilt: one arising from fear of an authority, and the other, later on, arising from fear of the super-ego. The first insists on a renunciation of instinctual satisfactions; the second, as well as doing this, presses for punishment, since the continuance of the forbidden wishes cannot be concealed from the super-ego. . . . Thus, in spite of the renunciation that has been made, a sense of guilt comes about. . . . A threatened external unhappiness—loss of love and punishment on the part of the external authority—has been exchanged for a permanent internal unhappiness, for the tension of the sense of guilt.

In *Reading 3* Freud discusses guilt at greater length. One of his main points is that since we so often feel like acting on the aggressive and sexual desires that society and our superego forbid, we constantly feel guilt. This is the true cause of our unhappiness. There is no escape from it, since humanity cannot return to its primitive condition in nature without suffering even more. The best we can do, for Freud, is for society to evolve a better balance between our instincts and the demands of cooperative living.

God and Immortality

Freud is an **atheist.** For him, there is no God and no life after this one. The question that interests him is that if God is merely a human creation and exists only in the minds of human beings, then why do so many people continue to believe in

God? We may have begun to believe as children who accept what their parents tell them, but why do we persist in our belief as we mature? If there is no God, should this belief that there is not have been given up long ago by each of us, and by humanity in general, like the belief in Santa Claus? For Freud, the widespread and persistent belief in God can be explained by the nature and function of the belief itself. Belief in God as an all powerful, all good, all wise father, is a special sort of belief, one which Freud calls an *illusion.*

An illusion is not to be understood as a hallucination or some other distorted form of our perception of reality. An illusion is a belief based upon a desire or a wish; it is a type of *wish fulfillment.* Freud tells us that people cling to their belief in God, even in the absence of evidence, because their desire to believe is so strong that the object of their belief becomes real for them. As a lonely person may create an imaginary friend to keep him company, so the human race has created God, our heavenly father, to fulfill many of its desires. Each of us who are believers continues to believe in God because we have lots of needs and desires that are satisfied by considering such a father figure to be real. People feel better if they can think of an all good, all powerful, heavenly father who watches over them, as once did their biological fathers. God for them is a heavenly father who protects them, loves them, and gives meaning and purpose to their lives. He is a heavenly father, moreover, who promises happiness, eternal happiness, in exchange for a good life led in this world of unhappiness.

For Freud, just as a patient undergoing psychoanalysis may be "cured" of her problem once she sees it for what it is, so also the human race, once they see that belief in God is nothing but a form of wish fulfillment, will be able to give it up and face the stark truth of a world empty of God. Freud believes that it is more healthy to be true to unpleasant facts than to wallow in comforting fiction. Religion is nothing but a crutch that a healthy individual no longer needs.

Gender

Freud finds few friends among feminist writers. One reason for this is that he has a lot less to say about female sexual development than he does about the sexual development of males. Another, more important reason, is that when he does discuss the sexuality of women, it is to assign to it a negative role in personality development. He claims that the personality of a woman is generally less fully equipped to deal with life in a mature way because of her sexual nature, and especially because of what he refers to as **penis envy.**

The story goes like this. The healthy male child who travels through the Oedipus complex represses his desire for his mother from fear of his rival, his father. Freud says that this fear is really fear of being castrated by his father. Once he arrives at puberty, no longer attached to the mother, he then seeks out females other than his mother. The "healthy" female child travels through a different version of the Oedipus complex. Some have called this the *Electra* complex,[6] after the Greek heroine who kills her mother and her mother's lover to revenge her father's murder. According to Freud's description, from three to five years of age the female child develops a romantic interest in her father and begins to resent her mother, to whom she previously had been primarily attached. Why the resentment? Because she sees herself as incomplete. She sees complete people as those with penises and she has no penis. Hers is missing. She believes that she had one but her mother cut it off from jealousy over the relationship between her and her father.

The trouble is that belief in this imaginary castration stunts the development of the female personality. She does identify with the mother insofar as she wants to have children of her own. But this is just to satisfy her need for a penis. She never does outgrow her dependence upon her father, however, and as a result is less mature in any number of ways than males. Freud says that since women never really get to separate from their fathers and complete their version of the Oedipus complex, their drives are less under their control, making women in general more irrational and emotional than men. The moral development of women lags behind that of men as well, since their feelings of being defective make them more concerned with acceptance than with justice. Because little girls never get fully through the Oedipus complex, Freud believes that they simply have less mature and less well-adjusted natures than men.

Readings

1. The Instincts

THE POWER OF THE ID expresses the true purpose of the individual organism's life. This consists in the satisfaction of its innate needs. No such purpose as that of keeping itself alive or of protecting itself from dangers by means of anxiety can be attributed to the id. That is the task of the ego, whose business it also is to discover the most favourable and least perilous method of obtaining satisfaction, taking the external world into account. The super-ego may bring fresh needs to the fore, but its main function remains the limitation of satisfactions.

The forces which we assume to exist behind the tensions caused by the needs of the id are called *instincts.* They represent the somatic demands upon the mind. Though they are the ultimate cause of all activity, they are of a conservative

nature; the state, whatever it may be, which an organism has reached gives rise to a tendency to re-establish that state so soon as it has been abandoned. It is thus possible to distinguish an indeterminate number of instincts, and in common practice this is in fact done. For us, however, the important question arises whether it may not be possible to trace all these numerous instincts back to a few basic ones. We have found that instincts can change their aim (by displacement) and also that they can replace one another—the energy of one instinct passing over to another. This latter process is still insufficiently understood. After long hesitancies and vacillations we have decided to assume the existence of only two basic instincts, *Eros* and *the destructive instinct.* (The contrast between the instincts of self-preservation and the

---

From Sigmund Freud, An Outline of Psychoanalysis, *trans. by James Strachey (New York: W. W. Norton, 1949), pp. 5–8. Reprinted with permission.*

preservation of the species, as well as the contrast between ego-love and object-love, fall within Eros.) The aim of the first of these basic instincts is to establish ever greater unities and to preserve them thus—in short, to bind together; the aim of the second is, on the contrary, to undo connections and so to destroy things. In the case of the destructive instinct we may suppose that its final aim is to lead what is living into an inorganic state. For this reason we also call it the *death instinct*. If we assume that living things came later than inanimate ones and arose from them, then the death instinct fits in with the formula we have proposed to the effect that instincts tend towards a return to an earlier state. In the case of Eros (or the love instinct) we cannot apply this formula. To do so would presuppose that living substance was once a unity which had later been torn apart and was now striving towards re-union.

In biological functions the two basic instincts operate against each other or combine with each other. Thus, the act of eating is a destruction of the object with the final aim of incorporating it, and the sexual act is an act of aggression with the purpose of the most intimate union. This concurrent and mutually opposing action of the two basic instincts gives rise to the whole variegation of the phenomena of life. The analogy of our two basic instincts extends from the sphere of living things to the pair of opposing forces—attraction and repulsion—which rule in the inorganic world.

Modifications in the proportions of the fusion between the instincts have the most tangible results. A surplus of sexual aggressiveness will turn a lover into a sex-murderer, while a sharp diminution in the aggressive factor will make him bashful or impotent.

There can be no question of restricting one or the other of the basic instincts to one of the provinces of the mind. They must necessarily be met with everywhere. We may picture an initial state as one in which the total available energy of Eros, which henceforward we shall speak of as 'libido', is present in the still undifferentiated ego-id and serves to neutralize the destructive tendencies which are simultaneously present. (We are

without a term analogous to 'libido' for describing the energy of the destructive instinct.) At a later stage it becomes relatively easy for us to follow the vicissitudes of the libido, but this is more difficult with the destructive instinct.

So long as that instinct operates internally, as a death instinct, it remains silent; it only comes to our notice when it is diverted outwards as an instinct of destruction. It seems to be essential for the preservation of the individual that this diversion should occur; the muscular apparatus serves this purpose. When the super-ego is established, considerable amounts of the aggressive instinct are fixated in the interior of the ego and operate there self-destructively. This is one of the dangers to health by which human beings are faced on their path to cultural development. Holding back aggressiveness is in general unhealthy and leads to illness (to mortification). A person in a fit of rage will often demonstrate how the transition from aggressiveness that has been prevented to self-destructiveness is brought about by diverting the aggressiveness against himself: he tears his hair or beats his face with his fists, though he would evidently have preferred to apply this treatment to someone else. Some portion of self-destructiveness remains within, whatever the circumstances; till at last it succeeds in killing the individual, not, perhaps, until his libido has been used up or fixated in a disadvantageous way. Thus it may in general be suspected that the *individual* dies of his internal conflicts but that the *species* dies of its unsuccessful struggle against the external world if the latter changes in a fashion which cannot be adequately dealt with by the adaptations which the species has acquired.

It is hard to say anything of the behaviour of the libido in the id and in the super-ego. All that we know about it relates to the ego, in which at first the whole available quota of libido is stored up. We call this state absolute, primary *narcissism*. It lasts till the ego begins to cathect the ideas of objects with libido, to transform narcissistic libido into object-libido. Throughout the whole of life the ego remains the great reservoir from which libidinal cathexes are sent out to objects and into which they are also once more withdrawn, just as an amoeba behaves with its pseudopodia. It is only when a person is completely in love that the main quota of libido is transferred on to the object and the object to some extent takes the place of the ego. A characteristic of the libido which is important in life is its *mobility*, the facility with which it passes from one object to another. This must be contrasted with *the fixation* of the libido to particular objects, which often persists throughout life.

There can be no question but that the libido has somatic sources, that it streams to the ego from various organs and parts of the body. This is most clearly seen in the case of that portion of the libido which, from its instinctual aim, is described as sexual excitation. The most prominent of the parts of the body from which this libido arises are known by the name of '*erotogenic zones*', though in fact the whole body is an erotogenic zone of this kind. The greater part of what we know about Eros—that is to say, about its exponent, the libido—has been gained from a study of the sexual function, which, indeed, on the prevailing view, even if not according to our theory, coincides with Eros. We have been able to form a picture of the way in which the sexual urge, which is destined to exercise a decisive influence on our life, gradually develops out of successive contributions from a number of component instincts, which represent particular erotogenic zones.

2. The Early Development of Sexuality

ACCORDING TO THE PREVAILING VIEW human sexual life consists essentially in an endeavour to bring one's own genitals into contact with those of someone of the opposite sex. With this are associated, as accessory phenomena and introductory acts, kissing this extraneous body, looking at it and touching it. This endeavour is supposed to make its appearance at puberty—that is, at the age of sexual maturity— and to serve the purposes of reproduction. Nevertheless, certain facts have always been known which do not fit into the narrow framework of this view. (1) It is a remarkable fact that there are people who are only attracted by individuals of their own sex and by their genitals. (2) It is equally remarkable that there are people whose desires behave exactly like sexual ones but who at the same time entirely disregard the sexual organs or their normal use; people of this kind are known as 'perverts'. (3) And lastly it is a striking thing that some children (who are on that account regarded as degenerate) take a very early interest in their genitals and show signs of excitation in them.

It may well be believed that psycho-analysis provoked astonishment and denials when, partly on the basis of these three neglected facts, it contradicted all the popular opinions on sexuality. Its principal findings are as follows:

(*a*) Sexual life does not begin only at puberty, but starts with plain manifestations soon after birth.

(*b*) It is necessary to distinguish sharply between the concepts of 'sexual' and 'genital'. The former is the wider concept and includes many activities that have nothing to do with the genitals.

(*c*) Sexual life includes the function of obtaining pleasure from zones of the body—a function which is subsequently brought into the service of reproduction. The two functions often fail to coincide completely.

The chief interest is naturally focused on the first of these assertions, the most unexpected of all. It has been found that in early childhood there are

From Sigmund Freud, An Outline of Psychoanalysis, *trans. by James Strachey (New York: W. W. Norton, 1949), pp. 9–13. Reprinted with permission.*

signs of bodily activity to which only an ancient prejudice could deny the name of sexual and which are linked to psychical phenomena that we come across later in adult erotic life—such as fixation to particular objects, jealousy, and so on. It is further found, however, that these phenomena which emerge in early childhood form part of an ordered course of development, that they pass through a regular process of increase, reaching a climax towards the end of the fifth year, after which there follows a lull. During this lull progress is at a standstill and much is unlearnt and there is much recession. After the end of this period of latency, as it is called, sexual life advances once more with puberty; we might say that it has a second efflorescence. And here we come upon the fact that the onset of sexual life is *diphasic,* that it occurs in two waves—something that is unknown except in man and evidently has an important bearing on hominazation. It is not a matter of indifference that the events of this early period, except for a few residues, fall a victim to *infantile amnesia.* Our views on the aetiology of the neuroses and our technique of analytic therapy are derived from these conceptions; and our tracing of the developmental processes in this early period has also provided evidence for yet other conclusions.

The first organ to emerge as an erotogenic zone and to make libidinal demands on the mind is, from the time of birth onwards, the mouth. To begin with, all psychical activity is concentrated on providing satisfaction for the needs of that zone. Primarily, of course, this satisfaction serves the purpose of self-preservation by means of nourishment; but physiology should not be confused with psychology. The baby's obstinate persistence in sucking gives evidence at an early stage of a need for satisfaction which, though it originates from and is instigated by the taking of nourishment, nevertheless strives to obtain pleasure independently of nourishment and for that reason may and should be termed *sexual.*

During this oral phase sadistic impulses already occur sporadically along with the appearance of the teeth. Their extent is far greater in the second phase, which we describe as the sadistic-anal one, because satisfaction is then sought in aggression and in the excretory function. Our justification for including aggressive urges under the libido is based on the view that sadism is an instinctual fusion of purely libidinal and purely destructive urges, a fusion which thenceforward persists uninterruptedly.

The third phase is that known as the phallic one, which is, as it were, a forerunner of the final form taken by sexual life and already much resembles it. It is to be noted that it is not the genitals of both sexes that play a part at this stage, but only the male ones (the phallus). The female genitals long remain unknown: in children's attempts to understand the sexual processes they pay homage to the venerable cloacal theory—a theory which has a genetic justification.

With the phallic phase and in the course of it the sexuality of early childhood reaches its height and approaches its dissolution. Thereafter boys and girls have different histories. Both have begun to put their intellectual activity at the service of sexual researches; both start off from the premiss of the universal presence of the penis. But now the paths of the sexes diverge. The boy enters the Oedipus phase; he begins to manipulate his penis and simultaneously has phantasies of carrying out some sort of activity with it in relation to his mother, till, owing to the combined effect of a threat of castration and the sight of the absence of a penis in females, he experiences the greatest trauma of his life and this introduces the period of latency with all its consequences. The girl, after vainly attempting to do the same as the boy, comes to recognize her lack of a penis or rather the inferiority of her clitoris, with permanent effects on the development of her character; as a result of this first disappointment in rivalry, she often begins by turning away altogether from sexual life.

It would be a mistake to suppose that these three phases succeed one another in a clear-cut fashion. One may appear in addition to another; they may overlap one another, may be present alongside of one another. In the early phases the different component instincts set about their pursuit of pleasure independently of one another; in the phallic phase there are the beginnings of an organization which subordinates the other urges to the primacy of the genitals and signifies the start of a co-ordination of the general urge towards pleasure into the sexual function. The complete organization is only achieved at puberty, in a fourth, genital phase. A state of things is then established in which (1) some earlier libidinal cathexes are retained, (2) others are taken into the sexual function as preparatory, auxiliary acts, the satisfaction of which produces what is known as fore-pleasure, and (3) other urges are excluded from the organization, and are either suppressed altogether (repressed) or are employed in the ego in another way, forming character-traits or undergoing sublimation with a displacement of their aims.

This process is not always performed faultlessly. Inhibitions in its development manifest themselves as the many sorts of disturbance in sexual life. When this is so, we find fixations of the libido to conditions in earlier phases, whose urge, which is independent of the normal sexual aim, is described as *perversion*. One such developmental inhibition, for instance, is homosexuality when it is manifest. Analysis shows that in every case a homosexual object-tie was present and in most cases persisted in a *latent* condition. The situation is complicated by the fact that as a rule the processes necessary for bringing about a normal outcome are not completely present or absent, but *partially* present, so that the final result remains dependent on these *quantitative* relations. In these circumstances the genital organization is, it is true, attained, but it lacks those portions of the libido which have not advanced with the rest and have remained fixated to pregenital objects and aims. This weakening shows itself in a tendency, if there is an absence of genital satisfaction or if there are difficulties in the real external world, for the libido to hark back to its earlier pregenital cathexes (*regression*).

During the study of the sexual functions we have been able to gain a first, preliminary conviction, or rather a suspicion, of two discoveries which will later be found to be important over the whole of our field. Firstly, the normal and abnormal manifestations observed by us (that is, the phenomenology of the subject) need to be described from the point of view of their dynamics and economics (in our case, from the point of view of the quantitative distribution of the libido). And secondly, the aetiology of the disorders which we study is to be looked for in the individual's developmental history—that is to say, in his early life.

3. The Social Function of Guilt

WHY DO THE ANIMALS, KIN to ourselves, not manifest any such cultural struggle? Oh, we don't know. Very probably certain of them, bees, ants, termites, had to strive for thousands of centuries before they found the way to those state institutions, that division of functions, those restrictions upon individuals, which we admire them for to-day. It is characteristic of our present state that we know by our own feelings that we should not think ourselves happy in any of these communities of the animal world, or in any of the rôles they delegate to individuals. With other animal species it may be that a temporary deadlock has been reached between the influences of their environment and the instincts contending within them, so that a cessation of development has taken place. In primitive man a fresh access of libido may have kindled a new spurt of energy on the part of the instinct of destruction. There are a great many questions in all this to which as yet we have no answer.

Another question concerns us more closely now. What means does civilization make use of to hold in check the aggressiveness that opposes it, to make it harmless, perhaps to get rid of it? Some of

From Sigmund Freud, Civilization and Its Discontents *(New York: Cape and Smith Publishers, 1930), pp. 105–122. Reprinted with permission.*

these measures we have already come to know, though not yet the one that is apparently the most important. We can study it in the evolution of the individual. What happens in him to render his craving for aggression innocuous? Something very curious, that we should never have guessed and that yet seems simple enough. The aggressiveness is introjected, 'internalized'; in fact, it is sent back where it came from, *i.e.* directed against the ego. It is there taken over by a part of the ego that distinguishes itself from the rest as a super-ego, and now, in the form of 'conscience', exercises the same propensity to harsh aggressiveness against the ego that the ego would have liked to enjoy against others. The tension between the strict super-ego and the subordinate ego we call the sense of guilt; it manifests itself as the need for punishment. Civilization therefore obtains the mastery over the dangerous love of aggression in individuals by enfeebling and disarming it and setting up an institution within their minds to keep watch over it, like a garrison in a conquered city.

As to the origin of the sense of guilt, analysts have different views from those of the psychologists; nor is it easy for analysts to explain it either. First of all, when one asks how a sense of guilt arises in anyone, one is told something one cannot dispute: people feel guilty (pious people call it 'sinful') when they have done something they know to be 'bad.' But then one sees how little this answer tells one. Perhaps after some hesitation one will add that a person who has not actually committed a bad act, but has merely become aware of the intention to do so, can also hold himself guilty, and then one will ask why in this case the intention is counted as equivalent to the deed. In both cases, however, one is presupposing that wickedness has already been recognized as reprehensible, as something that ought not to be put into execution. How is this judgement arrived at? One may reject the suggestion of an original—as one might say, natural—capacity for discriminating between good and evil. Evil is often not at all that which would injure or endanger the ego; on the contrary, it can also be something that it desires, that would give it pleasure. An extraneous influence is evidently at work; it is this that decides what is to be called good and

bad. Since their own feelings would not have led men along the same path, they must have had a motive for obeying this extraneous influence. It is easy to discover this motive in man's helplessness and dependence upon others; it can best be designated the dread of losing love. If he loses the love of others on whom he is dependent, he will forfeit also their protection against many dangers, and above all he runs the risk that this stronger person will show his superiority in the form of punishing him. What is bad is, therefore, to begin with, whatever causes one to be threatened with a loss of love; because of the dread of this loss, one must desist from it. That is why it makes little difference whether one has already committed the bad deed or only intends to do so; in either case the danger begins only when the authority has found it out, and the latter would behave in the same way in both cases.

We call this state of mind a 'bad conscience' but actually it does not deserve this name, for at this stage the sense of guilt is obviously only the dread of losing love, 'social' anxiety. In a little child it can never be anything else, but in many adults too it has only changed in so far as the larger human community takes the place of the father or of both parents. Consequently such people habitually permit themselves to do any bad deed that procures them something they want, if only they are sure that no authority will discover it or make them suffer for it; their anxiety relates only to the possibility of detection.[1] Present-day society has to take into account the prevalence of this state of mind.

A great change takes place as soon as the authority has been internalized by the development of a super-ego. The manifestations of conscience are then raised to a new level; to be accurate, one should not call them conscience and sense of guilt before this.[2] At this point the

---

[1]One is reminded of Rousseau's famous mandarin!

[2]Every reasonable person will understand and take into account that in this descriptive survey things that in reality occur by gradual transitions are sharply differentiated and that the mere existence of a super-ego is not the only factor concerned, but also its relative strength and sphere of influence. All that has been said above in regard to conscience and guilt, moreover, is common knowledge and practically undisputed.

dread of discovery ceases to operate and also once for all any difference between doing evil and wishing to do it, since nothing is hidden from the super-ego, not even thoughts. The real seriousness of the situation has vanished, it is true: for the new authority, the super-ego, has no motive, as far as we know, for ill-treating the ego with which it is itself closely bound up. But the influence of the genetic derivation of these things, which causes what has been outlived and surmounted to be re-lived, manifests itself so that on the whole things remain as they were at the beginning. The super-ego torments the sinful ego with the same feelings of dread and watches for opportunities whereby the outer world can be made to punish it.

At this second stage of development, conscience exhibits a peculiarity which was absent in the first and is not very easy to account for. That is, the more righteous a man is the stricter and more suspicious will his conscience be, so that ultimately it is precisely those people who have carried holiness farthest who reproach themselves with the deepest sinfulness. This means that virtue forfeits some of her promised reward; the submissive and abstemious ego does not enjoy the trust and confidence of its mentor, and, as it seems, strives in vain to earn it. Now, to this some people will be ready to object that these difficulties are artificialities. A relatively strict and vigilant conscience is the very sign of a virtuous man, and though saints may proclaim themselves sinners, they are not so wrong, in view of the temptations of instinctual gratifications to which they are peculiarly liable—since, as we know, temptations do but increase under constant privation, whereas they subside, at any rate temporarily, if they are sometimes gratified. The field of ethics is rich in problems, and another of the facts we find here is that misfortune, *i.e.* external deprivation, greatly intensifies the strength of conscience in the super-ego. As long as things go well with a man, his conscience is lenient and lets the ego do all kinds of things; when some calamity befalls, he holds an inquisition within, discovers his sin, heightens the standards of his conscience, imposes abstinences on himself and punishes himself with

penances.[3] Whole peoples have acted in this way and still do so. But this is easily explained from the original infantile stage of conscience which, as we thus see, is not abandoned after the introjection into the super-ego, but persists alongside and behind the latter. Fate is felt to be a substitute for the agency of the parents: adversity means that one is no longer loved by this highest power of all, and, threatened by this loss of love, one humbles oneself again before the representative of the parents in the super-ego which in happier days one had tried to disregard. This becomes especially clear when destiny is looked upon in the strictly religious sense as the expression of God's will and nothing else. The people of Israel believed themselves to be God's favourite child, and when the great Father hurled visitation after visitation upon them, it still never shook them in this belief or caused them to doubt His power and His justice; they proceeded instead to bring their prophets into the world to declare their sinfulness to them and out of their sense of guilt they constructed the stringent commandments of their priestly religion. It is curious how differently a savage behaves! If he has had bad fortune, he does not throw the blame on himself, but on his fetish, who has plainly not done his duty by him, and he belabours it instead of punishing himself.

Hence we know of two sources for feelings of guilt: that arising from the dread of authority and the later one from the dread of the super-ego. The first one compels us to renounce instinctual gratification; the other presses over and above this towards punishment, since the persistence of forbidden wishes cannot be concealed from the super-ego. We have also heard how the severity of the super-ego, the rigour of conscience, is to be explained. It simply carries on the severity of external authority which it has succeeded and to some extent replaced. We see now how renunciation of

[3]This increased sensitivity of morals in consequence of ill-luck has been illustrated by Mark Twain in a delicious little story: *The First Melon I ever Stole.* This melon, as it happened, was unripe. I heard Mark Twain tell the story himself in one of his lectures. After he had given out the title, he stopped and asked himself in a doubtful way: 'Was it the first?' This was the whole story.

instinctual gratification is related to the sense of guilt. Originally, it is true, renunciation is the consequence of a dread of external authority; one gives up pleasures so as not to lose its love. Having made this renunciation, one is quits with authority, so to speak; no feeling of guilt should remain. But with the dread of the super-ego the case is different. Renunciation of gratification does not suffice here, for the wish persists and is not capable of being hidden from the super-ego. In spite of the renunciations made, feelings of guilt will be experienced and this is a great disadvantage economically of the erection of the super-ego, or, as one may say, of the formation of conscience. Renunciation no longer has a completely absolving effect; virtuous restraint is no longer rewarded by the assurance of love; a threatened external unhappiness—loss of love and punishment meted out by external authority—has been exchanged for a lasting inner unhappiness, the tension of a sense of guilt.

These inter-relations are so complicated and at the same time so important that, in spite of the dangers of repetition, I will consider them again from another angle. The chronological sequence would thus be as follows: first, instinct-renunciation due to dread of an aggression by external authority—this is, of course, tantamount to the dread of loss of love, for love is a protection against these punitive aggressions. Then follows the erection of an internal authority, and instinctual renunciation due to dread of it—that is, dread of conscience. In the second case, there is the equivalence of wicked acts and wicked intentions; hence comes the sense of guilt, the need for punishment. The aggressiveness of conscience carries on the aggressiveness of authority. Thus far all seems to be clear; but how can we find a place in this scheme for the effect produced by misfortune (*i.e.* renunciations externally imposed), for the effect it has of increasing the rigour of conscience? how account for the exceptional stringency of conscience in the best men, those least given to rebel against it? We have already explained both these peculiarities of conscience, but probably we still have an impression that these explanations do not go to the root of the matter, and that they leave something still unexplained. And here at last comes in an idea which is quite peculiar to psycho-analysis and alien to ordinary ways of thinking. Its nature enables us to understand why the whole matter necessarily seemed so confused and obscure to us. It tells us this: in the beginning conscience (more correctly, the anxiety which later became conscience) was the cause of instinctual renunciation, but later this relation is reversed. Every renunciation then becomes a dynamic fount of conscience; every fresh abandonment of gratification increases its severity and intolerance; and if we could only bring it better into harmony with what we already know about the development of conscience, we should be tempted to make the following paradoxical statement: Conscience is the result of instinctual renunciation, or: Renunciation (externally imposed) gives rise to conscience, which then demands further renunciations.

The contradiction between this proposition and our previous knowledge about the genesis of conscience is not in actual fact so very great and we can see a way in which it may be still further reduced. In order to state the problem more easily, let us select the example of the instinct of aggression, and let us suppose that the renunciation in question is always a renunciation of aggression. This is, of course, merely a provisional assumption. The effect of instinctual renunciation on conscience then operates as follows: every impulse of aggression which we omit to gratify is taken over by the super-ego and goes to heighten its aggressiveness (against the ego). It does not fit in well with this that the original aggressiveness of conscience should represent a continuance of the rigour of external authority, and so have nothing to do with renunciation. But we can get rid of this discrepancy if we presume a different origin for the first quantum of aggressiveness with which the super-ego was endowed. When authority prevented the child from enjoying the first but most important gratifications of all, aggressive impulses of considerable intensity must have been evoked in it, irrespective of the particular nature of the instinctual deprivations concerned. The child must necessarily have had to give up the satisfaction of these revengeful aggressive wishes. In this situation, in which it is economically so hard pressed, it has recourse to certain mechanisms well known to us; by the process of identification it absorbs into itself the invulnerable authority, which then becomes the super-ego and comes into possession of all the aggressiveness which the child would gladly have exercised against it. The child's ego has to content itself with the unhappy rôle of the authority—the father—who has been thus degraded. It is, as so often, a reversal of the original situation, 'If I were father and you my child, I would treat *you* badly.' The relation between superego and ego is a reproduction, distorted by a wish, of the real relations between the ego, before it was subdivided, and an external object. That is also typical. The essential difference, however, is that the original severity of the superego does not—or not so much—represent the severity which has been experienced or anticipated from the object, but expresses the child's own aggressiveness towards the latter. If this is correct, one could truly assert that conscience is formed in the beginning from the suppression of an aggressive impulse and strengthened as time goes on by each fresh suppression of the kind.

Now, which of these two theories is the true one? The earlier, which seemed genetically so unassailable, or the new one, which rounds off our theories in such a welcome manner? Clearly, they are both justified, and by the evidence, too, of direct observation; they do not contradict each other, and even coincide at one point, for the child's revengeful aggressiveness will be in part provoked by the amount of punishing aggression that it anticipates from the father. Experience has shown, however, that the severity which a child's super-ego develops in no way corresponds to the severity of the treatment it has itself experienced.[4] It seems to be independent of the latter; a child which has been very leniently treated can acquire a very strict conscience. But it would also be wrong to exaggerate this independence; it is not difficult to assure oneself that strict upbringing also has a strong influence on the formation of a child's super-ego. It comes to this, that the formation of

the super-ego and the development of conscience are determined in part by innate constitutional factors and in part by the influence of the actual environment; and that is in no way surprising—on the contrary, it is the invariable aetiological condition of all such processes.[5]

It may also be said that when a child reacts to the first great instinctual deprivations with an excessive aggressiveness and a corresponding strictness of its super-ego, it is thereby following a phylogenetic prototype, unheedful of what reaction would in reality be justified; for the father of primitive times was certainly terrifying, and one may safely attribute the utmost degree of aggressiveness to him. The differences between the two theories of the genesis of conscience are thus still further diminished if one passes from individual to phylogenetic development. But then, on the other hand, we find a new important difference between the two processes. We cannot disregard the conclusion that man's sense of guilt has its origin in the Oedipus complex and was acquired when the father was killed by the association of the brothers. At that time the aggression was not suppressed but carried out, and it is this same act of aggression whose suppression in the child we regard as the source of feelings of guilt. Now, I should not be surprised if a reader were to cry out angrily: 'So it makes no difference whether one does kill one's father or does not, one gets a feeling of guilt in

---

[4]As has rightly been emphasized by Melanie Klein and other English writers.

[5]In his *Psychoanalyse der Gesamtpersönlichkeit*, 1927, Franz Alexander has, in connection with Aichhorn's study of dissocial behaviour in children, discussed the two main types of pathogenic methods of training, that of excessive severity and of spoiling. The 'unduly lenient and indulgent' father fosters the development of an over-strict super-ego because, in face of the love which is showered on it, the child has no other way of disposing of its aggressiveness than to turn it inwards. In neglected children who grow up without any love the tension between ego and super-ego is lacking; their aggressions can be directed externally. Apart from any constitutional factor which may be present, therefore, one may say that a strict conscience arises from the co-operation of two factors in the environment: the deprivation of instinctual gratification which evokes the child's aggressiveness, and the love it receives which turns this aggressiveness inwards, where it is taken over by the super-ego.

either case! Here I should think one may be allowed some doubts. Either it is not true that guilt is evoked by suppressed aggressiveness or else the whole story about the father-murder is a romance, and primeval man did not kill his father any more often than people do nowadays. Besides this, if it is not a romance but a plausible piece of history, it would only be an instance of what we all expect to happen, namely, that one feels guilty because one has really done something which cannot be justified. And what we are all waiting for is for psycho-analysis to give us an explanation of this reaction, which at any rate is something that happens every day.'

This is true, and we must make good the omission. There is no great mystery about it either. When one has feelings of guilt after one has committed some crime and because of it, this feeling should more properly be called *remorse*. It relates only to the one act, and clearly it presupposes that *conscience*, the capacity for feelings of guilt, was already in existence before the deed. Remorse of this kind can, therefore, never help us to find out the source of conscience and feelings of guilt in general. In these everyday instances the course of events is usually as follows: an instinctual need acquires the strength to achieve fulfilment in spite of conscience, the strength of which also has its limits, whereupon the inevitable reduction of the need after satisfaction restores the earlier balance of forces. Psycho-analysis is quite justified, therefore, in excluding the case of a sense of guilt through remorse from this discussion, however frequently it may occur and however great its importance may be practically.

But if man's sense of guilt goes back to the murder of the father, that was undoubtedly an instance of 'remorse', and yet are we to suppose that there were no conscience and feelings of guilt before the act on that occasion? If so, where did the remorse come from then? This instance must explain to us the riddle of the sense of guilt and so make an end of our difficulties. And it will do so, as I believe. This remorse was the result of the very earliest primal ambivalence of feelings towards the father: the sons hated him, but they loved him too; after their hate against him had been satisfied by their aggressive acts, their love came to expression in their remorse about the deed, set up the super-ego by identification with the father, gave it the father's power to punish as he would have done the aggression they had performed, and created the restrictions which should prevent a repetition of the deed. And since impulses to aggressions against the father were repeated in the next generations, the feelings of guilt, too, persisted, and were further reinforced every time an aggression was suppressed anew and made over to the super-ego. At this point, it seems to me, we can at last clearly perceive the part played by love in the origin of conscience and the fatal inevitableness of the sense of guilt. It is not really a decisive matter whether one has killed one's father or abstained from the deed; one must feel guilty in either case, for guilt is the expression of the conflict of ambivalence, the eternal struggle between Eros and the destructive or death instinct. This conflict is engendered as soon as man is confronted with the task of living with his fellows; as long as he knows no other form of life in common but that of the family, it must express itself in the Oedipus complex, cause the development of conscience and create the first feelings of guilt. When mankind tries to institute wider forms of communal life, the same conflict continues to arise—in forms derived from the past—and intensified so that a further reinforcement of the sense of guilt results. Since culture obeys an inner erotic impulse which bids it bind mankind into a closely-knit mass, it can achieve this aim only by means of its vigilance in fomenting an ever-increasing sense of guilt. That which began in relation to the father ends in relation to the community. If civilization is an inevitable course of development from the group of the family to the group of humanity as a whole, then an intensification of the sense of guilt—resulting from the innate conflict of ambivalence, from the eternal struggle between the love and the death trends—will be inextricably bound up with it, until perhaps the sense of guilt may swell to a magnitude that individuals can hardly support. One is reminded of the telling accusation made by the great poet against the 'heavenly forces':

> Ye set our feet on this life's road,
> Ye watch our guilty, erring courses,
> Then leave us, bowed beneath our load,
> For earth its every debt enforces.[6]

[6]Goethe, *Wilhelm Meister.* The Song of the Harper.

And one may heave a sigh at the thought that it is vouchsafed to a few, with hardly an effort, to salve from the whirlpool of their own emotions the deepest truths, to which we others have to force our way, ceaselessly groping amid torturing uncertainties.

Study Questions

1. Describe the five phases of Freud's intellectual and professional development.

2. What does it mean to say that Freud was a materialist but not a reductionist?

3. What is the difference between sublimation and repression?

4. What does Freud mean by the id, the ego, and the superego? Explain how they interact to form our personality.

5. Describe Freud's five phases of psychological development.

6. Explain the difference of the passage of girls and boys through the Oedipus complex.

7. Explain what Freud means by a defense mechanism. Define the following defense mechanisms: regression, fixation, projection, reaction formation, and displacement.

8. For Freud, how was society first formed?

9. What is the source of "discontent" in society?

10. What does Freud mean when he says that belief in God is a form of wish-fulfillment?

Chapter 10

Standard Equipment 1: Sociobiology and Evolutionary Psychology

Introduction

In this chapter we will describe the theory of evolution as it was developed by Charles Darwin. We then consider the implications of evolutionary theory for our understanding of human nature, especially as this has been developed by the newly emerging sciences of human nature, sociobiology, and evolutionary psychology. The general theme throughout is that one of the products of evolution has been a human species that comes equipped with many innate tendencies to behave in one way or another. We are all born with various types of "standard equipment"[1] that shapes what we are and how we act.

Just as my border collie has a nature, a set of particular innate tendencies to behave that have been bred into him, so we have a *human* nature, certain ways of behaving that have been designed by evolution to adapt us to the environment. Various cultures, what we learn, may shape and direct these natural ways of behaving in one direction or another, just as my dog's herding instincts may be directed at sheep, cattle, ducks, or even small children. Nevertheless, despite our cultural differences, a central assumption of the new sciences of human nature is that at our core humans are all alike. We have all been fashioned in the same way by nature. We all have the same natures, the same natural tendencies to behave in one way rather than another. The new sciences of human nature study the various elements which compose this core, and draw for us a picture of what it means to be a human being. Because what they say is so significant for our discussion of human nature, this chapter will be longer than most in this text.

Worldview

Denial of the "Blank Slate" View of Human Nature

When the "standard equipment" view of human nature began to be developed in the late 1970s, the prevailing scientific view of human nature was based on the theories of human behavior developed especially by B. F. (Burrhus Frederic) Skinner (1904–1990). Skinner took his lead from John Watson (1879–1958), another American psychologist, who is often credited with being the true founder of this view, called **behaviorism.**

For Skinner and Watson before him, if psychology was to be a science it had to stop studying subjective mental events and focus instead on publicly observable behavior. To understand what intelligence is, for example, it is not helpful to ask intelligent people what is going on in their minds when they act intelligently.

Even if they could find something in their minds to report about, their responses would vary from time to time and from person to person. If psychology is to be a science its subject matter must be publicly observable. Only then can there be agreement among psychologists, only then can there be objectivity in psychology, only then can it become scientific. Just as we can study the intelligence of animals without ever knowing anything about their mental states, so also we can study human intelligence by observing the intelligent behavior of human beings. The same is true for other mental states as well, even for feelings and emotions.

For behaviorists, what we want to know about behavior is what causes it and how it can be altered. What causes it is always going to be something in the environment, not something in the mind. In fact, there is no mind for the behaviorist, at least in the sense that Descartes thought there was a mind. There is no non-physical substance that thinks, feels, and desires. Nor is there a physical substance, the brain, that performs "mental" actions. The "mind" is not a thing but rather is just a collection of mental events. These "mental" events are not states of the mind or the brain, rather they are each simply a collection of publicly observable behaviors. To be intelligent is to behave well on intelligence tests, to solve problems, and in general to be good at figuring things out. To desire something is not to have an internal conscious urge, but is simply to be inclined to pursue the object of desire. Even being in pain is not to be thought of as a conscious event, but instead it is to be understood as a collection of pain behaviors.

It is not that behaviorists believe that there is nothing going on between the ears, there is. But what is going on that is important is not a mental state, conscious, unconscious, or even preconscious. Rather it is something called a **conditioned reflex.** Just as we are born with innate reflex responses to the environment, such as sneezing and blinking, so when we learn something we associate a stimulus from the environment with a particular kind of response. This type of learning is called **conditioning,** and in one form or another it is at the heart of behaviorism.

Watson was influenced by the work of the great Russian physiologist, Ivan Pavlov (1849–1936). Pavlov conducted experiments with dogs, who normally salivate when food is present. Pavlov conditioned dogs to salivate even when food was not present by ringing a bell every time he brought them food. In this way they learned to associate food with the sound of the bell. Later, when he rang the bell in the absence of food, they still salivated. They were conditioned to associate the bell with food, so that the bell produced the same behavior as the food. According to this model, called **classical conditioning,** learning means to form a habit of association, a link between a particular type of stimulus and a certain kind of behavioral response. Learning is building up S-R (stimulus-response) connections.

Skinner modified this model of conditioning by focusing more on the reinforcement of desired behaviors and the elimination of undesirable ones. This approach to learning, called **operant conditioning,** did not rely on natural associations and was thus a more flexible form of behavior shaping. It is through these various processes of conditioning that we all learn the rules, behaviors, and ideas commonly called our **culture.** For behaviorists, just as the software of a computer determines how it responds to various types of input, so we are "programmed" by our parents and by society in general to behave as we do. Our culture is passed on to us by those who manipulate the stimuli, enforce the punishments, and bestow the rewards required to elicit the responses that they desire. The results of this manipulation are a set of internal conditioned reflexes, or learned habits, which link the environment with appropriate behavior. Just as we condition (train) animals to behave in certain ways when we give them certain commands, we condition (teach) humans to behave in ways that society finds desirable.

According to this view of behavior, what we were born with, our innate tendencies and powers, determines very little of our behavior. Beyond our reflexes, our senses, and other biological equipment, such as the mechanisms of respiration and circulation, we have no innate tendencies. Instead, we are born as what John Locke called a *tabula rasa*, or "blank slate." It is upon this blank slate that the natural and social environments write to make us what we are. Everything that we do is caused by the forces within these environments that create through conditioning of one sort or another the very types of persons that we are. Watson went so far as to claim that if he had control of a child from infancy onward, he could shape its behavior in any way he decided to. He could create a doctor, lawyer, criminal, good man, or evil man—just because he could control the environmental causes that make the man.

Skinner went on to develop behaviorism in much greater detail than had his predecessors. Under his direction, not only did behaviorism become an extremely successful approach to the study of animal behavior, it also became the leading theory of human behavior and the leading scientific theory of human nature. It became a standard doctrine not only of psychology, but also of the many social sciences, that human behavior is shaped by cultural forces alone. It is what we learn, our **nurture,** that makes us who we are. We have no free will to resist these forces, nor are there any inborn natural ways of behaving—and thus no **nature** at all.

The Influence of Darwin

Most of the theories discussed in this chapter accept a materialist view of reality and a scientific view of knowledge. Instead of discussing materialism and the scientific method once again, the primary *reality* to be discussed in this section is that described by the theory of evolution, and the central type of *knowledge* discussed is the evidence used to support it. Sociobiologists and evolutionary psychologists accept the theory of evolution as developed by Charles Darwin. They add to it an understanding of the mechanism of change that was unknown to Darwin, the modern theory of genetics. They also have the benefit of more evidence to support the theory of evolution than Darwin had, especially in the form of a more extensive fossil record. However, since the theory of evolution as developed by Darwin is simpler to understand than its more sophisticated contemporary versions, we will focus in this section on the nature and evidence for Darwin's version of the theory.

Charles Darwin (1809–1882) was born of a well-to-do family in Shropshire, England. In his youth he loved being outside, riding, fishing, hunting, and especially collecting insects and other creatures. He claimed to have been a born naturalist. At the time, someone who was interested in what today would be called botany was called a naturalist. Those who collected various species and fossils showing the development of species were often called natural historians. Such an interest was considered to be more of a hobby than a science in 1825, when Darwin was sent by his physician father to the University of Edinburgh, in Scotland, to study medicine. Finding this experience unsatisfactory, he transferred in 1828 to Cambridge University, where for three years he studied for the Anglican ministry. Once again, his studies were a disappointment to him. What was satisfying to him was his growing love of naturalism. During his six years of studying medicine and theology he had trained himself to be a first-rate natural historian.

In order to pursue this interest, Darwin signed on to the crew of the *HMS Beagle*, a royal ship whose five-year mission was to survey the coastline and uninhabited islands of South America. On this journey he was able to spend a great deal of his time on shore collecting and classifying various species and fossils of insects, fish, and mammals. Many of these were collected during the month that he spent on the Galapagos Islands, a small group of volcanic islands 600 miles off the coast of Ecuador. The data gathered on this trip provided the empirical basis for his theory of evolution, which he was to develop over the next twenty years.

The notion that species evolved was not new. It was in the air at Darwin's time and accepted by many scientists. What was unknown was *how* evolution occurred, what was the mechanism of change. The development of Darwin's answer was influenced by several sources, including Thomas Malthus (1766–1835), who wrote about the geometrical growth of populations. Also important was the work of Charles Lyell (1797–1875), an early geologist whose ideas about the considerable age of the Earth, and especially about the various layers of rock formations corresponding to its various ages, inspired Darwin's explorations for buried fossils. In addition, Darwin's work was also influenced by Alfred Russell Wallace (1823–1913).

In a letter to Darwin, Wallace proposed a hypothesis that Darwin had already formulated himself, that the mechanism of change is natural selection. Darwin previously had been reluctant to publish his ideas for fear of a negative reaction from scientists, religious leaders, and the general public. With Wallace to support him, he presented a paper on the theory of evolution by natural selection to the Royal Linnean Society of London. This was followed in 1859 with the publication of the text that dramatically changed how we understand the origin of life, *On the Origin of Species by Means of Natural Selection*. Darwin said little about the evolution of human life in this text, but in 1871 wrote a book in which he described human beings as the product of evolution. This book, which dramatically changed how we think of ourselves, was called *The Descent of Man*.

Prior to the theory of evolution, the prevailing view of how the various living species that inhabit this planet were created was that found in the Old Testament account of creation found in the Book of Genesis. According to this view, all creatures were created a little over six thousand years ago. They were created within six days by God, and they were created then as they are now. Some species may have been lost through various sorts of catastrophes since that time, but no species exists now that did not get created by God directly during the initial six days of creation. According to an evolutionary account, on the other hand, the process of creation was very different from that described in the story of Genesis.

We know today, for example, that the universe is about 13 billion years old, and that it began with the Big Bang. Gases from this initial explosion cooled to form stars and planets. The Earth and the entire solar system of which it is a part was probably formed from the explosion of a giant star about 4.5 billion years ago. Bacteria began to exist on Earth about 3.5 million years ago, while the first cells with nuclei (from which all organisms other than bacteria are built) began to exist about 2 billion years ago. Vertebrates first appeared about half a billion years ago, mammals about 250 million years ago, and birds about 150 million years ago. The common ancestor of both apes (bonobo, gorilla, chimpanzee, and orangutan) and humans, *australopithecus,* a small ape-like creature, roamed the plains of Africa some 5 million years ago. *Homo sapiens,* or modern humans, began to appear a mere four hundred thousand years ago.

We also know this: that the various forms of life that exist now, or have existed in the past on the Earth, all evolved from lower forms of life. According to the Genesis account, there was no evolving, or changing, of one species into another species. According to theory of evolution, however, this is exactly what happened. Darwin's great contribution was to explain how it could have happened, how one form of life could have arisen from another. He called his explanation of evolution **natural selection.** Here in a nutshell is his five-step description of natural selection. The first step is called *geometric increase.* He observed that all living things reproduce great numbers of themselves. If all the seeds produced by plants and all the eggs produced by various types of animals were to survive, the planet would quickly be overrun with life. But this does not happen. So what keeps the populations of various species in check?

Darwin's answer, and his second point, is called the *struggle for existence.* The resources required for existence (food, water, space, and so on) are limited. They can only support a limited number of offspring. This is what limits population growth. All those reproduced must struggle for these limited resources, they must compete with members of their own species, and only some will survive. What determines which ones will survive? To answer this question first requires an understanding of Darwin's third point, *variation.* Within each species there are slight variations. Some giraffes may have necks that are slightly longer than other giraffes, for example, or some individual plants may be slightly more brilliantly colored than others. Today we know that the variations are usually caused by small differences in the genes. Darwin knew little about genes, so he did not understand what caused variations in a species. He did observe them, however, and he understood that they were the key to explaining which individuals win the struggle for existence.

Darwin's fourth point is called the *survival of the fittest.* The individuals that survive are those that are the fittest, the ones who are most capable of winning the struggle for existence. What makes them more fit to survive than others is that their differences, how they vary from other members of the species, allow them to adapt better to the environment. To adapt better means to acquire more successfully the resources required for survival. Giraffes with longer necks can reach leaves higher up the tree, for example. Since this allows them to have more food and thus to be more likely to survive, they are able to reproduce and to pass on this trait to their offspring. If the environment remains the same, the offspring will retain the survival advantage and continue to pass it on. It now becomes more and more widely spread, until all members of the species have the trait. In a similar manner, the trait of the more brilliantly colored plant will survive because it attracts bees more readily, which will spread its pollen and increase its chances of reproduction.

This is how natural selection works. Accidental variations "select," or fit some organisms to the environment better than others. The ones selected by nature pass on their traits to their offspring, while those less fit die out. If the environment remains constant, then the species will change little. Those with the original adaptations will continue to be the fittest. If the environment changes, however, then traits that were adaptive may no longer continue to be so. Organisms with what were more adaptive traits may themselves die out, to be replaced by fitter versions. If tall trees disappeared, for example, and only short ones remained, giraffes with shorter necks may be more adaptive, and thus reproduce more offspring, gradually replacing long-neck giraffes. In this way nature continually selects for survival and reproduction those organisms that best fit their environments. It involves interaction between the variation of inherent characteristics of organisms and the environmental conditions in which they exist. Darwin's fifth point builds upon this process to explain the *origin of species*. It is the process of natural selection, the survival and reproduction of those organisms with adaptive variations, that explains the appearance of new species. New species evolve from previous ones as the result of a gradual process of variation and selection.

It is important to note that natural selection is not the only possible explanation for evolution. One interesting alternative was presented by a scientist who attempted to explain evolution well before Darwin, John Baptiste Lamarck (1744–1829). Lamarck proposed that evolution resulted from acquiring new traits. Lamark argued that giraffes, for example, have long necks because they need them to reach leaves on the high branches of trees. They gradually stretch their necks to greater and greater heights, causing them to grow longer and longer. Since long necks are adaptive, the giraffes with them survive and pass them on to their offspring. Unfortunately for Lamarck's hypothesis, even if giraffes could acquire longer necks, acquired traits cannot be transmitted to the next generation. Lamarckian evolution may be a good account of cultural evolution, since cultures seem to change by acquiring new traits and passing them on to the next generation. We will return to this theme later. Other forces that may affect the course of evolution include the immigration of new genes into a species, or a large number of mutations of its genes. While these processes do affect the evolution of traits, however, natural selection remains the dominant force.

Natural selection remains today as the leading explanation of evolution, but the focus on what it is that evolves, what is "fit," is placed less on the organism and its traits, what biologists call its **phenotype,** and more on its hereditary constitution, its collection of genes, called its **genotype.** *Genetic fitness* is a measure of how many copies of the genotype are passed on or inherited by other organisms. From this perspective, phenotypic traits are adaptive because of genetic fitness, and thus the biological "purpose" of an organism is to pass on its genes. A genotype may even be thought of, somewhat metaphorically, as building an organism as a vehicle for transmitting itself to the next generation. The genotypes that survive, the fittest ones, are those that build the most adaptive organisms. These are the organisms which are the most capable of survival and reproduction in their given environments.

The *evidence* for evolution, that life evolved over a period of several billion years, comes from many sources.[2] One available to Darwin, and even more richly available to us today, are the *fossil records* which show the history of life on Earth. Many of these fossils are found in various layers of rock. The age of the rock layer, and thus the fossils captured within them, can be dated. In this way it is possible to discover which forms of life existed at which periods in the Earth's history. When fossils of similar types from various ages were lined up in a temporal sequence, Darwin observed that there were slight modifications from one time period to the next. When looked at as a whole, the tree of life itself started to become evident to him. That is, it could be observed how groups of organisms come into existence, how they change into various forms, how some continued on to form new species and even new classes of organisms (reptiles into birds, for example), and how some, such as dinosaurs, become extinct. For Darwin as well as for others at his time, this temporal sequence was a sign of evolution or, as he called it, "descent with modification."

Another source of evidence, also available to Darwin, is *comparative anatomy*. That various structural components of different organisms resemble each other was not unnoticed by Darwin. He asks, for example:[3]

> What can be more curious than that the hand of a man, formed for grasping, that of a mole for digging, the leg of the horse, the paddle of the porpoise, and the wing of the bat, should all be constructed on the same pattern, and should include the same bones, in the same relative positions?

Once again, this was a sign of evolution for Darwin. In addition, he pointed out that the *distribution of different forms of life* in different parts of the world also was evidence for evolution, especially for evolution through natural selection. The considerable differences in the life forms found on the Galapagos Islands or in Australia, for example, are a product of their isolation and of their different environments. It is these environmental differences that have led, by natural selection, to the formation of wildly different life forms from those found elsewhere.

Evidence that exists today which was unknown to Darwin especially includes that associated with advances in molecular biology. In particular, the discovery of the DNA molecule and a fuller understanding of how *genes* work to produce phenotypic traits has allowed various species to be compared more precisely. The similarities in DNA between chimps and humans, for example, is quite striking. We share at least 98 percent of our genes with chimpanzees. Close similarities such as these between different species is taken as evidence of evolution. The existence of evidence such as fossil records, comparative anatomy, geographical distribution, and DNA evidence plainly shows that the "theory" of evolution is not just a theory in the sense that this term is often used in daily life. It is not just a guess or a hunch or an untested hypothesis, for example. Evolution is a well-established scientific theory, just as are the sciences of classical physics, chemistry, or anatomy. There are gaps to be filled in for sure, but the evidence gathered thus far provides a firm foundation for the belief that all life evolved. Plants, animals, and even human beings themselves all evolved from single cell organisms over a period of 4.5 billion years. Thus all forms of life on this planet, including human life, are related to all other forms of life.

The belief that humans are also the product of evolution was the chief subject of Darwin's *The Descent of Man*. Darwin summarizes his views of how this happened in *Reading 1*. The exact picture of how this happened was unknown to Darwin, as the title of his first chapter indicates, "Development of Man from Some Lower Form." Today we have a better, though not a complete, idea of the path that this evolution took.[4] Early humans and apes had a common ancestor, *australopithecus*, a small ape-like creature, as we said earlier. The descendants of *australopithecus* evolved in two directions. One led to the evolution of apes, while the other branch spawned early humans. The first early humans appeared about 2.5 million years ago and were called *homo habilis* ("handy man"). This species had large brains, walked upright, and made stone tools. From *homo habilis*, somewhere between 1.5 million and 2 million years ago, evolved *homo erectus*, a species with an even larger brain and even more sophisticated tools.

The *homo erectus* line then branched into two directions. One led to the Neanderthals, who lived from about one hundred and fifty thousand to thirty thousand years ago, then went extinct. The other led to *homo sapiens*, the oldest versions of which appeared four hundred thousand years ago. Modern humans are members of the species of *homo sapiens*. The earlier versions of us had brains about 20 percent smaller than ours are today. Those with brains about the same size as ours began to appear about one hundred and twenty thousand years ago. Since that time until now there has been little change in our biological features. An interesting point to note is that the apes which are our closest relatives, chimpanzees and bonobos, did not evolve from their branch of the *australopithecus* line until about half a million years ago, well past the 2.5 million years that the various human species began their evolution. We did not evolve from chimps or any other living species of apes or monkeys. Our simian ancestors are all extinct.

Human Nature

In principle at least, Darwin's theory of evolution by natural selection is neutral on the subject of human nature. It is possible that any theory of human nature might be the one that evolved. Skinner's minimalist view that we are blank slate general learning machines is as compatible with evolution as is Freud's, or even Plato's, for that matter. Only an empirical investigation will determine which human nature, in fact, did evolve. In this section we will examine some such investigations which appear in the form of new sciences, or at least new branches of established sciences. Despite their differences in method and scope, they share the belief that all life on Earth evolved through natural selection, and the common task of discovering what this means for our understanding of human nature. Darwin himself had some thoughts on this matter and it is to his ideas that we first turn our attention.

Darwin on Human Nature

Throughout this text we have spoken of both the structure of human nature and our innate tendencies to behave. Darwin clearly claims many things about the *structure* of human nature. We are purely material beings for one thing. For another, given our origins, we are animals; very special animals to be sure, but animals nonetheless. What about our *innate tendencies* to behave? Has evolution built into us behavior, as well as structure? Has it even selected for certain "social" behaviors that bestow adaptability? Darwin seemed to think that there are behaviors that have been selected for by nature, behaviors that contribute to our survival and especially to our ability to reproduce. Central among these behaviors, he speculated, are moral sentiments, kin selection, and sex selection.

Darwin seems to think that certain **moral sentiments** may have been selected for. These include not only certain moral virtues but also the feeling of guilt and the motivation of praise that accompany their enforcement. About the moral virtues of central importance he says:[5]

> In order that the primeval men, or the ape-like progenitors of man, should become social, they must have acquired the same instinctive feelings, which impel other animals to live in a body; and they no doubt exhibited the same general disposition. They would have felt uneasy when separated from their comrades, for whom they would have felt some degree of love; they would have warned each other of danger, and have given mutual aid in attack or defense. All this implies some degree of sympathy, fidelity and courage. Such social qualities, the paramount importance of which to the lower animals is disputed by no one, were no doubt acquired by the progenitors of man in a similar manner, namely, through natural selection, aided by inherited habitat.

The trouble with the belief that morality is inherited, however, especially the willingness to sacrifice for the survival of one's fellow group members, is that it seems to refute Darwin's own theory of natural selection. It seems that if Darwinian theory is correct, such members of the colony should not exist. They should have died out long ago. If natural selection drives us to reproduce our*selves,* then why should there be any sacrifice at all for the group? If evolution by natural selection favors those who can survive and reproduce, then Darwin's puzzle becomes one of explaining why those who sacrifice their lives for others and cannot reproduce end up being selected, and thus "fit."

The idea of **kin selection** is used by Darwin to explain how sacrificing behaviors are compatible with his theory of natural selection. He introduces it first on the level of the social behavior of insects. For example, colonies of ants, termites, and bees have evolved elaborate systems of social behavior that make them more adaptive to the environment, and thus more likely to pass on their genes. Some of the members of these insect colonies, for example, are sterile. In addition to being unable to pass on their genes, they are altruistic. That is, they are willing to give up their lives for the sake of the survival of the colony. The key to explaining this today is to say that "fit" means genetic fitness. Since the sterile caste of a colony shares many of the same genes with other members, their kin, their genes do go on even if they as individual organisms do not reproduce. In fact, their genes have a better chance of being passed on because they sacrifice for the colony.

Darwin, even in the absence of an understanding of genes, recognized that the unit of fitness is the family, not the individual. It is kin that are selected for. For some, the best way to ensure perpetuation of one's own genes is to sacrifice for the survival and reproductive success of relatives. If you are a sterile termite, then to give your life in battle against hostile forces better ensures that your genes are passed on by fertile near relations. In this way, "heroic" termites contribute to the success of the perpetuation of their own genes, as required by natural selection. Darwin seems to believe that the trait of kin selection made its way up the evolutionary ladder to humans, because it bestows greater fitness upon them. He says:[6]

> It must not be forgotten that although a high standard of morality gives but slight or no advantage to each individual man and his children over the other men of the same tribe, yet that an increase in the number of well-endowed men and an advancement in the standard of morality will certainly give an immense advantage to one tribe over another. A tribe including many members who, from possessing in a high degree the spirit of patriotism, fidelity, obedience, courage, and sympathy, were always ready to aid one another, and to sacrifice themselves for the common good, would be victorious over most other tribes; and this would be natural selection. At all times throughout the world tribes have supplanted other tribes; and as morality is one important element in their success, the standard of morality and the number of well-endowed men will thus everywhere tend to rise and increase.

In addition to moral sentiments and kin selection being part of our nature, Darwin seemed to think that we have also inherited some forms of **sex selection** behaviors. He believed especially that some of our forms of courtship behavior are inherited from lower forms of life, and not learned. Darwin held this belief for two reasons. First, because our relatives among the apes and other lower forms of animals have courtship behaviors similar to ours, and second because such behaviors seem to bestow a reproductive advantage. He spoke a great deal about patterns of sex selection in *The Descent of Man*, whose full title is *The Descent of Man and Selection in Relation to Sex.*

The starting point in describing which of our sex selection behaviors are produced by natural selection is the recognition that males and females contribute differently to reproduction. Women invest a great deal in each pregnancy and are capable of only a limited number of them. Men, on the other hand, may contribute to a great many fertilizations. Given this biological reality, it becomes in the interest of men to compete for access to many females. Winning such competitions bestows an evolutionary advantage, since the more females with which a male mates the greater the chances that his genes will be passed on to the next generation. For females, on the other hand, the important thing in selecting a mate is to be discriminating, to choose the male who will be most likely to protect and provide for her children. More will be said about this important topic of sex selection later. Now we turn to the modern sciences of human nature, all of which are heavily indebted to Darwin.

Sociobiology and Human Nature

Sociobiology is defined by E. O. Wilson, the Harvard entomologist who first developed this new science, as the *systematic study of the biological basis of all social behavior*. It claims that the principles of Darwin's theory of natural selection, suitably interpreted in terms of modern genetics, can explain not only the structural features of organisms but also their behavior, especially their social behavior. The social behavior of ants and bees and other animals is performed from instinct, not learning. These instincts are rooted in the genes. Genes, then, determine both the structure and the natural ways of behaving—the nature—of animals. Throughout the animal world, nature has selected those genes which lead to the types of structures and behaviors that make animals more able to survive and reproduce.

In his massive *Sociobiology: The New Synthesis* (1975),[7] which is thought of as the "Bible" of sociobiology, Wilson claims that nature has also selected patterns of behavior for human animals. He agrees with Darwin that not only is our biological structure the product of evolution, but natural selection has also endowed us with innate tendencies to behave. Natural selection first created human nature in our *homo habilis* and *homo sapiens* ancestors, a nature that fit them to the environmental conditions of their hunter-gatherer environments hundreds of thousands of years ago. Little evolution by natural selection has occurred since that time. We retain the same natures today as were adaptive for them in the past. We do not come into the world as behavioral blank slates, but rather we arrive with a great many tendencies to behave in one way rather than another. We are born with a human nature fashioned by evolution. Though *Sociobiology* spends most of its time on the social behavior of animals, its last chapter discusses some specific social behaviors of human beings that Wilson considers to be the product of natural selection. His next book on the subject, *On Human Nature*[8] (1978), focused entirely on human nature. *Reading 2*, a selection from this book, explains in general Wilson's highly influential version of the standard equipment view.

But how does Wilson know that the behaviors he identifies in these two books are natural and not simply learned? How does he know which behaviors are the products of evolution and which the products of culture? One way to tell if a behavior is natural and not learned is to see if it is universal across human cultures, especially cultures that have had little contact with others. In addition, if the behavior is shared with closely related species, and if it promotes survival and reproduction, then it is to be considered as part of our nature. Among the behaviors that fit into this category Wilson includes many that were mentioned by Darwin before him, such as the avoidance of incest, sex selection, kin selection, altruism, and various forms of aggressive behavior such as defending territory, warfare, fighting for dominance in a group, male dominance, and the division of labor between males and females. He also adds such behaviors as homosexuality and, perhaps surprisingly, he lists ethical behavior, aesthetic appreciation, religion, and even culture itself as behaviors caused by natural selection.

There was an immediate outcry from those in the humanities and social sciences against these claims of Wilson and other sociobiologists. Feminists were upset as well, since Wilson made several claims about the biological basis for many differences in behavior between men and women. Even some of Wilson's fellow biologists were strongly opposed to his views. Much of the criticism expressed by these groups was directed against what they perceived to be the political consequences of the idea of a biologically based human nature. If our social behavior, *all* of it, as Wilson seemed to say, is grounded in a human nature that is the product of evolutionary forces, then this behavior seems not to be susceptible to change. Those who criticized Wilson favored the opposing view that society could be molded by reason and by the manipulation of cultural forces. In this way societies could be produced that were more free and equitable.

Other criticism focused more on the following two points that Wilson seemed to leave unexplained in his first two books. The first one concerns cultural diversity. There are remarkable differences between cultures past and present. There are even remarkable differences between individuals within a culture. Social scientists explain these differences by referring to different environments, the different things that people have learned. In the humanities reference is also made to reason and choice as underlying explanations of differences. But Wilson seems unable to explain this widespread variation. If a tendency to behave in a certain way is part of our nature, this seems to mean that we must behave in accordance with its dictates. If our behavior is determined by our genes, and if we have genes for aggression, religion, ethics, and aesthetic appreciation, then the behaviors which they control seem to be as fixed and as inevitable as the color of our eyes. If there is a rigid connection between genes and behavior, however, then cultures should be quite similar. In fact, Wilson seems to say that they are, and their differences are merely apparent. In *On Human Nature* he claims that our cultures may vary a bit, but only within the boundaries of human nature.[9]

> Human nature is, moreover, a hodgepodge of special genetic adaptations to an environment largely vanished, the world of the Ice-Age hunter-gatherer. Modern life, as rich and rapidly changing as it appears to those caught in it, is nevertheless only a mosaic of cultural hypertrophies [excessive growth] of the archaic behavioral adaptations.

The second problem pointed out by critics is that Wilson did not explain the role played by the mind in shaping behavior and culture. His critics believe that the mind is not controlled by evolutionary forces. If it evolved at all, it evolved only into a general problem-solving mechanism quite adept at creating new cultures of any sort to fit our changing needs. In his early writings, Wilson gave the appearance that the primary causal connection is between genes and the cultures that they produced. He seemed to think, as Skinner had before him, that it was not necessary to include reference to the mind to explain how and why we live as we do.

Wilson responded to these two objections in several additional publications, including *Genes, Mind and Culture* (1981). In the opening paragraph of the preface of this work he spells out the task before him.[10]

> This book contains the first attempt to trace development all the way from genes through the mind to culture. Many have sought the grail of a unifying theory of biology and the social sciences. In recent years the present authors have come to appreciate the probable existence of some form of coupling between genetic and cultural evolution, and we have undertaken our effort with the conviction that the time is ripe for the discovery of its nature. The key, we feel, lies in the ontogenetic development of mental activity and behavior and particularly the form of epigenetic rules, which can be treated as "molecular units" that assemble the mind midway along the developmental path between genes and culture.

In this work Wilson appeals to the mind, which he thinks of as primarily the brain, to answer both of the objections just mentioned. He shows both how the mind shapes behavior and how it promotes variation in cultures. In doing so, however, he does not agree with his critics that the mind can work independently of its biological basis to create various cultures of just any sort. Instead, he continues to claim that nature is the cause of culture, but now by building minds according to the instructions of the genes which evolution has selected. In this way he hopes to explain the role that biology should play in understanding culture.

The basic idea had already been expressed in the first page of *Sociobiology*. Here Wilson says that "the organism is only DNA's way of making more DNA." From an evolutionary perspective, genes that have been selected for are those that can build an organism which allows for their survival and reproduction. Part of what the genes build in the human organism is a brain. This brain is filled with what Wilson calls **epigenetic rules.** The brain is an information processor, like a computer, and these rules function as its programs. Each of these rules, each of these functions of the brain, has been selected for by selecting for the genes that produce it. They control not only the biological functions of the body, but also its emotions, desires, cognitive abilities, and behavioral tendencies. In this way Wilson explains the role of the mind in shaping behavior while keeping the nature of mind firmly rooted in biology.

To answer the "cultural diversity" objection, Wilson focuses on the fact that many of our innate behavioral tendencies are flexible. We may respond in more than one way as various cultural choices present themselves. I may defend my territory with a gun or a lawsuit, for example. I may compete for a mate by fist-fighting, or becoming rich, or getting a Ph.D. Once societies got larger and more choices became available, this built-in flexibility led to greater variation of behavior. This is why, for the past ten thousand years or so, cultural variation has been much more significant in shaping behavior than genetic variation. In addition, and perhaps more importantly, our innate cognitive structures, which will be discussed in the next chapter on "cognitive science," are also flexible. We are not general purpose problem solvers, as the blank slate view holds. Our intelligence comes in many forms, all of which have been shaped by natural selection.

Nevertheless, even though our cognitive structures are designed for specific types of tasks, there are so many of them that the result is that we are flexible problem solvers. Different people use this flexibility to learn in different ways to adapt to and improve their environments. This is why there are differences between cultures, and even differences among individuals within the same culture. By including minds in his evolutionary account of the human species, Wilson not only can answer his critics, but now can also use minds to *explain* cultural diversity, not just describe it as he claims the social sciences do. He believes that if the social sciences are to do more than describe the superficial differences between cultures, if they are to explain why people behave as they do, they must necessarily adopt the perspective of natural selection and the findings of sociobiology.

More will be said about the relationship between biology and culture later in this chapter. The point for now is to see that the social behavior of human beings is both shaped by the mind and flexible at the same time. Thus the two objections are met. However, the mind's flexibility is still limited by natural selection. We are still biased by the genes, to learn in particular ways and to choose some types of behaviors over others. Though there may be different ways to exhibit them in various cultures, ways of learning and various types of behaviors such as defending territory, mate selection, altruism, and so on, are wired into our brains, and thus are an inescapable part of human nature. Wilson's oft quoted phrase is that our genes hold culture "on a leash."

Evolutionary Psychology and Human Nature

According to some, **evolutionary psychology** is just another name for sociobiology. A name change was felt to be necessary by people working in the field because of the widespread, often ill-informed, usually negative reaction that sociobiology provoked. However, others distinguish between the two sciences by thinking of one as a subset of the other. Though there is dispute about which has the broader scope, it will be accepted here that evolutionary psychology is a part of sociobiology. It is the part that focuses especially on *human* social behavior, where sociobiology focuses on the social behavior of all animals. Evolutionary psychology is a subset of sociobiology not only because it has a similar subject matter, but also because it accepts the same theoretical framework. It assumes, for example, that the human mind has evolved according to the principles of natural selection. Not everyone accepts this assumption. It was even questioned by Alfred Wallace, who thought that the mind can do too much, well beyond that required for survival and reproduction, to be a product of evolution. While many continue to believe that our bodies may have been created by evolution, but our minds are the product of God, evolutionary psychologists see our minds—by which they mean our *brains*, as the products of nature.

Evolutionary psychologists also share the belief with sociobiologists that the mind is not one single thing, but rather is composed of various "parts" or functions. While Wilson calls these epigenetic rules, evolutionary psychology refers to these innate structures of the mind as **psychological adaptations.** That they are indeed adaptive is another belief of evolutionary psychology. The mind evolved as it has because each of its functions contributed to survival and reproduction. The period of time when most of the psychological adaptations which form our minds occurred was the Late Stone Age, from 1.8 million to about two hundred thousand years ago. For convenience, we will simply say that it was about a million years ago that our human nature was shaped in our hominid ancestors. It was to the environmental conditions present at that time that our inborn structures and functions, our human nature, adapted. Evolutionary psychologists assume that there has been little evolutionary progress, little change in human nature, in the past million or so years. The human nature that was shaped in the Stone Age is more or less the one that we find today. Most of the differences between humans today and then is attributed to cultural evolution, to the ways that we have learned to adapt to the changing conditions of the environment.

The basic goal of evolutionary psychology, is to discover the elements of a universal human nature, the functions of the human mind, how it is designed. It pursues this goal using the following two-step method. First, it determines which tendencies of human beings appear to be universal, that is, appear to be possessed by all human beings across all cultures and historical periods. Second, it considers these tendencies to be the product of evolution, and thus part of human nature, if explanations can be found for how they promoted survival and especially reproduction a million years ago.

In addition to the list contributed by Darwin, Wilson, and other sociobiologists, evolutionary psychologists have discovered many more ways that the mind has been designed. Sexual attraction and jealousy, for example, find their explanations as part of human nature in the dynamics of *reproduction*. Sexual attraction clearly promotes reproduction, though it is not immediately clear why feelings of jealousy do. The explanation is that jealousy helps to retain a mate and prevent infidelity, which in turn helps to ensure the passing on of one's own genes. Other psychological adaptations such as altruism and aggression help to promote *survival*. Sharing food, for example, as well as being aggressive in the face of danger, both contribute to survival and thus are fixed in human nature. As these examples show, for an evolutionary psychologist a scientific account of human nature is to be developed by identifying widespread current tendencies to behave and explaining how they could have been adaptive in the Late Stone Age. If a plausible story can be told about the way that the behavior enhances survival or reproduction, then it can be counted as part of human nature. If not, then it is to be considered learned behavior and not part of human nature.

An example from our ordinary lives may help to explain how such a story might be constructed. Suppose it seems to be universal across cultures that men are attracted to women with a certain type of figure. In particular, they like a certain hip-to-waist ratio. Is that an innate trait, or is it caused by learning, by watching ads on television, for example, which portray what are supposed to be attractive women? To answer this question requires a story to be told about the psychological adaptiveness of such a behavior. In this case, the story must show that it makes reproduction, the passing on of one's genes, more likely than alternative behaviors. Indeed it does, according to evolutionary psychologists, because they believe that women with just these sorts of figures turn out to be more fertile.

Much of what evolutionary psychologists explain is common, everyday behavior. They believe that most of us are blind to our innate tendencies to behave precisely because they are so familiar to us that they go unnoticed. One of the early developers of evolutionary psychology, Leda Cosmides, says:[11]

> . . . our natural competences—our ability to see, to speak, to find someone beautiful, to reciprocate a favor, to fear disease, to fall in love, to initiate an attack, to experience moral outrage, to navigate a landscape, and myriad others—only are possible because there is a vast and heterogeneous array of complex computational machinery (psychological adaptations) supporting and regulating these activities. This machinery works so well that we don't even realize that it exists. We all suffer from instinct blindness.

For an interesting example of such blindness in the presence of a psychological adaptation, consider the following.[12] We all assume that we know things about other people's mental states. We know if another is in pain, for example, when we see him hit his finger with a hammer and cry out. We know when people are depressed, happy, and fearful; we know when they are thinking, planning, hoping; and even sometimes what they are thinking about, and planning and hoping for. But how do we know this? We cannot observe the minds of others, only their behavior. For all we know, they might be like robots, behaving outwardly as we do in similar environmental circumstances, but with no mind on the inside.

To "know" that others have mental states, say evolutionary psychologists, is for us to construct a low-level theory about their minds. This theory amounts to the general hypothesis that they have minds in the first place. The basic "laws" of this theory say that when in certain circumstances others behave in a certain way, they have a mental state that is similar to mine when I behave that way in the same set of circumstances. When confronted by a saber-toothed tiger, for example, I get frightened and want to run away, so they must be frightened and want to flee when they see such a beast. In this way we can "read" the minds of others. We all do this all the time and simply take it for granted. It is part of our nature. But why is this so? Because being able to tell with a certain degree of probability what is going on in another's mind would have bestowed an advantage on our hunter-gatherer ancestors. The ones who had this psychological adaptation would be more likely to survive if they knew, for example, that an enemy was fearful. Since we do have this adaptation today, it did bestow such an advantage to them, and thus allowed more of those who developed it to pass it on in their genes.

The main point to make as we close this discussion on the core question of human nature is that sociobiology and evolutionary psychology together make a strong case for the existence of a universal human nature. Their central claim is that evolution has seen to it that we have been programmed with hundreds, even thousands of innate structures and innate tendencies to act in one way or another. These inborn structures and functions, our shared human nature, make us more fit to survive, reproduce, and understand the world in which we live.

Consequences

Freedom

Perhaps the fiercest criticism that the standard equipment view of human nature generated was of what seemed to many to be its unavoidable political consequences. They argued that social evils such as sexism, violence, and war seemed to be inevitable on the standard equipment view, since our minds come preprogrammed with aggression, selfishness, male dominance, and other relatively nasty inclinations. If our minds come with standard equipment such as this, then it seems that the standard equipment view dooms us to an imperfect social life. This is quite the opposite belief from Marx and Skinner, who thought that the "blank slate" of human nature was moldable into a more perfect condition. The new Darwinian sciences of man are dangerous, the critics argued, since they might lead people to abandon social reform as a hopeless enterprise.

At the root of this criticism lies the belief that the standard equipment view is committed to **genetic determinism.** This is the belief that human beings are merely puppets dancing on genetic strings. If we have genes for particular diseases and particular physical traits, such as the color of our hair and eyes, then we get those diseases and we get that hair and eye color. In the same way, the critics argued, if we have genes for certain types of behavior, we must also have to behave that way. To say, as Wilson did, that genes do not cause behavior, but that the epigenetic rules embedded in our minds do, seems to make little difference. After all, it is our genes that construct the epigenetic rules, including our psychological adaptations and our cognitive functions, which then lead to our social and individual behaviors. But does the standard equipment view really lead to the conclusion that we are genetically determined, and thus not any more free to act than, say, our computers?

The analogy between minds and computers may be helpful to clarify the issue of genetic determinism. Some rejected the standard equipment view because they want to return to the more traditional view of human nature. They had not been happy with the environmental determinism of Skinner before, and were now even less happy with the genetic determinism of Wilson. This is because they are not happy with any form of determinism. Instead, they prefer to understand the central elements of human nature to be reason and free will. Instinct may determine animal behavior, but reason and free will are what determine human behavior. For them, the human mind is not like a computer at all. Instead, it is like the operator of a computer. It stands outside of the forces of nature, and thus is able to change its course "at will." It can learn from experience, channel emotions into reasonable behavior, choose which desires to act upon, and initiate all sorts of behaviors. Our bodies may be machines that have been programmed by evolution, but our minds lie outside of nature and thus are free to act as reason suggests.

Others who rejected genetic determinism, including behaviorists, most social scientists, and even some biologists, nevertheless accepted environmental determinism. For them, the mind did evolve, but what it evolved into is a sort of general conditioning mechanism. It does not contain the many specific and specialized cognitive and behavioral functions that the standard equipment advocates claim for it. Instead, it is like a computer that comes with only the operating system hardwired in. Everything it does with this operating system, all of its behavior, is determined by the programs that get installed later. Its programs are the "software" acquired by learning, by being conditioned to act in accordance with the many aspects of our culture. Genes determine only our general ability to learn through various forms of conditioning, not what we learn and certainly not how we behave. The incredible flexibility of our behavior and the widespread variations among cultures seem to attest to that.

The standard equipment view, on the other hand, claims that we are like computers whose operating system *and* many, many specialized programs are all hardwired in. These programs most assuredly have been designed by the genes that were selected for the fitness of our hunter-gatherer ancestors. In this sense, genetic determinism is true. Genes do build our bodies and minds. They are the ultimate explanation for why we are as we are, and for why we have the tendencies to behave as we do. However, genes alone do not explain our behavior. Genes alone are merely the blueprint for the construction of a human being. They do nothing on their own. Many other bodily processes from the level of cells to the central nervous system itself must cooperate with these instructions for the human body to be designed. We will skip the long story, usually told by **behavioral genetics,** of the links between genes and cells and proteins and hormones and neural circuitry and so on. It is enough to say that many more things besides having genes must go right in the body before a mind with behavioral tendencies is built.

More importantly, the human nature that gets created is at most a collection of tendencies or dispositions to behave. The proper environmental conditions must exist for these behaviors to be elicited. Language learning behavior may be wired in, for example, but in the absence of linguistic stimuli language would not be developed. So behavior is at the very least the result of both environment and the genetically constructed mind; both nature and nurture are required for any behavior. Curiously enough, since the genes that we inherited were formed in reaction to the hunter-gatherer environment in which they evolved, it might even be said by the standard equipment advocate that the environment is the ultimate cause of human nature, and thus behavior.

The main thing that the foes of the standard equipment view of human nature fear is the lack of flexibility of our behavior that it seems to accept. However, the standard equipment view is not committed to such a view. It does recognize that human behavior is flexible, and explains this in two ways. First, the many specialized programs we have built into us are themselves what makes us flexible. Instead of seeing our innate tendencies to behave as restrictions on behavior, they may be viewed instead as opportunities to behave in many different ways. To understand this change of perspective note, for example, that we must have oxygen to live, and that we have developed lungs to breath it in from the environment. We do not say because of this that we are *determined* to breath in certain ways, that our breathing behavior is restricted and inflexible. Rather we say that having lungs gives us the ability to breath. In the same way, having minds that contain functions designed by nature that dispose us to behave in certain ways should be viewed less as a restriction on behavior, and more as the root of its flexibility. We can do many things because we have many wired in, specialized programs.

In addition, and most importantly, most of those who hold the standard equipment view understand that our innate tendencies may be expressed in various ways in various cultural environments. Almost everyone who accepts that the framework of evolutionary biology applies also to human behavior admits that cultural evolution has become more important in determining how we behave than biological evolution. They admit that we are intelligent beings and that we can learn from our experience of both the natural and the human environments which we inhabit. We especially can learn new behaviors relatively quickly by absorbing the wisdom found in our culture, and thus acquire a vastly more rich and complex repertoire of behaviors than nature alone designed for us so long ago. Think of all the things that you have learned so far in life—including language, science, math, personal relations skills, law, morality, sports, religion, business, entertainment, and all the manners and the customs of daily life—all part of culture and all knowledge that expands our repertoire of behavior. Possessing a culture vastly extends the variation of responses available to us beyond those which were available to our Stone Age ancestors.

Since our hunter-gatherer ancestors had to deal with the unpredictable behavior of their fellow hominids, and not just the relatively inflexible patterns of nature, such flexibility would have been adaptive then, as it is now. Especially in the past ten thousand years or so, since people began living in large groups, culture has been by far the most important cause of our behavior. Our genes may dispose us to build cultures of a certain sort. Not just any types of behaviors will mesh with our innate tendencies. But these tendencies to behavior may be expressed in a wide range of behaviors. For example, selecting a mate in the twenty-first century may be biologically and psychologically similar to doing so a million years ago. It may stem from the same innate tendencies now as it did then. However, it is significantly more complex and varied than it was for our ancient ancestors, since it is driven today by many culturally acquired desires as well. Even if there is such a thing as "the" correct hip-to-waist ratio, for example, males learn that their mates should have many more desirable qualities than simply the correct figure. Intelligence, kindness, and shared interests are equally as important. In addition, while aggression in a male may have been an important quality in the selection of a mate by a female in the Stone Age, too much of it today is seen as a negative quality. Just as important today is sensitivity and intelligence.

The details which explain the balance between our obvious flexibility and our innate tendencies are not yet fully worked out by these relatively new sciences. However the balance is finally understood, it should be clear that the standard equipment view is compatible with the flexibility of human behavior. This does not mean that it has a place for free will, however. At most it allows for a version of **soft determinism.** According to the "determinism" part of this view, for an action to be free means that it comes from you, not from external forces. You decided to do it; no one had a gun at your head. In general, to be free means to do what *you* want to. What you want to do, however, is itself caused, for the standard equipment view, by a combination of genes and environment. It is never the result of something called free will. We have no free will, only freedom of action.

The "soft" part of soft determinism holds that we are, nevertheless, responsible for our actions. To be responsible, however, simply means that our behavior is subject to the punishments and rewards that may be used to shape it, as Skinner, Freud, and so many others believed. We are not inflexible automatons, we are not like rocks and trees, incapable of alternative behaviors. We are flexible beings, whose behavior may be molded by environmental conditions. Among these conditions are included the praise and blame that awaits us after performing certain types of actions. If we know that blame, especially harsh punishment, for example, will be the outcome of an action, then we will refrain from performing it. On the other hand, we will be motivated to perform actions that promise rewards. In addition to the sorts of praise and blame that exist in ethics and the justice system, our ability to behave in a variety of ways also allows us to shape our behavior on an even grander scale. We do this by designing cultures which promote the behaviors that we desire and deter those that we oppose.

Ethics

We have seen many times in this text that ethics is about the nature of the good life and the nature of right and wrong. According to Darwin, Wilson, and other proponents of the standard equipment view of human nature, our ethical systems, the ones that we actually use, are not created by society. Rather, they have evolved to enable those of our hunter-gatherer ancestors who possessed them to pass on their genes more successfully than those who did not. But what is the nature of this system, and how might it best be described? Did evolution pass on a utilitarian view, a Kantian view, an Aristotelean view? What sort of ethics does evolutionary biology favor and why?

One answer to this question was called **Social Darwinism,** a view developed by a contemporary of Darwin, Herbert Spencer (1820–1903). It claimed that the proper ethical theory, the one that fits human nature best, comes directly from Darwinian principles. Spencer collectively called these principles "the survival of the fittest." Here the good life is the life of those with the highest social status, the morally acceptable actions are pretty much whatever it takes to get there. As the fittest animals are the ones that get to reproduce, the fittest (best) humans are the ones that are the richest and most influential.

According to this view, nature had selected the rich and the poor according to their characteristics to be in the station of life in which they found themselves. Since the results of social class were supposed to be caused by a process of nature, it was used to justify the callous and indifferent treatment of the poor by the rich. If nature had selected the strongest to rise to the top, and if this was the right thing to do, then why care about the poor whose condition was also determined by natural forces? Many of society's privileged few, especially in the United States, championed this doctrine. However, this was a distortion of Darwin's views and was rejected by Darwin himself. Nature selected as the fittest those organisms that were best able to pass on their genes; Spencer selected as the fittest those who happened, often by ruthless and immoral means, to be the richest and most powerful.

Wilson rejects social Darwinism and argues instead that the ethical perspective most compatible with evolution by natural selection is a type of **ethical subjectivism.** According to this view, the goal of life (the good life) is survival, and anything that promotes this is morally acceptable. Each of the moral rules that we follow, such as "do not murder," "do not commit adultery," and so on, are just so many ways to promote survival and reproduction.

So right and wrong are not determined by reason guiding us to a higher mode of existence, as Kant or Aristotle might say, but rather our moral obligations flow from a set of feelings that evolved because they enhanced our genetic fitness. Moral rules primarily present themselves as urges within us, as "gut reactions" to various situations. That is why Wilson refers to morality as "subjective." Perhaps later we give reasons for why we have the rules that we do. But these reasons, such as appeals to moral principles, are merely rationalizations of a deeper process. We consider actions to be wrong simply because we *feel* that they are wrong. The ones that we feel are wrong turn out to be the very ones selected to be opposed by evolution. For us to say that some actions are wrong, then, simply means that we do not approve of them, and that we will punish those who perform them. In the end, ethics reduces to feelings that are the product of natural selection.

Wilson allows that just because a feeling was adaptive a million years ago, and thus is natural, does not always mean that acting on it today should be considered to be right. Simply having a set of evolved moral feelings does not justify acting upon them. Being biologically adaptive does not mean that a behavior is advantageous today. Something like aggression that helped our hunter-gatherer ancestors pass on their genes may be a trait that is harmful today, and thus needs to be controlled by the power of both moral and legal rules. We may sometimes feel that we want to punch or shoot our neighbor, but we realize that rules which prohibit such actions are better suited for both the individual and the common good. We may have the same urges that our remote ancestors did. We may even feel required to act upon them in *some* way. Fortunately, as a result of living within cultures rich with choices, we have many different, more morally acceptable avenues to express these feelings today. Instead of killing our neighbor, for example, we can argue with him and then play or watch a game of football.

Society

There are several questions about society that may be asked of the standard equipment view. For example, it might be interesting to know if one type of society is to be preferred over another, given the human natures that we have. We may also ask about the origin of society. The answer would be a story about how our ancestors changed from a hunter-gatherer mode of existence to an agricultural one. This allowed for society to grow larger and for the emergence of the division of labor. Instead of asking about the nature or origin of society, however, the most interesting question to ask of the standard equipment view is *how our human nature relates to culture.* The answer provided by the standard equipment view is a long one, and it builds upon its response to the genetic determinism question discussed earlier. A shorter version of their answer goes something like this.

Culture is a collection of all of our shared beliefs, technologies, customs, and values that are learned. The prevailing view of culture adopted by the blank slate view is that culture should be thought of as a system that is independent of human minds. It is a system that we might call "society" and its role is to shape human minds. It is the source of our beliefs and the behaviors that follow from them; it is the source of our selves. We have no particular way to be prior to becoming socialized into a particular culture, no preexisting sort of self, no human nature. The cultural systems and subsystems in which we have been immersed define us. From this it follows that if you change the culture, you change the nature of society and thus you change the self.

One advantage of this story about the primacy of culture is that it seems to account for the speed with which cultures may change, or evolve. Cultural changes cannot be caused by natural selection, which usually work only over vast amounts of time to change behavior. Since human behavior has changed dramatically in the past ten thousand relative short years of our existence, it is because we learn how to adapt to our environments. If cultural changes come about so rapidly, it seems to follow that it is culture, not the painstakingly long evolution of our biology, that makes us who we are. It is learning, or *nurture,* that makes the person, not our *nature.* If the standard equipment view maintains that all humans come into this world with tendencies to behave that define us, and that these natural behaviors are shaped by millions of years of natural selection, then how can it explain the immense role that cultural evolution plays in shaping our lives, a culture that seems separate from our biology?

The standard equipment view agrees that it is cultural evolution, not natural selection, that has shaped us for at least the past ten thousand years. Our human nature has remained fixed during this time, because we have adapted to environmental changes by learning how to do so. If it got colder, we made warmer clothes; if hunting became more difficult, we grew food; if a drought hit us, we found water beneath the earth. While it is true that learning is now the primary shaper of behavior, however, it is only because evolution has shaped our cognitive, emotional, and moral faculties that we can learn in the first place, and that we can form cohesive societies which pass this knowledge on from one generation to the next. Our intellectual faculties have taken over the process of evolution. However, these faculties, as well as their emotional and moral accompaniments, themselves have their roots in natural selection. It is only by understanding what our various forms of standard equipment are like that we can understand the cultures that spring from them.

Seeing culture as embedded in human nature allows the standard equipment view to actually explain it. According to the standard equipment view, the social sciences explain nothing about behavior. They simply start with culture and then describe *how* it causes people to behave. It does not explain *why* we have the cultures that we do. In some respects this social science approach parallels that of Descartes' view of the mind. Culture for the blank slate view is like the Cartesian mind that is independent of the body. Because it is independent of the body, it must be studied by methods that are different from those used to study nature. The standard equipment view wants to join the mind and body once again. It wants to connect our biology with our beliefs and behaviors, and use our natures to explain our cultures. One way that it does this is by pointing out that the very thing that makes culture possible, our cognitive ability, has itself evolved to fit our hunter-gatherer ancestors to their environments. Because of this, there are now cognitive abilities of various sorts. We have various types of intelligence that allow us to learn various ways to adapt to our environments. We were shaped by natural selection to be problem solvers in various areas of life, to figure out different ways of doing things when old patterns break down. According to Howard Gardner, for example, we have seven different types of intelligence as part of our modular minds: linguistic, musical, interpersonal, intrapersonal, bodily, logical, and spatial.[13]

If we see culture not as an arbitrary way of living, but rather as a means to help us live our lives according to our evolved adaptive strategies, then the standard equipment view can begin to explain not only the diversity and importance of culture, but also its very existence. Cultures arise from minds shaped by evolution and they contain, despite their apparent diversity, patterns which reflect the innate structures and tendencies of these minds. Much of the diversity between cultures is superficial, just so many different ways to reflect similar tendencies to behave. All cultures, however, reflect the core of our hunter-gatherer minds. We do well to acknowledge this, especially if we want to discourage some of the behaviors that were adaptive a million years ago, but now are harmful. Changing how we ought to behave must begin with the recognition of our human nature as it is.

God

Two issues will be discussed very briefly in this section. One concerns the origin of religion, while the other examines one of the popular ways that some religions express their opposition to evolutionary biology. Concerning the origin of religion, Wilson points out that one of the virtually universal elements of all cultures, past and present, is **religion.** As did Freud and others before, some advocates of the standard equipment view, such as Wilson, attempt to explain religion in scientific terms. According to Wilson,[14]

> The enduring paradox of religion is that so much of its substance is demonstrably false, yet it remains a driving force in all societies.

While most religious believers think of God as creating the universe, Wilson thinks that the universe created God. That is, the practice of religion evolved because it serves many needs for individuals and societies.[15]

> Religions . . . provide rules and incentives to regulate the socially disruptive, egoistic strivings of individuals and mobilize them toward common goals that require cooperation and reciprocity. Religious rituals also supply a sense of community with the past as well as sanctifying the milestones of life: birth, puberty, marriage, and death. They nurture billions of people with love and hope and provide a spiritual release that is both real and comforting.

The second idea to discuss in this section is the "creation science" or **creationist** view. Many religions have little trouble these days accepting evolution as the way that God created the various species on Earth. Creationists, however, are usually members of fundamentalist sects, who accept the creation story as told in Genesis as literally true. This in itself would pose little concern, since people have a right to believe what they want to. However, many creationists actively oppose the teaching of evolutionary theory in high schools. Others at least insist that creationism be taught as well, as a competing view deserving the same respect. They often say such things as evolution "is just a theory," implying by this that it is only a "hunch" and that their account deserves equal consideration. Evolution, however, is a well-established scientific theory which is backed by a great deal of evidence. Scientists may disagree about the details, but the overall theory enjoys widespread acceptance in the scientific community. Creationism deserves to be respected as a belief of its adherents, but it does not deserve respect as a scientific theory. This is because it is not a scientific theory. No scientific theory is allowed to appeal to the supernatural to explain natural phenomena.

These two views, evolution and direct creation, may be reconciled by saying that the Genesis account is to be taken as a metaphor, whose central lesson is that God created us and that we are dependent upon God for our very existence. It is not a literal account of the creation of life, it is not a scientific treatise. It is instead an admonition for the faithful to recognize and to adore their creator. In some respects, the existence of human species as explained by evolution may be seen as even more miraculous than direct creation. If God took the trouble to create human beings by this complex process, one could argue, then God must have thought of us indeed as the "center" of creation.

Gender

Today, many feminist theorists still accept the blank slate concept of human nature, which is very much at odds with the standard equipment view of human nature that has been developed in this chapter. Here, in the clash between these two views, lies the contemporary version of the **nature versus nurture** debate. On the one hand there are those who believe that it is culture alone that shapes our behavior, while on the other hand there are those who believe that our evolved natures determine much of our behavior. According to the former view, our minds and our behavior are the products of the roles which are imposed upon us by society. This view is assumed to be true by many feminists.[16]

> . . . much contemporary feminist research has been directed toward demonstrating that observed psychological differences between the sexes are not innate but rather are the result of what researchers often call "sex-role conditioning." Many feminist writers document the ways in which girls and boys are treated differently almost from the moment of birth . . . [T]he liberal feminist position seems to be that male and female natures seem to be identical; or to put it more accurately, that there is no such thing as male and female nature . . .

Those who continue to follow the lead of behaviorism do not believe that there are differences in the "natures" of men and women beyond obvious biological differences, since they do not believe in human nature at all. Instead, all differences between boys and girls, and between adult men and women, may be attributed entirely to the ways that each have been socialized. *If* men are better CEOs than women it is because men play competitive team sports as children, for example, while women play cooperative games. *If* men excel at math, it is not because of any inherent talent for math that they have inherited. Rather, it is because girls are directed by society away from math and science in their adolescent years. *If* women are better caregivers than men it is because they are trained by their mothers to care for family members, while boys are not given that job. It is not because girls are better caregivers by nature. Skinner believes that if boys and girls were socialized in the same ways, and if these periods of early training were reinforced by the culture at large, then there would be no differences between the "minds" and the behavior of men and women. Each group would have the same sorts of feelings and emotions, would be equally talented as leaders, equally skilled in science and math, and equally good caregivers.

Since the goal of feminism is equality—the political, legal, and moral equality of men and women—many feminist writers argue that such equality will be achieved only when these social roles are rewritten. If the differences between men and women that some people believe constitute sufficient grounds for unequal treatment of the sexes are themselves merely social constructs, then they can be changed. The goal of those feminists who accept this view is to point out the discriminatory effect of these roles and to encourage their replacement with ones that produce more equitable results. In *Reading 3* Susan Moller Okin argues that gender differences between men and women are not grounded in biology, but rather are simply inventions of and perpetuated by a male dominated society. Further, the social roles that society imposes on males and females lead to unfair and harmful treatment of women. She develops this theme in the context of criticizing leading (usually male) political theorists for neglecting gender issues, especially in the context of the family.

On the other hand, many scientists today, including many women scientists, accept the themes developed in this chapter about human nature. They believe that we are born with natural ways of behaving, ways that are the products of evolution, ways that are not learned and cannot be changed. They also believe that we have many more of these innate tendencies than anyone had previously thought, and that these innate tendencies must be identified and acknowledged if human behavior is to be understood correctly. According to many evolutionary psychologists, the blank slate approach to understanding gender differences is both false and harmful.

> . . . (feminist authors) are bound by a common thread: none is interested in the well-grounded study of human nature, of the male and female minds. By "well-grounded study of human nature" I mean . . . grounded in comprehension of the process that designed human beings: natural selection. Specifically, the field of inquiry that I commend to feminists, and that they seem loathe to explore, is a science called evolutionary psychology. Evolutionary psychology sees (among other things) some clear differences between the male and female minds . . . (which) feminists fear will be used to justify oppression as "natural," as "in our genes" as beyond our control. That's certainly a danger but it's not inevitable. And besides, it's not necessarily worse than the alternative danger: that feminism . . . will falter under the weight of its doctrinal absurdities; and that the laudable ideals it started with . . . will begin to whither for lack of honest support.[17]

These competing views of human nature very much influence the current debate about the differences between men and women. Proponents of the blank slate view have been accused of ignoring evolutionary psychology, while those who champion the standard equipment view have been accused by many feminist writers of being sexist. Women have been fighting for decades for equality, and many feminists see the idea of men and women having different natures as one more threat, one more obstacle, that stands between them and achieving this goal. If the debate about the nurture/nature origin of gender differences is to be resolved, it is important first to understand what evolutionary psychology claims to be the different types of behavior that natural selection has bestowed upon males and females. Keep in mind, as we identify these differences, that evolutionary psychologists are not attempting either to justify them or to claim that they are inevitable. From our discussion of freedom and society earlier, we know that humans do not have to act on the impulses with which nature has programmed them. But it is important to be aware of them, since knowing what are our natural tendencies is the first step in bringing them under control.

Since natural selection designs organisms for reproduction, many of the differences in the innate dispositions to behave between men and women stem from their different reproductive tasks. In particular, because men and women have different reproductive organs, they have different degrees of investment in promoting the survival of their offspring. Since females grow and nourish their offspring within their body, then nurse and protect it after it is born, theirs is the heavier investment. Because of this they are choosy with whom they mate, selecting only the males who they believe will feed and protect their children. Males on the other hand are not selective. Their reproductive success is heightened if they reproduce with as many females as possible. Males compete for females, with the strongest gaining greater access to them.

Many additional behavioral traits follow from this basic picture. Men are by nature more interested in several sexual partners than women. They are not completely indiscriminate, however. While women prefer men who are strong and good providers, men prefer women who are young and beautiful. Beauty is measured by having average size, good hair, a handsome face with red lips and smooth skin, a certain hip-to-waist ratio, and the like. For our ancestors, these were all signs of health and fertility, and thus would have enhanced their reproductive success. Once having mated with a woman a man becomes intensely jealous if he suspects infidelity. Women become intensely jealous as well, especially when their interests are threatened. Since women must raise their children, the work of supplying food is left to the men. This division of labor is natural as a way to aid survival. In addition, since males must compete for females, defend against hostile intruders, defend their territory and hunt, they are naturally more aggressive than women. These types of behavioral differences are just some of many that have been pointed out by Darwin himself, and by sociobiologists and evolutionary psychologists since then. Many of them are discussed by Steven Pinker in *Reading 4.*

One area of recent controversy that has sharply divided blank slate and standard equipment proponents is the claim by some defenders of the standard equipment view that forced reproduction, what we call rape today, may also be a male adaptive strategy. It seems that this is the case for some of our simian relatives. If we think of our hunter-gatherer ancestors as living in relatively small groups with some of the males having access to many females, then it would have been in their reproductive interests to force sex on unwilling females. Once again, what evolutionary psychologists say about rape is not intended to justify it today. Rather it is said in order to understand it, and ultimately to control the behavior which springs from its urgings. However, this view of rape flies completely in the face of the current thinking of some blank slate feminists about rape. Not only do they not want to think of it as "natural," but they do not even want to think of it as sexual. That is, rape is more of a way for a man to exercise power over a woman than it is a sexual act. If the standard equipment view is correct, which is a matter of intense debate, then in the primitive brains of males rape *is* about sex and reproduction.

When extreme views clash, the truth of the contested matter may lie somewhere between their boundaries. So it may be with the current "nature/nurture" debate, which pits the extremes of the standard equipment's view of human nature against that of the blank slate. Which of these two views represents the best way to understand ourselves and our differences, especially the differences between men and women? Clearly, both genes and culture have a hand in shaping us, but to what degree does each do its work and, perhaps more importantly, just what work do they do? The answer to these questions are not yet in.

Perhaps, as the authors of *Reading 5* claim, a balanced approach to answering it is best. Instead of claiming one theory of human nature to the exclusion of the other, it may be best to include the insights of each and then to allow further empirical research to determine the outcome of the debate.

The sort of empirical research that would matter includes both the study of how and to what degree both the environment and our genes shape human behavior. This is especially important when there are conflicting explanations from each for the same behavior.[18]

> For instance, in one experiment women and men at a university campus were approached by attractive members of the opposite sex and invited to have sex. Many more men than women accepted the offer. Evolutionary psychology cites this as proof that men are programmed to pursue sex indiscriminately, while women have evolved to be more cautious. But another explanation is available: perhaps the women were tempted but were also afraid that they would be attacked or raped, especially by someone so strange as to suggest sex with a passer-by.

In cases such as these, if we are to understand just how much evolution has shaped our behavior, it is important to construct experiments to determine which explanation is most likely.

Also, it is important to know more accurately just what sorts of behaviors evolution has shaped. Some evolutionary psychologists, for example, do not agree with some of the components of the "standard" view of the differences between men and women. For example, Sarah Hrdy, who studies primate behavior as a clue to human behavior, claims that[19]

> There has been a prevailing bias among evolutionary theorists in favor of stressing sexual competition among males for access to females at the expense of careful scrutiny of what females in their own right were doing. Among their recurring themes are the male's struggle for pre-eminence and his quest for "sexual variety" in order to inseminate as many females as possible. Visionaries of male-male competition stressed the imagery of primate females herded by tyrannical male consorts: sexually cautious females safeguarding their fertility until the appropriate male partner arrives; women waiting at campsites for their men to return, and, particularly, females so preoccupied with motherhood that they have little respite to influence their species' social organization. Alternative possibilities were neglected: that selection favored females who were assertive, sexually active, or highly competitive, who adroitly manipulated male consorts, or who were as strongly motivated to gain high social status as they were to hold and carry babies.

These alternative possibilities have in fact been observed in female primates, our closest relatives. Many of these observations were made by female scientists who, according to Hrdy, are more sensitive to these possibilities and less biased that they might exist. As the process of careful, unbiased observation continues, we ought to learn more not only about how the environment directs and shapes our evolved natures, but also what these evolved natures themselves are really like.

Readings

1. The Origin of Man

A BRIEF SUMMARY WILL BE sufficient to recall to the reader's mind the more salient points in this work. Many of the views which have been advanced are highly speculative, and some no doubt will prove erroneous: but I have in every case given the reasons which have led me to one view rather than to another. It seemed worth while to try how far the principle of evolution would throw light on some of the more complex problems in the natural history of man. False facts are highly injurious to the progress of science, for they often endure long; but false views, if supported by some evidence, do little harm, for every one takes a salutary pleasure in proving their falseness: and when this is done, one path towards error is closed and the road to truth is often at the same time opened.

The main conclusion here arrived at, and now held by many naturalists who are well competent to form a sound judgment is that man is descended from some less highly organized form. The grounds upon which this conclusion rests will never be shaken, for the close similarity between man and the lower animals in embryonic development, as well as in innumerable points of structure and constitution, both of high and of the most trifling importance,—the rudiments which he retains, and the abnormal reversions to which he is occasionally liable,—are facts which cannot be disputed. They have long been known, but until recently they told us nothing with respect to the origin of man. Now when viewed by the light of our knowledge of the whole organic world, their meaning is unmistakable. The great principle of evolution stands up clear and firm, when these groups or facts are considered in connection with others, such as the mutual affinities of the members of the same group, their geographical distribution in past and present times, and their geological succession. It is incredible that all these facts should speak falsely. He who is not content to look, like a savage, at the phenomena of nature as disconnected, cannot any longer believe that man is the work of a separate act of creation. He will he forced to admit that the close resemblance of the embryo of man to that, for instance, of a dog—the construction of his skull, limbs and whole frame on the same plan with that of other mammals, independently of the uses to which the parts may be put—the occasional re-appearance of various structures, for instance of several muscles, which man does not normally possess, but which are common to the Quadrumana—and a crowd of analogous facts—all point in the plainest manner to the conclusion that man is the co-descendant with other mammals of a common progenitor.

We have seen that man incessantly presents individual differences in all parts of his body and in his mental faculties. These differences or variations seem to be induced by the same general causes, and to obey the same laws as with the lower animals. In both cases similar laws of inheritance prevail. Man tends to increase at a greater rate than his means of subsistence; consequently he is occasionally subjected to a severe struggle for existence, and natural selection will have effected whatever lies within its scope. A succession of strongly-marked variations of a similar nature is by no means requisite; slight fluctuating differences in the individual suffice for the work of natural selection: not that we have any reason to suppose that in the same species, all parts of the organization tend to vary to the same degree. We

---

From Charles Darwin, "The Descent of Man," Great Books, vol. 49 (Chicago: Encyclopaedia Brittanica, 1952), chap. XXI. Reprinted with permission.

may feel assured that the inherited effects of the long-continued use or disuse of parts will have done much in the same direction with natural selection. Modifications formerly of importance, though no longer of any special use, are long-inherited. When one part is modified, other parts change through the principle of correlation, of which we have instances in many curious cases of correlated monstrosities. Something may be attributed to the direct and definite action of the surrounding conditions of life, such as abundant food, heat or moisture; and lastly, many characters of slight physiological importance, some indeed of considerable importance, have been gained through sexual selection. . . .

The high standard of our intellectual powers and moral disposition is the greatest difficulty which presents itself, after we have been driven to this conclusion on the origin of man. But every one who admits the principle of evolution, must see that the mental powers of the higher animals, which are the same in kind with those of man, though so different in degree, are capable of advancement. Thus the interval between the mental powers of one of the higher apes and of a fish, or between those of an ant and scale-insect, is immense; yet their development does not offer any special difficulty; for with our domesticated animals, the mental faculties are certainly variable, and the variations are inherited. No one doubts that they are of the utmost importance to animals in a state of nature. Therefore the conditions are favorable for their development through natural selection. The same conclusion may be extended to man: the intellect must have been all-important to him, even at a very remote period, as enabling him to invent and use language, to make weapons, tools, traps, &c., whereby with the aid of his social habits, he long ago became the most dominant of all living creatures.

A great stride in the development of the intellect will have followed, as soon as the half-art and half-instinct of language came into use; for the continued use of language will have reacted on the brain and produced an inherited effect; and this again will have reacted on the improvement of language. As Mr. Chauncey Wright has well remarked, the largeness of the brain in man relatively to his body, compared with the lower animals, may be attributed in chief part to the early use of some simple form of language,—that wonderful engine which affixes signs to all sorts of objects and qualities, and excites trains of thought which would never arise from the mere impression of the senses, or if they did arise could not be followed out. The higher intellectual powers of man, such as those of ratiocination, abstraction, self-consciousness, &c., probably follow from the continued improvement and exercise of the other mental faculties.

The development of the moral qualities is a more interesting problem. The foundation lies in the social instincts, including under this term the family ties. These instincts are highly complex, and in the case of the lower animals give special tendencies towards certain definite actions: but the more important elements are love, and the distinct emotion of sympathy. Animals endowed with the social instincts take pleasure in one another's company, warn one another of danger, defend and aid one another in many ways. These instincts do not extend to all the individuals of the species, but only to those of the same community. As they are highly beneficial to the species, they have in all probability been acquired through natural selection.

A moral being is one who is capable of reflecting on his past actions and their motives—of approving of some and disapproving of others; and the fact that man is the one being who certainly deserves this designation, is the greatest of all distinctions between him and the lower animals. But in the fourth chapter I have endeavored to show that the moral sense follows, firstly, from the enduring and ever-present nature of the social instincts; secondly, from man's appreciation of the approbation and disapprobation of his fellows; and thirdly, from the high activity of his mental faculties, with past impressions extremely vivid; and in these latter respects he differs from the lower animals. Owing to this condition of mind, man cannot avoid looking both backwards and forwards, and comparing past impressions. Hence after some temporary desire or passion has mastered his social instincts, he reflects and compares the now weakened impression of such past impulses with the ever-present social instincts; and he then feels that sense of dissatisfaction which all unsatisfied instincts leave behind them, he therefore resolves to act differently for the future,—and this is conscience. Any instinct, permanently stronger or more enduring than another, gives rise to a feeling which we express by saying that it ought to be obeyed. A pointer dog, if able to reflect on his past conduct, would say to himself, I ought (as indeed we say of him) to have pointed at that hare and not have yielded to the passing temptation of hunting it.

Social animals are impelled partly by a wish to aid the members of their community in a general manner, but more commonly to perform certain definite actions. Man is impelled by the same general wish to aid his fellows; but has few or no special instincts. He differs also from the lower animals in the power of expressing his desires by words, which thus become a guide to the aid required and bestowed. The motive to give aid is likewise much modified in man: it no longer consists solely of a blind instinctive impulse, but is much influenced by the praise or blame of his fellows. The appreciation and the bestowal of praise and blame both rest on sympathy; and this emotion, as we have seen, is one of the most important elements of the social instincts. Sympathy, though gained as an instinct, is also much strengthened by exercise or habit. As all men desire their own happiness, praise or blame is bestowed on actions and motives, according as they lead to this end; and as happiness is an essential part of the general good, the greatest happiness principle indirectly serves as a nearly safe standard of right and wrong. As the reasoning powers advance and experience is gained, the remoter effects of certain lines of conduct on the character of the individual, and on the general good, are perceived; and then the self-regarding virtues come within the scope of public opinion, and receive praise, and their opposites blame. But with the less civilized nations reason often errs, and many bad customs and base superstitions come within the same scope, and are then esteemed as high virtues, and their breach as heavy crimes.

The moral faculties are generally and justly esteemed as of higher value than the intellectual powers. But we should bear in mind that the activity of the mind in vividly recalling past impressions is one of the fundamental though secondary bases of conscience. This affords the strongest argument for educating and stimulating in all possible ways the intellectual faculties of every human being. No doubt a man with a torpid mind, if his social affections and sympathies are well developed, will be led to good actions, and may have a fairly sensitive conscience. But whatever renders the imagination more vivid and strengthens the habit of recalling and comparing past impressions, will make the conscience more sensitive, and may even somewhat compensate for weak social affections and sympathies.

The moral nature of man has reached its present standard, partly through the advancement of his reasoning powers and consequently of a just public opinion, but especially from his sympathies having been rendered more tender and widely diffused through the effects of habit, example, instruction, and reflection. It is not improbable that after long practice virtuous tendencies may be inherited. With the more civilized races, the conviction of the existence of an all-seeing Deity has had a potent influence on the advance of morality. Ultimately man does not accept the praise or blame of his fellows as his sole guide, though few escape this influence, but his habitual convictions, controlled by reason, afford him the safest rule. His conscience then becomes the supreme judge and monitor. Nevertheless the first foundation or origin of the moral sense lies in the social instincts, including sympathy; and these instincts no doubt were primarily gained, as in the case of the lower animals, through natural selection.

The belief in God has often been advanced as not only the greatest, but the most complete of all the distinctions between man and the lower animals. It is however impossible, as we have seen, to maintain that this belief is innate or instinctive in man. On the other hand a belief in all-pervading spiritual agencies seems to be universal; and apparently follows from a considerable advance in man's reason, and from a still greater advance in his faculties of imagination, curiosity and wonder. I am aware that the assumed instinctive belief in God has been used by many persons as an argument for His existence. But this is a rash argument, as we should thus be compelled to believe in the existence of many cruel and malignant spirits, only a little more powerful than man: for the belief in them is far more general than in a beneficent Deity. The idea of a universal and beneficent Creator does not seem to arise in the mind of man, until he has been elevated by long-continued culture.

He who believes in the advancement of man from some low organized form, will naturally ask how does this bear on the belief in the immortality of the soul. The barbarous races of man, as Sir J. Lubbock has shown, possess no clear belief of this kind, but arguments derived from the primeval beliefs of savages are, as we have just seen, of little or no avail. Few persons feel any anxiety from the impossibility of determining at what precise period in the development of the individual, from the first trace of a minute germinal vesicle, man becomes an immortal being; and there is no greater cause for anxiety because the period cannot possibly be determined in the gradually ascending organic scale.

I am aware that the conclusions arrived at in this work will be denounced by some as highly irreligious; but he who denounces them is bound to show why it is more irreligious to explain the origin of man as a distinct species by descent from some lower form, through the jaws of variation and natural selection, than to explain the birth of the individual through the laws of ordinary reproduction. The birth both of the species and of the individual are equally parts of that grand sequence of events, which our minds refuse to accept as the result of blind chance. The understanding revolts at such a conclusion, whether or not we are able to believe that every slight variation of structure,—the union of each pair in marriage,—the dissemination of each seed,—and other such events, have all been ordained for some special purpose.

Sexual selection has been treated at great length in this work: for, as I have attempted to show, it has played an important part in the history of the organic world. I am aware that much remains doubtful, but I have endeavored to give a fair view of the whole case. In the lower divisions of the ani-

mal kingdom, sexual selection seems to have done nothing: such animals are often affixed for life to the same spot, or have the sexes combined in the same individual, or what is still more important, their perceptive and intellectual faculties are not sufficiently advanced to allow of the feelings of love and jealousy, or of the exertion of choice. When, however, we come to the Arthropoda and Vertebrata, even to the lowest classes in these two great sub-kingdoms, sexual selection has effected much.

In the several great classes of the animal kingdom,—in mammals, birds, reptiles, fishes, insects, and even crustaceans,—the differences between the sexes follow nearly the same rules. The males are almost always the wooers: and they alone are armed with special weapons for fighting with their rivals. They are generally stronger and larger than the females, and are endowed with the requisite qualities of courage and pugnacity. They are provided, either exclusively or in a much higher degree than the females, with organs for vocal or instrumental music, and with odoriferous glands. They are ornamental with infinitely diversified appendages, and with the most brilliant or conspicuous colors, often arranged in elegant patterns, whilst the females are unadorned. When the sexes differ in more important structures, it is the male which is provided with special sense-organs for discovering the female, with locomotive organs for reaching her, and often with prehensile organs for holding her. These various structures for charming or securing the female are often developed in the male during only part of the year, namely the breeding season. They have in many cases been more or less transferred to the females: and in the latter case they often appear in her as mere rudiments. They are lost or never gained by the males after emasculation. Generally they are not developed in the male during early youth, but appear a short time before the age for reproduction. Hence in most cases the young of both sexes resemble each other: and the female somewhat resembles her young offspring throughout life. In almost every great class a few anomalous cases occur, where there has been an almost complete transposition of the characters proper to the two sexes; the females assuming characters which properly belong to the males. This surprising uniformity in the laws regulating the differences between the sexes in so many and such widely separated classes, is intelligible if we admit the action of one common cause, namely sexual selection.

Sexual selection depends on the success of certain individuals over others of the same sex, in relation to the propagation of the species; whilst natural selection depends on the success of both sexes, at all ages, in relation to the general conditions of life. The sexual struggle is of two kinds: in the one it is between individuals of the same sex, generally the males, in order to drive away or kill their rivals, the females remaining passive; whilst in the other, the struggle is likewise between the individuals of the same sex, in order to excite or charm those of the opposite sex, generally the females, which no longer remain passive, but select the more agreeable partners. This latter kind of selection is closely analogous to that which man unintentionally, yet effectually, brings to bear on his domesticated productions, when he preserves during a long period the most pleasing or useful individuals, without any wish to modify the breed.

The laws of inheritance determine whether characters gained through sexual selection by either sex shall be transmitted to the same sex, or to both; as well as the age at which they shall be developed. It appears that variations arising late in life are commonly transmitted to one and the same sex. Variability is the necessary basis for the action of selection, and is wholly independent of it. It follows from this, that variations of the same general nature have often been taken advantage of and accumulated through sexual selection in relation to the propagation of the species, as well as through natural selection in relation to the general purposes of life. Hence secondary sexual characters, when equally transmitted to both sexes can be distinguished from ordinary specific characters only by the light of analogy. The modifications acquired through sexual selection are often so strongly pronounced that the two sexes have frequently been ranked as distinct species, or even as distinct genera. Such strongly-marked differences must be in some manner highly important: and we know that they have been acquired in some

instances at the cost not only of inconvenience, but of exposure to actual danger.

The belief in the power of sexual selection rests chiefly on the following considerations. Certain characters are confined to one sex: and this alone renders it probable that in most cases they are connected with the act of reproduction. In innumerable instances these characters are fully developed only at maturity, and often during only a part of the year, which is always the breeding-season. The males (passing over a few exceptional cases) are the more active in courtship; they are the better armed, and are rendered the more attractive in various ways. It is to be especially observed that the males display their attractions with elaborate care in the presence of the females; and that they rarely or never display them excepting during the season of love. It is incredible that all this should be purposeless. Lastly we have distinct evidence with some quadrupeds and birds, that the individuals of one sex are capable of feeling a strong antipathy or preference for certain individuals of the other sex.

Bearing in mind these facts, and the marked results of man's unconscious selection, when applied to domesticated animals and cultivated plants, it seems to me almost certain that if the individuals of one sex were during a long series of generations to prefer pairing with certain individuals of the other sex, characterized in some peculiar manner, the offspring would slowly but surely become modified in this same manner. I have not attempted to conceal that, excepting when the males are more numerous than the females, or when polygamy prevails, it is doubtful how the more attractive males succeed in leaving a large number of offspring to inherit their superiority in ornaments or other charms than the less attractive males; but I have shown that this would probably follow from the females,—especially the more vigorous ones, which would be the first to breed,— preferring not only the more attractive but at the same time the more vigorous and victorious males.

Although we have some positive evidence that birds appreciate bright and beautiful objects, as with the bower-birds of Australia, and although they certainly appreciate the power of song, yet I fully admit that it is astonishing that the females of many birds and some mammals should be endowed with sufficient taste to appreciate ornaments, which we have reason to attribute to sexual selection; and this is even more astonishing in the case of reptiles, fish, and insects. But we really know little about the minds of the lower animals. It cannot be supposed, for instance, that male birds of paradise or peacocks should take such pains in erecting, spreading, and vibrating their beautiful plumes before the females for no purpose. We should remember the fact given on excellent authority in a former chapter, that several peahens, when debarred from an admired male, remained widows during a whole season rather than pair with another bird.

Nevertheless I know of no fact in natural history more wonderful than that the female Argus pheasant should appreciate the exquisite shading of the ball-and-socket ornaments and the elegant patterns on the wing-feathers of the male. He who thinks that the male was created as he now exists must admit that the great plumes, which prevent the wings from being used for flight, and which are displayed during courtship and at no other time in a manner quite peculiar to this one species, were given to him as an ornament. If so, he must likewise admit that the female was created and endowed with the capacity of appreciating such ornaments. I differ only in the conviction that the male Argus pheasant acquired his beauty gradually, through the preference of the females during many generations for the more highly ornamented males; the aesthetic capacity of the females having been advanced through exercise or habit, just as our own taste is gradually improved. In the male through the fortunate chance of a few feathers being left unchanged, we can distinctly trace how simple spots with a little fulvous shading on one side may have been developed by small steps into the wonderful ball-and-socket ornaments; and it is probable that they were actually thus developed.

Everyone who admits the principle of evolution, and yet feels great difficulty in admitting that female mammals, birds, reptiles, and fish, could have acquired the high taste implied by the beauty of the males, and which generally coincides with our own standard, should reflect that the nerve-cells of the brain in the highest as well as in the lowest members of the vertebrate series, are derived from those of the common progenitor of this great kingdom. For we can thus see how it has come to pass that certain mental faculties, in various and widely distinct groups of animals, have been developed in nearly the same manner and to nearly the same degree.

The reader who has taken the trouble to go through the several chapters devoted to sexual selection, will be able to judge how far the conclusions at which I have arrived are supported by sufficient evidence. If he accepts these conclusions he may, I think, safely extend them to mankind; but it would be superfluous here to repeat what I have so lately said on the manner in which sexual selection apparently has acted on man, both on the male and female side, causing the two sexes to differ in body and mind, and the several races to differ from each other in various characters, as well as from their ancient and lowly-organized progenitors.

He who admits the principle of sexual selection will be led to the remarkable conclusion that the nervous system not only regulates most of the existing functions of the body, but has indirectly influenced the progressive development of various bodily structures and of certain mental qualities. Courage, pugnacity, perseverance, strength and size of body, weapons of all kinds, musical organs, both vocal and instrumental, bright colors and ornamental appendages, have all been indirectly gained by the one sex or the other, through the exertion of choice, the influence of love and jealousy, and the appreciation of the beautiful in sound, colour or form; and these powers of the mind manifestly depend on the development of the brain.

Man scans with scrupulous care the character and pedigree of his horses, cattle, and dogs before he matches them: but when he comes to his own marriage he rarely, or never, takes any such care. He is impelled by nearly the same motives as the lower animals, when they are left to their own free choice, though he is in so far superior to them that he highly values mental charms and virtues. On the other hand he is strongly attracted by mere wealth or rank. Yet he might by selection do something not only for the bodily constitution and frame of his offspring, but for their intellectual and moral qualities. Both sexes ought to refrain from marriage if they are in any marked degree inferior in body or mind; but such hopes are Utopian and will never be even partially realized until the laws of inheritance are thoroughly known. Everyone does good service, who aids towards this end. When the principles of breeding and inheritance are better understood, we shall not hear ignorant members or our legislature rejecting with scorn a plan for ascertaining whether or not consanguineous marriages are injurious to man.

The advancement of the welfare of mankind is a most intricate problem: all ought to refrain from marriage who cannot avoid abject poverty for their children; for poverty is not only a great evil, but tends to its own increase by leading to recklessness in marriage. On the other hand, as Mr. Galton has remarked, if the prudent avoid marriage, whilst the reckless marry, the inferior members tend to supplant the better members of society. Man, like every other animal, has no doubt advanced to his present high condition through a struggle for existence consequent on his rapid multiplication: and if he is to advance still higher, it is to be feared that he must remain subject to a severe struggle. Otherwise he would sink into indolence, and the more gifted men would not be more successful in the battle of life than the less gifted. Hence our natural rate of increase, though leading to many and obvious evils, must not be greatly diminished by any means. There should be open competition for all men; and the most able should not be prevented by laws or customs from succeeding best and rearing the largest number of offspring. Important as the struggle for existence has been and even still is, yet as far as the highest part of man's nature is concerned there are other agencies more important. For the moral qualities are advanced, either directly or indirectly, much more through the effects of habit, the reasoning powers, instruction, religion, &c., than through natural selection: though to this latter agency may be safely attributed the social instincts, which afforded the basis for the development of the moral sense.

The main conclusion arrived at in this work, namely, that man is descended from some lowly organized form, will, I regret to think, be highly distasteful to many. But there can hardly be a doubt that we are descended from barbarians. The astonishment which I felt on first seeing a party of Fuegians on a wild and broken shore will never be forgotten by me, for the reflection at once rushed into my mind—such were our ancestors. These men were absolutely naked and bedaubed with paint, their long hair was tangled, their mouths frothed with excitement, and their expression was wild, startled, and distrustful. They possessed hardly any arts, and like wild animals lived on what they could catch; they had no government, and were merciless to every one not of their own small tribe. He who has seen a savage in his native land will not feel much shame, if forced to acknowledge that the blood of some more humble creature flows in his veins. For my own part I would as soon be descended from that heroic little monkey, who braved his dreaded enemy in order to save the life of his keeper, or from that old baboon, who descending from the mountains, carried away in triumph his young comrade from a crowd of astonished dogs—as from a savage who delights to torture his enemies, offers up bloody sacrifices, practices infanticide without remorse, treats his wives like slaves, knows no decency, and is haunted by the grossest superstitions.

Man may be excused for feeling some pride at having risen, though not through his own exertions, to the very summit of the organic scale; and the fact of his having thus risen, instead of having been aboriginally placed there, may give him hope for a still higher destiny in the distant future. But we are not here concerned with hopes or fears, only with the truth as far as our reason permits us to discover it; and I have given the evidence to the best of my ability. We must, however, acknowledge, as it seems to me, that man with all his noble qualities, with sympathy which feels for the most debased, with benevolence which extends not only to other men but to the humblest living creature, with his god-like intellect which has penetrated into the movements and constitution of the solar system—with all these exalted powers—Man still bears in his bodily frame the indelible stamp of his lowly origin.

2. The Biological Basis of Human Nature

THESE ARE THE CENTRAL QUESTIONS that the great philosopher David Hume said are of unspeakable importance: How does the mind work, and beyond that why does it work in such a way and not another, and from these two considerations together, what is man's ultimate nature?

We keep returning to the subject with a sense of hesitancy and even dread. For if the brain is a machine of ten billion nerve cells and the mind can somehow be explained as the summed activity of a finite number of chemical and electrical reactions, boundaries limit the human prospect—we are biological and our souls cannot fly free. If humankind evolved by Darwinian natural selection, genetic chance and environmental necessity, not God, made the species. Deity can still be sought in the origin of the ultimate units of matter, in quarks and electron shells (Hans Küng was right to ask atheists why there is something instead of nothing) but not in the origin of species. However much we embellish that stark conclusion with metaphor and imagery, it remains the philosophical legacy of the last century of scientific research.

No way appears around this admittedly unappealing proposition. It is the essential first hypothesis for any serious consideration of the human condition. Without it the humanities and social sciences are the limited descriptors of surface phenomena, like astronomy without physics, biology without chemistry, and mathematics without algebra. With it, human nature can be laid open as an object of fully empirical research, biology can be put to the service of liberal education, and our self-conception can be enormously and truthfully enriched.

But to the extent that the new naturalism is true, its pursuit seems certain to generate two great spiritual dilemmas. The first is that no species, ours included, possesses a purpose beyond the imperatives created by its genetic history. Species may have vast potential for material and mental progress but they lack any immanent purpose or guidance from agents beyond their immediate environment or even an evolutionary goal toward which their molecular architecture automatically steers them. I believe that the human mind is constructed in a way that locks it inside this fundamental constraint and forces it to make choices with a purely biological instrument. If the brain evolved by natural selection, even the capacities to select particular esthetic judgments and religious beliefs must have arisen by the same mechanistic process. They are either direct adaptations to past environments in which the ancestral human populations evolved or at most constructions thrown up secondarily by deeper, less visible activities that were once adaptive in this stricter, biological sense.

The essence of the argument, then, is that the brain exists because it promotes the survival and multiplication of the genes that direct its assembly. The human mind is a device for survival and reproduction, and reason is just one of its various techniques. Steven Weinberg has pointed out that physical reality remains so mysterious even to physicists because of the extreme improbability that it was constructed to be understood by the human mind. We can reverse that insight to note with still greater force that the intellect was not constructed to understand atoms or even to understand itself but to promote the survival of human genes. The reflective person knows that his life is in some incomprehensible manner guided through a biological ontogeny, a more or less fixed order of life stages. He senses that with all the drive, wit, love, pride, anger, hope, and anxiety that characterize the species he will in the end be sure only of helping to perpetuate the same cycle. Poets have

From E. O. Wilson, On Human Nature *(Cambridge, Mass.: Harvard University Press, 1978), pp. 1–13. Reprinted with permission of the publisher. Copyright © 1978 by the President and Fellows of Harvard.*

defined this truth as tragedy. Yeats called it the coming of wisdom:

> Though leaves are many, the root is one;
> Through all the lying days of my youth
> I swayed my leaves and flowers in the sun;
> Now I may wither into the truth.

The first dilemma, in a word, is that we have no particular place to go. The species lacks any goal external to its own biological nature. It could be that in the next hundred years humankind will thread the needles of technology and politics, solve the energy and materials crises, avert nuclear war, and control reproduction. The world can at least hope for a stable ecosystem and a well-nourished population. But what then? Educated people everywhere like to believe that beyond material needs lie fulfillment and the realization of individual potential. But what is fulfillment, and to what ends may potential be realized? Traditional religious beliefs have been eroded, not so much by humiliating disproofs of their mythologies as by the growing awareness that beliefs are really enabling mechanisms for survival. Religions, like other human institutions, evolve so as to enhance the persistence and influence of their practitioners. Marxism and other secular religions offer little more than promises of material welfare and a legislated escape from the consequences of human nature. They, too, are energized by the goal of collective self-aggrandizement. The French political observer Akin Peyrefitte once said admiringly of Mao Tse-tung that "the Chinese knew the narcissistic joy of loving themselves in him. It is only natural that he should have loved himself through them." Thus does ideology bow to its hidden masters the genes, and the highest impulses seem upon closer examination to be metamorphosed into biological activity.

The more somber social interpreters of our time, such as Robert Heilbroner, Robert Nisbet, and L. S. Stavrianos, perceive Western civilization and ultimately mankind as a whole to be in immediate danger of decline. Their reasoning leads easily to a vision of post-ideological societies whose members will regress steadily toward self-indulgence. "The will to power will not have vanished entirely,"

Gunther Stent writes in *The Coming of the Golden Age,*

but the distribution of its intensity will have been drastically altered. At one end of this distribution will be the minority of the people whose work will keep intact the technology that sustains the multitude at a high standard of living. In the middle of the distribution will be found a type, largely unemployed, for whom the distinction between the real and the illusory will still be meaningful . . . He will retain interest in the world and seek satisfaction from sensual pleasures. At the other end of the spectrum will be a type largely unemployable, for whom the boundary of the real and the imagined will have been largely dissolved, at least to the extent compatible with his physical survival.

Thus the danger implicit in the first dilemma is the rapid dissolution of transcendental goals toward which societies can organize their energies. Those goals, the true moral equivalents of war, have faded; they went one by one, like mirages, as we drew closer. In order to search for a new morality based upon a more truthful definition of man, it is necessary to look inward, to dissect the machinery of the mind and to retrace its evolutionary history. But that effort, I predict, will uncover the second dilemma, which is the choice that must be made among the ethical premises inherent in man's biological nature.

At this point let me stare in briefest terms the basis of the second dilemma, while I defer its supporting argument to the next chapter: innate censors and motivators exist in the brain that deeply and unconsciously affect our ethical premises; from these roots, morality evolved as instinct. If that perception is correct, science may soon be in a position to investigate the very origin and meaning of human values, from which all ethical pronouncements and much of political practice flow.

Philosophers themselves, most of whom lack an evolutionary perspective, have not devoted much time to the problem. They examine the precepts of ethical systems with reference to their consequences and not their origins. Thus John Rawls opens his influential *A Theory of Justice* (1971) with a proposition he regards as beyond dispute:

"In a just society the liberties of equal citizenship are taken as settled; the rights secured by justice are not subject to political bargaining or to the calculus of social interests." Robert Nozick begins *Anarchy, State, and Utopia* (1974) with an equally firm proposition: "Individuals have rights, and there are things no person or group may do to them (without violating their rights). So strong and far-reaching are these rights they raise the question of what, if anything, the state and its officials may do." These two premises are somewhat different in content, and they lead to radically different prescriptions. Rawls would allow rigid social control to secure as close an approach as possible to the equal distribution of society's rewards. Nozick sees the ideal society as one governed by a minimal state, empowered only to protect its citizens from force and fraud, and with unequal distribution of rewards wholly permissible. Rawls rejects the meritocracy; Nozick accepts it as desirable except in those cases where local communities voluntarily decide to experiment with egalitarianism. Like everyone else, philosophers measure their personal emotional responses to various alternatives as though consulting a hidden oracle.

That oracle resides in the deep emotional centers of the brain, most probably within the limbic system, a complex array of neurons and hormone-secreting cells located just beneath the "thinking" portion of the cerebral cortex. Human emotional responses and the more general ethical practices based on them have been programmed to a substantial degree by natural selection over thousands of generations. The challenge to science is to measure the tightness of the constraints caused by the programming, to find their source in the brain, and to decode their significance through the reconstruction of the evolutionary history of the mind. This enterprise will be the logical complement of the continued study of cultural evolution.

Success will generate the second dilemma, which can be stated as follows: Which of the censors and motivators should be obeyed and which ones might better be curtailed or sublimated? These guides are the very core of our humanity. They and not the belief in spiritual apartness distinguish us from electronic computers. At some time in the future we will have to decide how human we wish to remain—in this ultimate, biological sense—because we must consciously choose among the alternative emotional guides we have inherited. To chart our destiny means that we must shift from automatic control based on our biological properties to precise steering based on biological knowledge.

Because the guides of human nature must be examined with a complicated arrangement of mirrors, they are a deceptive subject, always the philosopher's deadfall. The only way forward is to study human nature as part of the natural sciences, in an attempt to integrate the natural sciences with the social sciences and humanities. I can conceive of no ideological or formulistic shortcut. Neurobiology cannot be learned at the feet of a guru. The consequences of genetic history cannot be chosen by legislatures. Above all, for our own physical well-being if nothing else, ethical philosophy must not be left in the hands of the merely wise. Although human progress can be achieved by intuition and force of will, only hard-won empirical knowledge of our biological nature will allow us to make optimum choices among the competing criteria of progress.

The important initial development in this analysis will be the conjunction of biology and the various social sciences—psychology, anthropology, sociology, and economics. The two cultures have only recently come into full sight of one another. The result has been a predictable mixture of aversions, misunderstandings, overenthusiasm, local conflicts, and treaties. The situation can be summarized by saying that biology stands today as the antidiscipline of the social sciences. By the word "antidiscipline" I wish to emphasize the special adversary relation that often exists when fields of study at adjacent levels of organization first begin to interact. For chemistry there is the antidiscipline of many-body physics; for molecular biology, chemistry; for physiology, molecular biology; and so on upward through the paired levels of increasing specification and complexity.

In the typical early history of a discipline, its practitioners believe in the novelty and uniqueness of their subject. They devote lifetimes to special entities and patterns and during the early period of exploration they doubt that these phenomena can be reduced to simple laws. Members of the antidiscipline have a different attitude. Having chosen as their primary subject the units of the lower level of organization, say atoms as opposed to molecules, they believe that the next discipline above can and must be reformulated by their own laws: chemistry by the laws of physics, biology by the laws of chemistry, and so on downward. Their interest is relatively narrow, abstract, and exploitative. P. A. M. Dirac, speaking of the theory of the hydrogen atom, could say that its consequences would unfold as mere chemistry. A few biochemists are still content in the belief that life is "no more" than the actions of atoms and molecules.

It is easy to see why each scientific discipline is also an antidiscipline. An adversary relationship is probable because the devotees of the two adjacent organizational levels—such as atoms versus molecules—are initially committed to their own methods and ideas when they focus on the upper level (in this case, molecules). By today's standards a broad scientist can be defined as one who is a student of three subjects: his discipline (chemistry in the example cited), the lower antidiscipline (physics), and the subject to which his specialty stands as antidiscipline (the chemical aspects of biology). A well-rounded expert on the nervous system, to take a second, more finely graded example, is deeply versed in the structure of single nerve cells, but he also understands the chemical basis of the impulses that pass through and between these cells, and he hopes to explain how nerve cells work together to produce elementary patterns of behavior. Every successful scientist treats differently each of the three levels of phenomena surrounding his specialty.

The interplay between adjacent fields is tense and creative at the beginning, but with the passage of time it becomes fully complementary. Consider the origins of molecular biology. In the late 1800s the microscopic study of cells (cytology) and the study of chemical processes within and around the cells (biochemistry) grew at an accelerating pace. Their relationship during this period was complicated, but it broadly fits the historical schema

I have described. The cytologists were excited by the mounting evidence of an intricate cell architecture. They had interpreted the mysterious choreography of the chromosomes during cell division and thus set the stage for the emergence of modern genetics and experimental developmental biology. Many biochemists, on the other hand, remained skeptical of the idea that so much structure exists at the microscopic level. They thought that the cytologists were describing artifacts created by laboratory methods of fixing and staining cells for microscopic examination. Their interest lay in the more "fundamental" issues of the chemical nature of protoplasm, especially the newly formulated theory that life is based on enzymes. The cytologists responded with scorn to any notion that the cell is a "bag of enzymes."

In general, biochemists judged the cytologists to be too ignorant of chemistry to grasp the fundamental processes, while the cytologists considered the methods of the chemists inappropriate for the idiosyncratic structures of the living cell. The revival of Mendelian genetics in 1900 and the subsequent illumination of the roles of the chromosomes and genes did little at first to force a synthesis. Biochemists, seeing no immediate way to explain classical genetics, by and large ignored it.

Both sides were essentially correct. Biochemistry has now explained so much of the cellular machinery on its own terms as to justify its most extravagant early claims. But in achieving this feat, mostly since 1950, it was partially transformed into the new discipline of molecular biology, which can be defined as biochemistry that also accounts for the particular spatial arrangements of such molecules as the DNA helix and enzyme proteins. Cytology forced the development of a special kind of chemistry and the use of a battery of powerful new techniques, including electrophoresis, chromatography, density-gradient centrifugation, and x-ray crystallography. At the same time cytology metamorphosed into modern cell biology. Aided by the electron microscope, which magnifies objects by hundreds of thousands of times, it has converged in perspective and language toward molecular biology. Finally, classical genetics, by switching from fruit flies and mice to bacteria and viruses, has incorporated biochemistry to become molecular genetics.

Progress over a large part of biology has been fueled by competition among the various perspectives and techniques derived from cell biology and biochemistry, the discipline and its antidiscipline. The interplay has been a triumph for scientific materialism. It has vastly enriched our understanding of the nature of life and created materials for literature more powerful than any imagery of prescientific culture.

I suggest that we are about to repeat this cycle in the blending of biology and the social sciences and that as a consequence the two cultures of Western intellectual life will be joined at last. Biology has traditionally affected the social sciences only indirectly through technological manifestations, such as the benefits of medicine, the mixed blessings of gene splicing and other techniques of genetics, and the specter of population growth. Although of great practical importance, these matters are trivial with reference to the conceptual foundation of the social sciences. The conventional treatments of "social biology" and "social issues of biology" in our colleges and universities present some formidable intellectual challenges, but they are not addressed to the core of social theory. This core is the deep structure of human nature, an essentially biological phenomenon that is also the primary focus of the humanities.

It is all too easy to be seduced by the opposing view: that science is competent to generate only a few classes of information, that its cold, clear Apollonian method will never be relevant to the full Dionysian life of the mind, that single-minded devotion to science is dehumanizing. Expressing the mood of the counterculture, Theodore Roszak suggested a map of the mind "as a spectrum of possibilities, all of which properly blend into one another . . . At one end, we have the hard, bright lights of science; here we find information. In the center we have the sensuous hues of art; here we find the aesthetic shape of the world. At the far end, we have the dark, shadowy tones of religious experience, shading off into wave lengths beyond all perception; here we find meaning."

No, here we find obscurantism! And a curious underestimate of what the mind can accomplish. The sensuous hues and dark tones have been produced by the genetic evolution of our nervous and sensory tissues; to treat them as other than objects of biological inquiry is simply to aim too low.

The heart of the scientific method is the reduction of perceived phenomena to fundamental, testable principles. The elegance, we can fairly say the beauty, of any particular scientific generalization is measured by its simplicity relative to the number of phenomena it can explain. Ernst Mach, a physicist and forerunner of the logical positivists, captured the idea with a definition: "Science may be regarded as a minimal problem consisting of the completest presentation of facts with the least possible expenditure of thought."

Although Mach's perception has an undeniable charm, raw reduction is only half of the scientific process. The remainder consists of the reconstruction of complexity by an expanding synthesis under the control of laws newly demonstrated by analysis. This reconstitution reveals the existence of novel, emergent phenomena. When the observer shifts his attention from one level of organization to the next, as from physics to chemistry or from chemistry to biology, he expects to find obedience to all the laws of the levels below. But to reconstitute the upper levels of organization requires specifying the arrangement of the lower units and this in turn generates richness and the basis of new and unexpected principles. The specification consists of particular combinations of units, as well as particular spatial arrangements and histories of the ensembles of these elements. Consider the following simple example from chemistry. The ammonia molecule consists of a negatively charged nitrogen atom bonded to a triangle of three positively charged hydrogen atoms. If the atoms were locked in one position the ammonia molecule would have an opposite charge at each end (a dipole moment) in apparent contradiction to the symmetry laws of nuclear physics. Yet the molecule manages to behave properly: it neutralizes its dipole moment by passing the nitrogen atom back and forth through the triangle of hydrogen atoms at a frequency of thirty billion times per second. However, such symmetry is absent in the case of sugar and other large organic molecules, which are too large and complex in structure to invert themselves. They break but do not repeal the laws of physics. This specification may not be greatly interesting to nuclear physicists, but its consequences redound throughout organic chemistry and biology.

Consider a second example, closer to our subject, from the evolution of social life in the insects. In the Mesozoic Era, about 150 million years ago, primitive wasps evolved the sex-determining trait of haplodiploidy, in which fertilized eggs produced females and those left unfertilized produced males. This simple method of control may have been a specific adaptation that permitted females to choose the sex of their offspring according to the nature of the prey insects they were able to subdue. In particular, smaller prey might have been assigned to the male offspring, which require less protein in their development. But whatever its initial cause, haplodiploidy represented an evolutionary event that quite accidentally predisposed these insects to develop advanced forms of social life. The reason is that haplodiploidy causes sisters to be more closely related to each other than mothers are to daughters, and so females may derive genetic profit from becoming a sterile caste specialized for the rearing of sisters. Sterile castes engaged in rearing siblings are the essential feature of social organization in the insects. Because of its link to haplodiploidy, insect social life is almost limited to the wasps and their close relatives among the bees and ants. Further-

more, most cases can be classified either as matriarchies, in which queens control colonies of daughters, or as sisterhoods, in which sterile daughters control the egg-laying mothers. The societies of wasps, bees, and ants have proved so successful that they dominate and alter most of the land habitats of the Earth. In the forests of Brazil, their assembled forces constitute more than 20 percent of the weight of all land animals, including nematode worms, toucans, and jaguars. Who could have guessed all this from a knowledge of haplodiploidy?

Reduction is the traditional instrument of scientific analysis, but it is feared and resented. If human behavior can be reduced and determined to any considerable degree by the laws of biology, then mankind might appear to be less than unique and to that extent dehumanized. Few social scientists and scholars in the humanities are prepared to enter such a conspiracy, let alone surrender any of their territory. But this perception, which equates the method of reduction with the philosophy of diminution, is entirely in error. The laws of a subject are necessary to the discipline above it, they challenge and force a mentally more efficient restructuring, but they are not sufficient for the purposes of the discipline. Biology is the key to human nature, and social scientists cannot afford to ignore its rapidly tightening principles. But the social sciences are potentially far richer in content. Eventually they will absorb the relevant ideas of biology and go on to beggar them. The proper study of man is, for reasons that now transcend anthropocentrism, man.

3. The Social Construction of Gender

WE AS A SOCIETY PRIDE ourselves on our democratic values. We don't believe people should be constrained by innate differences from being able to achieve desired positions of influence to improve their well-being; equality of opportunity is our

professed aim. The Preamble to our Constitution stresses the importance of justice, as well as the general welfare and the blessings of liberty. The Pledge of Allegiance asserts that our republic preserves "liberty and justice for all."

Yet substantial inequalities between the sexes still exist in our society. In economic terms, full-time working women (after some very recent improvement) earn on average 71 percent of the earnings of full-time working men. One-half of poor and three-fifths of chronically poor households with dependent children are maintained by a single female parent. The poverty rate for elderly women is nearly twice that for elderly men. On the political front, two out of one hundred U.S. senators are women, one out of nine justices seems to be considered sufficient female representation on the Supreme Court, and the number of men chosen in each congressional election far exceeds the number of women elected in the entire history of the country. Underlying and intertwined with all of these inequalities is the unequal distribution of the unpaid labor of the family.

The typical current practices of family life, structured to a large extent by gender, are not just. These are not matters of natural necessity, as some people would believe. Surely nothing in our natures dictates that men should not be equal participants in the rearing of their children. Nothing in the nature of work makes it impossible to adjust it to the fact that people are parents as well as workers. That these things have not happened is part of the historically, socially constructed differentiation between the sexes that feminists have come to call *gender*. We live in a society that has over the years regarded the innate characteristic of sex as one of the clearest legitimizers of different rights and restrictions, both formal and informal. While the legal sanctions that uphold male dominance have begun to be eroded in the past century, and more rapidly in the last twenty years, the heavy weight of tradition, combined with the effects of socialization, still works powerfully to reinforce sex roles that are commonly regarded as of unequal prestige and worth. The sexual division of labor has not only been a fundamental part of the marriage contract, but so deeply influences us in our formative years that feminists of both sexes who try to reject it can find themselves struggling against it with varying degrees of ambivalence. Based on this linchpin, "gender"—by which I mean *the deeply entrenched institutionalization of sexual difference*—still permeates our society.

THE CONSTRUCTION OF GENDER

Due to feminism and feminist theory, gender is coming to be recognized as a social factor of major importance. Indeed, the new meaning of the word reflects the fact that so much of what has traditionally been thought of as sexual difference is now considered by many to be largely socially produced. Feminist scholars from many disciplines and with radically different points of view have contributed to the enterprise of making gender fully visible and comprehensible. At one end of the spectrum are those whose explanations of the subordination of women focus primarily on biological difference as causal in the construction of gender, and at the other end are those who argue that biological difference may not even lie at the core of the social construction that is gender; the views of the vast majority of feminists fall between these extremes. The rejection of biological determinism and the corresponding emphasis on gender as a social construction characterize most current feminist scholarship. Of particular relevance is work in psychology, where scholars have investigated the importance of female primary parenting in the formation of our gendered identities, and in history and anthropology, where emphasis has been placed on the historical and cultural variability of gender. Some feminists have been criticized for developing theories of gender that do not take sufficient account of differences *among* women, especially race, class, religion, and ethnicity. While such critiques should always inform our research and improve our arguments, it would be a mistake to allow them to detract our attention from gender itself as a factor of significance. Many injustices are experienced by women *as women*, whatever the differences among them and whatever other injustices they also suffer from. The past and present gendered nature of the family, and the ideology that surrounds it, affects virtually all women, whether or not they live or ever lived in traditional families. Recognizing this is not to deny or de-emphasize the fact that gender may affect different subgroups of women to a different extent and in different ways.

The potential significance of feminist discoveries and conclusions about gender for issues of social justice cannot be overemphasized. They undermine centuries of argument that started with the notion that not only the distinct differentiation of women and men but the domination of women by men, being natural, was therefore inevitable and not even to be considered in discussions of justice. As I shall make clear . . . such notions cannot stand up to rational scrutiny.

During the same two decades in which feminists have been intensely thinking, researching, analyzing, disagreeing about, and rethinking the subject of gender, our political and legal institutions have been increasingly faced with issues concerning the injustices of gender and their effects. These issues are being decided within a fundamentally patriarchal system, founded in a tradition in which "individuals" were assumed to be male heads of households. Not surprisingly, the system has demonstrated a limited capacity for determining what is just, in many cases involving gender. Sex discrimination, sexual harassment, abortion, pregnancy in the workplace, parental leave, childcare, and surrogate mothering have all become major and well-publicized issues of public policy, engaging both courts and legislatures. Issues of family justice, in particular—from child custody and divorce terms to physical and sexual abuse of wives and children—have become increasingly visible and pressing, and are commanding increasing attention from the police and court systems. There is clearly a major "justice crisis" in contemporary society arising from issues of gender.

THEORIES OF JUSTICE AND THE NEGLECT OF GENDER

During these same two decades, there has been a great resurgence of theories of social justice. Political theory, which had been sparse for a period before the late 1960s except as an important branch of intellectual history, has become a flourishing field, with social justice as its central concern. Yet, remarkably, major contemporary theorists of

justice have almost without exception ignored the situation just described. They have displayed little interest in or knowledge of the findings of feminism. They have largely bypassed the fact that the society to which their theories are supposed to pertain is heavily and deeply affected by gender, and faces difficult issues of justice stemming from its gendered past and present assumptions. Since theories of justice are centrally concerned with whether, how, and why persons should be treated differently from one another, this neglect seems inexplicable. These theories are *about* which initial or acquired characteristics or positions in society legitimize differential treatment of persons by social institutions, laws, and customs. They are *about* how and whether and to what extent beginnings should affect outcomes. The division of humanity into two sexes seems to provide an obvious subject for such inquiries. But, as we shall see, this does not strike most contemporary theorists of justice, and their theories suffer in both coherence and relevance because of it. . . . "How just is gender?"

Why is it that when we turn to contemporary theories of justice, we do not find illuminating and positive contributions to this question? How can theories of justice that are ostensibly about people in general neglect women, gender, and all the inequalities between the sexes? One reason is that most theorists *assume*, though they do not discuss, the traditional, gender-structured family.

Counting Women In

When we turn to the great tradition of Western political thought with questions about the justice of the treatment of the sexes in mind, it is to little avail. Bold feminists like Mary Astell, Mary Wollstonecraft, William Thompson, Harriet Taylor, and George Bernard Shaw have occasionally challenged the tradition, often using its own premises and arguments to overturn its explicit or implicit justification of the inequality of women. But John Stuart Mill is a rare exception to the rule that those who hold central positions in the tradition almost never question the justice of the subordination of women. This phenomenon is undoubtedly due in part to the fact that Aristotle, whose theory of justice has been so influential, relegated women to a sphere of "household justice"—populated by persons who are not fundamentally equal to the free men who participate in political justice, but inferiors whose natural function is to serve those who are more fully human. The liberal tradition, despite its supposed foundation of individual rights and human equality, is more Aristotelian in this respect than is generally acknowledged. In one way or another, almost all liberal theorists have assumed that the "individual" who is the basic subject of the theories is the male head of a patriarchal household.

Theories of justice must apply to all of us, and to all of human life, instead of *assuming* silently that half of us take care of whole areas of life that are considered outside the scope of social justice. In a just society, the structure and practices of families must afford women the same opportunities as men to develop their capacities, to participate in political power, to influence social choices, and to be economically as well as physically secure. . . .

The family is a crucial determinant of our opportunities in life, of what we "become." It has frequently been acknowledged by those concerned with real equality of opportunity that the family presents a problem. But though they have discerned a serious problem, these theorists have underestimated it because they have seen only half of it. They have seen that the disparity among families in terms of the physical and emotional environment, motivation, and material advantages they can give their children has a tremendous effect upon children's opportunities in life. We are not born as isolated, equal individuals in our society, but into family situations: some in the social middle, some poor and homeless, and some super-affluent; some to a single or soon-to-be-separated parent, some to parents whose marriage is fraught with conflict, some to parents who will stay together in love and happiness. Any claims that equal opportunity exists are therefore completely unfounded. Decades of neglect of the poor, especially of poor black and Hispanic households, accentuated by the policies of the Reagan years,

have brought us farther from the principles of equal opportunity. To come close to them would require, for example, a high and uniform standard of public education and the provision of equal social services—including health care, employment training, job opportunities, drug rehabilitation, and decent housing—for all who need them. In addition to redistributive taxation, only massive reallocations of resources from the military to social services could make these things possible. . . .

But even if all these disparities were somehow eliminated, we would still not attain equal opportunity for all. This is because what has not been recognized as an equal opportunity problem, except in feminist literature and circles, is the disparity *within* the family, the fact that its gender structure is itself a major obstacle to equality of opportunity. This is very important in itself, since one of the factors with most influence on our opportunities in life is the social significance attributed to our sex. The opportunities of girls and women are centrally affected by the structure and practices of family life, particularly by the fact that women are almost invariably primary parents. What nonfeminists who see in the family an obstacle to equal opportunity have *not* seen is that the extent to which a family is gender-structured can make the sex we belong to a relatively insignificant aspect of our identity and our life prospects or an all-pervading one. This is because so much of the social construction of gender takes place in the family and particularly in the institution of female parenting.

. . . In a just society, the structure and practices of families must give women the same opportunities as men to develop their capacities, to participate in political power and influence social choices, and to be economically secure. But in addition, families must be just because of the vast influence they have on the moral development of children. The family is the primary institution of formative moral development. And the structure and practices of the family must parallel those of the larger society if the sense of justice is to be fostered and maintained.

4. The Biological Basis of Gender Differences

IN HER BOOK *Who Stole Feminism?* the philosopher Christina Hoff Sommers draws a useful distinction between two schools of thought. *Equity feminism* opposes sex discrimination and other forms of unfairness to women. It is part of the classical liberal and humanistic tradition that grew out of the Enlightenment, and it guided the first wave of feminism and launched the second wave. *Gender feminism* holds that women continue to be enslaved by a pervasive system of male dominance, the gender system, in which "bi-sexual infants are transformed into male and female gender personalities, the one destined to command, the other to obey." It is opposed to the classical liberal tradition and allied instead with Marxism, postmodernism, social constructionism, and radical science. It has became the credo of some women's studies programs, feminist organizations, and spokespeople for the women's movement.

Equity feminism is a moral doctrine about equal treatment that makes no commitments regarding open empirical issues in psychology or biology. Gender feminism is an empirical doctrine committed to three claims about human nature. The first is that the differences between men and women have nothing to do with biology but are socially constructed in their entirety. The second is that humans possess a single social motive—power—and that social life can be understood only in terms of how it is exercised. The third is that human interactions arise not from the motives of people dealing with each other as individuals but from the motives of *groups* dealing with other groups—in this case, the male gender dominating the female gender.

In embracing these doctrines, the genderists are handcuffing feminism to railroad tracks on which a train is bearing down. As we shall see,

neuroscience, genetics, psychology, and ethnography are documenting sex differences that almost certainly originate in human biology. And evolutionary psychology is documenting a web of motives other than group-against-group dominance (such as love, sex, family, and beauty) that entangle us in many conflicts and confluences of interest with members of the same sex and of the opposite sex. Gender feminists want either to derail the train or to have other women join them in martyrdom, but the other women are not cooperating. Despite their visibility, gender feminists do not speak for all feminists, let alone for all women. . . .

All this is an essential background to the discussions to come. To say that women and men do not have interchangeable minds, that people have desires other than power, and that motives belong to individual people and not just to entire genders is not to attack feminism or to compromise the interests of women, despite the misconception that gender feminism speaks in their name. . . .

Why are people so afraid of the idea that the minds of men and women are not identical in every respect? . . . The fear, of course, is that different implies unequal—that if the sexes differed in any way, then men would have to be better, or more dominant, or have all the fun.

Nothing could be farther from biological thinking. . . . From a gene's point of view, being in the body of a male and being in the body of a female are equally good strategies, at least on average (circumstances can nudge the advantage somewhat in either direction). Natural selection thus tends toward an equal investment in the two sexes: equal numbers, an equal complexity of bodies and brains, and equally effective designs for survival. Is it better to be the size of a male baboon and have six-inch canine teeth or to be the size of a female baboon and not have them? Merely to ask the question is to reveal its pointlessness. A biologist would say that it's better to have the male adaptations to deal with male problems and the female adaptations to deal with female problems.

So men are not from Mars nor are women from Venus. Men and women are from Africa, the cradle of our evolution, where they evolved together as a single species. Men and women have all the same genes except for a handful on the Y chromosome, and their brains are so similar that it takes an eagle-eyed neuroanatomist to find the small differences between them. Their average levels of general intelligence are the same, according to the best psychometric estimates, and they use language and think about the physical and living world in the same general way. They feel the same basic emotions, and both enjoy sex, seek intelligent and kind marriage partners, get jealous, make sacrifices for their children, compete for status and mates, and sometimes commit aggression in pursuit of their interests.

But of course the minds of men and women are not identical, and recent reviews of sex differences have converged on some reliable differences. Sometimes the differences are large, with only slight overlap in the bell curves. Men have a much stronger taste for no-strings sex with multiple or anonymous partners, as we see in the almost all-male consumer base for prostitution and visual pornography. Men are far more likely to compete violently, sometimes lethally, with one another over stakes great and small (as in the recent case of a surgeon and an anesthesiologist who came to blows in the operating room while a patient lay on the table waiting to have her gall bladder removed). Among children, boys spend far more time practicing for violent conflict in the form of what psychologists genteelly call "rough-and-tumble play." The ability to manipulate three-dimensional objects and space in the mind also shows a large difference in favor of men.

With some other traits the differences are small on average but can be large at the extremes. That happens for two reasons. When two bell curves partly overlap, the farther out along the tail you

go, the larger the discrepancies between the groups. For example, men on average are taller than women and the discrepancy is greater for more extreme values. At a height of five foot ten, men outnumber women by a ratio of thirty to one; at a height of six feet, men outnumber women by a ratio of two thousand to one. Also, confirming an expectation from evolutionary psychology, for many traits the bell curve for males is flatter and wider than the curve for females. That is, there are proportionally more males at the extremes. Along the left tail of the curve, one finds that boys are far more likely to be dyslexic, learning disabled, attention deficient, emotionally disturbed, and mentally retarded (at least for some types of retardation). At the right tail, one finds that in a sample of talented students who score above 700 (out of 800) on the mathematics section of the Scholastic Assessment Test, boys outnumber girls by thirteen to one, even though the scores of boys and girls are similar within the bulk of the curve.

With still other traits, the average values for the two sexes differ by smaller amounts and in different directions for different traits. Though men, on average, are better at mentally rotating objects and maps, women are better at remembering landmarks and the positions of objects. Men are better throwers; women are more dexterous. Men are better at solving mathematical word problems, women at mathematical calculation. Women are more sensitive to sounds and smells, have better depth perception, match shapes faster, and are much better at reading facial expressions and body language. Women are better spellers, retrieve words more fluently, and have a better memory for verbal material.

Women experience basic emotions more intensely, except perhaps anger. Women have more intimate social relationships, are more concerned about them, and feel more empathy toward their friends, though not toward strangers. (The common view that women are more empathic toward everyone is both evolutionarily unlikely and untrue.) They maintain more eye contact, and smile and laugh far more often. Men are more likely to compete with one another for status using violence or occupational achievement, women more likely to use derogation and other forms of verbal aggression.

Men have a higher tolerance for pain and a greater willingness to risk life and limb for status, attention, and other dubious rewards. The Darwin Awards, given annually to "the individuals who ensure the long-term survival of our species by removing themselves from the gene pool in a sublimely idiotic fashion," almost always go to men. Recent honorees include the man who squashed himself under a Coke machine after tipping it forward to get a free can, three men who competed over who could stomp the hardest on an antitank mine, and the would-be pilot who tied weather balloons to his lawn chair, shot two miles into the air, and drifted out to sea (earning just an honorable mention because he was rescued by helicopter).

Women are more attentive to their infants' everyday cries (though both sexes respond equally to cries of extreme distress) and are more solicitous toward their children in general. Girls play more at parenting and trying on social roles, boys more at fighting, chasing, and manipulating objects. And men and women differ in their patterns of sexual jealousy, their mate preferences, and their incentives to philander.

Many sex differences, of course, have nothing to do with biology. Hair styles and dress vary capriciously across centuries and cultures, and in recent decades participation in universities, professions, and sports has switched from mostly male to fifty-fifty or mostly female. For all we know, some of the current sex differences may be just as ephemeral. But gender feminists argue that *all* sex differences, other than the anatomical ones, come from the expectations of parents, playmates, and society. The radical scientist Anne Fausto-Sterling wrote:

> The key biological fact is that boys and girls have different genitalia, and it is this biological difference that leads adults to interact differently with different babies whom we conveniently color-code in pink or blue to make it unnecessary to go peering into their diapers for information about gender.

But the pink-and-blue theory is becoming less and less credible. Here are a dozen kinds of evidence that suggest that the difference between men and women is more than genitalia-deep.

- Sex differences are not an arbitrary feature of Western culture, like the decision to drive on the left or on the right. In all human cultures, men and women are seen as having different natures. All cultures divide their labor by sex, with more responsibility for childrearing by women and more control of the public and political realms by men. (The division of labor emerged even in a culture where everyone had been committed to stamping it out, the Israeli kibbutz.) In all cultures men are more aggressive, more prone to stealing, more prone to lethal violence (including war), and more likely to woo, seduce, and trade favors for sex. And in all cultures one finds rape, as well as proscriptions against rape.

- Many of the psychological differences between the sexes are exactly what an evolutionary biologist who knew only their physical differences would predict. Throughout the animal kingdom, when the female has to invest more calories and risk in each offspring (in the case of mammals, through pregnancy and nursing), she also invests more in nurturing the offspring after birth, since it is more costly for a female to replace a child than for a male to replace one. The difference in investment is accompanied by a greater competition among males over opportunities to mate, since mating with many partners is more likely to multiply the number of offspring of a male than the number of offspring of a female. When the average male is larger than the average female (as is true of men and women), it bespeaks an evolutionary history of greater violent competition by males over mating opportunities. Other physical traits of men, such as later puberty, greater adult strength, and shorter lives, also indicate a history of selection for high-stakes competition.

- Many of the sex differences are found widely in other primates, indeed, throughout the mammalian class. The males tend to compete more aggressively and to be more polygamous; the females tend to invest more in parenting. In many mammals a greater territorial range is accompanied by an enhanced ability to navigate using the geometry of the spatial layout (as opposed to remembering individual landmarks). More often it is the male who has the greater range, and that is true of human hunter-gatherers. Men's advantage in using mental maps and performing 3-D mental rotation may not be a coincidence.

- Geneticists have found that the diversity of the DNA in the mitochondria of different people (which men and women inherit from their mothers) is far greater than the diversity of the DNA in Y chromosomes (which men inherit from their fathers). This suggests that for tens of millennia men had greater variation in their reproductive success than women. Some men had many descendants and others had none (leaving us with a small number of distinct Y chromosomes), whereas a larger number of women had a more evenly distributed number of descendants (leaving us with a larger number of distinct mitochondrial genomes). These are precisely the conditions that cause sexual selection, in which males compete for opportunities to mate and females choose the best-quality males.

- The human body contains a mechanism that causes the brains of boys and the brains of girls to diverge during development. The Y chromosome triggers the growth of testes in a male fetus, which secrete androgens, the characteristically male hormones (including testosterone). Androgens have lasting effects on the brain during fetal development, in the months after birth, and during puberty, and they have transient effects at other times. Estrogens, the characteristically female sex hormones, also affect the brain throughout life. Receptors for the sex hormones are found in the hypothalamus, the hippocampus, and the amygdala in the limbic system of the brain, as well as in the cerebral cortex.

- The brains of men differ visibly from the brains of women in several ways. Men have larger brains with more neurons (even correcting for body size), though women have a higher percentage of gray matter. (Since men and women are equally intelligent overall, the significance of these differences is unknown.) The interstitial nuclei in the anterior hypothalamus, and a nucleus of the stria terminalis, also in the hypothalamus, are larger in men; they have been implicated in sexual behavior and aggression. Portions of the cerebral commissures, which link the left and right hemispheres, appear to be larger in women, and their brains may function in a less lopsided manner than men's. Learning and socialization can affect the microstructure and functioning of the human brain, of course, but probably not the size of its visible anatomical structures.

- Variation in the level of testosterone among different men, and in the same man in different seasons or at different times of day, correlates with libido, self-confidence, and the drive for dominance. Violent criminals have higher levels than nonviolent criminals; trial lawyers have higher levels than those who push paper. The relations are complicated for a number of reasons. Over a broad range of values, the concentration of testosterone in the bloodstream doesn't matter. Some traits, such as spatial abilities, peak at moderate rather than high levels. The effects of testosterone depend on the number and distribution of receptors for the molecule, not just on its concentration. And one's psychological state can affect testosterone levels as well as the other way around. But there is a causal relation, albeit a complicated one. When women preparing for a sex-change operation are given androgens, they improve on tests of mental rotation and get worse, on tests of verbal fluency. The journalist Andrew Sullivan whose medical condition had lowered his testosterone levels, describes the effects of injecting it: "The rush of a T shot is not unlike the rush of going on a first date or speaking before an audience. I feel braced. After one injection, I almost got in a public brawl for the first time in my life. There is always a lust peak—every time it takes me unaware." Though testosterone levels in men and women do not overlap, variations in level have similar kinds of effects in the two sexes. High-testosterone women smile less often and have more extramarital affairs, a stronger social presence, and even a stronger handshake.

- Women's cognitive strengths and weaknesses vary with the phase of their menstrual cycle. When estrogen levels are high, women get even better at tasks on which they typically do better than men, such as verbal fluency. When the levels are low, women get better at tasks on which men typically do better, such as mental rotation. A variety of sexual motives, including their taste in men, vary with the menstrual cycle as well.

- Androgens have permanent effects on the developing brain, not just transient effects on the adult brain. Girls with congenital adrenal hyperplasia overproduce androstenedione, the androgen hormone made famous by the baseball slugger Mark McGwire. Though their hormone levels are brought to normal soon after birth, the girls grow into tomboys, with more rough-and-tumble play, a greater interest in trucks than dolls, better spatial abilities, and, when they get older, more sexual fantasies and attractions involving other girls. Those who are treated with hormones only later in childhood show male patterns of sexuality when they become young adults, including quick arousal by pornographic images, an autonomous sex drive centered on genital stimulation, and the equivalent of wet dreams.

- The ultimate fantasy experiment to separate biology from socialization would be to take a baby boy, give him a sex-change operation, and have his parents raise him as a girl and other people treat him as one. If gender is socially constructed, the child should have the mind of a normal girl; if it depends on prenatal hormones, the child should feel like a boy trapped in a girl's body. Remarkably, the experiment has been done in real life—not out of scientific curiosity, of course, but as a result of disease and accidents. One study looked at twenty-five boys who were born without a penis (a birth defect known as cloacal exstrophy) and who were then castrated and raised as girls. *All* of them showed male patterns of rough-and-tumble play and had typically male attitudes and interests. More than half of them spontaneously declared they were boys, one when he was just five years old.

In a famous case study, an eight-month-old boy lost his penis in a botched circumcision (not by a mohel, I was relieved to learn, but by a bungling doctor). His parents consulted the famous sex researcher John Money, who had maintained that "Nature is a political strategy of those committed to maintaining the status quo of sex differences." He advised them to let the doctors castrate the baby and build him an artificial vagina, and they raised him as a girl without telling him what had happened. I learned about the case as an undergraduate in the 1970s, when it was offered as proof that babies are born neuter and acquire a gender from the way they are raised. A *New York Times* article from the era reported that Brenda (nee Bruce) "has been sailing contentedly through childhood as a genuine girl." The facts were suppressed until 1997, when it was revealed that from a young age Brenda felt she was a boy trapped in a girl's body and gender role. She ripped off frilly dresses, rejected dolls in favor of guns, preferred to play with boys, and even insisted on urinating standing up. At fourteen she was so miserable that she decided either to live her life as a male or to end it, and her father finally told her the truth. She underwent a new set of operations, assumed a male identity, and today is happily married to a woman.

- Children with Turner's syndrome are genetically neuter. They have a single X chromosome, inherited from either their mother or their father, instead of the usual two X chromosomes of a girl (one from her mother, the other from her father) or the X and Y of a boy (the X from his mother, the Y from his father). Since a female body plan is the default among mammals, they look and act like girls. Geneticists have discovered that parents' bodies can molecularly imprint genes on the X chromosome so they become more or less active in the developing bodies and brains of their children. A Turner's syndrome girl who gets her X chromosome from her father may have genes that are evolutionarily optimized for girls (since a paternal X always ends up in a daughter). A Turner's girl who gets her X from her mother may have genes that are evolutionarily optimized for boys (since a maternal X, though it can end up in either sex, will act unopposed only in a son, who has no counterpart to the X genes on his puny Y chromosome). And in fact Turner's girls do differ psychologically depending on which parent gave them their X. The ones with an X from their father (which is destined for a girl) were better at interpreting body language, reading emotions, recognizing faces, handling words, and getting along with other people compared to the ones with an X from their mother (which is fully active only in a boy).

- Contrary to popular belief, parents in contemporary America do not treat their sons and daughters very differently. A recent assessment of 172 studies involving 28,000 children found that boys and girls are given similar amounts of encouragement, warmth, nurturance, restrictiveness, discipline, and clarity of communication. The only substantial difference was that about two-thirds of the boys were discouraged from playing with dolls, especially by their fathers, out of a fear that they would become gay. (Boys who prefer girls' toys often do turn out gay, but forbidding them the toys does not change the outcome.) Nor do differences between boys and girls depend on their observing masculine behavior in their fathers and feminine behavior in their mothers. When Hunter has two mommies, he acts just as much like a boy as if he had a mommy and a daddy.

Things are not looking good for the theory that boys and girls are born identical except for their genitalia, with all other differences coming from the way society treats them. If that were true, it would be an amazing coincidence that in every society the coin flip that assigns each sex to one set of roles would land the same way (or that one fateful flip at the dawn of the species should have been maintained without interruption across all the upheavals of the past hundred thousand years). It would be just as amazing that, time and again, society's arbitrary assignments matched the predictions that a Martian biologist would make for our species based on our anatomy and the distribution of our genes. It would seem odd that the hormones that make us male and female in the first place also modulate the characteristically male and female mental traits, both decisively in early brain development and in smaller degrees throughout our lives. It would be all the more odd that a second genetic mechanism differentiating the sexes (genomic imprinting) also installs characteristic male and female talents. Finally, two key predictions of the social construction theory—that boys treated as girls will grow up with girls' minds, and that differences between boys and girls can be traced to differences in how their parents treat them—have gone down in flames.

Of course, just because many sex differences are rooted in biology does not mean that one sex is superior, that the differences will emerge for all people in all circumstances, that discrimination against a person based on sex is justified, or that people should be coerced into doing things typical of their sex. But neither are the differences without consequences.

5. Nature and Nurture

WHAT SORT OF DIFFERENCE?

Is the difference between men and women natural, or is it produced by culture? Here is another false antithesis. In other fields today this one is usually nailed as false quite quickly, being unkindly referred to as "the old nature-nurture controversy." In most contexts, people now see that any aspect of human affairs can in principle have some biological sources in the genetic constitution of the species, and also some in recent culture and history. The two sets do not compete. The job of working out their details and relative importance is done by empirical enquiry, not by dying on the barricades.

Many feminists, however, still tend to resist this open-minded approach strongly. In the early stages of the movement they often dismissed any suggestion of natural sex differences as not only mistaken but wicked. Thus Kate Millett, complaining of "the threadbare tactic of justifying social and temperamental differences by biological ones," writes: "The sexes are inherently in everything alike, save reproductive systems, secondary sexual characteristics, orgasmic capacity, and genetic and morphological structure. Perhaps the only things they can uniquely exchange are semen and transudate." The extraordinary assumption that everything physical (the whole "genetic and morphological structure") could be different and yet everything mental could remain the same was rather widespread at that time among social scientists. Although every cell in our bodies is sexed, and although there are marked sex differences in the structure of the brain and working of the nervous system, the human spirit was treated as a separate entity, somehow immune to such gross influences. This attitude, which is luckily less common now, will be our business shortly. We must notice first, however, that Kate Millett's position cannot stand in any case because

it is inconsistent with some ideas central to feminism itself.

In itself, it is understandable as a reaction to confused male theorists, who have repeatedly justified local customs in this area which were just crude devices to protect masculine interests, or which were plain foolish, as laws fixed by unalterable dictates of nature. If what we want is merely to find food for satire and indignation, shooting them down can keep us occupied for a long time. But we do not only want that. Moreover, feminists need to be careful about shooting in this direction, since they may hit their own windows.

The assumption of natural causes is such a deep-rooted one that even those who officially disown it often find that they are using it. There are two prominent feminist concepts which seem to depend on that assumption. One is the idea of the natural superiority of women, either in general or in certain special respects. (It will be remembered that the strict, exclusive definition of feminism, to which Janet Radcliffe Richards referred, included belief in "the inherent equality of the sexes *or the superiority of the female.*" (Italics ours.) These two alternatives may look alike to the casual eye, but they call for opposite views on innateness.) The other is *sisterhood,* considered—as it usually seems to be—not just as an external community in misfortune, but as a natural bond of sympathy, resting on intrinsic likeness.

Neither of these ideas makes sense without the assumption of distinct, innate dispositions in the two sexes. We shall see that there is in fact nothing alarming in this suggestion. Innate difference does not have to be inferiority; it is just difference. And as we have already seen, people do not need to be standard, indistinguishable units like frozen peas, "in everything alike," in order to be political equals. They need just enough minimal likeness to

Selections from Mary Midgley and Judith Hughes, Women's Choices *(New York: St. Martin's Press, 1984), pp. 59–62.* Reprinted with permission.

make them members of the community. We shall lose nothing by jettisoning the dogma that the two sexes have to be inherently indistinguishable. And if we want to retain the use of these two feminist concepts, we must jettison it. The use and standing of these concepts remains to be discussed. They are mentioned here just to point out that the question of natural difference is not a simple one, settled at once by reference to what is politically edifying. There are, too, some influential feminists, such as Elaine Morgan, for whom biological considerations are central.

The issue is in any case a bit too serious for dogmatic bickering. We need the truth. In examining current attitudes to the sex difference and working to humanize them, we need the fullest understanding we can get of its real sources. To rule out the possibility of genetic ones in advance, simply because that area has been put to bad use in the past, is arbitrary. If there are such sources, even minor ones, we need to know about them. There is no substitute for this open-minded temper. Questions of fact cannot be settled in the lump on political grounds. If certain facts are dangerous, the remedy is, as usual, not suppression but more facts.

The Fear of Fatalism

All this may in general be admitted. But there is a special difficulty which apparently stops people from even considering propositions about human nature as candidates for belief. This is the suspicion of fatalism, usually described now as "biological determinism" or "genetic determinism." People feel that, if our conduct had any genetically determined causes, we would be condemned to the status of automata, doomed to stick helplessly in our grooves. Must we not therefore believe instead only in social causes, so as to give ourselves the option of initiating change?

It is a very mysterious point about this way of thinking that it treats social causes as so much less compelling than genetic ones. As is often remarked, we are all "conditioned by our culture."

This belief, however, is not thought to turn us into automata. Yet the account of social conditioning can be built up, quite as easily as that of physi-

cal causes, in such a way as to make us seem like robots. And it has the extra disadvantage that it makes social change seem impossible. Since, however, we know that social change continually takes place, there must be something wrong with this notion of conditioning—which is, indeed, a very crude one. Human beings are not lumps of putty, passively accepting a mould, but active creatures with their own individual natures, able to select among the suggestions which they get, and to transform customs, gradually and cumulatively, by their distinctive responses. It is our individual natures, and the use we make of them, which save us from the tyranny of culture.

There is no fatalism here. Fatalism is the belief that there are, not just causes, but overwhelming and unmanageable causes, opposing and dooming the enterprises that we value. In fact, originally fatalism is the belief in unbeatable hostile beings who are bound to get us whatever we do, as in the story of Oedipus. This is something quite different from determinism, which is just the modest assumption that events in the world may be expected to be regular. This assumption is needed for everyday science, though apparently not for the study of quantum mechanics. It need not rest on private information from heaven that events actually *are* regular. It is simply a convenient assumption, made for the sake of getting on with enquiry. Deterministic calculations can indeed sometimes be depressing, because they point out awkward facts about the world which we would have wished otherwise—such as that we are probably not going to be able to invent anti-gravity, so that weights will go on being heavy to lift. But we need to know these things. And just as often they point out welcome facts, such as the reliable good qualities of the plants and animals on which we depend. And in our observations of human conduct we depend on this calculation for our general expectations of good and evil alike. Human conduct is not random and unpredictable. . . .

The impression that biology, and physical science in general, constitutes a threat seems to be a response to a certain kind of illicit scientific reductionism which brings out with an air of triumph, as if exposing a fraudulent medium, the claim that we are "nothing but" certain scientific entities. About the physical basis of thought and feeling, this is usually done by claiming that the physical phenomena—secretions and the like—which accompany our experiences are their only real causes, and concluding that people are therefore really only the pawns or playthings of their secretions. The reducer's point is to exclude souls, vital force and other extras from the scientific scene, and this he is quite entitled to do. But to suggest that this shows ordinary experience to be unreal is sheer meaningless melodrama. Certainly we think and feel by means of our brains and nervous systems. If they fail us, our thought falters. But that is true of our hearts and livers as well, and is part of our general dependence on the physical world.

As whole beings, we think with our brains just as we jump with our legs. But to understand what we are doing requires much more than the physical sciences; it calls for a grasp of our purposes and the facts in the world to which they relate, all of which are perfectly real—indeed, their reality is far less problematical than that of, say, the basic entities of physics. The neurological explanation cannot therefore be the only one—or in some sense the only "real" one—and the reduction fails. So, and more resoundingly, does the still odder and more recent sociobiological one, which says that all we are really doing is maximizing the spread of our genes ("the organism is only DNA's way of making more DNA"). This is not biology, it is rhetoric.

What is needed in order to prevent causes from looking like fates is a full recognition of their complexity. This will show the presence of genetic causes to be inoffensive in both the areas where it impinges on left-wing thought generally and feminism in particular. . . .

Sisterhood and Motherhood

The degree to which male dominance is a general feature of [human cultures] has been questioned. But there is no doubt about something else, which has to be happening before that question can even arise—namely, why would the universal division of men and women into separate groups, with distinct social roles happen if they did not differ in

character? It is no use accounting for this as a case of the strong oppressing the weak, because that can be done without any division of roles at all. Some women, too, are stronger than some men, and in any case many of the differences do not seem to have anything to do with oppression. They are just differences, not tyrannies.

This notion of a natural, irremovable likeness binding women and distinguishing them from men is taken for granted as underlying the notion of sisterhood, which has been so important to the women's movement. It is scarcely possible to think of that bond as just a link connecting fellow-sufferers from a particular kind of deceptive or distorting treatment—a conditioning which has persuaded women that they were different. If that were the idea, women's groups would surely want to *cure* them of the illusion, and send them out into the world as individuals who would no longer specially need each other's company. Far from this, women cultivate their own distinctness, and find great relief in discovering not just that other women share their misfortunes, but that they respond to them similarly. This cannot possibly just mean that, as behaviorism requires, they have been stamped in the same mill.

The thinking of the women's movement, then, already agrees with the anthropological evidence which indicates that women and men are not a single standard item. . . .

Was there a total change—a miraculous Rise of Man, in which our species levitated away from the physical world altogether—when this whole instinctive mechanism vanished and was replaced by the radically different workings of social conditioning? Or did advanced intellect and culture emerge rather as a further development, enriching and organizing these simpler motivations into a new and splendid whole, not needing to destroy them first?

The first idea, which treats nature and culture as sharply exclusive alternatives, . . . is still popular among some social scientists; but no adequate reason for it, or plausible story about how it could occur, has ever been given. And in any detailed application it produces endless difficulties, of which the batch concerning motherhood are typical. How is it really supposed to work? Are the hormonal arrangements (which in human beings are very similar to those in the higher apes) supposed to have lost their function, become idle and ceased to be connected with the emotions? Or do they stay connected but only one way round—are they now passive, accepting social conditioning from outside but contributing nothing of their own? Is there now one-way causation? If this strange state of affairs were really working, nobody surely ought to be able to have emotions which their society did not demand of them. But they do. . . .

Those who are determined to admit only social causes usually deal with this kind of evidence by saying that the conditioning must have been more complex than it looked—that there has been counter-conditioning at a deeper level, producing the conflicting motives. At this point, however, the notion of conditioning stops being an empirical one at all. If unnoticed conditioning can always be invoked as a hidden cause, anything goes.

Study Questions

1. Explain how, according to Darwin, various species evolve from others according to the principle of natural selection.

2. Describe the various types of evidence there are which support evolution by natural selection.

3. What sorts of human social behavior did Darwin believe were caused by natural selection?

4. What is sociobiology, and why did its theories create such a negative reaction?

5. What are epigenetic rules, how do they arise, and what role do they play in causing social behavior?

6. According to evolutionary psychology, when did human nature evolve?

7. Explain what "reading the minds of others" means, and say why that is a psychological adaptation.

8. Is the standard equipment view guilty of genetic determinism? Explain.

9. How does the standard equipment view explain the relationship between human nature and culture?

10. Explain why many feminists are opposed to the standard equipment view.

Chapter 11

Standard Equipment 2: Cognitive Science

Introduction

Ever since psychology became a science in the early part of the twentieth century, people have looked to it more than to philosophy to define human nature. The dominant approach in psychology today is cognitive psychology. Behaviorism still has a great deal of influence as the method of choice for animal studies and provides a basis for some types of therapy, but cognitive psychology has replaced it as the leading way to understand the nature of the mind and human behavior. Its approach to understanding the mind has been supplemented by the findings of other sciences as well, sciences collectively called **cognitive sciences,** each of which, in its own way, studies the human mind.

Among the cognitive sciences are various neurosciences (neurophysiology and neurobiology, for example), computer science, linguistics, and cognitive psychology. Philosophy is also included, especially certain areas of philosophy such as logic and especially the philosophies of mind, language, and knowledge. The neurosciences, sometimes called the *brain* sciences, study the structure and function of the brain. The others, called the *mind* sciences, study the way the mind is designed to perform cognitive functions such as perception, memory, the formation of concepts and beliefs, and the like. Computer scientists, especially those who work in the field of artificial intelligence, are part of the mind sciences and study how human cognitive structures might be modeled in a computer.

For the most part, cognitive science accepts the neo-Darwinian view that the mind has evolved, and that it comes packed with a host of innate tendencies to behave. Cognitive science has a narrower subject matter than evolutionary psychology. Evolutionary psychology studies all of the evolved adaptive functions of the human mind, while cognitive science focuses especially on the nature of our evolved *cognitive* functions. While there is this difference between them in scope, cognitive science shares many common assumptions with evolutionary psychology, such as the belief that the mind is the brain or the way that the brain works, and that the mind evolved according to the principles of natural selection.

Especially important is the belief of cognitive scientists that the mind is not one seamless entity, but is composed of many parts or **modules,** each of which has a specific function. These modules are often understood as programs that the brain runs, just as a computer runs various specific programs. The purpose of these modules, or cognitive functions, is to transform input from the environment to appropriate behavioral responses. If the input from the environment is called *information,* the mind is then thought of as an **information processor.** Computers are commonly referred to as information processors. A computer's word processing program, for example, may be thought of as processing or transforming keyboard input into appropriate text on a screen.

In a similar manner, human cognitive functions work on input from the environment to process it into intelligent behavior, behavior appropriate to the environmental circumstances. Cognitive scientists study what the behaviorists left out—what goes on between our ears, between the environmental input and our behavioral output. It is what goes on in our minds that organizes the input and shapes the output that interests them most. Far from considering us to be "empty" on the inside, they see the connections between environment and behavior as possible only because of the intervening role of the various modules or functions of the mind.

Most cognitive scientists believe that many of these information processing modules, the collection of which constitute our minds, are part of the standard equipment with which we are born. We are not born as blank slates, waiting for the environment alone to shape our intelligent activity. Instead, just as sociobiologists have shown us that we are born with social instincts, and evolutionary psychologists have shown us that we have tendencies to behave in certain ways that increase our chances of survival and reproduction, so most cognitive scientists accept as well what the standard equipment view endorses—that many of our cognitive functions are part of a universal human nature. How we see, remember, form concepts, reason from one belief to another, and even how we acquire a language, are all functions that are hardwired into our minds by evolution. These and many other types of cognitive activity are part of our nature. Just as a snake, or a frog, or a bird, or any species processes information according to their own standard equipment, so human beings acquire, store, and act on information in their world according to the type of information processors with which we come equipped. It is the nature and function of the cognitive parts of this human "computer" called our minds, that is of primary interest to cognitive scientists.

Worldview

Most cognitive scientists accept a materialist view of reality, though not all do so completely. Most also accept the scientific method as the best way to know the world and ourselves. Instead of discussing materialism and the scientific method once again, the discussion of reality in this section will focus on the human mind, and the primary types of knowledge to be discussed are the various methods used by the different cognitive sciences to understand it. We start first with a discussion of the various methods of *knowledge* used by cognitive scientists.

The brain is a three-pound organ with 100 billion neurons, each of which has hundreds, even thousands of fibers linking it to other neurons. The sciences that study it are called **neurosciences,** sometimes referred to as the *brain* sciences. They include neurophysiology, which studies the electrical activities of the brain and nervous system; neurobiology, which studies the origin and structure of the brain and the structure and function of neurons; neurochemistry, which studies the biochemistry of the brain; and neurophysics, which studies the subatomic particles of the brain. They also include various subsets of these fields. Neuroscientists use many methods to gather information, but chief among them today are a number of relatively new brain scanning technologies. Using techniques such as CAT (computer assisted tomography) and PET (positron emission tomography) and SQUID (superconducting quantum interference device) scanners, a detail structural and functional map of the brain is beginning to emerge. This map locates what occurs in the brain when certain mental states occur, and identifies which areas of the brain are responsible for which functions.

By means of these scanners scientists may observe which parts of the brain are active when a person performs a specific mental event, such as seeing something, remembering something, or recognizing someone's face, and from this data begin to build a map of the structure and function of the brain. Such a map is currently in its infancy, but enough of it has been drawn to say with confidence that mental states have a physical basis. Someday, with a more complete, more detailed, and more reliable map, one created with the help of new and more precise brain scanners, another person may be able to "read our minds" by observing the brain activity which we associate with specific mental events. Perhaps a particular network of firing neurons will simply be taken to be the thought of going to Chicago, or the memory of Grandma's face, or the smell of a rose. For now, it can at least be said with confidence that there is a neurological basis for all mental states.

The *mind* cognitive sciences do not study the brain, but rather study the mind. The "mind" is understood by cognitive scientists as a collection of mental events, such as thoughts, sensations, feelings, and memories. But what does the thinking, sensing, feeling, and remembering? Most cognitive scientists think of the mind as a collection of functions of the brain, not as the product of some nonphysical substance. However, because what they study directly are these functions, apart from whatever it is that performs them, they can study what it is to think, sense, feel, and remember without studying the brain directly. Just as the software of a computer may be described apart from the hardware that runs it, so, too, cognitive scientists believe that the way the mind works, the "software" it runs, also may be studied apart from whatever it is that runs them.

The goal of the mind sciences is to identify cognitive functions and to show how they work. In this way they attempt to discover the *design* of the mind. One of the problems in achieving this goal is that we are not conscious of what much of the mind does. We cannot simply look inside ourselves and see what goes on when we, for example, remember where we left our keys. We just remember or not; we do not observe directly *how* we remember. The cognitive scientist, and from here on we will mean the "mind" cognitive scientist, is in a position similar to a person trying to figure out what is going on inside a factory when metal and paint and computers and other materials go in one end, and cars come out the other. The person cannot look inside the factory. Instead, he must construct hypotheses about what sorts of things happen to the materials to shape them into cars, and then figure out how to tell if these hypotheses, these guesses, are correct.

The Influence of Kant and Artificial Intelligence (AI)

Instead of using direct observation, the method that a mind scientist, such as a cognitive psychologist, uses to learn about the mind is very much like the method that Kant used to understand the mind (see Chapter 6).[1] Kant called his method **the transcendental deduction.** This is actually a form of inductive reasoning that today is referred to as "reasoning to the best explanation." It works like this. Like the man observing the automobile factory from the outside, the researcher begins with an observation, such as our ability to remember where we left our keys. Since we do not observe how it is that we remember where our keys have been left, we have to reason how we are able to perform this function. The next step is to consider various hypotheses which explain how we do this.

For example, does our mind run a serial search of all the places our keys might be and try to match it with a memory, or does it first rank the possible places where they are likely to be in order of importance and search one at a time? Or maybe it uses an entirely different method to recall its past experiences. After forming various hypotheses about how we remember something, the next step is to test them to see if any are true. This is done in two ways. The first is by arranging appropriate experiments. If remembering is a type of serial search, for example, it should take longer than a ranked search, and experiments can be constructed to test for these temporal variables.

Another method of testing how it is that we remember various things or events, or how we perform any mental acts for that matter, is to enlist the aid of computer science, especially the area called **artificial intelligence, or AI.** Those who work in this field attempt to produce in computers of various sorts the same types of intelligent behavior that human minds produce. The basic idea behind using AI to test a hypothesis about the workings of the human mind is this: if a program that duplicates human intelligent behavior can be constructed and successfully run on a machine, then it is likely to duplicate the way that human minds work. If a program works to create an artificial version of memory like that displayed by human beings, for example, then it is accepted as confirmation of the design of human memory.

The central assumption of AI research is that there is a useful analogy to be drawn between computers and the mind. The research program that this assumption defines is the twofold one that the design of the human mind can be duplicated on a computer, and that the building of intelligent computers often reveals the design of the human mind. When robots are to be built that can talk and see and remember, for example, the model for constructing them is often what humans do when they perform these functions. On the other hand, when machines are designed that solve complex mathematical problems, diagnose illnesses, plan vacations, and even beat champion chess masters, they offer fruitful hypotheses for how human beings may accomplish the same tasks. The important point for us at this time is to understand that duplicating the function of a particular mental event on a computer is simply taken as evidence by cognitive scientists for how the human mind works.

Cognitive scientists are not content simply with identifying mental events. Descartes did that four hundred years earlier. We can do that for ourselves through introspection. Instead, cognitive scientists want to *explain* as well as describe what the mind does. If to explain something is to point to what causes it, then cognitive scientists want to show how the various mental events of which we are conscious are caused by the simpler processes, largely unconscious, that produce them. The mind is like an iceberg; most of what it does is not accessible to us through introspection. Only the final results of its teeming and churning activity come to the surface as conscious mental events. To understand the design of the mind is to start from these conscious mental events and work backwards to discover how they are produced by the many smaller functions, or modules, that unite to create them.

Just as the movement of my arm can be broken down into the movement of various muscle groups, and these into the contraction of various muscle fibers, and these into movements of various molecules, and these into the activity of various atoms, and so on, so each mental act is created by progressively smaller and smaller modules of activity. A mental act is explained only when it is broken down into its various components, its subfunctions. The goal of the mind sciences, then, is to understand the mind by reducing its various mental acts into simpler and ever simpler functions. The hope is that at the point where the simplest possible functions are discovered, there will be located the connection between the brain and the mind sciences. This is because the simplest functions will be most likely to be reducible to a pattern of neuronal activity. As the brain sciences discover the various patterns of neurons correlated with various types of mental acts, and as the mind sciences discover the simpler functions that constitute these mental acts, the way then becomes clear to connect—and even identify—the activity of the mind with that of the brain.

It is now time to discuss the central problem of *reality* within the worldview of the cognitive scientist. We call it a problem because the question of the nature of the mind has more than one answer. It is a philosophical problem, not a scientific one, and may be expressed in the following two questions: (1) What is a mind? and (2) How do minds relate to brains? These questions combine to form what philosophers call the **mind-brain problem.** Remember that philosophical problems go beyond facts to interpretations of the facts. They are solved by providing reasons why one interpretation is to be preferred over another. The mind-body problem is a philosophical problem because cognitive sciences at most discover how the mind and the brain are *correlated.* That is, they show which brain events occur when certain mental events do. But showing this correlation leaves open the question of the nature of the mind. Is the mind a nonphysical substance closely correlated with the brain? Or is the mind the brain itself, and thus the correlations are identities between mental states and brain states? Or does the brain somehow produce mental states, which nevertheless are not brain states, in addition to producing neurological states? The scientific facts, as you can see, are open to various interpretations. It is the job of the philosopher to clarify and to examine the case for and against these and other various interpretations of the facts about the mind and how it relates to the brain. What follows is a very brief survey of some of the most important attempts to solve the elusive mind-body problem.

The Mind-Body Problem

Substance dualism is the view of Descartes, as well as many other philosophers before and after Descartes. It claims that the brain is one type of thing and the mind quite another. The mind is not physical, and thus we are creatures composed of two different sorts of stuff, minds and bodies. Happenings in the nonphysical mind are correlated and even causally related to brain events, to be sure, but they are not identical with them. There cannot be mental events such as perception, memory, and thought without the brain events which underlie them, but the two types of events are different in kind, as are each of the substances which produce them. We have previously examined the case for and against this view in Chapter 5 and will not revisit it here. It is enough to say that the reasons against substance dualism are so compelling that few if any cognitive scientists accept its claims today.

Behaviorism also offers a solution to the mind-body problem that finds few adherents today. It claims that the mind is neither a nonphysical substance nor a physical substance. In fact, there are no "things" called minds at all, only mental events. Each mental event, moreover, is simply a pattern of overt behavior. We have introduced this view briefly in Chapter 10 and will not examine its strengths and weaknesses here. It is a view that has fallen out of favor, mostly because it denies the existence of so much of what we all consider to be quite real—our inner, subjective lives.

The **identity theory,** on the other hand, is a very popular solution to the mind-body problem today. It says, essentially, that the mind is identical with the brain. The mind is the brain; every mental event is nothing but a brain event. The major evidence for this view is that as science is finding out more and more about our brains, as it maps in ever more detail the neurological events that are correlated with our mental events, there is no longer any reason to see minds and brains as separate, distinct entities. Brains (with the aid of the rest of the body) can sense, perceive, remember, think, feel, and desire. So why do we also need nonphysical minds to do these things? This solution is a type of **materialism** (sometimes called physicalism), which claims that we are entirely physical beings. It is also a type of **reductionism,** since it claims that the mind can be reduced to, or is nothing more than, the brain.

While this solution to the mind-body problem looks good at first glance, it has some serious problems that have caused most scientists to reject it. For example, some have objected to identifying mental states with brain states because both have different properties, and two things with different properties cannot be the same things. Thoughts, for example, are not in space, have no mass, no chemical or electrical properties, and so on. Neurological events, however, do have these properties, so it would appear they cannot be identical with thoughts. Much the same could be said for the properties of all mental states. Pains, for example, are sometimes intense and throbbing. Neurological events are not. But the identity theory has an answer for this objection, one that we have seen already. The differences referred to are differences in how we come to *know* mental states and brain states, not differences in what they are. Brain states may be known in two different ways, through brain scanners, for example, and through introspection. They are, nevertheless, identical.

To understand a more serious problem for the identity theorist requires that we first understand the difference between what philosophers call *types* and *tokens*. An example may help here. When physicists say that lightning is an electrical discharge, they are claiming that one type of thing is the same as another type of thing. In the same way, when the identity theorist says that a particular type of pain, say a toothache in the third molar, is identical with the firing of particular neurons in a specific region of the brain, she is identifying a type of pain with a certain type of brain state. The kind of identity that the identity theory holds is thus called **type-type** identity. It says that certain kinds, or types, of mental states are identical with certain types of brain states.

However, statements that certain types of mental states are identical with certain types of brain states are simply false. The reason is that when different people report having the same kind of mental event, they do not always have the same kind of brain states. My third molar toothache will produce a different PET scan than yours, for example, because my thought that "I love the smell of red roses," is carried out by different types of processes in my brain than occur in yours when you think the very same thought. Unlike computers of the same type, one human brain is not wired in exactly the same way as another. In addition to this, animals with very different neurological structures than humans seem to have mental events. Some of them surely feel pain, for example. It would make no sense to describe them as being in pain, however, if pain is the firing of specific patterns of neurons in *human* brains. Finally, suppose we were to encounter a race of alien beings with a different biochemistry from us, one that did not include brains composed of neurons. Suppose further that they cried out and otherwise pain behaved when they smashed their fingers with hammers. We would have to say that they had no feeling of pain if the identity theory is correct, because they had no neurons firing at all.

The way around this is for the identity theorist to switch to **token-token** identity. "Tokens" are individual instances of general types. According to this view, individual mental states (Harry's third molar toothache, not third molar toothaches in general) are identical with *some* neurological event in Harry's brain (not a specific kind of neurological event). These individual tokens, Harry's toothache and a specific brain state that shows up on Harry's PET scan, are what are identical. So Harry's toothache may not appear on a PET scan in exactly the same way as mine does, but for each of us, and for animals and alien beings too, having a toothache is identical with some brain state.

Unfortunately, this strategy will not do either. According to token-token identity, my thought that "it is a nice day" *is* the brain state that shows up on my PET scan when I think that thought. Your very same thought that "it is a nice day" is nothing but the brain state that shows up on your PET scan. If the thought is the brain state, and if there is no one kind of brain state shared by all who think the same thought, then what makes these thoughts the *same* thoughts? If there are no identical brain states that everyone shares when they are in the same mental state, and if mental states are brain states, then the identity theorist cannot explain the obvious fact that different people have the same mental events—the same thoughts, feelings, desires, memories, and so on. For many, this is an insurmountable objection to the identity theory and a good reason to move on to other possible solutions.

Eliminative materialism, defended in *Reading 1,* is a view that is popular with some cognitive scientists, especially some neuroscientists.[2] It is a view that is seen by many as a way to think of the mind as the brain, without having to go through the nearly impossible project of reducing mental events to brain events that is required of the identity theorist. Since eliminativism is a form of materialism, it denies the existence of a nonphysical mind. But, unlike the identity theory, it is not reductionist. It does not claim that the mind is identical with the brain, or that mental states may be reduced to brain states. Instead, it makes the radical claim that the knowledge we have of the mind in our everyday lives will be eliminated and replaced in the future solely by knowledge and descriptions of brain events.

Just as we no longer refer to possession by demons to explain psychotic events, so in the future we will no longer speak of beliefs, desires, memories, and the like to explain our behavior. Instead, we will refer only to neurological events. The eliminativist thinks that the reason why mental states will not accurately map onto brain states (the central objection to the identity theory) is because our ordinary understanding of our minds is very much misguided. They propose that our ordinary way of thinking about mental states, which psychologists call "folk psychology," should be eliminated entirely and replaced solely with a neurological understanding of ourselves. For example, we should no longer talk about a desire for X being nothing but a brain state X. Instead, we should just refer to brain states themselves.

In essence, eliminativism presents us with a research proposal. It says that the study of the mind should be directed at the level of biology, not psychology. We may still speak in our daily lives of mental events, for convenience perhaps. But science should not study mental events or their subfunctions any more than psychiatrists should study demonic possession. There is no world of demons; chemical imbalances and hallucinations are enough to explain psychotic behavior. For the eliminativist, there are no mental events either. Brain states are enough to explain human behavior. Since it studies mental events, cognitive psychology ought to be replaced by the neurosciences. Only time and the success of the neurosciences in understanding the brain will tell if the eliminativists are right. In the meantime, they ask a lot from us, almost as much as the behaviorist does. They want us to act and think and speak as though all of our experience of our mental lives is somehow misguided, and to consider it very likely that there are no such things as the collections of mental events that we call our minds, that we even call our selves. For many, this is far too much to ask.

Functionalism

So far, various solutions have claimed that the mind is a nonphysical substance, or that it does not exist, or that it is the brain. By far the most widely accepted solution to the mind-body problem, almost the official theory in the field of cognitive science, is **functionalism.** Because of its importance in cognitive science, we will take some time here to explain this tricky concept. Functionalism comes in at least two forms. On the one hand, it is the name for a *method* used in cognitive science, especially in cognitive psychology.

To clarify the basic claims of this method the first thing to say is that functionalists do not identify the mind with either a physical substance or a nonphysical substance. Like the behaviorist, functionalists do not identify the mind with any sort of "thing." Instead, they think of the mind as a *collection* of mental events. Psychologists generally believe that there is some substance that produces these mental events; something that does the thinking, the planning, the hoping and so on. Functionalism is neutral, however, on just what this substance is, and thus is neutral on the mind-body problem. It offers no solution; it avoids the problem. Maybe it's the brain that produces mental events; maybe it's a nonphysical substance; maybe it is something entirely unknown to us. Whatever it is, it is the collection of mental events which it produces that they are interested in. It is what they study and what they refer to as the mind.

Second, functionalists deny that we can directly observe mental events. We cannot study them with scanners or through introspection, for example. This is clearly true in the case of the mental events of others. I cannot observe your thoughts or pains, for example, but can only know about them through their expression in behavior. More dramatically, the functionalist claims that the same is true for our knowledge of our own mental events, and especially for the many subfunctions of which they are composed. We have no direct knowledge of our thoughts, for example. We know them only by the words which we use to express them. Because of this, we do not know what thoughts are made of or what sorts of properties they have. They could be brain events, they could be nonphysical events, they could even be made from something about which we know very little. All we know about our mental events, and thus all we know about our minds, is what they *do*—not what they are. Another way to say this is that we have only *functional knowledge* of mental events.

To have functional knowledge of something is to know what it does or how it functions. We sometimes contrast functional knowledge of something with knowledge of its intrinsic nature. To have knowledge of the intrinsic nature of something is to know what sort of material it is made of and especially to know what are its essential properties. Sometimes we may have both sorts of knowledge about an object. Even though we may understand what something is really like, we may also refer to it simply by its function. To have functional knowledge of an iron, for example, is to know that it is something that takes wrinkles out of clothes. In the case of irons, we also know what properties they have. They are usually made of metal, are heated by electricity, have handles, steam, and so on. This is knowledge of their intrinsic natures, of their essential properties, of what they are.

Functionalists claim that while we have no direct knowledge of what mental events are really like, we do have indirect knowledge of what they do. In general, what mental events do is to connect the environment with our behavior. Our thoughts, for example, make our behavior appropriate to the conditions around us. We may see something, relate it to other experiences from the past, form current beliefs about it, and then decide to act. We may not know what thoughts are really made of, but we do know when they are occurring and we do know how to tell one from another by the outward signs associated with them. These outward signs are the *causes* that produce them (what I saw and remembered, for example) and the observable *effects* that they produce (what I did or said in response). The important point here is that mental events are to be identified not by their intrinsic properties, but solely by reference to what causes them and to what sorts of behavior they produce. Once identified, they may be further studied, as we said earlier, by breaking them down into their simpler and simpler functions.

Third, if minds are collections of mental events, and mental events are known to us only as functional events, then the mind is to be understood by the functionalist as a *collection of functions.* Functionalists claim to be neutral on what sort of thing produces mental functions, but they are clear that the mind is a way that this something works. They often use the analogy of a computer to clarify this important point, especially by distinguishing between the software and hardware of a computer. The software of a computer is a set of functions. It is what the hardware of the computer does. The software is not some "thing" in addition to the hardware. In the same way, the mind is not some "thing." As talking about software is just a way to describe what some thing does, so the functionalist thinks that talking about the mind is just a way to talk about what some thing does.

While functionalism as a method is neutral about what this "thing" that performs these functions really is, what we will call **brain functionalism,** is not. Brain functionalism makes a claim not only about the proper method to be used in psychology (functionalism), but also makes a claim about what really exists. It is a type of materialism. It identifies the "hardware" of the mind with the brain. The brain functionalist claims that it is the brain that produces mental events. It is the brain that thinks and remembers and deliberates, for example. This does not mean that the mind is the brain. The brain functionalist denies that. Instead, the mind is simply the way that the brain functions. It is what the brain does. It is the collection, if you will, of all the software or programs run by all the modules of the brain. This is how the brain functionalist solves the mind-body problem: the mind is the way that the brain works, and it is related to the brain as the software of a computer is related to its hardware.

In order to get a clearer idea of the brain functionalist's notion of the mind, it may be helpful to examine further the analogy between the hardware and software of a computer. To say that the mind is the "software" of the brain is both to deny that it is the brain (the hardware) and also to deny that it is any "thing" more than the brain, such as a nonphysical substance. Instead, it is just an abstract way to refer to what the brain does, as discussing the software of a computer is an abstract way to discuss what a computer does. To say that these are abstract ways of thinking means that a functional property is considered "apart from" its physical embodiment.

In the same way, the mental events produced by our computer—the brain— may also be understood apart from their physical embodiments in particular brain states. This is what the mind is. It is the collection of all the ways that the brain works to connect environmental causes to behavioral effects. While the brain sciences understand the brain as it is, the mind sciences understand it abstractly, as it functions. As running is something that a runner does, and adding is something that a calculator does, so for the brain functionalist, thinking and perceiving and remembering are things that a brain does. When these functions of the brain are understood apart from the brain and collectively called the mind, it looks like we have a mystery about what minds are. There is no more mystery, however, than there is with the distinction between a computer's hardware and its software.

Brain functionalism has some serious problems that will be mentioned later. But for now it is important to notice one of its many benefits. In particular, it is important to notice that it is not a reductionist view. Because it does not try to identify mental states with brain states, it allows for the brain and the mind to be studied in different ways, even if the mind is not some "thing" over and above the brain. Since understanding the mind requires only functional knowledge, understanding the mind does not require an understanding of the brain. Just as knowledge of a certain program does not require us to be electrical engineers, to know the intimate details of the electrical circuitry of the computer, so understanding our mental states does not require a degree in neuroscience. In this sense the "mind" sciences, such as psychology, artificial intelligence, linguistics, and philosophy, for example, do study something different from the brain. They do not study some "thing" that is different from the brain, however. Instead, in studying mental events they study the programs that the brain runs, or how the brain functions, leaving the intrinsic nature of the brain to be studied by the various neurosciences.

Human Nature

The worldview assumed by cognitive science is dominated at present by brain functionalism. As we have seen, brain functionalism makes claims both about the nature of the mind and claims about how the mind is to be studied. It claims first that our minds are information processors, particular types of computers. It also claims that what is important to know about our minds is how these computers work to direct input from the environment into appropriate behavior. There is much more to be said than this about what it means to be a human being, of course. We all differ from each other in many ways. Even if we all had the same types of computers running the same programs we still all have different environments. As the same word processing program may be used by different individuals to write very different stories, the same sort of cognitive structures may be used by different individuals to process very different sorts of information. Further, we all acquire various programs, especially various ways of thinking or understanding, from our environment as part of the learning process. When we learn math and physics, for example, we learn new ways to interpret our experience. In this sense, we may acquire new "programs," new cognitive functions, to add to our collection of those that have been hardwired into us by evolution.

Despite these environmental differences, the cognitive scientist asserts that at the very core of what it means to be a human being is found our minds, and our minds are essentially information processors, and these information processors come with standard equipment, with built-in programs that are run by our brains. If this is the general *structure* of human nature, if we are essentially very special sorts of computers, we still have to know more about what sorts of computers we are and how they *function* if we are to have a clear idea of the cognitive scientist's notion of human nature. We have to know more about what these programs are like, how they are designed, if we want to know more about what kinds of beings we are. We begin our deeper investigation of the function of minds with a discussion of a central concept, though one not shared by all cognitive scientists, that concerns the degree to which our minds are a single entity.

The Mind Is Modular

For the brain functionalist, the mind is the way that the brain functions, and the brain is modular, so the mind is **modular** as well. To say that the mind is modular means that it is not one entity, as Descartes thought. It is a collection of mental events, each of which is itself composed of many different "parts" or modules. Each mental state is produced by a host of separate functions, each doing its own thing *independently of the other functions.* The brain is wired less like a digital computer, where steps are carried out in one long sequence, and more like parallel processors, which run smaller programs simultaneously and then weave together their results to produce a finished product. It appears that "the" mind is really lots of separate "minds," each of which does its own job in isolation from the rest. Then, somehow, the results get pooled with all the others to form a mental event. Just as automobiles are produced on an assembly line by lots of robots performing separate specific tasks, so, too, our minds are composed of various subsections, each of which works in parallel with, but independently from, the others, to produce a final result like seeing an orange on the table, or remembering Sally's face. Examples of this modularity will be discussed later in this section, when we talk about what it means to process information. For now, however, it is important to consider three important implications of the modularity thesis.

First, if the mind is modular, it is no longer possible to think of the mind as a unified, single subject. Instead, the modularity model forces us to think of the mind as a *collection* of a vast array of complex programs, each churning away in isolation from the rest. The mind is a collection of mental states, where each mental state is itself a collection of simpler programs, functions, or modules. We have no introspective experience of these simpler programs which constitute most of what goes on in our minds. So it seems to us that our minds are a single, unified entity; or, at the very least, a single, coordinated collection of mental events. This is because we are conscious only of the final results of lots of information processing. But the conscious mind is merely a small part of our minds. The vast majority of its incessant activity, activity that sometimes produces conscious mental events, remains in hiding. Through introspection, the knowledge we have of our minds is only a fraction of that which we have from cognitive science. This latter knowledge tells us that our minds are modular, that they are more like a "committee" of independently operating members than they are like a single person.

Second, if the mind is modular, then a startling conclusion follows about the nature of our selves. If we identify our selves, as most of us do, with the collection of our conscious mental states, the collection of all of our thoughts and feelings and memories, and so on, then it follows that our self is not our mind. It is only a small portion of our mind. Further, if we identify our selves with the conscious mind, then it follows from the modularity of mind thesis that thinking of our selves as single subjects that remain the same through time—as we do—is something of an illusion. There simply is no single subject tying all of our mental events together. There is no central observer of our mental states. There is no "me" of whom it might be said that these mental events are "mine." There is no one thing that is me. The modularity of the mind rules out that there is a simple, solitary subject called the self.

That we believe our selves to be single, enduring subjects is merely an illusion. How and why such an illusion arises needs to be explained, to be sure. One such attempt[3] claims that the illusion of the self arises from language. As a particular novel is one and the same novel because it is told by the same narrator throughout, so we tell ourselves a continuous story over the years, holding our experience together under the same narration. Whether this explanation, which is discussed in some detail in *Reading 2*, works or not to capture our experience of ourselves is questionable. Much more needs to be explained about how the brain generates a self, and especially why it does so. It would be important to know what evolutionary value this has. Here is one attempt at a general explanation:[4]

> Evolutionary biology . . . suggests a *very* general answer to the question of *why* brains might construct a self-concept: it plays a role in the neuronal organization used to coordinate movement with needs, perceptions, and memories. Such coordination is essential to an animal's survival and well-being. Coordination of functions ensures that inconsistent behaviors—fleeing and feeding, for example, are not attempted at the same time. It ensures that a hungry animal does not eat itself. For organisms with higher-level cognition, self-representational capacities constructed on the more fundamental platform help us to think about the future, make useful plans, and organize knowledge.

The central point for us is that according to the brain functionalist, the self as a single subject enduring through time does not really exist. It is an illusion created by the mind for reasons such as those mentioned in this quote.

Third, there are enormous implications for our conceptions of *knowledge and reality* if the mind is a modular information processor. We can no longer think of our minds as a single blank slate that the world writes on through our senses. In fact, it is no longer possible to think of our knowledge of the world as a "copy" of the external environment in any sense. Rather, it appears that Kant was on the right track. As processors of information, our minds now have to be thought of as "grinding up" data received from the environment and transforming it into the sorts of information that "fit" the processors of the brain.

Through programs that are hardwired into our brains, and those that we learn, we create from patterns of light waves, sound waves, and other forms of sensory input, the commonsense world of our experience. Some features of this world we may attribute to the environment, but most of its structure is contributed by us, by how we process environmental inputs. The modular mind is loaded with cognitive structures to which the information received from the environment must conform. We process it in separate programs and subprograms, the results of which are then combined to form conscious mental events such as seeing, hearing, and tasting. The interaction of the modules of the mind with the information received from the environment produces the world as we know it. Other species, with different brains and different types of sensory equipment, process information differently from the ways that we humans do, and thus are aware of a different world than we are. Because the mind is a modular information processor, we are aware of the world only as it has been molded by us, and not as it is in itself.

Information Processing

If we are to understand ourselves as modular information processors we need to know more about information processing. First, a word about the **processing** part of information processing. The brain processes information somewhat as a computer does. A computer follows rules, called *algorithms.* Simply put, an algorithm instructs the computer to take information from one place to another, to transform it from its input state to internal states of the computer, and finally to an output state. For example, if someone types "2896*345 =" on a keyboard and presses the "enter" key, then "999120" appears on the screen. This happened because the keyboard input caused an electrical state to arise within the computer, which then computed or processed the input information according to a particular algorithm, one that instructs it to carry out a particular operation or set of operations. In this case the operation was multiplication. This first internal state then gave rise to (caused) a second internal state, which produced the display on the screen. Of course, "first" state and "second" state are simplistic ways of speaking. In truth, there are any number of internal states involved in even the simplest acts of information processing. The important point is that processing information involves the transformation of information from one state to another according to rules. These rules are the collection of algorithms possessed by the computer. These determine what the computer does, and are usually referred to as its programs.

In a similar way, the mind processes information from the environment according to rules. These rules are the programs of the mind, its cognitive functions that nature has designed to adapt us better to the environment. The main point to understand if we are to understand ourselves as information processors is not only the design of these rules, the way the mind works, but also the nature of the **information** that it processes. If our knowledge is to be "of" the world, then it is especially important to see how this information arises from the environment. The quick answer is that what it means for the human mind to process information is for the brain to undergo a series of causally related states. These causally related states transform sensory stimuli into various internal brain states and, ultimately, into behavior that is adaptive to the environment. The key to understanding what information means on this level is to see the various causal steps of processing as each containing parts that are related in a pattern. The pattern in each *is* the information being processed. In the case of visual perception, for example, the molecular pattern of the object(s) we see produces patterns of light waves. These, in turn, cause retinal patterns (patterns of rods and cones), which cause optic nerve patterns (bioelectrical patterns), which cause patterns in the columns of neurons in the visual cortex. Finally, in a way as yet to be understood, this bursts forth into a conscious event of seeing an orange on the table, which may cause us to move toward the orange, and maybe even to eat it.

This is how we are to understand the concept of information on one level, as a pattern embedded in various physical stages which is preserved through its many causal transformations. But the concept of information is understood in other ways as well, by the cognitive sciences, depending upon the perspective that is taken, or the level at which it is understood. One well-known cognitive scientist, the philosopher, Daniel Dennett, has most carefully discussed these levels and named them the physical stance, the design stance, and the intentional stance levels of explanation.[5] "Information" means something different on each of these levels, and it is worth the effort to see just what the differences amount to. To understand how these distinctions are used to clarify the concept of information, it will be helpful to see first how they are used to understand the concept of information in an electronic computer.

In an electronic computer, information may be understood on the most basic level, the *physical stance* level, as the pattern of electronic gates that are wired on a chip, that happen to be open or closed. What determines which particular gates are open or closed is the program that the computer is running at the time. In such a program, at its lowest level of detail, an open gate is represented by a "1" and a closed gate by a "0." These are called binary numbers. Strings of these numbers are called binary codes. They form a type of language called **machine language,** in which are written the programs for the computer to follow. These instructions determine how the hardware of the computer, its electronic circuitry, is to configure or pattern itself in the presence of various types of input. On the physical stance level of understanding, the information being processed may be thought of as these patterns of binary code, realized in the electrical circuitry of the machine. This corresponds to the physical stance level of understanding the concept of information in human beings, the level we have just discussed, where information is identified with patterns embedded in various sensory and neurological states.

On the next level, the *design stance* level of understanding, information physically packaged in binary code is understood to represent letters, or numbers, or lines of various shapes, or colors, and so on. Collections of these are understood to be equations or sentences or graphics or rules. On this level of understanding, information processing in a computer is described in a **programming language,** a language that attributes to collections of binary code meaningful cognitive functions, such as adding, drawing, storing, and comparing information. On this level a programming instruction may say, for example, "For any N, add 2 + N." Physically, this instruction gets translated into binary code and directs the operation of the electrical patterns produced by the machine's hardware. Nothing has been added to the physical level. But now various chunks of binary code instructions are understood as functions that are meaningful to *us.* On this level, the information processed by the computer is understood to be things like numbers or text or graphics.

Understanding a human being on the design stance level is similar. Here, the information that the brain represents in its various stages of processing is studied in a more abstract way. Instead of studying the causal processes that hold between brain states, a job for the neurosciences, we may step back a bit and study what all this processing signifies to us. In other words, we may study how the *mind* processes information in ways that are meaningful to us. Just as we can describe the software of a computer in functional terms ("it is adding," "it is remembering," and so on), we can describe in functional terms what the brain is doing with the information it has received from the environment. This is the level on which the mind sciences operate. On this level we study not brain states, but the higher level of organization found in mental states. Here mental states are not understood in terms of their intrinsic natures (collections of brain states), but in terms of the functions that they perform which are meaningful to us, such as "seeing," "remembering," and "thinking."

The explanations given on this level are called **functional explanations.** The ultimate goal of a functional explanation is to identify all the subfunctions involved in a mental event and to reduce each of them to simpler and simpler functions. Ideally, such explanations go all the way down to functions that are so simple that they perform only one repetitive task. For example, memory may be reduced to searching, comparing, and matching functions. Searching, in turn, may be reduced to running through a series, and making comparisons of each item in the series with a standard. Making comparisons may be reduced to the individual comparisons that are made, and these to simpler functions, and so on. The explanation is complete once the level of the most simple functions has been reached.

Cognitive sciences do not take their explanations past simple functions, all the way down to the brain processes that realize these functions. These would be physical stance explanations, a task for the neurophysiologists, biologists, chemists, and physicists. But by reducing mental states to simpler functions, they go most of the way. Because of their simple and routine natures, these simple functions can often be modeled on a computer, and this model may then be used to understand what the brain is doing when it processes information that is associated with the mental state in question.

If information processing on the physical stance level is understood to be the transformation of patterns of energy from one physical medium to another, on the design stance level it is understood to be the churning away of various mechanisms of the mind to produce the full-fledged mental states of which we are conscious. "Compare this with that," "Search for this in memory," "Examine the syntactical structure of the sentence," might be how we would express such functions. All these sorts of functions, and the smaller ones into which they are dissolved, are examples of programs or processing or algorithms. What is processed, the information, is thought of in different ways as the functions get simpler. On the highest level, that of a conscious mental state such as seeing an orange on a table, information is thought of as the *content* of the mental state. The mental state is the "act" of seeing; the content of this act of visual perception is "what" is seen—the orange on the table. Even for the simpler functions into which visual perception may be analyzed, such as "seeing its texture" or "being aware of its color" or "recognizing its shape" and so on, information is still thought of as content, as what the subfunction is about—texture, color, shape.

Functional explanations of mental states ignore questions about what embodies these mechanisms of the mind. However, in going beyond the method of functionalism to make a metaphysical claim, brain functionalism holds that the processing is done by the brain. What the brain processes is explained on the physical stance level as various patterns of neurons, produced by environmental stimuli. Just as "adding $2+2$" in a computer may be described in machine language, so mental events and the simpler functions which constitute them are reducible to patterns of neurons in the brain. We may study cognitive functions and subfunctions independently of any knowledge of the brain on the design stance level, but design stance explanations are just higher level ways to explain what gets explained on the physical stance level—the brain and how it works. Design stance explanations describe how the brain works at a level that is meaningful to us, the level of the mind.

We have stepped back from the computer's hardware and its binary code instructions, and stepped up to the design stance level of description. Here we describe the same physical processes that exist on the physical stance level in ways that are meaningful to us. We now understand what the computer is doing as processing numbers and text and graphics. In the same way, we may step even further back from the hardware and the detail, and describe the computer as a single system which is working toward a goal; a goal such as solving a mathematical problem, or playing chess, or constructing a new graphic design. This is to understand the computer on the *intentional stance* level. We act as though it had intentions and did things in meaningful ways, ways that may be understood as various means to achieve its specific goals. When the computer is seen as acting for a purpose, we describe its behavior in an **intentional language.** We attribute meaning to the computer's behavior by referring to its goals and objectives and action plans. We now talk about it as processing such information as beliefs and memories, and we think of it as solving problems, and performing tasks, and reasoning as we do.

Unlike physical stance and design stance explanations, intentional stance explanations of mental events are not causal explanations. Instead, they are purposive, or goal-directed explanations. Purposive explanations account for events by referring to the purposes or goals of someone or something. We explain why someone does something (study for a philosophy exam), for example, by referring to what they want to achieve (to do well in the course). Purposive explanations of mental events are not directed at the subfunctions that produce them, let alone the physical processes and structures that embody them, but rather are directed at the roles played by particular mental states in achieving a person's goals. On this level, the level on which we operate in our everyday lives, and the level on which most philosophers talk about the mind, we use ordinary ways of speaking about mental states to describe how they contribute to our overall goals.

For example, I may explain why I am going out at midnight by referring to various mental events (in italics). I am going out because I am *hungry,* and I *want* something to eat. I *know* there is a pizza shop still open, and I am going to buy one and eat it, and then I will *feel* better. On the intentional stance level, each mental state is understood solely in terms of its role in achieving the overall goal of the person. On the intentional stance level of explanation, individual mental states are seen as states of a single subject, and as forming a single system (a mind), which has purposes and goals beyond those of individual mental states. In the same way as we speak in an intentional language about a computer playing chess, or solving a mathematical problem, we also speak about ourselves as having purposes for our behavior, or as doing things for a reason (goal).

Information on this level is thought of as the "content" of our mental states, as it was on the design stance level. We can distinguish between mental activity (thinking, for example) and the what it is that we think about (thoughts). As we have the activity of remembering, so also we have memories (what we remember); as we can hear, so also we have the sounds heard; as we can imagine, so also we have images, and so on. On the intentional stance level, we think of the information that our brains process as these contents of our mental events, as our thoughts, and feelings, and images, and so on. The mental events themselves are the processing mechanisms of the mind, the thinking, the feeling, the imagining. This information processing forms a system of mental events that work together to achieve a particular goal of the system that we call our selves.

In sum, brain functionalism claims that just as the workings of a computer may be described and explained on different levels and in different ways, so our brains may be described and explained on different levels and in different ways. On the physical stance level, neuroscientists understand what the brain is and how it works on the level of neuronal activity. This is similar to understanding a computer on the level of its machine language. When we move to the design stance level, we now describe brain processing abstractly, as mental events, each of which is a set of functions that make sense to us. This is similar to our descriptions of the software of a computer as what the computer does. We are not describing any new kind of reality on this level that was not present on the physical stance level. We are just giving it a different type of description.

When we reach the intentional stance level, we talk about the mind itself, as a single system of mental events, and understand this higher system in terms of its purposes and goals. Once again, we have not found a new kind of being on this level, a mind. The mind is not some "thing" over and above the brain, but is just another way to describe the functioning of the brain in an even more abstract way, as we might talk about a computer playing chess or solving a mathematical problem. For brain functionalism, there is only one reality, the brain, a reality that may be studied at three different levels.

Let us use an example of an *army* to drive this last point home. An army may be viewed as a collection of individual men and women, and as a collection of vehicles and weapons. We may explain what the bodies of these men and women are composed of and how they work when they do various things, which muscles contract and which sensory receptors are stimulated in which ways, and what temperatures cause perspiration, and so on. We may also study the design and materials of the trucks and tanks and other weapons used by this army. This would be a physical stance explanation of an army. On the other hand, we could also study what each of these components do, what their roles are, in ways that are intelligible to us. This man loads shells. This woman flies jet planes. This weapon fires rifle bullets. This would be a design stance explanation of an army. Each of these roles could be broken down into the simpler ones that make up the identified function, moreover, such as the steps involved in flying a jet plane.

Finally, we could step back even further from the elements that compose this army, and even from the specific roles that individuals play. From this broader perspective we might see the collection of all of these parts and functions as composing some one system called an army, something whose purpose is to defend a nation against attack, and even sometimes to wage war. In a similar way, the brain may be examined up close or further back. It is called the brain when we view it up close, mental events when seen further back, and the mind when we see it from the broadest perspective. For brain functionalism, there are not three things called the brain, mental events, and the mind, rather there are three ways of understanding the same thing, the brain.

This is a summary sketch of how cognitive science generally views human beings, especially the human cognitive mind. Many of the various sciences that constitute cognitive science are still in their infancy, and many important debates and questions remain. There is much discussion, for example, about just what sorts of computers we are. Certainly we are not like any computer that exists today. Also, it seems that if we are like computers, and if computers do not understand what they do, then we cannot explain how *we* understand what it is that we do either. In his famous example of the "Chinese room," found in *Reading 3*, John Searle discusses this problem.

Another important issue that cries out for further understanding is how the brain computes not only our "selves," an issue mentioned previously, but any conscious mental event at all. If our minds are a set of programs or functions, and if we built a computer with the same functions—if it could do everything that we can do—it still would not be conscious. It would not *experience* sweet smells, brilliant colors, delicious tastes, or the beautiful sounds of music. These experiences philosophers call **qualia,** and spend a great deal of time trying to explain how we can have them if we are simply material beings. They cannot understand how our brains can create these types of conscious experiences. If we were only material beings, they argue, we would be like zombies, dead on the "inside." Because of the apparent inability of brain functionalism, or any form of materialism, to explain consciousness, many people who reject both materialism and substance dualism have adopted a position called property dualism.

Property Dualism

There are several types of **property dualism.** One of its older versions is called **epiphenomenalism.** If we think of the qualia of conscious experience as the facts or "phenomena" to be explained, and if we understand the Greek prefix "epi-" to mean "above," then epiphenomenalism is the view that qualia are "above" the physical phenomena of the brain. What does this mean? It means several things. First, it means that qualia are to be understood as *nonphysical* properties. Second, even though they are not physical, they are nevertheless properties of the *brain*. They are produced by the brain, they reside in the brain—but in its nonphysical states, not its physical states. Just as the brain has physical properties, such as electrochemical properties, so also does it have nonphysical properties, properties like the feeling of a pain, or the smelling of a rose, or having an urge to eat a very large pizza.

The question of how brains produce qualia is often answered by classifying qualia as **emergent properties**—because they "emerge" only when the brain reaches a certain level of complexity. The various elements of the complex unite to form something not possessed by any of them individually, as enough colored grains of sand might collectively produce a picture of something. But no one really knows how these nonphysical properties "emerge" from the brain. No one knows how the brain produces an inner, private, world of conscious experience that most of us identify with our selves. But it does, claims the property dualist, and the world of consciousness that it produces is a world of nonphysical properties. Why not look at things this way? After all, there *are* such conscious experiences. We are aware of them every waking second of every day, and they are surely nothing like brain states. Since property dualists believe that there is no nonphysical substance to do the job of producing these properties, they must therefore be thought of as nonphysical properties that are produced by the brain.

It is important to note that for the epiphenomenalist version of property dualism, mental states have *no causal power*. When I feel a toothache, for example, the feeling of pain is not what makes me moan and groan, and clutch my jaw, and call the dentist. Instead, the brain does *all* the work. It receives information from the environment, in this case an internal bodily event, processes this information, and then produces behavioral responses. Conscious phenomena are "above" all of this hard work. They are like the shadow cast by a runner's body as she races toward the finish line. It may accompany her step for step, but the shadow does no work. In the same way, brains may cause conscious experiences to arise, but these experiences themselves cause nothing to happen. For the epiphenomenalist, they are simply "by-products" of what goes on in the brain. As a sufficiently complex brain goes about its business of information processing, it "emits" conscious experiences, casting them as "shadows" in the brain, shadows that we identify as our minds, as our selves.

Moreover, not only do conscious experiences play no role in behavior, they also play no role in causing other conscious events. A feeling of joy upon seeing my beloved's face is not caused by the conscious experience of seeing her face, for example. Instead, the brain processes that produce a "seeing her face" conscious experience also cause another brain process to occur which, in turn, gives rise to a conscious feeling of joy. Conscious experience plays no causal role in the public world of physical objects and events, and none in the private world of conscious mental states. All the action is in the physical world. The nonphysical world of conscious experiences merely mirror this action. The startling conclusion of this is that I would act in exactly the same way as I currently do, even if I had no conscious experience at all! If our behavior would be the same whether our private, subjective "minds" exist or not, then consciousness is unnecessary. It is something "extra" thrown into nature by God or evolution.

Why would anyone hold such a strange view, one that makes the two improbable claims that (1) nonphysical states can be produced, in some mysterious way, by a physical brain, and (2) that what I think and feel and see and decide makes no difference to either my behavior or other mental events? Part of the reason to be an epiphenomenalist is that it allows for a rigorously scientific account of human behavior. It lets science do the job of understanding us in terms of physical events. The other reason is that it seems true to the data of introspection, especially that our subjective conscious experiences, our selves, are very different from brain states. However, many have turned away from epiphenomenalism because it so blatantly denies the causal role of our conscious experience. After all, is it not the *feeling* of pain that causes me to cry out? Such a role seems so obvious that some have embraced a version of property dualism that allows for this two-way causality, **interactionist property dualism.**

According to this view, not only does the brain cause mental states, but mental states also cause brain states, as well as other mental states. The main problem with such a view, however, is that it appears to make the understanding of human behavior scientifically impossible, since now some of the events that cause behavior are beyond scientific study. They are private, they have no physical properties, and some of them, free choices for example, do not follow the causal laws studied by science. In addition, while this view seems truer to our experience than materialistic views, it leaves us, once again, with all the mysteries of mind-brain interaction that led to the ruin of substance dualism (again, see Chapter 5).

So we have what appears to be a dilemma. If we are true to scientific accounts of behavior, we have to deny the nonphysical status of conscious experiences. If we are true to our experience, on the other hand, we have to admit the reality of conscious experiences that appear to be nonphysical in nature. In addition, we have to admit to their causal role in producing behavior. This, in turn, forces us to admit that science is incapable, now and forever, of understanding the conscious human mind, the core of our selves.

Resolving this dilemma is not a problem for many. Some dualists agree whole-heartedly that the subjective self is beyond the study of science. We simply are different kinds of beings than those which science studies. In particular, we are not purely physical beings. Others, on the other side, pointing to how much we have learned recently about the physical basis of minds, are confident that it is only a matter of time before neuroscience is in a position to offer explanations for all the secrets of the mind, even consciousness itself. Some even appear to think that the major problems of explaining consciousness have already been solved. At the other extreme, there are some who believe that the secret of consciousness can never be unraveled, and that this dimension of our human nature lies beyond comprehension.[6] Perhaps. One thing is for certain, however: there is much work to be done before we can confidently say that we understand what it means to be a human being.

Consequences

In this section we usually consider some of the consequences that would seem to follow if the particular view of human nature being discussed was adopted. We usually discuss the implications that the particular view of human nature has for our understanding of freedom, ethics, society, God, and immortality and gender. Cognitive science is fairly open to many different beliefs about ethics and God. It is also compatible with a variety of views about how societies ought to be constructed, and even matters of gender. Its idea of freedom is generally a form of soft determinism, though it is often a more sophisticated form than we have previously discussed.[7] Instead of considering these usual consequences here, we focus instead in our remaining space on an issue that has been largely deferred until now and yet is important to many people—the belief in immortality.

Immortality

The question before us is this: Is the materialistic version of cognitive science compatible with the belief that we might continue to survive after our death? We can generalize the question and ask if adopting any form of materialism, and there have been many forms discussed in this text, rules out life after death?

Obviously we can believe what we want to, whether it is reasonable to do so or not. But what we want to know is *whether or not belief in life after death is compatible with materialism.* Does it make any sense to say that we are thoroughly physical beings yet somehow we may survive the death of our bodies, or do we need to think of ourselves as partly spiritual beings in order to believe in the possibility of life after death?

At first glance it appears that life after death is only possible if we are essentially spiritual beings—souls, to use the religious term. After all, how could there be life after death if we are purely material beings? It appears to be necessary for any version of materialism to hold the belief that when our bodies die at the end of this life, then we die. A closer look at the requirements for life after death, however, shows that such a belief is not incompatible with materialism. Let us spend a little time with this idea, the idea that you can be a materialist and still rationally believe in life after death.

We begin by pointing out that no one *knows* if there is life after death or not. There is no good evidence to justify such a claim. Some of this evidence is discussed in *Reading 4.* The evidence that has been offered includes accounts of "life after death" experiences as told by patients who have been clinically dead for a brief period. It also includes tales of the paranormal, where people describe their experiences of the dead appearing to them privately or through a special "medium." While experiences of both types may be powerfully convincing for those who have them, they may also be interpreted in other ways and are therefore not clearly experiences of the dead. "Life after death" experiences, for example, have been associated with physiological changes in the frontal lobes of the brain, brought on by a lack of oxygen.

If we cannot know that there is life after death, we also cannot know that there is not. This seems to leave the question open, to be decided by our own preferences, especially by our hopes and desires. However, if we are going to be rational, it must at least be *possible* that there could be life after death for us to believe it, or even hope or desire that such a belief is true. If it is not even possible, then believing or hoping or desiring that it is true would itself be as irrational as hoping to discover a square circle. By examining what must be true for there to be life after death, we will see that life after death is no less possible if you adopt a materialist view of the person than it is if you adopt a substance dualist view.

For life after death to be possible it is *necessary for God to exist and for miracles to occur on a regular basis.* If you are a substance dualist (as Descartes was) you may see life after death as simply the survival of the soul, apart from the body. But how did souls arise in the first place from a universe in which life evolved from lifeless matter? The standard answer is that God created a unique soul in each of us at birth—the "miracle" of life. If God must exist and if God must produce a miracle to create each human being, then it is just as easy to imagine the miracle being performed at the end of this life as it is to imagine it being performed at its beginning. God could have made us purely material beings, with magnificent brains which allow us to think and create and love one another. When we die, God could re-create us in a form which allows us to survive in a "life after death" state, whatever that might be like.

There is a great deal more to be said about life after death. We might talk about the difficulty of imagining what a disembodied soul would be like, and how it might recognize and communicate with other souls. We might also point out that such a soul is not truly who we are. Rather it is what is "in" the soul that defines us—our thoughts, memories, plans, and the like. These are the things that must make the trip to the next life if we are to continue *our* lives there—not our bare souls. As the information stored electronically on a disk might be transferred to a hard drive, so the contents of our minds need to be transferred to another type of medium in the next life for us to survive as the selves that we are now.

However the form that the next life takes might be imagined, the point for now is that it is not necessary to be a substance dualist in order to believe that there is life after death. Such a belief is just as compatible with materialism as it is with substance dualism. Since both perspectives require belief in God *and* in miracles, it may be argued that neither are rational. However, the point once again is that it is no *more* difficult to believe in life after death if you are a materialist, than it is if you are a substance dualist.

Readings

1. In Defense of Eliminative Materialism

THE IDENTITY THEORY WAS CALLED into doubt not because the prospects for a materialist account of our mental capacities were thought to be poor, but because it seemed unlikely that the arrival of an adequate materialist theory would bring with it the nice one-to-one match-ups, between the concepts of folk psychology and the concepts of theoretical neuroscience, that intertheoretic reduction requires. The reason for that doubt was the great variety of quite different physical systems that could instantiate the required functional organization. *Eliminative materialism* also doubts that the correct neuroscientific account of human capacities will produce a neat reduction of our common-sense framework, but here the doubts arise from a quite different source.

As the eliminative materialists see it, one-to-one match-ups will not be found and our common-sense psychological framework will not enjoy an intertheoretic reduction, *because our common-sense psychological framework is a false and radically misleading conception of the causes of human behavior and the nature of cognitive activity.* On this view, folk psychology is not just an incomplete representation of our inner natures; it is an outright misrepresentation of our internal states and activities. Consequently, we cannot expect a truly adequate neuroscientific account of our inner lives to provide theoretical categories that match-up nicely with the categories of our common-sense framework. Accordingly, we must expect that the older framework will simply be eliminated, rather than be reduced, by a matured neuroscience.

HISTORICAL PARALLELS

As the identity theorist can point to historical cases of successful intertheoretic reduction, so the eliminative materialists can point to historical cases of the outright elimination of the ontology of an older theory in favor of the ontology of a new and superior theory. For most of the eighteenth and nineteenth centuries, learned people believed that heat was a subtle *fluid* held in bodies, much in the way water is held in a sponge. A fair body of moderately successful theory described the way this fluid substance—called "caloric"—flowed within a body, or from one body to another, and how it produced thermal expansion, melting, boiling and so forth. But by the end of the last century it had become abundantly clear that heat was not a substance at all, but just the energy of motion of the trillions of jostling molecules that make up the heated body itself. The new theory—the "corpuscular/kinetic theory of matter and heat"—was much more successful than the old in explaining and predicting the thermal behavior of bodies. And since we were unable to *identify* caloric fluid with kinetic energy (according to the old theory, caloric is a material *substance;* according to the new theory, kinetic energy is a form of *motion*), it was finally agreed that there is *no such thing* as caloric. Caloric was simply eliminated from our accepted **ontology.**

A second example. It used to be thought that when a piece of wood burns, or a piece of metal rusts, a spiritlike substance called "phlogiston" was being released: briskly in the former case, slowly in the latter. Once gone, that "noble" substance left only a base pile of ash or rust. It later came to be appreciated that both processes involve, not the loss of something, but the *gaining* of a substance taken from the atmosphere: oxygen. Phlogiston emerged, not as an incomplete description of what was going on, but as a radical misdescription. Phlogiston was therefore not suitable for reduction to or identification with some notion from within the new oxygen chemistry, and it was simply eliminated from science.

Admittedly, both these examples concern the elimination of something nonobservable, but our history also includes the elimination of certain widely accepted "observables." Before Copernicus' view became available, almost any human who ventured out at night could look up at the *starry sphere of the heavens,* and if he stayed for more than a few minutes he could also see that it turned, around an axis through Polaris. What the sphere

was made of (crystal?) and what made it turn (the gods?) were theoretical questions that exercised us for over two millennia. But hardly anyone doubted the existence of what they could observe with their own eyes. In the end, however, we learned to reinterpret our visual experience of the night sky within a very different conceptual framework, and the turning sphere evaporated.

Witches provide another example. Psychosis is a fairly common affliction among humans, and in earlier centuries its victims were standardly seen as cases of demonic possession, as instances of Satan's spirit itself, glaring malevolently out at us from behind the victims' eyes. That witches exist was not a matter of controversy. One would occasionally see them, in any city or hamlet, engaged in incoherent, paranoid, or even murderous behavior. But observable or not, we eventually decided that witches simply do not exist. We concluded that the concept of a witch is an element within a conceptual framework that misrepresents so badly the phenomenon to which it was standardly applied that literal application of the notion should be permanently withdrawn. Modern theories of mental dysfunction led to the elimination of witches from our serious ontology.

The concepts of folk psychology—belief, desire, fear, sensation, pain, joy, and so on—await a similar fate, according to the view at issue. And when neuroscience has matured to the point where the poverty of our current conceptions is apparent to everyone, and the superiority of the new framework is established, we shall then be able to set about *re*conceiving our internal states as activities, within a truly adequate conceptual framework at last. Our explanations of one another's behavior will appeal to such things as our neuropharmacological states, the neural activity in specialized anatomical areas, and whatever other states are deemed relevant by the new theory. Our private introspection will also be transformed, and may be profoundly enhanced by reason of the more accurate and penetrating framework it will have to work with—just as the astronomer's perception of the night sky is much enhanced by the detailed knowledge of modern astronomical theory that he or she possesses.

The magnitude of the conceptual revolution here suggested should not be minimized: it would be enormous. And the benefits to humanity might be equally great. If each of us possessed an accurate neuroscientific understanding of (what we now conceive dimly as) the varieties and causes of mental illness, the factors involved in learning, the neural basis of emotions, intelligence, and socialization, then the sum total of human misery might be much reduced. The simple increase in mutual understanding that the new framework made possible could contribute substantially toward a more peaceful and humane society. Of course, there would be dangers as well: increased knowledge means increased power, and power can always be misused.

ARGUMENTS FOR ELIMINATIVE MATERIALISM

The arguments for eliminative materialism are diffuse and less than decisive, but they are stronger than is widely supposed. The distinguishing feature of this position is its denial that a smooth intertheoretic reduction is to be expected—even a species-specific reduction—of the framework of folk psychology to the framework of a matured neuroscience. The reason for this denial is the eliminative materialist's conviction that folk psychology is a hopelessly primitive and deeply confused conception of our internal activities. But why this low opinion of our common-sense conceptions?

There are at least three reasons. First, the eliminative materialist will point to the widespread explanatory, predictive, and manipulative failures of folk psychology. So much of what is central and familiar to us remains a complete mystery from within folk psychology. We do not know what *sleep* is, or why we have to have it, despite spending a full third of our lives in that condition. (The answer, "For rest," is mistaken. Even if people are allowed to rest continuously, their need for sleep is undiminished. Apparently, sleep serves some deeper functions, but we do not yet know what they are.) We do not understand how *learning* transforms each of us from a gaping infant to a cunning adult, or how differences in *intelligence* are grounded. We have not the slightest idea

how *memory* works, or how we manage to retrieve relevant bits of information instantly from the awesome mass we have stored. We do not know what *mental illness* is, nor how to cure it.

In sum, the most central things about us remain almost entirely mysterious from within folk psychology. And the defects noted cannot be blamed on inadequate time allowed for their correction, for folk psychology has enjoyed no significant changes or advances in well over 2,000 years, despite its manifest failures. Truly successful theories may be expected to reduce, but significantly unsuccessful theories merit no such expectation.

This argument from explanatory poverty has a further aspect. So long as one sticks to normal brains, the poverty of folk psychology is perhaps not strikingly evident. But as soon as one examines the many perplexing behavioral and cognitive deficits suffered by people with damaged brains, one's descriptive and explanatory resources start to claw the air. . . . As with other humble theories asked to operate successfully in unexplored extensions of their old domain (for example, Newtonian mechanics in the domain of velocities close to the velocity of light, and the classical gas law in the domain of high pressures or temperatures), the descriptive and explanatory inadequacies of folk psychology become starkly evident.

The second argument tries to draw an inductive lesson from our conceptual history. Our early folk theories of motion were profoundly confused, and were eventually displaced entirely by more sophisticated theories. Our early folk theories of the structure and activity of the heavens were wildly off the mark, and survive only as historical lessons in how wrong we can be. Our folk theories of the nature of fire, and the nature of life, were similarly cockeyed. And one could go on, since the vast majority of our past folk conceptions have been similarly exploded. All except folk psychology, which survives to this day and has only recently begun to feel pressure. But the phenomenon of conscious intelligence is surely a more complex and difficult phenomenon than any of those just listed. So far as accurate understanding is concerned, it would be a *miracle* if we had got *that* one right the very first time, when we fell down so badly on all the others. Folk psychology has survived for so very long, presumably not because it is basically correct in its representations, but because the phenomena addressed are so surpassingly difficult that any useful handle on them, no matter how feeble, is unlikely to be displaced in a hurry.

A third argument attempts to find an a priori advantage for eliminative materialism over the identity theory and functionalism. It attempts to counter the common intuition that eliminative materialism is distantly possible, perhaps, but is much less probable than either the identity theory or functionalism. The focus again is on whether the concepts of folk psychology will find vindicating match-ups in a matured neuroscience. The eliminativist bets no; the other two bet yes. (Even the functionalist bets yes, but expects the match-ups to be only species-specific, or only person specific. Functionalism, recall, denies the existence only of *universal* type/type identities.)

The eliminativist will point out that the requirements on a reduction are rather demanding. The new theory must entail a set of principles and embedded concepts that mirrors very closely the specific conceptual structure to be reduced. And the fact is, there are vastly many more ways of being an explanatorily successful neuroscience while *not* mirroring the structure of folk psychology. Accordingly, the a priori probability of eliminative materialism is not lower, but substantially *higher* than that of either of its competitors. One's initial intuitions here are simply mistaken.

Granted, this initial a priori advantage could be reduced if there were a very strong presumption in favor of the truth of folk psychology—true theories are better bets to win reduction. But according to the first two arguments, the presumptions on this point should run in precisely the opposite direction.

ARGUMENTS AGAINST ELIMINATIVE MATERIALISM

The initial plausibility of this rather radical view is low for almost everyone, since it denies deeply entrenched assumptions. That is at best a question-begging complaint, of course, since those assumptions are precisely what is at issue. But the following line of thought does attempt to mount a real argument.

Eliminative materialism is false, runs the argument, because one's introspection reveals directly the existence of pains, beliefs, desires, fears, and so forth. Their existence is as obvious as anything could be.

The eliminative materialist will reply that this argument makes the same mistake that an ancient or medieval person would be making if he insisted that he could just see with his own eyes that the heavens form a turning sphere, or that witches exist. The fact is, all observation occurs within some system of concepts, and our observation judgments are only as good as the conceptual framework in which they are expressed. In all three cases—the starry sphere, witches, and the familiar mental states—precisely what is challenged is the integrity of the background conceptual frameworks in which the observation judgments are expressed. To insist on the validity of one's experiences, *traditionally interpreted,* is therefore to beg the very question at issue. For in all three cases, the question is whether we should reconceive the nature of some familiar observational domain.

A second criticism attempts to find an incoherence in the eliminative materialist's position. The bald statement of eliminative materialism is that the familiar mental states do not really exist. But that statement is meaningful, runs the argument, only if it is the expression of a certain *belief,* and an *intention* to communicate, and a *knowledge* of the language, and so forth. But if the statement is true, then no such mental states exist, and the statement is therefore a meaningless string of marks or noises, and cannot be true. Evidently, the assumption that eliminative materialism is true entails that it cannot be true.

The hole in this argument is the premise concerning the conditions necessary for a statement to be meaningful. It begs the question. If eliminative materialism is true, then meaningfulness must have some different source. To insist on the "old" source is to insist on the validity of the very framework at issue. Again an historical parallel may be helpful here. Consider the medieval theory that being biologically *alive* is a matter of being ensouled by an immaterial *vital spirit*. And consider the following response to someone who has expressed disbelief in that theory.

> My learned friend has stated that there is no such thing as vital spirit. But this statement is incoherent. For if it is true, then my friend does not have vital spirit, and must therefore be *dead*. But if he is dead, then his statement is just a string of noises, devoid of meaning or truth. Evidently, the assumption that antivitalism is true entails that it cannot be true! Q.E.D.

This second argument is now a joke, but the first argument begs the question in exactly the same way.

A final criticism draws a much weaker conclusion, but makes a rather stronger case. Eliminative materialism, it has been said, is making mountains out of molehills. It exaggerates the defects of folk psychology, and underplays its real successes. Perhaps the arrival of a matured neuroscience will require the elimination of the occasional folk-psychological concept, continues the criticism, and a minor adjustment in certain folk-psychological principles may have to be endured. But the large-scale elimination forecast by the eliminative materialist is just an alarmist worry or a romantic enthusiasm.

Perhaps this complaint is correct. And perhaps it is merely complacent. Whichever, it does bring out the important point that we do not confront two simple and mutually exclusive possibilities here: pure reduction versus pure elimination. Rather these are the end points of a smooth spectrum of possible outcomes, between which there are mixed cases of partial elimination and partial reduction. Only empirical research . . . can tell us where on that spectrum our own case will fall. Perhaps we should speak here, more liberally, of "revisionary materialism," instead of concentrating on the more radical possibility of an across-the-board elimination. Perhaps we should. But it has been my aim in this section to make at least intelligible to you that our collective conceptual destiny lies substantially toward the revolutionary end of the spectrum.

2. The Illusion of Self

WHAT IS A SELF? I will try to answer this question by developing an analogy with something much simpler, something which is nowhere near as puzzling as a self, but has some properties in common with selves.

What I have in mind is *the centre of gravity* of an object. This is a well-behaved concept in Newtonian physics. But a centre of gravity is not an atom or a subatomic particle or any other physical item in the world. It has no mass; it has no colour; it has no physical properties at all, except for spatio-temporal location. It is a fine example of what Hans Reichenbach would call an *abstractum*. It is a purely abstract object. It is, if you like, a theorist's fiction. It is not one of the real things in the universe in addition to the atoms. But it is a fiction that has a nicely defined, well-delineated and well-behaved role within physics.

Let me remind you how robust and familiar the idea of a centre of gravity is. Consider a chair. Like all other physical objects, it has a centre of gravity. If you start tipping it, you can tell more or less accurately whether it would start to fall over or fall back in place if you let go of it. We are all quite good at making predictions involving centres of gravity and devising explanations about when and why things fall over. Place a book on the chair. It, too, has a centre of gravity. If you start to push it over the edge, we know that at some point it will fall. It will fall when its centre of gravity is no longer directly over a point of its supporting base (the chair seat). Notice that that statement is itself virtually tautological. The key terms in it are all interdefinable. And yet it can also figure in explanations that appear to be causal explanations of some sort. We ask "Why doesn't that lamp tip over?" We reply "Because its centre of gravity is so low." Is this a causal explanation? It can compete with explanations that are clearly causal, such as "Because it's nailed to the table," and "Because it's supported by wires."

We can manipulate centres of gravity. For instance, I change the centre of gravity of a water-pitcher easily, by pouring some of the water out. So, although a centre of gravity is a purely abstract object, it has a spatio-temporal career, which I can affect by my actions. It has a history, but its history can include some rather strange episodes. Although it moves around in space and time, its motion can be discontinuous. For instance, if I were to take a piece of bubble-gum and suddenly stick it on the pitcher's handle, that would shift the pitcher's centre of gravity from point A to point B. But the centre of gravity would not have to move through all the intervening positions. As an abstractum, it is not bound by all the constraints of physical travel.

Consider the centre of gravity of a slightly more complicated object. Suppose we wanted to keep track of the career of the centre of gravity of some complex machine with lots of turning-gears and camshafts and reciprocating rods—the engine of a steam-powered unicycle, perhaps. And suppose our theory of the machine's operation permitted us to plot the complicated trajectory of the centre of gravity precisely. And suppose—most improbably—that in this particular machine the trajectory of the centre of gravity was precisely the same as the trajectory of a particular iron atom in the crank-shaft. Even if this were discovered, we would be wrong even to *entertain* the hypothesis that the machine's centre of gravity was (identical with) that iron atom. That would be a category mistake. A centre

of gravity is *just* an abstractum. It's just a fictional object. But when I say it's a fictional object, I do not mean to disparage it; it's a wonderful fictional object, and it has a perfectly legitimate place within serious, sober, *echt* physical science.

A self is also an abstract object, a theorist's fiction. The theory is not particle physics but what we might call a branch of people-physics; it is more soberly known as a phenomenology or hermeneutics, or soul-science (*Geisteswissenschaft*). The physicist does an interpretation, if you like, of the chair and its behavior, and comes up with the theoretical abstraction of a centre of gravity, which is then very useful in characterizing the behavior of the chair in the future, under a wide variety of conditions. The hermeneuticist or phenomenologist—or anthropologist—sees some rather more complicated things moving about in the world (human beings and animals) and is faced with a similar problem of interpretation. It turns out to be theoretically perspicuous to organize the interpretation around a central abstraction: each person has a self (in addition to a centre of gravity). In fact we have to posit selves for ourselves as well. The theoretical problem of self-interpretation is at least as difficult and important as the problem of other-interpretation.

Now how does a self differ from a centre of gravity? It is a much more complicated concept. I will try to elucidate it via an analogy with another sort of fictional object: fictional characters in literature. Pick up *Moby Dick* and open it up to page one. It says, "Call me Ishmael." Call whom Ishmael? Call Melville Ishmael? No. Call Ishmael Ishmael. Melville has created a fictional character named Ishmael. As you read the book you learn about Ishmael, about his life, about his beliefs and desires, his acts and attitudes. You learn a lot more about Ishmael than Melville ever explicitly tells you. Some of it you can read in by implication. Some of it you can read in by extrapolation. But beyond the limits of such extrapolation fictional worlds are simply indeterminate. Thus, consider the following question (borrowed from David Lewis's "Truth and Fiction," *American Philosophical Quarterly*, 1978). Did Sherlock Holmes have three nostrils? The answer of course is no, but not because Conan Doyle ever says that he doesn't, or that he has two, but because we are entitled to make that extrapolation. In the absence of evidence to the contrary, Sherlock Holmes's nose can be supposed to be normal. Another question: Did Sherlock Holmes have a mole on his left shoulder-blade? The answer to this question is neither yes nor no. Nothing about the text or about the principles of extrapolation from the text permits an answer to that question. There is simply no fact of the matter. Why? Because Sherlock Holmes is merely a fictional character, created by, or constituted out of, the text and the culture in which that text resides.

This indeterminacy is a fundamental property of fictional objects which strongly distinguishes them from another sort of object scientists talk about: theoretical entities, or what Reichenbach called *illata*—inferred entities, such as atoms, molecules and neutrinos. A logician might say that the "principle of bivalence" does not hold for fictional objects. That is to say, with regard to any actual man, living or dead, the question of whether or not he has or had a mole on his left shoulder-blade has an answer, yes or no. Did Aristotle have such a mole? There is a fact of the matter even if we can never discover it. But with regard to a fictional character, that question may have no answer at all.

We can imagine someone, a benighted literary critic, perhaps, who doesn't understand that fiction is fiction. This critic has a strange theory about how fiction works. He thinks that something literally magical happens when a novelist writes a novel. When a novelist sets down words on paper, this critic says (one often hears claims like this, but not meant to be taken completely literally), the novelist actually creates a world. A litmus test for this bizarre view is the principle of bivalence: when our imagined critic speaks of a fictional world he means a strange sort of real world, a world in which the principle of bivalence holds. Such a critic might seriously wonder whether Dr. Watson was really Moriarty's second cousin, or whether the conductor of the train that took Holmes and Watson to Aldershot was also the conductor of the train that brought them back to London. That sort of question can't properly arise

if you understand fiction correctly, of course. Whereas analogous questions about historical personages have to have yes or no answers, even if we may never be able to dredge them up.

Centres of gravity, as fictional objects, exhibit the same feature. They have only the properties that the theory that constitutes them endowed them with. If you scratch your head and say, "I wonder if maybe centres of gravity are really neutrinos!" you have misunderstood the theoretical status of a centre of gravity.

Now how can I make the claim that a self—your own real self, for instance—is rather like a fictional character? Are all fictional selves not dependent for their very creation on the existence of real selves? It may seem so, but I will argue that this is an illusion. Let's go back to Ishmael. Ishmael is a fictional character, although we can certainly learn all about him. One might find him in many regards more real than many of one's friends. But, one thinks, Ishmael was created by Melville, and Melville is a real character—was a real character. A real self. Does this not show that it takes a real self to create a fictional self? I think not, but if I am to convince you, I must push you through an exercise of the imagination.

First of all, I want to imagine something some of you may think incredible: a novel-writing machine. We can suppose it is a product of artificial intelligence research, a computer that has been designed or programmed to write novels. But it has not been designed to write any particular novel. We can suppose (if it helps) that it has been given a great stock of whatever information it might need, and some partially random and hence unpredictable ways of starting the seed of a story going, and building upon it. Now imagine that the designers are sitting back, wondering what kind of novel their creation is going to write. They turn the thing on and after a while the high-speed printer begins to go clickety-clack and out comes the first sentence. "Call me Gilbert," it says. "What follows is the apparent autobiography of some fictional Gilbert. Now Gilbert is a fictional, created self but its creator is no self. Of course there were human designers who designed the machine, but they didn't design Gilbert. Gilbert is a product of a design or invention process in which there aren't any selves at all. That is, I am stipulating that this is not a conscious machine, not a "thinker." It is a dumb machine, but it does have the power to write a passable novel. (If you think this is strictly impossible I can only challenge you to show why you think this must be so, and invite you to read on; in the end you may not have an interest in defending such a precarious impossibility-claim.)

So we are to imagine that a passable story is emitted from the machine. Notice that we can perform the same sort of literary exegesis with regard to this novel as we can with any other. In fact if you were to pick up a novel at random out of a library, you could not tell with certainty that it wasn't written by something like this machine. (And if you're a New Critic you shouldn't care.) You've got a text and you can interpret it, and so you can learn the story, the life and adventures of Gilbert. Your expectations and predictions, as you read, and your interpretative reconstruction of what you have already read, will congeal around the central node of the fictional character, Gilbert.

But now I want to twiddle the knobs on this thought experiment. So far we've imagined the novel, *The Life and Times of Gilbert*, clanking out of a computer that is just a box, sitting in the corner of some lab. But now I want to change the story a little bit and suppose that the computer has arms and legs—or better: wheels. (I don't want to make it too anthropomorphic.) It has a television eye, and it moves around in the world. It also begins its tale with "Call me Gilbert," and tells a novel, but now we notice that if we do the trick that the New Critics say you should never do, and look outside the text, we discover that there's a truth-preserving interpretation of that text in the real world. The adventures of Gilbert, the fictional character, now bear a striking and presumably non-coincidental relationship to the adventures of this robot rolling around in the world. If you hit the robot with a baseball bat, very shortly thereafter the story of Gilbert includes his being hit with a baseball bat by somebody who looks like you. Every now and then the robot gets locked in the closet and then says "Help me!" Help whom? Well, help Gilbert, presumably. But who is Gilbert? Is Gilbert the robot, or merely the fictional self created by the

robot? If we go and help the robot out of the closet, it sends us a note: "Thank you. Love, Gilbert."

At this point we will be unable to ignore the fact that the fictional career of the fictional Gilbert bears an interesting resemblance to the "career" of this mere robot moving through the world. We can still maintain that the robot's brain, the robot's computer, really knows nothing about the world; it's not a self. It's just a clanky computer. It doesn't know what it's doing. It doesn't even know that it's creating a fictional character. (The same is just as true of your brain; it doesn't know what it's doing either.) Nevertheless, the patterns in the behavior that is being controlled by the computer are interpretable, by us, as accreting biography—telling the narrative of a self. But we are not the only interpreters. The robot novelist is also, of course, an interpreter; a self-interpreter, providing its own account of its activities in the world.

I propose that we take this analogy seriously. "Where is the self?" a materialist philosopher or neuroscientist might ask. It is a category mistake to start looking around for the self in the brain. Unlike centres of gravity, whose sole property is their spatio-temporal position, selves have a spatio-temporal position that is only grossly defined. Roughly speaking, in the normal case if there are three human beings sitting on a park bench, there are three selves there, all in a row and roughly equidistant from the fountain they face. Or we might use a rather antique turn of phrase and talk about how many souls are located in the park. ("All twenty souls in the starboard lifeboat were saved, but those that remained on deck perished.")

Brain research may permit us to make some more fine-grained localizations, but the capacity to achieve *some* fine-grained localization does not give one grounds for supposing that the process of localization can continue indefinitely and that the day will finally come when we can say, "That cell there, right in the middle of the hippocampus (or wherever)—that's the self!"

There's a big difference, of course, between fictional characters and our own selves. One I would stress is that a fictional character is usually encountered as a *fait accompli*. After the novel has been written and published, you read it. At that point it is too late for the novelist to render determinate anything indeterminate that strikes your curiosity. Dostoevsky is dead; you can't ask him what else Raskolnikov thought while he sat in the police station. But novels don't have to be that way. John Updike has written three novels about Rabbit Angstrom: *Rabbit Run*, *Rabbit Redux* and *Rabbit is Rich*. Suppose that those of us who particularly like the first novel were to get together and compose a list of questions for Updike—things we wished he had talked about in that first novel, when Rabbit was a young former basketball star. We could send our questions to Updike and ask him to consider writing another novel in the series, only this time not continuing the chronological sequence. Like Lawrence Durrell's *Alexandria Quartet*, the Rabbit series could include another novel about Rabbit's early days when he was still playing basketball, and this novel could answer our questions.

Notice what we would not be doing in such a case. We would not be saying to Updike, "Tell us the answers that you already know, the answers that are already fixed to those questions. Come on, let us know all those secrets you've been keeping from us." Nor would we be asking Updike to do research, as we might ask the author of a multi-volume biography of a real person, we would be asking him to write a new novel, to invent some more novel for us, on demand. And if he acceded, he would enlarge and make more determinate the character of Rabbit Angstrom in the process of writing the new novel. In this way matters which are indeterminate at one time can become determined later by a creative step.

I propose that this imagined exercise with Updike getting him to write more novels on demand to answer our questions, is actually a familiar exercise. That is the way we treat each other; that is the way we are. We cannot undo those parts of our pasts that are determinate, but our selves are constantly being made more determinate as we go along in response to the way the world impinges on us. Of course it is also possible for a person to engage in auto-hermeneutics, interpretation of one's self, and in particular to go back and think about one's past, and one's memories, and to rethink them and rewrite them. This process does change the "fictional" character, the character that you are, in much the way that Rabbit

Angstrom, after Updike writes the second novel about him as a young man, comes to be a rather different fictional character, determinate in ways he was never determinate before. This would be an utterly mysterious and magical prospect (and hence something no one should take seriously) if the self were anything but an abstractum.

I want to bring this out by extracting one more feature from the Updike thought experiment. Updike might take up our request but then he might prove to be forgetful. After all, it's been many years since he wrote *Rabbit Run*. He might not want to go back and re-read it carefully; and when he wrote the new novel it might end up being inconsistent with the first. He might have Rabbit being in two places at one time, for instance. If we wanted to settle what the true story was, we'd be falling into error; there is no true story. In such a circumstance there would simply be a failure of coherence of all the data that we had about Rabbit. And because Rabbit is a fictional character we wouldn't smite our foreheads in wonder and declare "Oh my goodness! There's a rift in the universe; we've found a contradiction in nature!" Nothing is easier than contradiction when you're dealing with fiction; a fictional character can have contradictory properties because it's just a fictional character. We find such contradictions intolerable, however, when we are trying to interpret something or someone, even a fictional character, so we typically bifurcate the character to resolve the conflict.

Something like this seems to happen to real people on rare occasions. Consider the putatively true case-histories recorded in Corbett H. Thigpen and Hervey Cleckly's *The Three Faces of Eve* (1957), and Flora Rheta Schreiber's *Sybil* (1973). Eve's three faces were the faces of three distinct personalities, it seems, and the woman portrayed in *Sybil* had many different selves, or so it seems. How can we make sense of this? Here is one way—a solemn, skeptical way favoured by some of the psychotherapists with whom I've talked about such cases: when Sybil went in to see her therapist the first time, she wasn't several different people rolled onto one body; she was a novel-writing machine that fell in with a very ingenious questioner, a very eager reader. And together they collaborated—innocently—to write many, many chapters of a new novel. And, of course, since Sybil was a sort of living novel, she went out and engaged in the world with these new selves, more or less created on demand, under the eager suggestion of a therapist.

I now believe that this is overly skeptical. The population explosion of new characters that typically follows the onset of psychotherapy for sufferers of Multiple Personality Disorder (MPD) is probably to be explained along just these lines, but there is quite compelling evidence in some cases that some multiplicity of selves (two or three or four, let us say) had already begun laying down biography before the therapist came along to do the "reading." And in any event, Sybil is only a strikingly pathological case of something quite normal, a behavior pattern we can find in ourselves. We are all, at times, confabulators, telling and retelling ourselves the story of our own lives, with scant attention to the question of truth. Why, though, do we behave this way? Why are we all such inveterate and inventive autobiographical novelists? As Umberto Maturana has (uncontroversially) observed: "Everything said is said by a speaker to another speaker that may be himself." But why should one talk to oneself? Why isn't that an utterly idle activity, as systematically futile as trying to pick oneself up by one's own bootstraps?

A central clue comes from the sort of phenomena uncovered by Michael Gazzaniga's research on those rare individuals—the "split-brain subjects"—whose *corpus callosum* has been surgically severed, creating in them two largely independent cortical hemispheres that can, on occasion, be differently informed about the current scene. Does the operation split the self in two? After it, patients normally exhibit no signs of psychological splitting, appearing to be no less unified than you or I except under particularly contrived circumstances. But on Gazzaniga's view, this does not so much show that the patients have preserved their pre-surgical unity as that the unity of normal life is an illusion.

According to him, the normal mind is not beautifully unified, but rather a problematically yoked-together bundle of partly autonomous systems. All parts of the mind are not equally accessible to each other at all times. These modules or systems sometimes have internal communication problems which they solve by various ingenious and devious routes. If this is true (and I think it is), it may provide us with an answer to a most puzzling question about conscious thought: what good is it? Such a question begs for an evolutionary answer, but it will have to be speculative, of course. (It is not critical to my speculative answer, for the moment, where genetic evolution and transmission break off and cultural evolution and transmission take over.)

In the beginning—according to Julian Jaynes (*The Origins of Consciousness in the Breakdown of the Bicameral Mind*, 1976), whose account I am adapting—were speakers, our ancestors, who weren't really conscious. They spoke, but they just sort of blurted things out, more or less the way bees do bee dances, or the way computers talk to each other. That is not conscious communication, surely. When these ancestors had problems, sometimes they would "ask" for help (more or less like Gilbert saying "Help me!" when he was locked in the closet), and sometimes there would be somebody around to hear them. So they got into the habit of asking for assistance and, particularly, asking questions. Whenever they couldn't figure out how to solve some problem, they would ask a question, addressed to no one in particular, and sometimes whoever was standing around could answer them. And they also came to be designed to be provoked on many such occasions into answering questions like that—to the best of their ability—when asked.

Then one day one of our ancestors asked a question in what was apparently an inappropriate circumstance: there was nobody around to be the audience. Strangely enough, he heard his own question, and this stimulated him, cooperatively, to think of an answer, and sure enough the answer came to him. He had established, without realizing what he had done, a communication link between two parts of his brain, between which there was, for some deep biological reason, an accessibility problem. One component of the mind had confronted a problem that another component could solve; if only the problem could be posed for the latter component. Thanks to his habit of asking questions, our ancestor stumbled upon a route via the ears. What a discovery! Sometimes talking and listening to yourself can have wonderful effects, not otherwise obtainable. All that is needed to make sense of this idea is the hypothesis that the modules of the mind have different capacities and ways of doing things, and are not perfectly interaccessible. Under such circumstances it could be true that the way to get yourself to figure out a problem is to tickle your ear with it, to get that part of your brain which is best stimulated by hearing a question to work on the problem. Then sometimes you will find yourself with the answer you seek on the tip of your tongue.

This would be enough to establish the evolutionary endorsement (which might well be only culturally transmitted) of the behavior of talking to yourself. But as many writers have observed, conscious thinking seems—much of it—to be a variety of a particularly efficient and private talking to oneself. The evolutionary transition to thought is then easy to conjure up. All we have to suppose is that the route, the circuit that at first went via mouth and ear, got shorter. People "realized" that the actual vocalization and audition was a rather inefficient part of the loop. Besides, if there were other people around who might overhear it, you might give away more information than you wanted. So what developed was a habit of subvocalization, and this in turn could be streamlined into conscious, verbal thought.

In his posthumous book *On Thinking* (1979), Gilbert Ryle asks: "What is *Le Penseur* doing?" For behaviorists like Ryle this is a real problem. One bit of chin-on-fist-with-knitted-brow looks pretty much like another bit, and yet some of it seems to arrive at good answers and some of it doesn't. What can be going on here? Ironically, Ryle, the arch-behaviorist, came up with some very sly suggestions about what might be going on. Conscious thought, Ryle claimed, should be understood on the model of self-teaching, or better, perhaps: self-schooling or training. He had little to say about how this self-schooling might actually work, but we can get some initial understanding of it on the supposition that we are not the captains of our ships; there is no conscious self that is unproblematically in command of the mind's resources. Rather, we are somewhat disunified. Our compo-

nent modules have to act in opportunistic but amazingly resourceful ways to produce a modicum of behavioral unity, which is then enhanced by an illusion of greater unity.

What Gazzaniga's research reveals, sometimes in vivid detail, is how this must go on. Consider some of his evidence for the extraordinary resourcefulness exhibited by (something in) the right hemisphere when it is faced with a communication problem. In one group of experiments, split-brain subjects reach into a closed bag with the left hand to feel an object, which they then identify verbally. The sensory nerves in the left hand lead to the right hemisphere, whereas the control of speech is normally in the left hemisphere, but for most of us, this poses no problem. In a normal person, the left hand can know what the right hand is doing thanks to the *corpus callosum,* which keeps both hemispheres mutually informed. But in a split-brain subject, this unifying link has been removed; the right hemisphere gets the information about the touched object from the left hand, but the left, language-controlling, hemisphere must make the identification public. So the "part which can speak" is kept in the dark, while the "part which knows" cannot make public its knowledge.

There is a devious solution to this problem, however, and split-brain patients have been observed to discover it. Whereas ordinary tactile sensations are represented contralaterally—the signals go to the opposite hemisphere—pain signals are also represented ipsilaterally. That is, thanks to the way the nervous system is wired up, pain stimuli go to both hemispheres. Suppose the object in the bag is a pencil. The right hemisphere will sometimes hit upon a very clever tactic: hold the pencil in your left hand so its point is pressed hard into your palm; this creates pain, and lets the left hemisphere know there's something sharp in the bag, which is enough of a hint so that it can begin guessing; the right hemisphere will signal "getting warmer" and "got it" by smiling or other controllable signs, and in a very short time "the subject"— the apparently unified "sole inhabitant" of the body—will be able to announce the correct answer.

Now either the split-brain subjects have developed this extraordinarily devious talent as a reaction to the operation that landed them with such a radical accessibility problem, or the operation reveals but does not create—a virtuoso talent to be—found also in normal people. Surely, Gazzaniga claims, the latter hypothesis is the most likely one to investigate. That is, it does seem that we are all virtuoso novelists, who find ourselves engaged in all sorts of behavior, more or less unified, but sometimes disunified, and we always put the best "faces" on if we can. We try to make all of our material cohere into a single good story. And that story is our autobiography.

The chief fictional character at the centre of that autobiography is one's self. And if you still want to know what the self really is, you're making a category mistake. After all, when a human being's behavioral control system becomes seriously impaired, it can turn out that the best hermeneutical story we can tell about that individual says that there is more than one character "inhabiting" that body. This is quite possible on the view of the self I have been presenting; it does not require any fancy metaphysical miracles. One can discover multiple selves in a person just as unproblematically as one could find Early Young Rabbit and Late Young Rabbit in the imagined Updike novels: all that has to be the case is that the story doesn't cohere around one self, one imaginary point, but coheres (coheres much better, in any case) around two different imaginary points.

We sometimes encounter psychological disorders, or surgically created disunities, where the only way to interpret or make sense of them is to posit in effect two centres of gravity, two selves. One isn't creating or discovering a little bit of ghost stuff in doing that. One is simply creating another abstraction. It is an abstraction one uses as part of a theoretical apparatus to understand, and predict, and make sense of, the behavior of some very complicated things. The fact that these abstract selves seem so robust and real is not surprising. They are much more complicated theoretical entities than a centre of gravity. And remember that even a centre of gravity has a fairly robust presence, once we start playing around with it. But no one has ever seen or ever will see a centre of gravity. As David Hume noted, no one has ever seen a self, either.

For my part, when I enter most intimately into what I call *myself*, I always stumble on some particular perception or other, of heat or cold, light or shade, love or hatred, pain or pleasure. I never can catch *myself* at any time without a perception, and never can observe anything but the perception. . . . If anyone, upon serious and unprejudiced reflection, thinks he has a different notion of *himself*, I must confess I can reason no longer with him. All I can allow him is, that he may be in the right as well as I, and that we are essentially different in this particular. He may, perhaps, perceive something simple and continued, which he calls *himself*; though I am certain there is no such principle in me. [*Treatise on Human Nature,* I, IV, sec. 6.]

3. The Chinese Room

WHAT PSYCHOLOGICAL AND PHILOSOPHICAL SIGNIFICANCE should we attach to recent efforts at computer simulations of human cognitive capacities? In answering this question, I find it useful to distinguish what I will call "strong" AI from "weak" or "cautious" AI (artificial intelligence). According to weak AI, the principal value of the computer in the study of the mind is that it gives us a very powerful tool. For example, it enables us to formulate and test hypotheses in a more rigorous and precise fashion.

Selections from John Searle, "Minds, Brains, and Programs," The Behavioral and Brain Sciences, *vol. 3, pp. 417–424 (Cambridge: Cambridge University Press, 1980). Reprinted with permission from Cambridge University Press.*

But according to strong AI, the computer is not merely a tool in the study of the mind; rather, the appropriately programmed computer really *is* a mind, in the sense that computers given the right programs can be literally said to *understand* and have other cognitive states. In strong AI, because the programmed computer has cognitive states, the programs are not mere tools that enable us to test psychological explanations; rather, the programs are themselves the explanations.

I have no objection to the claims of weak AI, at least as far as this article is concerned. My discussion here will be directed at the claims I have defined as those of strong AI, specifically the claim that the appropriately programmed computer literally has cognitive states and that the programs thereby explain human cognition. When I hereafter refer to AI, I have in mind the strong version, as expressed by these two claims.

I will consider the work of Roger Schank and his colleagues at Yale (Schank and Abelson 1977), because I am more familiar with it than I am with any other similar claims, and because it provides a very clear example of the sort of work I wish to examine. But nothing that follows depends upon the details of Schank's programs. The same arguments would apply to Winograd's SHRDLU (Winograd 1973), Weizenbaum's ELIZA (Weizenbaum 1965), and indeed any Turing machine simulation of human mental phenomena. [See "Further Reading" for Searle's references.]

Very briefly, and leaving out the various details, one can describe Schank's program as follows: The aim of the program is to simulate the human ability to understand stories. It is characteristic of human beings' story-understanding capacity that they can answer questions about the story even though the information that they give was never explicitly stated in the story. Thus, for example, suppose you are given the following story: "A man went into a restaurant and ordered a hamburger. When the hamburger arrived it was burned to a crisp, and the man stormed out of the restaurant angrily, without paying for the hamburger or leaving a tip." Now, if you are asked "Did the man eat the hamburger?" you will presumably answer, "No, he did not." Similarly, if you are given the following

story: "A man went into a restaurant and ordered a hamburger; when the hamburger came he was very pleased with it; and as he left the restaurant he gave the waitress a large tip before paying his bill," and you are asked the question, "Did the man eat the hamburger?" you will presumably answer, "Yes, he ate the hamburger." Now Schank's machines can similarly answer questions about restaurants in this fashion. To do this, they have a "representation" of the sort of information that human beings have about restaurants, which enables them to answer such questions as those above, given these sorts of stories. When the machine is given the story and then asked the question, the machine will print out answers of the sort that we would expect human beings to give if told similar stories. Partisans of strong AI claim that in this question and answer sequence the machine is not only simulating a human ability but also (1) that the machine can literally be said to *understand* the story and provide the answers to questions, and (2) that what the machine and its program do *explains* the human ability to understand the story and answer questions about it.

Both claims seem to me to be totally unsupported by Schank's work, as I will attempt to show in what follows. (I am not, of course, saying that Schank himself is committed to these claims.)

One way to test any theory of the mind is to ask oneself what it would be like if my mind actually worked on the principles that the theory says all minds work on. Let us apply this test to the Schank program with the following *Gedankenexperiment.* Suppose that I'm locked in a room and given a large batch of Chinese writing. Suppose furthermore (as is indeed the case) that I know no Chinese, either written or spoken, and that I'm not even confident that I could recognize Chinese writing as Chinese writing distinct from, say, Japanese writing or meaningless squiggles. To me, Chinese writing is just so many meaningless squiggles. Now suppose further that after this first batch of Chinese writing I am given a second batch of Chinese script together with a set of rules for correlating the second batch with the first batch. The rules are in English, and I understand these rules as well as any other native speaker of English. They enable me to correlate one set of formal symbols with another set of formal symbols, and all that "formal" means here is that I can identify the symbols entirely by their shapes. Now suppose also that I am given a third batch of Chinese symbols together with some instructions, again in English, that enable me to correlate elements of this third batch with the first two batches, and these rules instruct me how to give back certain Chinese symbols with certain sorts of shapes in response to certain sorts of shapes given me in the third batch. Unknown to me, the people who are giving me all of these symbols call the first batch a "script," they call the second batch a "story," and they call the third batch "questions." Furthermore, they call the symbols I give them back in response to the third batch "answers to the questions," and the set of rules in English that they gave me, they call the "program." Now just to complicate the story a little, imagine that these people also give me stories in English, which I understand, and they then ask me questions in English about these stories, and I give them back answers in English. Suppose also that after a while I get so good at following the instructions for manipulating the Chinese symbols and the programmers get so good at writing the programs that from the external point of view—that is, from the point of view of somebody outside the room in which I am locked—my answers to the questions are absolutely indistinguishable from those of native Chinese speakers. Nobody just looking at my answers can tell that I don't speak a word of Chinese. Let us also suppose that my answers to the English questions are, as they no doubt would be, indistinguishable from those of other native English speakers, for the simple reason that I am a native English speaker. From the external point of view—from the point of view of someone reading my "answers"—the answers to the Chinese questions and the English questions are equally good. But in the Chinese case, unlike the English case, I produce the answers by manipulating uninterpreted formal symbols. As far as the Chinese is concerned, I simply behave like a computer; I perform computational operations on formally specified elements. For the purposes of the Chinese, I am simply an instantiation of the computer program.

Now the claims made by strong AI are that the programmed computer understands the stories and that the program in some sense explains human understanding. But we are now in a position to examine these claims in light of our thought experiment.

1. As regards the first claim, it seems to me quite obvious in the example that I do not understand a word of the Chinese stories. I have inputs and outputs that are indistinguishable from those of the native Chinese speaker, and I can have any formal program you like, but I still understand nothing. For the same reasons, Schank's computer understands nothing of any stories, whether in Chinese, English, or whatever, since in the Chinese case the computer is me, and in cases where the computer is not me, the computer has nothing more than I have in the case where I understand nothing.

2. As regards the second claim, that the program explains human understanding, we can see that the computer and its program do not provide sufficient conditions of understanding since the computer and the program are functioning, and there is no understanding. But does it even provide a necessary condition or a significant contribution to understanding? One of the claims made by the supporters of strong AI is that when I understand a story in English, what I am doing is exactly the same—or perhaps more of the same—as what I was doing in manipulating the Chinese symbols. It is simply more formal symbol manipulation that distinguishes the case in English, where I do understand, from the case in Chinese, where I don't. I have not demonstrated that this claim is false, but it would certainly appear an incredible claim in the example. Such plausibility as the claim has derives from the supposition that we can construct a program that will have the same inputs and outputs as native speakers, and in addition we assume that speakers have some level of description where they are also instantiations of a program. On the basis of these two assumptions we assume that even if Schank's program isn't the whole story about understanding, it may be part of the story. Well, I suppose that is an empirical possibility, but not the slightest reason has so far been given to believe that it is true, since what is suggested—though certainly not demonstrated—

by the example is that the computer program is simply irrelevant to my understanding of the story. In the Chinese case I have everything that artificial intelligence can put into me by way of a program, and I understand nothing; in the English case I understand everything, and there is so far no reason at all to suppose that my understanding has anything to do with computer programs, that is, with computational operations on purely formally specified elements. As long as the program is defined in terms of computational operations on purely formally defined elements, what the example suggests is that these by themselves have no interesting connection with understanding. They are certainly not sufficient conditions, and not the slightest reason has been given to suppose that they are necessary conditions or even that they make a significant contribution to understanding. Notice that the force of the argument is not simply that different machines can have the same input and output while operating on different formal principles—that is not the point at all. Rather, whatever purely formal principles you put into the computer, they will not be sufficient for understanding, since a human will be able to follow the formal principles without understanding anything. No reason whatever has been offered to suppose that such principles are necessary or even contributory, since no reason has been given to suppose that when I understand English I am operating with any formal program at all.

Well, then, what is it that I have in the case of the English sentences that I do not have in the case of the Chinese sentences? The obvious answer is that I know what the former mean, while I haven't the faintest idea what the latter mean. But in what does this consist and why couldn't we give it to a machine, whatever it is? I will return to this question later, but first I want to continue with the example.

I have had the occasions to present this example to several workers in artificial intelligence, and, interestingly, they do not seem to agree on what the proper reply to it is. I get a surprising variety of replies, and in what follows I will consider the most common of these (specified along with their geographic origins).

But first I want to block some common misunderstandings about "understanding": In many of these discussions one finds a lot of fancy footwork about the word "understanding." My critics point out that there are many different degrees of understanding; that "understanding" is not a simple two-place predicate; that there are even different kinds and levels of understanding, and often the law of excluded middle doesn't even apply in a straightforward way to statements of the form "*x* understands *y*"; that in many cases it is a matter for decision and not a simple matter of fact whether *x* understands *y*; and so on. To all of these points I want to say: of course, of course. But they have nothing to do with the points at issue. There are clear cases in which "understanding" literally applies and clear cases in which it does not apply; and these two sorts of cases are all I need for this argument. I understand stories in English; to a lesser degree I can understand stories in French; to a still lesser degree, stories in German; and in Chinese, not at all. My car and my adding machine, on the other hand, understand nothing: they are not in that line of business. We often attribute "understanding" and other cognitive predicates by metaphor and analogy to cars, adding machines, and other artifacts, but nothing is proved by such attributions. We say, "The door *knows* when to open because of its photoelectric cell," "The adding machine *knows how* (*understands how*, is *able*) to do addition and subtraction but not division," and "The thermostat *perceives* changes in the temperature." The reason we make these attributions is quite interesting, and it has to do with the fact that in artifacts we extend our own intentionality; our tools are extensions of our purposes, and so we find it natural to make metaphorical attributions of intentionality to them; but I take it no philosophical ice is cut by such examples. The sense in which an automatic door "understands instructions" from its photoelectric cell is not at all the sense in which I understand English. If the sense in which Schank's programmed computers understand stories is supposed to be the metaphorical sense in which the door understands, and not the sense in which I understand English, the issue would not be worth discussing. But Newell and Simon (1963) write that the kind of cognition they claim for computers is exactly the same as for human beings. I like the straightforwardness of this claim, and it is the sort of claim I will be considering. I will argue that in the literal sense the programmed computer understands what the car and the adding machine understand, namely, exactly nothing. The computer understanding is not just (like my understanding of German) partial or incomplete; it is zero.

Now to the reply:

1. **The Systems Reply (Berkeley).** "While it is true that the individual person who is locked in the room does not understand the story, the fact is that he is merely part of a whole system, and the system does understand the story. The person has a large ledger in front of him in which are written the rules, he has a lot of scratch paper and pencils for doing calculations, he has 'data banks' of sets of Chinese symbols. Now, understanding is not being ascribed to the mere individual; rather it is being ascribed to this whole system of which he is a part."

4. Life After Death

INTRODUCTION

Progress in science in general, as well as in neuroscience in particular, has had an impact on a range of traditional philosophical issues, including the nature of the mind, the nature of the universe, and the nature of life. One metaphysical matter that looms large for many people concerns supernatural beings, and the existence of God in particular. Is there anything we have learned about the brain that bears upon questions of spirituality?

At the heart of reflections on religion and the brain are three questions: (1) Does God exist? (2) Is there life after death? (3) What happens to morality if God does not exist? One and all, these questions are ancient; one and all, they remain highly current topics of discussion. I raise them here partly because some developments in cognitive neuroscience have an impact on how we formulate possible answers. These questions have both a metaphysical and epistemological dimension, and addressing them pulls together many of the ideas discussed in earlier chapters. Certainly, they are preeminently *philosophical* questions, and the historical tradition is rich with arguments, replies, reformulations, and refutations. In this respect, it resembles the historical tradition of *natural philosophy* generally, as humans struggled to figure out the nature of physical reality and whether their beliefs about fire, life, the Earth, and the mind are likely to be true.

As one's understanding of the world expands, conflicts between beliefs are a regular feature of cognitive life. Some of these beliefs are humdrum (e.g., it looks like the Moon is about as big as a barn; the data show it actually has a diameter of 2,000 miles and is 240,000 miles away). Some are more momentous (e.g., one believes that autism is caused by cold mothering and then discovers that it has a genetic basis). Some have tumultuous personal effects (e.g., you believe that your enduring melancholia is a character flaw and then discover that you have a serotonin deficiency).

Some discoveries bear upon the belief that there is a life after death. More specifically, there is tension between (a) the idea of the *self* as an immaterial *and* immortal soul, created by God, and (b) the idea that the mind is what the brain does, that the human brain is a product of natural selection, and that disintegration of one's brain in disease and death entails disintegration of one's mind. For

From Patricia Churchland, Brain-Wise (Cambridge, Mass.: MIT Press, 2002), pp. 373–374; 393–396. Copyright 2002 Massachusetts Institute of Technology. Reprinted with permission.

most of us, it matters how we resolve these tensions, and it matters that we resolve them in a way that is intellectually satisfying rather than flippant or ideological. . . .

IS THERE LIFE AFTER DEATH?

As discussed in earlier chapters, the preponderance of evidence supports the hypothesis that mental states are brain states and mental processes are brain processes. On this hypothesis, what thing exists to survive the death of the brain? What kind of substance would it be, and how could it have the emotions, knowledge, preferences, and memories that the brain had when it was alive? How can it be related to those activities in the brain that make me *me?* Reasonable answers need to be forthcoming if the hypothesis that there is life after death is to win credibility.

So far as I can determine, there are no answers that cohere enough to make some sense of the life-after-death hypothesis. The preponderance of the evidence indicates that when the brain degenerates, mental functions are compromised, and when the brain dies, mental functions cease. The suggestion that the whole body is resurrected after death does address the problem, but so far the evidence for resurrection is not persuasive. Old graves contain old bones, and decaying flesh is devoured by scavengers.

Is there any positive evidence that *something,* we know not what, does in fact live on after the death of the brain? There are, certainly, many reports that purport to provide confirming evidence. Because I cannot consider them all here, I shall restrict myself to the following pertinent observations. So many of the claims that rest on the intervention of a psychic medium have been shown to be fraudulent that a general suspicion of these claims is as prudent as the general suspicion one has toward get-rich-quick investments. Many claims to a previous life are either openly concocted, confabulated, or a matter of unwitting selectivity of evidence. By "selectivity of evidence," I mean that one pays attention to events that, with suitable interpretation, could be construed as confirming one antecedently favored

hypothesis, while ignoring or explaining away in ad hoc fashion events that could be disconfirming.

For a made-up illustration of selectivity of evidence concerning an afterlife and a previous life, consider this story. A child draws a picture of a scene with a farmhouse, apple trees in the yard, a dog sleeping under the tree, and so forth. It reminds his mother of Great Grandfather Smith's house. Indeed, little Billy has some of Great Grandfather Smith's physical traits, including his curly red hair and his hot temper. The mother asks the child about his picture, and the source of his ideas. "Do you remember ever seeing a place like this?" she queries. If she *prompts* him, the child will begin to agree, as psychologists have repeatedly shown, that he remembers this place, remembers the dog, and so forth. Later he may quite innocently embellish all these "memories" with details from parental conversation, family albums, and so forth. Billy may even discover, perhaps without conscious knowledge, that he is encouraged to *confabulate* his earlier life, where his confabulations get conceptualized as the *recovery of hidden memories.*

Great Grandfather Smith, in Billy's "recovered memories," killed a grizzly with a mere bowie knife, built a snow house in a blizzard, and talked to quail and coyote. Nobody else remembers these events, but that is not troubling, since Grandfather was somewhat reserved. His mother, we may imagine, does not work hard to test the hypothesis that Billy is the reincarnation of Great Grandfather Smith. When she does ask a question about Great Grandfather Smith's life that Billy *cannot* answer, this is soothingly explained away by saying that Billy has forgotten that particular of his previous life. She ignores countervailing evidence, she tends to notice or remember only confirming evidence. This is not because she is openly mendacious. Quite the contrary. She is inadvertently fooling *herself.* She *wants* to believe. This fable illustrates selectivity in considering evidence, and it is something to which we all are prone. Consequently, we have to work hard to be as tough-minded with respect to hypotheses we *hope* are true as we are with respect to those we *fear* are true.

Whether all accounts of reincarnation share the weaknesses illustrated in the fable is not known, but because so many that have been studied do, and because one does not want to be gullible, we need to exercise careful scrutiny, case by individual case. Why do we not all enthusiastically believe Shirley McLaine's claims of her earlier, colorful lives? Partly, I think, because her accounts seem to suffer from the selectivity-of-evidence problem just outlined, partly because her claims are conveniently untestable, but also because they have the indelible stamp of fantasy. Her "earlier lives" are enviably glamorous; they are not the lives of a poor peasant grubbing about with running sores and bent back. Typically, reports of previous lives are replete with storybook appeal: handsome heroes, beautiful queens, and romantic deeds. Surely, there were many more hungry, stooped peasants than there were pining, gothic princesses, yet these tend not to be the "previous lives" channeling reveals. Or is it perhaps that only glamorous persons are reincarnated and the humble ones stay dead?

Recently, evocative descriptions provided by patients who very nearly died have become a source of interest to our question. Visual experiences involving tunnels with shimmering lights at the far end, feelings of great peacefulness, feelings that one is being led on a journey, and sometimes the experience of seeming to see one's body below on a gurney are typical of experiences called "near-death experiences." These experiences are alleged to be evidence that the patients have experienced the otherworld of the afterlife. As always, we must weigh the evidence for and against, and reflect on whether there might be more down-to-earth explanations.

Several obstacles suggest that caution is in order. First, these experiences seem to be somewhat unusual (about 35 percent) among those patients who are very close to death but who revive. *Selectivity of evidence* makes them seem to confirm an afterlife, despite the existence of other cases where the resuscitated patient reports no such experiences.

Second, the conditions are not those of a controlled experiment, and one wants to know whether any of these patients are *encouraged* to "remember" events that, in their current stressful circumstances, they attribute to experiences "while dead."

Third, the reports are reports from patients whose brains are under great stress; they are anoxic (oxygen deprived) and awash in norepinephrine, precisely *because* they are close to death. Brains under stress may produce many abnormal activities, including involuntary movements, strange speech, unusual eye movements, and unusual experiences. Severe anoxia, for example in drowning, is known to result in feelings of peacefulness, once the panic phase has passed. Some people have used self-strangulation as a means of inducing anoxic ecstasy. Anoxia resulting from breathing nitrous oxide (so-called laughing gas) can produce ecstatic feelings and feelings of having glimpsed profound truths. William James says he experienced "metaphysical illuminations" while intoxicated on nitrous oxide, though what he wrote on these occasions was, by his admission, sheer gibberish. Nitrous oxide stimulates neurons that release endorphins (the brain's endogenous opiates), which is why it can be used as an anesthetic. Endogenous endorphin release, along with some suggestibility perhaps, is the probable cause of ecstatic effects. In this respect, therefore, the problem is similar to the problem with the reports from the cases of temporal-lobe epileptics who experience "religious feelings" during a seizure.

Fourth, as noted in chapter 3, out-of-body experiences, as well as other disorienting and depersonalizing experiences, can be produced artificially, for example with the anesthetic ketamine or with LSD. It is not unlikely that the neuronal explanations for the ketamine experiences and the near-death experiences are very similar. Moreover, as Francis Crick has pointed out in conversation, the out-of-body claims could be tested a little more directly by asking whether the patient saw an object that could be seen only if he was where he said he was, such as floating out the hospital window. So far as I can tell, this sort of test has not been systematically undertaken.

Although the skepticism and caution with respect to claims about past and future lives are justified, we should keep an open mind about the possibility that a genuinely testable case will emerge. If a prima facie case does emerge, it will indeed be of the greatest importance to examine it carefully and systematically, to avoid inadvertent contamination of memory, to do everything possible to rule out fraud, to check the claims against what is known about the facts, to consider other possible explanations, and so forth. The record of examined cases makes one less than optimistic that such a case will survive scrutiny, but one must not rule out the possibility that it will.

But is the prospect of extinction not unsettling? Is it not disappointing and frightening? It may be all these things, but it need not be. One can live a richly purposeful life of love and work—of family, community, wilderness, music, and so forth— cognizant that it makes sense to make the best of *this* life. Arguably, it is less painful to accept that miseries are just a part of life than that they are punishment or trials or that one's prayers are being ignored. Arguably, it is comforting to assume that matters of justice and desert need to be addressed in the here and now, not deferred to an afterlife. Finding peaceful solutions, redressing wrongs, seeking reconciliation and compromise, expressing love, maximizing the significance of each day that one is alive—these things may make more sense than pinning too much hope on an iffy hereafter. When all is said and done, the truth is still the truth, however grim it turns out to be. If there is no life after death—if that *is* the truth—then wishing it were otherwise will not make it otherwise.

Study Questions

1. What is cognitive science?

2. Explain the differences in subject matter and method between the "brain" cognitive sciences and the "mind" cognitive sciences.

3. Explain how Kant and computer science influenced the methods of the mind cognitive sciences.

4. What is the general view of the mind accepted by brain functionalists?

5. Explain what it means to say that the mind is "modular."

6. What does it mean for a cognitive scientist to say that the mind is an "information processor"?

7. How does the "processing" part of "information processing" work in a computer?

8. Explain what "information" means on the physical, design, and intentional levels of explanation.

9. Why do many cognitive sciences believe that the experience of a unified self is an illusion? If it is an illusion, how is it created?

10. Is materialism compatible with the belief in life after death?

Notes

Introduction

1. I have taken this approach in previous textbooks. See my *Thinking Critically About Philosophical Problems*, Wadsworth, 2001, and *Thinking Critically About Moral Problems*, Wadsworth, 2003.

2. From Plato, *The Apology*. In *Plato: The Collected Dialogues*, ed. E. Hamilton and H. Cairns. Princeton, NJ: Princeton University Press, 1961.

3. Bertrand Russell, *Problems in Philosophy*. New York: Galaxy, 1959.

Chapter 1

1. For a brief, easily accessible history of Buddhism see *The History of Buddhism*, C. George Boeree at http://www.ship.edu/~cgboeree/buddhahist.html.

2. See John Hutchison, *Paths of Faith*. New York: McGraw Hill, 1991, p. 217 f.

3. Ibid., p. 225 f.

Chapter 3

1. Aristotle, *Metaphysics*, translated by Richard McKeon. NY: Random House, 1941. Book A (1), p. 689.

2. For a good account of Aquinas on abstraction, see F. C. Copleston, *Aquinas*. Baltimore: Penguin Books, 1955, pp. 175–77.

3. Aristotle, *Nicomachean Ethics*, Bk III (1) 1110a., translated by Richard McKeon. NY: Random House, 1941.

4. Ibid., Bk III (1) 1110b.

5. Aristotle, *Politics*, translated by Richard McKeon. NY: Random House, 1941.

Chapter 4

1. St. Augustine, *Confessions*, trans. by Edward Pusey, New York: Washington Square Press, 1962. p. 1.

2. St. Thomas Aquinas, *Summa Theologica*, Q 94, Art. 1 trans. by the Fathers of the English Domincan Province. New York: Benziger Bros., 1947.

Chapter 5

1. Descartes, *Meditations on First Philosophy*, trans. by John Veitch. New York: Open Court, 1901.

2. Ibid.

3. Gilbert Ryle, *The Concept of Mind*. New York: Barnes and Noble, 1949.

4. Allison Jaggar, "Feminist Ethics," in Lawrence Becker, ed., *Encyclopedia of Ethics*. New York: Garland, 1992.

Chapter 6

1. David Hume, *An Enquiry Concerning Human Understanding*, ed. L. A. Selby-Bigge. Oxford: Clarendon Press, 1902, section II.

2. Carol Gilligan, *In a Different Voice: Psychological Theory and Women's Development*. Cambridge: Harvard University Press, 1982.

Chapter 7

1. Thomas Hobbes developed his political philosophy in his *Leviathan*. London: Oxford University Press, 1998.

2. See John Locke's, *Two Treatises of Government*, first published in 1690. Cambridge: Cambridge University Press, 1988.

3. Jean-Jacques Rousseau, *The Social Contract*. New York: Penguin, 1968.

4. Leo Huberman and Paul Sweezy, *Introduction to Socialism*. NY: Modern Reader Paperbacks, 1968.

5. Herbert Marcuse, *One Dimensional Man*. Boston: Beacon Press, 1964.

Chapter 8

1. Barrett, *Irrational Man*. Doubleday, 1962.

2. Kelly James Clark and Ann Poortenga, *The Story of Ethics: Fulfilling Our Human Nature*. Upper Saddle River, NJ: Prentice Hall, 2003.

3. *Nausea*, p. 133. NY: New Directions Publishing, 1964.

Chapter 9

1. Ernest Jones, *The Life and Work of Sigmund Freud.* NY: Basic Books, 1953.

2. Franz Alexander and Sheldon Selesnick, *The History of Psychiatry.* NY: New American Library, 1966.

3. *Totem and Taboo,* in *The Complete Psychological Works of Sigmund Freud,* V. 13. London: The Hogarth Press, 1955.

4. *Civilization and Its Discontents,* ibid., v. 21.

5. Ibid.

6. Nina Rosenstand, *The Human Condition.* NY: McGraw-Hill, 2002.

Chapter 10

1. This phrase is used in Steven Pinker, *The Blank Slate: A Modern Denial of Human Nature.* NY: Viking, 2002.

2. For a more thorough account of this evidence see Goldsmith and Zimmerman, *Biology, Evolution, and Human Nature.* NY: Wiley, 2001.

3. Charles Darwin, *The Origin of Species, Great Books, Encyclopaedia Britannica.* Chicago, 1952.

4. Goldsmith (ibid.).

5. Charles Darwin, *Descent of Man, Great Books, Encyclopaedia Britannica.* Chicago, 1952.

6. Ibid.

7. E. O. Wilson, *Sociobiology.* Cambridge: Harvard University Press, 1975.

8. *On Human Nature.* Cambridge, Harvard University Press, 1978.

9. Ibid., p. 196.

10. E. O. Wilson and Charles Lumsden, *Genes, Mind and Culture.* Cambridge, Harvard University Press, 1981.

11. Leda Cosmides and John Tooby, *An Evolutionary Psychology Primer.* Find this at http://www.psych.ucsb.edu/research/cep/primer.html.

12. See Owen Flanagan, *The Science of the Mind.* Cambridge: MIT Press, 1991.

13. Howard Gardner, *Frames of Mind: The Idea of Multiple Intelligences.* New York: Basic Books, 1983.

14. Wilson, *Sociobiology,* p. 561.

15. Goldsmith, p. 346.

16. Alison Jaggar, *Feminist Politics and Human Nature.* New Jersey: Roman and Allanheld, 1983.

17. Robert Wright, "Feminists, Meet Mr. Darwin," *The New Republic,* November 28, 1994, 34–46.

18. Sophia Elliot Connell, "Feminism and Evolutionary Psychology." http://orlando.women.it/cyberarchive/files/elliot.htm.

19. Sarah Hrdy, *The Woman That Never Evolved.* Cambridge: Harvard University Press, 1981.

Chapter 11

1. For a good account of the influence of Kantian thought on cognitive science see Owen Flanagan, *The Science of the Mind.* Cambridge: MIT Press, 1991.

2. An early proponent of this view was Richard Rorty. See his, "Mind-Body Identity, Privacy, and Categories," *The Review of Metaphysics,* 19, 1965 (24–54). The view is sometimes defended today by Paul Churchland and Patricia Churchland. See her *Neurophilosophy.* Cambridge, MIT Press, 1986.

3. See Daniel Dennett, *Consciousness Explained.* Boston: Little Brown, 1991.

4. Patricia Churchland, *Brain-Wise: Studies in Neurophilosophy.* Cambridge, Mass.: MIT Press, 2002.

5. Dennett, *The Intentional Stance.* Cambridge, Mass., MIT Press, 1987.

6. There are a group of philosophers, dubbed the "New Mysterians," who hold this view. They are, along with some of their most famous works, Thomas Nagel, "What's it like to be a bat?" *Philosophical Review, 83,* 435–50; Colin McGinn, *The Character of Mind.* Oxford University Press, 1997; and, to a lesser extent, David Chalmers, *The Conscious Mind,* Oxford, 1996.

7. See especially the discussions of freedom by Daniel Dennett, both in his *Elbow Room,* Cambridge, Mass., MIT Press, 1984, and in his more recent book, *Freedom Evolves,* New York, Viking Press, 2003. Also see Patricia Churchland's discussion of freedom in *Brain-Wise: Studies in Neurophilosophy.*

Index